Microsoft® Office 2007

ILLUSTRATED, Windows Vista™ Edition

INTRODUCTORY

Beskeen/Cram/Duffy/Friedrichsen/Reding

COURSE TECHNOLOGY
CENGAGE Learning™

Australia • Brazil • Japan • Korea • Mexico • Singapore • Spain • United Kingdom • United States

COURSE TECHNOLOGY
CENGAGE Learning™

Microsoft® Office 2007—Illustrated Introductory, Windows Vista™ Edition
Beskeen/Cram/Duffy/Friedrichsen/Reding

Senior Acquisitions Editor: Marjorie Hunt

Senior Product Manager: Christina Kling Garrett

Associate Product Manager: Rebecca Padrick

Editorial Assistant: Michelle Camisa

Senior Marketing Manager: Joy Stark

Marketing Coordinator: Jennifer Hankin

Contributing Authors: Katherine T. Pinard, Harry Phillips, Rachel Biheller Bunin

Developmental Editors: Rachel Biheller Bunin, Barbara Clemens, Pamela Conrad, MT Cozzola, Jeanne Herring, Robin Romer, Lisa Ruffolo

Production Editors: Summer Hughes, Jill Klaffky, Daphne Barbas

Copy Editors: Harold Johnson, Gary Michael Spahl

QA Manuscript Reviewers: Nicole Ashton, John Frietas, Serge Palladino, Jeff Schwartz, Danielle Shaw, Marianne Snow, Teresa Storch, Susan Whalen

Cover Designers: Elizabeth Paquin, Kathleen Fivel

Cover Artist: Mark Hunt

Composition: GEX Publishing Services

For product information and technology assistance, contact us at
Cengage Learning Customer & Sales Support, 1-800-354-9706
For permission to use material from this text or product, submit all requests online at **cengage.com/permissions**
Further permissions questions can be emailed to
permissionrequest@cengage.com

Soft Cover
ISBN-10: 1-4239-0559-8
ISBN-13: 978-1-4239-0559-2

Hard Cover
ISBN-10: 1-4239-0514-8
ISBN-13: 978-1-4239-0514-1

Course Technology
25 Thomson Place
Boston, Massachusetts 02210
USA

Cengage Learning is a leading provider of customized learning solutions with office locations around the globe, including Singapore, the United Kingdom, Australia, Mexico, Brazil, and Japan. Locate your local office at:
international.cengage.com/region

Cengage Learning products are represented in Canada by Nelson Education, Ltd.

For your lifelong learning solutions, visit **course.cengage.com**

Visit our corporate website at **cengage.com**

Trademarks:
Some of the product names and company names used in this book have been used for identification purposes only and may be trademarks or registered trademarks of their respective manufacturers and sellers.

Microsoft and the Office logo are either registered trademarks or trademarks of Microsoft Corporation in the United States and/or other countries. Thomson Course Technology is an independent entity from Microsoft Corporation, and not affiliated with Microsoft in any manner.

Credit List
Essential Computer Concepts Unit

Figure	Credit Line
A-1	Courtesy of Acer America, Inc.
A-2	Courtesy of Hewlett-Packard Company
A-3	Courtesy of IBM Corporation
A-4	Courtesy of Intel Corporation
A-5	Courtesy of AMD
A-6a	*drawing - no credit*
A-6b	Courtesy of Microsoft Corporation
A-7 a & b	Courtesy of Logitech
A-8a	Courtesy of Hewlett-Packard Company
A-8b	Courtesy of IBM Corporation
A-9 a & b	Courtesy of Hewlett-Packard Company
A-10a & b	Courtesy of Hewlett-Packard Company
A-15	Courtesy of SanDisk Corporation
A-17	Courtesy of Hewlett-Packard Company
A-18	Courtesy of Belkin Corporation
A-27	Courtesy of Hewlett-Packard Company

PowerPoint Units

Figure	Credit Line
C-6	Courtesy of Jennifer L. Beskeen
C-12	Courtesy of Barbara Clemens
D-5	Courtesy of Christopher Garrett

Printed in the United States of America
2 3 4 5 6 7 8 9 11 10 09 08

About This Book

Welcome to *Microsoft Office 2007 Illustrated Introductory, Windows Vista Edition*! Since the first edition of this book was published in 1995, close to one million students have used various editions of it to master Microsoft Office. We are proud to bring you this latest edition on the most exciting version of Microsoft Office ever to release.

As you probably have heard by now, Microsoft completely redesigned this latest version of Office from the ground up. No more menus! No more toolbars! The software changes Microsoft made were based on years of research during which they studied users' needs and work habits. The result is a phenomenal and powerful new version of the software that will make you and your students more productive and help you get better results faster.

Before we started working on this new edition, we also conducted our own research. We reached out to nearly 100 instructors like you who have used previous editions of this book. Some of you responded to one of our surveys; others of you generously spent time with us on the phone, telling us your thoughts. Seven of you agreed to serve on our Advisory Board and guided our every decision in developing this new edition.

As a result of all the feedback you gave us, we have preserved the features that you love, and made improvements that you suggested and requested. And of course we have covered all the key features of the new software. (For more details on what's new in this edition, please read the Preface.) We are confident that this book and all its available resources will help your students master Microsoft Office 2007.

Advisory Board

We thank our Advisory Board who enthusiastically gave us their opinions and guided our every decision on content and design from beginning to end. They are:

Kristen Callahan, Mercer County Community College
Paulette Comet, Assistant Professor, Community College of Baltimore County
Barbara Comfort, J. Sargeant Reynolds Community College
Margaret Cooksey, Tallahassee Community College
Rachelle Hall, Glendale Community College
Hazel Kates, Miami Dade College
Charles Lupico, Thomas Nelson Community College

Author Acknowledgments

David Beskeen Experience, dedication, hard work, and attention-to-detail with a little humor thrown in are the qualities of a great editor and Rachel Biheller Bunin is truly a great editor—thank you so much! To all of the professionals at Course Technology, led by Christina Kling Garrett, thanks for your hard work. I would also like to especially thank Marjorie Hunt, who fifteen years ago, gave me my first opportunity to use my knowledge of PowerPoint to help others learn. Finally, a special thanks to my wife, Karen, and the "J's", for always being there.

Carol Cram A big thank you to my developmental editor Barbara Clemens for her patience, good humor, and insight! And, as always, everything I do is made possible by Gregg and Julia. They make everything worthwhile.

Jennifer Duffy Many talented people at Course Technology helped to shape this book — thank you all. I am especially indebted to Pam Conrad for her precision editing, sage encouragement, and endless good cheer throughout the many months of writing. On the home front, I am ever grateful to my husband and children for their patience and support.

Lisa Friedrichsen The Access portion is dedicated to my students, and all who are using this book to teach and learn about Access. Thank you. Also, thank you to all of the professionals who helped me create this book.

Elizabeth Eisner Reding Creating a book of this magnitude is a team effort. I would like to thank my husband, Michael, as well as Christina Kling Garrett, the project manager, and my development editor, MT Cozzola, for her suggestions and corrections. I would also like to thank the production and editorial staff for all their hard work that made this project a reality.

Preface

Welcome to *Microsoft Office 2007, Illustrated Introductory, Windows Vista Edition*. If this is your first experience with the Illustrated series, you'll see that this book has a unique design: each skill is presented on two facing pages, with steps on the left and screens on the right. The layout makes it easy to digest a skill without having to read a lot of text and flip pages to see an illustration.

This book is an ideal learning tool for a wide range of learners—the rookies will find the clean design easy to follow and focused with only essential information presented, and the hot-shots will appreciate being able to move quickly through the lessons to find the information they need without reading a lot of text. The design also makes this a great reference after the course is over! See the illustration on the right to learn more about the pedagogical and design elements of a typical lesson.

What's New in This Edition

We've made many changes and enhancements to this edition to make it the best ever. Here are some highlights of what's new:

- **New Getting Started with Microsoft Office 2007 Unit**—This unit begins the Office section and gets students up to speed on features of Office 2007 that are common to all the applications, such as the Ribbon, the Office button, and the Quick Access toolbar.

- **Real Life Independent Challenge**—The new Real Life Independent Challenge exercises offer students the opportunity to create projects that are meaningful to their lives, such as a personal letterhead, a database to track personal expenses, or a budget for buying a house.

- **New Case Study**—A new case study featuring Quest Specialty Travel provides a practical and fun scenario that students can relate to as they learn skills. This

Each two-page spread focuses on a single skill.

Concise text introduces the basic principles in the lesson and integrates a real-world case study.

UNIT D
Word 2007

Dividing a Document into Sections

Dividing a document into sections allows you to format each section of the document with different page layout settings. A **section** is a portion of a document that is separated from the rest of the document by section breaks. **Section breaks** are formatting marks that you insert in a document to show the end of a section. Once you have divided a document into sections, you can format each section with different column, margin, page orientation, header and footer, and other page layout settings. By default, a document is formatted as a single section, but you can divide a document into as many sections as you like. You insert a section break to divide the document into two sections, and then format the text in the second section in two columns. First, you customize the status bar to display section information.

STEPS

QUICK TIP
Use the Customize Status bar menu to turn on and off the display of information in the status bar.

1. **Right-click the status bar, click Section on the Customize Status Bar menu that opens (if it is not already checked), then click the document to close the menu**
   The status bar indicates the insertion point is located in section 1 of the document.

2. **Click the Home tab, then click the Show/Hide ¶ button ¶ in the Paragraph group**
   Turning on formatting marks allows you to see the section breaks you insert in a document.

QUICK TIP
When you insert a section break at the beginning of a paragraph, Word inserts the break at the end of the previous paragraph. A section break stores the formatting information for the preceding section.

3. **Place the insertion point before the headline QST Launches New Tours to South Africa, click the Page Layout tab, then click the Breaks button in the Page Setup group**
   The Breaks menu opens. You use this menu to insert different types of section breaks. See Table D-1.

4. **Click Continuous**
   Word inserts a continuous section break, shown as a dotted double line, above the headline. The document now has two sections. Notice that the status bar indicates the insertion point is in section 2.

5. **Click the Columns button in the Page Setup group**
   The columns menu opens. You use this menu to format text in one, two, or three columns of equal width, or to create two columns of different widths, one narrow and one wider. To create columns with custom widths and spacing, you click More Columns on the Columns menu.

QUICK TIP
When you delete a section break, you delete the section formatting of the text before the break. That text becomes part of the following section, and it assumes the formatting of that section.

6. **Click Two**
   Section 2 is formatted in two columns of equal width, as shown in Figure D-3. The text in section 1 remains formatted in a single column. Notice that the status bar now indicates the document is four pages long. Formatting text in columns is another way to increase the amount of text that fits on a page.

7. **Click the View tab, click the Two Pages button in the Zoom group, scroll down to examine all four pages of the document, press [Ctrl][Home], then save the document**
   The text in section 2—all the text below the continuous section break—is formatted in two columns. Text in columns flows automatically from the bottom of one column to the top of the next column.

TABLE D-1: Types of section breaks

section	function
Next page	Begins a new section and moves the text following the break to the top of the next page
Continuous	Begins a new section on the same page
Even page	Begins a new section and moves the text following the break to the top of the next even-numbered page
Odd page	Begins a new section and moves the text following the break to the top of the next odd-numbered page

Word 80   Formatting Documents

Hints as well as troubleshooting advice, right where you need it—next to the step itself.

Tables are quickly accessible summaries of key terms, toolbar buttons, or keyboard alternatives connected with the lesson material. Students can refer easily to this information when working on their own projects at a later time.

fictional company offers a wide variety of tours around the world.

- **Content Improvements**—All of the content in the book has been updated to cover Office 2007 and also to address instructor feedback. See the instructor resource CD for details on specific content changes for each application section.

Assignments

The lessons use Quest Specialty Travel, a fictional adventure travel company, as the case study. The assignments on the light purple pages at the end of each unit increase in difficulty. Data files and case studies provide a variety of interesting and relevant business applications. Assignments include:

- **Concepts Reviews** consist of multiple choice, matching, and screen identification questions.

- **Skills Reviews** provide additional hands-on, step-by-step reinforcement.

- **Independent Challenges** are case projects requiring critical thinking and application of the unit skills. The Independent Challenges increase in difficulty, with the first one in each unit being the easiest. Independent Challenges 2 and 3 become increasingly open-ended, requiring more independent problem solving.

- **Real Life Independent Challenges** are practical exercises in which students create documents to help them with their every day lives.

- **Advanced Challenge Exercises** set within the Independent Challenges provide optional steps for more advanced students.

- **Visual Workshops** are practical, self-graded capstone projects that require independent problem solving.

Every lesson features large, full-color representations of what the screen should look like as students complete the numbered steps.

Brightly colored tabs indicate which section of the book you are in.

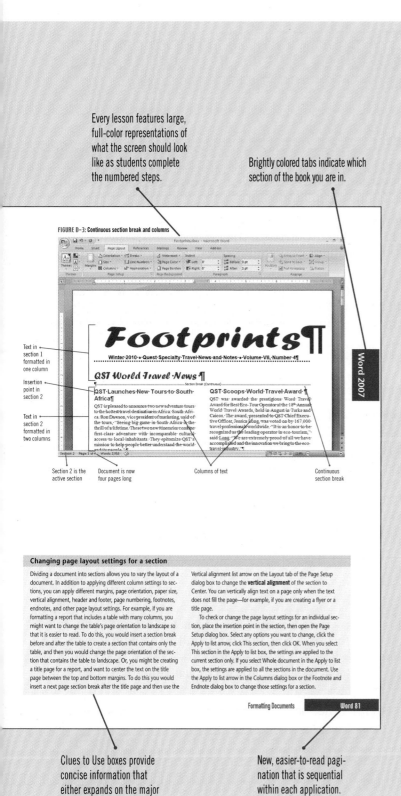

FIGURE D-3: Continuous section break and columns

Word 2007

Text in section 1 formatted in one column

Insertion point in section 2

Text in section 2 formatted in two columns

Section 2 is the active section

Document is now four pages long

Columns of text

Continuous section break

Changing page layout settings for a section

Dividing a document into sections allows you to vary the layout of a document. In addition to applying different column settings to sections, you can apply different margins, page orientation, paper size, vertical alignment, header and footer, page numbering, footnotes, endnotes, and other page layout settings. For example, if you are formatting a report that includes a table with many columns, you might want to change the table's page orientation to landscape so that it is easier to read. To do this, you would insert a section break before and after the table to create a section that contains only the table, and then you would change the page orientation of the section that contains the table to landscape. Or, you might be creating a title page for a report, and want to center the text on the title page between the top and bottom margins. To do this you would insert a next page section break after the title page and then use the

Vertical alignment list arrow on the Layout tab of the Page Setup dialog box to change the **vertical alignment** of the section to Center. You can vertically align text on a page only when the text does not fill the page—for example, if you are creating a flyer or a title page.

To check or change the page layout settings for an individual section, place the insertion point in the section, then open the Page Setup dialog box. Select any options you want to change, click the Apply to list arrow, click This section, then click OK. When you select This section in the Apply to list box, the settings are applied to the current section only. If you select Whole document in the Apply to list box, the settings are applied to all the sections in the document. Use the Apply to list arrow in the Columns dialog box or the Footnote and Endnote dialog box to change those settings for a section.

Formatting Documents

Word 81

Clues to Use boxes provide concise information that either expands on the major lesson skill or describes an independent task that in some way relates to the major lesson skill.

New, easier-to-read pagination that is sequential within each application.

v

Assessment & Training Solutions

SAM 2007

SAM 2007 helps bridge the gap between the classroom and the real world by allowing students to train and test on important computer skills in an active, hands-on environment.

SAM 2007's easy-to-use system includes powerful interactive exams, training, or projects on critical applications such as Word, Excel, Access, PowerPoint, Outlook, Windows, the Internet, and much more. SAM simulates the application environment, allowing students to demonstrate their knowledge and think through the skills by performing real-world tasks.

Designed to be used with the Illustrated series, SAM 2007 includes built-in page references so students can print helpful study guides that match the Illustrated textbooks used in class. Powerful administrative options allow instructors to schedule exams and assignments, secure tests, and run reports with almost limitless flexibility.

Student Edition Labs

Our Web-based interactive labs help students master hundreds of computer concepts, including input and output devices, file management and desktop applications, computer ethics, virus protection, and much more. Featuring up-to-the-minute content, eye-popping graphics, and rich animation, the highly interactive Student Edition Labs offer students an alternative way to learn through dynamic observation, step-by-step practice, and challenging review questions. Also available on CD at an additional cost.

Online Content — Blackboard

Blackboard is the leading distance learning solution provider and class-management platform today. Course Technology has partnered with Blackboard to bring you premium online content. Instructors: Content for use with *Microsoft Office 2007—Illustrated Introductory, Windows Vista Edition* is available in a Blackboard Course Cartridge and may include topic reviews, case projects, review questions, test banks, practice tests, custom syllabi, and more.

Course Technology also has solutions for several other learning management systems. Please visit *www.course.com* today to see what's available for this title.

Instructor Resources

The Instructor Resources CD is Course Technology's way of putting the resources and information needed to teach and learn effectively into your hands. With an integrated array of teaching and learning tools that offer you and your students a broad range of technology-based instructional options, we believe this CD represents the highest quality and most cutting edge resources available to instructors today. Many of these resources are available at *www.course.com*. The resources available with this book are:

- **Instructor's Manual**—Available as an electronic file, the Instructor's Manual includes detailed lecture topics with teaching tips for each unit.

- **Sample Syllabus**—Prepare and customize your course easily using this sample course outline.

- **PowerPoint Presentations**—Each unit has a corresponding PowerPoint presentation that you can use in lecture, distribute to your students, or customize to suit your course.

- **Figure Files**—The figures in the text are provided on the Instructor Resources CD to help you illustrate key topics or concepts. You can create traditional overhead transparencies by printing the figure files. Or you can create electronic slide shows by using the figures in a presentation program such as PowerPoint.

- **Solutions to Exercises**—Solutions to Exercises contains every file students are asked to create or modify in the lessons and end-of-unit material. Also provided in this section, there is a document outlining the solutions for the end-of-unit Concepts Review, Skills Review, and Independent Challenges. An Annotated Solution File and Grading Rubric accompany each file and can be used together for quick and easy grading.

- **Data Files for Students**—To complete most of the units in this book, your students will need Data Files. You can post the Data Files on a file server for students to copy. The Data Files are available on the Instructor Resources CD-ROM, the Review Pack, and can also be downloaded from www.course.com. In this edition, we have included a lesson on downloading the Data Files for this book, see page xxiv.

Instruct students to use the Data Files List included on the Review Pack and the Instructor Resources CD. This list gives instructions on copying and organizing files.

- **ExamView**—ExamView is a powerful testing software package that allows you to create and administer printed, computer (LAN-based), and Internet exams. ExamView includes hundreds of questions that correspond to the topics covered in this text, enabling students to generate detailed study guides that include page references for further review. The computer-based and Internet testing components allow students to take exams at their computers, and also saves you time by grading each exam automatically.

CourseCasts—Learning on the Go. Always available...always relevant.

Want to keep up with the latest technology trends relevant to you? Visit our site to find a library of podcasts, CourseCasts, featuring a "CourseCast of the Week," and download them to your mp3 player at *http://coursecasts.course.com*.

Our fast-paced world is driven by technology. You know because you're an active participant—always on the go, always keeping up with technological trends, and always learning new ways to embrace technology to power your life.

Ken Baldauf, a faculty member of the Florida State University Computer Science Department, is responsible for teaching technology classes to thousands of FSU students each year. He knows what you know; he knows what you want to learn. He's also an expert in the latest technology and will sort through and aggregate the most pertinent news and information so you can spend your time enjoying technology, rather than trying to figure it out.

Visit us at http://coursecasts.course.com to learn on the go!

Brief Contents

Brief Contents

Contents

WINDOWS VISTA

Unit B: Understanding File Management   25

INTERNET EXPLORER

Unit A: Getting Started with Internet Explorer 7   1

WORD 2007   **Unit B: Editing Documents**   **25**

WORD 2007   **Unit C: Formatting Text and Paragraphs**   **49**

Unit B: Working with Formulas and Functions   25

Unit C: Formatting a Worksheet   51

| POWERPOINT 2007 | **Unit A: Creating a Presentation in PowerPoint 2007** | **1** |

| POWERPOINT 2007 | **Unit B: Modifying a Presentation** | **25** |

POWERPOINT 2007 **Unit C: Inserting Objects into a Presentation** **49**

POWERPOINT 2007 **Unit D: Finishing a Presentation** **73**

INTEGRATION

Unit C: Integrating Word, Excel, Access, and PowerPoint — 33

OUTLOOK 2007

Unit A: Getting Started with E-Mail — 1

Read This Before You Begin

Frequently Asked Questions

What are Data Files?

A Data File is a partially completed Word document, Excel workbook, Access database, PowerPoint presentation, or another type of file that you use to complete the steps in the units and exercises to create the final document that you submit to your instructor. Each unit opener page lists the Data Files that you need for that unit.

Where are the Data Files?

Your instructor will provide the Data Files to you or direct you to a location on a network drive from which you can download them. Alternatively, you can follow the instructions on the next page to download the Data Files from this book's Web page.

What software was used to write and test this book?

This book was written and tested using a typical installation of Microsoft Office 2007 on a computer with a typical installation of Microsoft Windows Vista.

The browser used for any steps that require a browser is Internet Explorer 7.

Do I need to be connected to the Internet to complete the steps and exercises in this book?

Some of the exercises in this book assume that your computer is connected to the Internet. If you are not connected to the Internet, see your instructor for information on how to complete the exercises.

What do I do if my screen is different from the figures shown in this book?

This book was written and tested on computers with monitors set at a resolution of 1024 × 768. If your screen shows more or less information than the figures in the book, your monitor is probably set at a higher or lower resolution. If you don't see something on your screen, you might have to scroll down or up to see the object identified in the figures.

The Ribbon—the blue area at the top of the screen—in Microsoft Office 2007 adapts to different resolutions. If your monitor is set at a lower resolution than 1024 × 768, you might not see all of the buttons shown in the figures. The groups of buttons will always appear, but the entire group might be condensed into a single button that you need to click to access the buttons described in the instructions. For example, the figures and steps in this book assume that the Editing group on the Home tab in Word looks like the following:

1024 × 768 Editing Group

Editing Group on the
Home Tab of the
Ribbon at 1024 × 768

If your resolution is set to 800 × 600, the Ribbon in Word will look like the following figure, and you will need to click the Editing button to access the buttons that are visible in the Editing group.

800 × 600 Editing Group

Editing Group
on the Home Tab of the
Ribbon at 800 × 600

800 × 600 Editing Group Clicked

Editing Group on the Home Tab of the Ribbon at
800 × 600 is selected to show available buttons

Downloading Data Files for This Book

In order to complete many of the lesson steps and exercises in this book, you are asked to open and save Data Files. A **Data File** is a partially completed Word document, Excel workbook, Access database, PowerPoint presentation, or another type of file that you use as a starting point to complete the steps in the units and exercises. The benefit of using a Data File is that it saves you the time and effort needed to create a file; you can simply open a Data File, save it with a new name (so the original file remains intact), then make changes to it to complete lesson steps or an exercise. Your instructor will provide the Data Files to you or direct you to a location on a network drive from which you can download them. Alternatively, you can follow the instructions in this lesson to download the Data Files from this book's Web page.

1. Start Internet Explorer, type www.course.com in the address bar, then press [Enter]

2. When the Course.com Web site opens, click the Student Downloads link

3. On the Student Downloads page, click in the Search text box, type 9781423905592, then click Go

> **QUICK TIP**
>
> You can also click Student Downloads on the right side of the product page.

4. When the page opens for this textbook, in the left navigation bar, click the Download Student Files link, then, on the Student Downloads page, click the Data Files link

5. If the File Download – Security Warning dialog box opens, click Save. (If no dialog box appears, skip this step and go to Step 6)

> **TROUBLE**
>
> If a dialog box opens telling you that the download is complete, click Close.

6. If the Save As dialog box opens, click the Save in list arrow at the top of the dialog box, select a folder on your USB drive or hard disk to download the file to, then click Save

7. Close Internet Explorer and then open My Computer or Windows Explorer and display the contents of the drive and folder to which you downloaded the file

8. Double-click the file 905592.exe in the drive or folder, then, if the Open File – Security Warning dialog box opens, click Run

> **QUICK TIP**
>
> By default, the files will extract to C:\ CourseTechnology\ 905592

9. In the WinZip Self-Extractor window, navigate to the drive and folder where you want to unzip the files to, then click Unzip

10. When the WinZip Self-Extractor displays a dialog box listing the number of files that have unzipped successfully, click OK, click Close in the WinZip Self-Extractor dialog box, then close Windows Explorer or My Computer

You are now ready to open the required files.

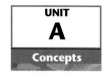

Understanding Essential Computer Concepts

Computers are essential tools in almost all kinds of activity in virtually every type of business. In this unit, you will learn about computers and their components. You will learn about input and output, how a computer processes data and stores information, how information is transmitted, and ways to secure that information. Finally, you will learn about system and application software. Quest Specialty Travel is expanding its North American offices and just purchased Sheehan Tours, an established travel agency in Boston, Massachusetts. Sheehan Tours has been in business for over 40 years and has a large customer base. Unfortunately, its computer system is tremendously outdated. Its office contains a hodgepodge of computer equipment, most of which has been purchased used. The office staff still carries data between computers on floppy disks, and only one computer is connected to the Internet. Kevin O'Brien, the manager of the New York office, has been sent to the new Boston office to help them switch to Quest's business practices. He has already ordered and installed new computer equipment. His next task is to teach the staff how to use the new equipment.

OBJECTIVES

Investigate types of computers
Examine computer systems
Examine input devices
Examine output devices
Investigate data processing
Understand memory
Understand storage media
Explore data communications
Learn about networks
Learn about security threats
Understand system software
Understand application software

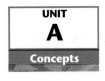

Investigating Types of Computers

A **computer** is an electronic device that accepts information and instructions from a user, manipulates the information according to the instructions, displays the information in some way, and stores the information for retrieval later. Computers are classified by their size, speed, and capabilities. ⬛⬛⬛⬛ Most of the staff at Sheehan Tours do not know anything about computers except for the ones that sit on their desks, so Kevin decides to start with a basic explanation of the types of computers available.

DETAILS

The following list describes various types of computers:

- **Personal computers** are computers typically used by a single user, for use in the home or office. Personal computers are used for general computing tasks such as word processing, manipulating numbers, working with photographs or graphics, exchanging e-mail, and accessing the Internet.

- A personal computer is available as a **desktop computer**, which is designed to sit compactly on a desk; as a **notebook computer** (also referred to as a **laptop computer**), which is small, lightweight, and designed for portability; or as a **tablet PC**, which is also designed for portability, but includes the capability of recognizing ordinary handwriting on the screen. Figure A-1 shows a notebook computer. Desktop personal computers can be purchased for as little as $300, but high-end notebooks can cost more than $3500. A notebook computer with similar capability is usually more expensive than a desktop computer, and tablet PCs are generally more expensive than notebook computers. Many computer users spend between $800 and $1500 when purchasing a new personal computer.

- **Hand-held computers** are small computers that fit in the palm of your hand. Hand-held computers have more limited capabilities than personal computers.

  - **PDAs** (**personal digital assistants**) are generally used to maintain an electronic appointment book, address book, calculator, and notepad. See Figure A-2. High-end PDAs are all-in-one devices that can send and receive e-mails and make phone calls.
  - **MP3 players** are hand-held computers that are primarily used to store and play music, although some models can also be used to play digital movies or television shows.
  - Cell phones are another type of hand-held computer. In addition to being used to make telephone calls, cell phones store contact information. Many cell phones can take and store digital photos and video and play and store music. Most cell phones have additional capabilities such as built-in calculator programs. High-end cell phones can also perform many of the same functions as a PDA.

- **Mainframe computers** are used by larger businesses and government agencies to provide centralized storage, processing, and management for large amounts of data. The price of a mainframe computer varies widely, from several hundred thousand dollars to several million dollars.

- The largest and fastest computers, called **supercomputers**, are used by large corporations and government agencies when the tremendous volume of data would seriously delay processing on a mainframe computer. A supercomputer, like the one shown in Figure A-3, can cost tens of millions of dollars.

Understanding terminals

When an organization uses mainframes or supercomputers, each user inputs processing requests and views output through a **terminal** or a **terminal emulator**. A terminal has a keyboard for input and a monitor for output, but processes little or no data on its own. A terminal emulator is a personal computer, workstation, or server that uses special software to imitate a terminal so that the PC can communicate with the mainframe or supercomputer for complex data processing.

FIGURE A-1: Notebook computer

FIGURE A-2: PDA

FIGURE A-3: Supercomputer

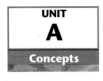

Examining Computer Systems

A **computer system** includes computer hardware and software. **Hardware** refers to the physical components of a computer. **Software** refers to the intangible components of a computer system, particularly the **programs**, or lists of instructions, that the computer needs to perform a specific task. Kevin explains how computers work and points out the main components of a computer system.

DETAILS

The following list provides an overview of computer system components and how they work:

- The design and construction of a computer is referred to as its **architecture** or **configuration**. The technical details about each hardware component are called **specifications**. For example, a computer system might be configured to include a printer; a specification for that printer might be a print speed of eight pages per minute or the capacity to print in color.

- The hardware and the software of a computer system work together to process data. **Data** refers to the words, numbers, figures, sounds, and graphics that describe people, events, things, and ideas. Modifying data is referred to as **processing**.

- In a computer, processing tasks occur on the **motherboard**, which is located inside the computer and is the main electronic component of the computer. The motherboard is a **circuit board**, which is a rigid piece of insulating material with **circuits**, electrical paths, on it that control specific functions. See Figure A-4. The motherboard contains the following processing hardware:

  - The **microprocessor**, also called the **processor** or the **central processing unit** (CPU), consists of transistors and electronic circuits on a silicon **chip** (an integrated circuit embedded in semiconductor material). See Figure A-5. The processor is mounted on the motherboard and is responsible for executing instructions to process information.
  - **Cards** are removable **circuit boards** that are inserted into slots in the motherboard to expand the capabilities of the motherboard. For example, a sound card translates the digital audio information from the computer into analog sounds that the human ear can hear.

- The data or instructions you type into the computer are called **input**. The result of the computer processing input is referred to as **output**. The computer itself takes care of the processing functions, but it needs additional components, called **peripheral devices**, to accomplish the input, output, and storage functions.

  - You use an **input device**, such as a keyboard or a mouse, to enter data and issue commands. **Commands** are input instructions that tell the computer how to process data. For example, you might want to center the title and double-space the text of a report. You use the appropriate commands in the word processing program that instruct the computer to modify the data you have input so the report text is double-spaced and the report title is centered.
  - Output can be in many different forms, including reports, documents, graphs, sounds, and pictures. Computers produce output using **output devices**, such as a monitor or printer.
  - The output you create using a computer can be stored either inside the computer itself or on an external storage device, such as a DVD. You will learn more about storage devices later in this unit.

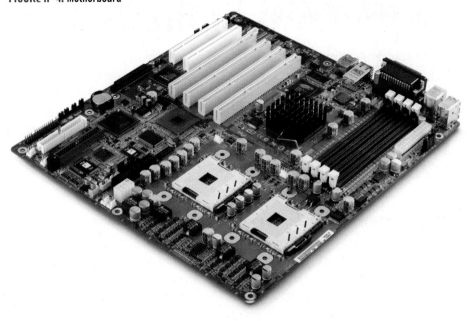

FIGURE A-5: Microprocessor (front and back views)

Concepts

Comparing microprocessor speeds

How fast a computer can process instructions depends partially on the speed of the microprocessor, which is determined by its clock speed, word size, and cache size, and whether it is single or dual core. **Clock speed** is measured in **megahertz (MHz)**, millions of cycles per second, or in **gigahertz (GHz)**, billions of cycles per second. **Word size** refers to the amount of data that is processed at one time. Finally, a **dual-core processor**, one that has two processors on a single chip, can process information up to twice as fast as a **single-core processor**, one with one processor on the chip.

Examining Input Devices

Before a computer can produce useful information, people must get data into the computer. This is accomplished by using input devices. In a typical personal computer system, you input data and commands by using an input device such as a keyboard or a mouse. Computers can also receive input from a storage device. You will learn about storage devices later in this unit. ▰▰▰▰ As Kevin explains peripheral devices to the Sheehan Tours staff, they ask several questions about input devices. For example, one person doesn't understand the difference between a mouse and a trackball. Kevin continues his explanation with a discussion of various input devices.

DETAILS

There are many types of input devices, as described below:

QUICK TIP

Another way to avoid repetitive motion injuries is to take frequent breaks when working at a computer and stretch your hands and wrists.

- One of the most frequently used input devices is a **keyboard**. The top keyboard in Figure A-6 is a standard keyboard. The bottom keyboard in Figure A-6 is **ergonomic**, which means that it has been designed to fit the natural placement of your hands and should reduce the risk of repetitive-motion injuries. It also has several additional keys programmed as shortcut keys to commonly used functions.

- Another common input device is a **pointing device**, which controls the **pointer**, a small arrow or other symbol on the screen. Pointing devices are used to select commands and manipulate text or graphics on the screen.

    - The most popular pointing device for a desktop computer is a **mouse**, such as the one shown on the left side in Figure A-7. An ordinary mouse has a rolling ball on its underside, and an optical mouse has a tiny camera on its underside that takes pictures as the mouse is moved. You control the pointer by moving the entire mouse. A mouse usually has two or more buttons for clicking commands. A mouse might also have a **scroll wheel** that you roll to scroll the page on the screen and that may function as one of the buttons.

    - The **trackball**, such as the one shown on the right side in Figure A-7, is similar to a mouse except that the rolling ball is on the top side and you control the movement of the pointer by moving only the ball.

    - Notebook computers are usually equipped with a touch pad or a pointing stick. See Figure A-8. A **touch pad** is a touch-sensitive device that you drag your finger over to control the pointer. The buttons are located in front of the touch pad. A **pointing stick** is a small, eraser-like device embedded among the typing keys that you push up, left, right, or down to move the pointer. Two buttons equivalent to mouse buttons are located in front of the spacebar.

- A **scanner** is a device that transfers the content on a piece of paper into memory. To do this, you place a piece of paper on the glass, a beam of light moves across the glass similar to a photocopier, and stores the image or words on the paper as digital information. You can scan a document or a photo and save it as an image file, or you can scan a document and have the text "read" by the scanner and saved in a document file for editing later.

- Microphones are another type of input device. You can use them to record sound for certain types of files, or, if you have the voice-recognition software, you can use them to input data and commands.

- Input devices can be connected to the computer with cables or wirelessly. Wireless input devices connect to the computer using infrared or radio frequency technology, similar to a remote control for a television.

Using assistive devices

People with physical impairments or disabilities can use computers because of advances in making computers accessible to everyone. For example, people who cannot use their arms or hands instead can use foot, head, or eye movements to control the pointer. People with poor vision can use keyboards with large keys for input, screen enlargers to enlarge the type and images on the monitor, or screen readers to read the content of the screen aloud. Computers are being developed that can be controlled by a person's thoughts, that is, the brain's electromagnetic waves.

FIGURE A-6: Keyboards

Editing keypad

Function keys

Main keyboard

Numeric keypad

Traditional keyboard

Ergonomic keyboard

FIGURE A-7: Personal computer pointing devices

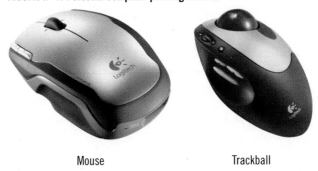

Mouse   Trackball

FIGURE A-8: Notebook pointing devices

Touch pad   Pointing Stick

Examining Output Devices

As stated earlier, output is the result of processing data; output devices show you those results. The most commonly used output devices are monitors and printers. Kevin continues his discussion of peripheral devices with an explanation of output devices.

Output devices are described below:

QUICK TIP

Flat panel monitors are more expensive than CRT monitors.

- The **monitor** displays the output from a computer.

  - The monitor shown on the left in Figure A-9 is a **flat panel monitor**, a lightweight monitor that takes up very little room on the desktop. Most flat panel monitors use **LCD** (**liquid crystal display**) technology, which creates the image you see on the screen by manipulating light within a layer of liquid crystal. A **CRT** (**cathode ray tube**) **monitor**, shown on the right in Figure A-9, uses gun-like devices that direct beams of electrons toward the screen to activate dots of color to form the image you see on the screen. CRT monitors require much more desk space than flat-panel display monitors.

  - Monitor **screen size** is the diagonal measurement from one corner of the screen to the other. In general, monitors on desktop computers range in size from 15" to 30", whereas monitors on notebook computers range in size from 12" to 20".

  - Most monitors have a **graphics display**, which divides the screen into a matrix of small dots called **pixels**. **Resolution** is the number of pixels the monitor displays. Standard resolutions range from 640×480 to 1600×1200. If your screen is small, a 1600×1200 resolution will make the objects on the screen too small to see clearly. **Dot pitch** (**dp**) measures the distance between pixels, so a smaller dot pitch means a sharper image. A .28 or .26 dot pitch is typical for today's monitors.

  - To display graphics, a computer must have a **graphics card**, also called a **video display adapter** or **video card**. The graphics card is installed on the motherboard, and controls the signals the computer sends to the monitor.

QUICK TIP

The speed of laser and inkjet printers is measured in **pages per minute (ppm)**. The speed of dot matrix printers is measured in **characters per second (cps)**.

- A **printer** produces a paper copy, often called **hard copy**, of the text or graphics processed by the computer. There are three popular categories of printers: laser printers, inkjet printers, and dot matrix printers.

  - **Laser printers**, like the one shown on the left in Figure A-10, are popular for business use because they produce high-quality output quickly and efficiently. In a laser printer, a temporary laser image is transferred onto paper with a powdery substance called **toner**.

  - **Inkjet printers**, such as the one shown on the right in Figure A-10, are popular printers for home use. These printers spray ink onto paper and produce output whose quality is comparable to that of a laser printer.

  - **Dot matrix printers** transfer ink to the paper by striking a ribbon with pins. A 24-pin dot matrix printer produces better quality print than a 9-pin. Dot matrix printers are most often used when a large number of pages need to be printed fairly quickly or when a business needs to print multi-page continuous forms.

- Speakers, like speakers on a sound system, allow you to hear sounds from the computer. Speakers can be separate peripheral devices attached to the computer, or they can be built in to the monitor.

- Like input devices, output devices can be connected to a computer using cables or a wireless connection.

FIGURE A-9: Monitors

Flat panel monitor   CRT monitor

FIGURE A-10: Printers

Laser printer   Inkjet printer

Concepts

Investigating Data Processing

In order to understand how data is processed in a computer, you first need to learn how the computer represents and stores data. All data and programs are stored as files. A computer **file** is a named collection of stored data. An **executable file** contains the instructions that tell a computer how to perform a specific task; for instance, the files that are used while the computer starts are executable. A **data file** is created by a user, usually with software. For instance, a report that you write with a word processing program is data, and must be saved as a data file if you want to access it later. 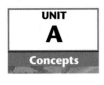 Kevin gives a basic description of how information is represented inside a computer.

The following information will help you understand data processing:

- The characters used in human language are meaningless to a computer. Like a light bulb, the computer must interpret every signal as either "on" or "off." A computer represents data as distinct or separate numbers. Specifically, it represents "on" with a 1 and "off" with a 0. These numbers are referred to as **binary digits**, or **bits**.

- A series of eight bits is called a **byte**. As Figure A-11 shows, the byte that represents the integer value 0 is 00000000, with all eight bits "off" or set to 0. The byte that represents the integer value 1 is 00000001, and the byte that represents 255 is 11111111.

- A **kilobyte** (**KB** or simply **K**) is 1024 bytes, or approximately one thousand bytes. A **megabyte** (**MB**) is 1,048,576 bytes, or about one million bytes. A **gigabyte** (**GB**) is 1,073,741,824 bytes, or about one billion bytes. A **terabyte** (**TB**) is 1,024 GB, or approximately one trillion bytes.

- Personal computers commonly use the ASCII system to represent character data. **ASCII** (pronounced "ASK-ee") stands for **American Standard Code for Information Interchange**. Each ASCII number represents an English character. Computers translate ASCII into binary data so that they can process it.

  - The original ASCII system used 7 bits to represent the numbers 0 (0000000) through 127 (1111111) to stand for 128 common characters and nonprinting control characters. Because bits are usually arranged in bytes, the eighth bit is reserved for error checking.
  - Extended ASCII uses eight bits and includes the numbers 128 (10000000) through 255 (11111111) to represent additional characters and symbols. Extended ASCII was developed to add codes for punctuation marks, symbols, such as $ and ©, and additional characters, such as é and ü, that were not included in the original 128 codes.
  - Most computers use the original ASCII definitions, but not all computers use the same definitions for Extended ASCII. Computers that run the Windows operating system use the set of Extended ASCII definitions defined by the American National Standards Institute (ANSI). Figure A-12 shows sample ASCII code with ANSI standard Extended ASCII characters.

FIGURE A-11: Binary representation of numbers

Number	Binary representation
0	00000000
1	00000001
2	00000010
3	00000011
4	00000100
5	00000101
6	00000110
7	00000111
8	00001000
⋮	⋮
253	11111101
254	11111110
255	11111111

FIGURE A-12: Sample ASCII code representing letters and symbols

Character	ASCII Code	Binary Number
(space)	32	00100000
$	36	00100100
A	65	01000001
B	66	01000010
a	97	01100001
b	98	01100010
?	129	10000001
£	163	10100011
®	217	11011001
é	233	11101001

Concepts

Understanding Memory

In addition to the microprocessor, another important component of personal computer hardware is the **memory**, which stores instructions and data. Memory is different from permanent storage in a computer. Your computer has five types of memory: random access memory, cache memory, virtual memory, read-only memory, and complementary metal oxide semiconductor memory. ⬛⬛⬛⬛ Kevin realizes that most of the Sheehan Tours staff don't understand the difference between memory types, so he explains the different types of memory.

DETAILS

Types of memory include the following:

QUICK TIP

When the computer is off, RAM is empty.

- **Random access memory** (**RAM**) temporarily holds programs and data while the computer is on and allows the computer to access that information randomly; in other words, RAM doesn't need to access data in the same sequence in which it was stored. For example, if you are writing a report, the microprocessor temporarily copies the word processing program you are using into RAM so the microprocessor can quickly access the instructions that you will need as you type and format your report. The characters you type are also stored in RAM, along with the fonts, graphics, and other objects that you might use. RAM consists of chips on cards that plug into the motherboard.

  - Most personal computers use **synchronous dynamic random access memory** (**SDRAM**), which is synchronized with the processor to allow faster access to its contents.
  - RAM is sometimes referred to as **volatile memory** or **temporary memory** because it is constantly changing as long as the computer is on and is cleared when the computer is turned off.
  - **Memory capacity**, sometimes referred to as **storage capacity**, is the amount of data that the computer can handle at any given time and is measured in megabytes or gigabytes. For example, a computer that has 512 MB of RAM has the capacity to temporarily store more than 512 million bits of data at one time.

- **Cache memory**, sometimes called **RAM cache** or **CPU cache**, is a special, high-speed memory chip on the motherboard or CPU itself that stores frequently accessed and recently accessed data and commands.

QUICK TIP

You can often add more RAM to a computer by installing additional memory cards on the motherboard. You cannot add ROM; it is permanently installed on the motherboard.

- **Virtual memory** is space on the computer's storage devices that simulates additional RAM. It enables programs to run as if your computer had more RAM by moving data and commands from RAM to the hard drive and swapping in the new data and commands. See Figure A-13. Virtual memory, however, is much slower than RAM.

- **Read-only memory** (**ROM**) is a chip on the motherboard that has been prerecorded with data. ROM permanently stores the set of instructions that the computer uses to check the computer system's components to make sure they are working and to activate the essential software that controls the processing function when you turn the computer on.

QUICK TIP

The act of turning on the computer is sometimes called **booting up**.

  - ROM contains a set of instructions called the **BIOS** (**basic input/output system**), which tells the computer to initialize the motherboard, how to recognize the peripherals, and to start the boot process. The **boot process** is the set of events that occurs between the moment you turn on the computer and the moment you can begin to use the computer. The set of instructions for executing the boot process is stored in ROM.
  - ROM never changes and it remains intact when the computer is turned off; therefore, it is called **nonvolatile memory** or **permanent memory**.

- **Complementary metal oxide semiconductor** (**CMOS**, pronounced "SEE-moss") **memory** is a chip installed on the motherboard that is activated during the boot process and identifies where essential software is stored.

  - A small rechargeable battery powers CMOS so its contents are saved when the computer is turned off. CMOS changes every time you add or remove hardware on your computer system.
  - CMOS, often referred to as **semipermanent memory**, changes when hardware is added or removed, but doesn't empty when the computer is shut off.
  - Because CMOS retains its contents when the computer is turned off, the date and time are stored there.

FIGURE A-13: How virtual memory works

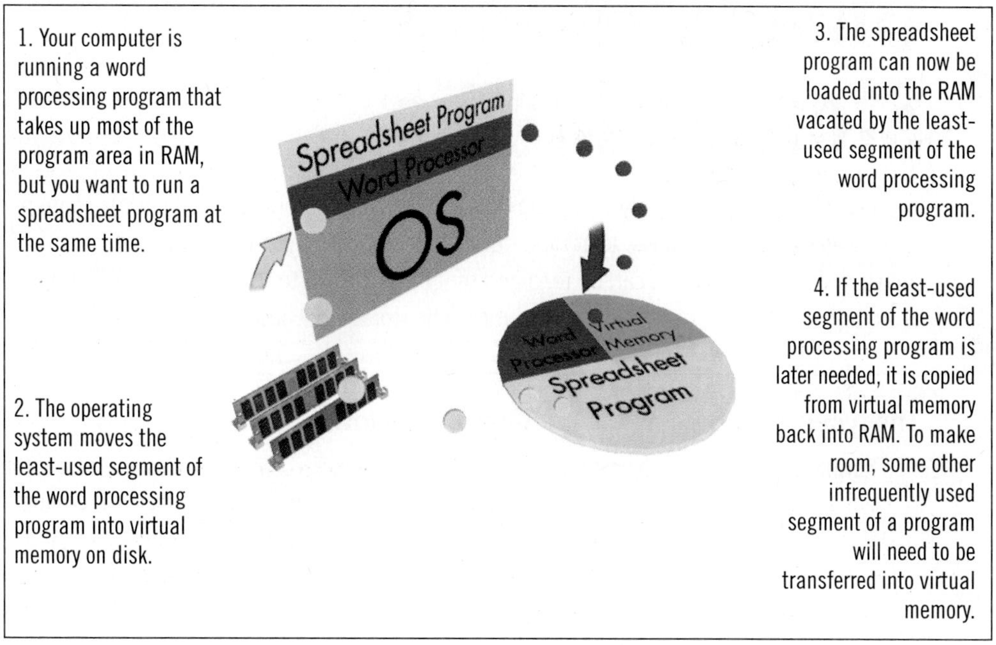
1. Your computer is running a word processing program that takes up most of the program area in RAM, but you want to run a spreadsheet program at the same time.
Spreadsheet Program
Word Processor
OS
Word Processor
Virtual Memory
Spreadsheet Program
2. The operating system moves the least-used segment of the word processing program into virtual memory on disk.
3. The spreadsheet program can now be loaded into the RAM vacated by the least-used segment of the word processing program.
4. If the least-used segment of the word processing program is later needed, it is copied from virtual memory back into RAM. To make room, some other infrequently used segment of a program will need to be transferred into virtual memory.

Upgrading RAM

One of the easiest ways to make a computer run faster is to add more RAM. This enables the computer to access instructions and data stored in RAM very quickly. The more RAM a computer has, the more instructions and data can be stored there. Currently, you can buy from 64 MB to 1 GB RAM cards, and usually, you can add more than one card. You need to check your computer's specifications to see what size RAM cards the slots on your motherboard will accept.

Understanding Storage Media

Because RAM retains data only while the power is on, your computer must have a more permanent storage option. As Figure A-14 shows, a storage device receives data from RAM and writes it on a storage medium, such as a CD. Later the data can be read and sent back to RAM to use again. Kevin explains the types of storage media available. He starts with magnetic storage because almost all computers have a hard disk.

DETAILS

The types of storage media are discussed below:

- **Magnetic storage devices** store data as magnetized particles on mylar, a plastic, which is then coated on both sides with a magnetic oxide coating. Common magnetic storage devices are hard disks, tape, and floppy disks.

  - A **hard disk** is the most common type of magnetic storage media. It contains several magnetic oxide-covered metal platters that are usually sealed in a case inside the computer.
  - **Tape** is another type of magnetic storage media. Tape storage is much too slow to be used for day-to-day computer tasks; therefore, tapes are used to make backup copies of data stored on hard disks. Tape provides inexpensive, though slow, archival storage for large companies who need to back up large quantities of data.
  - A **floppy disk** is a flat circle of magnetic oxide-coated mylar enclosed in a hard plastic case; a floppy disk can store 1.44 MB of data. Floppy disks are sometimes called 3½" disks because of the size of the hard plastic case. The floppy disk has almost become obsolete, and most personal computers are now manufactured without a floppy disk drive.

QUICK TIP

Optical storage devices, such as CDs and DVDs, are much more durable than magnetic storage media.

- **Optical storage devices** are polycarbonate discs coated with a reflective metal on which data is recorded using laser technology as a trail of tiny pits or dark spots in the surface of the disc. The data that these pits or spots represent can then be "read" with a beam of laser light.

  - The first standard optical storage device available for personal computers was the **CD** (**compact disc**). One CD can store 700 MB of data.
  - A **DVD**, though the same size as a CD, currently stores between 4.7 and 15.9 GB of data, depending on whether data is stored on one or two sides of the disc, and how many layers of data each side contains. The term *DVD* is no longer an acronym, although it was originally an acronym for *digital video disc* and later was sometimes updated to *digital versatile disc*.
  - New formats of optical storage include Blu-ray Discs and HD-DVD, which are capable of storing between 15 and 50 GB of data. They are used for storing high-definition video. Different companies support each format and it remains to be seen if one dominates the market.

- **Flash memory** is similar to ROM except that it can be written to more than once. **Flash memory cards** are small, portable cards encased in hard plastic to which data can be written and rewritten. They are used in digital cameras, handheld computers, video game controllers, and other devices.

- A popular type of flash memory is a **USB flash storage device**, also called a **USB drive** or a **flash drive**. See Figure A-15.

QUICK TIP

There is only one way to insert a flash drive, so if you're having problems inserting the drive into the slot, turn the drive around and try again.

  - USB drives for personal computers are available in a wide range of sizes; they currently range from drives capable of holding 32 MB of data to drives capable of holding 16 GB of data. They are becoming more popular for use as a secondary or backup storage device for data typically stored on a hard disk drive.
  - USB drives plug directly into the USB port of a personal computer; the computer recognizes the device as another disk drive. The location and letter designation of USB ports varies with the brand and model of computer you are using, but the physical port may be on the front, back, or side of a computer.
  - USB flash storage devices are about the size of a pack of gum and often have a ring that you can attach to your key chain.

FIGURE A-14: Storage devices and RAM

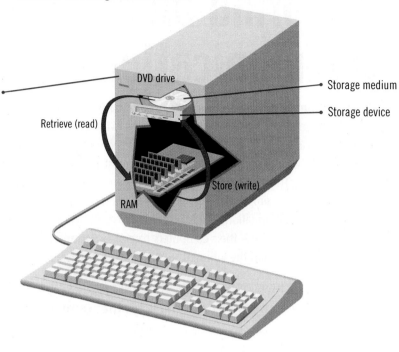

A storage device receives information from RAM, writes it on the storage medium, and reads and sends it back to RAM

DVD drive

Storage medium

Storage device

Retrieve (read)

Store (write)

RAM

FIGURE A-15: Flash storage device

Erasing and rewriting on CDs and DVDs

CD-ROM stands for **compact disc read-only memory**. CDs that you buy with software or music already on them are CD-ROMs—you can read from them, but you cannot record additional data onto them. In order to record data on a CD, you need a **CD-R** (**compact disc recordable**) or **CD-RW** (**compact disc rewritable**) drive and a CD-R or CD-RW disk. On CD-ROMs, data is stored in pits made on the surface of the disk; when you record data on a CD-R or -RW, a laser changes the reflectivity of a dye layer on a blank disk, creating dark spots on the disk's surface that represent the data. On a CD-R, once the data is recorded, you cannot erase or modify it, but you can add new data to the disk, as long as the disk has not been finalized. In

contrast, you can re-record a CD-RW. CD-R disks can be read by a standard CD-ROM drive or a DVD drive; CD-RW disks can be read only by CD-RW drives or CD-ROM drives labeled "multi-read." Recordable DVD drives are also available. As with CDs, you can buy a DVD to which you can record only once, or a rewritable DVD to which you can record and then re-record data. Recordable and rewriteable DVDs come in several formats; for example, recordable DVDs are available as DVD-R and DVD+R. Make sure you know which type of DVD your DVD drive uses. Newer DVD drives are capable of reading from and writing to both -RW and +RW DVDs and CDs, as well as DVDs with two layers.

Exploring Data Communications

Data communications is the transmission of data from one computer to another or to a peripheral device. The computer that originates the message is the **sender**. The message is sent over some type of **channel**, such as a telephone or coaxial cable. The computer or peripheral at the message's destination is the **receiver**. The rules that establish an orderly transfer of data between the sender and the receiver are called **protocols**. The transmission protocol between a computer and its peripheral devices is handled by a **device driver**, or simply **driver**, which is a computer program that can establish communication because it contains information about the characteristics of your computer and of the device. ▰▰▰▰ The Sheehan Tours staff will use their computers to connect to the computers at the Quest headquarters in California as well as to surf the Internet, so Kevin next explains how computers communicate.

DETAILS

The following describes some of the ways that computers communicate:

- The data path between the microprocessor, RAM, and the peripherals along which communication travels is called the **data bus**. Figure A-16 illustrates the data bus that connects a printer to a computer.

- An external peripheral device must have a corresponding **port** and **cable** that connect it to the computer. Inside the computer, each port connects to a **controller card**, sometimes called an **expansion card** or **interface card**. These cards plug into electrical connectors on the motherboard called **expansion slots** or **slots**. Personal computers can have several types of ports, including parallel, serial, SCSI, USB, MIDI, and Ethernet. Figure A-17 shows the ports on one desktop personal computer.

    - A **parallel port** transmits data eight bits at a time. Parallel transmissions are relatively fast, but they have an increased risk for interference. A **serial port** transmits data one bit at a time.
    - One **SCSI** (**small computer system interface**, pronounced "scuzzy") **port** provides an interface for one or more peripheral devices at the same port. The first is connected directly to the computer through the port, and the second device is plugged into a similar port on the first device.
    - A **USB** (**Universal Serial Bus**) **port** is a high-speed serial port which allows multiple connections at the same port. The device you install must have a **USB connector**, a small rectangular plug, as shown in Figure A-18. When you plug the USB connector into the USB port, the computer recognizes the device and allows you to use it immediately. You can connect multiple devices to a single USB port by "daisy chaining" them or by using a hub. USB flash storage devices plug into USB ports. For most USB devices, power is supplied via the port, so there is no need for extra power cables.
    - The port for a sound card usually includes jacks for speakers and a microphone, which are designed to work with a **MIDI** (**Musical Instrument Digital Interface**, pronounced "middy") **card**.
    - You can connect to another computer, a LAN, a modem, or sometimes directly to the Internet using an **Ethernet port**. Ethernet ports allow data to be transmitted at high speeds.

- An internal peripheral device such as a hard disk drive may plug directly into the motherboard, or it may have an attached controller card.

- Notebook computers may also include a **portable computer card** (**PC Card**). PC Cards are credit card-sized cards that plug directly into the PC Card slot and can contain additional RAM, a fax modem, or a hard disk drive (similar to a USB flash storage device).

QUICK TIP

Typically, a printer that is near the computer is connected to a parallel port, and the mouse, keyboard, and modem are connected to serial ports.

QUICK TIP

FireWire is another standard for transferring information between digital devices similar to USB.

Understanding Essential Computer Concepts

FIGURE A-16: Components needed to connect a printer to a computer

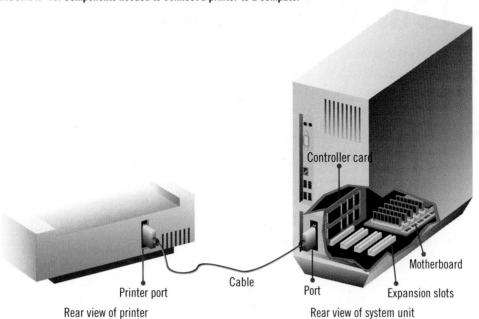

Controller card

Motherboard

Printer port

Cable

Port

Expansion slots

Rear view of printer

Rear view of system unit

FIGURE A-17: Computer ports and connections

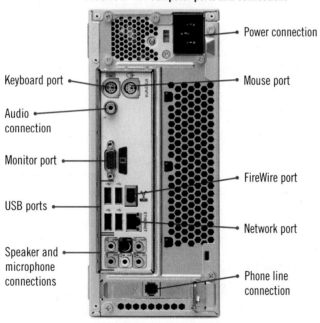

Power connection

Keyboard port

Mouse port

Audio connection

Monitor port

FireWire port

USB ports

Network port

Speaker and microphone connections

Phone line connection

FIGURE A-18: USB connector

Concepts

Learning about Networks

A **network** connects one computer to other computers and peripheral devices, enabling you to share data and resources with others. There are a variety of network configurations; however, any type of network has some basic characteristics and requirements that you should know. Kevin continues his discussion of how computers communicate with an explanation of networking.

Types of networks are described below:

- Each computer that is part of the network must have a **network interface card** (**NIC**) installed. This card creates a communications channel between the computer and the network. A cable is used to connect the NIC port to the network.

- **Network software** is also essential, establishing the communications protocols that will be observed on the network and controlling the "traffic flow" as data travels throughout the network.

- Some networks have one or more computers, called **servers**, that act as the central storage location for programs and provide mass storage for most of the data used on the network. A network with a server and computers dependent on the server is called a **client/server network**. The dependent computers are the **clients**.

- When a network does not have a server, all the computers essentially are equal, and programs and data are distributed among them. This is called a **peer-to-peer network**.

- A personal computer that is not connected to a network is called a **standalone computer**. When it is connected to the network, it becomes a **workstation**. You have already learned that a terminal has a keyboard and monitor used for input and output, but it is not capable of processing on its own. A terminal is connected to a network that uses mainframes as servers. Any device connected to the network is called a **node**. Figure A-19 illustrates a typical network configuration.

- In a **local area network** (**LAN**), computers and peripheral devices are located relatively close to each other, generally in the same building.

- A **wide area network** (**WAN**) is more than one LAN connected together. The Internet is the largest example of a WAN.

- In a **wireless local area network** (**WLAN**), computers and peripherals use high-frequency radio waves instead of wires to communicate and connect in a network. **Wi-Fi** (short for **wireless fidelity**) is the term created by the nonprofit Wi-Fi Alliance to describe networks connected using a standard radio frequency established by the Institute of Electrical and Electronics Engineers (IEEE). Wi-Fi is used over short distances to connect computers to a LAN.

- A **personal area network** (**PAN**) is a network that allows two or more devices located close to each other to communicate or to connect a device to the Internet. In a PAN, devices are connected with cables or wireless.

    - **Infrared technology** uses infrared light waves to beam data from one device to another. The devices must be compatible, and they must be positioned close to each other with their infrared ports pointed at each other for this to work. This is the technology used in TV remote controls.
    - **Bluetooth** uses short range radio waves to connect a device wirelessly to another device or to the Internet. The devices must each have a Bluetooth transmitter, but unlike infrared connections, they can communicate around corners or through walls.

- **WiMAX** (short for **Worldwide Interoperability for Microwave Access**), another standard defined by the IEEE, allows computer users to connect over many miles to a LAN. A WiMAX tower sends signals to a WiMAX receiver built or plugged into a computer. WiMAX towers can communicate with each other or with an Internet service provider.

Workstation

Server

Printer

Workstation

Your local workstation

Understanding telecommunications

Telecommunications means communicating over a comparatively long distance using a phone line or some other data conduit. When it is not possible to connect users on one network, telecommunications allows you to send and receive data over the telephone lines. To make this connection, you must use a communications device called a modem. A **modem**, which stands for *mo*dulator-*dem*odulator, is a device that connects your computer to a standard telephone jack. The modem converts the **digital**, or stop-start, **signals** your computer outputs into **analog**, or continuous wave, **signals** (sound waves) that can traverse ordinary phone lines. Figure A-20 shows the telecommunications process, in which a modem converts

digital signals to analog signals at the sending site (modulates) and a second modem converts the analog signals back into digital signals at the receiving site (demodulates). Most computers today come with a built-in 56 K modem and/or NIC (network interface card). 56 K represents the modem's capability to send and receive about 56,000 **bits per second** (**bps**). Actual speed may be reduced by factors such as distance, technical interference, and other issues. People who want to use a high-speed connection either over phone lines, such as a **DSL** (**digital subscriber line**), or over a cable connection, usually need to purchase an external DSL or cable modem separately.

FIGURE A-20: Using modems to send and receive data

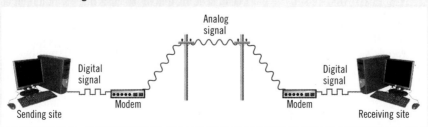

Concepts

Learning about Security Threats

Security refers to the steps a computer owner takes to prevent unauthorized use of or damage to the computer. Once a computer is connected to a network, it is essential that the computer be protected against possible threats from people intent on stealing information or causing malicious damage. Kevin explains how important it is to be vigilant about keeping the office computers secure and reviews ways to do this.

Several types of security threats are discussed below:

- **Malware** is a broad term that describes any program that is intended to cause harm or convey information to others without the owner's permission.

  QUICK TIP

  Some specific types of viruses are called worms; another type is a Trojan horse. Antivirus software usually protects against both types.

  - Unscrupulous programmers deliberately construct harmful programs, called **viruses**, which instruct your computer to perform destructive activities, such as erasing a disk drive. Some viruses are more annoying than destructive, but some can be harmful, erasing data or causing your hard disk to require reformatting. **Antivirus software**, sometimes referred to as **virus protection software**, searches executable files for the sequences of characters that may cause harm and disinfects the files by erasing or disabling those commands. Figure A-21 shows the screen that appears after AVG Anti-Virus Free Edition finished scanning a computer.

  - Some software programs contain other programs called **spyware** that track a computer user's Internet usage and send this data back to the company or person that created it. Most often, this is done without the computer user's permission or knowledge. **Anti-spyware software** can detect these programs and delete them.

  QUICK TIP

  Adware is software installed with another program usually with the user's permission that generates advertising revenue for the program's creator by displaying targeted ads to the program's user.

- A **firewall** is like a locked door on a computer. It prevents other computers on the Internet from accessing a computer and prevents programs on a computer from accessing the Internet without the computer user's permission. A firewall can be either hardware or software.

  - A hardware firewall provides strong protection against incoming threats. A **router**, a device that controls traffic between network components, usually has a built-in firewall.

  - Software firewalls track all incoming and outgoing traffic. If a program that never accessed the Internet before attempts to do so, the user is notified and can choose to forbid access. There are several free software firewall packages available. Figure A-22 shows an alert from Zone Alarm, a software firewall.

- Criminals are getting more aggressive as they try to figure out new ways to access computer users' personal information and passwords.

  - A Web site set up to look exactly like another Web site, such as a bank's Web site, but which does not actually belong to the organization portrayed in the site, is a **spoofed** site. The site developer creates a **URL** (address on the Web) that looks similar to a URL from the legitimate site. Usually, spoofed sites are set up to try to convince customers of the real site to enter personal information, such as credit card numbers, Social Security numbers, and passwords, so that the thief collecting the information can use it to steal the customer's money or identity.

  QUICK TIP

  Never click a URL in a phishing message. Open your browser and type the URL of the organization into the Address or Location bar instead.

  - **Phishing** refers to the practice of sending e-mails to customers or potential customers of a legitimate Web site asking them to click a link in the e-mail. The link leads to a spoofed site where the user is asked to verify or enter personal information.

  - Sometimes a criminal can break into a **DNS server** (a computer responsible for directing Internet traffic) and redirect any attempts to access a particular Web site to the criminal's spoofed site. This is called **pharming**.

FIGURE A-21: Completed antivirus scan

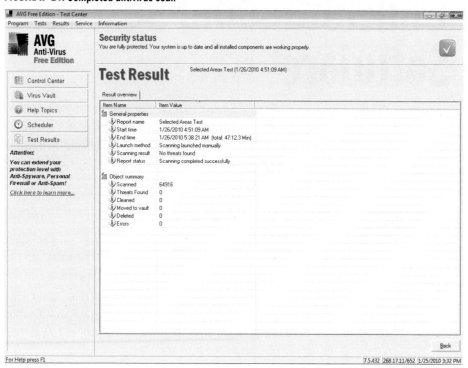

FIGURE A-22: Security alert from a software firewall

Protecting information with passwords

You can protect data on your computer by using passwords. You can set up accounts on your computer for multiple users and require that all users sign in with a user name and password before they can use the computer. This is known as **logging in**. You can also protect individual files on your computer so that people who try to open or alter a file need to type the password before they are allowed access to the file. Many Web sites require a user name and password in order to access the information stored on it. To prevent anyone from guessing your password, you should always create and use strong passwords. A **strong password** is at least eight characters of upper and lowercase letters and numbers. Avoid using common personal information, such as birthdays and addresses.

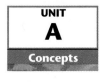
Understanding System Software

Sometimes the term software refers to a single program, but often the term refers to a collection of programs and data that are packaged together. **System software** helps the computer carry out its basic operating tasks. ▓▓▓▓ Before Kevin describes the various types of software that people use to accomplish things like writing memos, he needs to describe system software.

DETAILS

The components of system software are described below:

- System software manages the fundamental operations of your computer, such as loading programs and data into memory, executing programs, saving data to disks, displaying information on the monitor, and transmitting data through a port to a peripheral device. There are four types of system software: operating systems, utilities, device drivers, and programming languages.

- An **operating system** allocates system resources, manages storage space, maintains security, detects equipment failure, and controls basic input and output. **Input and output**, or **I/O**, is the flow of data from the microprocessor to memory to peripherals and back again.

    - The operating system allocates system resources so programs run properly. A **system resource** is any part of the computer system, including memory, storage devices, and the microprocessor, that can be used by a computer program.
    - The operating system is also responsible for managing the files on your storage devices. Not only does it open and save files, but it also keeps track of every part of every file for you and lets you know if any part is missing.
    - While you are working on the computer, the operating system is constantly guarding against equipment failure. Each electronic circuit is checked periodically, and the moment a problem is detected, the user is notified with a warning message on the screen.
    - Microsoft Windows, used on many personal computers, and the MAC OS, used exclusively on Macintosh computers, are referred to as **operating environments** because they provide a **graphical user interface** (**GUI**, pronounced "goo-ey") that acts as a liaison between the user and all of the computer's hardware and software. Figure A-23 shows the starting screen on a computer using Microsoft Windows Vista.

- **Utilities** are another category of system software that augment the operating system by taking over some of its responsibility for allocating hardware resources.

- As you learned earlier in the discussion of ports, device drivers handle the transmission protocol between a computer and its peripherals. When you add a device to an existing computer, part of its installation includes adding its device driver to the computer's configuration.

- Computer **programming languages**, which a programmer uses to write computer instructions, are also part of the system software. The instructions are translated into electrical signals that the computer can manipulate and process.

> **QUICK TIP**
> The operating system's responsibility to maintain security may include requiring a username and password or checking the computer for virus infection.

> **QUICK TIP**
> Some examples of popular programming languages are BASIC, Visual Basic, C, C++, C#, Java, and Delphi.

FIGURE A-23: Windows Vista starting screen

Icon (You might see additional icons on your screen)

Gadgets (small programs; you might see additional or different gadgets on your screen)

Start button

Taskbar

Quick Launch toolbar

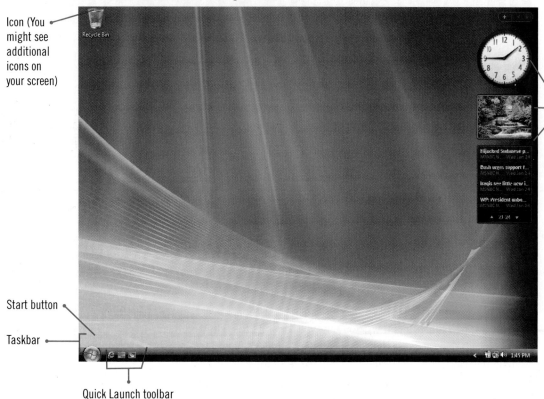

Examining Windows Vista hardware requirements

Windows Vista, the successor to Windows XP, requires more memory and hard drive space and a faster processor than Windows XP. To take full advantage of all of the features and capabilities of Windows Vista, you need a computer with a 1 GHz processor, 1 GB of RAM, a DirectX 9 graphics processor, 128 MB of specialized graphics RAM, and a 40 GB hard drive with at least 15 GB of available space. To run Windows Vista without all of its features, you need a computer with an 800 MHz processor, 512 MB of RAM, a graphics processor that is DirectX 9 capable (most computers come with this type of graphics processor), and 20 GB hard drive with at least 15 GB of available space. Keep in mind that these are the minimum recommendations. To prevent your computer from slowing to a crawl, you should consider upgrading the amount of RAM and the processor speed.

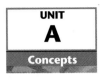

Understanding Application Software

Application software enables you to perform specific computer tasks. Some examples of tasks that are accomplished with application software are document production, spreadsheet calculations, database management, and giving presentations. ▨▨▨▨▨ Now that the Sheehan Tours staff understands operating systems, Kevin describes some common application software.

DETAILS

Typical application software includes the following:

- **Document production software** includes word processing software, desktop publishing software, e-mail editors, and Web authoring software. All of these production tools have a variety of features that assist you in writing and formatting documents, including changing the **font** (the style of type). Most offer **spell checking** to help you avoid typographical and spelling errors, as shown in Figure A-24.

- **Spreadsheet software** is a numerical analysis tool. Spreadsheet software creates a **worksheet**, composed of a grid of columns and rows. You can type data into the cells, and then enter mathematical formulas into other cells that reference the data. Figure A-25 shows a typical worksheet that includes a simple calculation and the data in the spreadsheet represented as a simple graph.

- **Database management software** lets you collect and manage data. A **database** is a collection of information stored on one or more computers organized in a uniform format of records and fields. A **record** is a collection of data items in a database. A **field** is one piece of information in the record. An example of a database is the online catalog of books at a library; the catalog contains one record for each book in the library, and each record contains fields that identify the title, the author, and the subjects under which the book can be classified.

- **Graphics** and **presentation software** allow you to create illustrations, diagrams, graphs, and charts that can be projected before a group, printed out for quick reference, or transmitted to remote computers. You can also use **clip art**, simple drawings that are included as collections with many software packages.

- **Photo editing software** allows you to manipulate digital photos. You can make the images brighter, add special effects to the photo, add additional images to a photo, or crop the photo to include only relevant parts of the image.

- **Multimedia authoring software** allows you to record digital sound files, video files, and animations that can be included in presentations and other documents.

- **Information management software** keeps track of schedules, appointments, contacts, and "to-do" lists. Most e-mail software allows users to add all the information about contacts to the list of e-mail addresses. In addition, some software, such as Microsoft Outlook, combines a contact list with information management components, such as a calendar and to-do list. The main screen of Microsoft Outlook is shown in Figure A-26.

- **Web site creation and management software** allows you to create and manage Web sites. They allow you to see what the Web pages will look like as you create them.

Understanding object linking and embedding (OLE)

Many programs allow users to use data created in one application in a document created by another application. **Object linking and embedding (OLE)** refers to the ability to use data from another file, called the **source**. **Embedding** occurs when you copy and paste the source data in the new file. **Linking** allows you to create a connection between the source data and the copy in the new file. The link updates the copy every time a change is made to the source data. The seamless nature of OLE among some applications is referred to as **integration**.

FIGURE A-24: Spell checking a document

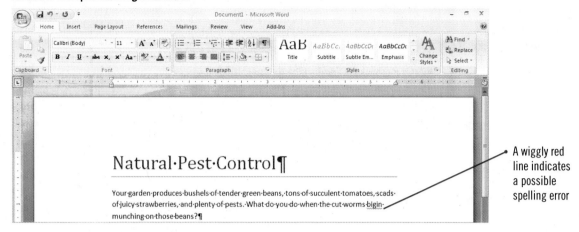

A wiggly red line indicates a possible spelling error

FIGURE A-25: Typical worksheet with numerical data and a graph

Cell B5 contains result of calculation performed by spreadsheet software

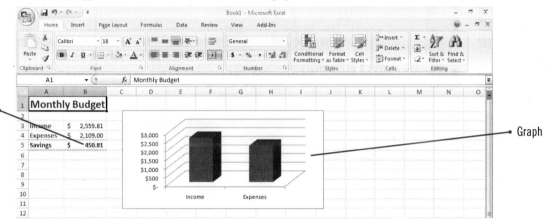

Graph

FIGURE A-26: Information management software

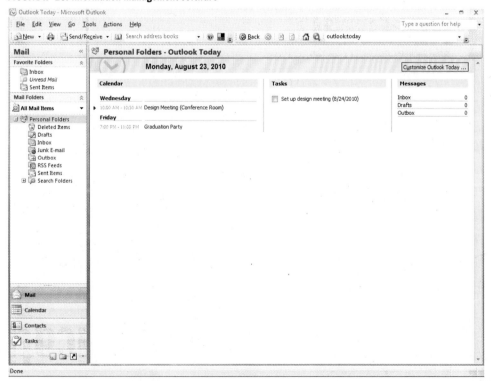

Concepts

Practice

If you have a SAM user profile, you may have access to hands-on instruction, practice, and assessment of the skills covered in this unit. Log in to your SAM account (http://sam2007.course.com) to launch any assigned training activities or exams that relate to the skills covered in this unit.

▼ CONCEPTS REVIEW

Label each component of the desktop personal computer shown in Figure A-27.

FIGURE A-27

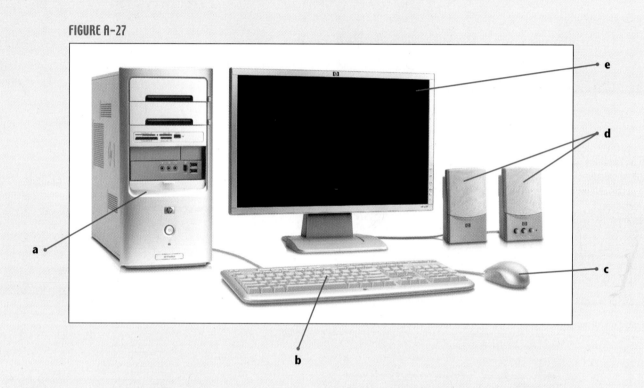

1. Which component do you use to point to items on the screen?
2. Which component displays output?
3. Which component is used to enter text?
4. Which component processes data?
5. Which component transmits audio output?

Match each term with the statement that best describes it.

6. **configuration**
7. **byte**
8. **RAM**
9. **hard disk**
10. **expansion slot**
11. **server**
12. **spyware**
13. **operating system**
14. **font**

a. Software that allocates resources, manages storage space, maintains security, and controls I/O

b. The style of type

c. The design and construction of a computer

d. Magnetic storage media that is usually sealed in a case inside the computer

e. Series of eight bits

f. A computer on a network that acts as the central storage location for programs and data used on the network

g. A program that tracks a user's Internet usage without the user's permission

h. A slot on the motherboard into which a controller card for a peripheral device is inserted

i. Temporarily holds data and programs while the computer is on

Select the best answer from the list of choices.

15. **Which one of the following would not be considered a personal computer?**
    a. Desktop
    b. Notebook
    c. Mainframe
    d. Tablet PC

16. **The intangible components of a computer system, including the programs, are called _____.**
    a. software
    b. hardware
    c. price
    d. peripherals

17. **What part of the computer is responsible for executing instructions to process information?**
    a. Card
    b. Processor
    c. Motherboard
    d. Peripheral device

18. **What are the technical details about each hardware component called?**
    a. Configuration
    b. Circuits
    c. Specifications
    d. Cards

19. **Keyboards, monitors, and printers are all examples of which of the following?**
    a. Input devices
    b. Output devices
    c. Software
    d. Peripheral devices

20. **Which of the following is a pointing device that allows you to control the pointer by moving the entire device around on a desk?**
    a. Mouse
    b. Trackball
    c. Touch pad
    d. Pointing stick

21. **In order to display graphics, a computer needs a monitor and a _____.**
    a. parallel port
    b. network card
    c. graphics card
    d. sound card

22. **What do you call each 1 or 0 used in the representation of computer data?**
    a. A bit
    b. A byte
    c. An ASCII
    d. A pixel

23. **Another way to refer to 1024 bytes is a _____.**
    a. byte
    b. kilobyte
    c. megabyte
    d. binary

24. **Which of the following is a chip installed on the motherboard that is activated during the boot process and identifies where essential software is stored?**
    a. RAM
    b. CMOS
    c. CPU cache
    d. ROM

25. **Which of the following is space on the computer's storage devices that simulates additional RAM?**
    a. Cache memory
    b. Virtual memory
    c. Read-only memory
    d. Volatile memory

26. **Which of the following permanently stores the set of instructions that the computer uses to activate the software that controls the processing function when you turn the computer on?**
    a. RAM
    b. CMOS
    c. CPU cache
    d. ROM

27. **Which of the following storage media is not a magnetic storage device?**
    a. Hard disk
    b. Floppy disk
    c. DVD
    d. Tape

28. **The transmission protocol between a computer and its peripheral devices is handled by a _____.**
    a. channel
    b. data bus
    c. driver
    d. controller card

29. **Which of the following is the data path between the microprocessor, RAM, and the peripherals?**
    a. Data bus
    b. Data channel
    c. Data port
    d. Cable

30. **The computer that originates a message to send to another computer is called the _____.**
   a. channel
   b. sender
   c. receiver
   d. driver

31. **A personal computer that is connected to a network is called a _____.**
   a. desktop
   b. workstation
   c. terminal
   d. PDA

32. **Which of the following acts as a locked door on a computer?**
   a. Antivirus software
   b. Firewall
   c. DNS server
   d. Spyware

33. **A _____ consists of connected computers and peripheral devices that are located relatively close to each other.**
   a. LAN
   b. WAN
   c. WLAN
   d. PAN

34. **The term that describes networks connected using a standard radio frequency established by the IEEE is _____.**
   a. WiMAX
   b. WAN
   c. WLAN
   d. Wi-Fi

35. **A Web site set up to look exactly like another Web site, such as a bank's Web site, but which does not actually belong to the organization portrayed in the site, is a _____ site.**
   a. malware
   b. phished
   c. spoofed
   d. served

▼ INDEPENDENT CHALLENGE 1

This Independent Challenge requires an Internet connection. In order to run the newest software, many people need to upgrade their existing computer system or buy a brand new one. What do you do with your old computer when you purchase a new one? Most municipalities have enacted laws regulating the disposal of electronics. Research these laws in your city and state and write a brief report describing them.

   a. Start your browser, go to your favorite search engine, then search for information about laws regarding the disposal of electronics in your city and state. Try finding your city's Web site and searching it for the information, or use **electronics disposal laws** followed by your city name as a search term and then repeat that search with your state's name in place of your city's name.
   b. Open each Web site that you find in a separate tab or browser window.
   c. Read the information on each Web site. Can some components be thrown away? Are there laws that apply only to monitors?

▼ INDEPENDENT CHALLENGE 1 (CONTINUED)

Advanced Challenge Exercise

- Search for organizations to which you can donate your computer.
- How do these organizations promise to protect your privacy?
- Can you take a deduction on your federal income tax for your donation?

d. Write a short report describing your findings. Include the URLs for all relevant Web sites. (*Hint*: If you are using a word processor to write your report, you can copy the URLs from your browser and paste them into the document. Drag to select the entire URL in the Address or Location bar in your browser. Right-click the selected text, then click Copy on the shortcut menu. Position the insertion point in the document where you want the URL to appear, then press [Ctrl][V].)

▼ INDEPENDENT CHALLENGE 2

This Independent Challenge requires an Internet connection. New viruses are discovered on an almost daily basis. If you surf the Internet or exchange e-mail, it is important to use updated anti-virus software. Research the most current virus threats and create a table listing the threats and details about them.

a. Start your browser, go to Symantec's Web site at **www.symantec.com**, then click the Latest Threats link. (If you don't see that link, type **threat explorer** in the Search box on the page, then click the link to Threat Explorer in the list of search results. On the Threat Explorer page, click the Latest tab.)

b. Click links to the first five latest threats.

c. Open a new word processing document and create a table listing each virus threat, a description of what each virus does, how widely it is distributed (the Wild value), and how damaging it is (the Damage Level value).

d. In your browser, go to the Security Advisor on CA's Web site at **www3.ca.com/securityadvisor**, and then click the Virus Information Center link. If any of the first five latest virus threats are different from the ones on the Symantec site, add them to your table. (*Hint*: After you click a virus name, check the "Also known as" list.)

e. For any viruses that are already in your table because they were on the Symantec site, read the CA description to see if there is any additional information describing how the virus could damage your system. Add this information to your table.

f. Save the word processing document as **Latest Threats** to the drive and folder where you store your Data Files.

▼ INDEPENDENT CHALLENGE 3

This Independent Challenge requires an Internet connection. One of the keyboards shown in this unit is an ergonomic keyboard. Ergonomics is the study of the design of a workspace so that the worker can work efficiently and avoid injury. The U.S. Occupational Safety and Health Administration (OSHA) has developed guidelines that describe a healthy computer work environment. Research these guidelines and evaluate your workspace.

a. Start your browser, and then go to **www.osha.gov/SLTC/etools/computerworkstations**.

b. Read the information on the main page. Follow links to descriptions of the best arrangement for equipment you use when working on a computer. (*Hint*: Look for the Workstation Components link, and point to it to open a submenu of links.)

c. Locate and print the checklist for evaluating your workspace. (*Hint*: Click the Checklist link, then click the View/Print the Evaluation Checklist PDF link. A new tab or window opens and the checklist opens in Adobe Acrobat Reader, a program that displays PDF files. If a dialog box opens telling you that you need to install Acrobat Reader to continue, ask your instructor or technical support person for help.)

d. Using the checklist, evaluate each of the conditions listed. If a condition does not apply to you, write N/A (not applicable) in the Yes column.

▼ INDEPENDENT CHALLENGE 3 (CONTINUED)

Advanced Challenge Exercise

- Use the OSHA Web site or a search engine to research repetitive motion injuries to which computer users are susceptible.
- Evaluate your risk for at least three common injuries.
- On the OSHA checklist, note what injury or injuries each applicable item or behavior will help prevent.

▼ REAL LIFE INDEPENDENT CHALLENGE

You are buying a new desktop computer. You want the computer to run Windows Vista and Microsoft Office 2007, and you want to make sure you are protected against security threats. You would like a large flat panel monitor and you need a printer. However, you have a limited budget, and can spend no more than $800 for everything (all hardware and software).

a. To help you organize your information, create the table shown in Figure A-28.

FIGURE A-28

	Your Requirements	Computer Retailer #1	Computer Retailer #2	Computer Retailer #3
Windows Vista (Edition)				
Office 2007 (Edition)				
Brand of computer				
Processor (brand and speed)				
RAM (amount)				
Video RAM (amount)				
Hard disk (size)				
Monitor (type and size)				
Printer (type and speed)				
Speakers				
Antivirus software				
Firewall (software or router with built-in firewall)				
System price				
Additional costs				
Total price				

b. Decide which edition of Windows Vista you want, Windows Vista Home Basic, Windows Vista Home Premium, Windows Vista Business, or Windows Vista Ultimate, and enter it in the Your Requirements column of the table. To read a description of the available editions, go to www.microsoft.com and search the Microsoft Web site for information about the Windows Vista Editions.

c. Research the hardware requirements for running the edition of Windows Vista you selected. Search the Microsoft Web site again for the minimum and recommended hardware requirements for running Windows Vista.

d. Decide which edition of Office 2007 you want and enter it in the first column of the table. Search the Microsoft Web site to find a description of the software included with each edition of Office 2007, and then search for the hardware requirements for running the edition of Office 2007 that you chose. If necessary, change the hardware requirements in the table.

e. Research the cost of your new computer system. To begin, visit local stores, look at advertisements, or search the Web for computer system retailers. Most computer retailers sell complete systems that come with all the necessary hardware, an operating system, and additional software already installed. In the Computer Retailer #1 column of the table, fill in the specifications for the system you chose. If any item listed as a minimum requirement is not included with the system you chose, find the cost of adding that item and enter the price in the table. Repeat this process with systems from two other retailers, entering the specifications in the Computer Retailer #2 and Computer Retailer #3 columns.

f. If the system you chose does not come with a printer, search the Web for an inexpensive color inkjet printer.

g. If the system you chose does not come with antivirus software, search the Web for the cost, if any, of an antivirus software package. Make sure you look up reviews of the package you chose. Decide whether to purchase this software or download a free one, and enter this cost in the table.

h. If you decide you need a router with a built-in firewall, search the Web for the price of one. Enter this information in the table.

i. Total the costs you entered in the table for the various items. Is the total cost $800 or less? If not, revisit some of the items. Can you get a less expensive printer? Do you need to downgrade to a less expensive monitor? Likewise, if you are under budget, upgrade a part of your system. For example, if the system you chose meets only the minimum requirements for running Windows Vista, see if you can afford a system that will be able to run Windows Vista with all of its features. Or perhaps you can afford to upgrade the monitor to a larger, flat panel monitor. Reevaluate your choices if necessary and try to get your total cost close to $800.

j. Submit your completed table to your instructor.

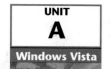

Getting Started with Windows Vista

Microsoft Windows Vista, or **Windows**, is an **operating system**—software that manages the complete operation of your computer. When you start a computer, Windows sets it up for use and then displays the **desktop**—a graphical user interface (GUI) that you use to interact with Windows and the other software on your computer. The Windows desktop displays **icons**, or small images, that represent items such as the Recycle Bin and Computer. When you open a program or document, Windows displays the program or document in a rectangular-shaped work area known as a **window**. Windows helps you organize **files** (collections of stored electronic data, such as text, pictures, video, music, and programs) in **folders** (containers for files) so that you can easily find them later. Windows also keeps all the computer hardware and software working together properly. As a new Oceania tour guide for Quest Specialty Travel (QST), you need to develop basic Windows skills to keep track of all the tour files on your company laptop computer.

OBJECTIVES

Start Windows Vista

Use a pointing device

Start a program

Move and resize windows

Use menus, toolbars, and
  keyboard shortcuts

Use dialog boxes

Use scroll bars

Use Windows Help and Support

End a Windows Vista session

Starting Windows Vista

When you start your computer, Windows steps through a process called **booting** to get the computer up and running. During this time, you might need to select your user account and enter your password. This information identifies you to Windows as an authorized user of the computer and helps keep your computer secure. After booting is complete, Windows displays the Windows desktop. The desktop, shown in Figure A-1, provides a way for you to interact with Windows Vista and to access its tools. The desktop appears with preset, or **default**, settings; however, you can change these settings to suit your needs. The image that fills the desktop background is called **wallpaper**. The desktop contains an icon for the Recycle Bin, which stores deleted files and folders. The desktop also displays **gadgets** (mini-programs for performing everyday tasks, such as a Clock) on the **Sidebar**. The **taskbar**, the horizontal bar at the bottom of the screen, displays information about open programs, folders, and files. You click the **Start button** on the left side of the taskbar to start programs, find and open files, access Windows Help and Support, and more. The **Quick Launch toolbar**, located on the taskbar, includes buttons for showing the desktop when it is not currently visible, switching between windows (the work areas for open programs), and starting the Internet Explorer Web browser. Table A-1 identifies the default icons and elements found on a desktop. 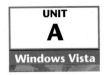 Your supervisor, Nancy McDonald, Oceania's tour developer, asks you to become familiar with Windows Vista and its features before your upcoming tour.

STEPS

1. **If your computer and monitor are turned off, press the** Power button **on the front of the system unit, then press the** Power button **on the monitor**

   After your computer starts, you see either a **Welcome screen** with icons for each user account on the computer or the Windows desktop. If you see the Welcome screen, continue with Step 2. If you see the Windows desktop, compare it to the one shown in Figure A-1, then continue with Step 4.

2. **If necessary, click the icon for your user account**

   If you use a password with your user account, Windows prompts you for the password. If not, continue with Step 4.

3. **If prompted for a password, type your password in the Password box, then click the** Next button

   After Windows verifies your password, you see the Windows desktop. See Figure A-1. Your Windows desktop may look slightly different.

> **TROUBLE**
>
> If you don't know your password, ask your instructor or technical support person. If you don't use a password, leave the Password box empty and click the Next button

4. **If the Welcome Center opens, click the** Close button ⊠ **in the upper-right corner of the Welcome Center window**

TABLE A-1: Common desktop components

desktop element	icon	allows you to
Recycle Bin	🗑	Store folders and files you delete from your hard drive(s) and restore them
Windows Sidebar (or Sidebar)		View the current time on a clock, view a slide show, and more
Taskbar		Switch between open programs, folders, and files; and resize windows
Notification area		Check the time, adjust the volume of your speakers, connect to the Internet, check problems identified by Windows Vista, and more
Quick Launch toolbar		Show the desktop, switch between windows, and open the Internet Explorer Web browser
Start button	⊞	Start programs, search for files, open documents, view pictures, listen to music, play games, get help, and more

FIGURE A-1: Windows Vista desktop

Icon

Wallpaper (background image)

Quick Launch toolbar

Start button

Gadgets on the Sidebar

Taskbar

Notification area

Using Windows Vista with Aero

Some editions of Windows Vista support **Windows Aero**, a new graphical user-interface feature that enhances the transparency (referred to as **translucency**) of the Start menu, taskbar, windows, and dialog boxes, as shown in Figure A-2. These transparency features also enable you to locate content by seeing through one window to the next window. **Windows Flip** allows you to display a set of thumbnails or miniature images of all open windows. **Windows Flip 3D** allows you to display stacked windows at a three-dimensional angle to see even more of the content of all open windows. Likewise, **live taskbar thumbnails** display the content within open, but not visible, windows, including live content such as video. These features provide three different ways to quickly view, locate, and select windows with the content you need. To view these effects, your version of Windows Vista and your computer's hardware must support the use of Windows Aero.

FIGURE A-2: Windows Aero features

Translucent Start menu

Translucent window frame and borders

Live thumbnail

Live taskbar thumbnail for a minimized window

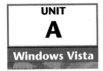

Using a Pointing Device

The most common way to interact with your computer and the software you are using is with a **pointing device**, such as a mouse, trackball, touch pad, or pointing stick, as shown in Figure A-3. If touch input is available on your computer, you can also use an onscreen **touch pointer** to perform pointing operations with a finger. As you move your pointing device, a small arrow or other symbol on the screen, called a **pointer**, moves in the same direction. Table A-2 illustrates common pointer shapes and their functions. You press the left and right buttons on the pointing device to select and move objects (such as icons and desktop windows); open programs, windows, folders, and files; and select options for performing specific tasks, such as saving your work. Table A-3 lists the five basic ways in which you can use a pointing device. Pointing devices can work with your computer through a cable or through a wireless connection that transmits data using radio waves. You'll practice using your pointing device so you can work more efficiently.

STEPS

1. **Locate the pointer on the desktop, then move your pointing device**

    The pointer moves across the Windows desktop in the same direction as you move your pointing device.

2. **Move the pointer so the tip is directly over the Recycle Bin icon**

    Positioning the pointer over an item is called **pointing**. The Recycle Bin icon is highlighted and a **ToolTip**, or label, identifies its purpose.

3. **With the pointer over, press and release the left button on your pointing device**

    Pressing and releasing the left button, called **clicking** or **single-clicking**, selects an icon on the desktop or in a window and selects options and objects within a program. In this case, the Recycle Bin icon is selected.

4. **With still selected, press and hold down the left button on your pointing device, move your pointing device to another location on the desktop, then release the left button**

    A copy of the Recycle Bin icon moves with the pointer. When you release the left button on your pointing device, the Recycle Bin is placed on the desktop in a different location. You use this technique, called **dragging**, to move icons and windows.

5. **Drag back to its original desktop location**

6. **Position the pointer over, then press and release the right button on your pointing device**

    This action, called **right-clicking**, opens a shortcut menu, as shown in Figure A-4. A **shortcut menu** lists common commands for an object. A **command** is an instruction to perform a task, such as renaming an object. If a command is dimmed, such as "Empty Recycle Bin," it is not currently available for you to use.

7. **Click the desktop background**

    The shortcut menu closes and Windows selects the desktop background.

8. **Point to, then quickly press the left button on your pointing device twice and release it**

    Quickly clicking the left button twice is called **double-clicking**, which opens a window or a program. In this case, the Recycle Bin window opens to display any folders and files deleted from the hard disk.

9. **Click the Close button in the upper-right corner of the Recycle Bin window**

    The Recycle Bin window closes. Every window has a Close button; clicking it is the fastest way to close a window.

FIGURE A-3: Common pointing devices

Mouse

Trackball

Touch pointer

Touchpad

Pointing stick

FIGURE A-4: Shortcut menu

Selected object

Dimmed command is unavailable

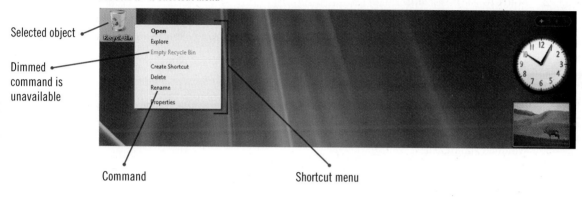

Command

Shortcut menu

TABLE A-2: Common pointer shapes

shape	name	description
	Normal Select	Points to an object and chooses a command
	Busy	Indicates that Windows or another program is busy and you must wait before continuing
	Working in Background	Indicates that Windows or another program is busy and the computer's response time is slower, but you can still perform other operations
	Text Select (also called I-Beam)	Identifies where you can type, select, insert, or edit text
	Link Select	Identifies a link you can click to jump to another location, such as a Help topic or a Web site

TABLE A-3: Basic pointing device techniques

technique	what to do
Pointing	Move the pointing device to position the tip of the pointer over an object, option, or item
Clicking	Quickly press and release the left button
Double-clicking	Quickly press and release the left button twice
Dragging	Point to an object, press and hold the left button, move the object to a new location, then release the left button
Right-clicking	Point to an object, then quickly press and release the right button

Starting a Program

From the Start menu, you can open programs or software products on your computer. In addition to other software that you purchase and install on the computer, Windows Vista includes a variety of programs, such as Windows Calendar, Windows Mail, Windows Movie Maker, and Windows Photo Gallery. Windows also comes with **accessories**, which are simple programs to perform specific tasks, such as the Windows Calculator accessory for performing quick calculations. Table A-4 describes the organization of the Start menu. ▓▓▓ Because you need to develop QST tour proposals and brochures with photographs of exotic Pacific islands, you want to try the Windows Photo Gallery.

STEPS

QUICK TIP
You can also press the Windows logo key to open or close the Start menu.

1. **Click the Start button** ⊕ **on the taskbar**

   The Start menu opens, as shown in Figure A-5. From the left pane, you can start programs installed on your computer. From the right pane, you can open specific folders, open Windows tools, change Windows settings, get Help and Support, and shut down Windows. Some of the options on your Start menu will differ.

2. **Point to** All Programs

   The All Programs menu opens in the left pane, with an alphabetical listing of the programs installed on your computer followed by groups of related programs, such as Accessories. See Figure A-6. Your list of programs will differ.

TROUBLE
If you see an Info Pane on the right side of the window, close it by clicking the Hide Info Pane button.

3. **Click** Windows Photo Gallery **on the All Programs menu**

   The Windows Photo Gallery window opens, displaying thumbnails of images in the Sample Pictures folder on your computer. See Figure A-7. A **thumbnail** is a smaller image of the actual contents of a file that contains a picture. Windows also displays a Windows Photo Gallery button on the taskbar for the now open Windows Photo Gallery.

4. **Leave the Photo Gallery window open for the next lesson**

TABLE A-4: Start menu components

component	description
Pinned Items List	Contains the two programs commonly used for a Web browser and e-mail: Internet Explorer and a version of Microsoft Outlook; you can change these two programs and you can add other programs to this list
Recently-opened Programs List	Lists programs you have recently opened so you can quickly return to them.
All Programs	Displays a list of programs installed on your computer
Search Box	Quickly locates programs, folders, and files, and shows the search results in the left pane of the Start menu
User Folders	Provides quick access to your Documents, Pictures, Music, and Games folders, plus the folder for your user account (your username at the top of the right pane)
Windows Tools	Search quickly locates programs, folders, and files Recent Items displays the names of up to 15 files you recently opened Computer opens a Windows Explorer window and shows the drives and other hardware on your computer Network provides access to computers and other hardware on your network Connect To shows your Internet and network connections
Settings & Help	Control Panel provides tools for viewing and changing Windows settings and installing hardware and software Default Programs lets you specify the programs and program settings you prefer to use Help and Support opens the Windows Help and Support Center to provide you with assistance and Help information
Power & Lock Buttons	Power button puts your computer to sleep (your computer appears off and uses very little power) Lock button locks your computer (a security measure for when you are not using the computer), and displays shut-down options

FIGURE A-5: Start menu

Pinned items list

Recently-opened programs

Power, Lock, and Lock menu buttons

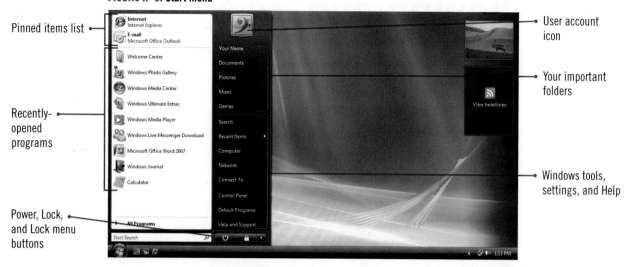

User account icon

Your important folders

Windows tools, settings, and Help

FIGURE A-6: All Programs menu

Installed programs (your list will differ)

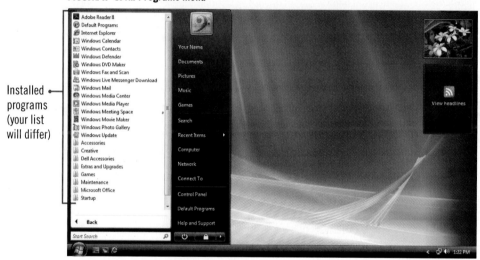

FIGURE A-7: Windows Photo Gallery window

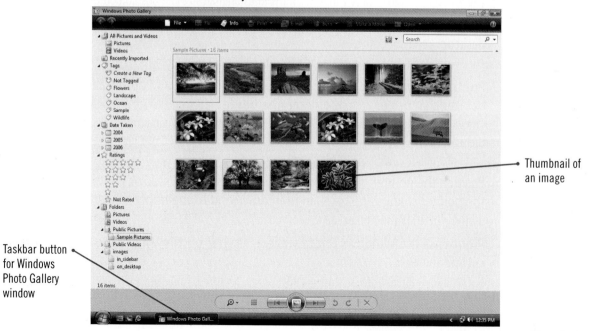

Thumbnail of an image

Taskbar button for Windows Photo Gallery window

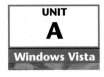

Moving and Resizing Windows

Each program you start opens in its own window. As you work, you will invariably need to move and resize windows so that you can see more of one window or view two or more windows at the same time. To resize a window, you use the **resizing buttons**—Maximize 🔲, Restore Down 🗗, and Minimize 🔲 —in the upper-right corner of the window. To adjust a window's height or width (or both), you drag a window border or window corner. To move a window, you drag its **title bar**—the area across the top of the window that displays the window name or program name. If you open more than one program at once, you are **multitasking**—performing several tasks at the same time—and each program appears in a different window. The **active window** is the window you are currently using. An **inactive window** is another open window that you are not currently using. ▓▓▓▓ As you examine photos for a new tour brochure, you need to move and resize the Windows Photo Gallery window.

STEPS

QUICK TIP
You can also maximize or restore down a window by double-clicking its title bar.

1. **If the Windows Photo Gallery window does not fill the desktop, click the Maximize button 🔲 in the upper-right corner of the Windows Photo Gallery window**

   The Windows Photo Gallery window is maximized. A **maximized window** fills your desktop and you cannot see its borders. After you maximize a window, the Maximize button changes to a Restore Down button.

2. **Click the Restore Down button 🗗 in the upper-right corner of the Windows Photo Gallery window**

   The Windows Photo Gallery window returns to its previous size and position on the desktop. The window borders are visible, and the Restore Down button changes to a Maximize button.

3. **Click the Minimize button 🔲 in the upper-right corner of the Windows Photo Gallery window**

   The Windows Photo Gallery window is still open, just not visible. See Figure A-8. A **minimized window** shrinks to a button on the taskbar. You can use this feature to hide a window that you are not currently using, but may use later.

4. **Click the Windows Photo Gallery taskbar button**

   The Windows Photo Gallery window returns to its original size and position on the desktop.

5. **Drag the title bar on the Windows Photo Gallery window to the upper-left corner of the desktop**

   The Windows Photo Gallery window is repositioned on the desktop.

6. **Position the pointer on the right border of the Windows Photo Gallery window until the pointer changes to ⟷, then drag the border left**

   The width of the Windows Photo Gallery window narrows. See Figure A-9. To widen the window, you drag the right window border to the right. To decrease or increase a window's height, you drag the bottom border up or down.

7. **Position the pointer on the lower-right corner of the Windows Photo Gallery window until the pointer changes to ⬉, then drag down and to the right**

   Both the height and width of the window change.

8. **Right-click the Windows Photo Gallery taskbar button, then click Close on the shortcut menu**

   The Windows Photo Gallery window closes.

FIGURE A-8: Minimized window

Windows Photo Gallery
is open, but not visible

FIGURE A-9: Restored down window being resized

Title bar

Close button

Maximize
button

Minimize
button

Side border
adjusts the
window's
width

Corner
adjusts the
window's
height and
width

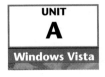

Using Menus, Toolbars, and Keyboard Shortcuts

A **menu** displays a list of commands you use to accomplish a task. Menus organize commands into groups of related tasks. In some program windows, you open menus from a **menu bar** located below the window's title bar. At other times, you open menus from a **toolbar**, a set of buttons you can click to open menus or select common commands that may also be available from a menu bar. Some menu commands and toolbar buttons have a **keyboard shortcut**, which is a key or a combination of keys that you press to perform a command. ▰▰▰ As you prepare for your first tour, Nancy recommends that you examine the Slide Show gadget and the Windows Photo Gallery.

TROUBLE

If you don't see the Sidebar, click the Start button, point to All Programs, click Accessories, then click Windows Sidebar. If you still don't see the Sidebar, click the Windows Sidebar icon in the taskbar Notification area.

1. **Point to the Slide Show gadget on the Sidebar, resting the pointer on the displayed image**

   The Slide Show toolbar appears at the bottom of the slide show image, and the Slide Show gadget toolbar appears to the right of the Slide Show gadget. See Figure A-10. The left border of the Sidebar is now visible.

2. **Click the View button 🖼 on the Slide Show toolbar**

   The Windows Photo Gallery window opens and displays an enlarged view of the image displayed in the Slide Show gadget. The title bar identifies the filename of the image and the name of the open program. A toolbar appears below the title bar, with options for working with the image.

3. **Click the File button 🗋 File ▾ on the toolbar**

   The File menu lists commands related to working with the files. See Figure A-11. A keyboard shortcut appears to the right of some commands.

4. **Click Exit**

   The Windows Photo Gallery window closes.

5. **Point to the Slide Show gadget on the Sidebar, then click 🖼 on the Slide Show toolbar**

   The Photo Gallery Viewer window opens again.

6. **Click the Play Slide Show button 🔘 on the Slide Show toolbar at the bottom of the window**

   Windows Photo Gallery displays a full-screen slide show of each image in your Sample Pictures folder, one at a time.

QUICK TIP

"Esc," an abbreviation for "Escape," is a standard keyboard shortcut for canceling an operation or backing up a step.

7. **Press [Esc]**

   The slide show stops and you return to the Windows Photo Gallery window.

8. **Press and hold [Alt], press and release [F4], then release [Alt]**

   The Windows Photo Gallery window closes. The keyboard shortcut [Alt][F4] closes any active window.

FIGURE A-10: Windows Sidebar

Add Gadget button

Slide Show gadget

View button

FIGURE A-11: File menu

File button

Commands on File menu

Play Slide Show button

Toolbar

Keyboard shortcut

Dimmed command is unavilable

Exit command

Using keyboard shortcuts

Keyboard shortcuts allow you to work more quickly and efficiently because you can keep your hands on the keyboard rather than moving between the keyboard and your pointing device. Many programs use the same keyboard shortcuts for common operations, such as [Ctrl][O] for opening a file and [Ctrl][S] for saving a file. Taking the time to learn the keyboard shortcuts for the actions you perform frequently will improve your productivity. Keyboard shortcuts are shown on menus with a plus sign separating the keys you need to press at the same time, such as Ctrl+S for saving a file. Remember, you do not press the plus sign when you use a keyboard shortcut

Using Dialog Boxes

When you select a command from a menu or toolbar, the program may perform the operation immediately. Or, it may open a **dialog box**, a type of window in which you specify how you want to complete the operation. Although dialog boxes are similar to a window, they do not contain Maximize, Minimize, and Restore Down buttons, and you usually cannot resize a dialog box. Figure A-12 shows a Print dialog box with two **tabs**—General and Options—that separate groups of settings into related categories. Dialog boxes provide different ways to select options. Table A-5 lists common types of options found in dialog boxes. ▨▨▨▨ You want to review the Sidebar default settings to determine whether they meet your needs while you work.

STEPS

1. **Right-click the background of the Sidebar under the last gadget, then click Properties**

   The Windows Sidebar Properties dialog box opens, as shown in Figure A-13. **Properties** are characteristics or settings of a component of the graphical user interface. The first setting in the dialog box is a check box for starting the Sidebar whenever Windows starts. A **check box** turns an option on (checked) or off (unchecked). You click the check box to change the option's status. As you can see from the check mark in the Start Sidebar when Windows starts check box, it is already turned on.

2. **Click the Sidebar is always on top of other windows check box**

   A check mark is added to the check box, which sets the Sidebar to remain visible when you open a window.

3. **In the Arrangement section, click the Left option button**

   You click one **option button** to select from several options. In this case, you clicked the option button to display the Sidebar on the left side of the desktop. You can select only one option button for a setting. The "Display Sidebar on monitor" button is a **drop-down list button** that you click to open a list that shows one or more options to choose. The **link** at the bottom of the Maintenance section opens a Help topic about how to customize the Sidebar. At the bottom of the dialog box are **command buttons**, which you click to complete or cancel any changes you make in the dialog box. Clicking OK closes the dialog box and applies the settings you selected. Clicking Apply applies the settings you selected, but keeps the dialog box open for additional changes. Clicking Cancel leaves the settings unchanged and closes the dialog box.

QUICK TIP
In a dialog box, pressing [Enter] is the same as clicking OK; pressing [Esc] is the same as clicking Cancel.

4. **Click Cancel**

   The dialog box closes without changing any of the settings for the Sidebar.

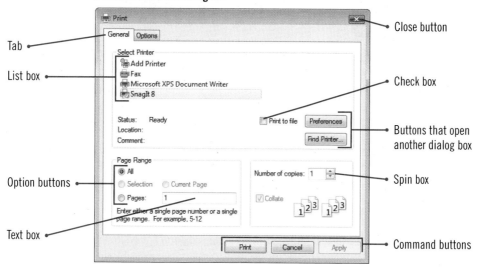

FIGURE A-12: Print dialog box

Tab • ·········· General | Options
Close button • ·········· Close button
List box • ·········· Select Printer
Check box • ·········· Print to file
Buttons that open another dialog box • ·········· Preferences / Find Printer...
Option buttons • ·········· Page Range
Spin box • ·········· Number of copies
Text box • ·········· Pages
Command buttons • ·········· Print / Cancel / Apply

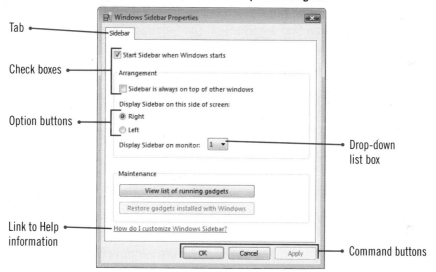

FIGURE A-13: Windows Sidebar Properties dialog box

Tab • ·········· Sidebar
Check boxes • ·········· Start Sidebar when Windows starts
Option buttons • ·········· Right / Left
Drop-down list box • ·········· Display Sidebar on monitor
Link to Help information • ·········· How do I customize Windows Sidebar?
Command buttons • ·········· OK / Cancel / Apply

TABLE A-5: Typical elements in a dialog box

element	description
Check box	A box that turns an option on when checked or off when unchecked
Collapse button	A button that shrinks a portion of a dialog box to hide some settings
Command button	A button that completes or cancels an operation
Drop-down list button	A button that displays a list of options from which you can choose
Expand button	A button that extends a dialog box to display additional settings
Link	A shortcut for opening a Help topic or a Web site
List box	A box that displays a list of options from which you can choose (you may need to adjust your view to see additional options in the list)
Option button	A small circle you click to select only one of two or more related options
Slider	A shape you drag along a bar to select a setting that falls within a range, such as between Slow and Fast
Spin box	A text box with up and down arrows; you can type a setting in the text box or click the arrows to increase or decrease a setting
Text box	A box in which you type text (such as a password)

Using Scroll Bars

When you cannot see all of the items available in a window, list box, or drop-down list box, you must **scroll**, or adjust your view. Scrolling is similar to taking a picture with a camera. You move the camera to select a view of a landscape in front of you. If you move the camera to the right or left or up or down, you see a different part of that same landscape. When a window on your computer contains more items than it can display at once, scroll bars appear so you can adjust your view in the window. **Scroll bars** are vertical and horizontal bars that appear along the right and bottom sides of a window when there is more content than can be displayed within the window. At each end of a scroll bar are **scroll arrow buttons** for shifting your view in small increments in either direction. Within each scroll bar is a **scroll box** you can drag to display a different part of a window. You can also click in a scroll bar on either side of the scroll box to shift your view in larger increments. Instead of using a pointing device to scroll, you can also use keyboard shortcuts to scroll, which can be faster. Table A-6 summarizes different ways to scroll. For each QST tour, you work with a large variety of files. To locate your files, and to view different pages within each file, you use scroll bars. You will practice scrolling using a Windows Vista accessory called Paint—a graphics program.

STEPS

1. **Point to the Slide Show gadget on the Sidebar, then click the View button on the Slide Show toolbar**

   An image from your Sample Pictures folder appears in the Windows Photo Gallery window.

2. **Click the Open button on the toolbar, then click Paint**

   The image opens in a Paint window for editing. Paint is one of the Windows Vista accessories.

TROUBLE

If you don't see scroll bars, drag the lower-right corner of the Paint window up and to the left until both scroll bars appear.

3. **If the Paint window fills the desktop, then click its Restore Down button**

   Because of the large size of the image, you can see only a portion of it within the window. However, Paint displays scroll bars on the right and bottom of the window so you can adjust your view. See Figure A-14. Your image and view may differ.

4. **Click the down scroll arrow in the vertical scroll bar**

   The window scrolls down to show another part of the image, and part of the image has now scrolled out of view.

5. **Drag the vertical scroll box slowly down the window to the bottom of the vertical scroll bar**

   The window view changes in larger increments, and the bottom part of the image is visible at the bottom of the window.

6. **Click the vertical scroll bar between the scroll box and the up scroll arrow**

   The view moves up approximately the height of one window.

7. **Click the right scroll arrow in the horizontal scroll bar three times**

   The window keeps scrolling right to show other views onto the image.

TROUBLE

If a dialog box opens asking if you want to save changes to the image, click Don't Save.

8. **Click the Close button on the Paint title bar**

   The Paint window closes.

9. **Click on the Windows Photo Gallery title bar**

   The Windows Photo Gallery window closes.

FIGURE A-14: Scroll bars

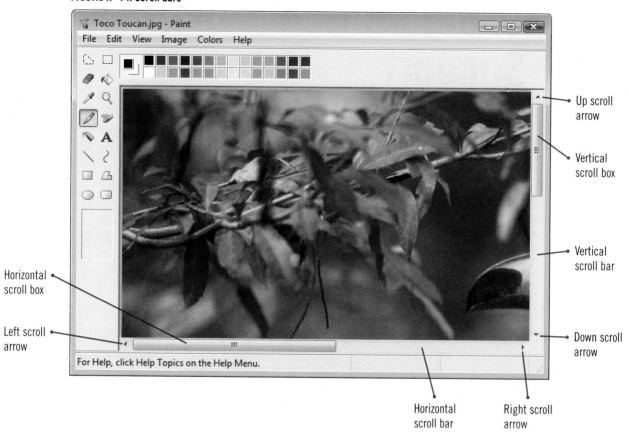

Up scroll arrow

Vertical scroll box

Vertical scroll bar

Down scroll arrow

Horizontal scroll box

Left scroll arrow

Horizontal scroll bar

Right scroll arrow

TABLE A-6: Using scroll bars

to	do this with the mouse
Move down a small increment or one line	Click the down scroll arrow at the bottom of the vertical scroll bar
Move up a small increment or one line	Click the up scroll arrow at the top of the vertical scroll bar
Move down about one window's height	Click between the scroll box and the down scroll arrow in the vertical scroll bar
Move up about one window's height	Click between the scroll box and the up scroll arrow in the vertical scroll bar
Move up a large distance	Drag the scroll box up the vertical scroll bar
Move down a large distance	Drag the scroll box down the vertical scroll bar
Move left or right a small distance	Click the left or the right scroll arrow in the horizontal scroll bar
Move to the left or right one window's width	Click between the scroll box and the left or right scroll arrow in the horizontal scroll bar
Move left or right a large distance	Drag the scroll box in the horizontal scroll bar to the left or right

Using Windows Help and Support

When you need assistance or more information about how to use Windows, you can use Help and Support. After you open Help and Support, you can browse Help by first selecting a general category, such as "Windows Basics," then a narrower category, such as "Desktop fundamentals," and finally a specific Help topic, such as "The desktop (overview)." Or, you can select a topic from a table of contents. You can also search Help and Support using one or more descriptive words called **keywords**, such as "Windows Sidebar gadgets," to obtain a list of search results for all the Help topics that include the word or phrase. In certain places within Help and Support, you can use Windows Media Player to watch video clips called Windows Vista demos that provide an overview of Windows features and how to use them. ▚▚▚▚ Because you often use the Sidebar and Windows Photo Gallery as a tour guide, you decide to review the information in Windows Help and Support on these two Windows features.

STEPS

TROUBLE

If the Help and Support dialog box opens, asking you if you want to get the latest online content, click No. If a warning appears that you have lost your connection to the Windows Help and Support Web site, you are not connected to the Internet. Continue with the remaining steps.

1. **Click the Start button ⊕ on the taskbar, click Help and Support, then click the Maximize button ▭ if the window doesn't fill the desktop**

   The Windows Help and Support window opens and fills the desktop. Figure A-15 identifies the various types of Help options. Table A-7 explains the purpose of the buttons on the Help toolbar in the upper-right corner of the window.

2. **Under Find an answer, click the Windows Basics icon**

   Windows Help and Support displays categories of Help topics about basic Windows features.

3. **Under Desktop fundamentals, click Windows Sidebar and gadgets (overview)**

   The Windows Sidebar and gadgets (overview) Help topic explains what the Sidebar is, how it works, why you would use it, and how to work with gadgets—including adding, removing, and organizing gadgets.

4. **Click in the Search Help text box, type edit my digital photos, then click the Search Help button 🔍**

   A list of search results appears for the keywords you specified. As shown in Figure A-16, the 30 best results for editing digital photos are listed.

QUICK TIP

If you click a topic under "In this article," the window automatically scrolls to that topic.

5. **Click Working with digital pictures in the list of Help topics**

   This Help topic explains how to get pictures from a camera into your computer—just what you need as a tour guide.

6. **In the second paragraph, click flash memory card (shown in green)**

   The definition of a flash memory card and how you can use this device appears.

7. **Click the Close button ❎ in the upper-right corner of the Windows Help and Support window**

   The Windows Help and Support window closes.

Using Windows Online Help

Windows Vista Help and Support provides answers on how to use basic and advanced Windows Vista features. You can get additional help from the Microsoft Windows Help and How-to Web site. On this Web site, you can find more information about basic and advanced Windows Vista features, view "how-to" videos, get help from other people in Windows Vista online discussion groups, read up-to-date articles on changes in Windows Vista, and get online support from Microsoft technical support staff. To open the Windows Online Help and Support Home page, click Windows Online Help in the Find an answer section of the Windows Help and Support window.

FIGURE A-15: Windows Help and Support window

Back button

Forward button

Help category

Home button

Options button

Ask button

Browse Help button

Print button

Online Help

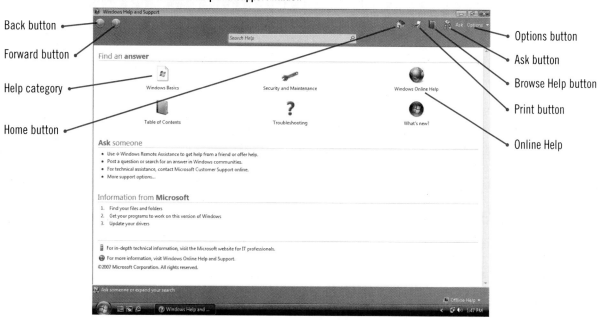

FIGURE A-16: Search results

Search keywords

Search results

Search Help button

Search Help text box

TABLE A-7: Windows Help and Support toolbar buttons

button icon	button name	purpose
	Back	Takes you back to previous Help topic(s)
	Forward	Returns you to Help topic(s) you just left (available only after you click the Back button)
	Home	Opens the Help and Support starting page
	Print	Prints a Help topic
	Browse Help	Displays a list of Help topics to browse
	Ask	Provides additional resources and tools for finding Help information
	Options	Lists options for printing, browsing Help, adjusting the Help text size, searching a Help topic page, and changing Help settings

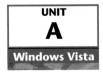

Ending a Windows Vista Session

When you finish working on your computer, you should save and close any open files, close any open programs, close any open windows, and shut down Windows. As shown in Table A-8, there are various options for ending your Windows sessions. Whichever option you choose, it's important to shut down your computer in an orderly manner. If you turn off the computer while Windows Vista is running, you could lose data or damage Windows Vista and your computer. If you are working in a computer lab, follow your instructor's directions and your lab's policies and guidelines for ending your Windows session. You have examined the basic ways in which you can use Windows Vista, so you are ready to end your Windows Vista session.

STEPS

1. **Click the Start button ⊞ on the taskbar**

   The Start menu has three buttons for ending a Windows session—the Power button, the Lock button, and the Lock menu button.

   QUICK TIP
   Some keyboards have Log Off and Sleep keys that you can press to perform these operations.

2. **Point to the Lock menu button ▶**

   The Lock menu lists all the shut-down options. See Figure A-17.

3. **If you are working in a computer lab, follow the instructions provided by your instructor or technical support person for ending your Windows Vista session; if you are working on your own computer, click Shut Down or the option you prefer for ending your Windows Vista session**

   After you shut down your computer, you may also need to turn off your monitor and other hardware devices, such as a printer, to conserve energy.

FIGURE A-17: Shut down Windows Vista options

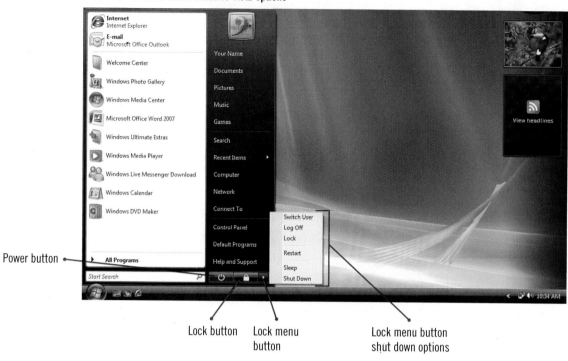

Power button

Lock button   Lock menu button

Lock menu button shut down options

TABLE A-8: Options for ending a Windows Vista session

option	description	click
Shut Down	Completely shuts down your computer.	Start button, Lock menu button, Shut Down
Log Off	Closes all windows, programs, and documents, then displays the Welcome screen.	Start button, Lock menu button, Log Off
Restart	Shuts down your computer, then restarts it.	Start button, Lock menu button, Restart
Switch User	Locks your user account and displays the Welcome screen so another user can log on.	Start button, Lock menu button, Switch User
Lock	Locks your user account, then displays the Welcome screen.	Start button, Lock button, OR Start button, Lock menu button, Lock
Sleep	Saves your work, turns off the monitor, then reduces power consumption to all hardware components in your computer so it appears off.	Start button, Power button, OR Start button, Lock menu button, Sleep
Hibernate	Saves your work, then turns off your computer.	Start button, Lock menu button, Hibernate

Practice

If you have a SAM user profile, you may have access to hands-on instruction, practice, and assessment of the skills covered in this unit. Log in to your SAM account (http://sam2007.course.com/) to launch any assigned training activities or exams that relate to the skills covered in this unit.

▼ CONCEPTS REVIEW

Identify each of the items labeled in Figure A-18.

FIGURE A-18

Match each statement with the term it describes.

12. A desktop object that displays buttons for open programs and windows
13. A desktop object that represents a program or Windows tool
14. A type of window that opens after you select a menu command so you can specify settings for completing the operation
15. A Windows component for adjusting your view within a window
16. The workspace within which you work with a program

a. dialog box
b. taskbar
c. scroll bar
d. window
e. icon

Select the best answer from the list of choices.

17. Operating system software is software that:
   a. Interferes with your use of a computer.
   b. Manages the operation of a computer.
   c. Performs a single task, such as connecting to the Internet.
   d. Creates documents, such as a resume.

18. When you right-click a pointing device such as a mouse, Windows:
   a. Opens a Windows tool or program.
   b. Moves an object, such as a desktop icon.
   c. Opens a shortcut menu.
   d. Deletes the object.

19. What portion of a window displays the name of the program you opened?

  a. Title bar   **c.** Toolbar

  b. Menu bar   **d.** Scroll bar

20. You use the Maximize button to:

  a. Restore a window to its previous size and location.   **c.** Temporarily hide a window.

  b. Expand a window to fill the entire desktop.   **d.** Scroll through a window.

21. When you put a computer to sleep, Windows:

  a. Completely shuts down the computer.   **c.** Restarts your computer.

  b. Provides an option for switching users.   **d.** Reduces power to the computer and its hardware.

▼ SKILLS REVIEW

1. Start Windows Vista and view the desktop.

  a. Turn on your computer, select your user account or enter your user name, then enter your password (if necessary).

  b. Identify and list as many components of the Windows Vista desktop as you can without referring to the lessons.

  c. Compare your results to Figure A-1 to make sure that you have identified all the desktop objects and icons.

2. Use a pointing device.

  a. Point to the Recycle Bin icon and display its ToolTip.

  b. Double-click the Recycle Bin icon, then restore down the Recycle Bin window if it is maximized.

  c. Drag the Recycle Bin window to the upper-left corner of the desktop, then close the window.

3. Start a program.

  a. Open the Start menu.

  b. Display a list of all programs.

  c. Start Windows Calendar.

4. Move and resize windows.

  a. If the Windows Calendar window is maximized, restore down the window.

  b. Adjust the height and width of the window in one operation.

  c. Maximize, minimize, then restore the Windows Calendar window.

5. Use menus, toolbars, and keyboard shortcuts.

  a. Open the View menu on the menu bar, then choose Month to display a calendar for the current month.

  b. Use the View button on the toolbar to display a calendar for the current day.

  c. In the mini-calendar in the Navigation pane on the left, click the date for the next day to view its schedule.

  d. Use the keyboard shortcut [Alt][F4] to close Windows Calendar.

6. Use dialog boxes.

  a. If you do not see the Sidebar on the desktop, open the Start menu, display the All Programs menu, and then choose Windows Sidebar from the Accessories menu (or click the Windows Sidebar icon in the Notification area).

  b. Right-click the Clock gadget, then click Options to view settings for the Clock gadget.

  c. Under the preview of a clock, use the Next button to advance through the eight options for viewing the Clock.

  d. Use the Previous button to return to the first (default) view for the Clock gadget.

  e. Click the Cancel button to close the Clock dialog box without making any changes to the settings.

7. Use scroll bars.

  a. From the Start menu, open Windows Help and Support and maximize the window (if necessary).

  b. Open the Windows Basics Help topic.

  c. Use the down scroll arrow in the vertical scroll bar to examine other Help topics.

  d. Use the up scroll arrow in the vertical scroll bar to view previously displayed Help topics.

  e. Use the scroll box in the vertical scroll bar to view the last Windows Basics Help topic.

8. Use Windows Help and Support.

  a. Open "The Start menu (overview)" Help topic.

  b. Read the information about the Start menu in the first two paragraphs (through the bulleted list).

  c. Use the Search Help box to locate help on gadgets.

▼ SKILLS REVIEW (CONTINUED)

d. Open the Help topic entitled "Windows Sidebar and gadgets (overview)."

e. Under "In this article," click "Adding and removing gadgets" to jump to this Help topic.

f. Click "To add a gadget to Sidebar" (shown in blue) to view the steps for this process, then click the "To remove a gadget from Sidebar" (shown in blue) to view the single step for this process.

g. Close the Windows Help and Support window.

9. End a Windows Vista session.

a. If you are working in a computer lab, follow the instructions provided by your instructor for using the Start menu to log off the computer, restart the computer, put the computer to sleep, or shut down the computer completely. If you are working on your own computer, use the Start menu to choose the shut-down option you prefer.

▼ INDEPENDENT CHALLENGE 1

You work as a teacher for ABC Computer Mentors. You need to prepare a set of handouts that provide an overview of some of the new desktop features in Windows Vista for individuals enrolled in an upcoming class on Computer Survival Skills.

a. Open Windows Help and Support, then open the Windows Basics Help topic.

b. Open the **Using menus, buttons, bars, and boxes** Help topic under Desktop Fundamentals.

c. Use the vertical scroll bar to read the entire Help topic.

d. Prepare a handwritten list of 10 new features that you learned about working with menus, buttons, bars, and boxes. Use the following title for your list: **Using Menus, Buttons, Bars, and Boxes**

e. Close Windows Help and Support, write your name on your list, and submit it to your instructor.

▼ INDEPENDENT CHALLENGE 2

You are a freelance photographer who takes photographs for magazine covers, articles, newsletters, and Web sites. You want to evaluate how the Windows Photo Gallery can be used to make simple changes to digital photos.

a. Open Windows Help and Support and search for tips on editing pictures in Windows Photo Gallery.

b. After reading the Tips for editing pictures Help topic, prepare a handwritten summary with the title **Tips for Editing Pictures**, listing the recommended workflow for editing pictures in Windows Photo Gallery. (*Hint*: Use the first figure in the Help topic on the recommended workflow in Photo Gallery to identify the four steps.)

c. Use Windows Help and Support to search for information on how to remove red eye from a picture.

d. Add to your summary a short paragraph that describes red eye and how you can correct this problem with Windows Photo Gallery.

e. Close Windows Help and Support, write your name on your summary, and submit it to your instructor.

▼ INDEPENDENT CHALLENGE 3

As a marketing analyst for Expert AI Systems, Ltd., in Great Britain, you contact and collaborate with employees at an Australian branch of the company. Because your colleagues live in a different time zone, you want to add another clock to your Sidebar and customize it to show the time in Australia. This way, you can quickly determine when to reach these employees at a convenient time during their workday hours.

a. If Windows does not display the Sidebar on the desktop, use the All Programs menu or the Windows Sidebar icon in the Notification area to display the Sidebar.

b. Use Windows Help and Support to search for information on how to customize the Windows Sidebar and how to change an individual gadget's options.

c. Use this Help information to view the settings for the Clock gadget on the Sidebar, then try each setting.

d. Click Cancel to close the Clock dialog box without changing the settings.

▼ INDEPENDENT CHALLENGE 3 (CONTINUED)

Advanced Challenge Exercise

- Point to the Gadgets toolbar at the top of the Sidebar, then click the Add Gadget button.
- Double-click the Clock gadget in the Add Gadgets dialog box, then close the Add Gadgets dialog box.
- Drag the new copy of the Clock gadget and place it below the last gadget on the Sidebar.
- Right-click the new Clock gadget, then click Options on the shortcut menu to view settings for the new Clock.
- Choose a different view for the clock and, in the Clock name text box, type **Australia**.
- Click the Time Zone list arrow to display a list of different time zones, then click the time zone for Canberra, Melbourne, and Sydney. (*Hint:* You want the GMT+10:00 time zone near the bottom of the list of time zones.)
- Add a check mark to the "Show the second hand" check box to enable this feature.
- Click OK to close the Clock dialog box.
- Right-click the new Clock gadget, then click Close Gadget on the shortcut menu to restore your Sidebar to its original state.

e. Prepare a handwritten summary entitled **Using Clock Gadgets** that describes what settings you examined and how you might use them in your daily life.

f. Write your name on your summary and submit it to your instructor.

▼ REAL LIFE INDEPENDENT CHALLENGE

In preparation for an upcoming convention to present new products produced by your company, Continental Saunas, Inc., you decide to prepare a slide show using the Windows Photo Gallery.

a. Open Windows Help and Support, then search for Help information on viewing your pictures as a slide show.

b. Read the Help information, studying the features of the Slide Show Controls toolbar and slide show themes.

c. Open the Photo Gallery Viewer from the Slide Show gadget on the Sidebar.

d. Use the Play Slide Show button to view a slide show of the photos in your Pictures folder.

Advanced Challenge Exercise

Note: To view the Slide Show Controls toolbar as well as certain themes and transitions, your computer must have a graphics card capable of displaying these features and special effects.

- After the slide show starts, move your pointing device to display the Slide Show Controls toolbar.
- Use the Slide Show Controls toolbar to perform the following operations during the slide show. Note the default setting for specific buttons, which options you choose, and what they do so that you can prepare a short written summary for co-workers who might use the Windows Photo Gallery for slide shows.
- Use the Themes pop-up list button to select and view other themes (or presentation formats) for slide shows. Note the default theme, try at least three other themes, then restore the default theme.
- Use the Slide Show Settings button to change the slide show speed and examine the Shuffle and Loop options, then restore the default slide show speed and Shuffle or Loop option.
- Use the Previous and Next buttons to view the previous and next image.
- Use the Exit button to end the slide show.

e. Prepare a one-page handwritten summary titled **Photo Gallery Slide Show** that describes what you have learned about the Windows Photo Gallery and how you might use it in your daily life.

f. Write your name on the summary and submit it to your instructor.

After returning from a Quest Specialty Travel tour, you want to print a copy of a digital photo to promote an upcoming trip. Use the skills you have learned in this lesson to print a copy of a digital photo:

• Use Windows Help and Support to search for information on how to print a picture using Windows Photo Gallery.

• Use the Slide Show gadget to open the Windows Photo Gallery, then choose the option to print a 4 x 6 inch copy of the image on letter-size paper, as shown in Figure A-19.

• Write your name on the printed copy and submit it to your instructor.

FIGURE A-19

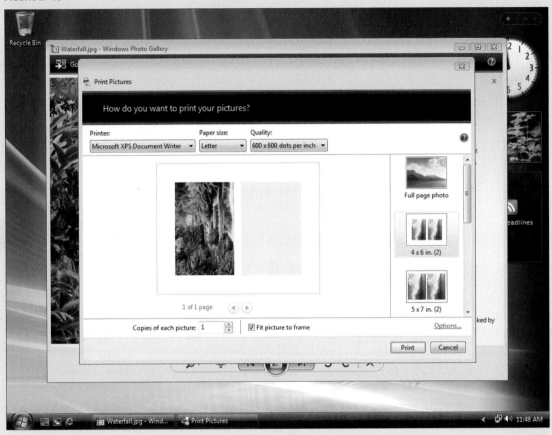

Understanding File Management

You use Windows Vista to access the drives where you store your folders and files. Each **drive** on your computer is a physical location for storing files. Most people store their files on the computer's hard disk drive and keep duplicate copies on other drives, such as a USB flash drive. The **hard disk** is a built-in, high-capacity, high-speed storage medium for all the software, folders, and files on a computer. When you create a document or other types of data with a program, you save the results in a file, which consists of stored electronic data such as text, a picture, a video, or music. Each file is stored in a folder, which is a container for a group of related files such as reports, correspondence, or e-mail contacts. As a tour guide for Quest Specialty Travel (QST), you want to better understand how you can use Windows Vista to manage the files you need for proposing, planning, organizing, and documenting QST tours.

OBJECTIVES

Manage folders and files

Open the Computer window

Create and save documents

Open the Documents folder

Copy files

Open, edit, and print files

Move and rename files

Search for files

Delete and restore files

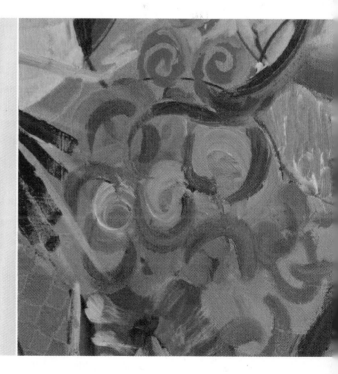

Managing Folders and Files

Most of the work you do on a computer involves using programs to create files, which you then store in folders. Over time, you create many folders and files and save them on different storage media. The process of organizing and finding your folders and files can become a challenge. It is helpful to develop a strategy for organizing your folders and files; these tasks are referred to as **file management**. Windows Vista provides a variety of file management tools to assist you in these tasks. ░▒▓ As a QST tour guide for destinations in the South Pacific, you work with many types of files. You want to review how Windows can help you track and organize your files.

DETAILS

You can use Windows Vista to:

- **Create folders for storing and organizing files**

  Folders provide a location for your important files and help you organize them into groups of related files so that you can easily locate a file later. You give each folder you create a unique, descriptive **folder name** that identifies the files you intend to place in the folder. A folder can also contain other folders, called **subfolders**, to help organize files into smaller groups. This structure for organizing folders and files is called a **file hierarchy** because it describes the logic and layout of the folder structure on a disk. Windows Vista provides the Documents folder in which you create folders and subfolders for saving your files on your hard disk drive. Most programs automatically open and use the Documents folder when you save or open files. Figure B-1 illustrates how you might organize your tour folders and files within the Documents folder. Windows Vista provides other folders dedicated to specific types of files, such as the Pictures folder for image files; the Music folder for music or sound files; the Contacts folder for e-mail addresses and other contact information, including names, addresses, and phone numbers; and the Favorites folder for Internet shortcuts to your preferred Web sites. Figure B-2 shows the standard folders that Windows Vista creates for each user.

- **Rename, copy, and move folders and files**

  If you want to change the name of a folder or file, you can rename it. For example, you might change the name of the "French Polynesia Tour Proposal" file to "French Polynesia Tour" after your supervisor approves the tour. If you need a duplicate of a file, you can copy it. For example, you could make a copy of the "French Polynesia Tour" file, rename the copy to "Fiji Islands Tour Proposal," then modify the file's content for a new tour location. You can also move a folder or file to another folder or disk and physically change its location.

- **Delete and restore folders and files**

  Deleting folders and files you no longer need frees up storage space on your disk and helps keep your files organized. Folders and files deleted from your hard disk are moved to a Windows folder called the Recycle Bin. If you accidentally delete an important folder or file, or if you change your mind and want to restore a deleted folder or file, you can retrieve it from the Recycle Bin. Folders or files deleted from a removable disk, such as a USB flash drive, are permanently removed and cannot be retrieved with Windows.

- **Locate folders and files quickly using Instant Search**

  Instant Search helps you quickly locate a folder or file if you forget where you stored it. If you can provide part of the folder or file name—or some other fact about the item, such as the author's name—Instant Search can easily locate it and save you a lot of time and effort.

- **Use shortcuts to access frequently used files and folders**

  As your file structure becomes more complex, a file or folder you use often might be located several levels down the file hierarchy and require multiple steps to open. To save time, you can create shortcuts on your desktop to the files and folders you use frequently. A **shortcut** is a link that gives you quick access to a folder, file, or Web site. As shown in Figure B-2, Windows uses shortcuts to folders that contain sample files, such as pictures, music, and videos. Also, each program listed on the All Programs menu is a shortcut to the actual program stored elsewhere on your computer.

FIGURE B-1: Sample folder and file hierarchy

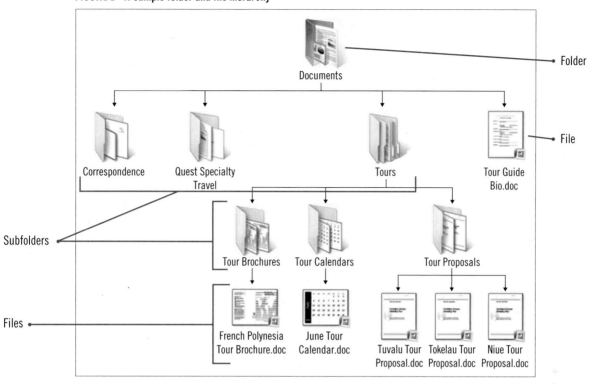

FIGURE B-2: Default user folders in Windows Vista

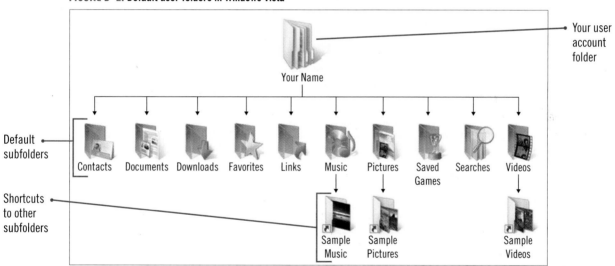

Organizing your folders and files efficiently

Good planning is essential for effective file management. First, identify the types of files you work with, such as images, music, and reports, then determine a logical system for organizing your files. The Pictures and Music folders are good places to store images and music. The Documents folder is the most common place to store all of your other files. Within each folder, use subfolders to better organize the files into smaller groups. For example, use subfolders in the Pictures folder to separate family photos from vacation photos, or to group them by year. In the Documents folder, you might group personal files in one subfolder and business files in another subfolder, then create additional subfolders to further distinguish sets of files. For example, your personal files might include subfolders for resumes, letters, and income tax returns, to name a few. Your business files might include subfolders for clients, projects, and invoices. You should periodically reevaluate your folder structure to ensure that it continues to meet your needs.

Opening the Computer Window

The **Computer window** shows the drives on your computer organized into two groups—Hard Disk Drives and Devices with Removable Storage. A **device** is a hardware component in your computer system. **Removable storage** refers to storage media that you can easily transfer from one computer to another, such as DVDs, CDs, or flash drives. **USB flash drives** (also called pen drives, jump drives, keychain drives, and thumb drives) are a popular removable storage device because of their ease of use and portability. When you attach a USB flash drive to a computer, a new drive icon appears under Devices with Removable Storage. To distinguish one drive from another, each drive has a unique **drive name** that consists of a letter followed by a colon, such as C: for the hard disk drive. Table B-1 lists examples of different drive types. Table B-2 lists commonly used terms to describe the storage capacities of different types of disks. ▄▄▄▄ Before you plan your next tour, you want to see what types of drives are available on your computer.

STEPS

1. **Start your computer and Windows Vista, logging onto your computer if necessary**

QUICK TIP

The **Navigation Pane** contains links to your personal folders, including the Documents, Pictures, and Music folders.

2. **Click the Start button 🅦 on the taskbar, click Computer on the right side of the Start menu, then click the Maximize button ⬜ if the Computer window does not fill the desktop**

   The Computer window opens, displaying icons for the hard disk drive and removable storage devices on your computer. Your computer may have more than one hard disk drive or other types of removable storage. You may also see icons for other types of hardware, such as a scanner or digital camera.

TROUBLE

If the Details Pane is hidden, click the Organize button on the toolbar, point to Layout, then click Details Pane.

3. **Under Hard Disk Drives, click the your hard disk drive icon**

   As shown in Figure B-3, the **Details Pane** at the bottom of the Computer window shows a friendly name for your hard disk drive (such as Local Disk), its actual drive name (C:), the total size or total storage capacity, the amount of free space, and a horizontal bar that shows the storage space already being used on the hard disk drive. When you select the hard disk drive (or some other drive), the options on the toolbar change to ones available for that drive.

4. **Click the Close button ❌ on the Computer window title bar**

   The Computer window closes.

TABLE B-1: Drive names and drive icons

drive type	drive icon	friendly name	drive name	referred to as
floppy disk drive	🖫	3½ Floppy	A:	drive A
hard disk drive	🖴	Local Disk	C:	drive C
CD drive	💿	CD-RW Drive, CD-R Drive, or CD-ROM Drive	next available drive letter; for example, D:	drive D
DVD drive	📀	DVD-RW Drive, DVD-R Drive, or DVD-ROM Drive	next available drive letter; for example, E:	drive E
USB flash drive	🖴	[varies with drive]	next available drive letter; for example, F:	drive F

FIGURE B-3: Computer window

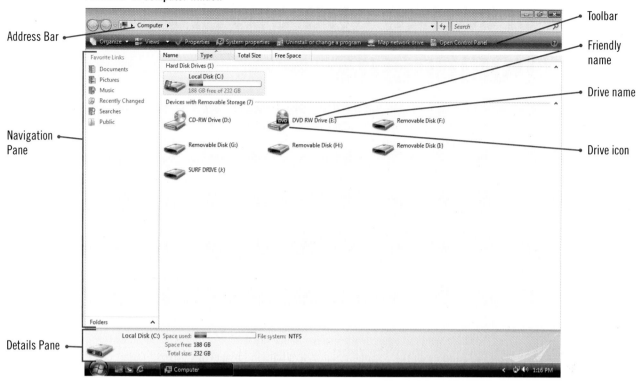

Address Bar

Navigation Pane

Details Pane

Toolbar

Friendly name

Drive name

Drive icon

TABLE B-2: Disk storage capacity terms

term	equals approximately	example	storage space
byte	one character of storage space on disk or in RAM (memory)	A simple text file with the phrase *To-Do List*	10 bytes; count all the characters in the phrase including the hyphen and the blank space between the two words (10 characters = 10 bytes of storage space)
kilobyte (KB or K)	one thousand bytes	A file with a 10-page term paper (approximately 3500 characters per page)	35 KB (approximately 35,000 bytes)
megabyte (MB or M)	one million bytes (or one thousand kilobytes)	512 MB USB flash drive	512 MB (approximately 512 million bytes)
gigabyte (GB or G)	one billion bytes (or one thousand megabytes)	350 GB hard disk	350 GB (approximately 350 billion bytes)
terabyte (TB or T)	one trillion bytes (or one thousand gigabytes)	1 TB hard disk drive	1 TB (approximately one trillion bytes)

Displaying the Computer icon on the desktop

By default, the Computer icon does not appear on the desktop. You can display the Computer icon on the desktop so you can open the Computer window in one step rather than from the Start menu, which involves several steps. To add the Computer icon to your desktop, click the Start button, right-click Computer, then click Show on Desktop. You can now quickly open the Computer window by double-clicking the Computer icon on the desktop. You can repeat these steps to remove the Computer icon from the desktop.

Creating and Saving Documents

Windows comes with easy-to-use programs called Accessories. For example, you can use the WordPad Accessory to create simple text documents such as a letter or to-do list. Any document you create with WordPad (or another program) is temporarily stored in your computer's **RAM (random access memory)**. Anything stored in RAM is lost when you turn off your computer or the power fails unexpectedly. Before you close a document or exit WordPad, you must create a permanent copy of the document by saving it as a file on a disk. You can save files in the **Documents folder** on your local hard disk drive (drive C) or on a removable storage device such as a USB flash drive. When you name a file, choose a **filename** that clearly identifies the file contents. Filenames can be no more than 255 characters, including spaces and can include letters, numbers, and certain symbols. ▨▨▨ You want to use WordPad to create a to-do list for your next tour, then save the file to the Documents folder. The To-Do List is shown in Figure B-4.

STEPS

1. **Click the Start button ☺ on the taskbar, point to All Programs, click Accessories, then click WordPad**

   The WordPad window opens with a new, blank document. Table B-3 identifies the components of the WordPad window. In the document window, a blinking **insertion point** indicates where the next character you type will appear.

   > **QUICK TIP**
   > If you make a typing mistake, press [Backspace] to delete the character to the left of the insertion point.

2. **Type To-Do List on the first line, then press [Enter] three times**

   Each time you press [Enter], WordPad inserts a new blank line and places the insertion point at the beginning of the line.

3. **Type the text shown in Figure B-4, pressing [Enter] at the end of each line**

   > **TROUBLE**
   > If the Documents folder is not displayed, click Documents in the Navigation Pane.

4. **Click File on the menu bar, click Save As, then click the Browse Folders button in the Save As dialog box**

   The Save As dialog box expands to show the contents of the Documents folder, as shown in Figure B-5.

5. **Click Document.rtf in the File name text box to select it, then type To-Do List**

   > **TROUBLE**
   > If a Confirm Save As dialog box asks if you want to replace a file with the same name, click Yes.

6. **Click Save in the Save As dialog box**

   WordPad saves the document in a file named "To-Do List" in the Documents folder and closes the Save As dialog box. The title bar displays "To-Do List.rtf"—the filename you entered followed by the file extension .rtf. A **file extension** identifies the type of file. Each program assigns a file extension to files you create, so you only need to enter a name for the file. Depending on how Windows is set up, you may not see the file extensions.

7. **Click the Close button ▨⊠ on the WordPad title bar**

FIGURE B-3: Components of the WordPad window

component	used to
Title bar	Display the name of the open document and program
Menu bar	Display menu names with commands for performing operations on a document and its contents and for specifying program settings
Toolbar	Display buttons for common menu commands, such as saving and printing
Format bar	Display buttons for formatting, or enhancing, the appearance of a document
Ruler	Mark a document's width in ⅛ths of an inch (also shows one-inch marks)
Document window	Display all or part of the open document
Status bar	Display simple Help information and tips

FIGURE B-4: WordPad document

Temporary filename

Program name

Insertion point

Toolbar

Format bar

Ruler

Document window

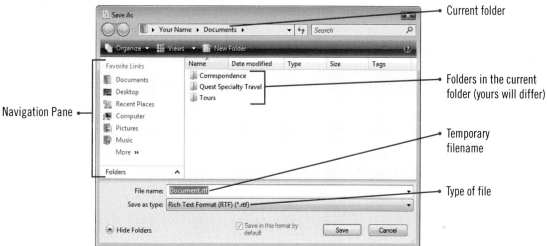

FIGURE B-5: Save As dialog box

Current folder

Navigation Pane

Folders in the current folder (yours will differ)

Temporary filename

Type of file

Using the Address Bar in the Save As dialog box

The **Address Bar** shows your current location in the computer's file hierarchy as a series of links separated by arrows. In Figure B-5, this series of links appears as an icon followed by "Your Name" (your user account folder name) then Documents. If you click the leftmost arrow in the Address Bar, you can use the drop-down list that opens to switch to the desktop, the Computer window, or other system folders. If you click the arrow after your user account name, you can use the list that opens to switch to any of your user account folders, such as Contacts, Music, Pictures, and Videos. If you click the arrow after Documents, you can use the list that opens to switch to a sub-folder in the Documents folder, as shown in Figure B-6.

FIGURE B-6: Address Bar drop-down menu

Address Bar

Address Bar arrow displays a drop-down list of subfolders within the Documents folder

Subfolders in the Documents folder

Opening the Documents Folder

The Documents folder is the most common place to store files you create or receive from others. From the Documents folder, you can examine your files, organize them into subfolders, or perform other common file management tasks such as renaming, copying, moving, or deleting a folder or file. 🖳🖱 You store all your QST tour files in the Documents folder on your computer. You want to organize the files in your Documents folder before you copy them to a USB flash drive.

1. **Click the Start button 🏵 on the taskbar, then click Documents**

   The Documents window opens and displays your folders and files, including the To-Do List.rtf file. Table B-4 identifies the components of the Documents window.

TROUBLE
If your view did not change, Windows Vista is already set to Large Icons view.

2. **Click the Views button arrow on the toolbar, then click Large Icons**

   Like some of the other views, Large Icons view displays folder icons with different icons for the types of files (such as a text document) contained in a folder or a **live view** of the actual content in files.

QUICK TIP
The Layout option on the Organize menu controls whether to display the Details, Preview, and Navigation panes.

3. **If you do not see the Preview Pane on the right side of the window, click the Organize button on the toolbar, point to Layout, then click Preview Pane**

   The **Preview Pane** shows the actual contents of the selected file, such as the WordPad file, without starting a program. Preview may not work for some types of files.

4. **Click the To-Do List.rtf file icon**

   The Preview Pane shows the actual contents of your To-Do List file, and the Details Pane lists information about the file itself, including the dates it was created and last modified, and its size. See Figure B-7.

5. **Leave the Documents window open for the next lesson**

TABLE B-4: Components of the Documents window

component	used to
Back button	Go back to previously viewed folders
Forward button	Return to the folders you just left
Address Bar	Display the name of the current folder and navigate to a different folder
Search box	Locate files or folders in the current folder
Toolbar	Perform common tasks on a folder or its contents (such as changing the view or e-mailing a file)
Navigation Pane	Navigate to another folder
File list	Display the subfolders and files in the current folder
Details Pane	View information about the folder or file you select in the File list
Preview Pane	View the actual content within some types of files

FIGURE B-7: Documents window

Forward button

Back button

Address Bar

Navigation Pane

Files list (shows folders and files in Large Icons view)

Search box

Toolbar

Preview Pane

Details Pane

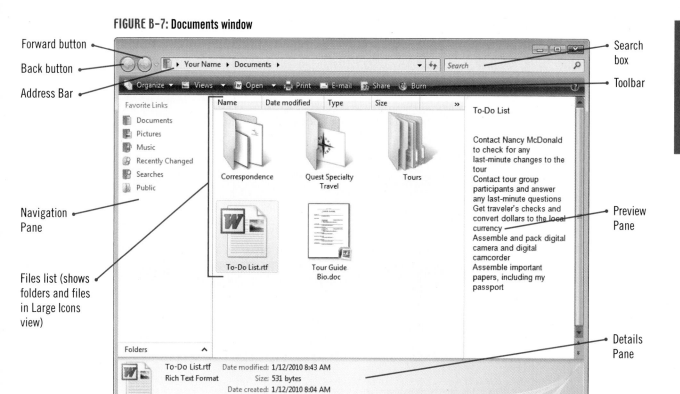

Changing views in a window

The Views button provides seven ways to display the folders and files in a window. Extra Large Icons, Large Icons, and Medium Icons views display rows of folder and file icons at different sizes, with their names displayed under the icon. Small Icons view displays rows of even smaller folder and file icons with the folder or filename to the right of the icon. List view displays columns of very small folder or filename icons with the names to the right of the icon. Tiles view is similar to Small Icons view, but displays larger icons and also lists the type of folder or file and the file size. Details view is similar to List view, but displays columns with the folder or filename, the date and time that a folder or file was modified, the type of folder or file, the size of files, and any tags assigned to a file. A **tag** is a word or phrase that reminds you of a file's content. You can use the Views button slider bar to scale icons to your preferred size between Small Icons and Extra Large Icons.

Copying Files

You can copy a file, a group of files, or a folder from one disk drive to another or from one folder to another. When you **copy** a file, the original file stays in its current location and a duplicate of the file is created in another location. This feature lets you make a backup of your important files. A **backup** is a copy of a file that is stored in another location. If you lose the original file, you can make a new working copy from your backup. You can use the Send To menu to quickly copy a file from the Documents folder to another disk drive. ▰▰▰▰ You want to copy your To-Do List.rtf file to your USB flash drive so you can work with the file as you travel.

STEPS

TROUBLE

If you are using a different storage device, insert the appropriate disk and substitute that device whenever you see USB flash drive in the steps.

1. **Attach your USB flash drive to your computer or to a cable connected to your computer, then, if the AutoPlay dialog box opens, click the Close button** ▣

   Your USB flash drive is ready to use.

2. **Right-click the To-Do List.rtf file icon, then point to Send To on the shortcut menu**

   A list of the available drives and locations where you can copy the file appears on the shortcut menu, as shown in Figure B-8. The options on your Send To menu will differ.

QUICK TIP

If you hold down [Shift] while you click a Send To option, Windows moves the file to that disk; it does not make another copy

3. **Click the USB flash drive option**

   Windows copies the To-Do List.rtf file to your USB flash drive. There are now two copies of the same file stored in two different locations.

4. **Click the first Address Bar arrow** ▶ **on the Address Bar, as shown in Figure B-9, then click Computer**

   The contents of the Computer folder appear in the window.

5. **Double-click the USB flash drive icon**

   The contents of your USB flash drive, including the To-Do List.rtf file you copied to this disk, appear in the window. See Figure B-10.

6. **Click the Close button** ▣ **on the Removable Disk window title bar**

Using the Send To menu

You can create a shortcut on the desktop to any folder or file you use frequently with the "Desktop (create shortcut)" option on the Send To menu. The Compressed (zipped) Folder option on the Send To menu creates a new compressed file using the same filename, but with the .zip file extension. For example, compressing To-Do List.rtf creates a new file named To-Do List.zip. Before you send a file by e-mail, especially a large file, it is a good idea to **compress** it, which makes the file smaller in size.

FIGURE B-8: Send To menu

Send To
option

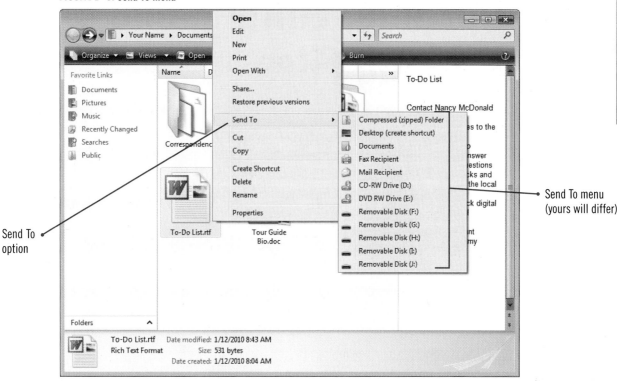

Send To menu
(yours will differ)

FIGURE B-9: Navigating with the Address Bar

Address Bar
arrow displays
a drop-down list
of locations

Switches to
the Computer
window

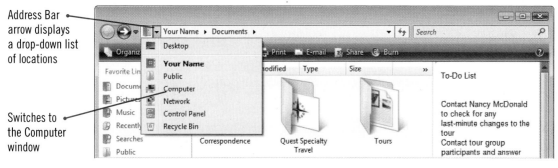

FIGURE B-10: Removable Disk window

Address Bar
arrows

Flash drive
(yours may be a
different letter)

Copy of the
original file

Opening, Editing, and Printing Files

Sometimes you create new files, as you did in the previous lesson. But often, you want to change a file that you or someone else already created. After you open an existing file stored on a disk, you can **edit**, or make changes, to it. For example, you might want to add or delete text, or change the **formatting** or appearance of the text. After you finish editing, you usually save the file with the same filename, which replaces the file with a new copy that contains all your most recent changes. If you want to keep the original file, you can save the edited file with a different filename; this keeps the original file without the edits and creates a new copy of the file with the most recent changes. When you want a **hard copy**, or paper copy of the file, you need to print it. ▰▰▰▰ You need to add two items to your To-Do List, so you want to open and edit the file you created in WordPad, then print the To-Do List.

STEPS

1. **Click the** Start button ⊕ **on the taskbar, point to** All Programs, **click** Accessories, **then click** WordPad

   The WordPad program window opens.

2. **Click the** Open button 📂 **on the WordPad toolbar, click** Computer **in the Navigation Pane, then double-click your** USB flash drive icon

   The Open dialog box displays the contents of your USB flash drive. See Figure B-11. You may see additional files.

   > **QUICK TIP**
   > You can also open a file by double-clicking it in the Open dialog box.

3. **Click** To-Do List.rtf **in the File list, then click** Open **in the Open dialog box**

   The Open dialog box closes and the To-Do List.rtf file appears in the WordPad window.

4. **Click at the beginning of the last blank line in the To-Do List, then type the two additional lines shown in Figure B-12, pressing [Enter] after each line**

5. **Click the** Save button 💾 **on the WordPad toolbar**

   WordPad saves the edited To-Do List.rtf file under the same filename on your USB flash drive.

   > **QUICK TIP**
   > You should always use Print Preview before you print to save time and effort as well as toner ink and paper.

6. **Click the** Print Preview button 🔍 **on the WordPad toolbar**

   Print Preview displays a full-page view of your document, as shown in Figure B-13, so you can check its layout before you print. Dotted lines separate the area on the page reserved for the document and the blank space reserved for the left, right, top, and bottom margins. If you need to make additional edits, click the Close button on the Print Preview toolbar (not the title bar), make your changes, then use Print Preview to check the document again before printing.

7. **Click the** Print button **on the Print Preview toolbar**

   Print Preview closes and the Print dialog box opens, so you can verify the print settings.

8. **Click** Print **in the Print dialog box, then retrieve your printed copy from the printer**

9. **Click the** Close button ✖ **on the WordPad title bar**

   WordPad closes.

Comparing Save and Save As

The File menu has two save options—Save and Save As. When you first save a file, the Save As dialog box opens (whether you choose Save or Save As) so you can select the drive and folder where you want to save the file and enter its filename. If you edit and save a previously saved file, you can save the file to the same location with the same filename, you can change the location or filename, or you can do both. Save updates the file stored on disk using the same location and filename without opening the Save As dialog box. Save As opens the Save As dialog box so you can save an updated copy of the file to another location or with a new filename.

FIGURE B-11: Open dialog box

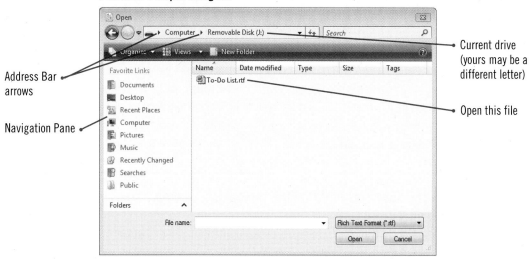

Address Bar arrows

Navigation Pane

Current drive (yours may be a different letter)

Open this file

FIGURE B-12: Edited To-Do List file

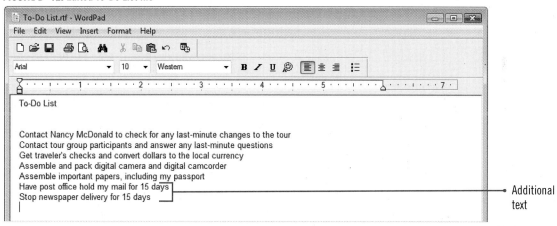

Additional text

FIGURE B-13: Print Preview

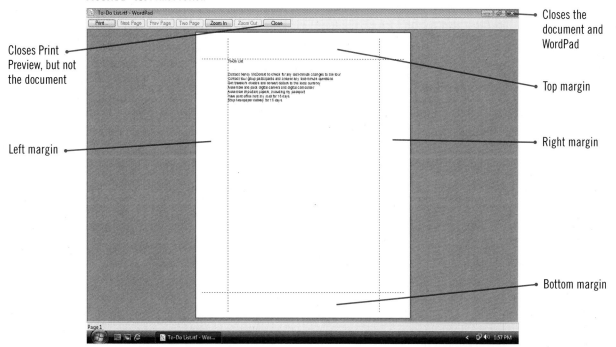

Closes Print Preview, but not the document

Left margin

Closes the document and WordPad

Top margin

Right margin

Bottom margin

Moving and Renaming Files

You can move a file, a group of files, or a folder to another location such as a different folder on the same drive or a different drive. When you **move** a file, the original file is stored in a different location. One of the fastest ways to move a file is with **drag and drop** (which uses a pointing device to drag a file or folder to a new location). You may also need to rename a file, giving it a name that more clearly describes the file's contents and how you intend to use the file. ▰▰▰▰ You want to move the To-Do List.rtf file to a new folder and rename it so you can update the list for your next tour.

STEPS

1. **Click the Start button ◉ on the taskbar, click Computer, then double-click your USB flash drive icon**

   The contents of your USB flash drive appear in the Computer window.

2. **Click the Views button arrow on the Computer window toolbar, then click Large Icons**

   The larger icons make it easier to work with folder and file icons as you move and rename files.

3. **Click the Organize button on the Computer window toolbar, then click New Folder**

   Windows creates a new folder named "New Folder," as shown in Figure B-14. The folder name is highlighted so you can type a more descriptive folder name.

   > **TROUBLE**
   >
   > If you cannot type a name for the new folder, press [F2] (the Rename key), then repeat Step 4.

4. **Type French Polynesia Tour as the folder name, then press [Enter]**

   Windows changes the name of the folder.

5. **Click the white background of the window, point to the To-Do List.rtf file, press and hold the left button on your pointing device, drag the To-Do List.rtf file icon on top of the French Polynesia Tour folder, then pause**

   As shown in Figure B-15, a smaller transparent copy of the To-Do List.rtf file icon appears over the French Polynesia Tour folder and a ToolTip describes the type of operation.

6. **Release the left button on your pointing device**

   The To-Do List.rtf file moves into the French Polynesia Tour folder.

7. **Double-click the French Polynesia Tour folder**

   The Address Bar shows the name of the open folder, French Polynesia Tour. The To-Do List.rtf file appears in this folder.

8. **Click the To-Do List.rtf file icon, click the Organize button, then click Rename**

   The first part of the filename is highlighted so you can type a new name for the file.

9. **Type Tour Preparation as the new filename, then press [Enter]**

   Windows renames the file. See Figure B-16.

10. **Click the Close button ▰✕▰ on the title bar**

Understanding File Management

FIGURE B-14: Creating a new folder

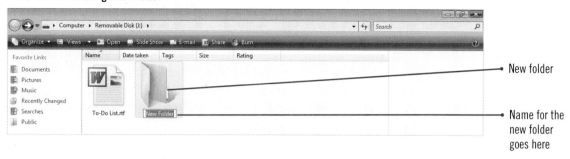

New folder

Name for the
new folder
goes here

FIGURE B-15: Moving a file using drag and drop

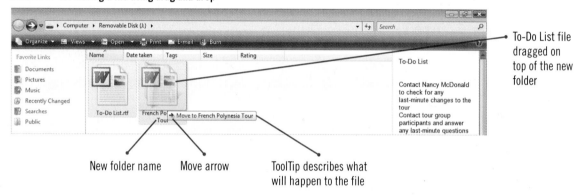

To-Do List file
dragged on
top of the new
folder

New folder name   Move arrow   ToolTip describes what
will happen to the file

FIGURE B-16: Renamed file

Current folder

Renamed file in the
new folder

Using drag and drop to copy and move files

If you drag and drop a file to a folder on the same drive, Windows moves the file into that folder. However, if you drag and drop a file to a folder on another drive, Windows copies the file instead. If you want to move a file to another drive, hold down [Shift] while you drag and drop. If you want to copy a file to another folder on the same drive, hold down [Ctrl] while you drag and drop.

Searching for Files

After creating, saving, deleting, and renaming folders and files, you may forget where you stored a particular folder or file, its name, or both. **Instant Search** helps you quickly find a folder or file on your computer. You must specify **search criteria** (one or more pieces of information that help Windows identify the file you want). You can search using all or part of the filename, a unique word in the file, or the file type such as document, picture, or music. Instant Search finds items only in your user account, not in other user accounts on the same computer. The **Boolean filters** shown in Table B-5 allow you to specify multiple criteria so that you have a greater chance of finding what you need quickly. When you use the Boolean filters AND, OR, and NOT, you must type them in uppercase so they work properly. ░░░░ You want to quickly locate the copy of the To-Do List for your next tour.

STEPS

1. **Click the Start button ⊕ on the taskbar, then click in the Start Search box**

QUICK TIP

Searches are not case sensitive, so you can use uppercase or lowercase letters when you type search criteria.

2. **Type To**

   The search results on the left side of the Start menu are organized by categories, as shown in Figure B-17. Your search results will differ; however, all of the search results will have the characters "To" somewhere in the name of each item in the search results. Under Files, you may see two listings for To-Do List.rtf. One is the file in your Documents folder. The other is a shortcut to the original file on the flash drive that you renamed. Windows Vista keeps a list of shortcuts to files you have used recently, even if that file no longer exists.

QUICK TIP

If you type "To-Do List" with quotation marks, Instant Search finds the To-Do List.rtf file and any shortcut or other files with the same name.

3. **Type -Do List after the word "To", then press [Spacebar]**

   The additional text you typed narrows the search results, as shown in Figure B-18. Now you see documents with "To," "Do," and "List" in the filename.

4. **Under Files, click To-Do List.rtf**

   The To-Do List.rtf file opens in Microsoft Word, WordPad, or another program that works with Rich Text Format files.

5. **Click the Close button ▣ in the program window's title bar**

TABLE B-5: Boolean filters

Boolean filter	example	how it works
AND	tour AND proposal	Finds all files that contain the word *tour* and the word *proposal*; the two words may or may not be located next to each other
OR	tour OR proposal	Finds all files that contain the word *tour* or the word *proposal* (or both)
NOT	tour NOT proposal	Finds all files that contain the word *tour* but not the word *proposal*
" " (quotation marks)	"tour proposal"	Finds all files that contain the exact phrase *tour proposal*

FIGURE B-17: Search results

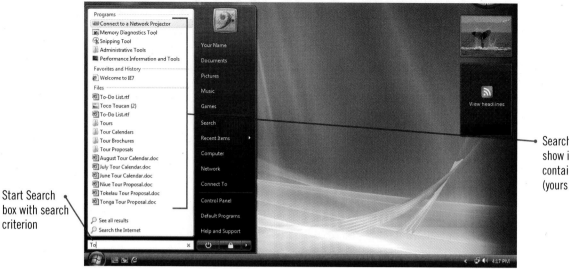

Start Search box with search criterion

Search results show items that contain "To" (yours will differ)

FIGURE B-18: Narrowed search results

Search found the file with the To-Do List

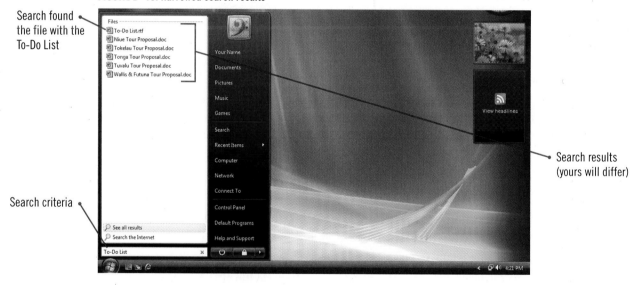

Search results (yours will differ)

Search criteria

Performing more advanced searches

If you want to search all your personal folders for a file, use the Start Search box on the Start menu. If you want to locate a file in a specific folder and all its subfolders (such as the Documents folder), open the folder and use the Search box in the folder. If you want to locate all files that have the same file extension (such as .rtf), type the file extension as your search criteria. If you want to locate files created by a certain person, use the first name, last name, or first and last name as your search criteria. If you want to locate files created on a certain date, type the date (for example, 7/9/2010) as your search criteria. If you remember the title in a document, type the title as your search criteria. If you have created e-mail contacts in your Contacts folder, you can type the person's name to find his or her e-mail address.

Deleting and Restoring Files

If you no longer need a folder or file, you can **delete** (or remove) it. If you delete a folder, Windows removes the folder as well as everything stored in it. Windows places folders and files you delete from your hard disk drive in the Recycle Bin. If you later discover that you need a deleted file or folder, you can restore it to its original location as long as you have not yet emptied the Recycle Bin. Emptying the Recycle Bin permanently removes the deleted folders and files from your computer. By deleting files and folders you no longer need and periodically emptying the Recycle Bin, you free up valuable storage space on your hard disk drive and keep your computer uncluttered. Be aware that files and folders you delete from a removable disk drive, such as a USB flash drive, are immediately and permanently deleted and cannot be restored by Windows. If you try to delete a file or folder that is too large for the Recycle Bin, Windows asks whether you want to permanently delete the file or folder. Choose Yes to delete the file or folder, or choose No to cancel the operation. ▰▰▰▰ You have the updated copy of the To-Do List.rtf file stored on your USB flash drive, so you want to delete the copy in the Documents folder.

STEPS

1. **Click the Start button ⊕ on the taskbar, click Documents, then click the To-Do List file in the Documents folder**

   After you select a folder or file, you can delete it.

QUICK TIP
You can also quickly delete a selected folder or file by pressing [Delete] or [Del].

2. **Click the Organize button on the toolbar, then click Delete**

   The Delete File dialog box opens so you can confirm the deletion, as shown in Figure B-19.

3. **Click Yes**

   The file moves from the Documents folder into the Recycle Bin.

4. **Click the Minimize button ▭ on the Documents window title bar and examine the Recycle Bin icon**

   The Recycle Bin icon contains wads of paper if the Recycle Bin contains deleted folders and files. If the Recycle Bin icon does not contain wads of paper, then it is empty and does not contain any deleted files or folders.

5. **Double-click the Recycle Bin icon 🗑**

   The Recycle Bin window opens and displays any deleted folders and files, including the To-Do List.rtf file, as shown in Figure B-20. Your Recycle Bin's contents may differ.

QUICK TIP
Windows keeps track of the original location of deleted subfolders and files so it can restore them later, recreating the original folder structure as needed.

6. **Click the To-Do List.rtf file to select it, then click the Restore this item button on the Recycle Bin toolbar**

   The file returns its original location and no longer appears in the Recycle Bin window.

7. **Click the Close button ✖ on the Recycle Bin title bar, then click the Documents taskbar button**

   The Recycle Bin window closes, and the Documents window opens. The Documents window contains the restored file. You decide to permanently delete this previous version of the To-Do List file.

8. **Click the To-Do List file, press [Delete], then click Yes in the Delete File dialog box**

   The To-Do List moves from the Documents folder to the Recycle Bin.

9. **Click the Close button ✖ on the Documents window title bar, then end your Windows session**

FIGURE B-19: Delete File dialog box

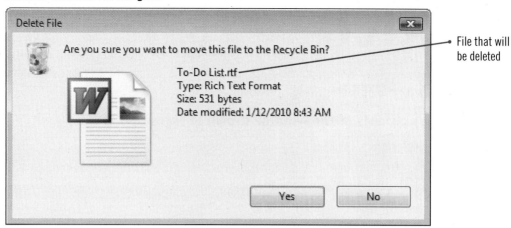

File that will
be deleted

FIGURE B-20: Recycle Bin folder

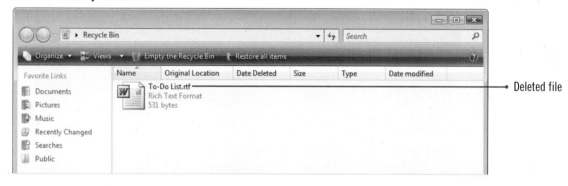

Deleted file

Emptying the Recycle Bin

If you are certain that you no longer need any of the deleted files and folders in your Recycle Bin, you can empty it. If the Recycle Bin folder is open, click the Empty the Recycle Bin button on the toolbar. If it is closed, right-click the Recycle Bin icon on the desktop, then click Empty Recycle Bin on the shortcut menu. In the Delete Multiple Items dialog box, choose Yes to confirm that you want to permanently delete all the items in the Recycle Bin, or choose No to cancel the operation.

Practice

If you have a SAM user profile, you may have access to hands-on instruction, practice, and assessment of the skills covered in this unit. Log in to your SAM account (http://sam2007.course.com/) to launch any assigned training activities or exams that relate to the skills covered in this unit.

▼ CONCEPTS REVIEW

Label each of the elements of the window shown in Figure B-21.

FIGURE B-21

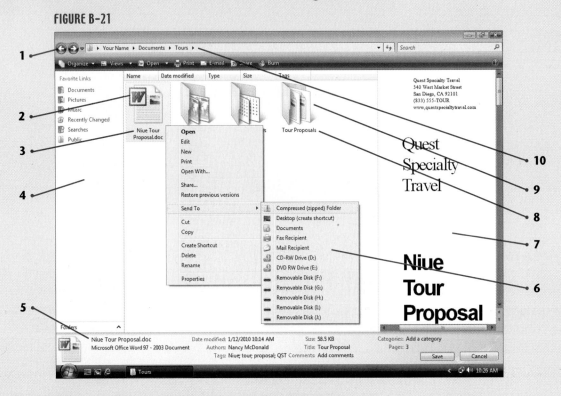

Match each statement with the term it best describes.

11. A container for related files
12. A link that provides quick access to a folder, file, or Web site
13. One or more pieces of information for locating a folder or file
14. Organizing and managing folders and files
15. The name that you assign to a file to identify its contents

a. file management
b. filename
c. folder
d. Search criteria
e. shortcut

Select the best answer from the list of choices.

16. One billion bytes of storage space on a disk is referred to as a:
    a. Kilobyte.
    b. Megabyte.
    c. Gigabyte.
    d. Terabyte.

17. To save a previously saved file with a new filename, you use the:
    a. Save command on the File menu.
    b. Save As command on the File menu.
    c. Save or Save As command on the File menu.
    d. Save button on the program's toolbar.

18. The blinking vertical bar in the WordPad application window is called the:
    a. Insertion point.
    b. Pointer.
    c. Ruler.
    d. Shortcut.

19. After you copy a file, you have:
    a. Only one copy of the file.
    b. A duplicate copy of the file in a different location.
    c. Moved the orginal file to a new location.
    d. Deleted the file.

20. **After you move a file, you have:**
   - **a.** A backup copy of that file.
   - **b.** A duplicate copy of the file in a different location.
   - **c.** The orginal file in a different location.
   - **d.** Deleted the file.

21. **When you delete a file from your hard disk drive, Windows:**
   - **a.** Puts the deleted file in the Recycle Bin.
   - **b.** Permanently deletes the file from the hard disk drive.
   - **c.** Stores a duplicate copy of the file in the Recycle Bin..
   - **d.** Moves the file to a removable disk.

▼ SKILLS REVIEW

1. **Manage folders and files.**
   - **a.** Assume you manage a small travel agency. How would you organize your business files using a hierarchical file structure?
   - **b.** What icon can you place on your desktop to quickly locate your flash drive where you store copies of important files?
   - **c.** What shortcuts would you place on your desktop for easier access to your business files?

2. **Open the Computer window. (If possible, use a different computer than you used for the lessons.)**
   - **a.** Attach your USB flash drive to your computer.
   - **b.** Open the Computer window from the Start menu.
   - **c.** Note the types of drives on this computer, their friendly names, and their actual drive names. Note the drive name assigned to your USB flash drive.
   - **d.** Select the hard disk drive icon, then view the information in the Details Pane about the hard disk drive's total size and free space.
   - **e.** Close the Computer window.

3. **Create and save documents.**
   - **a.** Open WordPad from the All Programs menu.
   - **b.** Type Oceania Tours as the title, followed by one blank line.
   - **c.** Type your name, followed by two blank lines.
   - **d.** Use WordPad to create the following list of current Oceania tours.

      Current Tours:

      1. French Poynesia

      2. Fiji Islands

      3. Pitcairn Islands

      4. Tonga

      5. Niue

      6. Tokelau
   - **e.** Save the WordPad file with the filename Oceania Tours in the Documents folder.
   - **f.** View the full filename in the WordPad title bar, then close WordPad.

4. **Open the Documents folder.**
   - **a.** Open the Documents folder from the Start menu.
   - **b.** If necessary, use the Views button to change the folder view to Large Icons.
   - **c.** Click the Oceania Tours.rtf file.
   - **d.** If necessary, use the Organize menu to display the Preview Pane.
   - **e.** View the contents of the Oceania Tours.rtf file in the Preview Pane.

5. **Copy files.**
   - **a.** Right-click the Oceania Tours.rft file, point to Send To on the shortcut menu, then send a copy of the WordPad file to your USB flash drive.
   - **b.** Use the Address Bar to change to the Computer window, then to your USB flash drive window.
   - **c.** Verify you successfully copied the Oceania Tours.rtf file to your USB flash drive, then close the USB flash drive window.

6. **Open, edit, and print files.**
   - **a.** Open WordPad from the Start menu.
   - **b.** Open the WordPad file named Oceania Tours.rtf from your USB flash drive (not from your Documents folder).

    c. Click at the beginning of the blank line after the last current tour, then add the names of two more tours on two separate lines: Palau and Tuvalu.

    d. Save the edited WordPad file.

    e. Use Print Preview to display a full-page view of the document.

    f. Print the Oceania Tours.rtf document and retrieve your printed copy from the printer, then close WordPad.

7. Move and rename files.

    a. Open a Computer window, then display the contents of your USB flash drive.

    b. If necessary, change your folder view to Large Icons.

    c. Use the Organize menu to create a new folder and name it Oceania Tours.

    d. Use drag and drop to move the Oceania Tours.rtf file into the new folder.

    e. Open the new folder and verify the move operation.

    f. Use the Organize menu to rename the moved WordPad file as Current Oceania Tours.

    g. Close the folder window.

8. Search for files.

    a. From the Start menu, enter Oceania in the Search box as the search criteria.

    b. Examine the Search results, then open the original Oceania Tours.rtf file.

    c. Close the program window.

9. Delete and restore files.

    a. Open the Documents folder from the Start menu.

    b. Select and delete your original WordPad file with the name Oceania Tours.rtf.

    c. Minimize the Documents window, then open the Recycle Bin.

    d. Select and restore the file named Oceania Tours.rtf that you just deleted, then close the Recycle Bin window.

    e. Use the Documents taskbar button to redisplay the Documents window.

    f. Verify Windows restored the file named Oceania Tours.rtf to the Documents folder.

    g. Select and delete this file again, then close the Documents window.

    h. Submit the printed copy of your revised WordPad document and your answers to Step 1 to your instructor.

▼ INDEPENDENT CHALLENGE 1

To meet the needs of high-tech workers in your town, you have opened an Internet café named Internet To-Go where your customers can enjoy a cup of fresh-brewed coffee and bakery goods while they check e-mail. To promote your new business, you want to develop a newspaper ad, flyers, and breakfast and lunch menus.

    a. Connect your USB flash drive to your computer, if necessary.

    b. Create a new folder named Internet To-Go on your USB flash drive.

    c. In the Internet To-Go folder, create three subfolders named Advertising, Flyers, and Menus.

    d. Use WordPad to create a short ad for your local newspaper that describes your business:

        • Use the name of the business as the title for your document.

        • Write a short paragraph about the business. Include a fictitious location, street address, and phone number.

        • After the paragraph, type your name.

    e. Save the WordPad document with the filename Newspaper Ad in the Advertising folder.

    f. Preview and then print your WordPad document.

▼ INDEPENDENT CHALLENGE 2

As a freelance writer for several national magazines, you depend on your computer to meet critical deadlines. Whenever you encounter a computer problem, you contact a computer consultant who helps you resolve the problem. This consultant asked you to document, or keep records of, your computer's current settings.

    a. Connect your USB flash drive to your computer, if necessary.

    b. Open the Computer window so that you can view information on your drives and other installed hardware.

▼ INDEPENDENT CHALLENGE 2 (CONTINUED)

c. Open WordPad and create a document with the title My Hardware Documentation and your name on separate lines.

d. List the names of the hard disk drive (or drives), devices with removable storage, and any other hardware devices, such as a digital camera, installed on the computer you are using. Also include the total size and amount of free space on your hard disk drive(s). (*Hint:* If you need to check the Computer window for this information, use the taskbar button for the Computer window to view your drives, then use the WordPad taskbar button to return to WordPad.)

e. Save the WordPad document with the filename My Hardware Documentation on your USB flash drive.

f. Preview your document, print your WordPad document, then close WordPad.

▼ INDEPENDENT CHALLENGE 3

As an adjunct, or part-time, instructor at Everhart College, you teach special summer classes for kids on how to use and create computer games, compose digital art, work with digital photographs, and compose digital music. You want to create a folder structure on your USB flash drive to store the files for each class.

a. Connect your USB flash drive to your computer, then open the Computer window to your USB flash drive.

b. Create a folder named Computer Games.

c. In the Computer Games folder, create a subfolder named Class 1.

Advanced Challenge Exercise

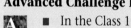

- In the Class 1 folder, create subfolders named Class Outline and Hands-On Lab.
- Rename the Class Outline folder to Class Handouts.
- Create a new folder named Interactive Presentations in the Class 1 subfolder.

d. Close the Class 1 folder window.

e. Use WordPad to create a document with the title Photocopying and your name on separate lines, and the following list of items that you need to photocopy for the first class:

Class 1:

Class 1 Topics & Resources

Hands-On Lab Assignment

On Your Own Exercise

Interactive Presentation Slides

f. Save the WordPad document with the filename Photocopying in the Class 1 folder. (*Hint:* After you switch to your USB flash drive in the Save As dialog box, open the Computer Games folder, then open the Class 1 folder before saving the file.)

g. Preview and print the Photocopying.rtf file, then close WordPad.

h. Draw a diagram of your new folder structure on the printed copy of your WordPad document.

▼ REAL LIFE INDEPENDENT CHALLENGE

This Real Life Independent Challenge requires an Internet connection. You want to open a small specialty shop for pottery, stained glass, handcrafts, and other consignments from local artists and craftspeople. First, you need to search for information on the Internet about preparing a business plan so that you can obtain financing from your local bank for the business.

a. Using the Start Search box on the Start menu, enter Preparing a Business Plan as the search criteria, then click the Search the Internet button in the Search Results pane.

b. From the list of Search results, locate a Web site that contains information on how to write a business plan.

c. Start WordPad and create a document in which you summarize in your own words the basic process for preparing a business plan. Include a title and your name in the document. At the bottom of your document, list the URL of the Web site or sites from which you prepared your WordPad document. (*Note:* You should not copy the exact content of a Web site, but instead summarize your findings in your own words because many sites copyright the content on their Web site. If you want to determine what content at a Web site is copyrighted and the conditions for using that content, scroll to the bottom of the Web site and click the link that covers copyright use and restrictions.)

d. Preview and print your WordPad document, then save the document on your USB flash drive.

▼ VISUAL WORKSHOP

As a technical support specialist at Advanced Robotic Systems, Ltd., in Great Britain, you need to respond to employee queries quickly and thoroughly. You decide that it is time to evaluate and reorganize the folder structure on your computer so you can quickly access the resources required for your job. Create the folder structure shown in Figure B-22 on your USB flash drive. As you work, use WordPad to prepare a simple outline of the steps you follow to create the folder structure. Include your name in the document, preview and print the document, then submit it to your instructor.

FIGURE B-22

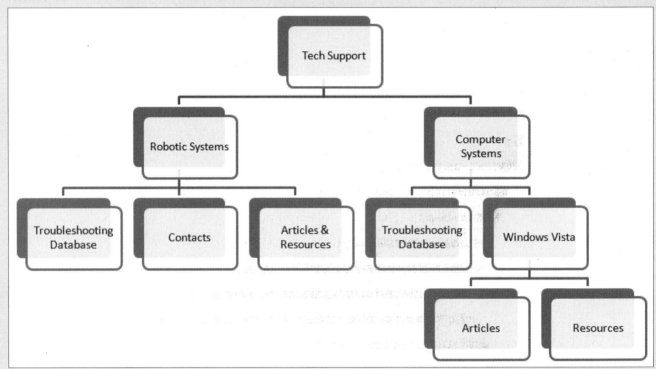

Getting Started with Internet Explorer 7

In this unit, you learn how to use the Internet Explorer 7 browser to find information on the World Wide Web (WWW or the Web). You will learn how to navigate to sites on the Web, how to navigate from one Web page to another, and how to search for information on the Web. You will also learn how to print Web pages and how to get helpful information about using Internet Explorer. You need to connect to the Internet to complete this unit. 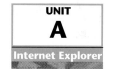 At Quest Specialty Travel (QST), the tour developers for each region have decided to provide laptop computers with mobile Internet technology to all tour guides. Guides can then use the Internet to research the latest information on local weather, events, and news while traveling with the groups. Each computer will have Internet Explorer 7 installed as the browser. Your job is to train the guides to use the Internet Explorer 7 browser and teach them how to take advantage of the information on the Internet during their tours.

OBJECTIVES

Understand Web browsers

Explore the browser

View and navigate Web pages

Use tabbed browsing

Save favorite Web pages

Print a Web page

Search for information

Get Help and exit Internet Explorer

Understanding Web Browsers

The **World Wide Web** (the **Web** or **WWW**) is the part of the Internet that contains linked Web pages. **Web pages** are documents that can contain text, graphics, sound, and video. **Web browsers (browsers)** are software programs used to access and display Web pages. You must use a browser to view Web pages that are on the Web. Browsers, such as Microsoft Internet Explorer, Opera, FireFox, and Netscape Navigator, make navigating the Web easy. When you view Web pages with a browser, you click words, phrases, or graphics called **hyperlinks**, or simply **links**, to connect to and view other Web pages. Links on a Web page can also open graphics files or play sound or video files. This unit features **Internet Explorer**, a popular browser that is part of the Microsoft Windows operating system. Figure A-1 shows a Web page from the U.S. government's White House Web site. 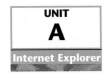 The tour developers have asked you to become familiar with Internet Explorer 7 and the Web so you can teach the guides how to find information for their tours. You discuss the features and benefits of using Internet Explorer.

DETAILS

- ### Display Web pages

  You can access Web sites from all over the world with a Web browser. A **Web site** is a group of Web pages focused on a particular subject. Web sites exist for individuals, businesses, museums, governments, charitable organizations, and educational institutions. There are Web sites for the arts, music, politics, education, sports, and commerce—for any topic, interest, or endeavor in the world. The QST tour guides can use the Web to get up-to-date information about the places they are touring. They can get maps and directions, explore shopping areas, find out about special events, determine currency conversion rates, get weather forecasts, read news, and view photographs.

- ### Use links to move from one Web page to another

  You can click the hyperlinks on a Web page to get more specific information about a business, city, or organization. For example, if a museum is on the tour, a guide can visit the Web site for the museum and click links to view different Web pages that describe current exhibits, visiting hours, or special tours.

- ### Play audio and video clips

  A Web browser can play audio and video clips if it has been configured to do so and your computer has the appropriate hardware, such as speakers. In their research, tour guides might find Web pages that include video clips of historic buildings, shopping trips, local stories and customs, or other information about a region.

- ### Search the Web for information

  A **search engine** is a special Web site that quickly searches the Internet for Web sites based on words or phrases that you enter. Tour guides can take advantage of search engines to look for Web sites that focus on a country, government, or region of travel, or on a specific topic of interest.

- ### Save a list of favorite Web pages

  You can save a list of links to Web pages that you might need to visit again, such as a page for a specific museum, city, or map. Internet Explorer makes it easy to compile a list of your favorite Web sites that is quickly accessible when you want to view those Web sites later. Tour guides can save pages for historic sites or museums for each city they visit with their groups.

- ### Print or save the text and graphics on Web pages

  If you want to keep a hard copy of the information or images you find on the Web, you can simply print the Web page, including any graphics. You can also save the text or graphics on a Web page or copy the information temporarily to the Clipboard, where it is available for pasting into other programs. Tour guides can print maps or informational paragraphs from the Web to hand out to the groups.

- ### E-mail Web pages

  If you want to share a Web page with a colleague, you can e-mail the link or the page directly from the browser window to another person who is set up for e-mail. The person receives the page or link to the page as part of an e-mail message.

FIGURE A-1: A sample Web page

The Internet, computer networks, and intranets

A **computer network** is the hardware and software that makes it possible for two or more computers to share information and resources. An **intranet** is a computer network that connects computers in a local area only, such as computers in a company's office. Users can dial into intranets from remote locations to share company information and resources. The **Internet** is a network of connected computers and computer networks located around the world. The Internet is an international community; Web pages exist from nearly every country in the world. There are over 200 million users worldwide currently connected to the Internet through telephone lines, cables, satellites, and other telecommunications media. Through the Internet, these computers can share many types of information, including text, graphics, sound, video, and computer programs. Anyone who has access to a computer and a connection to the Internet through a computer network or modem can use this rich information source.

The Internet has its roots in the U.S. Department of Defense Advanced Research Projects Agency Network (ARPANET), which began in 1969. In 1986 the National Science Foundation formed NSFNET, which replaced ARPANET. NSFNET expanded the foundation of the U.S. portion of the Internet with high-speed, long-distance lines. By the end of the 1980s, corporations began to use the Internet to communicate with each other and with their customers. In 1991, the U.S. Congress further expanded the Internet's capacity and speed and opened it to commercial use.

The World Wide Web was created in Switzerland in 1991 to allow links between documents on the Internet. The first graphical Web browser, Mosaic, was introduced at the University of Illinois in 1993, leading to the development of browsers such as Netscape Navigator and Internet Explorer. With the boom in the personal computer industry and the expanding availability of inexpensive desktop machines and powerful, network-ready servers, many companies were able to join the Internet for the first time in the early 1990s. The Web is now an integral component of corporate culture, educational institutions, and individuals' personal lives. The Web is used daily for commerce, education, and entertainment by millions of people around the world.

Exploring the Browser

Internet Explorer is a Web browser that connects your computer to the Web through an Internet connection. The browser lets you view, print, and search for information on the Web. You can customize elements of the window. You can choose to view the buttons on the toolbar with or without their corresponding text labels, with large icons, or with text labels on the right. You can also choose whether or not to display the menu bar. Typically, after Internet Explorer is installed, its icon appears on your Windows desktop and the Quick Launch section of the taskbar. You can double-click the desktop icon or click the Quick Launch icon to start Internet Explorer. ■■■■ Before you show the tour guides how to view Web pages and navigate from one page to another, you need to become more familiar with the components of the Internet Explorer browser window.

STEPS

QUICK TIP

If you use a modem and a telephone, follow your normal procedure to establish an Internet connection.

1. **Locate the** Internet Explorer icon 🌐 **on your Windows desktop**

    The location of the Internet Explorer icon shown in Figure A-2 might vary on different computers. You can start Internet Explorer by clicking the Start button on the taskbar, pointing to All Programs, then clicking Internet Explorer. Some computers have the Internet Explorer icon "pinned" to the Start menu, so you can click the Start button on the taskbar, then click Internet Explorer. You might also start Internet Explorer by clicking the Internet Explorer button on the Quick Launch toolbar.

TROUBLE

If an Internet Connection Wizard dialog box opens at any point, you either need to connect to the Internet or enter your Internet settings. Ask your technical support person for assistance.

2. **Double-click the** Internet Explorer icon 🌐 **on the Windows desktop, then if necessary, click the Maximize button** 🔲 **on the Internet Explorer title bar to maximize the program window**

    Internet Explorer opens and displays your home page. A **home page** is the first Web page that opens every time you start Internet Explorer. The term "home page" also applies to the main page that opens when you first go to a Web site. Figure A-3 shows the Quest Specialty Travel home page. Your home page may be different. Look at the home page on your screen and compare the elements described, using Figure A-3 as a guide.

The elements of the Internet Explorer browser window include the following:

- The **title bar** contains the name of the Web page currently displayed in the Web browser's active tab window.
- The **Address bar** displays the address of the Web page currently opened in the active tab. The **Uniform Resource Locator (URL)**, or the Web page's address, appears in the Address box on the Address bar after you open (or load) the page. If you click the Address box list arrow, you see a list of addresses you have recently entered in the Address box. The Address bar also has buttons to refresh a page, to stop the loading of a Web page, and to move forward and back from one Web page to another.
- The **Search box** is used along with the Address bar to help you search for Web sites about a particular topic. You can enter a keyword or words in the Search box, then click the Search button. Click the Search list arrow to specify the search engine to use. When the search is complete, a list of related Web sites opens in a search results Web page.
- The **menu bar** provides access to most of the browser's features through a series of menus.

QUICK TIP

To display toolbars, such as the menu bar and Links bar, click the Tools list arrow on the Command bar, click Menu Bar or point to Toolbars and then click the name of the bar you want to display.

- The **Links bar** is a convenient place to store links to Web pages that you use often. You can add a link to the Links bar by dragging the Internet Explorer icon that precedes the URL in the Address bar to the Links bar. Links placed in the Links bar are also found in the Links folder on the Favorites menu.
- The **Command bar** provides buttons for options, such as printing Web pages, adding Favorites, and searching for information on the Internet. Many commonly used commands available on menus are more quickly accomplished using the toolbar buttons. Depending on the programs installed on your computer, you may have additional buttons.
- The **Favorites Center** is used to store and organize the links to the Web pages that you want to revisit often. To open the Favorites Center, you click the Favorites Center button on the Command bar.
- The **browser window** is the specific area where the current Web page appears.

QUICK TIP

Click the tab for a Web page to display that Web page in front.

- The **tabs** identify the current Web page or pages open in the browser. **Tabbed browsing** allows you to open more than one Web page at a time in a browser window.
- The **vertical scroll bar** appears along the right side of a page if the page is longer than the window's viewable area. The **scroll box** indicates your relative position within the Web page.

FIGURE A-2: Starting Internet Explorer

Icon on desktop

Program pinned to Start menu

Icon on Quick Launch toolbar

FIGURE A-3: Elements of the Internet Explorer window

Title bar with name of Web page

Address bar with URL

Favorites Center Button

Menu bar (closed by default)

Status bar

Search box

Links bar

Command bar

Tabs for tabbed browsing

Scroll box

Browser window

Vertical scroll bar

Understanding the status bar

The status bar performs several functions. It displays information about your connection progress whenever you open a new Web page. It notifies you when you connect to another Web site. As the page loads, it identifies the percentage of information transferred from the Web server to your browser and then displays "Done" when the page is loaded. The status bar displays the Web addresses of any links on the Web page when you move your mouse pointer over them. When the phishing filter is active, the status bar identifies the status of the filter. The Zoom Level button is also located on the status bar. The status indicator, a green bar, is animated while a new Web page loads. You can hide or display the status bar by clicking View on the menu bar and then clicking Status Bar, or by right-clicking the Command bar and then clicking Status Bar.

Internet

Viewing and Navigating Web Pages

Moving between Web pages located at different addresses is simple with hyperlinks. **Hyperlinks** enable you to navigate to, or open, another location on the same Web page or to jump to an entirely different Web page. You can follow these links to obtain more information about a topic by clicking a linked word or phrase. In addition to links on Web pages themselves, you can use the navigation tools in Internet Explorer to move around the Web. You can navigate from page to page using the Forward and Back buttons, as well as the Home button. If you click the Recent Pages button to the right of the Forward button or the Address box list arrow on the Address bar, you see a list of recently viewed Web pages. You can click the name of the page you want to view. You look at the Library of Congress Web site for information for a tour traveling to Washington, D.C.

STEPS

1. **Click anywhere in the Address box on the Address bar**

   The current address is highlighted; any text you type replaces it.

TROUBLE

If the Microsoft Phishing Filter dialog box opens, you can turn on the filter, turn off the filter, or decide whether to turn it off or on later.

2. **Type www.loc.gov, then press [Enter]**

   After a few seconds, the home page for the Library of Congress opens in the browser window, as shown in Figure A-4, and the status bar displays "Done". Web pages change frequently. The Web page you load may look different from that shown in the figure. After you press [Enter], Internet Explorer automatically adds the "http://" protocol to the beginning of the address you type. If you have typed a specific address in the Address bar previously, the AutoComplete feature recognizes the first few characters you type. A list opens below the Address box containing the addresses in which the typed letters appear; you can click the URL in the list to open the page rather than complete the typing of the URL. As the page is loading, the status bar displays the connection process. The page contains both pictures and text, some of which are hyperlinks.

3. **Place your mouse pointer on the Visitors link in the Resources for section**

   When you place the pointer on a hyperlink, the pointer changes to �👆 and the URL for the hyperlink appears in the status bar. A ScreenTip may also appear, giving you more information about the linked page.

4. **Click the Visitors link**

   The Visitors page opens in your Web browser window, as shown in Figure A-5. The name of the Web page appears on the front tab in the browser window. A Web page icon appears to the left of the Web page name.

QUICK TIP

Move the pointer over the Back or Forward button to display a ScreenTip showing which page will appear when the button is clicked.

5. **Click the Back button ⬅ on the Address bar**

   The Web page that you viewed, the Library of Congress home page, opens in the browser window.

6. **Click the Forward button ➡ on the Address bar**

   The Forward button opens the Visitors page in the browser window again.

7. **Click the Home button 🏠 on the Command bar**

   Clicking the Home button opens the home page designated for your installation of Internet Explorer. Click the Refresh button ↻ on the Address bar to update a page that may have changed.

QUICK TIP

If you change your mind or if a page takes too long to load, you can click the Stop button on the Address bar to stop a new Web page from loading.

8. **Click the Recent Pages button ▾ to the right of the Forward button ➡ on the Address bar, then click The Library of Congress**

   The Recent Pages button displays a list of the last few pages that you visited.

FIGURE A-4: Home page for the Library of Congress

Back button

Forward button

URL

New Tab tab

Visitors link

FIGURE A-5: Visitors Web page at the Library of Congress Web site

Name of Web page
on the tab

Stop button

Refresh button

Home button

Setting the Home Page

When you click the Home button on the Command bar, the page that is specified as the home page opens in your Web browser window. Each time you start Internet Explorer, the first page that appears is your home page. When you install Internet Explorer, the default home page might have been the Welcome to MSN.com home page at the MSN Web site. You can easily select a different home page to open each time you start Internet Explorer. Simply go to the page that you want to be your home page, click the Home button list arrow on the Command bar, then click Add or Change Home Page to open the Add or Change Home Page dialog box. See Figure A-6. When the dialog box opens, select the option that identifies how you want to set the Web page as your home page. If you have more than one tab open, you will see all these options. You can also click Tools on the menu bar,

then click Internet Options to open the Internet Options dialog box. Click the General tab if necessary, click the Use current button in the Home page area to specify the current page as your home page.

FIGURE A-6: Add or Change Home Page dialog box

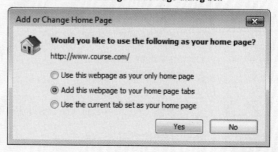

Internet

Using Tabbed Browsing

Tabbed browsing allows more than one Web page to open within the same browser window. Each window appears on a separate tab. This method for organizing Web pages while browsing makes navigation between Web pages fast and simple, and minimizes the number of windows you need open on your desktop as you browse the Web. You can open several Internet Explorer windows at the same time, each with its own series of Web pages accessible by tabs. You can also change the default settings for tabbed browsing: for example, you can have several pages open automatically for a Web site on several tabs, or you can bypass the tab settings to open pages in their own windows. Figure A-7 shows an Internet Explorer window with several pages from the Library of Congress Web site open in tabs. Table A-1 describes buttons that are available on the Command bar and the Address bar. 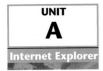 You want to show the tour guides how tabbed browsing will allow them to more easily compare events in a location by viewing the Web pages in one browsing session.

STEPS

1. **Type www.usa.gov in the Address bar, then press [Enter]**
   The Web page for the U.S. government opens. It is on the front tab in the browser window.

> **TROUBLE**
> If someone has clicked the Don't show this page again check box on the about:Tabs page, you will see a Web page rather than the Welcome to Tabbed Browsing page.

2. **Click the New Tab tab in the browser window**
   The about:Tabs Web page appears as a new tab in the browser window, as shown in Figure A-8.

3. **Click the Close Tab button in the Welcome to Tabbed Browsing tab**
   The usa.gov Web page is in the browser window.

4. **Right-click the State Government link, click Open in New Tab on the menu, then click the State and Territorial tab to display the Web page**

5. **Right-click any state link, click Open in New Tab on the menu, then click the state tab**
   Using tabbed browsing, you now have three Web pages open in one browser window.

6. **Position the mouse pointer over each tab to display the ScreenTip for each**
   Each ScreenTip tells you the name and URL of the Web page in the tab.

7. **Click the Quick Tabs button 🔠 to the left of the tabs**
   Thumbnail images of open tabs appear in Quick Tabs view, as shown in Figure A-9.

8. **Click the Close Tab button for the second and third thumbnails in Quick Tabs view, then click the USA.gov tab**
   Quick Tabs view closes and the USA.gov tab is open in the window.

TABLE A-1: Internet Explorer 7 buttons

button name	button	description	button name	button	description
Back	←	Opens previous page	Add to Favorites	⭐	Opens Add to Favorites menu and dialog box
Forward	→	Opens next page	Print	🖨	Prints current Web page
Recent Pages	▾	Displays list of recently viewed pages	View Feeds on this page	📶	Adds current RSS Feed to Favorites Center
Stop	✕	Stops loading new page	Page	Page ▾	Provides Page options
Refresh	↻	Refreshes the contents of current page	Help	❓	Displays Internet Explorer Help window
Home	🏠	Opens the home page	Tools	Tools ▾	Opens a menu of commands to manage settings for the Pop-up Blocker, Phishing Filter, Windows Update, and browsing history
Search	🔍	Searches for Web sites based on a keyword	Research	📖	Opens Research task pane
Favorites Center	⭐	Opens Favorites Center			

FIGURE A-7: Tabbed browsing

Tab list

New Tab tab

Three tabs open in one browser window

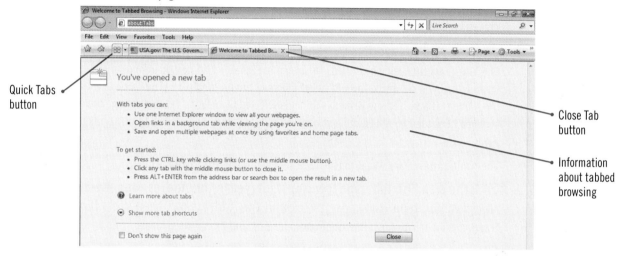

FIGURE A-8: New page in a second tab

Quick Tabs button

Close Tab button

Information about tabbed browsing

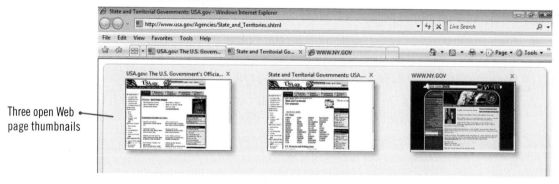

FIGURE A-9: Quick Tabs view

Three open Web page thumbnails

Exiting options when you have multiple tabs open

When you finish looking at Web pages using Internet Explorer, you may find that you have several tabs open. When you exit Internet Explorer and you have more than one tab open, a dialog box appears asking if you want to close all the tabs. If you want the same tabs to open the next time you start Internet Explorer, click Show Options, click Open these the next time I use Internet Explorer, then click Close Tabs.

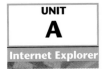

Saving Favorite Web Pages

The **Favorites Center** allows you to create your own list of frequently visited Web pages, or **favorites**. When you find a Web page that you know you will want to revisit, add the site address to the Favorites Center. You can then access the site by clicking a link in the Favorites Center. After you add a Web page to the Favorites Center, you can automatically access that page by clicking the Favorites Center button on the Command bar, by clicking Favorites on the menu bar and then clicking the link, or by clicking the icon on the Links bar if available. ▰▰▰▰ The tour guides will want to be able to revisit some travel site Web pages without having to write the URLs on a sheet of paper and typing the URLs in the Address bar each time.

STEPS

1. **Click the Address bar, type www.nps.gov/brca, then press [Enter]**
   The home page for Bryce Canyon National Park opens, as shown in Figure A-10.

> **QUICK TIP**
> Web pages change frequently. The PHOTOS & MULTIMEDIA link may be in a new location on the page.

2. **Click the PHOTOS & MULTIMEDIA link, read the information, then click the Back button ⬅ on the Address bar**
   This site offers information for adventure travelers. You want to save the link in the Favorites Center.

3. **Click the Add to Favorites button ⭐ on the Command bar, then click Add to Favorites**
   The Add a Favorite dialog box opens, as shown in Figure A-11. The Add a Favorite dialog box shows the folders in which you can place the URL for the Bryce Canyon Web page. The name of the Web page appears in the Name text box, and the Favorites folder is selected by default. You can change the default page name by typing a new name in the Name text box.

4. **Click Add**
   The name and URL are added to the Favorites Center and the Favorites menu.

5. **Click the New Tab tab, type www.nps.gov/yell in the Address bar, press [Enter], click the New Tab tab, type www.nps.gov/zion in the Address bar, then press [Enter]**
   You opened new tabs for Yellowstone National Park and Zion National Park.

6. **Click the Add to Favorites button ⭐ on the Command bar, click Add Tab Group to Favorites, type National Parks Tour West in the Tab Group Name text box, then click Add**
   You added all the open tabs in the window to a tab group in the Favorites Center.

> **QUICK TIP**
> The most recently added favorites appear at the bottom of the Favorites list.

7. **Close the second and third tabs, then click the Home button 🏠 on the Command bar to return to your home page**

8. **Click the Favorites Center button ⭐ on the Command bar**
   The Favorites Center opens. You see a list of Favorites, including the Bryce Canyon National Park favorite you just added and the National Parks Tour West tab group you added, listed as a folder.

> **QUICK TIP**
> Click the arrow to open all links in the group, each in its own tab.

9. **Click National Parks Tour West to open the list of links associated with that Folder, then click the Bryce Canyon National Park link in the Favorites Center**
   The Bryce Canyon home page opens in your Web browser window.

Understanding URLs

Every Web page has a unique address on the Web, also known as the **URL** for the page. Browser software locates a Web page based on its address. All Web page addresses begin with "http," which stands for Hypertext Transfer Protocol, the set of rules for exchanging files on the Web. This is followed by a colon and two forward slashes. Most pages begin with "www" (which indicates that the page is on the World Wide Web), followed by a dot, or period, and then the Web site's name, known as the **domain name**. Following the domain name is another dot and the top-level domain, such as com (for commercial sites), edu (for educational institutions), or org (for organizations). The **top-level domain** tells you the type of site you are visiting. After the top-level domain, another slash and one or more folder names and a filename might appear.

FIGURE A-10: Bryce Canyon National Park home page

Favorites Center button

Add to Favorites button

PHOTOS & MULTIMEDIA link

FIGURE A-11: Add a Favorite dialog box

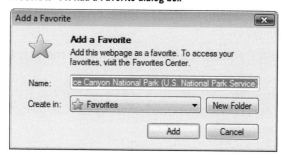

Creating and organizing favorites

Once you add a Web page to your Favorites Center, returning to that page is much easier. To keep your Favorites Center list manageable, only add pages that you expect to visit again. You can organize your list of favorites by placing them into folders by category. For example, you may want to create folders according to your interests, such as sports, cooking, and travel. You may want to create folders in which each member of a household can place his or her own favorites. Favorites can be listed individually or placed in folders in the Favorites Center or on the Favorites menu. To add a folder to your Favorites Center, click Add to Favorites on the Command bar, then click Organize Favorites. The Organize Favorites dialog box opens, as shown in Figure A-12. Click the New Folder button to add a new folder to the list of folders and favorites. You can move a favorite to a specific folder by clicking the favorite, clicking the Move button, and then selecting the folder or creating a new folder in which to add the favorite you want to move. You can also drag and drop a favorite into a folder, and you can rename favorites and folders. Information about a selected favorite appears below the list.

Links stored in the Links folder appear on the Links bar in the browser window. The Favorites Center also stores the links for RSS feeds and keeps the history of all Web pages visited.

FIGURE A-12: Organize Favorites dialog box

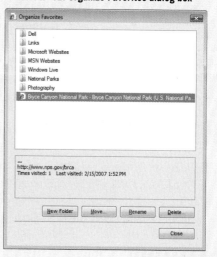

Internet

Printing a Web Page

When you print a Web page, its text and any graphics appear on the printed page. Internet Explorer provides ways to shrink text so that the contents of a Web page fit on one page. You can also adjust margins, change the page orientation, change headers and footers, and adjust the print space to best meet your printing needs. The options in the Print dialog box allow you to specify print options such as the number of copies and the page range. With Internet Explorer, you can preview a Web page prior to printing by using Print Preview, which is helpful because some Web pages are lengthy and you may only want to print the pages that have the information relevant to your task. ▨▨▨▨ You show the tour guides how to print a copy of a Web page so they can provide the information as handouts to the tour guests.

STEPS

QUICK TIP
To have your name appear on the printed page, type your name in the Header or Footer text box.

1. **Click the Address box on the Address bar, type www.nps.gov, press [Enter], then click the HISTORY & CULTURE link**
   The History & Culture page for the National Park Service opens.

2. **Click the Print button list arrow ▤ ▾ on the Command bar, then click Page Setup**
   The Page Setup dialog box opens. You can change the page size, margins, and orientation. You can also edit the footers and headers. By default, the current URL and the date and time are printed on the page, so people can see the URL and visit the Web site if they want to.

QUICK TIP
To print a Web page without previewing the page or changing any settings, click the Print button on the Command bar.

3. **Click Cancel, click the Print button list arrow ▤ ▾ , then click Print Preview**
   The Print Preview window opens. See Figure A-13. The default setting in the Change Print Size box is Shrink to Fit, which indicates that the Web page width will be adjusted to fit the width of one printed page. The Turn headers and footers on or off button on the toolbar determines whether the headers and footers are visible on the printed page.

4. **Click the Landscape button ▨ on the toolbar, then click the Portrait button ▨ on the toolbar**
   You confirm that Portrait orientation is best for the handout. If there are multiple pages to print, you can click the Show multiple pages list arrow on the toolbar and then click the number of pages that you prefer to view at once.

5. **Click the Print Document button ▨ on the toolbar**
   The Print dialog box opens, as shown in Figure A-14. Table A-2 explains printing options in more detail.

6. **Make sure 1 appears in the Number of copies text box, then click the Current Page option button in the Page Range area**
   These settings indicate that one copy of the current Web page will print using the default printer.

TROUBLE
If your computer is not connected to a printer or if an error message appears, ask your technical support person for assistance.

7. **Make sure that your computer is connected to a printer and that the printer is turned on and contains paper, then click Print**
   The Print dialog box closes, and one copy of the current Web page prints.

Copying information from a Web page

You can select text on a Web page and use the Copy and Paste commands to use the same information in another program, such as Microsoft Word or other Office programs. You can also save a graphic image from a Web page by right-clicking the image, clicking Save Picture As on the shortcut menu, then specifying where to save the image. If you just need to copy an image, click the Copy command on the shortcut menu. Using the Copy command saves the text or image to the Clipboard.

Keep in mind that the same laws that protect printed works generally protect information and graphics published on a Web page. Do not use material on a Web page without citing its source and checking the site carefully for any usage restrictions.

FIGURE A-13: Print Preview window

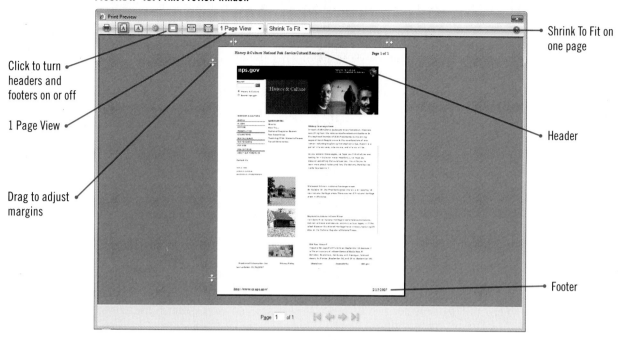

Click to turn headers and footers on or off

1 Page View

Drag to adjust margins

Shrink To Fit on one page

Header

Footer

FIGURE A-14: Print dialog box

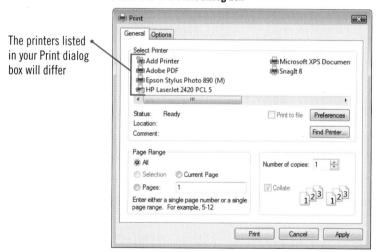

The printers listed in your Print dialog box will differ

TABLE A-2: Printing options

option	tab	description
Select Printer	General	Displays information about the name, status, type, and location of the printer
Page Range	General	Choose to print current page, all pages, a range of pages, or a selection
Number of copies	General	Indicates the number of copies of each page to print and their sequence
Print all linked documents	Options	Opens and prints each document referenced by a link on the current page
Print frames	Options	In a Web page containing frames, allows you to print frames as laid out, only the selected frame, or all frames individually
Print table of links	Options	Prints links in a table at the end of the document
Orientation	(Depends on printer)	Allows you to specify landscape or portrait page orientation

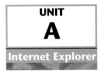

UNIT
A

Internet Explorer

Searching for Information

A vast and ever-increasing number of Web pages and other information sources are available through the Internet. A search for information using Internet Explorer's **Address bar** is based on criteria or **keywords**, which are words related to the topic for which you are searching. To search using the Address bar, you can enter a keyword or words in the Search box, then click the Search button to start the search. The **Search box** enables you to search in two ways: It can provide a list of links similar in content or topic to the Web page you are currently viewing, or you can use the Search box to search for information based on keywords. If you use Web **search engines** such as Windows Live, MSN Search, Google, or Yahoo! to locate information, the result is a list of links to Web sites related to your search topic. You can click one of the links in the list to go quickly to a site. ▓▓▓▓▓ You decide to show the tour guides how to look for adventure travel information by searching with the browser.

STEPS

> **QUICK TIP**
>
> Each search engine differs slightly in the way it formats information, the way it records the number of Internet sites in the database, and how often it updates the database.

1. **Click the Address bar, type www.google.com, then press [Enter]**

   The Google home page opens in the browser window. Google is a commercial company that runs a search engine. Search engines such as Yahoo!, Google, Ask, and Lycos routinely use software programs to methodically catalog, or crawl, through the entire Internet and create huge databases with links to Web pages and their URLs. When you enter a keyword or phrase, the search engine examines its database index for relevant information and displays a list of Web sites.

2. **Type adventure travel in the Search box, then click Google Search**

   Your search results appear as a list of links to related Web sites with a description of each site.

3. **Click any link to view a Web page, click the Back button ⊖ twice on the Address bar to return to the Google home page, then click the New Tab tab to open a new tab**

4. **Click the Search list arrow 🔍 ▾ on the Address bar**

   The default search engine for Internet Explorer 7 is Live Search. If another search engine is listed, such as Google, you can use that as well. You decide to investigate online photo-sharing, since tour guests like to exchange photos.

5. **Click Change Search Defaults**

   See Figure A-15. The Change Search Defaults dialog box is used to set another Web site as the default.

> **QUICK TIP**
>
> Topic searches, which limit the search to a specific subject such as travel, science, or history, are available through Web sites such as Expedia.com, About.com, and Wikipedia.com.

6. **Click Cancel in the Change Search Defaults dialog box, click in the Search box on the Address bar, type share photos online, then click the Search button 🔍 on the Address bar**

   The Web is searched on the keywords you entered using the default search engine. As shown in Figure A-16, your search results appear as a list of related Web sites in the Live Search Web page in the tab of the browser window. You can click any hyperlink to open a Web page or a list of Web pages relating to a specific category.

7. **Examine the results list by scrolling up or down, then right-click a hyperlink of your choice and click Open in New Tab**

   The related page containing information about a Web site that you can use to share photographs opens in the browser window. You want to compare these results with those of another search engine.

8. **Click the Google tab, type share photos online in the Google Search box, then click Google Search**

   You can click between the tabs to compare results and click the different Web pages to find the information.

9. **Review the list of results, press and hold [Ctrl], then click any hyperlink**

   The Web page opens in a new tab. You can click the tab to view the Web page. Based on your search, you see that there are many different Web sites with information about online photo-sharing.

10. **Close all open tabs except the first tab, then click the Home button 🏠**

    Your home page appears in the browser window.

FIGURE A-15: Change Search Defaults dialog box

FIGURE A-16: Search results

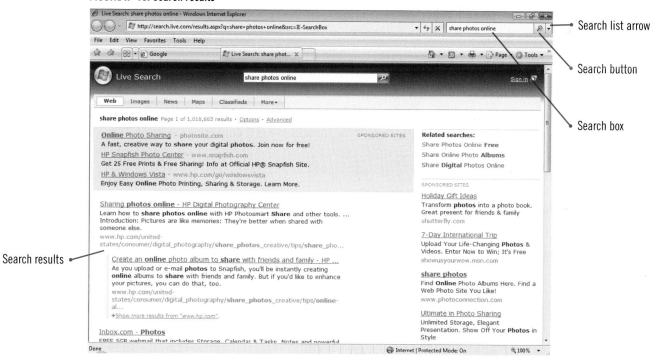

Search list arrow

Search button

Search box

Search results

Blocking pop-ups

Pop-ups are windows that open on your screen as you visit Web sites, generally to advertise products you may or may not want. Often they are annoying, so you might choose to block them. Internet Explorer comes with a built-in Pop-up Blocker. Click Tools on the Command bar, point to Pop-up Blocker, then click Turn Off Pop-up Blocker to turn it off if you want pop-ups, or click Pop-up Blocker Settings to open the Pop-up Blocker Settings dialog box to permit pop-ups from specific Web sites. You can also control notifications and set the filter level. Notifications will play a sound or show the Information Bar if a pop-up is blocked. Filter levels can be set to Low, Medium, or High.

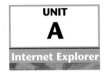
Getting Help and Exiting Internet Explorer

Internet Explorer provides a Help system with information and instructions on various features and commands. ▓▓▓▓▓ While demonstrating Internet Explorer, you were asked about the purpose of the Phishing Filter on the status bar. **Phishing** is an illicit activity where people send you fraudulent Web sites to gather your personal information for possible illegal purposes. You decide to demonstrate the Help system to the tour guides by finding out more about phishing and privacy protection as you use Internet Explorer.

STEPS

TROUBLE
If the Help button is not visible, click the More button ▾ on the Command bar, then click Help.

1. **Click the Help button 🔘 on the Command bar, then click Contents and Index**
   The Windows Help and Support window opens. You can type a keyword in the Search Help text box, or you can click links to access several Help features. The buttons at the top of the Window provide various avenues into the Help System. Refer to Figure A-17.

2. **Click the Browse Help button**
   The Contents page shows a list of common options.

3. **Click the Home button 🏠, type phishing in the Search Help text box, press [Enter], click Phishing Filter: frequently asked questions in the results list, then maximize the window if necessary**
   As shown in Figure A-18, the links in the Windows Help and Support window provide a list of frequently asked questions. Each question is a link to the answer.

QUICK TIP
Click Show All to display all the answers at once, then scroll as needed to read all the text.

4. **Click one question link and read the information**
   The question expands to reveal the answer to that question about phishing.

5. **Click the Close button ❌ in the upper-right corner of the Help window**
   The Help window closes. When you are ready to exit Internet Explorer, you can click the Close button in the upper-right corner of the browser window or click Close on the File menu. You do not need to save files before you exit.

6. **Click Add to Favorites ⭐ on the Command bar, click Organize Favorites, select each Favorite or Folder that you added in this unit, click Delete, click Yes in the confirmation dialog box, then click Close to close the Organize Favorites dialog box**

7. **Click the Close button ❌ on the title bar**
   The Internet Explorer browser window closes. If you have more than one tab open, you will see a dialog box like the one shown in Figure A-19, confirming that you want to close all tabs.

8. **If you connected to the Internet by telephone line, follow your normal procedure to close your connection**

Viewing sites in other languages

The Web is an international forum; as you surf the Web, you may find sites that display text in the native language of the country where the site originates. If you are a native English-speaking person, most Web sites have an English link somewhere on the site's home page that you can click to display the site in English.

FIGURE A-17: Windows Internet Explorer Help window

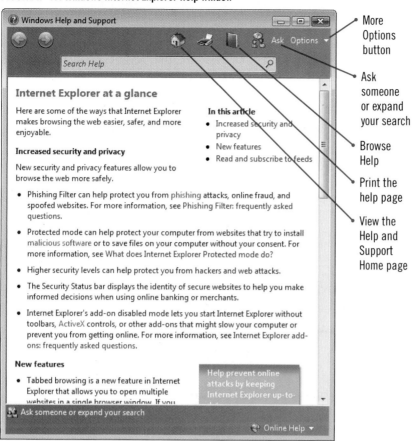

More Options button

Ask someone or expand your search

Browse Help

Print the help page

View the Help and Support Home page

FIGURE A-18: Phishing Filter FAQs

FIGURE A-19: Closing multiple tabs

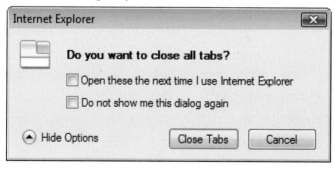

Saving or sending a Web page

Before exiting Internet Explorer, you may want to save a copy of the current page or send someone a copy of the page. If you want to use the menu bar, you can click File on the menu bar to open the File menu and access the Save and Send commands. If you want to use the Command bar, you can click the Page button list arrow to see the Save and Send commands. By selecting the Save As command, you can save the complete Web page, including any graphics—or just the text from the page—in a file on your computer. If you want to send the complete page to someone, use the Send Page By E-mail command, and then use your e-mail program to address and send the message to the intended recipient. If you want to send the Link only, not the whole page, use the Send Link by E-mail command.

Internet

Practice

If you have a SAM user profile, you may have access to hands-on instruction, practice, and assessment of the skills covered in this unit. Log in to your SAM account (http://sam2007.course.com/) to launch any assigned training activities or exams that relate to the skills covered in this unit.

▼ CONCEPTS REVIEW

Label each element of the Internet Explorer browser window shown in Figure A-20.

FIGURE A-20

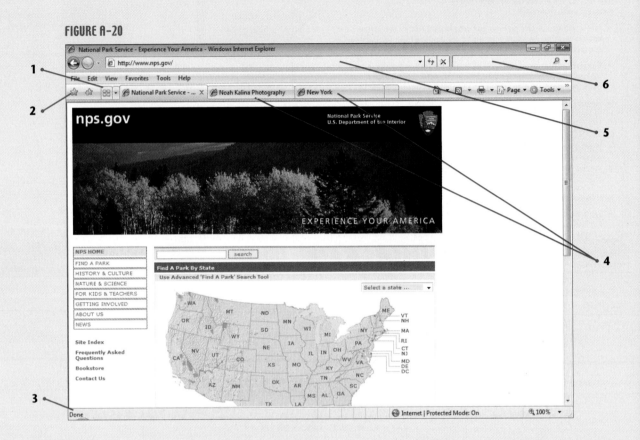

Match each term with the statement that best describes it.

7. **Hyperlink**

8. **Quick Tabs button**

9. **Favorites Center**

10. **Address box**

11. **Uniform Resource Locator (URL)**

a. Click to view a new Web page

b. Displays the URL for the currently displayed page

c. Use to display all open Web pages as thumbnails

d. Displays a list of saved Web pages

e. A Web page's address

Select the best answer from the list of choices.

12. Software programs such as Internet Explorer and FireFox are called _____.
   - **a.** Web companions
   - **b.** Web browsers
   - **c.** Web documents
   - **d.** Web windows

13. Which of the following functions is NOT available on the status bar?
   - **a.** Displays information about your connection progress
   - **b.** Notifies you when you connect to another Web site
   - **c.** Displays search results
   - **d.** Displays "Done" when the page is loaded

14. Click the _____ button to view the links of pages you have visited and saved.
   - **a.** Address
   - **b.** Link
   - **c.** Favorites Center
   - **d.** Back

15. _____ browsing allows you to open more than one Web page at a time in a browser window.
   - **a.** Tabbed
   - **b.** Web
   - **c.** Linked
   - **d.** Favorites

16. You can search for Web sites by category by entering a keyword in the Address bar, then clicking the _____.
   - **a.** Search button
   - **b.** Refresh button
   - **c.** Home button
   - **d.** Link button

17. The letters following the dot after the domain name are called the _____ domain and tell you the type of site you are visiting.
   - **a.** top-level
   - **b.** home-level
   - **c.** dot-com
   - **d.** main-level

18. Which button on the Command bar should you click if you want to view the previous Web page on your computer?
   - **a.** Home
   - **b.** Last
   - **c.** Back
   - **d.** Link

19. Words or graphics on a Web page that, when clicked, enable you to navigate to another Web page location are called _____.
   - **a.** Tabs
   - **b.** Web browsers
   - **c.** Hyperlinks
   - **d.** Buttons

20. Using the Internet to gather personal information without the knowledge or permission of the person who's information is being collected is called _____.
   - **a.** Phishing
   - **b.** Linking
   - **c.** Popping
   - **d.** Spam

21. When viewing a Web page, what method for clicking a link will NOT open a new page on a new tab?
   - **a.** Press and hold [Ctrl], then click
   - **b.** Right-click, then click Open in New Tab
   - **c.** Double-click the link
   - **d.** Press and hold [Ctrl], then press T

▼ SKILLS REVIEW

1. Start Internet Explorer.
   - **a.** Make sure your computer is connected to the Internet.
   - **b.** Start Internet Explorer.

2. Explore the browser window.
   - **a.** Identify the Command bar, menu bar, Address bar, Search box, Links bar, status bar, URL, browser window, and scroll bar.
   - **b.** Identify the buttons for printing, searching, viewing favorites, and returning to the home page.
   - **c.** Identify the complete URL of the current Web page.

Internet

3. View and navigate Web pages.

  a. Open the Web page www.llnl.gov using the Address bar to open the Web page shown in Figure A-21.

  b. Click a link on the Web page to view a new Web page.

  c. Return to the default home page for your browser.

  d. Click the Back button.

  e. Follow another link to investigate the content.

  f. Return to the default home page for your browser.

4. Use tabbed browsing.

  a. Open the Web page www.nytimes.com using the Address bar.

  b. Right-click a link on the Web page to open an article in a new tab.

  c. Click the New Tab tab to open a third tab in the browser window, then open www.cnn.com in the new tab using the Address bar.

  d. Press and hold [CTRL], then click a link on the CNN home page to open a fourth tab.

  e. Click the Quick Tabs button to view all four Web pages as thumbnails.

  f. Click the first thumbnail to view the Web page. Your screen should resemble Figure A-22.

  g. Close all tabs except for the New York Times tab.

5. Save favorite Web pages.

  a. Open the Web page www.nasa.gov using the Address bar.

  b. Add the Web page to your Favorites Center.

  c. Return to the default home page for your browser.

  d. Using the Favorites Center, return to the NASA home page.

6. Print a Web page.

  a. Click any link on the NASA home page that is interesting to you.

  b. Use Print Preview to preview the Web page in printed form.

  c. Verify that the Print Size is set to Shrink To Fit. If there is more than one page, look at 2 Page View, as shown in Figure A-23.

  d. Print one copy of the first page only.

  e. Close Print Preview.

FIGURE A-21

FIGURE A-22

FIGURE A-23

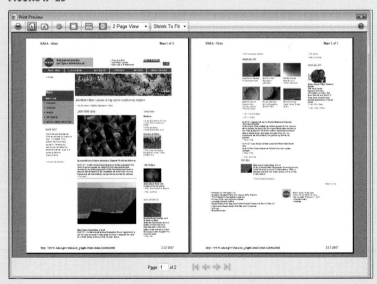

▼ SKILLS REVIEW (CONTINUED)

7. Search for information on the Web.

   a. Click the Search box in the Address bar.

   b. Type any keyword or phrase for which you would like to find information, then execute the search and review the results.

   c. Click any link in the Search results page and read the Web page.

   d. Enter the URL for a search engine in the Address Bar (you can use www.google.com, www.ask.com, www.live.com, or www.yahoo.com).

   e. Type any keyword or phrase for which you would like to find information, then start the search using the search engine.

   f. View the resulting list of links, then click a link and review the Web page.

   g. Return to the search results page, then explore some of the other hyperlinks you found.

8. Get Help.

   a. Open Microsoft Internet Explorer Help, then search for a topic of interest to you.

   b. Click any link for any topic you want to learn more about.

   c. Read the results.

   d. Close the Windows Internet Explorer Help window.

9. Exit Internet Explorer.

   a. Delete any Favorites you created using the Organize Favorites dialog box.

   b. Exit Internet Explorer.

▼ INDEPENDENT CHALLENGE 1

You are an aspiring journalist interested in understanding how different journalists approach the same story. You decide to use the Web to find some articles for comparison.

   a. Start Internet Explorer.

   b. Read and compare the coverage of a current international news story using two of the following sites:

   - CNN   www.cnn.com
   - MSNBC News   www.msnbc.com
   - National Public Radio   www.npr.org
   - ABC News   www.abcnews.com
   - CBS News   www.cbsnews.com

   c. Open each news story in its own tab in the browser window.

   d. Use the Page Setup dialog box to add your name as a footer to the printed page, then print one page of the same story from both sites that you chose using the Shrink to Fit option.

Advanced Challenge Exercise

You should be able to find many English-language versions of non-U.S. papers.

   - Use your favorite search engine to locate an online news media source from a country other than the United States. You can search on keywords such as "Asian newspapers" or "European newspapers."
   - See if you can find the news story you researched in Step b.
   - Read the article.
   - Use the Page Setup dialog box to add your name as a footer to the printed page, then print one page of the article from the site that you chose.

   e. Close all but one of the tabs, then exit Internet Explorer.

▼ INDEPENDENT CHALLENGE 2

You have been asked by your local community college to teach a short course on classic films from the 1940s and 1950s. The class will meet four times; each class will begin with a screening and be followed by a discussion. You decide to use the Web to research the material.

a. Start Internet Explorer.

b. Go to your favorite search engine, then use a keyword search to find a Web site that contains information about films made in the 1940s.

c. Find two films from the 1940s that you want to show as part of the course. View the information about each film in a separate tab in the browser window.

d. Click several links on the film site and review the online resources.

e. Search the film site to find two films from the 1950s. View the information about each film in a separate tab in the browser window.

f. Add the film site as a favorite to the Favorites Center.

g. Use the Page Setup dialog box to add your name as a footer to the printed page, then print one page for each film from the site.

Advanced Challenge Exercise

- Find one page that includes a link for media such as audio or video.
- Click the link and listen to the audio or play the video.
- After listening to or viewing the media file, close the window.

h. Delete the film site from the Favorites Center, then exit Internet Explorer.

▼ INDEPENDENT CHALLENGE 3

As a student of American political history, you want to learn about your representatives in the U.S. government. You decide to use the Web to get information about this topic.

a. Start Internet Explorer, then access the following government Web site: **www.thomas.gov**.

b. Explore the site to find information about members of Congress. Use the Page Setup dialog box to add your name as a footer to the printed page, then print one page from that site.

c. In a new tab, open the Web site **www.senate.gov**, the U.S. Senate home page, as shown in Figure A-24.

d. Click the Senators link, then find a link to a Web site for a senator who represents the state that you would most like to visit. Click the link, then print one page from that site.

e. Explore three links on the senator's Web site to learn more about those topics, opening each page in a new tab.

f. Use the Quick Tabs feature to navigate between the Web pages.

g. Use the Page Setup dialog box to add your name as a footer to the printed page, then print one page from one of the related sites.

h. Exit Internet Explorer.

FIGURE A-24

▼ REAL LIFE INDEPENDENT CHALLENGE

You would like to select a search engine to use consistently when you search the Web. You decide to compare several search engines to determine which one you like the most.

a. Start Internet Explorer. Using two of the search engines listed below, type **nobel prize winners** in the Search text box, and then search for the topic.
- Yahoo!   www.yahoo.com
- Live Search   www.live.com
- Google   www.google.com
- Ask   www.ask.com

b. Add your name as a footer to the printed page, then print the first page of the results from each search. Circle the name of the search engine and the number of results it produced.

c. On a sheet of paper, write which search engine you think is better and include a few reasons for your preference.

Advanced Challenge Exercise

- Create a folder in the Favorites Center called **Search Results**.
- Add the home page for your favorite search engine to the Favorites Center, in the Search Results folder.
- Return to your home page, then use the Favorites Center to go to the search engine home page.
- Delete the Search Results folder and search engine home page from the Favorites Center.

d. Exit Internet Explorer.

Internet

▼ VISUAL WORKSHOP

Graphics you find as you view pages on the Web can be static images, video, or animated graphics. Find two Web sites that include a video. You may be given the option to watch the video using a player such as Windows Media Player, as shown in Figure A-25. Other viewing options may include other players or viewing the video directly through the Web page. View at least one video on a news site and one video on a topic-specific Web site such as an organization or tourism site. Write a brief summary of the videos you watched. Did you have to load a special program to watch the video? Identify the Web sites on which the videos were located.

FIGURE A-25

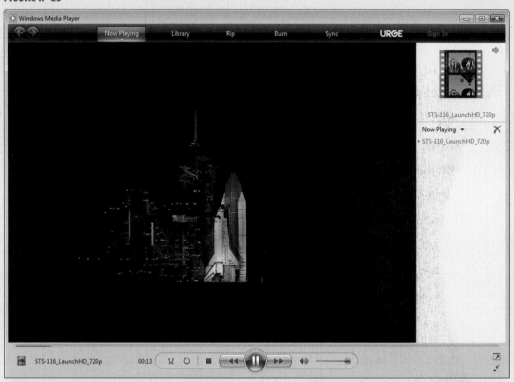

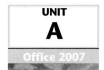

Getting Started with Microsoft Office 2007

Files You Will Need:

OFFICE A-1.xlsx

Microsoft Office 2007 is a group of software programs designed to help you create documents, collaborate with co-workers, and track and analyze information. Each program is designed so you can work quickly and efficiently to create professional-looking results. You use different Office programs to accomplish specific tasks, such as writing a letter or producing a sales presentation, yet all the programs have a similar look and feel. Once you become familiar with one program, you'll find it easy to transfer your knowledge to the others. This unit introduces you to the most frequently used programs in Office, as well as common features they all share.

OBJECTIVES

Understand the Office 2007 Suite

Start and exit an Office program

View the Office 2007 user interface

Create and save a file

Open a file and save it with a new name

View and print your work

Get Help and close a file

Understanding the Office 2007 Suite

Microsoft Office 2007 features an intuitive, context-sensitive user interface, so you can get up to speed faster and use advanced features with greater ease. The programs in Office are bundled together in a group called a **suite** (although you can also purchase them separately). The Office suite is available in several configurations, but all include Word and Excel. Other configurations include PowerPoint, Access, Outlook, Publisher, and/or others. ⬛⬛⬛⬛ Each program in Office is best suited for completing specific types of tasks, though there is some overlap in terms of their capabilities.

The Office programs covered in this book include:

- **Microsoft Office Word 2007**

  When you need to create any kind of text-based document, such as memos, newsletters, or multi-page reports, Word is the program to use. You can easily make your documents look great by inserting eye-catching graphics and using formatting tools such as themes. **Themes** are predesigned combinations of color and formatting attributes you can apply, and are available in most Office programs. The Word document shown in Figure A-1 was formatted with the Solstice theme.

- **Microsoft Office Excel 2007**

  Excel is the perfect solution when you need to work with numeric values and make calculations. It puts the power of formulas, functions, charts, and other analytical tools into the hands of every user, so you can analyze sales projections, figure out loan payments, and present your findings in style. The Excel worksheet shown in Figure A-1 tracks personal expenses. Because Excel automatically recalculates results whenever a value changes, the information is always up-to-date. A chart illustrates how the monthly expenses are broken down.

- **Microsoft Office PowerPoint 2007**

  Using PowerPoint, it's easy to create powerful presentations complete with graphics, transitions, and even a soundtrack. Using professionally designed themes and clip art, you can quickly and easily create dynamic slideshows such as the one shown in Figure A-1.

- **Microsoft Office Access 2007**

  Access helps you keep track of large amounts of quantitative data, such as product inventories or employee records. The form shown in Figure A-1 was created for a grocery store inventory database. Employees use the form to enter data about each item. Using Access enables employees to quickly find specific information such as price and quantity, without hunting through store shelves and stockrooms.

Microsoft Office has benefits beyond the power of each program, including:

- **Common user interface: Improving business processes**

  Because the Office suite programs have a similar **interface**, or look and feel, your experience using one program's tools makes it easy to learn those in the other programs. Office documents are **compatible** with one another, meaning that you can easily incorporate, or **integrate**, an Excel chart into a PowerPoint slide, or an Access table into a Word document.

- **Collaboration: Simplifying how people work together**

  Office recognizes the way people do business today, and supports the emphasis on communication and knowledge-sharing within companies and across the globe. All Office programs include the capability to incorporate feedback—called **online collaboration**—across the Internet or a company network.

FIGURE A-1: Microsoft Office 2007 documents

Word document

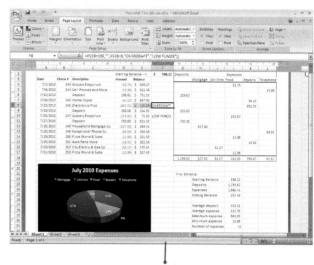

Excel worksheet

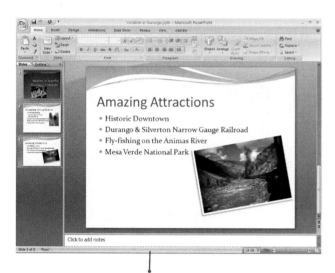

PowerPoint presentation

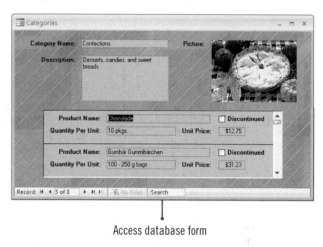

Access database form

Deciding which program to use

Every Office program includes tools that go far beyond what you might expect. For example, although Excel is primarily designed for making calculations, you can use it to create a database. So when you're planning a project, how do you decide which Office program to use? The general rule of thumb is to use the program best suited for your intended task, and make use of supporting tools in the program if you need them. Word is best for creating text-based documents, Excel is best for making mathematical calculations, PowerPoint is best for preparing presentations, and Access is best for managing quantitative data. Although the capabilities of Office are so vast that you *could* create an inventory in Excel or a budget in Word, you'll find greater flexibility and efficiency by using the program designed for the task. And remember, you can always create a file in one program, and then insert it in a document in another program when you need to, such as including sales projections (Excel) in a memo (Word).

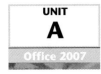
Starting and Exiting an Office Program

The first step in using an Office program is of course to open, or **launch**, it on your computer. You have a few choices for how to launch a program, but the easiest way is to click the Start button on the Windows taskbar, or to double-click an icon on your desktop. You can have multiple programs open on your computer simultaneously, and you can move between open programs by clicking the desired program or document button on the taskbar or by using the [Alt][Tab] keyboard shortcut combination. When working, you'll often want to open multiple programs in Office, and switch among them throughout the day. Begin by launching a few Office programs now.

STEPS

1. **Click the Start button 🏁 on the taskbar**

   The Start menu opens, as shown in Figure A-2. If the taskbar is hidden, you can display it by pointing to the bottom of the screen. Depending on your taskbar property settings, the taskbar may be displayed at all times, or only when you point to that area of the screen. For more information, or to change your taskbar properties, consult your instructor or technical support person.

2. **Point to All Programs, click Microsoft Office, then click Microsoft Office Word 2007**

   Microsoft Office Word 2007 starts and the program window opens on your screen.

3. **Click 🏁 on the taskbar, point to All Programs, click Microsoft Office, then click Microsoft Office Excel 2007**

   Microsoft Office Excel 2007 starts and the program window opens, as shown in Figure A-3. Word is no longer visible, but it remains open. The taskbar displays a button for each open program and document. Because this Excel document is **active**, or in front and available, the Microsoft Excel – Book1 button on the taskbar appears in a darker shade.

4. **Click Document1 – Microsoft Word on the taskbar**

   Clicking a button on the taskbar activates that program and document. The Word program window is now in front, and the Document1 – Microsoft Word taskbar button appears shaded.

5. **Click 🏁 on the taskbar, point to All Programs, click Microsoft Office, then click Microsoft Office PowerPoint 2007**

   Microsoft Office PowerPoint 2007 starts, and becomes the active program.

6. **Click Microsoft Excel – Book1 on the taskbar**

   Excel is now the active program.

7. **Click 🏁 on the taskbar, point to All Programs, click Microsoft Office, then click Microsoft Office Access 2007**

   Microsoft Office Access 2007 starts, and becomes the active program.

8. **Point to the taskbar to display it, if necessary**

   Four Office programs are open simultaneously.

9. **Click the Office button 🏁, then click Exit Access, as shown in Figure A-4**

   Access closes, leaving Excel active and Word and PowerPoint open.

FIGURE A-2: Start menu

FIGURE A-3: Excel program window and Windows taskbar

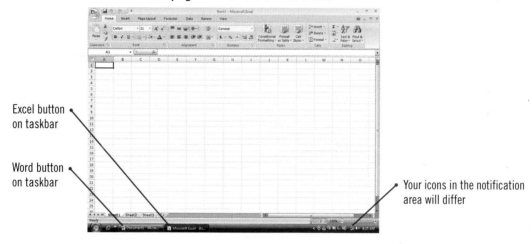

Excel button on taskbar

Word button on taskbar

Your icons in the notification area will differ

FIGURE A-4: Exiting Microsoft Office Access

Microsoft Office button

Exit Access button

Mouse pointer

Using shortcut keys to move between Office programs

As an alternative to the Windows taskbar, you can use a keyboard shortcut to move among open Office programs. The [Alt][Tab] keyboard combination lets you either switch quickly to the next open program, or choose one from a palette. To switch immediately to the next open program, press [Alt][Tab]. To choose from all open programs, press and hold [Alt], then press and release [Tab] without releasing [Alt]. A palette opens on screen, displaying the icon and filename of each open program and file. Each time you press [Tab] while holding [Alt], the selection cycles to the next open file. Release [Alt] when the program/file you want to activate is selected.

Viewing the Office 2007 User Interface

One of the benefits of using Office is that the programs have much in common, making them easy to learn and making it simple to move from one to another. Individual Office programs have always shared many features, but the innovations in the Office 2007 user interface mean even greater similarity among them all. That means you can also use your knowledge of one program to get up to speed in another. A **user interface** is a collective term for all the ways you interact with a software program. The user interface in Office 2007 includes a more intuitive way of choosing commands, working with files, and navigating in the program window. Familiarize yourself with some of the common interface elements in Office by examining the PowerPoint program window.

STEPS

1. **Click Microsoft PowerPoint – [Presentation1] on the taskbar**

   PowerPoint becomes the active program. Refer to Figure A-5 to identify common elements of the Office user interface. The **document window** occupies most of the screen. In PowerPoint, a blank slide appears in the document window, so you can build your slide show. At the top of every Office program window is a **title bar**, which displays the document and program name. Below the title bar is the **Ribbon**, which displays commands you're likely to need for the current task. Commands are organized into **tabs**. The tab names appear at the top of the Ribbon, and the active tab appears in front with its name highlighted. The Ribbon in every Office program includes tabs specific to the program, but all include a Home tab on the far left, for the most popular tasks in that program.

2. **Click the Office button**

   The Office menu opens. This menu contains commands common to most Office programs, such as opening a file, saving a file, and closing the current program. Next to the Office button is the **Quick Access toolbar**, which includes buttons for common Office commands.

3. **Click again to close it, then point to the Save button on the Quick Access toolbar, *but do not click it***

   You can point to any button in Office to see a description; this is a good way to learn the available choices.

4. **Click the Design tab on the Ribbon**

   To display a different tab, you click its name on the Ribbon. Each tab arranges related commands into **groups** to make features easy to find. The Themes group displays available themes in a **gallery**, or palette of choices you can browse. Many groups contain a **dialog box launcher**, an icon you can click to open a dialog box or task pane for the current group, which offers an alternative way to choose commands.

5. **Move the mouse pointer over the Aspect theme in the Themes group as shown in Figure A-6, *but do not click the mouse button***

   Because you have not clicked the theme, you have not actually made any changes to the slide. With the **Live Preview** feature, you can point to a choice, see the results right in the document, and then decide whether you want to make the change.

6. **Move away from the Ribbon and towards the slide**

   If you clicked the Aspect theme, it would be applied to this slide. Instead, the slide remains unchanged.

7. **Point to the Zoom slider on the status bar, then drag to the right until the Zoom percentage reads 166%**

   The slide display is enlarged. Zoom tools are located on the status bar. You can drag the slider or click the plus and minus buttons to zoom in/out on an area of interest. The percentage tells you the zoom effect.

8. **Drag the Zoom slider on the status bar to the left until the Zoom percentage reads 73%**

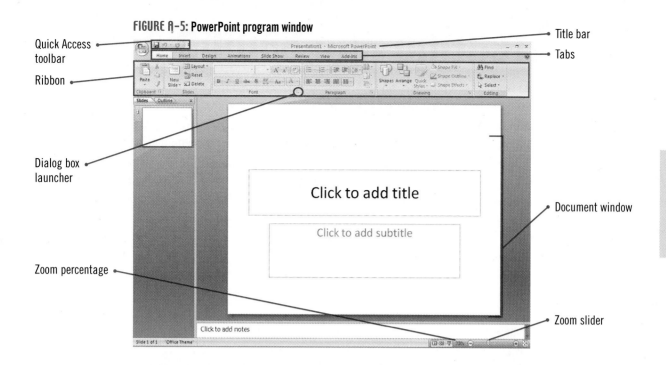

FIGURE A-5: PowerPoint program window

Quick Access toolbar

Ribbon

Dialog box launcher

Zoom percentage

Title bar

Tabs

Document window

Zoom slider

Click to add title

Click to add subtitle

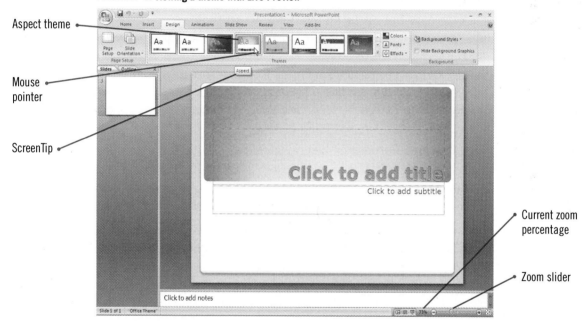

FIGURE A-6: Viewing a theme with Live Preview

Aspect theme

Mouse pointer

ScreenTip

Current zoom percentage

Zoom slider

Click to add title

Click to add subtitle

Customizing the Quick Access toolbar

You can customize the Quick Access toolbar to display your favorite commands. To do so, click the Customize Quick Access Toolbar button in the title bar, then click the command you want to add. If you don't see the command in the list, click More Commands to open the Customize tab of the Options dialog box. In the Options dialog box, use the Choose commands from list to choose a category, click the desired command in the list on the left, click Add to add it to the Quick Access toolbar, then click OK. To remove a button from the toolbar, click the name in the list on the right, then click Remove. To add a command to the Quick Access toolbar on the fly, simply right-click the button on the Ribbon, then click Add to Quick Access Toolbar on the shortcut menu. You can also use the Customize Quick Access Toolbar button to move the toolbar below the ribbon, by clicking Show Below the Ribbon, or to minimize the Ribbon so it takes up less space onscreen. If you click Minimize the Ribbon, the Ribbon is minimized to display only the tabs. When you click a tab, the Ribbon opens so you can choose a command; once you choose a command, the Ribbon closes again, and only the tabs are visible.

Creating and Saving a File

When working in a program, one of the first things you need to do is to create and save a file. A **file** is a stored collection of data. Saving a file enables you to work on a project now, then put it away and work on it again later. In some Office programs, including Word, Excel, and PowerPoint, a new file is automatically created when you start the program, so all you have to do is enter some data and save it. In Access, you must expressly create a file before you enter any data. You should give your files meaningful names and save them in an appropriate location, so they're easy to find. Use Microsoft Word to familiarize yourself with the process of creating and saving a document. First you'll type some notes about a possible location for a corporate meeting, then you'll save the information for later use.

STEPS

1. **Click** Document1 – Microsoft Word **on the taskbar**

2. **Type** Locations for Corporate Meeting, **then press [Enter] twice**
   The text appears in the document window, and a cursor blinks on a new blank line. The cursor indicates where the next typed text will appear.

3. **Type** Las Vegas, NV, **press [Enter], type** Orlando, FL, **press [Enter], type** Chicago, IL, **press [Enter] twice, then type your name**
   Compare your document to Figure A-7.

> **QUICK TIP**
> A filename can be up to 255 characters, including a file extension, and can include upper- or lowercase characters and spaces, but not ?, ", /, \, <, >, *, |, or :.

4. **Click the** Save button 🖫 **on the Quick Access toolbar**
   Because this is the first time you are saving this document, the Save As dialog box opens, as shown in Figure A-8. The Save As dialog box includes options for assigning a filename and storage location. Once you save a file for the first time, clicking 🖫 saves any changes to the file *without* opening the Save As dialog box, because no additional information is needed. In the Address bar, Office displays the default location for where to save the file, but you can change to any location. In the File name field, Office displays a suggested name for the document based on text in the file, but you can enter a different name.

> **QUICK TIP**
> You can create a desktop icon that you can double-click to both launch a program and open a document, by saving it to the desktop.

5. **Type** Potential Corporate Meeting Locations
   The text you type replaces the highlighted text.

6. **In the Save As dialog box, use the Address bar or Navigation pane to navigate to the drive and folder where you store your Data Files**
   Many students store files on a flash drive or Zip drive, but you can also store files on your computer, a network drive, or any storage device indicated by your instructor or technical support person.

> **QUICK TIP**
> To create a new blank file when a file is open, click the Office button, click New, then click Create.

7. **Click** Save
   The Save As dialog box closes, the new file is saved to the location you specified, then the name of the document appears in the title bar, as shown in Figure A-9. (You may or may not see a file extension.) See Table A-1 for a description of the different types of files you create in Office, and the file extensions associated with each. You can save a file in an earlier version of a program by choosing from the list of choices in the Save as type list arrow in the Save As dialog box.

TABLE A-1: Common filenames and default file extensions

File created in	is called a	and has the default extension
Excel	workbook	.xlsx
Word	document	.docx
Access	database	.accdb
PowerPoint	presentation	.pptx

FIGURE A-7: Creating a document in Word

Save button

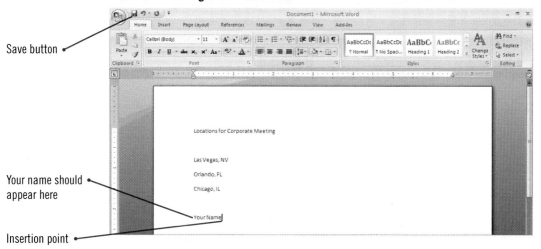

Your name should appear here

Insertion point

FIGURE A-8: Save As dialog box

Address bar

Navigation pane; your links and Folders setting may differ

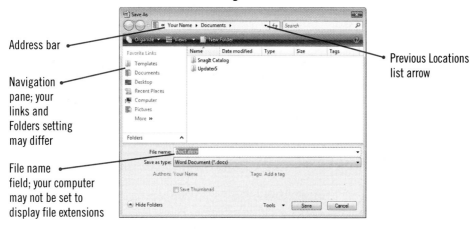

Previous Locations list arrow

File name field; your computer may not be set to display file extensions

FIGURE A-9: Named Word document

Name appears in title bar

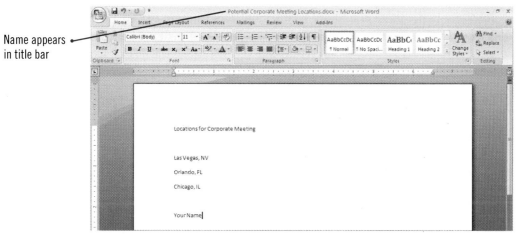

Using the Office Clipboard

You can use the Office Clipboard to cut and copy items from one Office program and paste them into others. The Clipboard can store a maximum of 24 items. To access it, open the Office Clipboard task pane by clicking the launcher in the Clipboard group in the Home tab. Each time you copy a selection, it is saved in the Office Clipboard. Each entry in the Office Clipboard includes an icon that tells you the program in which it was created. To paste an entry, click in the document where you want it to appear, then click the item in the Office Clipboard. To delete an item from the Office Clipboard, right-click the item, then click Delete.

Opening a File and Saving it with a New Name

In many cases as you work in Office, you start with a blank document, but often you need to use an existing file. It might be a file you or a co-worker created earlier as a work-in-progress, or it could be a complete document that you want to use as the basis for another. For example, you might want to create a budget for this year using the budget you created last year; you could type in all the categories and information from scratch, or you could open last year's budget, save it with a new name, and just make changes to update it for the current year. By opening the existing file and saving it with the Save As command, you create a duplicate that you can modify to your heart's content, while the original file remains intact. ✦✦✦✦✦ Use Excel to open an existing workbook file, and save it with a new name so the original remains unchanged.

STEPS

1. **Click Microsoft Excel – Book1 on the taskbar, click the Office button ⊕, then click Open**
   The Open dialog box opens, where you can navigate to any drive or folder location accessible to your computer to locate a file.

2. **In the Open dialog box, navigate to the drive and folder where you store your Data Files**
   The files available in the current folder are listed, as shown in Figure A-10. This folder contains one file.

3. **Click OFFICE A-1.xlsx, then click Open**
   The dialog box closes and the file opens in Excel. An Excel file is an electronic spreadsheet, so it looks different from a Word document or a PowerPoint slide.

4. **Click ⊕, then click Save As**
   The Save As dialog box opens, and the current filename is highlighted in the File name text box. Using the Save As command enables you to create a copy of the current, existing file with a new name. This action preserves the original file, and creates a new file that you can modify.

5. **Navigate to the drive and folder where your Data Files are stored if necessary, type Budget for Corporate Meeting in the File name text box, as shown in Figure A-11, then click Save**
   A copy of the existing document is created with the new name. The original file, Office A-1.xlsx, closes automatically.

6. **Click cell A19, type your name, then press [Enter], as shown in Figure A-12**
   In Excel, you enter data in cells, which are formed by the intersection of a row and a column. Cell A19 is at the intersection of column A and row 19. When you press [Enter], the cell pointer moves to cell A20.

7. **Click the Save button 💾 on the Quick Access toolbar**
   Your name appears in the worksheet, and your changes to the file are saved.

Exploring File Open options

You might have noticed that the Open button on the Open dialog box includes an arrow. In a dialog box, if a button includes an arrow you can click the button to invoke the command, or you can click the arrow to choose from a list of related commands. The Open button list arrow includes several related commands, including Open Read-Only and Open as Copy. Clicking Open Read-Only opens a file that you can only save by saving it with a new name; you cannot save changes to the original file. Clicking Open as Copy creates a copy of the file already saved and named with the word "Copy" in the title. Like the Save As command, these commands provide additional ways to use copies of existing files while ensuring that original files do not get inadvertently changed.

FIGURE A-10: Open dialog box

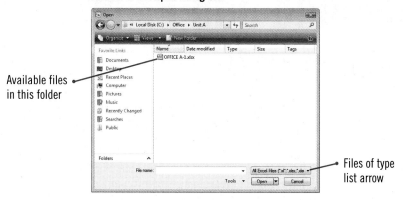

Available files in this folder

Files of type list arrow

FIGURE A-11: Save As dialog box

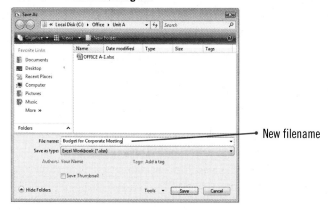

New filename

FIGURE A-12: Adding your name to the worksheet

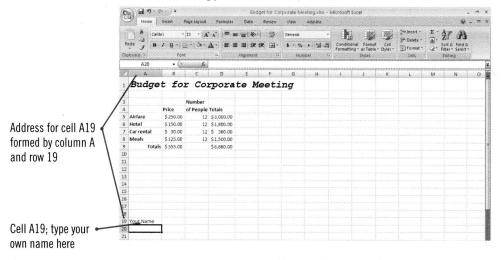

Address for cell A19 formed by column A and row 19

Cell A19; type your own name here

Working in Compatibility mode

Not everyone upgrades to the newest version of Office. As a general rule, new software versions are **backward-compatible**, meaning that documents saved by an older version can be read by newer software. The reverse is not always true, so Office 2007 includes a feature called Compatibility mode. When you open a file created in an earlier version of Office, "Compatibility Mode" appears in the title bar, letting you know the file was created in an earlier, but usable version of the program. If you are working with someone who may not be using the newest version of the software, you can avoid possible incompatibility problems by saving your file in

another, earlier format. To do this, click the Office button, point to the Save As command, then click a choice on the Save As submenu. For example, if you're working in Excel, click Excel 97-2003 Workbook format. When the Save As dialog box opens, you'll notice that the Save as type box reads "Excel 97-2003 Workbook" instead of the default "Excel Workbook." To see more file format choices, such as Excel 97-2003 Template or Microsoft Excel 5.0/95 Workbook, click Other Formats on the Save As submenu. In the Save As dialog box, click the Save as type button, click the choice you think matches what your co-worker is using, then click Save.

Viewing and Printing Your Work

If your computer is connected to a printer or a print server, you can easily print any Office document. Printing can be as simple as clicking a button, or as involved as customizing the print job by printing only selected pages or making other choices, and/or **previewing** the document to see exactly what a document will look like when it is printed. (In order for printing and previewing to work, a printer must be installed.) In addition to using Print Preview, each Microsoft Office program lets you switch among various **views** of the document window, to show more or fewer details or a different combination of elements that make it easier to complete certain tasks, such as formatting or reading text. You can also increase or decrease your view of a document, so you can see more or less of it on the screen at once. Changing your view of a document does not affect the file in any way, it affects only the way it looks on screen. ▓▓▓▓ Experiment with changing your view of a Word document, and then preview and print your work.

STEPS

1. **Click** Potential Corporate Meeting Locations – Microsoft Word **on the taskbar**
   Word becomes the active program, and the document fills the screen.

2. **Click the** View tab **on the Ribbon**
   In most Office programs, the View tab on the Ribbon includes groups and commands for changing your view of the current document. You can also change views using the View buttons on the status bar.

3. **Click** Web Layout button **in the Document Views group on the View tab**
   The view changes to Web Layout view, as shown in Figure A-13. This view shows how the document will look if you save it as a Web page.

> **QUICK TIP**
> You can also use the Zoom button in the Zoom group of the View tab to enlarge or reduce a document's appearance.

4. **Click the** Zoom in button ⊕ **on the status bar** eight times **until the zoom percentage reads** 180%
   Zooming in, or choosing a higher percentage, makes a document appear bigger on screen, but less of it fits on the screen at once; **zooming out**, or choosing a lower percentage, lets you see more of the document but at a reduced size.

5. **Drag the** Zoom slider ⬇ **on the status bar to the** center mark
   The Zoom slider lets you zoom in and out without opening a dialog box or clicking buttons.

6. **Click the** Print Layout button **on the View tab**
   You return to Print Layout view, the default view in Microsoft Word.

7. **Click the** Office button ⬤, **point to** Print, **then click** Print Preview
   The Print Preview presents the most accurate view of how your document will look when printed, displaying the entire page on screen at once. Compare your screen to Figure A-14. The Ribbon in Print Preview contains a single tab, also known as a **program** tab, with commands specific to Print Preview. The commands on this tab facilitate viewing and changing overall settings such as margins and page size.

> **QUICK TIP**
> You can open the Print dialog box from any view by clicking the Office button, then clicking Print.

8. **Click the** Print button **on the Ribbon**
   The Print dialog box opens, as shown in Figure A-15. You can use this dialog box to change which pages to print, the number of printed copies, and even the number of pages you print on each page. If you have multiple printers from which to choose, you can change from one installed printer by clicking the Name list arrow, then clicking the name of the installed printer you want to use.

9. **Click** OK, **then click the** Close Print Preview button **on the Ribbon**
   A copy of the document prints, and Print Preview closes.

FIGURE A-13: Web Layout view

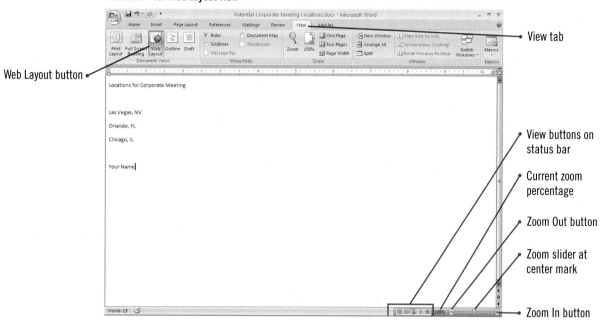

Web Layout button

View tab

View buttons on status bar

Current zoom percentage

Zoom Out button

Zoom slider at center mark

Zoom In button

FIGURE A-14: Print Preview screen

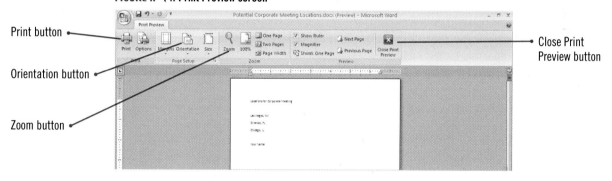

Print button

Orientation button

Zoom button

Close Print Preview button

FIGURE A-15: Print dialog box

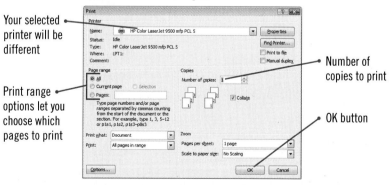

Your selected printer will be different

Print range options let you choose which pages to print

Number of copies to print

OK button

Using the Print Screen feature to create a screen capture

At some point you may want to create a screen capture. A **screen capture** is a snapshot of your screen, as if you took a picture of it with a camera. You might want to take a screen capture if an error message occurs and you want Technical Support to see exactly what's on the screen. Or perhaps your instructor wants to see what your screen looks like when you create a particular document. To create a screen capture, press [PrtScn]. (Keyboards differ, but you may find the [PrtScn] button on the Insert key in or near your keyboard's function keys. You may have to press the [F Lock] key to enable the Function keys.) Pressing this key places a digital image of your screen in the Windows temporary storage area known as the **Clipboard**. Open the document where you want the screen capture to appear, click the Home tab on the Ribbon (if necessary), then click Paste on the Home tab. The screen capture is pasted into the document.

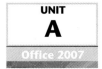

Getting Help and Closing a File

You can get comprehensive help at any time by pressing [F1] in an Office program. You can also get help in the form of a ScreenTip by pointing to almost any icon in the program window. When you're finished working in an Office document, you have a few choices regarding ending your work session. You can close a file or exit a program by using the Office button or by clicking a button on the title bar. Closing a file leaves a program running, while exiting a program closes all the open files in that program as well as the program itself. In all cases, Office reminds you if you try to close a file or exit a program and your document contains unsaved changes. Explore the Help system in Microsoft Office, and then close your documents and exit any open programs.

STEPS

1. **Point to the Zoom button on the View tab of the Ribbon**

   A ScreenTip appears that describes how the Zoom button works.

2. **Press [F1]**

   The Word Help window opens, as shown in Figure A-16, displaying the home page for help in Word. Each entry is a hyperlink you can click to open a list of related topics. This window also includes a toolbar of useful Help commands and a Search field. The connection status at the bottom of the Help window indicates that the connection to Office Online is active. Office Online supplements the help content available on your computer with a wide variety of up-to-date topics, templates, and training.

   > **QUICK TIP**
   > If you are not connected to the Internet, the Help window displays only the help content available on your computer.

3. **Click the Getting help link in the Table of Contents pane**

   The icon next to Getting help changes and its list of subtopics expands.

4. **Click the Work with the Help window link in the topics list in the left pane**

   The topic opens in the right pane, as shown in Figure A-17.

   > **QUICK TIP**
   > You can also open the Help window by clicking the Microsoft Office Help button 🔘 to the right of the tabs on the Ribbon.

5. **Click the Hide Table of Contents button 🔲 on the Help toolbar**

   The left pane closes, as shown in Figure A-18.

6. **Click the Show Table of Contents button 📖 on the Help toolbar, scroll to the bottom of the left pane, click the Accessibility link in the Table of Contents pane, click the Use the keyboard to work with Ribbon programs link, read the information in the right pane, then click the Help window Close button**

   > **QUICK TIP**
   > You can print the current topic by clicking the Print button 🖨 on the Help toolbar to open the Print dialog box.

7. **Click the Office button 🔘, then click Close; if a dialog box opens asking whether you want to save your changes, click Yes**

   The Potential Corporate Meeting Locations document closes, leaving the Word program open.

8. **Click 🔘, then click Exit Word**

   Microsoft Office Word closes, and the Excel program window is active.

9. **Click 🔘, click Exit Excel, click the PowerPoint button on the taskbar if necessary, click 🔘, then click Exit PowerPoint**

   Microsoft Office Excel and Microsoft Office PowerPoint both close.

FIGURE A-16: Word Help window

Help toolbar

Search field

Hide Table of
Contents
button

The colors
of your links
may differ

Connection status

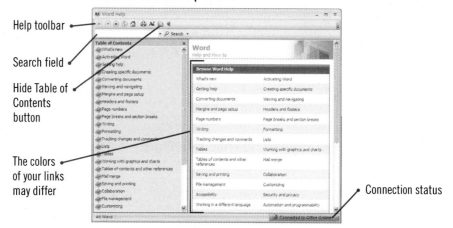

FIGURE A-17: Work with the Help window

Print button

Icon indicates
expanded topic

Work with
the Help
window link

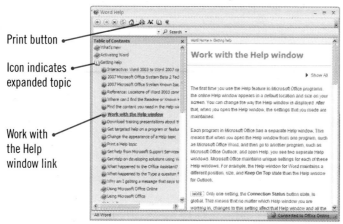

FIGURE A-18: Help window with Table of Contents closed

Show Table of
Contents button

Recovering a document

Sometimes while you are using Office, you may experience a power failure or your computer may "freeze," making it impossible to continue working. If this type of interruption occurs, each Office program has a built-in recovery feature that allows you to open and save files that were open at the time of the interruption. When you restart the program(s) after an interruption, the Document Recovery task pane opens on the left side of your screen displaying both original and recovered versions of the files that were open. If you're not sure which file to open (original or recovered), it's usually better to open the recovered file because it will contain the latest information. You can, however, open and review all versions of the file that were recovered and save the best one. Each file listed in the Document Recovery task pane displays a list arrow with options that allow you to open the file, save it as is, delete it, or show repairs made to it during recovery.

Practice

▼ CONCEPTS REVIEW

Label the elements of the program window shown in Figure A-19.

FIGURE A-19

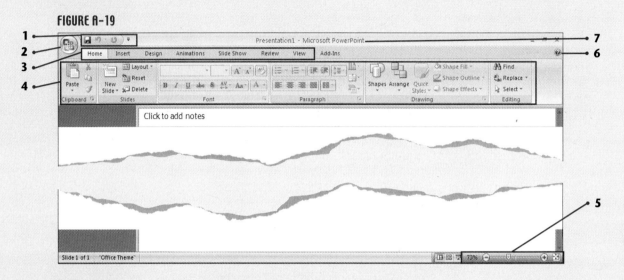

Match each project with the program for which it is best suited.

8. Microsoft Office PowerPoint

9. Microsoft Office Excel

10. Microsoft Office Word

11. Microsoft Office Access

a. Corporate expansion budget with expense projections

b. Business résumé for a job application

c. Auto parts store inventory

d. Presentation for Board of Directors meeting

▼ INDEPENDENT CHALLENGE 1

You just accepted an administrative position with a local car dealership that's recently invested in computers and is now considering purchasing Microsoft Office. You are asked to propose ways Office might help the dealership. You produce your proposal in Microsoft Word.

a. Start Word, then save the document as Microsoft Office Proposal in the drive and folder where you store your Data Files.

b. Type Microsoft Office Word, press [Enter] twice, type Microsoft Office Excel, press [Enter] twice, type Microsoft Office PowerPoint, press [Enter] twice, type Microsoft Office Access, press [Enter] twice, then type your name.

c. Click the line beneath each program name, type at least two tasks suited to that program, then press [Enter].

d. Save your work, then print one copy of this document.

Advanced Challenge Exercise

■ Press the [PrtScn] button to create a screen capture, then press [Ctrl][V].

■ Save and print the document.

e. Exit Word.

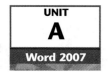

Creating Documents with Word 2007

Files You Will Need:

WD A-1.doc

Microsoft Office Word 2007 is a word processing program that makes it easy to create a variety of professional-looking documents, from simple letters and memos to newsletters, research papers, blog posts, business cards, résumés, financial reports, and other documents that include multiple pages of text and sophisticated formatting. In this unit, you will explore the editing and formatting features available in Word and create two documents. You have been hired to work in the Marketing Department at Quest Specialty Travel (QST), a tour company that specializes in cultural tourism and adventure travel. Shortly after reporting to your new office, Ron Dawson, the vice president of marketing, asks you to use Word to create a memo to the marketing staff and a fax to one of the tour developers.

OBJECTIVES

Understand word processing software

Explore the Word program window

Start a document

Save a document

Select text

Format text using the Mini toolbar

Create a document using a template

View and navigate a document

Understanding Word Processing Software

A **word processing program** is a software program that includes tools for entering, editing, and formatting text and graphics. Microsoft Word is a powerful word processing program that allows you to create and enhance a wide range of documents quickly and easily. Figure A-1 shows the first page of a report created using Word and illustrates some of the Word features you can use to enhance your documents. The electronic files you create using Word are called **documents**. One of the benefits of using Word is that document files can be stored on a hard disk, CD, flash drive, or other storage device, making them easy to transport, exchange, and revise. 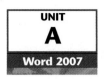 Before beginning your memo to the marketing staff, you explore the editing and formatting capabilities available in Word.

DETAILS

You can use Word to accomplish the following tasks:

- **Type and edit text**

  The Word editing tools make it simple to insert and delete text in a document. You can add text to the middle of an existing paragraph, replace text with other text, undo an editing change, and correct typing, spelling, and grammatical errors with ease.

- **Copy and move text from one location to another**

  Using the more advanced editing features of Word, you can copy or move text from one location and insert it in a different location in a document. You also can copy and move text between documents. Being able to copy and move text means you don't have to retype text that is already entered in a document.

- **Format text and paragraphs with fonts, colors, and other elements**

  The sophisticated formatting tools available in Word allow you to make the text in your documents come alive. You can change the size, style, and color of text, add lines and shading to paragraphs, and enhance lists with bullets and numbers. Formatting text creatively helps you highlight important ideas in your documents.

- **Format and design pages**

  The Word page-formatting features give you power to design attractive newsletters, create powerful résumés, and produce documents such as business cards, CD labels, and books. You can change the paper size and orientation of your documents, organize text in columns, and control the layout of text and graphics on each page of a document. For quick results, Word includes preformatted cover pages, pull quotes, and headers and footers, as well as galleries of coordinated text, table, and graphic styles that you can rely on to give documents a polished look.

- **Enhance documents with tables, charts, diagrams, and graphics**

  Using the powerful graphics tools available in Word, you can spice up your documents with pictures, photographs, lines, shapes, and diagrams. You also can illustrate your documents with tables and charts to help convey your message in a visually interesting way.

- **Use Mail Merge to create form letters and mailing labels**

  The Word Mail Merge feature allows you to send personalized form letters to many different people. You can also use Mail Merge to create mailing labels, directories, e-mail messages, and other types of documents.

- **Share documents securely**

  The Word Document Inspector feature makes it quick and easy to thoroughly remove comments, tracked changes, and unwanted personal information from your files before you share them with others. You can also add a digital signature to a document, convert a file to a format suitable for publishing on the Web, and easily recognize a document that might contain a potentially harmful macro.

FIGURE A-1: A report created using Word

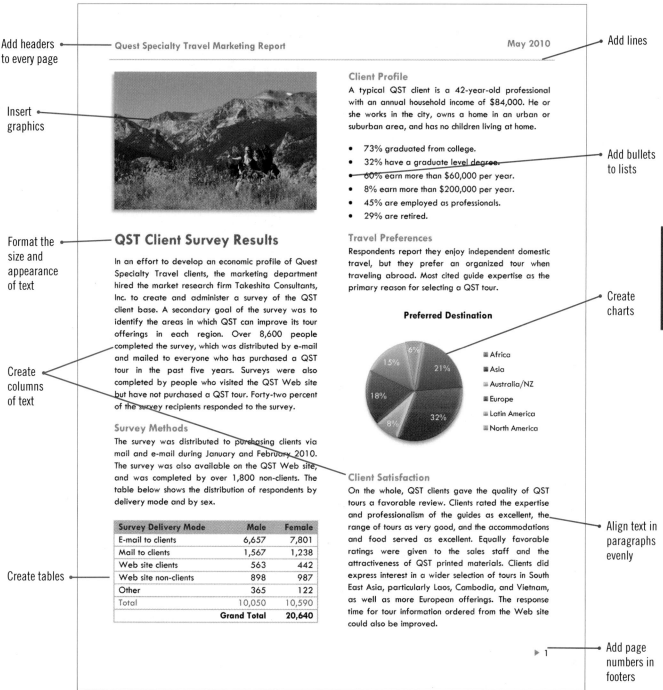

Add headers to every page

Insert graphics

Format the size and appearance of text

Create columns of text

Create tables

Add lines

Add bullets to lists

Create charts

Align text in paragraphs evenly

Add page numbers in footers

Quest Specialty Travel Marketing Report   May 2010

Client Profile

A typical QST client is a 42-year-old professional with an annual household income of $84,000. He or she works in the city, owns a home in an urban or suburban area, and has no children living at home.

- 73% graduated from college.
- 32% have a graduate level degree.
- 60% earn more than $60,000 per year.
- 8% earn more than $200,000 per year.
- 45% are employed as professionals.
- 29% are retired.

Travel Preferences

Respondents report they enjoy independent domestic travel, but they prefer an organized tour when traveling abroad. Most cited guide expertise as the primary reason for selecting a QST tour.

QST Client Survey Results

In an effort to develop an economic profile of Quest Specialty Travel clients, the marketing department hired the market research firm Takeshita Consultants, Inc. to create and administer a survey of the QST client base. A secondary goal of the survey was to identify the areas in which QST can improve its tour offerings in each region. Over 8,600 people completed the survey, which was distributed by e-mail and mailed to everyone who has purchased a QST tour in the past five years. Surveys were also completed by people who visited the QST Web site but have not purchased a QST tour. Forty-two percent of the survey recipients responded to the survey.

Preferred Destination

- Africa
- Asia
- Australia/NZ
- Europe
- Latin America
- North America

6% 21% 15% 18% 8% 32%

Survey Methods

The survey was distributed to purchasing clients via mail and e-mail during January and February 2010. The survey was also available on the QST Web site, and was completed by over 1,800 non-clients. The table below shows the distribution of respondents by delivery mode and by sex.

Client Satisfaction

On the whole, QST clients gave the quality of QST tours a favorable review. Clients rated the expertise and professionalism of the guides as excellent, the range of tours as very good, and the accommodations and food served as excellent. Equally favorable ratings were given to the sales staff and the attractiveness of QST printed materials. Clients did express interest in a wider selection of tours in South East Asia, particularly Laos, Cambodia, and Vietnam, as well as more European offerings. The response time for tour information ordered from the Web site could also be improved.

Survey Delivery Mode	Male	Female
E-mail to clients	6,657	7,801
Mail to clients	1,567	1,238
Web site clients	563	442
Web site non-clients	898	987
Other	365	122
Total	10,050	10,590
Grand Total		**20,640**

▶ 1

Planning a document

Before you create a new document, it's a good idea to spend time planning it. Identify the message you want to convey, the audience for your document, and the elements, such as tables or charts, you want to include. You should also think about the tone and look of your document—are you writing a business letter, which should be written in a pleasant, but serious tone and have a formal appearance, or are you creating a flyer that must be colorful, eye-catching, and fun to read? The purpose and audience for your document determines the appropriate design. Planning the layout and design of a document involves deciding how to organize the text, selecting the fonts to use, identifying the graphics to include, and selecting the formatting elements that will enhance the message and appeal of the document. For longer documents, such as newsletters, it can be useful to sketch the layout and design of each page before you begin.

Exploring the Word Program Window

When you start Word, a blank document appears in the document window. ▆▆▆ You examine the elements of the Word program window.

1. **Start** Word

    The **Word program window** opens, as shown in Figure A-2. The blinking vertical line in the document window is the **insertion point**. It indicates where text appears as you type. The blank document opens in Print Layout view. **Views** are different ways of displaying a document in the document window.

2. **Move the mouse pointer around the Word program window**

    The mouse pointer changes shape depending on where it is in the Word program window. You use pointers to move the insertion point or to select text to edit. Table A-1 describes common pointers in Word.

3. **Place the mouse pointer over a button on the Ribbon**

    When you place the mouse pointer over a button or some other elements of the Word program window, a ScreenTip appears. A **ScreenTip** is a label that identifies the name of the button or feature, briefly describes its function, conveys any keyboard shortcut for the command, and includes a link to associated help topics, if any.

Using Figure A-2 as a guide, find the elements described below in your program window.

*   The **title bar** displays the name of the document and the name of the program. Until you give a new document a different name, its temporary name is Document1. The title bar also contains resizing buttons and the program Close button. These buttons are common to all Windows programs.

*   Clicking the **Office button** opens a menu of commands related to managing and sharing documents, including opening, printing, and saving a document, creating a new document, and preparing a document for distribution. The Office button also provides access to the Word Options dialog box, which is used to customize the way you use Word.

*   The **Quick Access toolbar** contains buttons for saving a document and for undoing, redoing, and repeating a change. You can modify the Quick Access toolbar to include the commands you use most frequently.

QUICK TIP

To display a different tab, you simply click its name on the Ribbon.

*   The **Ribbon** contains the names of the Word tabs. Each **tab** includes buttons for commands, which are organized in **groups**. For example, the Home tab includes the Clipboard, Font, Paragraph, Styles, and Editing groups, each containing buttons related to editing and formatting text. The Ribbon also includes the **Microsoft Office Word Help button**, which you use to access the Word Help system.

*   The **document window** displays the current document. You enter text and format your document in the document window.

TROUBLE

Click the View Ruler button 🖳 at the top of the vertical scroll bar to display the rulers if they are not already displayed.

*   The rulers appear in the document window in Print Layout view. The **horizontal ruler** displays left and right document margins as well as the tab settings and paragraph indents, if any, for the paragraph in which the insertion point is located. The **vertical ruler** displays the top and bottom document margins.

*   The **vertical scroll bar** and the **horizontal scroll bar** are used to display different parts of the document in the document window. The scroll bars include **scroll boxes** and **scroll arrows**, which you can use to move easily through a document.

*   The **status bar** displays the page number of the current page, the total number of pages and words in the document, and the status of spelling and grammar checking. It also includes the view buttons, the Zoom level button, and the Zoom slider. You can customize the status bar to display other information.

*   The **view buttons** on the status bar allow you to display the document in Print Layout, Full Screen Reading, Web Layout, Outline, or Draft view.

*   The **Zoom level** button and the **Zoom slider** provide quick ways to enlarge and decrease the size of the document in the document window, making it easy to zoom in on a detail of a document or to view the layout of the document as a whole.

FIGURE A-2: Elements of the Word program window

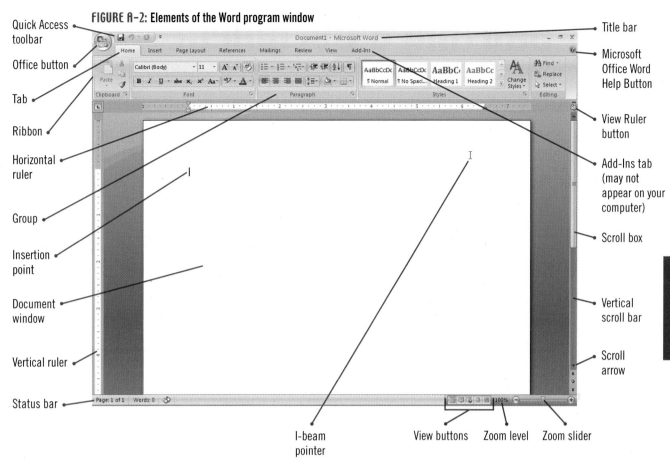

Quick Access toolbar

Office button

Tab

Ribbon

Horizontal ruler

Group

Insertion point

Document window

Vertical ruler

Status bar

I-beam pointer

View buttons   Zoom level   Zoom slider

Title bar

Microsoft Office Word Help Button

View Ruler button

Add-Ins tab (may not appear on your computer)

Scroll box

Vertical scroll bar

Scroll arrow

Word 2007

TABLE A-1: Common mouse pointers in Word

name	pointer	use to
I-beam pointer	I	Move the insertion point in a document or to select text
Click-and-type pointers: left-align click-and-type pointer; center-align click-and-type pointer	I≡ or I≡	Move the insertion point in a blank area of a document in Print Layout or Web Layout view; double-clicking with a Click and Type pointer automatically applies the paragraph formatting (alignment and indentation) required to position text or a graphic at that location in the document
Selection pointer	⩍	Click a button or other element of the Word program window; appears when you point to elements of the Word program window
Right-pointing arrow pointer	⩘	Select a line or lines of text; appears when you point to the left edge of a line of text in the document window
Hand pointer	🖑	Open a hyperlink; appears when you point to a hyperlink in a task pane or when you press [Ctrl] and point to a hyperlink in a document
Hide white space pointer	⇥⇤	Hide the white space in the top and bottom margins of a document in Print Layout view
Show white space pointer	⇥⇤	Show the white space in the top and bottom margins of a document in Print Layout view

Starting a Document

You begin a new document by simply typing text in a blank document in the document window. Word includes a **word-wrap** feature so that as you type Word automatically moves the insertion point to the next line of the document when you reach the right margin. You only press [Enter] when you want to start a new paragraph or insert a blank line. ▄▄▄▄▄ You type a quick memo to the marketing staff.

STEPS

1. **Type Memorandum, then press [Enter] twice**

   Each time you press [Enter] the insertion point moves to the start of the next line.

2. **Type TO:, then press [Tab] twice**

   Pressing [Tab] moves the insertion point several spaces to the right. You can use the [Tab] key to align the text in a memo header or to indent the first line of a paragraph.

3. **Type QST Managers, then press [Enter]**

   The insertion point moves to the start of the next line.

4. **Type: FROM: [Tab] [Tab] Ron Dawson [Enter]**
   DATE: [Tab] [Tab] July 12, 2010 [Enter]
   RE: [Tab] [Tab] Marketing Meeting [Enter] [Enter]

   Red or green wavy lines may appear under the words you typed, indicating a possible spelling or grammar error. Spelling and grammar checking is one of the many automatic features you will encounter as you type. Table A-2 describes several of these automatic features. You can correct any typing errors you make later.

5. **Type The next marketing staff meeting will be held on the 16th of July at 1 p.m. in the conference room on the ground floor., then press [Spacebar]**

   As you type, notice that the insertion point moves automatically to the next line of the document. You also might notice that Word automatically changed "16th" to "16th" in the memo. This feature is called **AutoCorrect**. AutoCorrect automatically makes typographical adjustments and detects and adjusts typing errors, certain misspelled words (such as "taht" for "that"), and incorrect capitalization as you type.

6. **Type Heading the agenda will be the launch of our new Mai Chau Mountain Tribal Trek, a ten-day walking and rafting tour of the sultry rivers, hidden villages, and misty forests of northern Vietnam, scheduled for February 2012.**

   When you type the first few characters of "February," the Word AutoComplete feature displays the complete word in a ScreenTip. **AutoComplete** suggests text to insert quickly into your documents. You can ignore AutoComplete for now. Your memo should resemble Figure A-3.

7. **Press [Enter], then type Wim Hoppengarth is in Hanoi hammering out the details. A preliminary draft of the tour brochure is attached. Bring your creative ideas for launch-ing this exciting new tour to the meeting.**

   When you press [Enter] and type the new paragraph, notice that Word adds more space between the para-graphs than it does between the lines within each individual paragraph. This is part of the default style for paragraphs in Word, called the Normal style.

8. **Position the I pointer after for (but before the space) in the last line of the first para-graph, then click**

   Clicking moves the insertion point after "for."

9. **Press [Backspace] three times, then type to depart in**

   Pressing [Backspace] removes the character before the insertion point.

10. **Move the insertion point before staff in the first sentence, then press [Delete] six times to remove the word staff and the space after it**

    Pressing [Delete] removes the character after the insertion point. Figure A-4 shows the revised memo.

FIGURE A-3: Memo text in the document window

Blank lines between paragraphs

Red, wavy underline indicates a possible spelling error

Text wraps to the next line

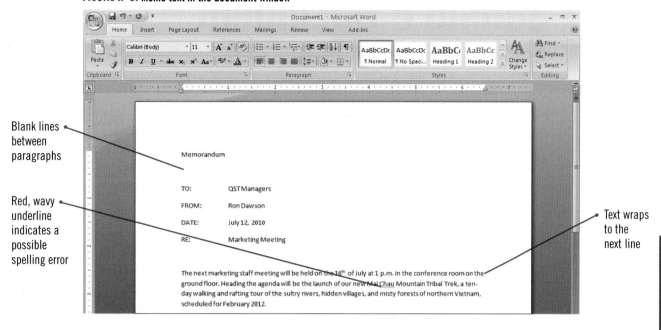

FIGURE A-4: Edited memo text

Text inserted in the memo

Normal style leaves more space between paragraphs than between lines

No Spacing button

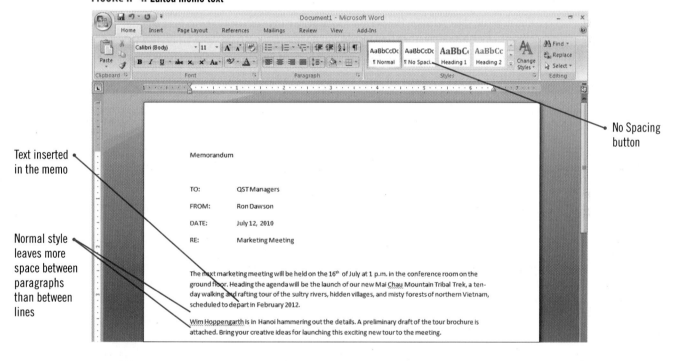

TABLE A-2: Automatic features that appear as you type in Word

feature	what appears	to use
AutoComplete	A ScreenTip suggesting text to insert appears as you type	Press [Enter] to insert the text suggested by the ScreenTip; continue typing to reject the suggestion
AutoCorrect	A small blue box appears when you place the pointer over text corrected by AutoCorrect; an AutoCorrect Options button ⟦☲⟧ appears when you point to the corrected text	Word automatically corrects typos, minor spelling errors, and capitalization, and adds typographical symbols (such as © and ™) as you type; to reverse an AutoCorrect adjustment, click the AutoCorrect Options list arrow, then click Undo or the option that will undo the action
Spelling and Grammar	A red wavy line under a word indicates a possible misspelling; a green wavy line under text indicates a possible grammar error	Right-click red- or green-underlined text to display a shortcut menu of correction options; click a correction to accept it and remove the wavy underline

Saving a Document

To store a document permanently so you can open it and edit it in the future, you must save it as a **file**. When you **save** a document you give it a name, called a **filename**, and indicate the location where you want to store the file. Files created in Word 2007 are automatically assigned the .docx file extension to distinguish them from files created in other software programs, including previous versions of Word. Files created in previous versions of Word carry the .doc file extension. You can save a document using the Save button on the Quick Access toolbar or the Save command on the Office menu. Once you have saved a document for the first time, you should save it again every few minutes and always before printing so that the saved file is updated to reflect your latest changes. 🖰🖮 You save your memo using a descriptive filename and the default file extension.

STEPS

TROUBLE

If you don't see the extension .docx as part of the filename, Windows is set not to display file extensions.

1. **Click the Save button 🖫 on the Quick Access toolbar**

   The first time you save a document, the Save As dialog box opens, as shown in Figure A-5. The default filename, Memorandum, appears in the File name text box. The default filename is based on the first few words of the document. The default file extension, .docx, appears in the Save as type list box. Table A-3 describes the functions of some of the buttons in the Save As dialog box.

2. **Type Vietnam Tour Memo in the File name text box**

   The new filename replaces the default filename. Giving your documents brief descriptive filenames makes it easier to locate and organize them later. You do not need to type .docx when you type a new filename.

TROUBLE

Click Browse Folders in the Save As dialog box to display the Navigation pane and folder window.

3. **Navigate to the drive and folder where you store your Data Files**

   You can navigate to a different drive or folder either by clicking a location in the Address bar to go directly to that location, or by clicking an arrow next to a location in the Address bar to open a list of subfolders, and then selecting a new location from the list. Click the double arrow in the Address bar to navigate to the next highest level in the folder hierarchy. You can also double-click a drive or folder in the Navigation pane or the folder window to change the active location. When you are finished, the drive or folder where you store your Data Files appears in the Address bar. Your Save As dialog box should resemble Figure A-6.

QUICK TIP

To save a document so it can be opened in a previous version of Word, click the Save as type list arrow, then click Word 97-2003 Document (*.doc).

4. **Click Save**

   The document is saved to the drive and folder you specified in the Save As dialog box, and the title bar displays the new filename, Vietnam Tour Memo.docx.

5. **Place the insertion point before ten-day in the second sentence, type rugged, then press [Spacebar]**

   You can continue to work on a document after you have saved it with a new filename.

6. **Click 🖫**

   Your change to the memo is saved. Saving a document after you give it a filename saves the changes you make to the document. You also can press [Ctrl][S] to save a document.

Working with XML and binary files

The default x suffix in the .docx file extension indicates a file is saved in the Office **XML format**, which is new to Word 2007. Earlier versions of Word employed a binary file format, signified by the familiar .doc file extension. To facilitate file sharing between the different versions of Office, Word 2007 allows you to open, edit, and save files in either XML or binary format. When you open a binary file in Word 2007, the words Compatibility Mode appear in the title bar next to the filename. You can also turn on Compatibility Mode by saving a copy of an XML file in Word 97-2003 format. When you are working in Compatibility Mode, some Word 2007 document features, including built-in document themes, margins, text boxes, SmartArt, bibliographies, mail merge data, and certain theme colors, fonts, and effects will be permanently changed or behave differently.

Converting a binary file to XML format is simple: click the Office button, click Convert on the Office menu, and then click OK in the Microsoft Office Word dialog box that opens. This turns off Compatibility Mode. Once a file is converted to XML, you can save the converted file, which replaces the original .doc file with a .docx file of the same filename, by clicking the Save button, or you can use the Save As command on the Office menu to create a new .docx file, preserving the original binary .doc file.

FIGURE A-5: Save As dialog box

Click an arrow in the Address bar to change the active folder or drive

Address bar

Active folder

Navigation pane

Click Folders button to display expandable list of folders in the Navigation pane

Default filename and file extension are selected

Click to hide the Navigation pane and folder window

Search for an item in the active location

Folder window displays the folders and files in the active folder or drive (yours will differ)

Click to change the file type

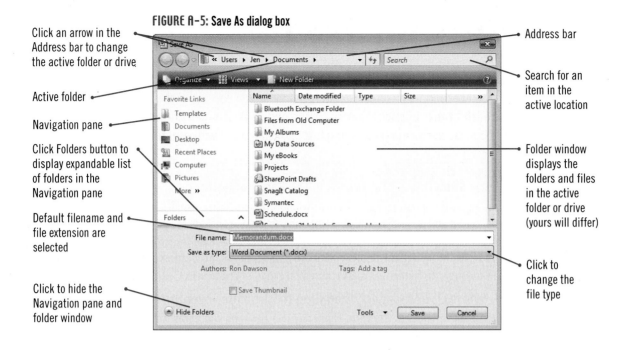

FIGURE A-6: File to be saved to the Unit A folder

Location of Data Files (yours might differ)

New filename

Your folder window might list the files and folders in the active location

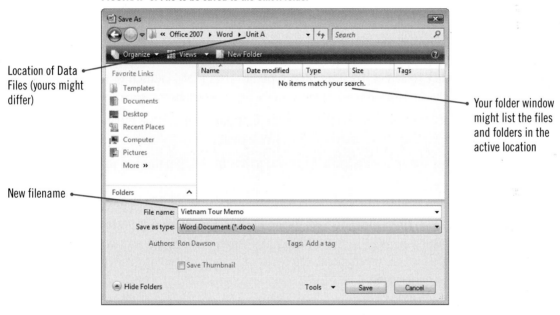

TABLE A-3: Save As dialog box buttons

button	use to
🔙 **Back**	Navigate back to the drive or folder that was previously active in the Address bar
🔜 **Forward**	Navigate forward to the drive or folder that was previously active in the Address bar
Organize ▾ **Organize**	Open a menu of commands related to organizing the selected file or folder, including Cut, Copy, Delete, Rename, and Properties
Views ▾ **Views**	Change the way folder and file information is shown in the folder window in the Save As dialog box; click the Views list arrow to open a menu of options
New Folder **New Folder**	Create a new folder in the current folder or drive

Selecting Text

Before deleting, editing, or formatting text, you must **select** the text. Selecting text involves clicking and dragging the I-beam pointer across text to highlight it. You also can click with the ⇗ pointer in the blank area to the left of text to select lines or paragraphs. Table A-4 describes the many ways to select text. You revise the memo by selecting text and replacing it with new text.

STEPS

1. **Click the Show/Hide ¶ button ¶ in the Paragraph group**

   Formatting marks appear in the document window. **Formatting marks** are special characters that appear on your screen and do not print. Common formatting marks include the paragraph symbol (¶), which shows the end of a paragraph—wherever you press [Enter]; the dot symbol (•), which represents a space—wherever you press [Spacebar]; and the arrow symbol (→), which shows the location of a tab stop—wherever you press [Tab]. Working with formatting marks turned on can help you to select, edit, and format text with precision.

   > **TROUBLE**
   > If you make a mistake, you can deselect the text by clicking anywhere in the document window.

2. **Click before QST Managers, then drag the I pointer over the text to select it**

   The words are selected, as shown in Figure A-7. For now you can ignore the faint toolbar that appears over text when you first select it.

3. **Type Marketing Staff**

   The text you type replaces the selected text.

4. **Double-click Ron, type your first name, double-click Dawson, then type your last name**

   Double-clicking a word selects the entire word.

   > **QUICK TIP**
   > If you delete text by mistake, immediately click the Undo button ↩ on the Quick Access toolbar to restore the deleted text to the document.

5. **Place the pointer in the margin to the left of the RE: line so that the pointer changes to ⇗, click to select the line, then type RE: [Tab][Tab] Launch of new Vietnam trekking tour**

   Clicking to the left of a line of text with the ⇗ pointer selects the entire line.

6. **Select sultry in the third line of the first paragraph, type meandering, select misty forests, then type stunning limestone peaks**

7. **Select the sentence Wim Hoppengarth is in Hanoi hammering out the details., then press [Delete]**

   Selecting text and pressing [Delete] removes the text from the document.

   > **QUICK TIP**
   > Always save before and after editing text.

8. **Click ¶, then click the Save button 💾 on the Quick Access toolbar**

   Formatting marks are turned off and your changes to the memo are saved. The Show/Hide ¶ button is a **toggle button**, which means you can use it to turn formatting marks on and off. The edited memo is shown in Figure A-8.

TABLE A-4: Methods for selecting text

to select	use the pointer to
Any amount of text	Drag over the text
A word	Double-click the word
A line of text	Click with the ⇗ pointer to the left of the line
A sentence	Press and hold [Ctrl], then click the sentence
A paragraph	Triple-click the paragraph or double-click with the ⇗ pointer to the left of the paragraph
A large block of text	Click at the beginning of the selection, press and hold [Shift], then click at the end of the selection
Multiple nonconsecutive selections	Select the first selection, then press and hold [Ctrl] as you select each additional selection
An entire document	Triple-click with the ⇗ pointer to the left of any text, press [Ctrl][A], or click the Select button in the Editing group on the Home tab, and then click Select All

FIGURE A-7: Text selected in the memo

Selected text

Left document margin

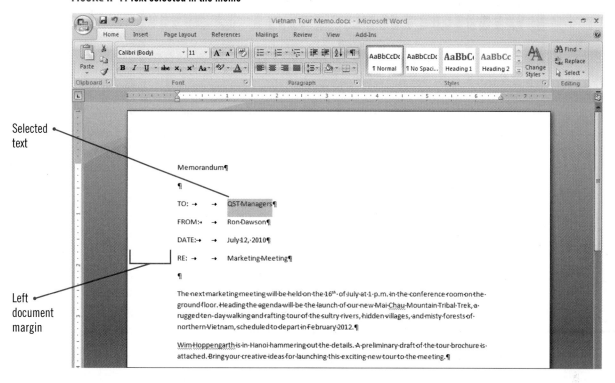

FIGURE A-8: Edited memo with replacement text

Replacement text

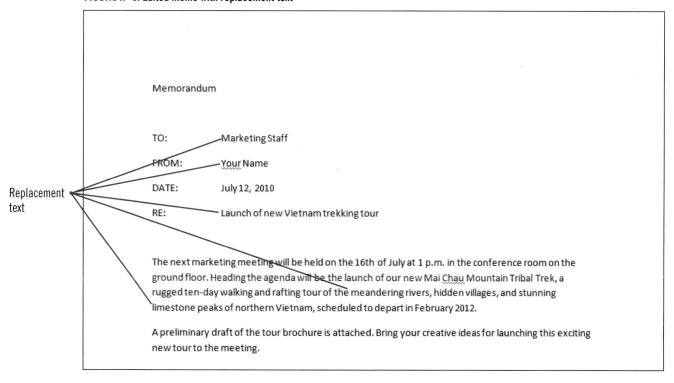

Formatting Text Using the Mini Toolbar

Changing the format of text is a fast and fun way to spruce up the appearance of a document and highlight important information. You can easily format text with fonts, colors, styles, borders, and other formatting options by selecting the text and clicking a command on the Home tab. The **Mini toolbar**, which appears faintly above text when you first select it, also includes the most commonly used text and paragraph formatting commands. Table A-5 describes the function of the buttons on the Mini toolbar. You enhance the appearance of the memo by formatting the text using the Mini toolbar. Before printing the finished memo, you preview it in Print Preview.

STEPS

1. **Double-click Memorandum**

   The Mini toolbar appears in ghosted fashion over the selected text. When you point to the Mini toolbar, it becomes solid, as shown in Figure A-9, and you can click a formatting option to apply it to the selected text.

2. **Click the Center button 📃 on the Mini toolbar**

   The word Memorandum is centered between the left and right document margins.

3. **Click the Grow Font button A˙ on the Mini toolbar eight times, then click the Bold button B on the Mini toolbar**

   Each time you click the Grow Font button the selected text is enlarged. Applying **bold** to the text makes it thicker and darker.

4. **Select TO:, click B , select FROM:, click B , select DATE:, click B , select RE:, then click B**

   Bold is applied to the heading text.

5. **Click the blank line between the RE: line and the body text, then click the Bottom Border button 📖 in the Paragraph group**

   A single-line border is added between the heading and the body text in the memo.

6. **Click the Office button 🔘, point to Print, then click Print Preview**

   The document appears in Print Preview. Before you print a document, it's a good habit to examine it carefully in **Print Preview** so you can identify and correct any problems before printing.

7. **Move the pointer over the memo text until it changes to 🔍, then click the word Memorandum**

   Clicking with the 🔍 pointer magnifies the document in the Print Preview window and changes the pointer to 🔍. The memo appears as it will look when printed, as shown in Figure A-10. Clicking with the 🔍 pointer reduces the size of the document in the Print Preview window.

8. **Click the Magnifier check box in the Preview group**

   Deselecting the Magnifier check box turns off the magnification feature and allows you to edit the document in Print Preview. In edit mode, the pointer changes to I.

9. **Examine your memo carefully for errors, correct any mistakes, then click the Close Print Preview button in the Preview group**

   Print Preview closes and the memo appears in the document window.

10. **Save the document, click 🔘, click Print, click OK in the Print dialog box, click 🔘, then click Close**

    A copy of the memo prints using the default print settings. You can use the Print dialog box to change the current printer, change the number of copies to print, select what pages of a document to print, and modify other printing options. After printing, the document closes, but the Word program window remains open.

Creating Documents with Word 2007

FIGURE A-9: Mini toolbar

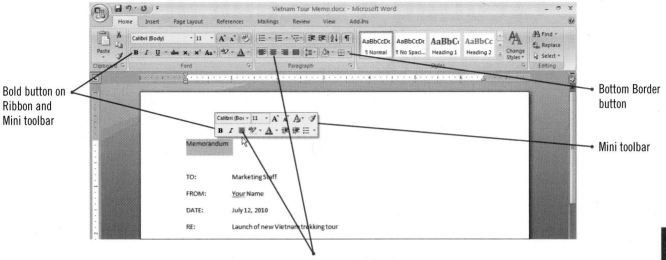

Bold button on Ribbon and Mini toolbar

Bottom Border button

Mini toolbar

Center button on Ribbon and Mini toolbar

FIGURE A-10: Completed memo in the Print Preview window

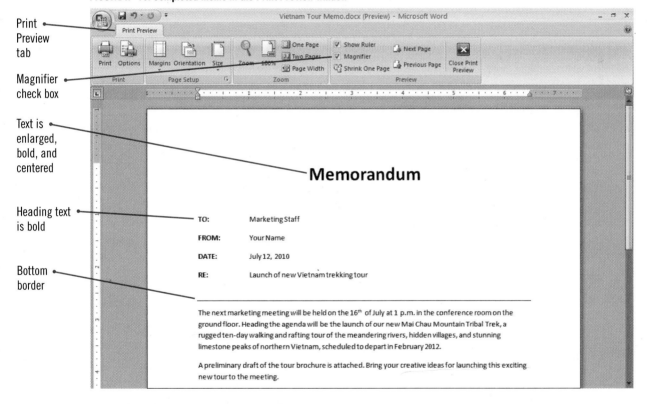

Print Preview tab

Magnifier check box

Text is enlarged, bold, and centered

Heading text is bold

Bottom border

TABLE A-5: Buttons on the Mini toolbar

button	use to	button	use to
Calibri (Boc ▾	Change the font of text	*I*	Italicize text
11 ▾	Change the font size of text	≣	Center text between the margins
A˄	Make text larger	aby ▾	Apply colored highlighting to text
A˅	Make text smaller	**A** ▾	Change the color of text
A	Apply a style to text	≣	Decrease the indent level of a paragraph
✎	Copy the formats applied to text to other text	≣	Increase the indent level of a paragraph
B	Apply bold to text	≣ ▾	Format paragraphs as a bulleted list

Creating a Document Using a Template

Word includes many templates that you can use to quickly create memos, faxes, letters, reports, brochures, and other professionally designed documents. A **template** is a formatted document that contains place-holder text, generic text that you replace with text specific to your needs. You use the New command on the Office menu to open a file that is based on a template. You then replace the placeholder text with your own text, and save the document with a new filename. ▓▓▓▓ You want to fax a draft of the Vietnam tour brochure to Wim Hoppengarth, the tour developer for Asia. You use a template to create a fax cover sheet.

1. **Click the Office button ◉, then click New**

   The New Document dialog box opens, as shown in Figure A-11.

2. **Click Installed Templates in the Templates Categories pane, scroll down the list of Installed Templates, then click Oriel Fax**

   A preview of the Oriel Fax template appears in the New Document dialog box.

3. **Click Create**

   The Oriel Fax template opens as a new document in the document window. It contains placeholder text, which you can replace with your own information.

4. **Click [Pick the date]**

   The placeholder text is selected and appears inside a content control. A **content control** is an interactive object that you use to customize a document with your own information. A content control might include placeholder text, a drop-down list of choices, or a calendar. To deselect a content control, you click a blank area of the document.

5. **Click the Pick the date list arrow**

   A calendar opens below the content control. You use the calendar to select the date you want to appear on your document—simply click a date on the calendar to enter that date in the document. You can use the arrows to the left and right of the month and year to scroll the calendar and display a different month.

6. **Click the Today button in the calendar**

   The current date replaces the placeholder text.

7. **Click [TYPE THE RECIPIENT NAME], type Wim Hoppengarth, Guest, click [Type the recipient fax number], then type 1-84-4-555-1510**

   You do not need to drag to select the placeholder text in a content control, you can simply click it. The text you type replaces the placeholder text.

8. **Click [Type the recipient phone number], press [Delete] twice, press [Backspace] seven times, then type HOTEL NIKKO HANOI, ROOM 1384**

   The recipient phone number content control is removed from the document.

9. **If the text In the From line is not your name, drag to select the text, then type your name**

   When the document is created, Word automatically enters the user name identified in the Word Options dialog box in the From line. This text is not placeholder text, so you have to drag to select it.

10. **Replace the remaining heading placeholder text with the text shown in Figure A-12, click ◉, click Save As, then save the document as Wim Fax to the drive and folder where you store your Data Files**

    The document is saved with the filename Wim Fax.

FIGURE A-11: New Document dialog box

Installed templates

Types of templates available with an active Internet connection

Select to create a blank document

Your list of recently used templates will differ or may not appear at all

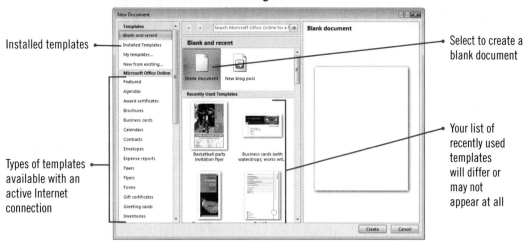

FIGURE A-12: Document created using the Oriel fax template

7/12/2010

TO: Wim Hoppengarth, Guest

FAX: 1-84-4-555-1510

HOTEL NIKKO HANOI, ROOM 1384

FROM: Your Name

FAX: 619-555-0937

PHONE: 619-555-1223

PAGES: 3, including cover sheet

RE: Mai Chau tour brochure

CC:

COMMENTS:
[Type comments]

FAX

[Type the sender company name] [Type the company address] [Type

Using the Undo, Redo, and Repeat commands

Word remembers the editing and formatting changes you make so that you can easily reverse or repeat them. You can reverse the last action you took by clicking the Undo button ![icon] on the Quick Access toolbar, or you can undo a series of actions by clicking the Undo list arrow ![icon] and selecting the action you want to reverse. When you undo an action using the Undo list arrow, you also undo all the actions above it in the list—that is, all actions that were performed after the action you selected. Similarly, you can keep the change you just reversed by using the Redo button ![icon] on the

Quick Access toolbar. The Redo button appears only immediately after clicking the Undo button to undo a change.

If you want to repeat an action you just completed, you can use the Repeat button ![icon] on the Quick Access toolbar. For example, if you just typed "thank you," clicking ![icon] inserts "thank you" at the location of the insertion point. If you just applied bold, clicking ![icon] applies bold to the currently selected text. You also can repeat the last action you took by pressing [F4].

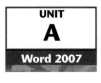

Viewing and Navigating a Document

The Word Zoom feature lets you enlarge a document in the document window to get a close-up view of a detail, or reduce the size of the document in the document window for an overview of the layout as a whole. You zoom in and out on a document using the tools in the Zoom group on the View tab and the Zoom level button and Zoom slider on the status bar. ⬛⬛⬛ You find it's helpful to zoom in and out on the document as you finalize the fax cover sheet.

STEPS

1. **Click the down scroll arrow at the bottom of the vertical scroll bar until COMMENTS: is at the top of your document window**

    The scroll arrows or scroll bars allow you to **scroll** through a document. You scroll through a document when you want to display different parts of the document in the document window. You can also scroll by clicking the scroll bar above and below the scroll box, or by dragging the scroll box up or down in the scroll bar. In longer documents, you can click the Previous Page button ⬛ or the Next Page button ⬛ on the scroll bar to display the document page by page.

2. **Click [Type comments], then type A draft copy of the Mai Chau tour brochure is attached. Please revise the text for accuracy. The photos are for placement only. Have you hired a photographer yet?**

QUICK TIP
You can also click the Zoom button in the Zoom group on the View tab to open the Zoom dialog box.

3. **Click the Zoom level button `100%` on the status bar**

    The Zoom dialog box opens. You use the Zoom dialog box to select a zoom level for displaying the document in the document window.

4. **Click the Whole page option button, then click OK**

    The entire document is displayed in the document window.

5. **Click the text at the bottom of the page to move the insertion point to the bottom of the page, click the View tab, then click the Page Width button in the Zoom group**

    The document is enlarged to the width of the document window. When you enlarge a document, the area where the insertion point is located appears in the document window.

6. **Click in the Urgent box, type x, then click the One Page button in the Zoom group**

    The entire document is displayed in the document window.

7. **Click Fax to move the insertion point to the upper-right corner of the page, then move the Zoom slider to the right until the Zoom percentage is 100%, as shown in Figure A-13**

    Moving the Zoom slider to the right enlarges the document in the document window. Moving the zoom slider to the left allows you to see more of the page at a reduced size. You can also move the Zoom slider by clicking a point on the Zoom slider, or by clicking the Zoom Out and Zoom In buttons.

8. **Click the Zoom In button ⊕ three times, click the vertical placeholder [Type the sender company name], press [Delete] twice, click [Type the company address], press [Delete] twice, click [Type the company phone number], then type Quest Specialty Travel, San Diego, CA**

    The text you type replaces the vertical placeholder text. You do not always need to replace the placeholder text with the type of information suggested in the content control.

9. **Preview the document in Print Preview, correct any errors, close Print Preview, click `130%`, click 100%, click OK, save the document, print it, close the file, then exit Word**

    The completed fax coversheet is shown in Figure A-14.

Creating Documents with Word 2007

FIGURE A-13: Zoom slider

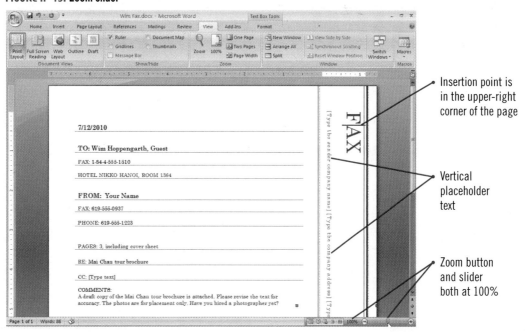

Insertion point is in the upper-right corner of the page

Vertical placeholder text

Zoom button and slider both at 100%

FIGURE A-14: Completed fax cover sheet

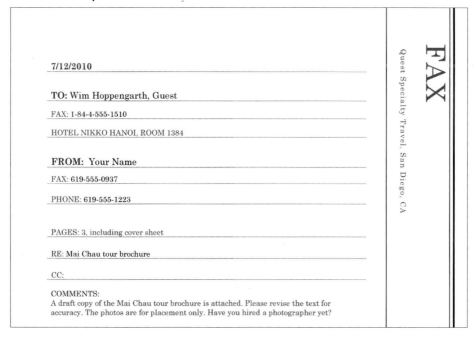

Using Word document views

Each Word view provides features that are useful for working on different types of documents. The default view, **Print Layout view**, displays a document as it will look on a printed page. Print Layout view is helpful for formatting text and pages, including adjusting document margins, creating columns of text, inserting graphics, and formatting headers and footers. Also useful is **Draft view**, which shows a simplified layout of a document, without margins, headers and footers, or graphics. When you want to quickly type, edit, and format text, it's often easiest to work in Draft view. Other Word views are helpful for performing specialized tasks. **Full Screen Reading view** displays document text so that it is easy to read and annotate. You can easily highlight content, add comments, and track and review changes in Full Screen Reading view. **Web Layout view** allows you to accurately format Web pages or documents that will be viewed on a computer screen. In Web Layout view, a document appears just as it will when viewed with a Web browser. Finally, **Outline view** is useful for editing and formatting longer documents that include multiple headings. Outline view allows you to reorganize text by moving the headings. You switch between views by clicking the view buttons on the status bar or by using the commands on the View tab. Changing views does not affect how the printed document will appear. It simply changes the way you view the document in the document window.

Practice

▼ CONCEPTS REVIEW

Label the elements of the Word program window shown in Figure A-15.

FIGURE A-15

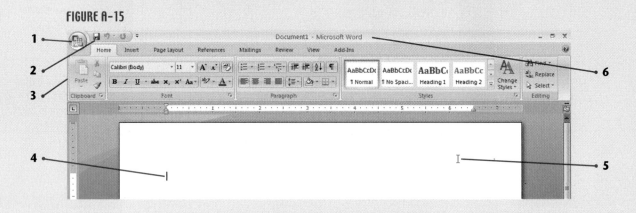

Match each term with the statement that best describes it.

7. Template
8. Formatting marks
9. Status bar
10. Ribbon
11. AutoComplete
12. Horizontal ruler
13. AutoCorrect
14. Zoom slider

a. Enlarges and reduces the document in the document window
b. Special characters that appear on screen but do not print
c. Provides access to Word commands
d. Displays tab settings and paragraph indents
e. A formatted document that contains placeholder text
f. Fixes certain errors as you type
g. Displays the number of pages in the current document
h. Suggests text to insert into a document

Select the best answer from the list of choices.

15. **Which of the following does not contain commands?**
    a. The Mini toolbar
    b. The status bar
    c. The Ribbon
    d. The Office menu

16. **Which tab includes buttons for formatting text?**
    a. Home
    b. Insert
    c. Page Layout
    d. View

17. **Which of the following is not included in a ScreenTip for a command?**
    a. Keyboard shortcut for the command
    b. Alternative location of the command
    c. Description of the function of the command
    d. Link to a help topic on the command

18. **Which element of the Word program window shows the settings for the top and bottom document margins?**
    a. View tab
    b. Status bar
    c. Vertical scroll bar
    d. Vertical ruler

19. What is the default file extension for a document created in Word 2007?

   a. .doc   **c.** .docx

   b. .dot   **d.** .dotx

20. Which view is best for annotating text with comments and highlighting?

   a. Draft view   **c.** Full Screen Reading view

   b. Outline view   **d.** Print Layout view

▼ SKILLS REVIEW

1. Explore the Word program window.

   a. Start Word.

   b. Identify as many elements of the Word program window as you can without referring to the unit material.

   c. Click the Office button, then drag the pointer through the menu commands, pointing to the arrow when commands include an arrow.

   d. Click each tab on the Ribbon, review the groups and buttons on each tab, then return to the Home tab.

   e. Point to each button on the Home tab and read the ScreenTips.

   f. Click the view buttons to view the blank document in each view, then return to Print Layout view.

   g. Use the Zoom slider to zoom all the way in and all the way out on the document, then return to 100%.

2. Start a document.

   a. In a new blank document, type FAX at the top of the page, then press [Enter] two times.

   b. Type the following, pressing [Tab] as indicated and pressing [Enter] at the end of each line:

      To: [Tab][Tab] Joanna Card

      From: [Tab] [Tab] Your Name

      Date: [Tab] [Tab] Today's date

      Re: [Tab] [Tab] Reservation confirmation

      Pages: [Tab] [Tab] 1

      Fax: [Tab] [Tab] (603) 555-5478

   c. Press [Enter] again, then type Thank you for your interest in our summer festival weekend package, which includes accommodations for three nights in downtown Montreal, continental breakfast, and a festival pass. Rooms are still available during the following festivals: International Jazz Festival, Just for Laughs Festival, Montreal Fringe Festival, and Le Festival des Arts du Village. Please see the attached schedule for festival dates and details.

   d. Press [Enter], then type To make a reservation, please call me at (514) 555-7482. I will need payment in full by the 3rd of June to hold a room. No one knows how to celebrate summer like Montrealers!

   e. Insert Grand Prix Festival, before International Jazz Festival.

   f. Using the [Backspace] key, delete 1 in the Pages: line, then type 2.

   g. Using the [Delete] key, delete festival in the last sentence of the first paragraph.

3. Save a document.

   a. Click the Save button on the Quick Access toolbar.

   b. Save the document as Card Fax with the default file extension to the drive and folder where you store your Data Files.

   c. After your name, type a comma, press [Spacebar], then type Global Montreal

   d. Save the document.

4. Select text.

   a. Turn on formatting marks.

   b. Select the Re: line, then type Re: [Tab] [Tab] Summer Festival Weekend Package

   c. Select three in the first sentence, then type two.

   d. Select 3rd of June in the second sentence of the last paragraph, type 15th of May, select room, then type reservation.

   e. Delete the sentence No one knows how to celebrate summer like Montrealers!

   f. Turn off the display of formatting marks, then save the document.

5. Format text using the Mini toolbar.

a. Select FAX, then click the Grow Font button on the Mini toolbar 11 times.

b. Apply bold to the word FAX, then center it on the page.

c. Apply a bottom border under the word FAX.

d. Apply bold to the following words in the fax heading: To:, From:, Date:, Re:, Pages:, and Fax:.

e. View the document in Print Preview.

f. Click the word FAX to zoom in on the document, then proofread the fax.

g. Switch to edit mode, then correct any typing errors in your document.

h. Close Print Preview, then save the document. Compare your document to Figure A-16.

i. Print the fax using the default print settings, then close the document.

6. Create a document using a template. This exercise requires an Internet connection.

a. Click the Office button, then click New to open the New Document dialog box.

b. Scroll down the list of Microsoft Office Online templates in the Templates pane, click Memos, select the Memo (Professional design) template, click Download, then click Continue. (*Note:* You must be working with an active Internet connection to download a template from Microsoft Office Online. Select a different memo template if the Professional design memo is not available to you.)

c. Type Louis Philippe Ouellette to replace the To placeholder text, type your name to replace the From placeholder text, then type Sold out summer festival packages to replace the Re placeholder text.

d. Select the Cc line, then press [Delete]. The date in the document should be the current date.

e. Click the Office button, click Convert, click OK, then save the document with the filename Sold Out Memo to the drive and folder where you store your Data Files.

7. View and navigate a document.

a. Scroll down until How to Use This Memo Template is at the top of your document window.

b. Delete the text How to Use This Memo Template.

c. Select the remaining placeholder body text, type Packages for the following summer festivals are sold out: First Peoples' Festival, Chamber Music Festival, and Dragon Boat Race Festival. We had expected these packages to be less popular than those for the bigger festivals, but interest has been high. Next year, we will increase our bookings for these festivals by 30%.

d. Use the Zoom dialog box to view the Whole Page.

e. Click Company Name Here to move the insertion point to the upper-right corner of the page, then use the Zoom slider to set the Zoom percentage at approximately 200%.

f. Replace Company Name Here with Global Montreal, then reduce the zoom percentage to 100%.

g. Preview the document in Print Preview, correct any errors, close Print Preview, save the document, print it, close the file, then exit Word. Compare your document to Figure A-17.

FIGURE A-16

FAX

To:	Joanna Card
From:	Your Name, Global Montreal
Date:	April 14, 2010
Re:	Summer Festival Weekend Package
Pages:	2
Fax:	(603) 555-5478

Thank you for your interest in our summer festival weekend package, which includes accommodations for two nights in downtown Montreal, continental breakfast, and a festival pass. Rooms are still available during the following festivals: Grand Prix Festival, International Jazz Festival, Just for Laughs Festival, Montreal Fringe Festival, and Le Festival des Arts du Village. Please see the attached schedule for dates and details.

To make a reservation, please call me at (514) 555-7482. I will need payment in full by the 15th of May to hold a reservation.

FIGURE A-17

Global Montreal

Memo

To:	Louis Philippe Ouellette
From:	Your Name
Date:	6/1/10
Re:	Sold out summer festival packages

Packages for the following summer festivals are sold out: First Peoples' Festival, Chamber Music Festival, and Dragon Boat Race Festival. We had expected these packages to be less popular than those for the bigger festivals, but interest has been high. Next year, we will increase our bookings for these festivals by 30%.

▼ INDEPENDENT CHALLENGE 1

Yesterday you interviewed for a job as U.S. marketing director at Edo Design Services. You spoke with several people at Edo, including Mayumi Suzuki, chief executive officer, whose business card is shown in Figure A-18. You need to write a follow-up letter to Ms. Suzuki, thanking her for the interview and expressing your interest in the company and the position. She also asked you to send her some samples of your marketing work, which you will enclose with the letter.

FIGURE A-18

a. Start Word and save a new blank document as **Edo Letter** to the drive and folder where you store your Data Files.

b. Begin the letter by clicking the No Spacing button in the Styles group. You use this button to apply the No Spacing style to the document so that your document does not include extra space between paragraphs.

c. Type a personal letterhead for the letter that includes your name, address, telephone number, and e-mail address. If Word formats your e-mail address as a hyperlink, right-click your e-mail address, then click Remove Hyperlink. (*Note*: Format the letterhead after you finish typing the letter.)

d. Three lines below the bottom of the letterhead, type today's date.

e. Four lines below the date, type the inside address, referring to Figure A-18 for the address information. Be sure to include the recipient's title, company name, and full mailing address in the inside address. (*Hint*: When typing a foreign address, type the name of the country in capital letters by itself on the last line.)

f. Two lines below the inside address, type the salutation.

g. Two lines below the salutation, type the body of the letter according to the following guidelines:

- In the first paragraph, thank her for the interview. Then restate your interest in the position and express your desire to work for the company. Add any specific details you think will enhance the power of your letter.

- In the second paragraph, note that you are enclosing three samples of your work and explain something about the samples you are enclosing.

- Type a short final paragraph.

h. Two lines below the last body paragraph, type a closing, then four lines below the closing, type the signature block. Be sure to include your name in the signature block.

i. Two lines below the signature block, type an enclosure notation. (*Hint*: An enclosure notation usually includes the word "Enclosures" or the abbreviation "Enc." followed by the number of enclosures in parentheses.)

j. Format the letterhead with bold, centering, and a bottom border.

k. Save your changes.

l. Preview and print the letter, then close the document and exit Word.

▼ INDEPENDENT CHALLENGE 2

Your company has recently installed Word 2007 on its company network. As the training manager, it's your responsibility to teach employees how to use the new software productively. Now that they have begun working with Word 2007, several employees have asked you about sharing Word 2007 documents with colleagues who are using an earlier version of Word. In response to their queries, you decide to write a memo to all employees explaining file compatibility issues between Word 2007 and previous versions of Word. Rather than write the memo from scratch, you revise a memo you wrote earlier on this topic to the department heads. That memo was written on your home office computer, which still has Word 2003 installed.

a. Start Word, open the file **WD A-1.doc** from the drive and folder where you store your Data Files, then read the memo to get a feel for its contents. The .doc file extension lets you know this file was created in a previous version of Word. Notice the words Compatibility Mode in the title bar. Compatibility Mode ensures that no new features in Word 2007 are available while you are working with the document so that the document will be fully accessible to people who use previous versions of Word.

b. Save the file in Word 97-2003 format as **XML Memo** to the drive and folder where you store your Data Files.

c. Replace the information in the memo header with the information shown in Figure A-19. Make sure to include your name in the From line and the current date in the Date line.

d. Apply bold to **To:**, **From:**, **Date:**, and **Re:**.

e. Increase the size of **WORD TRAINING MEMORANDUM** to match Figure A-19, center the text on the page, add a border below it, then save your changes.

FIGURE A-19

WORD TRAINING MEMORANDUM

To:	All employees
From:	Your Name, Training Manager
Date:	Today's date
Re:	File compatibility in Word 2007

---

f. In order to save the memo in XML format, click the Office button, click Convert, read the text in the Microsoft Office Word dialog box, then click OK. Notice the phrase Compatibility Mode no longer appears in the title bar. Compatibility Mode is turned off.

g. Click the Save button. Notice the file extension in the title bar changes to .docx if Windows is set to display file extensions on your computer.

Advanced Challenge Exercise

- Using the Font list on the Mini toolbar, apply a different font to **WORD TRAINING MEMORANDUM**. Make sure to select a font that is appropriate for a business memo.
- Using the Font Color button on the Mini toolbar, change the color of **WORD TRAINING MEMORANDUM** to an appropriate color.
- Save a copy of the memo in Word 97-2003 format as **XML Memo ACE** to the drive or folder where you store your Data Files. (*Hint*: Click the Office button, point to Save As, then click Word 97-2003 Document.)

h. Preview and print the memo, then close the document and exit Word.

▼ INDEPENDENT CHALLENGE 3

You are an expert on global warming. The president of the National Park Association, Jeremy Moynihan, has asked you to be the keynote speaker at an upcoming conference on the impact of climate change on the national parks, to be held in Glacier National Park. You use one of the Word letter templates to write a letter to Mr. Moynihan accepting the invitation and confirming the details. Your letter to Mr. Moynihan should reference the following information:

- The conference will be held June 4–6, 2010, at the Many Glacier Hotel in the park.
- You have been asked to speak for an hour on Saturday, June 5, followed by one half hour for questions.
- Mr. Moynihan suggested the lecture topic "Melting Glaciers, Changing Ecosystems."
- Your talk will include a 45-minute slide presentation.
- The National Park Association will make your travel arrangements.
- Your preference is to arrive at Glacier Park International Airport in Kalispell on the morning of Friday, June 4 and to depart on Monday, June 7. You would like to rent a car at the airport for the drive to the Many Glacier Hotel.
- You want to fly in and out of the airport closest to your home.

a. Start Word, open the New Document dialog box, click Installed Templates, and then select an appropriate letter template. Save the document as **Moynihan Letter** to the drive and folder where you store your Data Files.

b. Replace the placeholders in the letterhead with your personal information. Include your name, address, phone number, and e-mail address. Delete any placeholders that do not apply. (*Hints*: Depending on the template you choose, the letterhead might be located at the top or on the side of the document. You can press [Enter] when typing in a placeholder to add an additional line of text. You can also change the format of text typed in a placeholder.)

c. Use the Pick the date content control to select the current date.

d. Replace the placeholders in the inside address. Be sure to include Mr. Moynihan's title and the name of the organization. Make up a street address and zip code.

e. Type **Dear Mr. Moynihan:** for the salutation.

f. Using the information listed previously, type the body of the letter:

- In the first paragraph, accept the invitation to speak and confirm the important conference details.
- In the second paragraph, confirm your lecture topic and provide any relevant details.
- In the third paragraph, state your travel preferences.
- Type a short final paragraph.

g. Type **Sincerely,** for the closing, then include your name in the signature block.

h. Adjust the formatting of the letter as necessary. For example, remove bold formatting or change the font color of text to a more appropriate color.

Advanced Challenge Exercise

- Zoom in and out on the document, looking for spelling, grammar, and formatting errors.
- Correct your spelling and grammar errors, if any, by right-clicking any red- or green-underlined text and then choosing from the options on the shortcut menu.
- View the letter in Full Screen Reading view, then click the Close button to return to Print Layout view.

i. Proofread your letter, make corrections as needed, then save your changes.

j. Preview the letter, print the letter, close the document, then exit Word.

▼ REAL LIFE INDEPENDENT CHALLENGE

This Independent Challenge requires an Internet connection.

The computer keyboard has become as essential an office tool as the pencil. The more adept you become at touch typing—the fastest and most accurate way to type—the more comfortable you will be working with computers and the more saleable your office skills to a potential employer. The World Wide Web is one source of information on touch typing, and many Web sites include free typing tests and online tutorials to help you practice and improve your typing skills. In this independent challenge, you will take an online typing test to check your typing skills. You will then research the fundamentals of touch typing and investigate some of the ergonomic factors important to becoming a productive keyboard typist.

a. Use your favorite search engine to search the Web for information on typing. Use the keywords **typing** and **typing ergonomics** to conduct your search.

b. Review the Web sites you find. Choose a site that offers a free online typing test, take the test, then print the Web page showing the results of your typing test.

c. Start Word and save a new blank document as **Touch Typing** to the drive and folder where you store your Data Files.

d. Type your name at the top of the document.

e. Type a brief report on the results of your research. Your report should answer the following questions:

- What are the URLs of the Web sites you visited to research touch typing and keyboard ergonomics? (*Hint*: A URL is a Web page's address. An example of a URL is www.course.com.)
- What are some of the benefits of using the touch typing method?
- In touch typing, on which keys should the fingers of the left and right hands rest?
- What ergonomic factors are important to keep in mind while typing?

f. Save your changes to the document, preview and print it, then close the document and exit Word.

▼ VISUAL WORKSHOP

Create the cover letter shown in Figure A-20. Before beginning to type, click the No Spacing button in the Styles group on the Home tab. Add the bottom border to the letterhead after typing the letter. Save the document as **Wong Cover Letter** to the drive and folder where you store your Data Files, print a copy of the letter, then close the document and exit Word.

FIGURE A-20

Your Name

345 West 11th Avenue, Anchorage, AK 99501
Tel: 907-555-7283; Fax: 907-555-1445

June 28, 2010

Ms. Sylvia Wong
Wong Associates
2286 East Northern Lights Blvd.
Suite 501
Anchorage, AK 99514

Dear Ms. Wong:

I read of the opening for a public information assistant in the June 27 edition of adn.com, and I would like to be considered for the position. I am a recent graduate of Greater Anchorage Community College (GACC), and I am interested in pursuing a career in public relations.

My interest in a public relations career springs from my publicly acknowledged writing and journalism abilities. For example, at GACC, I was a reporter for the student newspaper and frequently wrote press releases for campus and community events.

I have a wealth of experience using Microsoft Word in professional settings. Last summer, I worked as an office assistant for the architecture firm Coleman & Greenberg, where I used Word to create newsletters, brochures, and financial reports. During the school year, I also worked part-time in the GACC Office of Community Relations, where I used the Word mail merge feature to create form letters and mailing labels.

My enclosed resume details my skills and experience. I welcome the opportunity to discuss the position and my qualifications with you. I can be reached at 907-555-7283.

Sincerely,

Your Name

Enc.

Editing Documents

The sophisticated editing features in Word make it easy to revise and polish your documents. In this unit, you learn how to revise an existing file by opening it, copying and moving text, and then saving the document as a new file. You also learn how to perfect your documents using proofing tools and how to quickly prepare a document for distribution to the public. You have been asked to edit and finalize a press release for a QST promotional lecture series. The press release should provide information about the series so that newspapers, radio stations, and other media outlets can announce it to the public. QST press releases are disseminated by fax and by e-mail. Before distributing the file electronically to your lists of press contacts and local QST clients, you add several hyperlinks and then strip the file of private information.

OBJECTIVES

Cut and paste text

Copy and paste text

Use the Office Clipboard

Find and replace text

Check spelling and grammar

Research information

Add hyperlinks

Prepare a document for distribution

Cutting and Pasting Text

The editing features in Word allow you to move text from one location to another in a document. The operation of moving text is often called **cut and paste**. When you cut text, it is removed from the document and placed on the **Clipboard**, a temporary storage area for text and graphics that you cut or copy from a document. To cut text, you select it and then click the Cut button in the Clipboard group on the Home tab. To insert the text from the Clipboard into the document, you place the insertion point where you want to insert the text, and then click the Paste button in the Clipboard group. You also can move selected text by dragging it to a new location using the mouse. This operation is called **drag and drop**. You open the press release that was drafted by a colleague, save it with a new filename, and then reorganize the information in the press release using the cut-and-paste and drag-and-drop methods.

STEPS

1. **Start** Word, **click the** Office button ⊞, **click** Open, **navigate to the drive and folder where you store your Data Files, click** WD B-1.docx, **then click** Open

   The document opens. Once you have opened a file, you can edit it and use the Save or the Save As command to save your changes. You use the **Save** command when you want to save the changes you make to a file, overwriting the file that is stored on a disk. You use the **Save As** command when you want to leave the original file intact and create a duplicate file with a different filename, file extension, or location.

2. **Click** ⊞, **click** Save As, **type** Wanderlust PR **in the File name text box, then click** Save

   You can now make changes to the press release file without affecting the original file.

3. **Replace** Ron Dawson **with your name, scroll down until the headline Katherine Quoss to Speak... is at the top of your document window, then click the** Show/Hide ¶ button ¶ **in the Paragraph group on the Home tab to display formatting marks**

4. **Select** Alaskan guide Gilbert Coonan, **(including the comma and the space after it) in the third paragraph, then click the** Cut button ✂ **in the Clipboard group**

   The text is removed from the document and placed on the Clipboard. Word uses two different clipboards: the **system Clipboard** (the Clipboard), which holds just one item, and the **Office Clipboard**, which holds up to 24 items. The last item you cut or copy is always added to both clipboards. You'll learn more about the Office Clipboard in a later lesson.

5. **Place the insertion point before** Serengeti **(but after the space) in the first line of the third paragraph, then click the** Paste button **in the Clipboard group**

   The text is pasted at the location of the insertion point, as shown in Figure B-1. The Paste Options button appears below text when you first paste it in a document. You'll learn more about the Paste Options button in the next lesson. For now, you can ignore it.

6. **Press and hold** [Ctrl], **click the sentence** Ticket prices include lunch. **in the fourth paragraph, then release** [Ctrl]

   The entire sentence is selected.

7. **Press and hold the mouse button over the selected text until the pointer changes to** ▭

   Notice the pointer's vertical line. You use this to indicate the location where you want the text to be inserted when you release the mouse button.

8. **Drag the pointer's vertical line to the end of the fifth paragraph (between the period and the paragraph mark) as shown in Figure B-2, then release the mouse button**

   The selected text is moved to the location of the insertion point. It is convenient to move text using the drag-and-drop method when the locations of origin and destination are both visible on the screen. Text is not placed on the Clipboard when you move it using drag-and-drop.

9. **Deselect the text, then click the** Save button 🖫 **on the Quick Access toolbar**

FIGURE B-1: Moved text with Paste Options button

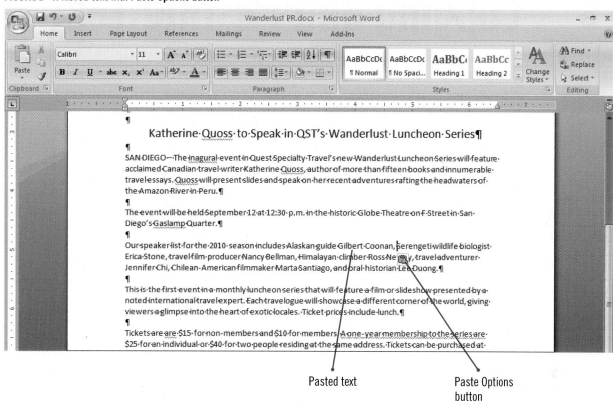

Pasted text

Paste Options button

FIGURE B-2: Text being dragged to a new location

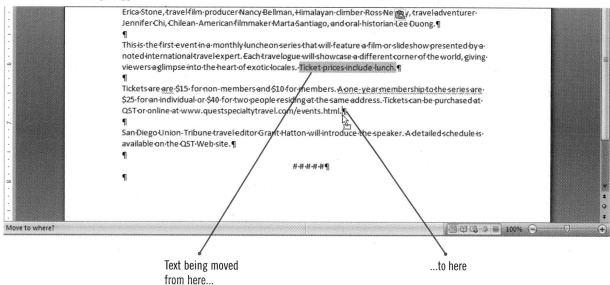

Text being moved from here...

...to here

Using keyboard shortcuts

Instead of using the Cut, Copy, and Paste commands to edit text in Word, you can use the **keyboard shortcuts** [Ctrl][X] to cut text, [Ctrl][C] to copy text, and [Ctrl][V] to paste text. A **shortcut key** is a function key, such as [F1], or a combination of keys, such as [Ctrl][S], that you press to perform a command. For example, you can press [Ctrl][S] to save changes to a document instead of clicking the Save button on the Quick Access toolbar or clicking Save on the Office menu. Becoming skilled at using keyboard shortcuts can help you to quickly accomplish many of the tasks you perform frequently in Word. If a keyboard shortcut is available for a command, then it is listed in the ScreenTip for the command.

Copying and Pasting Text

Copying and pasting text is similar to cutting and pasting text, except that the text you copy is not removed from the document. Rather, a copy of the text is placed on the Clipboard, leaving the original text in place. You can copy text to the Clipboard using the Copy button in the Clipboard group on the Home tab, or you can copy text by pressing [Ctrl] as you drag the selected text from one location to another. You continue to edit the press release by copying text from one location to another.

STEPS

QUICK TIP
You can also copy selected text by right-clicking it, and then clicking Copy on the Edit menu.

1. **Select Wanderlust Luncheon in the headline, then click the Copy button** 📋 **in the Clipboard group**

   A copy of the text is placed on the Clipboard, leaving the text you copied in place.

2. **Place the insertion point before season in the third body paragraph, then click the Paste button in the Clipboard group**

   "Wanderlust Luncheon" is inserted before "season," as shown in Figure B-3. Notice that the pasted text is formatted differently than the paragraph in which it was inserted.

QUICK TIP
If you don't like the result of a paste option, try another option or click the Undo button 🔄 and then paste the text again.

3. **Click the Paste Options button** 📋, **then click Match Destination Formatting**

   The Paste Options button allows you to change the formatting of pasted text. The formatting of "Wanderlust Luncheon" is changed to match the rest of the paragraph. The options available on the Paste Options menu depend on the format of the text you are pasting and the format of the surrounding text.

4. **Select www.questspecialtytravel.com in the fifth paragraph, press and hold [Ctrl], press and hold the mouse button until the pointer changes to** 🔲

5. **Drag the pointer's vertical line to the end of the last paragraph, placing it between site and the period, release the mouse button, then release [Ctrl]**

   The text is copied to the last paragraph. Since the formatting of the text you copied is the same as the formatting of the paragraph in which you inserted it, you can ignore the Paste Options button. Text is not copied to the Clipboard when you copy it using the drag-and-drop method.

6. **Place the insertion point before www.questspecialtytravel.com in the last paragraph, type at followed by a space, then save the document**

   Compare your document with Figure B-4.

Splitting the document window to copy and move items in a long document

If you want to copy or move items between parts of a long document, it can be useful to split the document window into two panes so that the item you want to copy or move is displayed in one pane and the destination for the item is displayed in the other pane. To split a window, click the Split button in the Window group on the View tab, drag the horizontal split bar that appears to the location you want to split the window, and then click. Once the document window is split into two panes, you can drag the split bar to resize the panes and use the scroll bars in each pane to display different parts of the document. To copy or move an item from one pane to another, you can use the Cut, Copy, and Paste commands, or you can drag the item between the panes. When you are finished editing the document, double-click the split bar to restore the window to a single pane, or click the Remove Split button in the Window group on the View tab.

FIGURE B-3: Text pasted in document

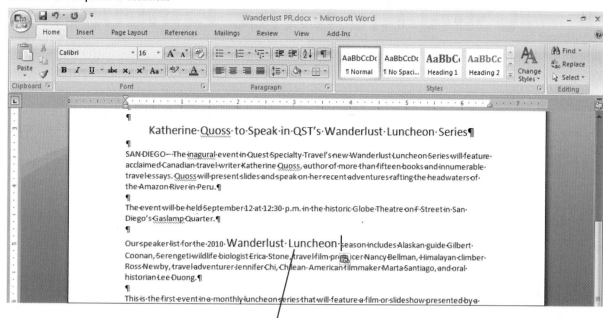

Formatting of the pasted
text matches the headline

FIGURE B-4: Copied text in document

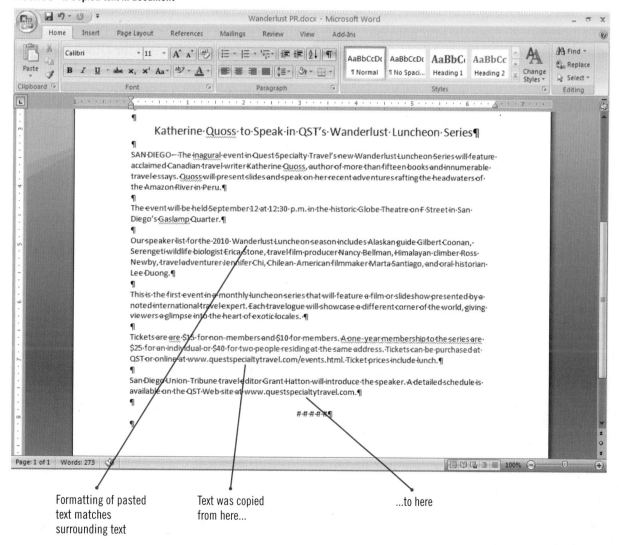

Formatting of pasted
text matches
surrounding text

Text was copied
from here...

...to here

Using the Office Clipboard

The Office Clipboard allows you to collect text and graphics from files created in any Office program and insert them into your Word documents. It holds up to 24 items and, unlike the system Clipboard, the items on the Office Clipboard can be viewed. To display the Office Clipboard, you simply click the launcher in the Clipboard group on the Home tab. You add items to the Office Clipboard using the Cut and Copy commands. The last item you collect is always added to both the system Clipboard and the Office Clipboard. You use the Office Clipboard to move several sentences in your press release.

STEPS

1. **Click the launcher ⟐ in the Clipboard group**

   The Office Clipboard opens in the Clipboard task pane. It contains the Wanderlust Luncheon item you copied in the last lesson.

2. **Select the sentence San Diego Union-Tribune travel editor ... (including the space after the period) in the last paragraph, right-click the selected text, then click Cut on the Edit menu**

   The sentence is cut to the Office Clipboard.

3. **Select the sentence A detailed schedule is... (including the ¶ mark), right-click the selected text, then click Cut**

   The Office Clipboard displays the items you cut or copied, as shown in Figure B-5. The icon next to each item indicates the items are from a Word document. The last item collected displays at the top of the Clipboard task pane. As new items are collected, the first items collected move down the task pane.

4. **Place the insertion point at the end of the second paragraph (after Quarter. but before the ¶ mark), then click the San Diego Union-Tribune... item on the Office Clipboard**

   Clicking an item on the Office Clipboard pastes the item in the document at the location of the insertion point. Items remain on the Office Clipboard until you delete them or close all open Office programs. Also, if you add a 25th item to the Office Clipboard, the first item is deleted.

5. **Place the insertion point at the end of the third paragraph (after Duong.), then click the A detailed schedule is... item on the Office Clipboard**

   The sentence is pasted in the document.

6. **Select the fourth paragraph, which begins with the sentence This is the first event... (including the ¶ mark), right-click the selected text, then click Cut**

   The paragraph is cut to the Office Clipboard.

7. **Place the insertion point at the beginning of the third paragraph (before Our...), right-click, click Paste on the Edit menu, then press [Backspace]**

   The sentences from the "This is the first..." paragraph are pasted at the beginning of the "Our speaker list..." paragraph. You can paste the last item collected using either the Paste command or the Office Clipboard.

8. **Place the insertion point at the end of the third paragraph (after www.questspecialtytravel.com and before the ¶ mark), then press [Delete] twice**

   The ¶ symbols and the extra blank lines between the third and fourth paragraphs are deleted.

9. **Click the Show/Hide ¶ button ¶ in the Paragraph group**

   Compare your press release with Figure B-6. Note that many Word users prefer to work with formatting marks on at all times. Experiment to see which method you prefer.

10. **Click the Clear All button on the Clipboard task pane to remove the items from the Office Clipboard, click the Close button on the Clipboard task pane, press [Ctrl][Home], then save the document**

    Pressing [Ctrl][Home] moves the insertion point to the top of the document.

FIGURE B-5: Office Clipboard in Clipboard task pane

Click to resize or move the Clipboard task pane

Clipboard task pane

Items stored on the Office Clipboard (yours may include additional items)

Click to change display options for the Office Clipboard

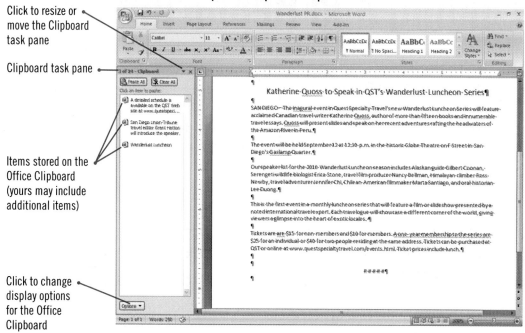

FIGURE B-6: Revised press release

Last item collected

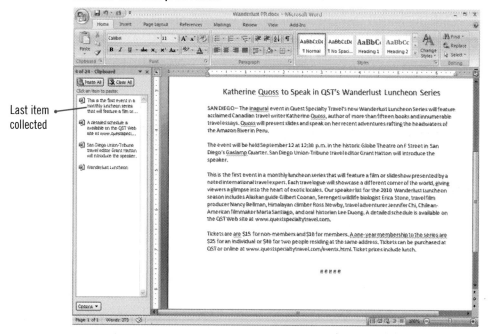

Copying and moving items between documents

The system and Office Clipboards also can be used to copy and move items between Word documents. To copy or cut items from one Word document and paste them into another, first open both documents and the Clipboard task pane in the program window. With multiple documents open, you can copy and move items between documents by copying or cutting the item(s) from one document and then switching to another document and pasting the item(s). To switch between open documents, click the button on the taskbar for the document you want to appear in the document window. You can also display both documents at the same time by clicking the Arrange All button or the View Side by Side button in the Window group on the View tab. The Office Clipboard stores all the items collected from all documents, regardless of which document is displayed in the document window. The system Clipboard stores the last item collected from any document.

Finding and Replacing Text

The Find and Replace feature in Word allows you to automatically search for and replace all instances of a word or phrase in a document. For example, you might need to substitute "tour" for "trip," and it would be very time-consuming to manually locate and replace each instance of "trip" in a long document. Using the Replace command you can automatically find and replace all occurrences of specific text at once, or you can choose to find and review each occurrence individually. You also can use the Find command to locate and select every occurrence of a specific word or phrase in a document. ▨▨▨ QST has decided to change the name of the lecture series from "Wanderlust Luncheon Series" to "Wanderlust Travelogue Series." You use the Replace command to search the document for all instances of "Luncheon" and replace them with "Travelogue."

STEPS

1. **Click the Replace button in the Editing group, then click More in the Find and Replace dialog box**

   The Find and Replace dialog box opens, as shown in Figure B-7.

2. **Type Luncheon in the Find what text box**

   "Luncheon" is the text that will be replaced.

3. **Press [Tab], then type Travelogue in the Replace with text box**

   "Travelogue" is the text that will replace "Luncheon."

4. **Click the Match case check box in the Search Options section to select it**

   Selecting the Match case check box tells Word to find only exact matches for the uppercase and lowercase characters you entered in the Find what text box. You want to replace all instances of "Luncheon" in the proper name "Wanderlust Luncheon Series." You do not want to replace "luncheon" when it refers to a lunchtime event.

5. **Click Replace All**

   Clicking Replace All changes all occurrences of "Luncheon" to "Travelogue" in the press release. A message box reports three replacements were made.

6. **Click OK to close the message box, then click Close in the Find and Replace dialog box**

   Word replaced "Luncheon" with "Travelogue" in three locations, but did not replace "luncheon."

7. **Click the Find button in the Editing group**

   The Find and Replace dialog box opens with the Find tab displayed. The Find command allows you to quickly locate all instances of text in a document. You can use it to verify that Word did not replace "luncheon."

8. **Type luncheon in the Find what text box, make sure the Match case check box is still selected, click Find in, click Main Document on the menu that opens, then click Close**

   The Find and Replace dialog box closes and "luncheon" is selected in the document, as shown in Figure B-8.

9. **Deselect the text, press [Ctrl][Home], then save the document**

Navigating a document using the Go To command

Rather than scrolling to move to a different place in a longer document, you can use the Go To command to quickly move the insertion point to a specific location. To move to a specific page, section, line, table, graphic, or other item in a document, click the Page number button on the status bar to open the Find and Replace dialog box with the Go To tab displayed. On the Go To tab in the Find and Replace dialog box, select the type of item you want to find in the Go to what list box, enter the relevant information about that item, and then click Go To or Next to move the insertion point to the item.

Editing Documents

FIGURE B-7: Find and Replace dialog box

Replace only exact matches of upper-case and lowercase characters

Find only complete words

Use wildcards (*) in a search string

Find words that sound like the Find what text

Find and replace all forms of a word

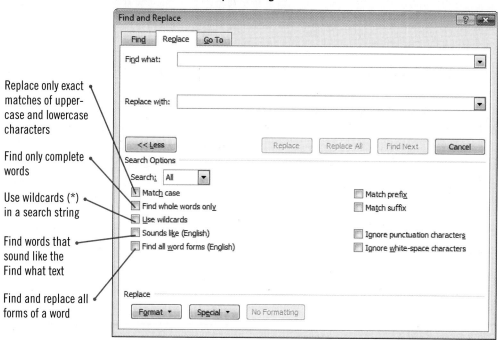

FIGURE B-8: Found text highlighted in document

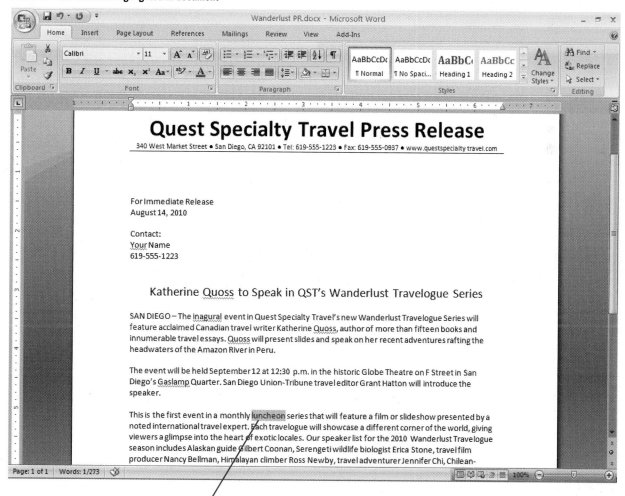

Found text is highlighted

Checking Spelling and Grammar

When you finish typing and revising a document, you can use the Spelling and Grammar command to search the document for misspelled words and grammar errors. The Spelling and Grammar checker flags possible mistakes, suggests correct spellings, and offers remedies for grammar errors such as subject-verb agreement, repeated words, and punctuation. ▚▚▚ You use the Spelling and Grammar checker to search your press release for errors. Before beginning the search, you set the Spelling and Grammar checker to ignore words, such as Quoss, that you know are spelled correctly.

1. **Right-click Quoss in the headline**

   A shortcut menu that includes suggestions for correcting the spelling of "Quoss" opens. You can correct individual spelling and grammar errors by right-clicking text that is underlined with a red or green wavy line and selecting a correction. Although "Quoss" is not in the Word dictionary, it is spelled correctly in the document.

2. **Click Ignore All**

   Clicking Ignore All tells Word not to flag "Quoss" as misspelled.

3. **Press [Ctrl][Home], click the Review tab, then click the Spelling and Grammar button in the Proofing group**

   The Spelling and Grammar: English (United States) dialog box opens, as shown in Figure B-9. The dialog box identifies "inagural" as misspelled and suggests possible corrections for the error. The word selected in the Suggestions box is the correct spelling.

4. **Click Change**

   Word replaces the misspelled word with the correctly spelled word. Next, the dialog box identifies "Gaslamp" as a misspelled word and suggests the correction "Gas lamp". The proper name "Gaslamp Quarter" is spelled correctly in the document.

5. **Click Ignore Once**

   Word ignores the spelling. Next, the dialog box indicates that "are" is repeated in a sentence.

6. **Click Delete**

   Word deletes the second occurrence of the repeated word. Next, the dialog box flags a subject-verb agreement error and suggests using "is" instead of "are," as shown in Figure B-10. The phrase selected in the Suggestions box is correct.

7. **Click Change**

   Word replaces "are" with "is" in the sentence and the Spelling and Grammar dialog box closes. Keep in mind that the Spelling and Grammar checker identifies many common errors, but you cannot rely on it to find and correct all spelling and grammar errors in your documents. Always proofread your documents carefully.

8. **Click OK to complete the spelling and grammar check, press [Ctrl][Home], then save the document**

FIGURE B-9: Spelling and Grammar: English (United States) dialog box

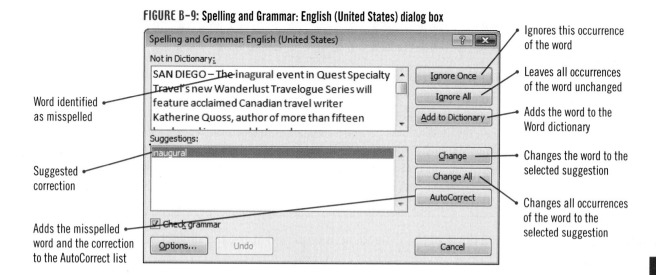

Ignores this occurrence of the word

Leaves all occurrences of the word unchanged

Adds the word to the Word dictionary

Changes the word to the selected suggestion

Changes all occurrences of the word to the selected suggestion

Word identified as misspelled

Suggested correction

Adds the misspelled word and the correction to the AutoCorrect list

FIGURE B-10: Grammar error identified in Spelling and Grammar dialog box

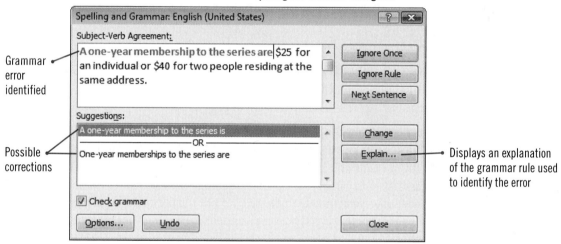

Grammar error identified

Possible corrections

Displays an explanation of the grammar rule used to identify the error

Inserting text with AutoCorrect

As you type, AutoCorrect automatically corrects many commonly misspelled words. By creating your own AutoCorrect entries, you can set Word to quickly insert text that you type often, such as your name or contact information, or to correct words you frequently misspell. For example, you could create an AutoCorrect entry so that the name "Ron Dawson" is automatically inserted whenever you type "rd" followed by a space. You create AutoCorrect entries and customize other AutoCorrect and AutoFormat options using the AutoCorrect dialog box. To open the AutoCorrect dialog box, click the Office button, click Word Options on the Office menu, click Proofing in the Word Options dialog box that opens, and then click

AutoCorrect Options. On the AutoCorrect tab in the AutoCorrect dialog box, type the text you want to be automatically corrected in the Replace text box (such as "rd"), type the text you want to be automatically inserted in its place in the With text box (such as "Ron Dawson"), and then click Add. The AutoCorrect entry is added to the list. Click OK to close the AutoCorrect dialog box, and then click OK to close the Word Options dialog box. Note that Word inserts an AutoCorrect entry in a document only when you press [Spacebar] after typing the text you want Word to correct. For example, Word will insert "Ron Dawson" when you type "rd" followed by a space, but not when you type "Mountain Rd."

Researching Information

The Word Research feature allows you to quickly search reference sources for information related to a word or phrase. Among the reference sources available in the Research task pane is a Thesaurus, which you can use to look up synonyms for awkward or repetitive words. When you are working with an active Internet connection, the Research task pane provides access to dictionary, encyclopedia, translation, and other reference sources, as well as third-party research services, such as medical and legal dictionaries. ▓▓▓▓ After proofreading your document for errors, you decide the press release would read better if several adjectives were more descriptive. You use the Thesaurus to find synonyms.

STEPS

QUICK TIP
You can also click the Research button in the Proofing group to open the Research task pane.

1. **Scroll down until the headline is displayed at the top of your screen**

2. **Select noted in the first sentence of the third paragraph, then click Thesaurus in the Proofing group**

   The Research task pane opens, as shown in Figure B-11. "Noted" appears in the Search for text box and possible synonyms for "noted" are listed under the Thesaurus: English (United States) heading in the task pane.

QUICK TIP
To look up synonyms for a different word, type the word in the Search for text box, then click the green Start searching button.

3. **Point to prominent in the list of synonyms**

   A box containing a list arrow appears around the word.

4. **Click the list arrow, click Insert on the menu that appears, then close the Research task pane**

   "Prominent" replaces "noted" in the press release.

5. **Right-click innumerable in the first sentence of the first paragraph, point to Synonyms on the Edit menu, then click numerous**

   "Numerous" replaces "innumerable" in the press release.

6. **Select the four paragraphs of body text (including the ¶ at the end of the last paragraph), then click the Word Count button 🔢 in the Proofing group**

   The Word Count dialog box opens, as shown in Figure B-12. The dialog box lists the number of pages, words, characters, paragraphs, and lines included in the selected text. Notice that the status bar also displays the number of words included in the selected text and the total number of words in the entire document. If you want to view the page, character, paragraph, and line count for the entire document, make sure nothing is selected in your document, and then click Word Count in the Proofing group.

QUICK TIP
To add or remove available reference sources, click Research options in the Research task pane.

7. **Click Close, press [Ctrl][Home], then save the document**

8. **Click the Office button 🏢, click Save As, type Wanderlust PR Public in the File name text box, then click Save**

   The Wanderlust PR file closes and the Wanderlust PR Public file is displayed in the document window. You will modify this file to prepare it for electronic release to the public.

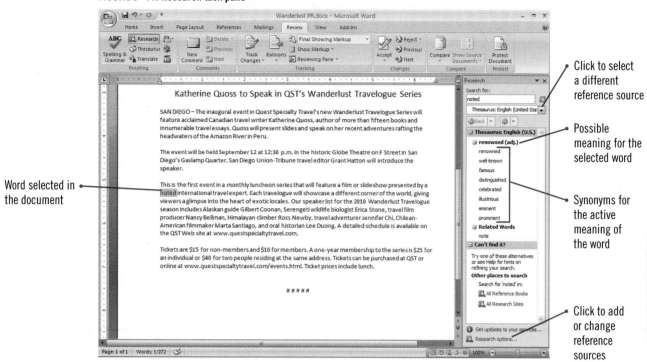

Click to select a different reference source

Possible meaning for the selected word

Synonyms for the active meaning of the word

Word selected in the document

Click to add or change reference sources

FIGURE B-12: Word Count dialog box

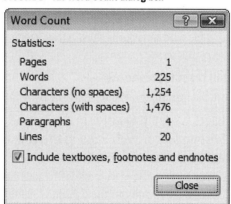

Publishing a blog directly from Word

A **blog**, which is short for weblog, is an informal journal that is cre-ated by an individual or a group and available to the public on the Internet. A blog usually conveys the ideas, comments, and opinions of the blogger and is written using a strong personal voice. The per-son who creates and maintains a blog, the **blogger**, typically updates the blog daily. If you have or want to start a blog, you can configure Word to link to your blog site, so that you can write, for-mat, and publish blog entries directly from Word. To create a blog

entry, click the Office button, click New, then double-click New blog post to open a predesigned blog post document that you can cus-tomize with your own text, formatting, and images. When you are ready to publish the entry to your blog, Word prompts you to log onto your personal blog account. To blog directly from Word, you must first obtain a blog account with a blog service provider. The Word Help system provides detailed information on obtaining and registering your personal blog account with Word.

Adding Hyperlinks

A **hyperlink** is text or a graphic that, when clicked, "jumps" the viewer to a different location or program. When a document is viewed on screen, hyperlinks allow readers to link (or "jump") to a Web page, an e-mail address, a file, or a specific location in a document. When you create a hyperlink in a document, you select the text or graphic you want to use as a hyperlink and then specify the location you want to jump to when the hyperlink is clicked. You create a hyperlink using the Hyperlink button in the Links group on the Insert tab. Text that is formatted as a hyperlink appears as colored, underlined text. ████████ Hundreds of people on your lists of press and client contacts will receive the press release by e-mail or Internet fax. To make it easier for these people to access additional information about the series, you add several hyperlinks to the press release.

STEPS

1. **Select your name, click the Insert tab, then click the Hyperlink button in the Links group**

   The Insert Hyperlink dialog box opens, as shown in Figure B-13. You use this dialog box to specify the location of the Web page, file, e-mail address, or position in the current document you want to jump to when the hyperlink—in this case, your name—is clicked.

2. **Click E-mail Address in the Link to section**

   The Insert Hyperlink dialog box changes so you can create a hyperlink to your e-mail address.

3. **Type your e-mail address in the E-mail address text box, type Wanderlust Travelogue Series in the Subject text box, then click OK**

   As you type, Word automatically adds mailto: in front of your e-mail address. After you close the dialog box, the hyperlink text—your name—is formatted in blue and underlined.

4. **Press and hold [Ctrl], then click the your name hyperlink**

   An e-mail message addressed to you with the subject "Wanderlust Travelogue Series" opens in the default e-mail program. People who receive the press release electronically can use the hyperlink to send you an e-mail message about the series.

5. **Close the e-mail message window**

   The hyperlink text changes to purple, indicating the hyperlink has been followed.

6. **Scroll down, select Gaslamp Quarter in the second paragraph, click the Hyperlink button, click Existing File or Web Page in the Link to section, type www.gaslamp.org in the Address text box, then click OK**

   As you type the Web address, Word automatically adds http:// in front of "www." The text "Gaslamp Quarter" is formatted as a hyperlink to the Gaslamp Quarter Association home page at www.gaslamp.org. When clicked, the hyperlink will open the Web page in the default browser window.

7. **Select detailed schedule in the last sentence of the third paragraph, click the Hyperlink button, type www.questspecialtytravel.com in the Address text box, then click OK**

   The text "detailed schedule" is formatted as a hyperlink to the QST Web site. If you point to a hyperlink in Word, the link to location appears in a ScreenTip. You can edit ScreenTip text to make it more descriptive.

8. **Right-click Quarter in the Gaslamp Quarter hyperlink, click Edit Hyperlink, click ScreenTip in the Edit Hyperlink dialog box, type Map, parking, and other information about the Gaslamp Quarter in the ScreenTip text text box, click OK, click OK, save your changes, then point to the Gaslamp Quarter hyperlink in the document**

   The ScreenTip you created appears above the Gaslamp Quarter hyperlink, as shown in Figure B-14.

9. **If you are working with an active Internet connection, press [Ctrl], click the Gaslamp Quarter hyperlink, close the browser window that opens, press [Ctrl], click the detailed schedule hyperlink, then close the browser window**

   Before distributing a document, it's important to test each hyperlink to verify it works as you intended.

FIGURE B-13: Insert Hyperlink dialog box

Create a hyperlink to a Web page or file

Create a hyperlink to a location in the current file

Create a hyperlink to a new blank document

Create a hyperlink to an e-mail address

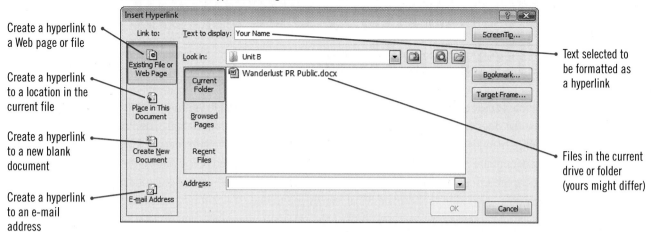

Text selected to be formatted as a hyperlink

Files in the current drive or folder (yours might differ)

FIGURE B-14: Hyperlinks in the document

Purple indicates the hyperlink has been followed

Hyperlinks are colored and underlined

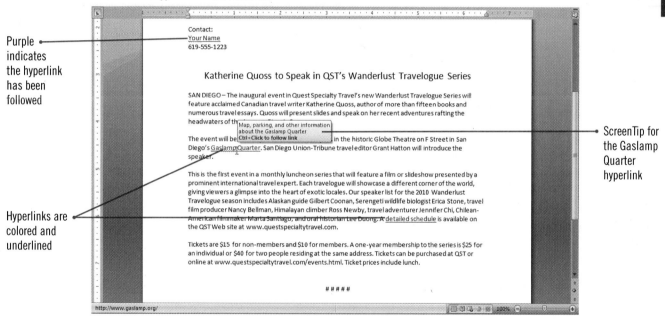

ScreenTip for the Gaslamp Quarter hyperlink

E-mailing and faxing documents directly from Word

Word includes several options for distributing and sharing documents over the Internet directly from within Word, including e-mailing and faxing documents. When you e-mail a document from within Word, the document is sent as an attachment to an e-mail message using your default e-mail program. To e-mail a file, open the file in Word, click the Office button, point to Send, and then click E-mail. A message window opens that includes the filename of the current file as the message subject and the file as an attachment. Type the e-mail address(es) of the recipient(s) in the To and Cc text boxes, any message you want in the message window, and then click Send on the message window toolbar to send the message. The default e-mail program sends a copy of the document to each recipient. It's also possible to fax a document directly from within Word, although faxing a document requires registration with a third-party Internet fax service. To fax a document, open it in Word, click the Office button, point to Send, click Internet Fax, click OK to find and select a fax service if you don't already have one, and then follow the on-screen instructions. Fax services generally charge a monthly or per page fee for sending and receiving faxes.

Preparing a Document for Distribution

Before you distribute a document electronically to people outside your organization, it's wise to make sure the file does not include embedded private or confidential information. The Prepare command on the Office menu includes tools for stripping a document of sensitive information, for securing its authenticity, and for guarding it from unwanted changes once it is distributed to the public. See Table B-1. One of these tools, the Document Inspector, detects and removes unwanted private or confidential information from a document. Another tool, Mark as Final, allows you to make a document read-only so it cannot be modified by viewers. ▓▓▓▓ Before sending the press release to the public, you remove all identifying information from the file and mark it as final.

STEPS

1. **Press [Ctrl][Home], click the Office button 🔘, point to Prepare, then click Properties**

   The Document Information panel opens above the document window, as shown in Figure B-15. It shows the standard document properties for the press release. **Document properties** are user-defined details about a file that describe its contents and origin, including the name of the author, the title of the document, and keywords that you can assign to help organize and search your files.

2. **Click 🔘, point to Prepare, click Inspect Document, then click Yes**

   The Document Inspector dialog box opens. You use this dialog box to indicate which private or identifying information you want to search for and remove from the document.

3. **Make sure all the check boxes are selected, then click Inspect**

   After a moment, the Document Inspector dialog box changes to indicate that the file contains document properties. You might not want this information to be available to the public.

4. **Click Remove All next to Document Properties, then click Close**

   The standard document property information is removed from the press release document.

5. **Click 🔘, point to Prepare, then click Mark as Final**

   A dialog box indicating that the document will be marked as final opens.

6. **Click OK, then click OK if a second message box opens**

   The document is saved automatically, "Final" appears in the Status text box in the Document Information panel, and the commands on the Insert tab are disabled, indicating that the document is marked as final and cannot be changed. The Marked as Final icon also appears in the status bar.

7. **Click the Close button in the Document Information panel, click 🔘, point to Print, click Quick Print, close the file, then exit Word**

   The press release prints. The completed press release is shown in Figure B-16.

TABLE B-1: Prepare command options

feature	use to
Properties	View and modify the standard document properties and open the Properties dialog box
Inspect Document	Detect and remove unwanted private or proprietary information from a document, including document properties, comments, revisions, annotations, personal information, custom XML data, and hidden text
Encrypt Document	Add encryption to a document to make it more secure
Add a Digital Signature	Add an invisible digital signature to a document to verify its authenticity and integrity
Mark as Final	Indicate to readers that a document is read-only and cannot be edited
Run Compatibility Checker	Check the document for features that are not supported by previous versions of Microsoft Word

FIGURE B-15: Document Information panel

Document properties assigned when the original file was created

Your file location will differ

Document Information panel

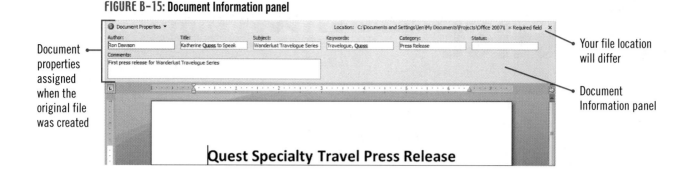

Quest Specialty Travel Press Release

FIGURE B-16: Completed press release for electronic distribution

Viewing and modifying advanced document properties

The Document Information panel includes summary information about the document that you enter to suit your needs. To view more detailed document properties, including those entered automatically by Word when the document is created, click the Document Properties list arrow in the Document Information panel, and then click Advanced Properties to open the Properties dialog box. The General, Statistics, and Contents tabs of the Properties dialog box display information about the file that is automatically created and updated by Word. The General tab shows the file type, location, size, and date and time the file was created and last modified; the Statistics tab displays information about revisions to the document along with the number of pages, words, lines, paragraphs, and characters in the file; and the Contents tab shows the title of the document. You can define other document properties using the Summary and Custom tabs of the Properties dialog box. The Summary tab shows information similar to the information shown in the Document Information panel. The Custom tab allows you to create new document properties, such as client, project, or date completed. To create a custom property, select a property name in the Name list box on the Custom tab, use the Type list arrow to select the type of data you want for the property, type the identifying detail (such as a project name) in the Value text box, and then click Add. When you are finished viewing or modifying the document properties, click OK to close the Properties dialog box, then click the Close button in the Document Information panel.

Practice

▼ CONCEPTS REVIEW

Label the elements of the Word program window shown in Figure B-17.

FIGURE B-17

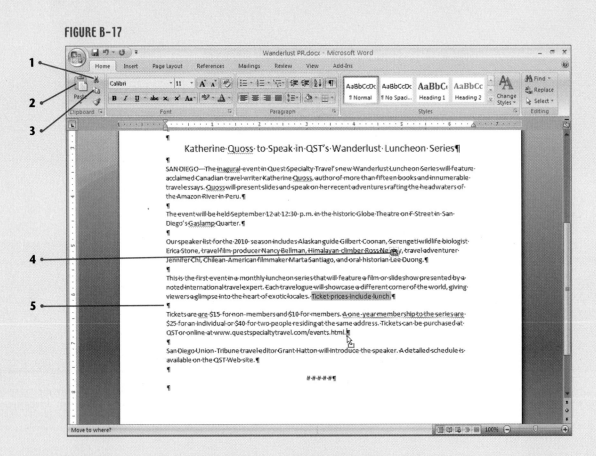

Match each term with the statement that best describes it.

6. **Hyperlink**

7. **Cut**

8. **Shortcut key**

9. **Document properties**

10. **Paste**

11. **Office Clipboard**

12. **System Clipboard**

13. **Blog**

14. **Thesaurus**

a. Command used to insert text stored on the Clipboard into a document

b. Temporary storage area for up to 24 items collected from Office files

c. Temporary storage area for only the last item cut or copied from a document

d. A function key or a combination of keys that perform a command when pressed

e. Text or a graphic that jumps the reader to a different location or program when clicked

f. An informal journal that is available to the public on the Internet

g. User-defined details about a file that describe its contents and origin

h. Feature used to suggest synonyms for words

i. Command used to remove text from a document and place it on the Clipboard

Select the best answer from the list of choices.

15. **What is the keyboard shortcut for the Paste command?**
    a. [Ctrl][C]   c. [Ctrl][X]
    b. [Ctrl][V]   d. [Ctrl][P]

16. **Which of the following statements is *not* true?**
    a. The Office Clipboard can hold more than one item.
    b. You can view the contents of the Office Clipboard.
    c. When you move text by dragging it, a copy of the text you move is stored on the system Clipboard.
    d. The last item cut or copied from a document is stored on the system Clipboard.

17. **To locate and select all instances of a word in a document, which command do you use?**
    a. Highlight   c. Find
    b. Replace   d. Search

18. **Which command is used to display a document in two panes in the document window?**
    a. New Window   c. Two Pages
    b. Split   d. Arrange All

19. **Which of the following is an example of a document property?**
    a. Keyword   c. URL
    b. Language   d. Permission

20. **A hyperlink *cannot* be linked to which of the following?**
    a. Web page   c. ScreenTip
    b. E-mail address   d. New blank document

▼ SKILLS REVIEW

1. **Cut and paste text.**
   a. Start Word, click the Office button, then open the file WD B-2.docx from the drive and folder where you store your Data Files.
   b. Save the document with the filename PAOS 2010 PR.
   c. Select Your Name and replace it with your name.
   d. Display paragraph and other formatting marks in your document if they are not already displayed.
   e. Use the Cut and Paste buttons to switch the order of the two sentences in the fourth paragraph (which begins New group shows...).
   f. Use the drag-and-drop method to switch the order of the second and third paragraphs.
   g. Adjust the spacing if necessary so that there is one blank line between paragraphs, then save your changes.

2. **Copy and paste text.**
   a. Use the Copy and Paste buttons to copy PAOS 2008 from the headline and paste it before the word map in the third paragraph.
   b. Change the formatting of the pasted text to match the formatting of the third paragraph, then insert a space between 2008 and map if necessary.
   c. Use the drag-and-drop method to copy PAOS from the third paragraph and paste it before the word group in the second sentence of the fourth paragraph, then save your changes.

3. **Use the Office Clipboard.**
   a. Use the launcher in the Clipboard group to open the Clipboard task pane.
   b. Scroll so that the first body paragraph is displayed at the top of the document window.
   c. Select the fifth paragraph (which begins Studio location maps...) and cut it to the Office Clipboard.
   d. Select the third paragraph (which begins Portsmouth is easily accessible...) and cut it to the Office Clipboard.
   e. Use the Office Clipboard to paste the Studio location maps... item as the new fourth paragraph.
   f. Use the Office Clipboard to paste the Portsmouth is easily accessible... item as the new fifth paragraph.
   g. Adjust the spacing if necessary so that there is one blank line between each of the six body paragraphs.
   h. Turn off the display of formatting marks, clear and close the Office Clipboard, then save your changes.

4. **Find and replace text.**

   a. Using the Replace command, replace all instances of 2008 with 2010.

   b. Replace all instances of the abbreviation st with street, taking care to replace whole words only when you perform the replace. (*Hint*: Deselect Match case if it is selected.)

   c. Use the Find command to find all instances of st in the document and to make sure no errors occurred when you replaced st with street. (*Hint*: Deselect the Find whole words only check box.)

   d. Save your changes to the press release.

5. **Check spelling and grammar and research information.**

   a. Switch to the Review tab.

   b. Move the insertion point to the top of the document, then use the Spelling and Grammar command to search for and correct any spelling and grammar errors in the press release. (*Hint*: Jumpin' is not misspelled.)

   c. Use the Thesaurus to replace thriving in the second paragraph with a different suitable word.

   d. Check the word count of the press release.

   e. Proofread your press release, correct any errors, then save your changes.

6. **Add hyperlinks.**

   a. Save the document as PAOS 2010 PR Public, then switch to the Insert tab.

   b. Select your name, then open the Insert Hyperlink dialog box.

   c. Create a hyperlink to your e-mail address with the subject PAOS 2010.

   d. Test the your name hyperlink, then close the message window that opens. (*Hint*: Press [Ctrl], then click the hyperlink.)

   e. Select NEA in the last paragraph of the press release, then create a hyperlink to the URL www.nea.gov.

   f. Right-click the NEA hyperlink, then edit the hyperlink ScreenTip to become Information on the National Endowment for the Arts.

   g. Point to the NEA hyperlink to view the new ScreenTip, then save your changes.

   h. If you are working with an active Internet connection, press [Ctrl], click the NEA hyperlink, view the NEA home page in the browser window, then close the browser window.

7. **Prepare a document for distribution.**

   a. Click the Office button, point to Prepare, then view the document properties for the press release.

   b. Use the Prepare command to run the Document Inspector.

   c. Remove the document property data, then save your changes.

   d. Use the Prepare command to mark the document as final. The finished press release is shown in Figure B-18.

   e. Print the press release, close the file, then exit Word.

FIGURE B-18

PRESS RELEASE

FOR IMMEDIATE RELEASE
September 7, 2010

Contact:
Your Name
603-555-2938

PAOS 2010
Portsmouth Artists Open Their Studios to the Public

PORTSMOUTH, NH -- The fall 2010 Open Studios season kicks off with Portsmouth Artists Open Studios on Saturday and Sunday, October 13 and 14, from 11 a.m. to 6 p.m. More than 60 Portsmouth artists will open their studios and homes to the public for this annual event, now in its tenth year.

Portsmouth is an historic and diverse city, long home to a flourishing community of artists. Quiet residential streets lined with charming Victorians edge a vibrant commercial and industrial zone, all peppered with the studios of printmakers, sculptors, painters, glass and jewelry makers, illustrators, potters, photographers, watercolorists, and other artists working in a wide range of mediums.

Internationally celebrated sculptor Eva Russo will display her new work in the rotunda of City Hall. New PAOS group shows will open at the Atlantic Gallery and at Jumpin' Jay's Fish Café, both on Congress Street.

Studio location maps will be available prior to the opening at businesses and public libraries, and on the days of the event at Market Square. Market Square is located at the junction of Congress Street and Pleasant Street in downtown Portsmouth.

Portsmouth is easily accessible from all points in the Northeast by car or bus, and from Boston and Portland by train. On Saturday, non-Portsmouth residents may park in permit-only areas provided they display a copy of the PAOS 2010 map on the dashboard. There are no parking restrictions on Sundays in Portsmouth.

PAOS 2010 receives funds from participating artists and from the Portsmouth Arts Council, the New Hampshire Cultural Council, and the NEA, with valuable support from local universities and businesses.

#####

▼ INDEPENDENT CHALLENGE 1

Because of your success in revitalizing a historic theatre in Wellington, New Zealand, you were hired as the director of The Hobart Lyric Theatre in Hobart, Tasmania, to breathe life into its theatre revitalization efforts. After a year on the job, you are launching your first major fund-raising drive. You'll create a fund-raising letter for the Lyric Theatre by modifying a letter you wrote for the theatre in Wellington.

a. Start Word, open the file WD B-3.docx from the drive and folder where you store your Data Files, then save it as Lyric Fundraising Letter.

b. Replace the theatre name and address, the date, the inside address, and the salutation with the text shown in Figure B-19.

c. Use the Replace command to replace all instances of Wellington with Hobart.

d. Use the Replace command to replace all instances of Town Hall with Lyric.

e. Use the Replace command to replace all instances of New Zealanders with Tasmanians.

f. Use the Find command to locate the word considerable, then use the Thesaurus to replace the word with a synonym.

g. Move the fourth body paragraph so that it becomes the second body paragraph.

h. Create an AutoCorrect entry that inserts Executive Director whenever you type exd.

i. Replace Your Name with your name in the signature block, select Title, then type exd followed by a space.

j. Use the Spelling and Grammar command to check for and correct spelling and grammar errors.

FIGURE B-19

The Hobart Lyric Theatre
60-62 Macquarie Street, Hobart, Tasmania 7001, Australia

November 10, 2010

Ms. Natasha Campbell
450 Elizabeth Street
North Hobart, TAS 7004

Dear Ms. Campbell:

Advanced Challenge Exercise

- Open the Document Information panel, change the title to Hobart Lyric Theatre, then add the keyword fund-raising.
- Open the Properties dialog box, add your name as author on the Summary tab, then review the paragraph, line, word, and character count on the Statistics tab.
- On the Custom tab, add a property named Project with the value Capital Campaign, then close the dialog box and the Document Information panel.

k. Proofread the letter, correct any errors, save your changes, print a copy, close the document, then exit Word.

▼ INDEPENDENT CHALLENGE 2

An advertisement for job openings in Toronto caught your eye and you have decided to apply. The ad, shown in Figure B-20, was printed in last weekend's edition of your local newspaper. Instead of writing a cover letter from scratch, you revise a draft of a cover letter you wrote several years ago for a summer internship position.

a. Read the ad shown in Figure B-20 and decide which position to apply for. Choose the position that most closely matches your qualifications.

b. Start Word, open WD B-4.docx from the drive and folder where you store your Data Files, then save it as Cover Letter.

c. Replace the name, address, telephone number, and e-mail address in the letterhead with your own information.

d. Remove the hyperlink from the e-mail address.

e. Replace the date with today's date, then replace the inside address and the salutation with the information shown in Figure B-20.

f. Read the draft cover letter to get a feel for its contents.

g. Rework the text in the body of the letter to address your qualifications for the job you have chosen to apply for:

- Delete the third paragraph.
- Adjust the first sentence of the first paragraph as follows: specify the job you are applying for, including the position code, and indicate where you saw the position advertised.
- Move the first sentence in the last paragraph, which briefly states your qualifications and interest in the position, to the end of the first paragraph, then rework the sentence to describe your current qualifications.
- Adjust the second paragraph as follows: describe your work experience and skills. Be sure to relate your experience and qualifications to the position requirements listed in the advertisement. Add a third paragraph if your qualifications are extensive.
- Adjust the final paragraph as follows: politely request an interview for the position and provide your phone number and e-mail address.

h. Include your name in the signature block.

i. When you are finished revising the letter, check it for spelling and grammar errors and correct any mistakes. Make sure to remove any hyperlinks.

j. Save your changes to the letter, print a copy, close the document, then exit Word.

FIGURE B-20

---

*Global*Dynamics

Career Opportunities in Toronto

Global Dynamics, an established software development firm with offices in North America, Asia, and Europe, is seeking candidates for the following positions in its Toronto facility:

Instructor
Responsible for delivering software training to our expanding Canadian customer base. Duties include delivering hands-on training, keeping up-to-date with product development, and working with the Director of Training to ensure the high quality of course materials. Successful candidate will have excellent presentation skills and be proficient in Microsoft PowerPoint and Microsoft Word. **Position B12C6**

Administrative Assistant
Proficiency with Microsoft Word a must! Administrative office duties include making travel arrangements, scheduling meetings, taking notes and publishing meeting minutes, handling correspondence, and ordering office supplies. Must have superb multitasking abilities, excellent communication, organizational, and interpersonal skills, and be comfortable working with e-mail and the Internet. **Position B16F5**

Copywriter
The ideal candidate will have marketing or advertising writing experience in a high tech environment, including collateral, newsletters, and direct mail. Experience writing for the Web, broadcast, and multimedia is a plus. Fluency with Microsoft Word required. **Position C13D4**

Positions offer salary, excellent benefits, moving expenses, and career growth opportunities.

Send resume and cover letter referencing position code to:

**Thomas Finlay
Director of Recruiting
Global Dynamics
330 University Avenue
Toronto, Ontario M5G 1R8
Canada**

▼ INDEPENDENT CHALLENGE 3

As administrative director of continuing education, you drafted a memo to instructors asking them to help you finalize the course schedule for next semester. Today you'll examine the draft and make revisions before distributing it as an e-mail attachment.

a. Start Word, open the file WD B-5.docx from the drive and folder where you store your Data Files, then save it as **Business Courses Memo**.

b. Replace Your Name with your name in the From line, then scroll down until the first body paragraph is at the top of the screen.

Advanced Challenge Exercise

- Use the Split command on the View tab to split the window under the first body paragraph, then scroll until the last paragraph of the memo is displayed in the bottom pane.
- Use the Cut and Paste buttons to move the sentence **If you are planning to teach…** from the first body paragraph to become the first sentence in the last paragraph of the memo.
- Double-click the split bar to restore the window to a single pane.

c. Use the [Delete] key to merge the first two paragraphs into one paragraph.

d. Use the Office Clipboard to reorganize the list of twelve-week courses so that the courses are listed in alphabetical order.

e. Use the drag-and-drop method to reorganize the list of one-day seminars so that the seminars are listed in alphabetical order, then clear and close the Office Clipboard.

f. Select Web site in the first paragraph, then create a hyperlink to the URL **www.course.com** with the ScreenTip **Spring 2011 Business Course**.

g. Select e-mail me in the last paragraph, then create a hyperlink to your e-mail address with the subject **Final Business Course Schedule**.

h. Use the Spelling and Grammar command to check for and correct spelling and grammar errors.

i. Use the Document Inspector to strip the document of document property information, ignore any other content that is flagged by the Document Inspector, then close the Document Inspector.

j. Proofread the memo, correct any errors, save your changes, print a copy, close the document, then exit Word.

▼ REAL LIFE INDEPENDENT CHALLENGE

This Independent Challenge requires an Internet connection.

Reference sources—dictionaries, thesauri, style and grammar guides, and guides to business etiquette and procedure—are essential for day-to-day use in the workplace. Much of this reference information is available on the World Wide Web. In this independent challenge, you will locate reference sources on the Web and use some of them to look up definitions, synonyms, and antonyms for words. Your goal is to familiarize yourself with online reference sources so you can use them later in your work.

a. Start Word, open the file WD B-6.docx from the drive and folder where you store your Data Files, then save it as **Web Reference Sources**. This document contains the questions you will answer about the Web reference sources you find. You will type your answers to the questions in the document.

b. Replace the placeholder text at the top of the Web Reference Sources document with your name and the date.

c. Use your favorite search engine to search the Web for grammar and style guides, dictionaries, and thesauri. Use the keywords **grammar**, **usage**, **dictionary**, **glossary**, and **thesaurus** to conduct your search.

d. Complete the Web Reference Sources document, then proofread it and correct any mistakes.

e. Save the document, print a copy, close the document, then exit Word.

Open WD B-7.docx from the drive and folder where you store your Data Files, then save the document as **Australian Visa Letter**. Replace the placeholders for the date, letterhead, inside address, salutation, and closing with the information shown in Figure B-21, then use the Office Clipboard to reorganize the sentences to match Figure B-21. Correct spelling and grammar errors, remove the document property information from the file, mark the document as final, then print a copy.

FIGURE B-21

Your Name
4637 Baker Street, Chicago, IL 60627; Tel: 630-555-2840

1/3/2010

Embassy of Australia
1601 Massachusetts Avenue NW
Washington, DC 20036

Dear Sir or Madam:

I am applying for a long-stay tourist visa to Australia, valid for four years. I am scheduled to depart for Sydney on March 13, 2010, returning to Chicago on September 8, 2010.

During my stay in Australia, I will be interviewing musicians and recording footage for a film I am making on contemporary Australian music. I would like a multiple entry visa valid for four years so I can return to Australia after this trip to follow up on my initial research. I will be based in Sydney, but I will be traveling frequently to film performances and to meet with musicians and producers.

Included with this letter are my completed visa application form, my passport, a passport photo, a copy of my return air ticket, and the visa fee. Please contact me if you need further information.

Sincerely,

Your Name

Enc: 5

Formatting Text and Paragraphs

Files You Will Need:

WD C-1.docx
WD C-2.docx
WD C-3.docx
WD C-4.docx
WD C-5.docx
WD C-6.docx

Formatting can enhance the appearance of a document, create visual impact, and help illustrate a document's structure. The formatting of a document can also set the tone of the document, allowing readers to know at a glance if the document is business-like, serious, formal, informal, or fun. In this unit you learn how to format text using different fonts and font-formatting options. You also learn how to change the alignment, indentation, and spacing of paragraphs, how to spruce up documents with borders, shading, bullets, and other paragraph-formatting effects, and how to add footnotes and endnotes to a document. The Word live preview feature simplifies formatting by allowing you to quickly preview the different formatting options in your document before you apply them. You have finished drafting the text for a two-page flyer advertising last minute specials for October tours. Now, you need to format the flyer so it is attractive and highlights the significant information. The flyer will be distributed to clients with the quarterly newsletter.

OBJECTIVES

Format with fonts

Copy formats using the Format Painter

Change line and paragraph spacing

Align paragraphs

Work with tabs

Work with indents

Add bullets and numbering

Add borders and shading

Add footnotes and endnotes

Formatting with Fonts

Formatting text with different fonts is a quick and powerful way to enhance the appearance of a document. A **font** is a complete set of characters with the same typeface or design. Arial, Times New Roman, Comic Sans, Courier, Tahoma, and Calibri are some of the more common fonts, but there are hundreds of others, each with a specific design and feel. Another way to alter the impact of text is to increase or decrease its **font size**, which is measured in points. A **point** is ½ of an inch. ▰▰▰▰ You change the font and font size of the body text, title, and headings in the flyer, selecting fonts and font sizes that enhance the sales tone of the document and help to visually structure the report for readers.

STEPS

1. **Start Word, open the file** WD C-1.docx **from the drive and folder where you store your Data Files, then save it as** Last Minute Deals

   Notice that the name of the font used in the document, Calibri, is displayed in the Font list box in the Font group. The word "(Body)" in the Font list box indicates Calibri is the font used for body text in the current theme, the default theme. A **theme** is a related set of fonts, colors, styles, and effects that is applied to an entire document to give it a cohesive appearance. The font size, 11, appears next to it in the Font Size list box.

2. **Scroll the document to get a feel for its contents, press** [Ctrl][Home], **press** [Ctrl][A] **to select the entire document, then click the** Font list arrow **in the Font group**

   The Font list, which shows the fonts available on your computer, opens as shown in Figure C-1. The font names are formatted in the font and can appear in more than one location on the font list.

3. **Drag the pointer slowly down the font names in the Font list, use the scroll box to scroll down the Font list, then click** Garamond

   Dragging the pointer down the font list allows you to preview how the selected text will look if the highlighted font is applied. Clicking a font name applies the font. The font of the flyer changes to Garamond.

4. **Click the** Font Size list arrow **in the Font group, drag the pointer slowly up and down the Font Size list, then click** 12

   Dragging the pointer over the font sizes allows you to preview how the selected text will look if the highlighted font size is applied. The font size of the selected text increases to 12 points.

5. **Select the title** Quest Specialty Travel Last Minute Travel Deals, **click the** Font list arrow, **click** Trebuchet MS, **click the** Font Size list arrow, **click** 22, **then click the** Bold button **B** **in the Font group**

   The title is formatted in 22-point Trebuchet MS bold.

6. **Click the** Font Color list arrow **A·** **in the Font group**

   A gallery of colors opens. It includes the set of theme colors in a range of tints and shades as well as a set of standard colors. You can point to a color in the gallery to preview it applied to the selected text.

7. **Click the** Blue, Accent 1 **color as shown in Figure C-2, then deselect the text**

   The color of the title text changes to blue. The active color on the Font Color button also changes to blue.

8. **Select the heading** Rajasthan Desert Safari, **then, using the Mini toolbar, click the** Font list arrow, **click** Trebuchet MS, **click the** Font Size list arrow, **click** 14, **click** A·, **click the** Dark Blue, Text 2 **color, click** B, **then deselect the text**

   The heading is formatted in 14-point Trebuchet MS bold with a dark blue color. Notice that when you use the buttons on the Mini toolbar to format text, you cannot preview the formatting options in the document.

9. **Press** [Ctrl][Home], **then click the** Save button 🖫 **on the Quick Access toolbar**

   Compare your document to Figure C-3.

Word 2007

FIGURE C-1: Font list

Font list arrow

Font Size list arrow

Fonts used in the default theme

Your list of recently used fonts will differ

Alphabetical list of all fonts on your computer

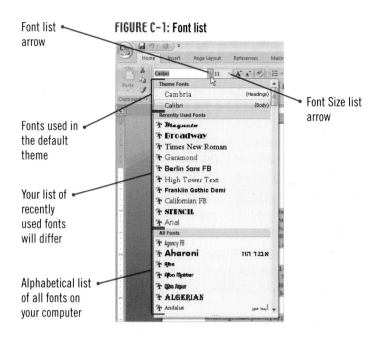

FIGURE C-2: Font Color gallery

Font Color list arrow

Name of color appears as a ScreenTip

Click to create a custom color

Live preview of Blue, Accent 1 color applied to text

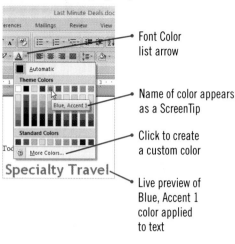

FIGURE C-3: Document formatted with fonts

Title formatted in 22-point Trebuchet MS, bold, blue

Body text formatted in 12-point Garamond

Heading formatted in 14-point Trebuchet MS, bold, dark blue

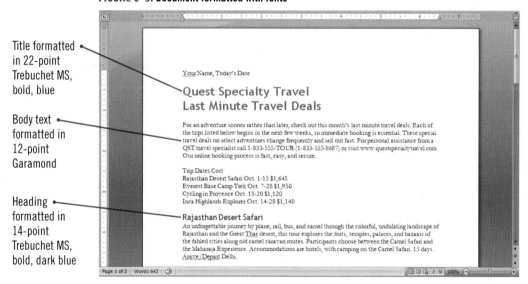

Adding a drop cap

A fun way to illustrate a document with fonts is to add a drop cap to a paragraph. A **drop cap** is a large initial capital letter, often used to set off the first paragraph of an article. To create a drop cap, place the insertion point in the paragraph you want to format, click the Insert tab, and then click the Drop Cap button in the Text group to open a menu of Drop cap options. Preview and select one of the options on the menu, or click Drop Cap Options to open the Drop Cap dialog box, shown in Figure C-4. In the Drop Cap dialog box, select the position, font, number of lines to drop, and the distance you want the drop cap to be from the paragraph text, and then click OK. The drop cap is added to the paragraph as a graphic object.

Once a drop cap is inserted in a paragraph, you can modify it by selecting it and then changing the settings in the Drop Cap dialog box. For even more interesting effects, enhance a drop cap with font color, font styles, or font effects, fill the graphic object with shading, or add a border around it. To enhance a drop cap, first select it, and then experiment with the formatting options available in the Font dialog box and in the Borders and Shading dialog box.

FIGURE C-4: Drop Cap dialog box

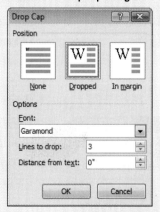

Copying Formats Using the Format Painter

You can dramatically change the appearance of text by applying different font styles, font effects, and character-spacing effects. For example, you can use the buttons in the Font group to make text darker by applying **bold** or to slant text by applying **italic**. You can also use the Font dialog box to apply font effects and character-spacing effects to text. When you are satisfied with the formatting of certain text, you can quickly apply the same formats to other text using the Format Painter. The **Format Painter** is a powerful Word feature that allows you to copy all the format settings applied to selected text to other text that you want to format the same way. ▰▰▰ You spice up the appearance of the text in the document by applying different font styles and effects. After formatting a heading and subheading, you use the Format Painter to apply the settings to other headings and subheadings.

1. **Select** immediate booking is essential **in the first body paragraph, click the** Bold button **B** **on the Mini toolbar, select the entire** paragraph, **then click the** Italic button **I** **on the Mini toolbar**

   "Immediate booking is essential" is bold and the entire paragraph is formatted in italic.

   QUICK TIP
   To change the case of selected text from lowercase to uppercase — and visa versa — click the Change Case button **Aa▾** in the Font group, and then select the case style you want to use.

2. **Select** Last Minute Travel Deals, **then click the** launcher ▣ **in the Font group**

   The Font dialog box opens, as shown in Figure C-5. You can use options on the Font tab to change the font, font style, size, and color of text, and to add an underline and apply font effects to text.

3. **Scroll down the Size list, click** 48, **click the** Font color list arrow, **click the** Red, Accent 2 **color in the Theme Colors, click the** Shadow check box, **click** OK, **then deselect the text**

   The text is larger, red, and has a shadow effect.

4. **Select** Last Minute Travel Deals, **right-click, click** Font **on the Edit menu, click the** Character Spacing tab, **click the** Scale list arrow, **click** 80%, **click** OK, **then deselect the text**

   You use the Character Spacing tab in the Font dialog box to change the scale, or width, of the selected characters, to alter the spacing between characters, or to raise or lower the characters. Decreasing the scale of the characters makes them narrower and gives the text a tall, thin appearance, as shown in Figure C-6.

5. **Scroll down, select the subheading** Camel Safari, **then, using the Mini toolbar, click the** Font list arrow, **click** Trebuchet MS, **click** **B**, **click** **I**, **click the** Font Color list arrow **A▾**, **click the** Red, Accent 2 **color in the Theme Colors, then deselect the text**

   The subheading is formatted in Trebuchet MS, bold, italic, and red.

   TROUBLE
   Move the pointer over the document text to see the 🖌I pointer.

6. **Select** Camel Safari, **then click the** Format Painter button 🖌 **in the Clipboard group**

   The pointer changes to 🖌I.

7. **Scroll down, select** Maharaja Experience **with the** 🖌I **pointer, then deselect the text**

   The subheading is formatted in Trebuchet MS, bold, italic, and red, as shown in Figure C-7.

8. **Scroll up as needed, select** Rajasthan Desert Safari, **then double-click** 🖌

   Double-clicking the Format Painter button allows the Format Painter to remain active until you turn it off. By keeping the Format Painter turned on you can apply formatting to multiple items.

   QUICK TIP
   You can also press [Esc] to turn off the Format Painter.

9. **Scroll down, select the headings** Everest Base Camp Trek, Cycling in Provence, **and** Inca Highlands Explorer **with the** 🖌I **pointer, click** 🖌 **to turn off the Format Painter, then save your changes**

   The headings are formatted in 14-point Trebuchet MS bold with a dark blue font color.

FIGURE C-5: Font tab in Font dialog box

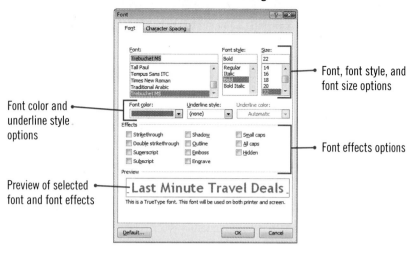

Font color and underline style options

Font, font style, and font size options

Font effects options

Preview of selected font and font effects

FIGURE C-6: Font and character spacing effects applied to text

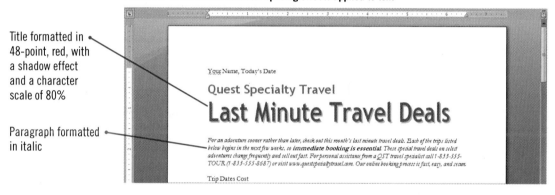

Title formatted in 48-point, red, with a shadow effect and a character scale of 80%

Paragraph formatted in italic

FIGURE C-7: Formats copied and applied using the Format Painter

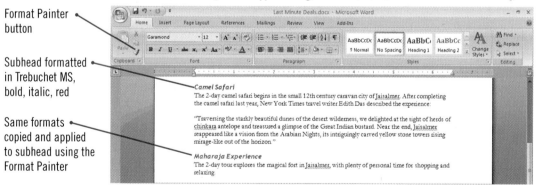

Format Painter button

Subhead formatted in Trebuchet MS, bold, italic, red

Same formats copied and applied to subhead using the Format Painter

Underlining text

Another creative way to call attention to text and to jazz up the appearance of a document is to apply an underline style to words you want to highlight. The Underline list arrow in the Font group displays straight, dotted, wavy, dashed, and mixed style underlines, along with a gallery of colors to choose from. To apply an underline to text, simply select it, click the Underline list arrow, and then select an underline style from the list. For a wider variety of underline styles, click More Underlines in the list, and then select an underline style in the Font dialog box. You can change the color of an underline at any time by selecting the underlined text, clicking the Underline list arrow, pointing to Underline Color, and then choosing from the options in the color gallery. If you want to remove an underline from text, select the underlined text, and then click the Underline button.

Changing Line and Paragraph Spacing

Increasing the amount of space between lines adds more white space to a document and can make it easier to read. Adding space before and after paragraphs can also open up a document and improve its appearance. You use the Line Spacing list arrow in the Paragraph group on the Home tab to quickly change line spacing. To change paragraph spacing, you use the Spacing options in the Paragraph group on the Page Layout tab. Line and paragraph spacing are measured in points. ██████ You increase the line spacing of several paragraphs and add extra space under each heading to give the report a more open feel. You work with formatting marks turned on, so you can see the paragraph marks (¶).

STEPS

1. **Press [Ctrl][Home], click the Show/Hide ¶ button** ¶ **in the Paragraph group, place the insertion point in the italicized paragraph under the title, then click the Line Spacing list arrow** ≣▾ **in the Paragraph group on the Home tab**

   The Line Spacing list opens. This list includes options for increasing the space between lines. The check mark on the Line Spacing list indicates the current line spacing.

2. **Click 1.15**

   The space between the lines in the paragraph increases to 1.15 lines. Notice that you do not need to select an entire paragraph to change its paragraph formatting; simply place the insertion point in the paragraph you want to format.

QUICK TIP

Word recognizes any string of text that ends with a paragraph mark as a paragraph, including titles, headings, and single lines in a list.

3. **Select the five-line list that begins with Trip Dates Cost, click** ≣▾, **then click 1.5**

   The line spacing between the selected paragraphs changes to 1.5. To change the paragraph-formatting features of more than one paragraph, you must select the paragraphs.

4. **Scroll down, place the insertion point in the heading Rajasthan Desert Safari, then click the Page Layout tab**

   The paragraph spacing settings for the active paragraph are shown in the Before and After text boxes in the Paragraph group on the Page Layout tab.

5. **Click the After up arrow in the Spacing section of the Paragraph group so that 6 pt appears**

   Six points of space are added after the Rajasthan Desert Safari heading paragraph.

QUICK TIP

Using [F4] is not the same as using the Format Painter. Pressing [F4] repeats only the last action you took. You can use the Format Painter at any time to copy multiple format settings.

6. **Scroll down, place the insertion point in the heading Everest Base Camp Trek, then press [F4]**

   Pressing [F4] repeats the last action you took, in this case, adding six points of space after the paragraph. Six points of space are added below the Everest Base Camp Trek heading.

7. **Scroll down, select Cycling in Provence, press and hold [Ctrl], select Inca Highlands Explorer, release [Ctrl], then press [F4]**

   When you press [Ctrl] as you select items, you can select and format multiple items at once. Six points of space are added after each heading.

8. **Press [Ctrl][Home], place the insertion point in Last Minute Travel Deals, click the Before up arrow in the Spacing section of the Paragraph group twice so that 12 pt appears**

   The second line of the title has 12 points of space before it. Compare your document with Figure C-8.

QUICK TIP

Adjusting the space between paragraphs is a more precise way to add white space to a document than inserting blank lines.

9. **Click the Home tab, click** ¶, **then save your changes**

FIGURE C-8: Line and paragraph spacing applied to document

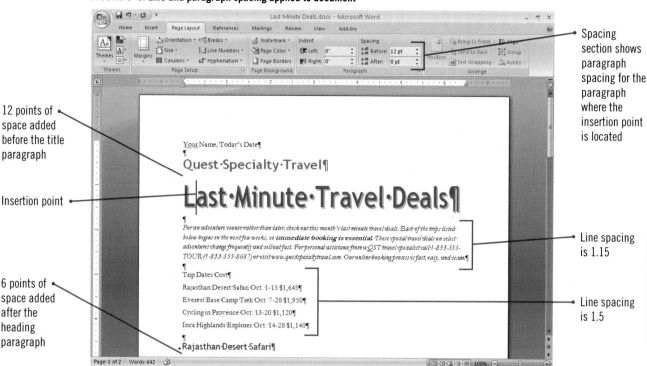

12 points of space added before the title paragraph

Insertion point

6 points of space added after the heading paragraph

Spacing section shows paragraph spacing for the paragraph where the insertion point is located

Line spacing is 1.15

Line spacing is 1.5

Word 2007

Formatting with Quick Styles

You can also apply multiple format settings to text in one step by applying a style. A **style** is a set of formats, such as font, font size, and paragraph alignment, that are named and stored together. Formatting a document with styles is a quick and easy way to give it a professional appearance. To make it even easier, Word includes sets of styles, called **Quick Styles**, that are designed to be used together in a document to make it attractive and readable. A Quick Style set includes styles for a title, several heading levels, body text, quotes, and lists. The styles in a Quick Style set use common fonts, colors, and formats, so that using the styles together in a document gives the document a cohesive look.

To view the active set of Quick Styles, click the More button ⤓ in the Styles group on the Home tab to expand the Quick Styles gallery, shown in Figure C-9. As you move the pointer over each style in the gallery, a preview of the style is applied to the selected text. To apply a style to the selected text, you simply click the button for that style in the Quick Styles gallery. To remove a style from selected text, you click the Clear Formatting button 🧽 in the Font group or in the Quick Styles gallery.

If you want to change the active set of Quick Styles to a Quick Style set with a different design, click the Change Styles button in the Styles group, point to Style Set, and then select the Quick Style set that best suits your document's content, tone, and audience. Distinctive, Traditional, Modern, Fancy, and Formal are some examples of the Quick Style sets you can choose to apply. When you

change the Quick Style set, a complete set of new fonts and colors is applied to the entire document. You can also change the color scheme or font used in the active Quick Style set by clicking the Change Styles button, pointing to Colors or to Fonts, and then selecting from the available color schemes or font options.

FIGURE C-9: Quick Styles gallery

AaBbCcDc	AaBbCcDc	AaBbCc	AaBbCc
¶ Normal	No Spacing	Heading 1	Heading 2
AaBbCcI	AaB	AaBbCc.	AaBbCcDc
Heading 3	Title	Subtitle	Subtle Em...
AaBbCcL	AABBCCDL	AaBbCcDc	AaBbCcDc
Emphasis	Intense E...	Strong	Quote
AaBbCcDc	AABBCCDC	AABBCCDC	AABBCCDL
Intense Q...	Subtle Ref...	Intense R...	Book Title
AaBbCcDc			
¶ List Para...			

Save Selection as a New Quick Style...

🧽 Clear Formatting

🔧 Apply Styles...

Aligning Paragraphs

Changing paragraph alignment is another way to enhance a document's appearance. Paragraphs are aligned relative to the left and right margins in a document. By default, text is **left-aligned**, which means it is flush with the left margin and has a ragged right edge. Using the alignment buttons in the Paragraph group, you can **right-align** a paragraph—make it flush with the right margin—or **center** a paragraph so that it is positioned evenly between the left and right margins. You can also **justify** a paragraph so that both the left and right edges of the paragraph are flush with the left and right margins. ▨▨▨ You change the alignment of several paragraphs at the beginning of the report to make it more visually interesting.

STEPS

1. **Replace** Your Name, Today's Date **with your name, a comma, and the date**

2. **Select your name, the comma, and the date, then click the** Align Text Right button 📰 **in the Paragraph group**

   The text is aligned with the right margin. In Page Layout view, the junction of the white and shaded sections of the horizontal ruler indicates the location of the left and right margins.

3. **Place the insertion point between your name and the comma, press** [Delete] **to delete the comma, then press** [Enter]

   The new paragraph containing the date is also right-aligned. Pressing [Enter] in the middle of a paragraph creates a new paragraph with the same text and paragraph formatting as the original paragraph.

4. **Select the two-line** title, **then click the** Center button 📰 **in the Paragraph group**

   The two paragraphs that make up the title are centered between the left and right margins.

5. **Scroll down as needed, place the insertion point in the** Rajasthan Desert Safari **heading, then click** 📰

   The Rajasthan Desert Safari heading is centered.

6. **Place the insertion point in the italicized paragraph under the title, then click the** Justify button 📰 **in the Paragraph group**

   The paragraph is aligned with both the left and right margins, as shown in Figure C-10. When you justify a paragraph, Word adjusts the spacing between words so that each line in the paragraph is flush with the left and the right margins.

7. **Place the insertion point in** Rajasthan Desert Safari, **then click the** launcher 🔲 **in the Paragraph group**

   The Paragraph dialog box opens, as shown in Figure C-11. The Indents and Spacing tab shows the paragraph format settings for the paragraph where the insertion point is located. You can check or change paragraph format settings using this dialog box.

8. **Click the** Alignment list arrow, **click** Left, **click** OK, **then save your changes**

   The Rajasthan Desert Safari heading is left-aligned.

FIGURE C-10: Modified paragraph alignment

- Right margin on the ruler
- View Ruler button
- Right-aligned
- Center-aligned
- Justified
- Left-aligned

FIGURE C-11: Indents and Spacing tab in Paragraph dialog box

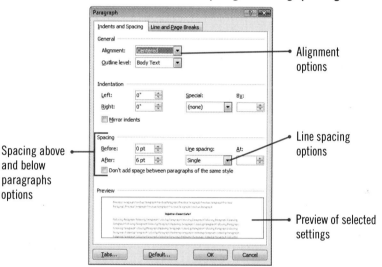

- Alignment options
- Line spacing options
- Spacing above and below paragraphs options
- Preview of selected settings

Formatting a document using themes

Changing the theme applied to a document is another powerful and efficient way to tailor a document's look and feel, particularly when a document is formatted with a Quick Style set. By default, all documents created in Word are formatted with the default Office theme—which uses Calibri as the font for the body text—but you can change the theme at any time to fit the content, tone, and purpose of a document. When you change the theme for a document, a complete set of new theme colors, fonts, and effects is applied to the whole document.

To preview how various themes look when applied to the current document, click the Themes button in the Themes group on the Page Layout tab, and then move the pointer over each theme in the gallery and notice how the document changes. When you click the theme you like, all document content that uses theme colors, all text

that is formatted with a style, including default body text, and all table styles and graphic effects change to the colors, fonts, and effects used by the theme. In addition, the gallery of colors changes to display the set of theme colors, and the active Quick Style set changes to employ the theme colors and fonts. Note that changing the theme does not affect the formatting of text to which font formatting has already been applied, nor does it change any standard or custom colors used in the document.

If you want to tweak the document design further, you can modify it by applying a different set of theme colors, heading and body text fonts, or graphic effects. To do this, simply click the Theme Colors, Theme Fonts, or Theme Effects button in the Themes group, move the pointer over each option in the gallery to preview it in the document, and then click the option you like best.

Word 2007

Working with Tabs

Tabs allow you to align text at a specific location in a document. A **tab stop** is a point on the horizontal ruler that indicates the location at which to align text. By default, tab stops are located every ½" from the left margin, but you can also set custom tab stops. Using tabs, you can align text to the left, right, or center of a tab stop, or you can align text at a decimal point or insert a bar character. Table C-1 describes the different types of tab stops. You set tabs using the horizontal ruler or the Tabs dialog box. ████ You use tabs to format the summary information on last minute tour deals so it is easy to read.

STEPS

1. **Scroll as needed, then select the five-line list beginning with Trip Dates Cost**

   Before you set tab stops for existing text, you must select the paragraphs for which you want to set tabs.

2. **Point to the tab indicator ⌊ at the left end of the horizontal ruler**

   The icon that appears in the tab indicator indicates the active type of tab; pointing to the tab indicator displays a ScreenTip with the name of the active tab type. By default, left tab is the active tab type. Clicking the tab indicator scrolls through the types of tabs and indents.

3. **Click the tab indicator to see each of the available tab and indent types, make Left Tab ⌊ the active tab type, click the 1" mark on the horizontal ruler, then click the 3½" mark on the horizontal ruler**

   A left tab stop is inserted at the 1" mark and the 3½" on the horizontal ruler. Clicking the horizontal ruler inserts a tab stop of the active type for the selected paragraph or paragraphs.

4. **Click the tab indicator twice so the Right Tab icon ⌋ is active, then click the 5" mark on the horizontal ruler**

   A right tab stop is inserted at the 5" mark on the horizontal ruler, as shown in Figure C-12.

5. **Place the insertion point before Trip in the first line in the list, press [Tab], place the insertion point before Dates, press [Tab], place the insertion point before Cost, then press [Tab]**

   Inserting a tab before Trip left-aligns the text at the 1" mark, inserting a tab before Dates left-aligns the text at the 3½" mark, and inserting a tab before Cost right-aligns Cost at the 5" mark.

6. **Insert a tab at the beginning of each remaining line in the list**

   The paragraphs left-align at the 1" mark.

7. **Insert a tab before each Oct. in the list, then insert a tab before each $ in the list**

   The dates left-align at the 3½" mark. The prices right-align at the 5" mark.

8. **Select the five lines of tabbed text, drag the right tab stop to the 5½" mark on the horizontal ruler, then deselect the text**

   Dragging the tab stop moves it to a new location. The prices right-align at the 5½" mark.

9. **Select the last four lines of tabbed text, click the launcher ▣ in the Paragraph group, then click Tabs in the Paragraph dialog box**

   The Tabs dialog box opens, as shown in Figure C-13. You can use the Tabs dialog box to set tab stops, change the position or alignment of existing tab stops, clear tab stops, and apply tab leaders to tabs. **Tab leaders** are lines that appear in front of tabbed text.

10. **Click 3.5" in the Tab stop position list box, click the 2 option button in the Leader section, click Set, click 5.5" in the Tab stop position list box, click the 2 option button in the Leader section, click Set, click OK, deselect the text, then save your changes**

    A dotted tab leader is added before each 3.5" and 5.5" tab stop in the last four lines of tabbed text, as shown in Figure C-14.

Formatting Text and Paragraphs

FIGURE C-12: Left and right tab stops on the horizontal ruler

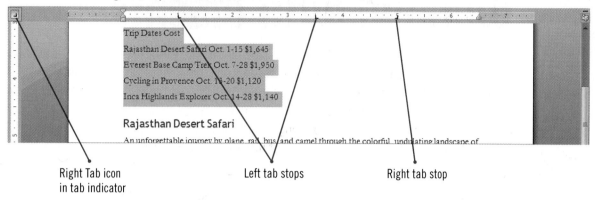

Right Tab icon
in tab indicator

Left tab stops

Right tab stop

FIGURE C-13: Tabs dialog box

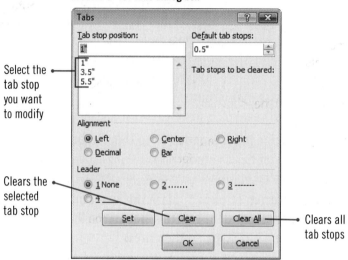

Select the
tab stop
you want
to modify

Clears the
selected
tab stop

Clears all
tab stops

FIGURE C-14: Tab leaders

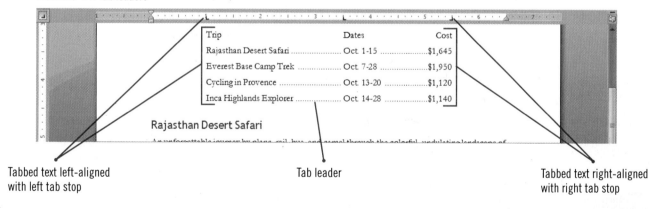

Tabbed text left-aligned
with left tab stop

Tab leader

Tabbed text right-aligned
with right tab stop

TABLE C-1: Types of tabs

tab	use to
Left tab	Set the start position of text so that text runs to the right of the tab stop as you type
Center tab	Set the center align position of text so that text stays centered on the tab stop as you type
Right tab	Set the right or end position of text so that text moves to the left of the tab stop as you type
Decimal tab	Set the position of the decimal point so that numbers align around the decimal point as you type
Bar tab	Insert a vertical bar at the tab position

Working with Indents

When you **indent** a paragraph, you move its edge in from the left or right margin. You can indent the entire left or right edge of a paragraph, just the first line, or all lines except the first line. The **indent markers** on the horizontal ruler indicate the indent settings for the paragraph in which the insertion point is located. Dragging an indent marker to a new location on the ruler is one way to change the indentation of a paragraph; changing the indent settings in the Paragraph group on the Page Layout tab is another; and using the indent buttons in the Paragraph group on the Home tab is a third. Table C-2 describes different types of indents and some of the methods for creating each. ▰▰▰▰ You indent several paragraphs in the report.

STEPS

QUICK TIP
Press [Tab] at the beginning of a paragraph to indent the first line ½".

1. **Press [Ctrl][Home], place the insertion point in the italicized paragraph under the title, then click the Increase Indent button ▤ in the Paragraph group on the Home tab**
   The entire paragraph is indented ½" from the left margin, as shown in Figure C-15. The indent marker ▲ also moves to the ½" mark on the horizontal ruler. Each time you click the Increase Indent button, the left edge of a paragraph moves another ½" to the right.

2. **Click the Decrease Indent button ▤ in the Paragraph group**
   The left edge of the paragraph moves ½" to the left, and the indent marker moves back to the left margin.

TROUBLE
Take care to drag only the First Line Indent marker. If you make a mistake, click the Undo button, then try again.

3. **Drag the First Line Indent marker ▽ to the ¾" mark on the horizontal ruler**
   Figure C-16 shows the First Line Indent marker being dragged. The first line of the paragraph is indented ¾". Dragging the First Line Indent marker indents only the first line of a paragraph.

4. **Scroll to the bottom of page 1, place the insertion point in the quotation, click the Page Layout tab, click the Indent Left text box in the Paragraph group, type .5, click the Indent Right text box, type .5, then press [Enter]**
   The left and right edges of the paragraph are indented ½" from the margins, as shown in Figure C-17.

5. **Press [Ctrl][Home], place the insertion point in the italicized paragraph, then click the launcher ▣ in the Paragraph group**
   The Paragraph dialog box opens. You can use the Indents and Spacing tab to check or change the alignment, indentation, and paragraph and line spacing settings applied to a paragraph.

6. **Click the Special list arrow, click (none), click OK, then save your changes**
   The first line indent is removed from the paragraph.

TABLE C-2: Types of indents

indent type: description	to create
Left indent: The left edge of a paragraph is moved in from the left margin	Enter the position you want the left edge of the paragraph to align in the Indent Left text box in the Paragraph group on the Page Layout tab; or drag the Left Indent marker ▭ on the ruler right to the position where you want the left edge of the paragraph to align
Right indent: The right edge of a paragraph is moved in from the right margin	Enter the position you want the right edge of the paragraph to align in the Indent Right text box in the Paragraph group on the Page Layout tab; or drag the Right Indent marker △ on the ruler left to the position where you want the right edge of the paragraph to end
First line indent: The first line of a paragraph is indented more than the subsequent lines	Drag ▽ on the ruler right to the position where you want the first line of the paragraph to begin; or activate the First Line Indent marker ▽ in the tab indicator, and then click the ruler at the position where you want the first line of the paragraph to begin
Hanging indent: The subsequent lines of a paragraph are indented more than the first line	Drag the Hanging Indent marker △ on the ruler right to the position where you want the hanging indent to begin; or activate the Hanging Indent marker △ in the tab indicator, and then click the ruler at the position where you want the second and remaining lines of the paragraph to begin
Negative indent (or Outdent): The left edge of a paragraph is moved to the left of the left margin	Enter the negative position you want the left edge of the paragraph to align in the Indent Left text box in the Paragraph group on the Page Layout tab; or drag the Left Indent marker ▭ on the ruler left to the position where you want the negative indent to begin

FIGURE C-15: Indented paragraph

First Line Indent marker

Hanging Indent marker

Left Indent marker

Indented paragraph

Right Indent marker

Increase Indent button

Decrease Indent button

FIGURE C-16: Dragging the First Line Indent marker

First Line Indent marker being dragged

Dotted line shows the position of indent in the document

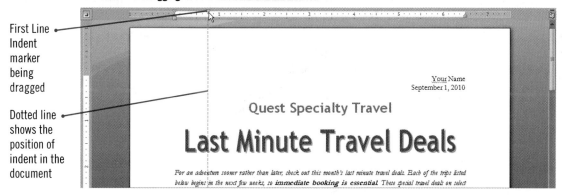

FIGURE C-17: Paragraph indented from the left and right

Paragraph indented ½" from left margin

Paragraph indented ½" from right margin

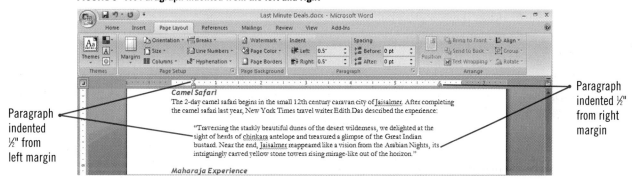

Clearing formatting

If you are unhappy with the way text is formatted, you can use the Clear Formatting command to return the text to the default format settings. The default format includes font and paragraph formatting: text is formatted in 11-point Calibri, and paragraphs are left-aligned with 1.15 point line spacing, 10 points of space below, and no indents. To clear formatting from text and return it to the default format, select the text you want to clear, and then click the Clear Formatting button in the Font group on the Home tab. If you prefer to return the text to the default font and remove all paragraph formatting, making the text 11-point Calibri, left-aligned, single spaced, with no paragraph spacing or indents, select the text and then simply click the No Spacing button in the Styles group on the Home tab.

Word 2007

Adding Bullets and Numbering

Formatting a list with bullets or numbering can help to organize the ideas in a document. A **bullet** is a character, often a small circle, that appears before the items in a list to add emphasis. Formatting a list as a numbered list helps illustrate sequences and priorities. You can quickly format a list with bullets or numbering by using the Bullets and Numbering buttons in the Paragraph group on the Home tab. You format the lists in your report with numbers and bullets.

STEPS

1. **Scroll until the Everest Base Camp Trek heading is at the top of your screen**

QUICK TIP

To change the style, font, number format, and alignment of the numbers in a list, right-click the list, point to Numbering, then click Define New Number Format.

2. **Select the three-line list of 3-day add-ons, click the Home tab, then click the Numbering list arrow ▤ ▾ in the Paragraph group**

   The Numbering Library opens, as shown in Figure C-18. You use this list to choose or change the numbering style applied to a list.

3. **Drag the pointer over different numbering styles, then click the numbering style shown in Figure C-18**

   Dragging the pointer over the numbering styles allows you to preview how the selected text will look if the highlighted numbering style is applied. After clicking, the paragraphs are formatted as a numbered list.

QUICK TIP

To remove a bullet or number, select the paragraph(s), then click ▤ or ▤.

4. **Place the insertion point after Pokhara — Valley of Lakes, press [Enter], then type Temples of Janakpur**

   Pressing [Enter] in the middle of the numbered list creates a new numbered paragraph and automatically renumbers the remainder of the list. Similarly, if you delete a paragraph from a numbered list, Word automatically renumbers the remaining paragraphs.

5. **Click 1 in the list**

   Clicking a number in a list selects all the numbers, as shown in Figure C-19.

6. **Click the Bold button ⓑ in the Font group**

   The numbers are all formatted in bold. Notice that the formatting of the items in the list does not change when you change the formatting of the numbers. You can also use this technique to change the formatting of bullets in a bulleted list.

QUICK TIP

To use a symbol or a picture for a bullet character, click Define New Bullet in the Bullet list, and then select from the options in the Define New Bullet dialog box.

7. **Select the list of items under Last minute participants in the Everest Base Camp trek..., then click the Bullets button ▤ in the Paragraph group**

   The four paragraphs are formatted as a bulleted list using the most recently used bullet style.

8. **Click a bullet in the list to select all the bullets, click the Bullets list arrow ▤ ▾ in the Paragraph group, click the check mark bullet style, then save your changes**

   The bullet character changes to a check mark, as shown in Figure C-20.

Creating multilevel lists

You can create lists with hierarchical structures by applying a multilevel list style to a list. To create a **multilevel list**, also called an outline, begin by applying a multilevel list style using the Multilevel List list arrow ▤ ▾ in the Paragraph group on the Home tab, then type your outline, pressing [Enter] after each item. To demote items to a lower level of importance in the outline, place the insertion point in the item, then click the Increase Indent button ▤ in the Paragraph group on the Home tab. Each time you indent a paragraph, the item is demoted to a lower level in the outline. Similarly, you can use the Decrease Indent button ▤ to promote an item to a higher level in the outline. You can also create a hierarchical structure in any bulleted or numbered list by using ▤ and ▤ to demote and promote items in the list. To change the multilevel list style applied to a list, select the list, click ▤ ▾, then select a new style.

FIGURE C-18: Numbering Library

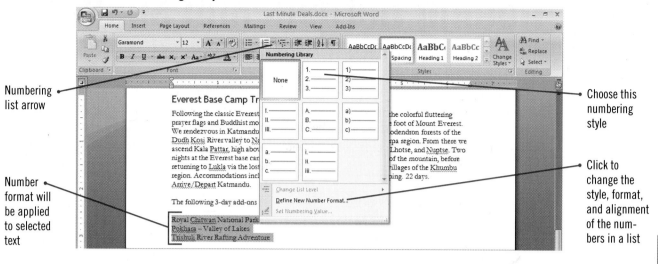

Numbering list arrow

Number format will be applied to selected text

Choose this numbering style

Click to change the style, format, and alignment of the numbers in a list

FIGURE C-19: Numbered list

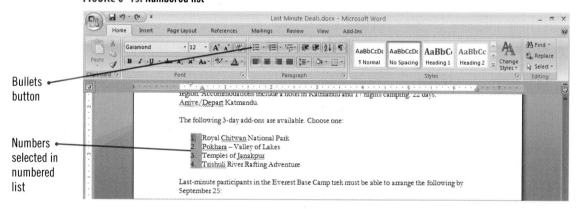

Bullets button

Numbers selected in numbered list

FIGURE C-20: Check mark bullets applied to list

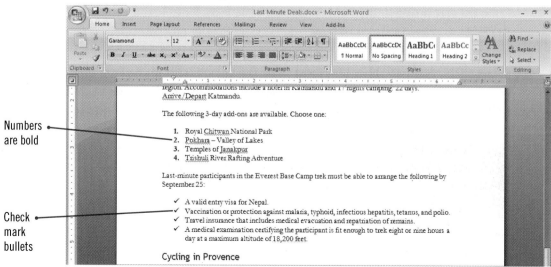

Numbers are bold

Check mark bullets

Adding Borders and Shading

Borders and shading can add color and splash to a document. **Borders** are lines you add above, below, to the side, or around words or paragraphs. You can format borders using different line styles, colors, and widths. **Shading** is a color or pattern you apply behind words or paragraphs to make them stand out on a page. You apply borders and shading using the Borders button and the Shading button in the Paragraph group on the Home tab. You enhance the tabbed text of the last minute tours schedule by adding shading to it. You also apply a border around the tabbed text to set it off from the rest of the document.

STEPS

1. **Press [Ctrl][Home], then scroll down until the tabbed text is at the top of your screen**

2. **Select the** five paragraphs **of tabbed text, click the** Shading list arrow ⬧ **in the Paragraph group on the Home tab, click the** Blue, Accent 1, Lighter 60% color, **then deselect the text**
    Light blue shading is applied to the five paragraphs. Notice that the shading is applied to the entire width of the paragraphs, despite the tab settings.

3. **Select the** five paragraphs, **drag the** Left Indent marker ⬚ **to the ¾" mark on the horizontal ruler, drag the** Right Indent marker ⬧ **to the 5¾" mark, then deselect the text**
    The shading for the paragraphs is indented from the left and right, which makes it look more attractive, as shown in Figure C-21.

4. **Select the** five paragraphs, **click the** Bottom Border list arrow ⬚ **in the Paragraph group, click** Outside Borders, **then deselect the text**
    A black outside border is added around the selected text. You can use the Borders list arrow to add a border above, below, to the side of, or around the selected text, among other options. The style of the border added is the most recently used border style, in this case the default, a thin black line.

5. **Select the** five paragraphs, **click the** Outside Borders list arrow ⬚, **click** No Border, **click the** No Border list arrow ⬚, **then click** Borders and Shading
    The Borders and Shading dialog box opens, as shown in Figure C-22. You use the Borders tab to change the border style, color, and width, and to add boxes and lines to words or paragraphs.

QUICK TIP
When creating custom borders, it's important to select the style, color, and width settings before applying the borders in the Preview section.

6. **Click the** Box box **in the Setting section, scroll down the Style list, click the** double line **style, click the** Color list arrow, **click the** Dark Blue, Text 2 color, **click the** Width list arrow, **click** 1½ pt, **click** OK, **then deselect the text**
    A 1½-point dark blue double line border is added around the tabbed text.

7. **Select the** five paragraphs, **click the** Bold button **B** **in the Font group, click the** Font Color list arrow **A** **in the Font group, click the** Dark Blue, Text 2 color, **then deselect the text**
    The text changes to bold dark blue.

8. **Select the first line in the tabbed text, click the** launcher ⬚ **in the Font group, click the** Font tab **if it is not the active tab, click** 14 **in the Size list, click the** Font Color list arrow, **click the** Red, Accent 2 color, **click the** Small caps check box **in the Effects section, click** OK, **deselect the text, then save your changes**
    The text in the first line of the tabbed text is enlarged and changed to red small caps, as shown in Figure C-23. When you change text to small caps, the lowercase letters are changed to uppercase letters in a smaller font size.

Formatting Text and Paragraphs

FIGURE C-21: Shading applied to the tabbed text

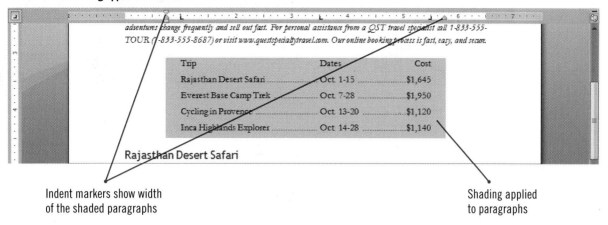

Indent markers show width
of the shaded paragraphs

Shading applied
to paragraphs

FIGURE C-22: Borders tab in Borders and Shading dialog box

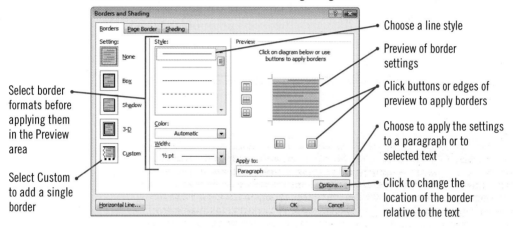

Choose a line style

Preview of border
settings

Click buttons or edges of
preview to apply borders

Choose to apply the settings
to a paragraph or to
selected text

Click to change the
location of the border
relative to the text

Select border
formats before
applying them
in the Preview
area

Select Custom
to add a single
border

FIGURE C-23: Border and font formatting applied to tabbed text

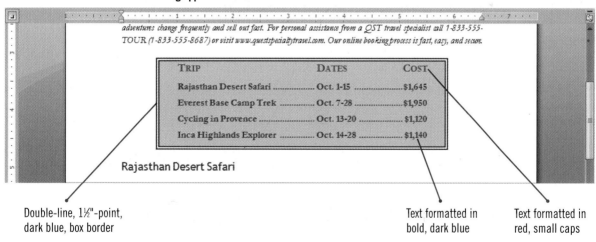

Double-line, 1½"-point,
dark blue, box border

Text formatted in
bold, dark blue

Text formatted in
red, small caps

Highlighting text in a document

The Highlight tool allows you to mark and find important text in a document. **Highlighting** is transparent color that is applied to text using the Highlight pointer ✍. To highlight text, click the Text Highlight Color list arrow 🔲 in the Font group on the Home tab, select a color, then use the I-beam part of the ✍ pointer to select the text. Click 🔲 to turn off the Highlight pointer. To remove highlighting, select the highlighted text, click 🔲, then click No Color. Highlighting prints, but it is used most effectively when a document is viewed on screen.

Adding Footnotes and Endnotes

Footnotes and endnotes are used in printed documents to provide further information, comment on, or supply references for text in a document. A **footnote** or **endnote** is an explanatory note that consists of two linked parts: the note reference mark that appears next to text to indicate that additional information is offered in a footnote or endnote, and the corresponding footnote or endnote text. Word places footnotes at the end of each page and endnotes at the end of the document. You insert and manage footnotes and endnotes in a document using the tools in the Footnotes group on the References tab. Before finalizing the document, you add several footnotes to expand upon the document information.

STEPS

1. **Place the insertion point after Cost in the top row of the tabbed text, click the References tab, then click the Insert Footnote button in the Footnotes group**

   A note reference mark, in this case a superscript 1, appears after Cost, and the insertion point moves below a separator line at the bottom of the page. A note reference mark can be a number, a symbol, a character, or a combination of characters.

2. **Type International flights, travel insurance, visas, and taxes are not included in the tour price.**

   The footnote text appears below the separator line at the bottom of page 1.

3. **Place the insertion point at the end of the quotation at the bottom of page 1, click the Insert Footnote button, then type April 12, 2009**

   The footnote text for the second footnote appears under the first footnote at the bottom of page 1, as shown in Figure C-24.

4. **Scroll to the middle of page 2, place the insertion point at the end of the second line in the bulleted list, click the Insert Footnote button, then type Vaccination requirements are subject to change and should be confirmed before departure.**

   The footnote text for the third footnote appears at the bottom of page 2.

5. **Scroll up, place the insertion point after the Everest Base Camp Trek heading, click the Insert Footnote button, then type Due to altitude, terrain, and distance walked, this trek is for strong mountain walkers only.**

   Notice that when you inserted a new footnote between existing footnotes, Word automatically renumbered the footnotes. The new footnote appears above the final footnote at the bottom of page 2.

6. **Press [Ctrl][Home], click the Next Footnote button in the Footnotes group**

   The insertion point moves to the first reference mark in the document.

7. **Click the Next Footnote button, press [Delete] to select the number 2 reference mark, then press [Delete] again**

   The reference mark and associated footnote are deleted from the document and the footnotes are automatically renumbered. You must select a reference mark to delete a footnote; you can not simply delete the footnote text itself.

8. **Scroll to the bottom of page 2, notice the remaining footnotes have been renumbered, press [Ctrl][Home], then save your changes**

   The completed document is shown in Figure C-25.

9. **Click the Office button, point to Print, click Quick Print, close the document, then exit Word**

   A copy of the flyer prints. Depending on your printer, colors might appear differently when you print. If you are using a black-and-white printer, colors will print in shades of gray.

FIGURE C-24: Footnotes in the document

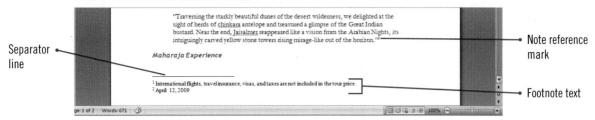

Separator line

Note reference mark

Footnote text

FIGURE C-25: Completed document

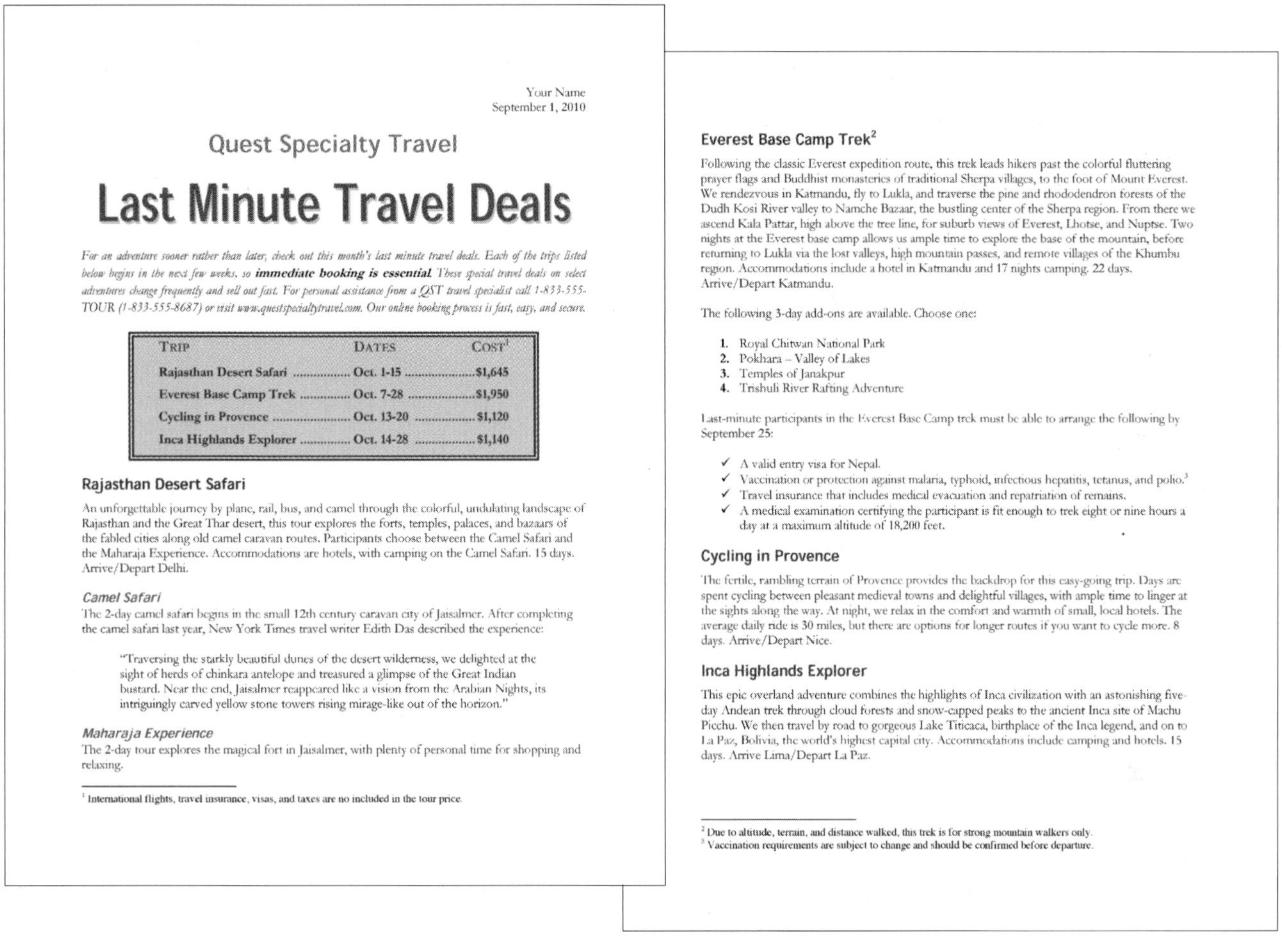

Creating a bibliography

Many documents require a **bibliography**, a list of sources that you consulted or cited in creating the document. The Word bibliography feature allows you to quickly create sources, add citations to a document, and automatically generate a bibliography based on the source information you provide for the document. Each time you create a new source, the source information is saved on your computer so that it is available for use in any document.

To add a citation and source to a document, begin by selecting the style you want to use for the citation and source using the Style list arrow in the Citations & Bibliography group on the References tab. APA, Chicago, and MLA are commonly used styles. Next, place the insertion point at the end of the sentence where you want to add the citation, click the Insert Citation button in the Citations & Bibliography group, click Add New Source, and then enter the relevant information about the reference source in the Create Source dialog box. When you have finished adding citations to a document and are ready to create a bibliography, place the insertion point where you want the bibliography, usually at the end of the document, click the Bibliography button in the Citations & Bibliography group, and then click a built-in bibliography style from the gallery, or click Insert Bibliography. The bibliography is inserted in the document as a field, and can be formatted any way you choose.

Practice

If you have a SAM user profile, you may have access to hands-on instruction, practice, and assessment of the skills covered in this unit. Log in to your SAM account (http://sam2007.course.com/) to launch any assigned training activities or exams that relate to the skills covered in this unit.

▼ CONCEPTS REVIEW

Label each element of the Word program window shown in Figure C-26.

FIGURE C-26

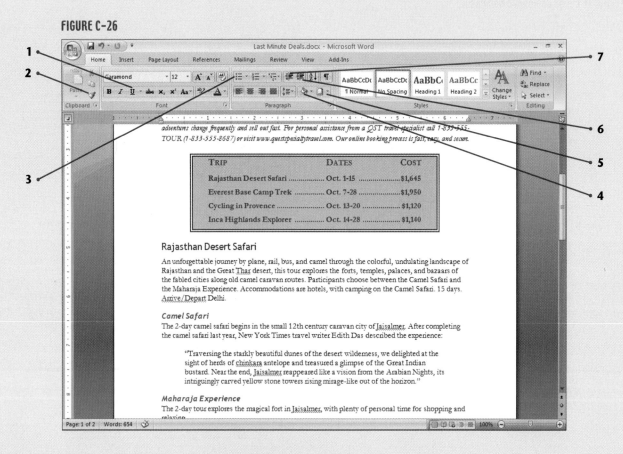

Match each term with the statement that best describes it.

8. **Footnote**

9. **Shading**

10. **Point**

11. **Style**

12. **Bibliography**

13. **Highlight**

14. **Bullet**

15. **Border**

a. Color or pattern that is applied behind text to make it look attractive

b. A note placed at the bottom of a page that comments on part of the document text

c. A list of sources consulted or cited in creating a document

d. A line that can be applied above, below, or to the sides of a paragraph

e. Transparent color that is applied to text to mark it in a document

f. A unit of measurement equal to ½ of an inch

g. A character that appears at the beginning of a paragraph to add emphasis

h. A set of format settings

Select the best answer from the list of choices.

16. **What is Garamond?**
    a. A character format
    b. A style
    c. A font
    d. A text effect

17. **What is the most precise way to increase the amount of white space between two paragraphs?**
    a. Change the before paragraph spacing for the second paragraph
    b. Indent the paragraphs
    c. Change the line spacing of the paragraphs
    d. Insert an extra blank line between the paragraphs

18. **In which type of indent are the subsequent lines of a paragraph indented more than the first line?**
    a. Hanging indent
    b. Negative indent
    c. First Line indent
    d. Right indent

19. **Which dialog box is used to change the scale of characters?**
    a. Paragraph
    b. Borders and Shading
    c. Tabs
    d. Font

20. **Which button is used to align a paragraph with both the left and right margins?**
    a. [icon]
    b. [icon]
    c. [icon]
    d. [icon]

▼ SKILLS REVIEW

1. **Format with fonts.**
    a. Start Word, open the file WD C-2.docx from the drive and folder where you store your Data Files, save it as Franklin EDA Report, then scroll through the document to get a feel for its contents.
    b. Press [Ctrl][A], then format the text in 12-point Californian FB. Choose a different serif font if Californian FB is not available to you.
    c. Press [Ctrl][Home], format the report title Town of Franklin Economic Development Authority Report Executive Summary in 26-point Berlin Sans FB. Choose a different sans serif font if Berlin Sans FB is not available to you.
    d. Change the font color of the report title to Purple, Accent 4, Darker 25%, then press [Enter] after Franklin in the title.
    e. Place the insertion point in the first body paragraph under the title, then add a two-line drop cap to the paragraph using the Dropped position.
    f. Format the heading Mission Statement in 14-point Berlin Sans FB with the Purple, Accent 4, Darker 25% font color.
    g. Press [Ctrl][Home], then save your changes to the report.

2. **Copy formats using the Format Painter.**
    a. Use the Format Painter to copy the format of the Mission Statement heading to the following headings: Guiding Principles, Issues, Proposed Actions.
    b. Show formatting marks, then format the paragraph under the Mission Statement heading in italic.
    c. Format Years Population Growth, the first line in the four-line list under the Issues heading, in bold, small caps, with Purple, Accent 4, Darker 50% font color.
    d. Change the font color of the next two lines under Years Population Growth to Purple, Accent 4, Darker 50%.
    e. Format the line Source: Office of State Planning in italic.

f. Scroll to the top of the report, then change the character scale of Town of Franklin Economic Development Authority Report to 90%.

g. Change the character scale of Executive Summary to 150%, then save your changes.

3. **Change line and paragraph spacing.**

a. Change the line spacing of the three-line list under the first body paragraph to 1.5 lines.

b. Add 24 points of space before and 6 points of space after the Executive Summary line in the title.

c. Add 12 points of space after the Mission Statement heading, then use the F4 key to add 12 points of space after each additional heading in the report (Guiding Principles, Issues, Proposed Actions).

d. Add 6 points of space after each paragraph in the list under the Guiding Principles heading.

e. Change the line spacing of the 4-line list under the Issues heading that begins with Years Population Growth to 1.15.

f. Add 6 points of space after each paragraph under the Proposed Actions heading.

g. Press [Ctrl][Home], then save your changes to the report.

4. **Align paragraphs.**

a. Press [Ctrl][A] to select the entire document, then justify all the paragraphs.

b. Center the three-line report title.

c. Press [Ctrl][End], type your name, press [Enter], type the current date, then right-align your name and the date.

d. Save your changes to the report.

5. **Work with tabs.**

a. Scroll up and select the four-line list of population information under the Issues heading.

b. Set left tab stops at the 2" mark and the 3¾" mark.

c. Insert a tab at the beginning of each line in the list.

d. In the first line, insert a tab before Population. In the second line, insert a tab before 4.5%. In the third line, insert a tab before 53%.

e. Select the first three lines, then drag the second tab stop to the 3" mark on the horizontal ruler.

f. Press [Ctrl][Home], then save your changes to the report.

6. **Work with indents.**

a. Indent the paragraph under the Mission Statement heading ½" from the left and ½" from the right.

b. Indent the first line of the paragraph under the Guiding Principles heading ½".

c. Indent the first line of the three body paragraphs under the Issues heading ½".

d. Press [Ctrl][Home], then save your changes to the report.

7. **Add bullets and numbering.**

a. Apply bullets to the three-line list under the first body paragraph. Change the bullet style to small black circles if necessary.

b. Change the font color of the bullets to Purple, Accent 4, Darker 25%.

c. Scroll down until the Guiding Principles heading is at the top of your screen.

d. Format the six-paragraph list under Guiding Principles as a numbered list.

e. Format the numbers in 14-point Berlin Sans FB, then change the font color to Purple, Accent 4, Darker 25%.

f. Scroll down until the Proposed Actions heading is at the top of your screen, then format the paragraphs under the heading as a bulleted list using check marks as the bullet style.

g. Change the font color of the bullets to Purple, Accent 4, Darker 25%, press [Ctrl][Home], then save your changes to the report.

8. Add borders and shading.

a. Change the font color of **Town of Franklin Economic Development Authority Report** to White, Background 1, then apply Orange, Accent 6 shading.

b. Add a 1-point Orange, Accent 6 border below the Mission Statement heading.

c. Use the F4 key to add the same border to the other headings in the report (Guiding Principles, Issues, Proposed Actions).

d. Under the Issues heading, select the first three lines of tabbed text, which are formatted in purple, then apply Purple, Accent 4, Lighter 60% shading to the paragraphs.

e. Select the first three lines of tabbed text again if necessary, then add a 1½ -point Orange, Accent 6 single line box border around the paragraphs.

f. Indent the shading and border around the paragraphs 1¾" from the left and 1¾" from the right, then save your changes.

9. Add footnotes and endnotes.

a. Place the insertion point at the end of item 5 under the Guiding Principles heading, insert an endnote, then type **A capital reserve fund was established in 2009.**

b. Place the insertion point at the end of item 3, insert an endnote, then type **See the Downtown District EDA Report.**

c. Place the insertion point at the end of the third item in the list under the Proposed Actions heading, insert an endnote, then type **Scheduled for February 2010.**

d. Locate and delete the first endnote from the document. Scroll to the end of the document and verify the endnotes are correct.

e. Press [Ctrl][Home], save your changes to the report, view the report in Print Preview, then print a copy. The formatted report is shown in Figure C-27.

f. Turn off formatting marks, close the file and exit Word.

FIGURE C-27

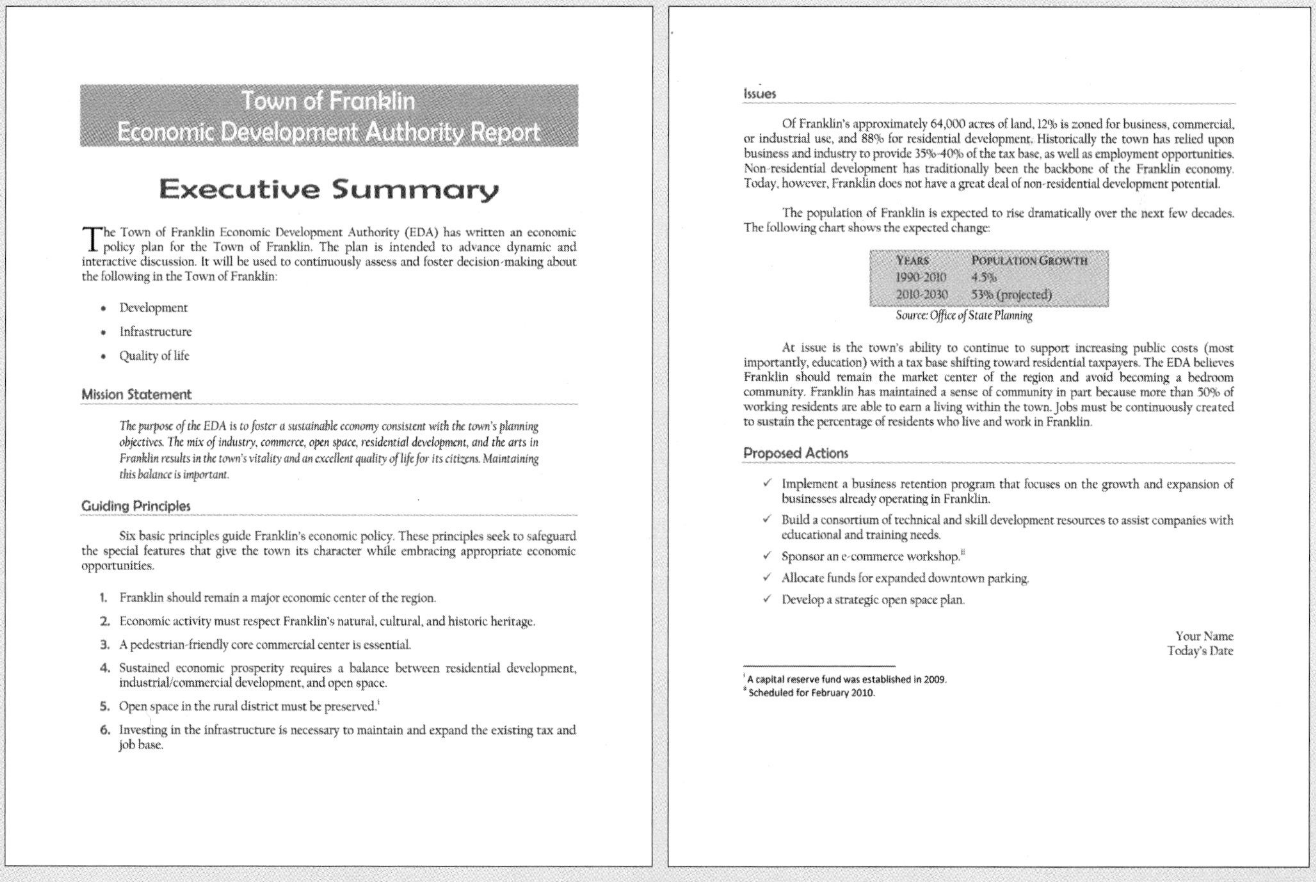

Town of Franklin
Economic Development Authority Report

Executive Summary

The Town of Franklin Economic Development Authority (EDA) has written an economic policy plan for the Town of Franklin. The plan is intended to advance dynamic and interactive discussion. It will be used to continuously assess and foster decision-making about the following in the Town of Franklin:

- Development
- Infrastructure
- Quality of life

Mission Statement

The purpose of the EDA is to foster a sustainable economy consistent with the town's planning objectives. The mix of industry, commerce, open space, residential development, and the arts in Franklin results in the town's vitality and an excellent quality of life for its citizens. Maintaining this balance is important.

Guiding Principles

Six basic principles guide Franklin's economic policy. These principles seek to safeguard the special features that give the town its character while embracing appropriate economic opportunities.

1. Franklin should remain a major economic center of the region.
2. Economic activity must respect Franklin's natural, cultural, and historic heritage.
3. A pedestrian-friendly core commercial center is essential.
4. Sustained economic prosperity requires a balance between residential development, industrial/commercial development, and open space.
5. Open space in the rural district must be preserved.[i]
6. Investing in the infrastructure is necessary to maintain and expand the existing tax and job base.

Issues

Of Franklin's approximately 64,000 acres of land, 12% is zoned for business, commercial, or industrial use, and 88% for residential development. Historically the town has relied upon business and industry to provide 35%-40% of the tax base, as well as employment opportunities. Non-residential development has traditionally been the backbone of the Franklin economy. Today, however, Franklin does not have a great deal of non-residential development potential.

The population of Franklin is expected to rise dramatically over the next few decades. The following chart shows the expected change:

YEARS	POPULATION GROWTH
1990-2010	4.5%
2010-2030	53% (projected)

Source: Office of State Planning

At issue is the town's ability to continue to support increasing public costs (most importantly, education) with a tax base shifting toward residential taxpayers. The EDA believes Franklin should remain the market center of the region and avoid becoming a bedroom community. Franklin has maintained a sense of community in part because more than 50% of working residents are able to earn a living within the town. Jobs must be continuously created to sustain the percentage of residents who live and work in Franklin.

Proposed Actions

- ✓ Implement a business retention program that focuses on the growth and expansion of businesses already operating in Franklin.
- ✓ Build a consortium of technical and skill development resources to assist companies with educational and training needs.
- ✓ Sponsor an e-commerce workshop.[ii]
- ✓ Allocate funds for expanded downtown parking.
- ✓ Develop a strategic open space plan.

Your Name
Today's Date

[i] A capital reserve fund was established in 2009.
[ii] Scheduled for February 2010.

▼ INDEPENDENT CHALLENGE 1

You are an estimator for Jermanok Construction in the Australian city of Wollongong. You have drafted an estimate for a home renovation job, and need to format it. It's important that your estimate have a clean, striking design, and reflect your company's professionalism.

a. Start Word, open the file WD C-3.docx from the drive and folder where you store your Data Files, save it as Jermanok Construction, then read the document to get a feel for its contents. Figure C-28 shows how you will format the letterhead.

FIGURE C-28

JERMANOK*Construction*

26-38 Corrimal Street, Wollongong, NSW 2500; Tel: 02-4225-3202; www.jermanok.com.au

b. Select the entire document, change the style to No Spacing, then change the font to 12-point Times New Roman.

c. In the first paragraph, format Jermanok in 24-point Arial Black and change the case to All caps. Format Construction in 24-point Arial, apply italic, then delete the space between the two words. (*Hint*: Select a similar font if Arial Black is not available to you.)

d. Format the next line in 10-point Arial, then right-align the two-line letterhead.

e. Add a 2¼ -point dotted black border below the address line paragraph.

f. With the insertion point in the address line, open the Borders and Shading dialog box, click Options to open the Border and Shading Options dialog box, change the Bottom setting to 5 points, then click OK twice to adjust the location of the border relative to the line of text.

g. Format the title Proposal of Renovation in 14-point Arial Black, then center the title.

h. Format the following headings (including the colons) in 11-point Arial Black: Date, Work to be performed for and at, Scope of work, Payment schedule, and Agreement.

i. Select the 14-line list under Scope of work that begins with Demo of all..., then change the paragraph spacing to add 4 points of space after each paragraph in the list. (*Hint*: Select 0 pt in the After text box, type 4, then press Enter.)

j. With the list selected, set a right tab stop at the 6¼" mark, insert tabs before every price in the list, then apply dotted line tab leaders.

k. Format the list as a numbered list, then apply bold to the numbers.

l. Apply bold to the two lines, Total estimated job cost... and Approximate job time... below the list.

m. Replace Your Name with your name in the signature block, select the signature block (Respectfully submitted through your name), set a left tab stop at the 3¼" mark, then indent the signature block using tabs.

n. Examine the document carefully for formatting errors and make any necessary adjustments.

o. Save and print the document, then close the file and exit Word.

▼ INDEPENDENT CHALLENGE 2

Your employer, The Lange Center for Contemporary Arts in Halifax, Nova Scotia, is launching a membership drive. Your boss has written the text for a flyer advertising Lange membership, and asks you to format it so that it is eye catching and attractive.

a. Open the file WD C-4.docx from the drive and folder where you store your Data Files, save it as **Membership Drive 2010**, then read the document. Figure C-29 shows how you will format the first several paragraphs of the flyer.

FIGURE C-29

MEMBERSHIP DRIVE
2010

What we do for ARTISTS

Since 1982, the artist residency program at the Lange Center for Contemporary Arts has supported the work of more than 1500 artists from all over Canada and from 40 other nations. The residency awards include studio and living space, a monthly stipend to help artists with their expenses, and use of specialized equipment for all types of visual and performance art. Each artist gives a public lecture or performance at the Lange.

b. Select the entire document, change the style to No Spacing, then change the font to 11-point Arial Narrow.

c. Center the first line, **Membership Drive**, and apply shading to the paragraph. Choose a dark custom shading color of your choice for the shading color. (*Hint*: Click More Colors, then select a color from the Standard or Custom tab.) Format the text in 26-point Arial Narrow, bold, with a white font color. Expand the character spacing by 10 points.

d. Format the second line, **2010**, in 36-point Arial Black. Expand the character spacing by 25 points and change the character scale to 250%. Center the line.

e. Format each **What we do for...** heading in 12-point Arial, bold. Change the font color to the same custom color used for shading the title. (*Note*: The color now appears in the Recent Colors section of the Font Color gallery.) Add a single line ½-point black border under each heading.

f. Format each subheading (**Gallery**, **Lectures**, **Library**, **All members...**, and **Membership Levels**) in 10-point Arial, bold. Add 3 points of spacing before each paragraph. (*Hint*: Select 0 in the Before text box, type 3, then press Enter.)

g. Indent each body paragraph ¼", except for the lines under the **What we do for YOU** heading.

h. Format the four lines under the All members... subheading as a bulleted list. Use a bullet symbol of your choice and format the bullets in the custom font color.

i. Indent the five lines under the Membership Levels heading ¼". For these five lines, set left tab stops at the 1¼" mark and the 2" mark on the horizontal ruler. Insert tabs before the price and before the word All in each of the five lines.

j. Format the name of each membership level (**Artistic**, **Conceptual**, etc.) in 10-point Arial, bold, italic, with the custom font color.

k. Format the **For more information** heading in 14-point Arial, bold, with the custom font color, then center the heading.

l. Format the last two lines in 11-point Arial Narrow, and center the lines. In the contact information, replace Your Name with your name, then apply bold to your name.

Advanced Challenge Exercise

- Change the font color of **2010** to a dark gray and add a shadow effect.
- Add a shadow effect to each **What we do for...** heading.
- Add a 3-point dotted black border above the **For more information** heading.

m. Examine the document carefully for formatting errors and make any necessary adjustments.

n. Save and print the flyer, then close the file and exit Word.

▼ INDEPENDENT CHALLENGE 3

One of your responsibilities as program coordinator at Solstice Mountain Sports is to develop a program of winter outdoor learning and adventure workshops. You have drafted a memo to your boss to update her on your progress. You need to format the memo so it is professional looking and easy to read.

a. Start Word, open the file WD C-5.docx from the drive and folder where you store your Data Files, then save it as Solstice Winter Memo.

b. Select the heading Solstice Mountain Sports Memorandum, apply the Quick Style Title to it, then center the heading. (*Hint*: Open the Quick Style gallery, then click the Title button.)

c. In the memo header, replace Today's Date and Your Name with the current date and your name.

d. Select the four-line memo header, set a left tab stop at the ¾" mark, then insert tabs before the date, the recipient's name, your name, and the subject of the memo.

e. Apply the Quick Style Strong to Date:, To:, From:, and Re:.

f. Apply the Quick Style Heading 2 to the headings Overview, Workshops, Accommodations, Fees, and Proposed winter programming.

g. Under the Fees heading, apply the Quick Style Emphasis to the words Workshop fees and Accommodations fees.

h. On the second page of the document, format the list under the Proposed winter programming heading as a multilevel list. Figure C-30 shows the hierarchical structure of the outline. (*Hint*: Apply a multilevel list style, then use the Increase Indent and Decrease Indent buttons to change the level of importance of each item.)

i. Change the outline numbering style to the bullet numbering style shown in Figure C-30, if necessary.

Advanced Challenge Exercise

- Zoom out on the memo so that two pages display in the document window, then, using the Change Styles button, change the style set to Modern.
- Using the Change Case button, change the title Solstice Mountain Sports Memorandum so that only the initial letter of each word is capitalized.
- Using the Themes button, change the theme applied to the document.
- Using the Theme Fonts button, change the fonts to a font set of your choice. Choose fonts that allow the document to fit on two pages.
- Using the Theme Colors button, change the colors to a color palette of your choice.
- Apply different styles and adjust other formatting elements as necessary to make the memo attractive, eye-catching, and readable.

j. Save and print the document, then close the file and exit Word.

FIGURE C-30

Proposed winter programming
- ❖ Skiing, Snowboarding, and Snowshoeing
  - ➢ Skiing and Snowboarding
    - ▪ Cross-country skiing
      - • Cross-country skiing for beginners
      - • Intermediate cross-country skiing
      - • Inn-to-inn ski touring
      - • Moonlight cross-country skiing
    - ▪ Telemarking
      - • Basic telemark skiing
      - • Introduction to backcountry skiing
      - • Exploring on skis
    - ▪ Snowboarding
      - • Backcountry snowboarding
  - ➢ Snowshoeing
    - ▪ Beginner
      - • Snowshoeing for beginners
      - • Snowshoeing and winter ecology
    - ▪ Intermediate and Advanced
      - • Intermediate snowshoeing
      - • Guided snowshoe trek
      - • Above tree line snowshoeing
- ❖ Winter Hiking, Camping, and Survival
  - ➢ Hiking
    - ▪ Beginner
      - • Long-distance hiking
      - • Winter summits
      - • Hiking for women
  - ➢ Winter camping and survival
    - ▪ Beginner
      - • Introduction to winter camping
      - • Basic winter mountain skills
      - • Building snow shelters
    - ▪ Intermediate
      - • Basic winter mountain skills II
      - • Ice climbing
      - • Avalanche awareness and rescue

▼ REAL LIFE INDEPENDENT CHALLENGE

The fonts you choose for a document can have a major effect on the document's tone. Not all fonts are appropriate for use in a business document, and some fonts, especially those with a definite theme, are appropriate only for specific purposes. In this Independent Challenge, you will use font formatting and other formatting features to design a letterhead and a fax coversheet for yourself or your business. The letterhead and coversheet should not only look professional and attract interest; the design should say something about the character of your business or your personality. Figure C-31 shows an example of a business letterhead.

FIGURE C-31

a. Start Word, and save a new blank document as **Personal Letterhead** to the drive and folder where you store your Data Files.

b. Type your name or the name of your business, your address, your phone number, your fax number, and your Web site or e-mail address.

c. Format your name or the name of your business in a font that expresses your personality or says something about the nature of your business. Use fonts, font colors, font effects, borders, shading, paragraph formatting, and other formatting features to design a letterhead that is appealing and professional.

d. Save your changes, print a copy, then close the file.

e. Open a new blank document and save it as **Personal Fax Coversheet**. Type FAX, your name or the name of your business, your address, your phone number, your fax number, and your Web site or e-mail address at the top of the document.

f. Type a fax header that includes the following: Date; To; From; Re; Number of pages, including cover sheet; and Comments.

g. Format the information in the fax coversheet using fonts, font effects, borders, shading, paragraph formatting, and other formatting features. Since a fax coversheet is designed to be faxed, all fonts and other formatting elements should be black. Format the fax header using tabs.

h. Save your changes, print a copy, close the file, then exit Word.

Open the file WD C-6.docx from the drive and folder where you store your Data Files. Create the menu shown in Figure C-32. (*Hints:* Use Harlow Solid Italic and Eras Light ITC or similar fonts. Change the font size of the heading to 48 points, the font size of Daily Specials to 20 points, the font size of the days and the specials to 16 points, and the font size of the descriptions to 12 points. Format the prices using tabs. Use paragraph spacing to adjust the spacing between paragraphs so that all the text fits on one page.) Save the menu as **Nina's Trackside**, then print a copy.

FIGURE C-32

Nina's Trackside Café

Daily Specials

Monday
  Chicken Cajun Bleu: Cajun chicken, chunky blue cheese, cucumbers, leaf lettuce, and tomato on our roasted garlic roll. $6.50

Tuesday
  Clam Chowder: Classic New England thick, rich, clam chowder in our peasant French bread bowl. Served with a garden salad. $5.95

Wednesday
  Veggie Chili: Hearty veggie chili with melted cheddar in our peasant French bread bowl. Topped with sour cream & scallions. $5.95

Thursday
  French Dip: Lean roast beef topped with melted cheddar on our roasted garlic roll. Served with a side of au jus and red bliss mashed potatoes. $6.95

Friday
  Turkey-Bacon Club: Double-decker roasted turkey, crisp bacon, leaf lettuce, tomato, and sun-dried tomato mayo on toasted triple seed. $6.50

Saturday
  Greek Salad: Our large garden salad with Kalamata olives, feta cheese, and garlic vinaigrette. Served with an assortment of rolls. $5.95

Sunday
  Hot Chicken and Gravy: Delicious chicken and savory gravy served on a thick slice of toasted honest white. Served with a garden salad. $6.95

Chef: Your Name

Formatting Documents

The page-formatting features of Word allow you to lay out and design the pages of your documents creatively. In this unit, you learn how to change the document margins, determine page orientation, add page numbers, and insert headers and footers. You also learn how to format text in columns and how to illustrate your documents with tables and clip art. You have written and formatted the text for the quarterly newsletter for QST clients. You are now ready to lay out and design the newsletter pages. You plan to organize the articles in columns and to enhance the visual appeal of the newsletter by adding a table and clip art.

OBJECTIVES

Set document margins

Divide a document into sections

Insert page breaks

Format columns

Insert page numbers

Add headers and footers

Edit headers and footers

Insert a table

Insert clip art

Setting Document Margins

Changing a document's margins is one way to change the appearance of a document and control the amount of text that fits on a page. The **margins** of a document are the blank areas between the edge of the text and the edge of the page. When you create a document in Word, the default margins are 1" at the top, bottom, left, and right sides of the page. You can adjust the size of a document's margins using the Margins command on the Page Layout tab, or using the rulers. ▰▰▰▱▱ The newsletter should be a four-page document when finished. You begin formatting the pages by reducing the size of the document margins so that more text fits on each page.

STEPS

TROUBLE
Click the View Ruler button 🔲 at the top of the vertical scroll bar to display the rulers if they are not already displayed.

1. **Start Word, open the file WD D-1.docx from the drive and folder where you store your Data Files, then save it as Footprints**

   The newsletter opens in Print Layout view.

2. **Scroll through the newsletter to get a feel for its contents, then press [Ctrl][Home]**

   The newsletter is currently five pages long. Notice that the status bar indicates the page where the insertion point is located and the total number of pages in the document.

3. **Click the Page Layout tab, then click the Margins button in the Page Setup group**

   The Margins menu opens. You can select predefined margin settings from this menu, or click Custom Margins to create different margin settings.

QUICK TIP
You can also click the launcher in the Page Setup group to open the Page Setup dialog box.

4. **Click Custom Margins**

   The Page Setup dialog box opens with the Margins tab displayed, as shown in Figure D-1. You can use the Margins tab to change the top, bottom, left, or right document margin, to change the orientation of the pages from portrait to landscape, and to alter other page layout settings. **Portrait orientation** means a page is taller than it is wide; **landscape orientation** means a page is wider than it is tall. This newsletter uses portrait orientation. You can also use the Orientation button in the Page Setup group on the Page Layout tab to change the orientation of a document.

5. **Click the Top down arrow three times until 0.7" appears, then click the Bottom down arrow until 0.7" appears**

   The top and bottom margins of the newsletter will be .7". Notice that the margins in the Preview section of the dialog box change as you adjust the margin settings.

QUICK TIP
The minimum allowable margin settings depend on your printer and the size of the paper you are using. Word displays a warning message if you set margins that are too narrow for your printer.

6. **Press [Tab], type .7 in the Left text box, press [Tab], then type .7 in the Right text box**

   The left and right margins of the newsletter will also be .7". You can change the margin settings by using the arrows or by typing a value in the appropriate text box.

7. **Click OK**

   The document margins change to .7", as shown in Figure D-2. The location of each margin (right, left, top, and bottom) is shown on the horizontal and vertical rulers at the intersection of the white and shaded areas. You can also change a margin setting by using the ⟷ pointer to drag the intersection to a new location on the ruler.

8. **Click the View tab, then click the Two Pages button in the Zoom group**

   The first two pages of the document appear in the document window.

9. **Scroll down to view all five pages of the newsletter, press [Ctrl][Home], click the Page Width button in the Zoom group, then save your changes**

Default margin settings

Select page orientation

Select part of document to apply settings to

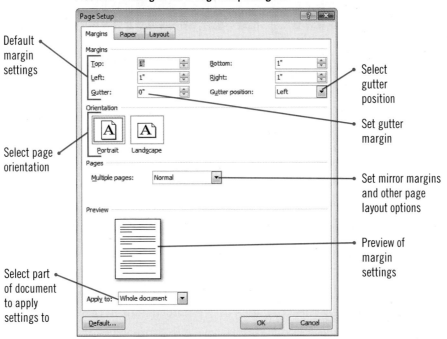

Select gutter position

Set gutter margin

Set mirror margins and other page layout options

Preview of margin settings

FIGURE D-2: Newsletter with smaller margins

Left margin on ruler

Top margin on ruler

Document margins are narrower

Page 1 is the active page

Right margin on ruler

Document is five pages long

Changing orientation, margin settings, and paper size

By default, the documents you create in Word use an 8½" × 11" paper size in portrait orientation with the default margin settings. You can change the orientation, margin settings, and paper size to common settings using the Orientation, Margins, and Size buttons in the Page Setup group on the Page Layout tab. You can also adjust these settings and others in the Page Setup dialog box. For example, to change the layout of multiple pages, use the Multiple pages list arrow on the Margins tab to create pages that use mirror margins, that include two pages per sheet of paper, or that are formatted like a folded booklet. **Mirror margins** are used in a document with facing pages, such as a magazine, where the margins on the left page of the document are a mirror image of the margins on the right page. Documents with mirror margins have inside and outside margins, rather than right and left margins. Another type of margin is a gutter margin, which is used in documents that are bound, such as books. A **gutter** adds extra space to the left, top, or inside margin to allow for the binding. Add a gutter to a document by adjusting the setting in the Gutter position text box on the Margins tab. To change the size of the paper used, use the Paper size list arrow on the Paper tab to select a standard paper size, or enter custom measurements in the Width and Height text boxes.

Dividing a Document into Sections

Dividing a document into sections allows you to format each section of the document with different page layout settings. A **section** is a portion of a document that is separated from the rest of the document by section breaks. **Section breaks** are formatting marks that you insert in a document to show the end of a section. Once you have divided a document into sections, you can format each section with different column, margin, page orientation, header and footer, and other page layout settings. By default, a document is formatted as a single section, but you can divide a document into as many sections as you like. ▰▰▰ You insert a section break to divide the document into two sections, and then format the text in the second section in two columns. First, you customize the status bar to display section information.

STEPS

QUICK TIP

Use the Customize Status bar menu to turn on and off the display of information in the status bar.

1. **Right-click the status bar, click Section on the Customize Status Bar menu that opens (if it is not already checked), then click the document to close the menu**
   The status bar indicates the insertion point is located in section 1 of the document.

2. **Click the Home tab, then click the Show/Hide ¶ button ¶ in the Paragraph group**
   Turning on formatting marks allows you to see the section breaks you insert in a document.

QUICK TIP

When you insert a section break at the beginning of a paragraph, Word inserts the break at the end of the previous paragraph. A section break stores the formatting information for the preceding section.

3. **Place the insertion point before the headline QST Launches New Tours to South Africa, click the Page Layout tab, then click the Breaks button in the Page Setup group**
   The Breaks menu opens. You use this menu to insert different types of section breaks. See Table D-1.

4. **Click Continuous**
   Word inserts a continuous section break, shown as a dotted double line, above the headline. The document now has two sections. Notice that the status bar indicates the insertion point is in section 2.

5. **Click the Columns button in the Page Setup group**
   The columns menu opens. You use this menu to format text in one, two, or three columns of equal width, or to create two columns of different widths, one narrow and one wider. To create columns with custom widths and spacing, you click More Columns on the Columns menu.

QUICK TIP

When you delete a section break, you delete the section formatting of the text before the break. That text becomes part of the following section, and it assumes the formatting of that section.

6. **Click Two**
   Section 2 is formatted in two columns of equal width, as shown in Figure D-3. The text in section 1 remains formatted in a single column. Notice that the status bar now indicates the document is four pages long. Formatting text in columns is another way to increase the amount of text that fits on a page.

7. **Click the View tab, click the Two Pages button in the Zoom group, scroll down to examine all four pages of the document, press [Ctrl][Home], then save the document**
   The text in section 2—all the text below the continuous section break—is formatted in two columns. Text in columns flows automatically from the bottom of one column to the top of the next column.

TABLE D-1: Types of section breaks

section	function
Next page	Begins a new section and moves the text following the break to the top of the next page
Continuous	Begins a new section on the same page
Even page	Begins a new section and moves the text following the break to the top of the next even-numbered page
Odd page	Begins a new section and moves the text following the break to the top of the next odd-numbered page

Formatting Documents

FIGURE D-3: Continuous section break and columns

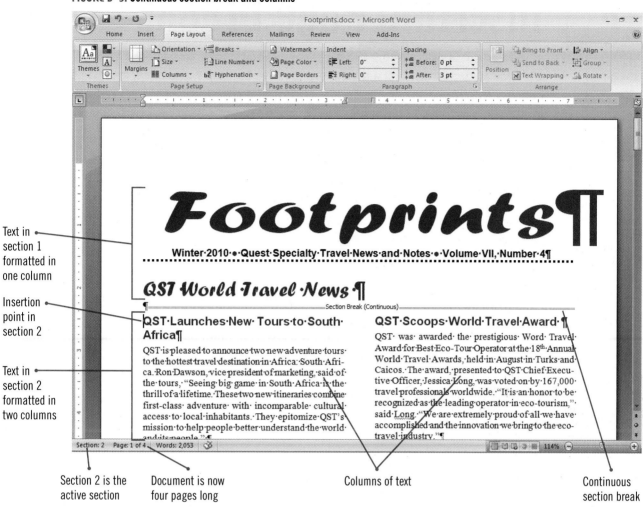

Text in section 1 formatted in one column

Insertion point in section 2

Text in section 2 formatted in two columns

Section 2 is the active section

Document is now four pages long

Columns of text

Continuous section break

Changing page layout settings for a section

Dividing a document into sections allows you to vary the layout of a document. In addition to applying different column settings to sections, you can apply different margins, page orientation, paper size, vertical alignment, header and footer, page numbering, footnotes, endnotes, and other page layout settings. For example, if you are formatting a report that includes a table with many columns, you might want to change the table's page orientation to landscape so that it is easier to read. To do this, you would insert a section break before and after the table to create a section that contains only the table, and then you would change the page orientation of the section that contains the table to landscape. Or, you might be creating a title page for a report, and want to center the text on the title page between the top and bottom margins. To do this you would insert a next page section break after the title page and then use the Vertical alignment list arrow on the Layout tab of the Page Setup dialog box to change the **vertical alignment** of the section to Center. You can vertically align text on a page only when the text does not fill the page—for example, if you are creating a flyer or a title page.

To check or change the page layout settings for an individual section, place the insertion point in the section, then open the Page Setup dialog box. Select any options you want to change, click the Apply to list arrow, click This section, then click OK. When you select This section in the Apply to list box, the settings are applied to the current section only. If you select Whole document in the Apply to list box, the settings are applied to all the sections in the document. Use the Apply to list arrow in the Columns dialog box or the Footnote and Endnote dialog box to change those settings for a section.

Inserting Page Breaks

As you type text in a document, Word inserts an **automatic page break** (also called a soft page break) when you reach the bottom of a page, allowing you to continue typing on the next page. You can also force text onto the next page of a document by using the Breaks command to insert a **manual page break** (also called a hard page break). ▰▰▰ You insert manual page breaks where you know you want to begin each new page of the newsletter.

STEPS

1. **Place the insertion point before the headline Spotlight on Japan on page 2, click the Page Layout tab, then click the Breaks button in the Page Setup group**

   The Breaks menu opens. You also use this menu to insert page, column, and text-wrapping breaks. Table D-2 describes these types of breaks.

   > **QUICK TIP**
   > Manual and automatic page breaks are always visible in Draft view.

2. **Click Page**

   Word inserts a manual page break before "Spotlight on Japan" and moves all the text following the page break to the beginning of the next page. The page break appears as a dotted line in Print Layout view when formatting marks are displayed. Page break marks are visible on the screen but do not print.

3. **Scroll down to pages 3 and 4, place the insertion point before the headline Language and Culture Immersion: Antigua, Guatemala, press and hold [Ctrl], then press [Enter]**

   Pressing [Ctrl][Enter] is a fast way to insert a manual page break. The headline is forced to the top of the fourth page, as shown in Figure D-4.

   > **QUICK TIP**
   > You can also double-click a page break to select it, and then press [Delete] to delete it.

4. **Place the insertion point before the headline Traveler's Corner on page 4, then press [Ctrl][Enter]**

   The headline is forced to the top of the fifth page.

5. **Press [Ctrl][Home], click to the left of the page break at the top of page 2 to select it, then press [Delete]**

   The manual page break is deleted and the text from pages 2 and 3 flows together. You can also click to the left of a section or a column break to select it.

   > **QUICK TIP**
   > To add line numbers in the margin to the left of each line on a page, in a section, or in a document, click the Line Numbers button in the Page Setup group, and then select an option.

6. **Click the Breaks button, then click Next Page**

   A next page section break is inserted at the top of page 2 and the text following the break is forced to the top of page 3, as shown in Figure D-5. The document now contains three sections.

7. **Place the insertion point in section 2 on page 1 (the body text), then save the document**

   The status bar indicates the insertion point is in section 2. In the next lesson you will format the columns in section 2 so that the entire section fits on the first page of the newsletter.

Controlling automatic pagination

Another way to control the flow of text between pages (or between columns) is to apply pagination settings to specify where Word positions automatic page breaks. For example, you might want to make sure an article appears on the same page as its heading, or you might want to prevent a page from breaking in the middle of the last paragraph of a report. To manipulate automatic pagination, simply select the paragraphs(s) or line(s) you want to control, click the launcher in the Paragraph group on the Home or Page Layout tab, click the Line and Page Breaks tab in the Paragraph dialog box, select one or more of the following settings from the Pagination section, and then click OK. Apply the Keep with next setting to any paragraph you want to appear together with the next paragraph on a single page, in order to prevent the page from breaking between the paragraphs. To prevent a page from breaking in the middle of a paragraph or between certain lines, select the paragraph or lines and apply the Keep lines together setting. Finally, to specify that a certain paragraph follows an automatic page break, apply the Page break before setting to the paragraph. Note that the Widow/Orphan control setting is turned on by default in the Pagination section of the dialog box. This setting ensures that at least two lines of a paragraph appear at the top and bottom of every page. In other words, it prevents a page from beginning with just the last line of a paragraph (a **widow**), and prevents a page from ending with only the first line of a new paragraph (an **orphan**).

FIGURE D-4: Manual page break in document

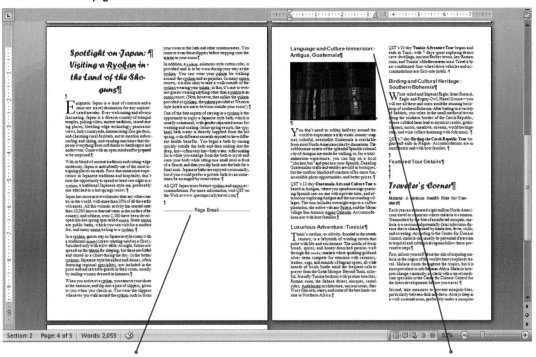

Hard page break

Text that follows break is forced onto the next page

FIGURE D-5: Next page section break in document

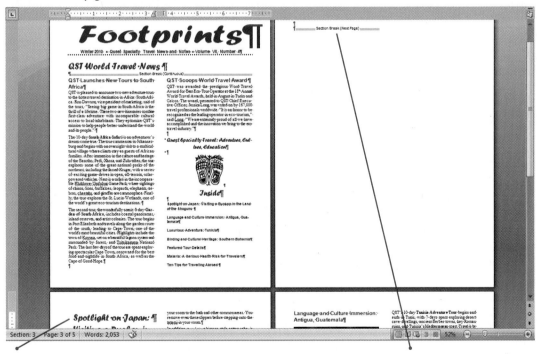

Text that follows break is forced onto the next page and is in a new section

Next page section break

TABLE D-2: Types of breaks

break	function
Page	Forces the text following the break to begin at the top of the next page
Column	Forces the text following the break to begin at the top of the next column
Text Wrapping	Forces the text following the break to begin at the beginning of the next line

Formatting Columns

Formatting text in columns often makes the text easier to read. You can apply column formatting to a whole document, to a section, or to selected text. The Columns command on the Page Layout tab allows you to quickly create columns of equal width and spacing, and to customize the width and spacing of columns. To control the way text flows between columns, you can insert a **column break**, which forces the text following the break to move to the top of the next column. You can also balance columns of unequal length on a page by inserting a continuous section break at the end of the last column on the page. ▓▓▓ You continue to format the newsletter using columns.

STEPS

1. **Make sure the insertion point is in section 2, click the Columns button in the Page Setup group, then click Right.**

    The text in section 2 is reformatted into two columns of unequal width. The formatting of the text in section 3 does not change. All the text now fits on four pages.

QUICK TIP

To change the width and spacing of existing columns, you can use the Columns dialog box or drag the column markers on the horizontal ruler.

2. **Select the headline Spotlight on Japan: Visiting a Ryokan in the Land of the Shoguns and the paragraph mark below it, click the Columns button, then click One**

    A continuous section break is added below the headline. The headline is formatted as a single column in its own new section, section 3, where the insertion point is located. The newsletter now contains 4 sections, each with different column formatting.

3. **Scroll down, place the insertion point before Malaria: A Serious... on page 4, click the Zoom Level button 52% on the status bar, click the Page width option button, click OK, click the Breaks button in the Page Setup group, then click Continuous**

    next after End A continuous section break is inserted before the Malaria headline, and the insertion point is in the new section, section 5.

QUICK TIP

To fit more text on the screen, you can hide the white space on the top and bottom of each page by moving the pointer between the pages until it changes to ⊞, and then double-clicking. To show the white space again, double-click with the ⊞ pointer.

4. **Click the Columns button, then click More Columns**

    The Columns dialog box opens, as shown in Figure D-6.

5. **Select Three in the Presets section, click the Spacing down arrow twice until 0.3" appears, select the Line between check box, then click OK**

    All the text in section 5 is formatted in three columns of equal width with a line between the columns, as shown in Figure D-7.

6. **Click the Zoom Level button 114% on the status bar, click the Whole page option button, then click OK**

    Page 4 would look better if the three columns were balanced—each the same length.

7. **Place the insertion point at the end of the third column (before the final paragraph mark), click the Breaks button, then click Continuous**

    The columns in section 5 adjust to become roughly the same length.

QUICK TIP

If a section contains a column break, you cannot balance the columns by inserting a continuous section break.

8. **Scroll up to page 3, place the insertion point before the heading Luxurious Adventure: Tunisia, click the Breaks button, then click Column**

    The text following the column break is forced to the top of the next column. The page looks cleaner when the Tunisia article does not break across the columns.

9. **Click the View tab, click the Two Pages button in the Zoom group, then save the document**

    The columns on pages 3 and 4 are formatted as shown in Figure D-8.

FIGURE D-6: Columns dialog box

Select a preset format for columns •——

Set custom widths and spacing for columns •——

Select to create columns of equal width •——

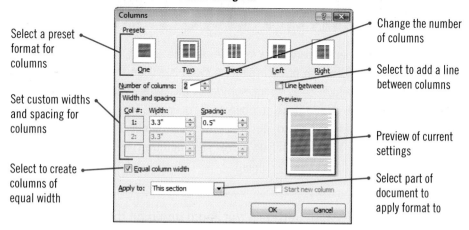

——• Change the number of columns

——• Select to add a line between columns

——• Preview of current settings

——• Select part of document to apply format to

FIGURE D-7: Text formatted in three columns

Section break at end of section 4 •——

Section 5 formatted in three columns •——

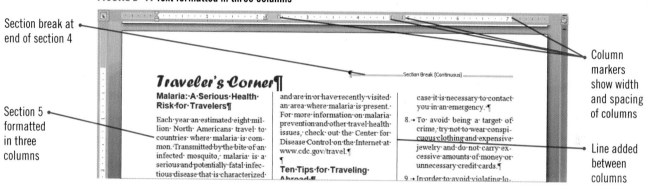

——• Column markers show width and spacing of columns

——• Line added between columns

FIGURE D-8: Columns on pages 3 and 4 of the newsletter

Text following column break forced to top of next column •——

Column break •——

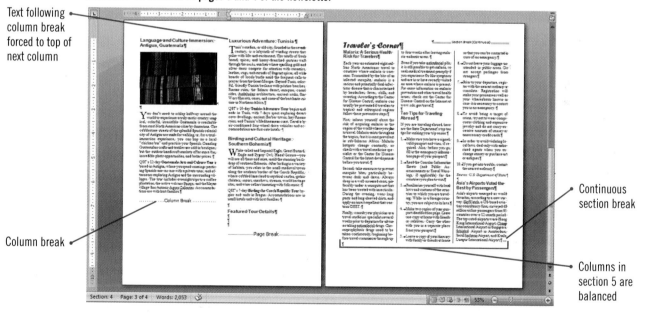

——• Continuous section break

——• Columns in section 5 are balanced

Hyphenating text in a document

Hyphenating a document is another way to control the flow of text in columns. Hyphens are small dashes that break words that fall at the end of a line. Hyphenation diminishes the gaps between words in justified text and reduces ragged right edges in left-aligned text. If a document includes narrow columns, hyphenating the text can help give the pages a cleaner look. To hyphenate a document automatically, click the Hyphenation button in the Page Setup group on the Page Layout tab, and then click Automatic. To set the hyphenation zone—the distance between the margin and the end of the last word in the line—click the Hyphenation button and then click Hyphenation Options to open the Hyphenation dialog box. A smaller hyphenation zone results in a greater number of hyphenated words.

Inserting Page Numbers

If you want to number the pages of a multiple-page document, you can insert a page number field in the top, bottom, or side margin of each page. A **field** is a code that serves as a placeholder for data that changes in a document, such as a page number or the current date. When you use the Page Number button on the Insert tab to add page numbers to a document, you insert the page number field at the top, bottom, or side of any page and Word automatically numbers all the pages in the document for you. You insert a page number field so that page numbers will appear centered between the margins at the bottom of each page in the document.

STEPS

QUICK TIP

Point to Current Position to insert a page number field at the location of the insertion point.

1. **Click the Page Width button in the Zoom group on the View tab, press [Ctrl][Home], click the Insert tab, then click the Page Number button in the Header & Footer group**

   The Page Number menu opens. You use this menu to select the position for the page numbers. If you choose to add a page number field to the top, bottom, or side of a document, a page number will appear on every page in the document. If you choose to insert it in the document at the location of the insertion point, the field will appear on that page only.

2. **Point to Bottom of Page**

   A gallery of formatting and alignment options for page numbers located at the bottom of a page opens, as shown in Figure D-9.

QUICK TIP

To change the location or formatting of page numbers, click the Page Number button, point to a page number location, then select a format from the gallery.

3. **Drag the scroll box down the gallery to view the options, scroll to the top of the gallery, then click Plain Number 2 in the Simple section**

   The page number 1 appears centered in the Footer area at the bottom of the first page, as shown in Figure D-10. The document text is gray, or dimmed, because the Footer area is open. Text that is inserted in a Footer area appears at the bottom of every page in a document.

4. **Double-click the document text, then scroll to the bottom of page 1**

   Double-clicking the document text closes the Footer area. The page number is now dimmed because it is located in the Footer area, which is no longer the active area. When the document is printed, the page numbers appear as normal text. You will learn more about working with the Footer area in the next lesson.

QUICK TIP

To remove page numbers from a document, click the Page Number button, then click Remove Page Numbers.

5. **Scroll down the document to see the page number at the bottom of each page**

   Word automatically numbered each page of the newsletter, and each page number is centered at the bottom of the page. If you want to change the numbering format or to start page numbering with a different number, you can simply click the Page Number button, click Format Page Numbers, and then choose from the options in the Page Number Format dialog box.

6. **Press [Ctrl][Home], then save the document**

Moving around in a long document

Rather than scrolling to move to a different place in a long document, you can use the Browse by Object feature to quickly move the insertion point to a specific location. Browse by Object allows you to browse to the next or previous page, section, line, table, graphic, or other item of the same type in a document. To do this, first click the Select Browse Object button ⊙ below the vertical scroll bar to open a palette of object types. On this palette, click the button for the type of item by which you want to browse, and then click the Next ⬇ or Previous ⬆ buttons to scroll through the items of that type in the document.

FIGURE D-9: Gallery of options for page numbers located at the bottom of the page

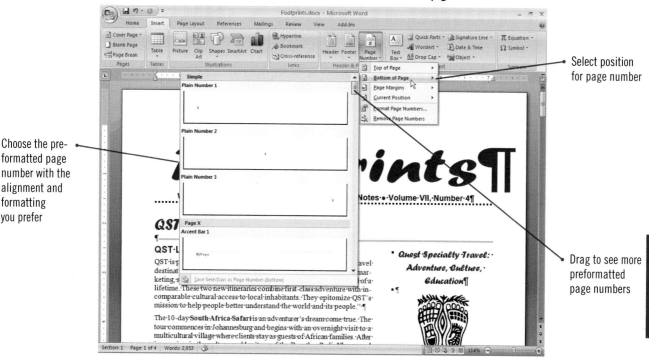

Choose the pre-formatted page number with the alignment and formatting you prefer

Select position for page number

Drag to see more preformatted page numbers

FIGURE D-10: Page number in document

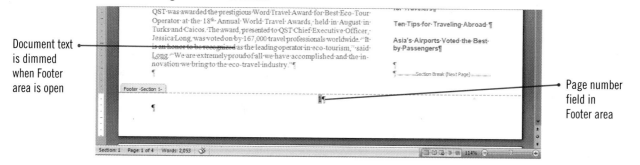

Document text is dimmed when Footer area is open

Page number field in Footer area

Inserting Quick Parts

The Word Quick Parts feature makes it easy to insert reusable pieces of content into a document quickly. The **Quick Parts** items you can insert include fields, such as for the current date or the total number of pages in a document; document property information, such as the author and title of a document; and building blocks, which are customized content that you create, format, and save for future use.

To insert a Quick Part into a document at the location of the insertion point, click the Quick Parts button in the Text group on the Insert tab (or, if headers and footers are open, click the Quick Parts button in the Insert group on the Header and Footer Tools Design tab), and then select the type of Quick Part you want to insert. To insert a field into a document, click Field on the Quick Parts menu that opens, click the name of the field you want to insert in the Field dialog box, and then click OK. Field information is updated automatically each time the document is opened or saved.

To insert a document property, point to Document Property on the Quick Parts menu and then click the property you want to insert. The property is added to the document as a content control and contains the document property information you entered in the Document Information panel. If you did not assign a document property, the content control contains a placeholder, which you can replace with your own text. Once you replace the placeholder text—or edit the document property information that appears in the content control—this text replaces the document property information in the Document Information panel.

To insert a building block, click Building Blocks Organizer on the Quick Parts menu, select the building block you want, and then click Insert. You will learn more about working with building blocks in later lessons.

Adding Headers and Footers

A **header** is text or graphics that appears at the top of every page of a document. A **footer** is text or graphics that appears at the bottom of every page. In longer documents, headers and footers often contain information such as the title of the publication, the title of the chapter, the name of the author, the date, or a page number. You can add headers and footers to a document by double-clicking the top or bottom margin of a document to open the Header and Footer areas, and then inserting text and graphics into them. You can also use the Header or Footer command on the Insert tab to insert predesigned headers and footers that you can modify to include your own information. ████████ You create a header that includes the name of the newsletter and the current date, and add the word "Page" to the footer.

STEPS

1. **Click the Insert tab, then click the Header button in the Header & Footer group**
   A gallery of built-in header designs opens.

2. **Scroll down the gallery to view the header designs, scroll to the top of the gallery, then click Blank**
   The Header and Footer areas open and the document text is dimmed. When the document text is dimmed, it cannot be edited. The Header & Footer Tools Design tab also opens and is the active tab, as shown in Figure D-11. This tab is available whenever the Header and Footer areas are open. The Header and Footer areas of a document are independent of the document itself and must be formatted separately. For example, if you select all the text in a document and then change the font, the header and footer font does not change.

3. **Type Footprints in the content control in the Header area, press [Spacebar] twice, then click the Date & Time button in the Insert group**
   The Date and Time dialog box opens. You use this dialog box to select the format for the date or time and to indicate whether you want the date or time inserted in the document as a field that is updated automatically, or as static text. Word uses the clock on your computer to compute the date and time.

4. **Make sure the Update Automatically check box is selected, then click OK**
   A date field is inserted into the header using the default month/date/year (M/d/yyyy) format. The word "Footprints" and the current date will appear at the top of every page in the document.

5. **Select Footprints and the date, click the Font list arrow on the Mini toolbar, click Forte, click the Center button ≡ on the Mini toolbar, then click in the Header area to deselect the text**
   The text is formatted in Forte and centered in the Header area. In addition to the alignment buttons, you can use the Insert Alignment Tab button in the Position group on the Header & Footer Tools Design tab to left-, center-, and right-align text in the Header and Footer areas with the document margins.

6. **Click the Go to Footer button in the Navigation group**
   The insertion point moves to the Footer area, where a page number field is centered in the Footer area. You can use the buttons in the Navigation group to move quickly between the Header and Footer areas on the current page or to a header or a footer in the previous or next section of the document.

7. **Verify that the insertion point is before the page number field, type Page, press [Spacebar], select the text and the field in the footer, click the Font list arrow on the Mini toolbar, click Forte, then click in the Footer area to deselect the text and field**
   The footer text is formatted in Forte.

8. **Click the Close Header and Footer button in the Close group, save the document, then scroll down until the bottom of page 1 and the top of page 2 appear in the document window**
   The Header and Footer areas close and the header and footer text is dimmed, as shown in Figure D-12.

FIGURE D-11: Header area open

Header & Footer Tools Design tab

Header area is open

Content control

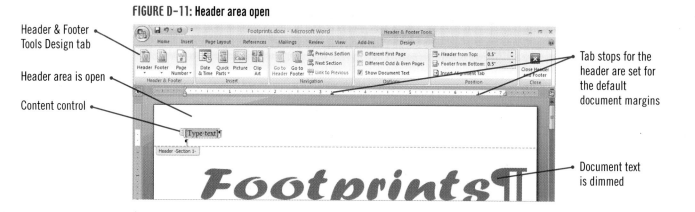

Tab stops for the header are set for the default document margins

Document text is dimmed

FIGURE D-12: Header and footer in document

Page number appears in footer on every page

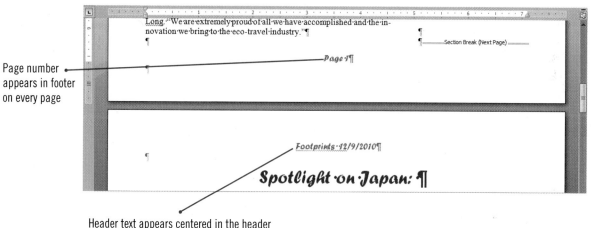

Header text appears centered in the header on every page (your date will differ)

Adding a custom header or footer to the gallery

When you design a header that you want to use again in other documents, you can add it to the Header gallery by saving it as a building block. **Building blocks** are reusable pieces of formatted content or document parts, including headers and footers, page numbers, and text boxes, that are stored in galleries. Building blocks include predesigned content that comes with Word, as well as content that you create and save for future use. For example, you might create a custom header that contains your company name and logo and is formatted using the fonts, border, and colors you use in all company documents.

To add a custom header to the Header gallery, select all the text in the header, including the last paragraph mark, click the Header button, and then click Save Selection to Header Gallery. In the

Create New Building Block dialog box that opens, type a unique name for the header in the Name text box, click the Gallery list arrow and select the appropriate gallery, verify that the Category is General, and then type a brief description of the new header design in the Description text box. This description appears in a ScreenTip when you point to the custom header in the gallery. When you are finished, click OK. The new header appears in the Header gallery under the General category.

To remove a custom header from the Header gallery, right-click it, click Organize and Delete, make sure the appropriate building block is selected in the Building Blocks Organizer that opens, click Delete, click Yes, and then click Close. You can follow the same process to add or remove a custom footer to the Footer gallery.

Editing Headers and Footers

To change header and footer text or to alter the formatting of headers and footers, you must first open the Header and Footer areas. You open headers and footers by using the Edit Header or Edit Footer command in the Header and Footer galleries, or by double-clicking a header or footer in Print Layout view. You modify the header by adding a small circle symbol between "Footprints" and the date. You also add a border under the header text to set it off from the rest of the page. Finally, you remove the header and footer text from the first page of the document.

STEPS

1. **Scroll down, place the insertion point at the top of page 2, position the pointer over the header text at the top of page 2, then double-click**

   The Header and Footer areas open. The insertion point is located in the Header area at the top of page 2.

2. **Place the insertion point between the two spaces after Footprints, click the Insert tab, click the Symbol button in the Symbols group, then click More Symbols in the gallery of recently used symbols**

   The Symbol dialog box opens and is similar to Figure D-13. **Symbols** are special characters, such as graphics, shapes, and foreign language characters, that you can insert into a document. The symbols shown in Figure D-13 are the symbols included with the (normal text) font. You can use the Font list arrow on the Symbols tab to view the symbols included with each font on your computer.

3. **Scroll the list of symbols if necessary to locate the bullet symbol shown in Figure D-13, select the bullet symbol, click Insert, then click Close**

   A bullet symbol is added at the location of the insertion point.

4. **With the insertion point in the header text, click the Home tab, click the Bottom Border list arrow in the Paragraph group, then click Borders and Shading**

   The Borders and Shading dialog box opens.

5. **Click the Borders tab if it is not already selected, click Custom in the Setting section, click the dotted line in the Style list box (the second line style), click the Width list arrow, click 2¼ pt, click the Bottom border button in the Preview section, make sure Paragraph is selected in the Apply to list box, click OK, double-click the document text to close the Header and Footer areas, then click the Show/Hide button ¶ in the Paragraph group**

   A dotted line border is added below the header text, as shown in Figure D-14.

6. **Press [Ctrl][Home] to move the insertion point to the beginning of the document**

   The newsletter already includes the name of the document at the top of the first page, making the header information redundant. You can modify headers and footers so that the header and footer text does not appear on the first page of a document or a section.

7. **Position the pointer over the header text at the top of page 1, then double-click**

   The Header and Footer areas open. The Options group on the Header & Footer Tools Design tab includes options for creating a different header and footer for the first page of a document or a section, and for creating different headers and footers for odd- and even-numbered pages. For example, in a document with facing pages, such as a magazine, you might want the publication title to appear in the left-page header and the publication date to appear in the right-page header.

8. **Click the Different First Page check box to select it, then click the Close Header and Footer button**

   The header and footer text is removed from the Header and Footer areas on the first page.

9. **Scroll to see the header and footer on pages 2, 3, and 4, then save the document**

Formatting Documents

FIGURE D-13: Symbol dialog box

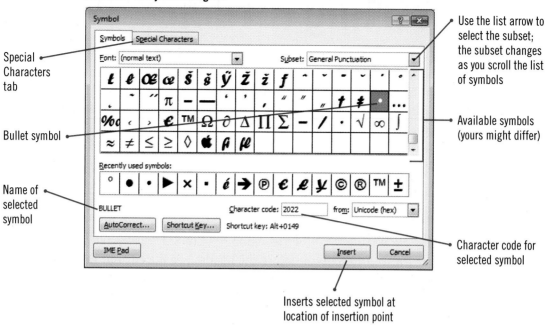

Special Characters tab

Use the list arrow to select the subset; the subset changes as you scroll the list of symbols

Bullet symbol

Available symbols (yours might differ)

Name of selected symbol

Character code for selected symbol

Inserts selected symbol at location of insertion point

FIGURE D-14: Symbol and border added to header

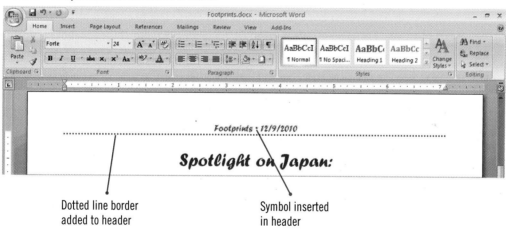

Dotted line border added to header

Symbol inserted in header

Creating an AutoText building block

AutoText is a type of building block that allows you to store text and graphics that you use frequently so that you can easily insert them in a document. AutoText entries are stored in the Building Blocks Organizer, and each AutoText entry has a unique name, so that you can find it when you need it. For example, you might want to store your company letterhead or a list of staff names and titles, so that you can easily insert them in a document without having to retype or reformat the information.

To create a custom AutoText entry, enter the text or graphic you want to store—such as a company letterhead or staff list—in a document, select it, click the Quick Parts button in the Text group on the Insert tab, and then click Save Selection to Quick Part Gallery. In the Create New Building Block dialog box that opens, enter a unique name for the new building block, select AutoText for the Gallery, enter any other relevant information, such as a description, and then click OK to save the text or graphic as an AutoText entry in the Building Blocks Organizer.

To insert an AutoText entry or any other building block into a document at the location of the insertion point, click the Quick Parts button, click Building Blocks Organizer, scroll the list of building blocks to find the building block you want, select it, and then click Insert.

Inserting a Table

Adding a table to a document is a useful way to illustrate information that is intended for quick reference and analysis. A **table** is a grid of columns and rows of cells that you can fill with text and graphics. A **cell** is the box formed by the intersection of a column and a row. The lines that divide the columns and rows of a table and help you see the grid-like structure of the table are called **borders**. A simple way to insert a table into a document is to use the Insert Table command on the Insert tab. This command allows you to determine the dimensions and format of a table before it is inserted. You add a table showing the details for the QST tours mentioned by name in the newsletter.

STEPS

1. **Click the Show/Hide button ¶ in the Paragraph group, then scroll until the heading Featured Tour Details on page 3 is at the top of your document window**

2. **Place the insertion point before the heading Featured Tour Details, click the Page Layout tab, click the Breaks button in the Page Setup group, then click Continuous**
   A continuous section break is inserted before the heading. The document now includes six sections, with the heading Featured Tour Details in the fifth section.

3. **Click the Columns button in the Page Setup group, then click One**
   Section 5 is formatted as a single column.

4. **Place the insertion point before the second paragraph mark below the heading, click the Insert tab, click the Table button in the Tables group, then click Insert Table**
   The Insert Table dialog box opens. You use this dialog box to create a blank table with a set number of columns and rows, and to choose an option for sizing the width of the columns in the table.

5. **Type 4 in the Number of columns text box, press [Tab], type 6 in the Number of rows text box, make sure the Fixed column width option button is selected, then click OK**
   A blank table with four columns and six rows is inserted in the document at the location of the insertion point. The insertion point is in the upper-left cell of the table, the first cell in the header row. When the insertion point is in a table, the Table Tools Design tab becomes the active tab.

6. **Type Tour in the first cell in the first row, press [Tab], type Season, press [Tab], type Length, press [Tab], type Cost, then press [Tab]**
   Pressing [Tab] moves the insertion point to the next cell in the row. At the end of a row, pressing [Tab] moves the insertion point to the first cell in the next row. You can also click in a cell to move the insertion point to it.

7. **Type the text shown in Figure D-15 in the table cells, pressing [Tab] to move from cell to cell**
   Don't be concerned if the text wraps to the next line in a cell as you type: you will adjust the width of the columns after you finish typing.

8. **Click the Table Tools Layout tab, click the AutoFit button in the Cell Size group, click AutoFit Contents, click the AutoFit button again, then click AutoFit Window**
   The width of the table columns is adjusted to fit the text and then the window. You modify the structure of a table using the commands on the Table Tools Layout tab. To edit the text in a table, simply place the insertion point in a cell and then type.

9. **Click the Table Tools Design tab, click the More button ▽ in the Table Styles group to expand the Table Styles gallery, click the Light List – Accent 2 style, then clear the First Column check box in the Table Style Options group**
   The Light List - Accent 2 style table style is applied to the table, as shown in Figure D-16. A **table style** includes format settings for the text, borders, and shading in a table.

10. **Click the View tab, click the Two Pages button, then save the document**
    Completed pages 3 and 4 are shown in Figure D-17.

Formatting Documents

FIGURE D-15: Text in table

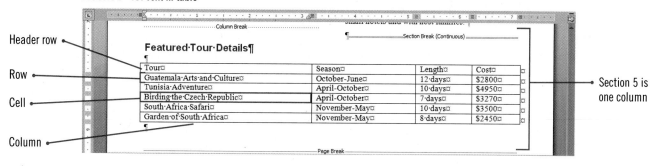

Header row → Featured Tour Details¶

Row →

Cell →

Column →

Section 5 is
one column →

FIGURE D-16: Completed table

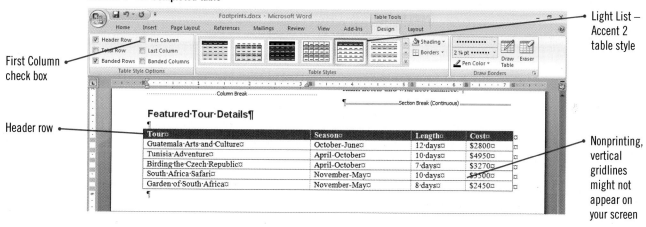

First Column
check box →

Light List –
Accent 2
table style →

Header row → Featured Tour Details¶

Nonprinting,
vertical
gridlines
might not
appear on
your screen →

FIGURE D-17: Completed pages 3 and 4

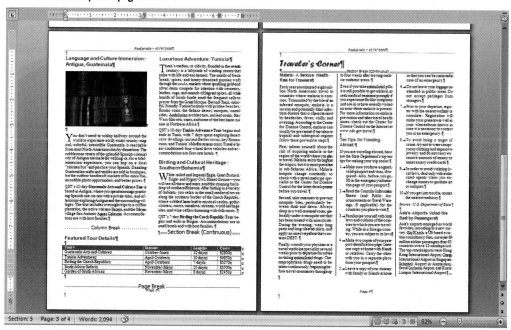

Inserting Clip Art

Clip art is a collection of graphic images that you can insert into a document. Clip art images are stored in the **Clip Organizer**, a library of the **clips**—media files such as graphics, photographs, sounds, movies, and animations—that come with Word. You can add a clip to a document using the Clip Art command on the Insert tab. Once you insert a clip art image, you can wrap text around it, resize it, enhance it, and move it to a different location. You illustrate the second page of the newsletter with a clip art image.

QUICK TIP

If you are working with an active Internet connection, your search results will include clips from the Microsoft Office Online Web site.

1. **Click the** Page Width button **in the Zoom group, scroll to the top of page 2, place the insertion point before the second body paragraph, which begins With its blend..., click the** Insert tab, **then click the** Clip Art button **in the Illustrations group**

   The Clip Art task pane opens. You can use this task pane to search for clips related to a keyword.

2. **Select the text in the Search for text box if necessary, type** pagoda, **click the** Search in list arrow, **make sure** Everywhere **has a check mark, click the** Results should be list arrow, **make sure** All media types **has a check mark, then click** Go

   Clips that include the keyword "pagoda" appear in the Clip Art task pane, as shown in Figure D-18.

TROUBLE

Select a different clip if the clip shown in Figure D-18 is not available to you. If you are not working with an active Internet connection, use the keyword "Asia".

3. **Point to the** clip **called out in Figure D-18, click the** list arrow **that appears next to the clip, click** Insert **on the menu, then close the Clip Art task pane**

   The clip is inserted at the location of the insertion point. When a graphic is selected, the active tab changes to the Picture Tools Format tab. This tab contains commands used to adjust, enhance, arrange, and size graphics. Until you apply text wrapping to a graphic, it is part of the line of text in which it was inserted (an **inline graphic**). To move a graphic independently of text, you must wrap the text around it to make it a **floating graphic**, which can be moved anywhere on a page.

4. **Click the** Position button **in the Arrange group, then click** Position in Middle Right with Square Text Wrapping

   The photo is moved to the middle right side of the page and the text wraps around it. The white circles that appear on the square edges of the graphic are the **sizing handles**. Applying text wrapping to the photo made it a floating graphic.

5. **Click the** Shape Width up arrow **in the Size group until** 3.8" **appears**

   The photo is enlarged. Notice that when you increased the width of the photo, the height increased proportionally. You can also resize a graphic proportionally by dragging a corner sizing handle.

QUICK TIP

To crop a graphic or to change its scale using precise measurements, click the launcher in the Size group, then adjust the settings on the Size tab in the Size dialog box.

6. **Scroll to the top of page 2, position the pointer over the graphic, when the pointer changes to ⬚ drag the graphic up and to the left so it is centered on the page and its top is just under the second line of text as shown in Figure D-19, then release the mouse button**

   The graphic is moved up and is roughly centered between the margins.

7. **Click the** Position button, **click** More Layout Options, **click the** Picture Position tab **if necessary, click the** Alignment option button **in the Horizontal section, click the** Alignment list arrow, **click** Centered, **then click** OK

   The Advanced Layout dialog box allows you to position a graphic using precise measurements.

8. **Click the** More button ⬇ **in the Picture Styles group, select the** Soft Edge Oval picture style, **click the** Text Wrapping button **in the Arrange group, click** Tight, **then deselect the graphic**

   A picture style is applied to the photo and the text wraps tight to the oval shape.

TROUBLE

If page 3 is a blank page or contains text continued from page 2, reduce the size of the graphic on page 2.

9. **Click the** View tab, **then click the** Two Pages button

   The completed pages 1 and 2 are displayed, as shown in Figure D-20.

10. **Click the** Page Width button, **press** [Ctrl][End], **press** [Enter], **type your name, save your changes, print the document, then close the document and exit Word**

FIGURE D-18: Clip Art task pane

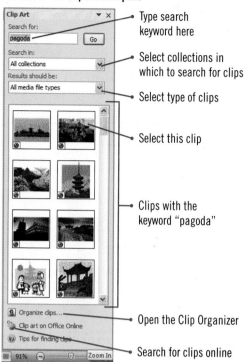

- Type search keyword here
- Select collections in which to search for clips
- Select type of clips
- Select this clip
- Clips with the keyword "pagoda"
- Open the Clip Organizer
- Search for clips online

FIGURE D-19: Graphic being moved to a new location

- Faded image shows graphic as it is being dragged; position the graphic as shown
- Sizing handles

FIGURE D-20: Completed pages 1 and 2 of newsletter

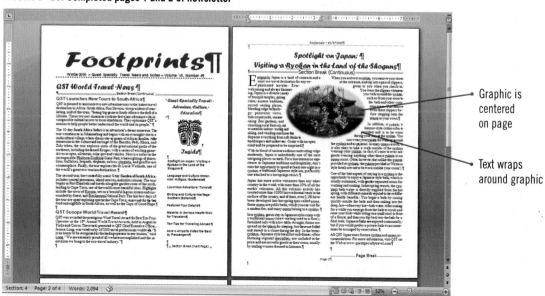

- Graphic is centered on page
- Text wraps around graphic

Practice

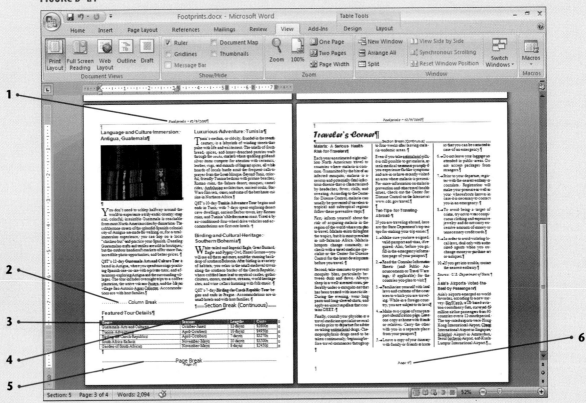

SAM

If you have a SAM user profile, you may have access to hands-on instruction, practice, and assessment of the skills covered in this unit. Log in to your SAM account (http://sam2007.course.com/) to launch any assigned training activities or exams that relate to the skills covered in this unit.

▼ CONCEPTS REVIEW

Label each element shown in Figure D-21.

FIGURE D-21

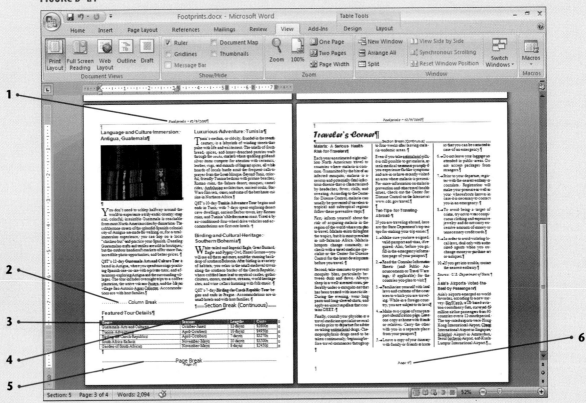

Match each term with the statement that best describes it.

7. **Footer**
8. **Header**
9. **Manual page break**
10. **Section break**
11. **Field**
12. **Inline graphic**
13. **Floating graphic**
14. **Margin**

a. An image that is inserted as part of a line of text

b. The blank area between the edge of the text and the edge of the page

c. A formatting mark that divides a document into parts that can be formatted differently

d. Text or graphics that appear at the bottom of every page in a document

e. A placeholder for information that changes

f. A formatting mark that forces the text following the mark to begin at the top of the next page

g. Text or graphics that appear at the top of every page in a document

h. An image to which text wrapping has been applied

Select the best answer from the list of choices.

15. **Which type of break can you insert if you want to force text to begin on the next page?**
    a. Automatic page break
    b. Continuous section break
    c. Text wrapping break
    d. Next page section break

16. **Which type of break do you insert if you want to balance the columns in a section?**
    a. Column break
    b. Continuous section break
    c. Manual page break
    d. Text wrapping break

17. **Which of the following cannot be inserted using the Quick Parts command?**
    a. AutoText building block
    b. Document property
    c. Page number field
    d. Page break

18. **Which of the following do documents with mirror margins always have?**
    a. Gutters
    b. Landscape orientation
    c. Inside and outside margins
    d. Different first page headers and footers

19. **What name describes formatted pieces of content that are stored in galleries?**
    a. Header
    b. Field
    c. Building Block
    d. Property

20. **What must you do to change an inline graphic to a floating graphic?**
    a. Apply text wrapping to the graphic
    b. Resize the graphic
    c. Anchor the graphic
    d. Move the graphic

▼ SKILLS REVIEW

1. **Set document margins.**
   a. Start Word, open the file WD D-2.docx from the drive and folder where you store your Data Files, then save it as Greenwood Fitness.
   b. Change the top and bottom margins settings to Moderate: 1" top and bottom, and .75" left and right.
   c. Save your changes to the document.

2. **Divide a document into sections.**
   a. Hide the white space in the document by moving the pointer to the top of a page, then double-clicking with the Hide White Space pointer that appears.
   b. Turn on the display of formatting marks, then customize the status bar to display sections if necessary.
   c. Scroll down, then insert a continuous section break before the Facilities heading.
   d. Format the text in section 2 in two columns, then save your changes to the document.

3. **Insert page breaks.**
   a. Insert a manual page break before the heading Welcome to the Greenwood Fitness Center!.
   b. Scroll down and insert a manual page break before the heading Services.
   c. Scroll down and insert a manual page break before the heading Membership.
   d. Show the white space in the document by moving the pointer over the thick black line that separates the pages, and then double-clicking with the Show White Space pointer that appears.
   e. Press [Ctrl][Home], then save your changes to the document.

4. **Format columns.**
   a. On page 2, select Facilities and the paragraph mark below it, use the Columns button to format the selected text as one column, then center Facilities on the page.
   b. Balance the columns on page 2 by inserting a continuous section break at the bottom of the second column.
   c. On page 3, select Services and the paragraph mark below it, format the selected text as one column, then center the text.
   d. Balance the columns on page 3.
   e. On page 4, select Membership and the paragraph mark below it, format the selected text as one column, then center the text.
   f. Insert a column break before the Membership Cards heading, press [Ctrl][Home], then save your changes to the document.

5. Insert page numbers.

   a. Insert page numbers in the document at the bottom of the page. Select the Plain Number 2 page number style from the gallery.

   b. Scroll through the document to view the page numbers on each page, then save your changes to the document.

6. Add headers and footers.

   a. Double-click the margin at the top of a page to open the Header and Footer areas.

   b. With the insertion point in the Header area, click the Quick Parts button in the Insert Group on the Header & Footer Tools Design tab, point to Document Property, then click Author.

   c. Replace the text in the Author content control with your name, press [End] to move the insertion point out of the content control, then press [Spacebar]. (*Note*: If your name does not appear in the header, right-click the Author content control, click Remove Content Control, then type your name in the header.)

   d. Click the Insert Alignment Tab button in the Position group, select the Right option button and keep the alignment relative to the margin, then click OK in the dialog box to move the insertion point to the right margin.

   e. Use the Insert Date and Time command in the Insert group to insert the current date as static text.

   f. Move the insertion point to the Footer area.

   g. Double-click the page number to select it, then format the page number in bold italic.

   h. Close headers and footers, view the header and footer on each page, then save your changes to the document.

7. Edit headers and footers.

   a. Open headers and footers, then apply italic to the text in the header.

   b. Move the insertion point to the Footer area, then change the footer style to Plain Number 3. (*Hint*: Click the Page Number button, point to Bottom of Page, then click the new style.)

   c. Use the Symbol command on the Insert tab to open the Symbol dialog box, insert a black right-pointing triangle symbol (character code: 25BA), then close the Symbol dialog box. (*Note*: Select a different symbol if 25BA is not available to you.)

   d. Use the Header & Footer Tools Design tab to create a different header and footer for the first page of the document.

   e. Scroll to the beginning of the document, type your name in the First Page Header area, then apply italic to your name.

   f. Close headers and footers, preview the header and footer on each page in Print Preview, close Print Preview, then save your changes to the document.

8. Insert a table.

   a. On page 4, select the word Table at the end of the Membership Rates section, press [Delete], open the Insert Table dialog box, then create a table with two columns and five rows.

   b. Apply the green Light List - Accent 3 table style to the table.

   c. Press [Tab] to leave the first cell in the header row blank, then type Rate.

   d. Press [Tab], then type the following text in the table, pressing [Tab] to move from cell to cell.

Enrollment/Individual	$100
Enrollment/Couple	$150
Monthly membership/Individual	$35
Monthly membership/Couple	$60

   e. With the insertion point in the table, right-click the table, use the AutoFit command to AutoFit to Contents, and then AutoFit to Window.

   f. Save your changes to the document.

9. Insert clip art.

a. On page 1, place the insertion point in the second blank paragraph below A Rehabilitation and Exercise Facility. (*Hint*: Place the insertion point to the left of the paragraph mark.)

b. Open the Clip Art task pane. Search for clips related to the keyword fitness.

c. Insert the clip shown in Figure D-22. (*Note*: An active Internet connection is needed to select the clip shown in the figure. Select a different clip if this one is not available to you. If you are working offline, you might need to search using a keyword such as sports.)

d. Select the graphic, then drag the lower-right sizing handle down and to the right so that the graphic is about 3.75" wide and 3.1" tall. Size the graphic so that all the text and the manual page break fit on page 1. You can use the Shape Height and Shape Width text boxes in the Size group on the Format tab to size the graphic precisely if necessary.

e. Apply a Drop Shadow Rectangle picture style to the graphic.

f. Move the insertion point to page 3, search for clips related to the keyword massage, then insert an appropriate clip. Select a clip that works with the design of the document.

g. Use the Position command to position the clip at the bottom center of the document with square text wrapping.

h. Save your changes to the document. Preview the document, print a copy, then close the document and exit Word.

Word 2007

FIGURE D-22

The Greenwood Fitness Center

A Rehabilitation and Exercise Facility

Member Services

Hours of Operation

Monday – Friday:
6:00 a.m. to 10:00 p.m.

Saturday:
7:00 a.m. to 10:00 p.m.

Sunday:
1:00 p.m. to 5:00 p.m.

▼ INDEPENDENT CHALLENGE 1

You are the owner of a small business in White Horse, Yukon Territory, called Blue Chair Catering. You have begun work on the text for a brochure advertising your business and are now ready to lay out the pages and prepare the final copy. The brochure will be printed on both sides of an 8½" × 11" sheet of paper, and folded in thirds.

a. Start Word, open the file WD D-3.docx from the drive and folder where you store your Data Files, then save it as **Blue Chair**. Read the document to get a feel for its contents.

b. Change the page orientation to landscape, and change all four margins to .6".

c. Format the document in three columns of equal width.

d. Insert a next page section break before the heading **Catering Services**.

e. On page 1, insert column breaks before the headings **Sample Tuscan Banquet Menu** and **Sample Indian Banquet Menu**.

f. Change the column spacing on the first page to .4", add lines between the columns on the first page, then center the text in the columns.

g. Double-click the bottom margin to open the footer area, create a different header and footer for the first page, then type **Call for custom menus designed to your taste and budget** in the First Page Footer area.

h. Center the text in the footer area, format it in 20-point Papyrus, with a Blue, Accent 1 font color, then close headers and footers.

i. On page 2, insert a column break before Your Name. Press [Enter] as many times as necessary to move the contact information to the bottom of the second column. Be sure all five lines of the contact information are in column 2 and do not flow to the next column.

j. Replace Your Name with your name, then center the contact information in the column.

k. Insert a column break at the bottom of the second column. Then, type the text shown in Figure D-23 in the third column and apply the No Spacing style. Refer to the figure as you follow the instructions for formatting the text in the third column.

l. Format Blue Chair Catering in 30-point Papyrus, bold.

m. Format the remaining text in 12-point Papyrus. Center the text in the third column.

n. Insert the clip art graphic shown in Figure D-23 or another appropriate clip art graphic. Do not wrap text around the graphic.

o. Resize the graphic and add or remove blank paragraphs in the third column of your brochure so that the spacing between elements roughly matches the spacing shown in Figure D-23.

Advanced Challenge Exercise

- Insert a different appropriate clip art graphic at the bottom of the first column on page 2.
- Apply text wrapping to the graphic, then resize the graphic and position it so it enhances the design of the brochure.
- Apply a suitable picture style to the graphic.

p. Save your changes, preview the brochure in Print Preview, then print a copy. If possible, print the two pages of the brochure back to back so that the brochure can be folded in thirds.

q. Close the document and exit Word.

FIGURE D-23

Blue Chair Catering

Complete catering services available for all types of events. Menus and estimates provided upon request.

▼ INDEPENDENT CHALLENGE 2

You work in the Campus Safety Department at Pacific State College. You have written the text for an informational flyer about parking regulations on campus, and now you need to format the flyer so it is attractive and readable.

a. Start Word, open the file WD D-4.docx from the drive and folder where you store your Data Files, then save it as **Pacific Parking FAQ**. Read the document to get a feel for its contents.

b. Change all four margins to .7".

c. Insert a continuous section break before **1. May I bring a car to school?** (*Hint:* Place the insertion point before May.)

d. Scroll down and insert a next page section break before **Sample Parking Permit**.

e. Format the text in section 2 in three columns of equal width with .3" of space between the columns.

f. Hyphenate the document using the automatic hyphenation feature. (*Hint:* If the Hyphenation feature is not installed on your computer, skip this step.)

g. Add a 3-point dotted-line bottom border to the blank paragraph under Pacific State College. (*Hint:* Place the insertion point before the paragraph mark under Pacific State College.)

h. Open the Header area and insert your name in the header. Right-align your name and format it in 10-point Arial.

i. Add the following text to the footer, inserting symbols between words as indicated:
Parking and Shuttle Service Office • 54 Buckley Street • Pacific State College • 942-555-2227.

j. Format the footer text in 9-point Arial Black and center it in the footer. Use a different font if Arial Black is not available to you. If necessary, adjust the font and font size so that the entire address fits on one line.

FIGURE D-24

k. Apply a 3-point dotted-line border above the footer text. Make sure to apply the border to the paragraph.

l. Balance the columns in section 2.

Frequently Asked Questions (FAQ)
Department of Campus Safety
Parking & Shuttle Service Office
Pacific State College

m. Add the clip art graphic shown in Figure D-24 (or another appropriate clip art graphic) to the upper-right corner of the document, above the border. Make sure the graphic does not obscure the border. (*Hint:* Apply text wrapping to the graphic before positioning it.)

n. Place the insertion point on page 2 (which is section 4). Change the left and right margins in section 4 to 1". Also change the page orientation of section 4 to landscape.

o. Change the vertical alignment of section 4 to center. (*Hint:* Use the Layout tab in the Page Setup dialog box.)

p. Apply a table style to the table similar to the style shown in Figure D-25.

q. Save your changes, preview the flyer in Print Preview, then print a copy. If possible, print the two pages of the flyer back to back.

r. Close the document and exit Word.

FIGURE D-25

Sample Parking Permit

Pacific State College
Office of Parking and Shuttle Service

2010-11 Student Parking Permit

License number:	VA 498 359
Make:	Subaru
Model:	Forester
Year:	2004
Color:	Red
Permit Issue Date:	September 8, 2010
Permit Expiration Date:	June 4, 2011

Restrictions:
Parking is permitted in the Pacific State College Greene Street lot 24 hours a day, 7 days a week. Shuttle service is available from the Greene Street lot to campus from 7 a.m. to 7 p.m. Monday through Friday. Parking is also permitted in any on-campus lot from 4:30 p.m. Friday to midnight Sunday.

▼ INDEPENDENT CHALLENGE 3

A book publisher would like to publish an article you wrote on stormwater pollution in Australia as a chapter in a forthcoming book called *Environmental Issues for the New Millennium*. The publisher has requested that you format your article like a book chapter before submitting it for publication, and has provided you with a style sheet.

a. Start Word, open the file WD D-5.docx from the drive and folder where you store your Data Files, then save it as Chapter 9.

b. Change the font of the entire document to 11-point High Tower Text. If this font is not available to you, select a different font suitable for the pages of a book. Change the alignment to justified.

c. Change the paper size to 6" × 9".

d. Create mirror margins. (*Hint*: Use the Multiple Pages list arrow.) Change the top and bottom margins to .8", change the inside margin to .4", change the outside margin to .6", and create a .3" gutter to allow room for the book's binding.

e. Change the Zoom level to Page Width, open the Header and Footer areas, then apply the setting to create different headers and footers for odd- and even-numbered pages.

f. In the odd-page header, type Chapter 9, insert a symbol of your choice, then type Stormwater Pollution in the Fairy Creek Catchment.

g. Format the header text in 9-point High Tower Text italic, then right-align the text.

h. In the even-page header, type your name, insert a symbol of your choice, then insert a date field that updates automatically. (*Hint*: Scroll down or use the Next Section button to move the insertion point to the even-page header.)

i. Change the format of the date to include just the month and the year. (*Hint*: Right-click the date field, click Edit Field, then type MMMM yyyy in the Date Formats text box.)

j. Format the header text in 9-point High Tower Text italic. The even-page header should be left-aligned.

k. Insert a left-aligned page number field in the even-page footer area, format it in 10-point High Tower Text, insert a right-aligned page number field in the odd-page footer area, then format it in 10-point High Tower Text.

l. Format the page numbers so that the first page of your chapter, which is Chapter 9 in the book, begins on page 135. (*Hint*: Select a page number field, click the Page Number button, then click Format Page Numbers.)

m. Go to the beginning of the document, press [Enter] 10 times, type Chapter 9: Stormwater Pollution in the Fairy Creek Catchment, press [Enter] twice, type your name, then press [Enter] twice.

n. Format the chapter title in 16-point Calibri bold, format your name in 14-point Calibri, then left-align the title text and your name, as shown in Figure D-26.

FIGURE D-26

Chapter 9 • Stormwater Pollution in the Fairy Creek Catchment

Chapter 9: Stormwater Pollution in the Fairy Creek Catchment

Your Name

Australia's beaches are a key component of its cultural identity, but this symbol is not as clean as could be. Beach pollution is—or should be—an issue of great concern to the beach-going public. There are many reasons why beaches become polluted. Oil spills, industrial discharge of toxic waste, trash, and even unsafe levels of treated sewage are well-known and obvious sources of pollution. However, according to the Environmental Protection Agency (EPA), the most common cause of beach pollution is contaminated stormwater.

The environmental movement's concern about beach pollution has shifted from sewerage to stormwater. This change in focus is in large part due to increased water quality testing, which has revealed stormwater as the major culprit. In response, in 1997 the state government created the Waterways Package, a plan to improve the quality of the state's waterways. The state mandated that every council have a stormwater management plan aimed at achieving clean, healthy waterways, and allocated $60 million as part of a stormwater trust fund to improve water quality.

Stormwater causes beach pollution because it becomes contaminated with pollutants as it travels through the stormwater system. These pollutants can include dog droppings, automobile fluids, cigarette butts, litter, runoff from streets, and anything that is washed into the stormwater system. Stormwater is then piped into catchments (areas of land that drain to a common point) that empty unfiltered into the sea. This problem is exacerbated by land development, which alters

135

▼ INDEPENDENT CHALLENGE 3 (CONTINUED)

Advanced Challenge Exercise

- Scroll to page 4 in the document, place the insertion point at the end of the paragraph above the Potential health effects... heading, press [Enter] twice, type **Table 1: Total annual pollutant loads per year in the Fairy Creek Catchment**, format the text as bold, then press [Enter] twice.
- Insert a table with four columns and four rows.
- Type the text shown in Figure D-27 in the table. Do not be concerned when the text wraps to the next line in a cell.
- Apply the Light List Table style. Make sure the text in the header row is bold, then remove any bold formatting from the text in the remaining rows.
- AutoFit the table to fit the contents, then AutoFit the table to fit the window.

FIGURE D-27

Area	Nitrogen	Phosphorus	Suspended solids
Fairy Creek	9.3 tonnes	1.2 tonnes	756.4 tonnes
Durras Arm	6.2 tonnes	.9 tonnes	348.2 tonnes
Cabbage Tree Creek	9.8 tonnes	2.3 tonnes	485.7 tonnes

o. Save your changes, preview the chapter in Print Preview, print the first four pages of the chapter, then close the document and exit Word.

▼ REAL LIFE INDEPENDENT CHALLENGE

One of the most common opportunities to use the page layout features of Word is when formatting a research paper. The format recommended by the *MLA Handbook for Writers of Research Papers*, a style guide that includes information on preparing, writing, and formatting research papers, is the standard format used by many schools, colleges, and universities. In this independent challenge, you will research the MLA (Modern Language Association) guidelines for formatting a research paper and use the guidelines you find to prepare a sample research report.

a. Use your favorite search engine to search the Web for information on the MLA guidelines for formatting a research report. Use the keywords **MLA Style** and **research paper format** to conduct your search.

b. Look for information on the proper formatting for the following aspects of a research paper: paper size, margins, title page or first page of the report, line spacing, paragraph indentation, and page numbers. Print the information you find.

c. Start Word, open the file WD D-6.docx from the drive and folder where you store your Data Files, then save it as **Research Paper**. Using the information you learned, format this document as a research report.

d. Adjust the margins, set the line spacing, and add page numbers to the document in the format recommended by the MLA. Use **The Maori History of New Zealand** as the title for your sample report, use your name as the author name, and make up information about the course and instructor, if necessary. Make sure to format the title page exactly as the MLA style dictates.

e. Format the remaining text as the body of the research report. Indent the first line of each paragraph rather than use quadruple spacing between paragraphs.

f. Save the document, print a copy, close the document, then exit Word.

Open the file WD D-7.docx from the drive and folder where you store your Data Files, then modify it to create the article shown in Figure D-28. (*Hint*: Change all four margins to .6". To locate the flower clip art image, search using the keyword **dahlias**, and be sure only the Photographs check box in the Results should be in list box in the Clip Art task pane has a check mark. Select a different clip if the clip shown in the figure is not available to you.) Save the document with the file-name **Gardener's Corner**, then print a copy.

FIGURE D-28

GARDENER'S CORNER

Putting a Perennial Garden to Bed

By Your Name

A certain sense of peace descends when a perennial garden is put to bed for the season. The plants are safely tucked in against the elements, and the garden is ready to welcome the first signs of life. When the work is done, you can sit back and anticipate the bright blooms of spring. Many gardeners are uncertain of how to close a perennial garden. This week's column demystifies the process.

Clean up

Garden clean up can be a gradual process—plants will deteriorate at different rates, allowing you to do a little bit each week.

- Edge beds and borders and remove stakes and other plant supports.
- Dig and divide irises, daylilies, and other early bloomers.
- Cut back plants when foliage starts to deteriorate, then rake all debris out of the garden and pull any weeds that remain.

Plant perennials

Fall is the perfect time to plant perennials! The warm, sunny days and cool nights provide optimal conditions for new root growth.

- Dig deeply and enhance soil with organic matter.
- Use a good starter fertilizer to speed up new root growth.
- Untangle the roots of new plants before planting.
- Water deeply after planting as the weather dictates, and keep plants moist for several days after planting.

Add compost

Organic matter is the key ingredient to healthy garden soil. Composting adds nutrients to the soil, helps the soil retain water and nutrients, and keeps the soil well aerated. If you take care of the soil, your plants will become strong and disease resistant. Before adding compost, use an iron rake to loosen the top few inches of soil. Spread a one to two inch layer of compost over the entire garden— the best compost is made up of yard waste and kitchen scraps—and then refrain from stepping on the area and compacting the soil.

To mulch or not to mulch?

Winter protection for perennial beds can only help plants survive the winter. Winter mulch prevents the freezing and thawing cycles, which cause plants to heave and eventually die. Here's what works and what doesn't:

- Always apply mulch after the ground is frozen.
- Never apply generic hay because is contains billions of weed seeds. Also, whole leaves and bark mulch hold too much moisture.
- Use a loose material to allow air filtration. Straw and salt marsh hay are excellent choices for mulch. If using leaves, use only stiff leaves such as Oak or Beech. Soft leaves, such as Maple, make it difficult for air and water to filtrate.
- Remove the winter mulch in the spring as soon as new growth begins.

For copies of earlier Gardener's Corner columns, call 1-800-555-3827.

Getting Started with Excel 2007

Files You Will Need:

EX A-1.xlsx

EX A-2.xlsx

EX A-3.xlsx

EX A-4.xlsx

EX A-5.xlsx

In this unit, you will learn how spreadsheet software helps you analyze data and make business decisions, even if you aren't a math pro. You'll become familiar with the different elements of a spreadsheet and learn your way around the Excel program window. You will also work in an Excel worksheet and make simple calculations. You have been hired as an assistant at Quest Specialty Travel (QST), a company offering tours that immerse travelers in regional culture. You report to Grace Wong, the vice president of finance. As Grace's assistant, you create worksheets to analyze data from various divisions of the company, so you can help her make sound decisions on company expansion and investments.

OBJECTIVES

Understand spreadsheet software

Tour the Excel 2007 window

Understand formulas

Enter labels and values and use AutoSum

Edit cell entries

Enter and edit a simple formula

Switch worksheet views

Choose print options

Understanding Spreadsheet Software

Microsoft Excel is the electronic spreadsheet program within Microsoft Office. An **electronic spreadsheet** is an application you use to perform numeric calculations and to analyze and present numeric data. One advantage of spreadsheet programs over pencil and paper is that your calculations are updated automatically, so you can change entries without having to manually recalculate. Table A-1 shows some of the common business tasks people accomplish using Excel. In Excel, the electronic spreadsheet you work in is called a **worksheet**, and is contained in a file called a **workbook**, which has the file extension .xlsx. 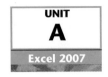 At Quest Specialty Travel, you use Excel extensively to track finances and manage corporate data.

When you use Excel, you have the ability to:

- **Enter data quickly and accurately**

  With Excel, you can enter information faster and more accurately than with pencil and paper. Figure A-1 shows a payroll worksheet created using pencil and paper. Figure A-2 shows the same worksheet created using Excel. Equations were added to calculate the hours and pay. You can copy the payroll deductions that don't change from quarter to quarter, then use Excel to calculate the gross and net payroll by supplying unique data and formulas for each quarter. You can also quickly create charts and other elements to help visualize how the payroll is distributed.

- **Recalculate data easily**

  Fixing typing errors or updating data is easy in Excel. In the payroll example, if you receive updated hours for an employee, you just enter the new hours and Excel recalculates the pay.

- **Perform what-if analysis**

  The ability to change data and quickly view the recalculated results gives you the power to make informed business decisions. For instance, if you're considering raising the hourly rate for an entry-level tour guide from $12.50 to $15.00, you can enter the new value in the worksheet and immediately see the impact on the overall payroll as well as on the individual employee. Any time you use a worksheet to ask the question "what if?" you are performing **what-if analysis**. Excel also includes a Scenario Manager where you can name and save different what-if versions of your worksheet.

- **Change the appearance of information**

  Excel provides powerful features for making information visually appealing and easier to understand. You can format text and numbers in different fonts, colors, and styles to make it stand out.

- **Create charts**

  Excel makes it easy to create charts based on worksheet information. Charts are updated automatically in Excel whenever data changes. The worksheet in Figure A-2 includes a 3-D pie chart.

- **Share information**

  It's easy for everyone at QST to collaborate in Excel, using the company intranet, the Internet, or a network storage device. For example, you can complete the weekly payroll that your boss, Grace Wong, started creating. You can also take advantage of collaboration tools such as shared workbooks, so that multiple people can edit a workbook simultaneously.

- **Build on previous work**

  Instead of creating a new worksheet for every project, it's easy to modify an existing Excel worksheet. When you are ready to create next week's payroll, you can open the file for last week's payroll, save it with a new filename, and modify the information as necessary. You can also use predesigned, formatted files called **templates** to create new worksheets quickly. Excel comes with many templates, that you can customize.

FIGURE A-1: Traditional paper worksheet

Quest Specialty Travel
Tour Guide Payroll Calculator

Name	Hours	O/T Hrs	Hrly Rate	Reg Pay	O/T Pay	Gross Pay
Brueghel, Pieter	40	4	15–	600–	120–	720–
Cortona, Livia	35	0	10–	350–	0–	350–
Klimt, Gustave	40	2	12⁵⁰	500–	50–	550–
Le Pen, Jean-Marie	29	0	15–	435–	0–	435–
Martinez, Juan	37	0	12⁵⁰	462.50	0–	462.50
Mioshi, Keiko	39	0	20–	780–	0–	780–
Sherwood, Burton	40	0	15–	600–	0–	600–
Strano, Riccardo	40	8	15–	600–	240–	840–
Wadsworth, Alicia	40	5	12⁵⁰	500–	125–	625–
Yamamoto, Johji	38	0	15–	570–	0–	570–

FIGURE A-2: Excel worksheet

Corporate logo →

3-D pie chart

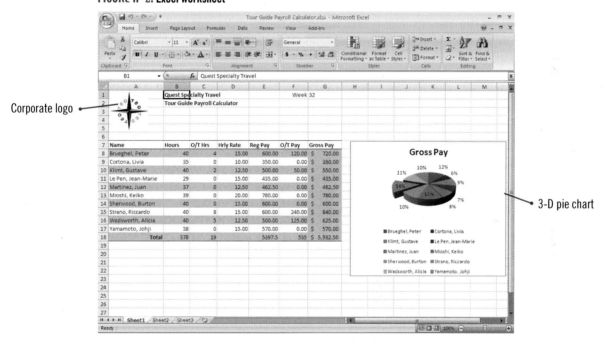

TABLE A-1: Business tasks you can accomplish using Excel

you can use spreadsheets to	by
Perform calculations	Adding formulas and functions to worksheet data; for example, adding a list of sales results or calculating a car payment
Represent values graphically	Creating charts based on worksheet data; for example, creating a chart that displays expenses
Generate reports	Creating workbooks that combine information from multiple worksheets, such as summarized sales information from multiple stores
Organize data	Sorting data in ascending or descending order; for example, alphabetizing a list of products or customer names, or prioritizing orders by date
Analyze data	Creating data summaries and short lists using PivotTables or AutoFilters; for example, making a list of the top 10 customers based on spending habits
Create what-if data scenarios	Using variable values to investigate and sample different outcomes, such as changing the interest rate or payment schedule on a loan

Touring the Excel 2007 Window

To start Excel, Microsoft Windows must be running. Similar to starting any program in Office, you can use the Start button on the Windows taskbar, or you may have a shortcut on your desktop you prefer to use. If you need additional assistance, ask your instructor or technical support person. ▰▰▰▰▰ You decide to start Excel and familiarize yourself with the worksheet window.

STEPS

QUICK TIP

For more information on starting a program or opening and saving a file, see the unit "Getting Started with Microsoft Office 2007."

TROUBLE

If you don't see the extension .xlsx on the filenames in the Open dialog box, don't worry; Windows can be set up to display or not to display the file extensions.

1. **Start Excel, click the** Microsoft Office button 🏷, **then click** Open

2. **In the Open dialog box, navigate to the drive and folder where you store your Data Files, click** EX A-1.xlsx, **then click** Open

3. **Click** 🏷, **then click** Save As

4. **In the Save As dialog box, navigate to the drive and folder where you store your Data Files if necessary, type** Tour Guide Payroll Calculator **in the File name text box, then click** Save

   Using Figure A-3 as a guide, identify the following items:
   - The **Name box** displays the active cell address. "A1" appears in the Name box.
   - The **formula bar** allows you to enter or edit data in the worksheet. The worksheet window contains a grid of columns and rows. Columns are labeled alphabetically and rows are labeled numerically. The worksheet window can contain a total of 1,048,576 rows and 16,384 columns.
   - The intersection of a column and a row is called a **cell**. Cells can contain text, numbers, formulas, or a combination of all three. Every cell has its own unique location or **cell address**, which is identified by the coordinates of the intersecting column and row.
   - The **cell pointer** is a dark rectangle that outlines the cell in which you are working. This cell is called the **active cell**. In Figure A-3, the cell pointer outlines cell A1, so A1 is the active cell. The column and row headings for the active cell are highlighted, making it easier to locate.
   - **Sheet tabs** below the worksheet grid let you switch from sheet to sheet in a workbook. By default, a workbook file contains three worksheets—but you can use just one, or have as many as 255, in a workbook. The Insert Worksheet button to the right of Sheet 3 allows you to add worksheets to a workbook. **Sheet tab scrolling buttons** let you navigate to additional sheet tabs when available.
   - You can use the **scroll bars** to move around in a document that is too large to fit on the screen at once.
   - The **status bar** is located at the bottom of the Excel window. It provides a brief description of the active command or task in progress. The **mode indicator** in the bottom-left corner of the status bar provides additional information about certain tasks.

5. **Click cell** A4

   Cell A4 becomes the active cell. To activate a different cell, you can click the cell or press the arrow keys on your keyboard to move to it.

6. **Click cell** B5, **press and hold the mouse button, drag** ✛ **to** cell B14, **then release the mouse button**

   You selected a group of cells and they are highlighted, as shown in Figure A-4. A selection of two or more cells such as B5:B14 is called a **range**; you select a range when you want to perform an action on a group of cells at once, such as moving them or formatting them. When you select a range, the status bar displays the average, count (or number of items selected), and sum of the selected cells as a quick reference.

FIGURE A-3: Open workbook

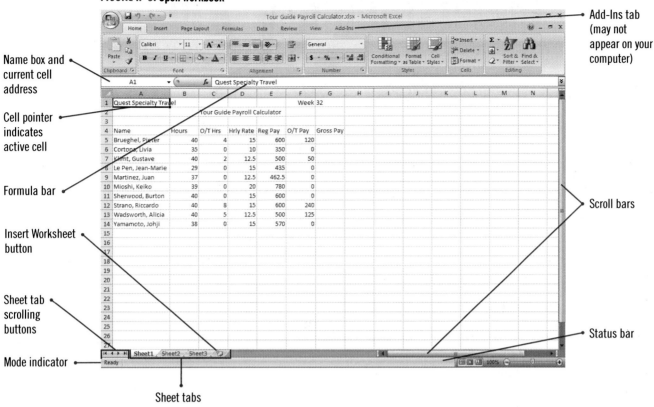

Add-Ins tab (may not appear on your computer)

Name box and current cell address

Cell pointer indicates active cell

Formula bar

Insert Worksheet button

Sheet tab scrolling buttons

Mode indicator

Scroll bars

Status bar

Sheet tabs

FIGURE A-4: Selecting a range

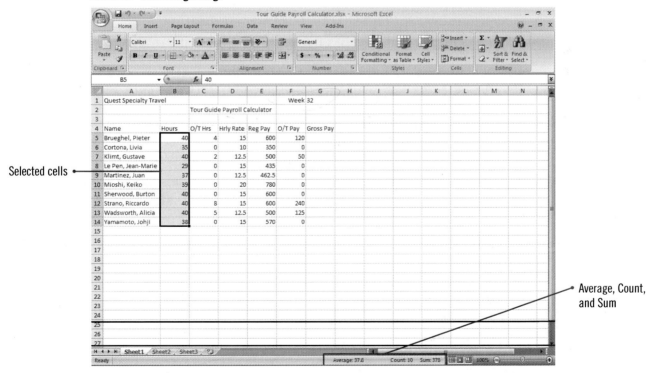

Selected cells

Average, Count, and Sum

Excel 2007

Understanding Formulas

Excel is a truly powerful program because users at every level of mathematical expertise can make calculations with accuracy. To do so, you use formulas. **Formulas** are equations in a worksheet. You use formulas to make calculations as simple as adding a column of numbers, or as complex as profit-and-loss projections for a global corporation. To tap into the power of Excel, you should understand how formulas work. 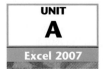 Managers at QST use the Tour Guide Payroll Calculator workbook to keep track of employee hours prior to submitting them to the Payroll Department. You'll be using this workbook regularly, so you need to understand the formulas it contains and how Excel calculates the results.

STEPS

1. **Click cell E5**

   The active cell contains a formula, which appears on the formula bar. All Excel formulas begin with the equal sign (=). If you wanted a cell to show the result of adding 4 plus 2, the formula in the cell would look like this: =4+2. If you wanted a cell to show the result of multiplying two values in your worksheet, such as the values in cells B5 and D5, the formula would look like this: =B5*D5, as shown in Figure A-5.

2. **Click cell F5**

   While you're entering a formula in a cell, the cell references and arithmetic operators appear on the formula bar. See Table A-2 for a list of common Excel arithmetic operators. When you're finished entering the formula, you can either click the Enter button on the formula bar, or press [Enter]. An example of a more complex formula is the calculation of overtime pay. At QST, overtime pay is calculated at twice the regular hourly rate times the number of overtime hours. The formula used to calculate overtime pay for the employee in row 5 is:
   O/T Hrs times (2 times Hrly Rate)
   In a worksheet cell, you would enter: =C5*(2*D5), as shown in Figure A-6.

   The use of parentheses creates groups within the formula and indicates which calculations to complete first—an important consideration in complex formulas. In this formula, the hourly rate is doubled, and that value is multiplied by the number of overtime hours. Because overtime is calculated at twice the hourly rate, managers are aware that they need to closely watch this expense.

DETAILS

In creating calculations in Excel, it is important to:

- **Know where the formulas should be**

  Excel formulas are created in the cell where they are viewed. This means that the formula calculating Gross Pay for the employee in row 5 will be entered in cell G5.

- **Know exactly what cells and arithmetic operations are needed**

  Don't guess; make sure you know exactly what cells are involved before creating a formula.

- **Create formulas with care**

  Make sure you know exactly what you want a formula to accomplish before it is created. An inaccurate formula may have far-reaching effects if the formula or its results are referenced by other formulas.

- **Use cell references rather than values**

  The beauty of Excel is that whenever you change a value in a cell, any formula containing a reference to that cell is automatically updated. For this reason, it's important that you use cell references in formulas, rather than actual values whenever possible.

- **Determine what calculations will be needed**

  Sometimes it's difficult to predict what data will be needed within a worksheet, but you should try to anticipate what statistical information may be required. For example, if there are columns of numbers, chances are good that both column and row totals should be present.

FIGURE A-5: Viewing a formula

Formula appears in formula bar

Result of formula appears in cell

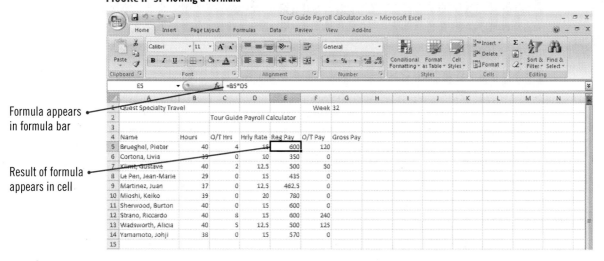

FIGURE A-6: Formula with multiple operators

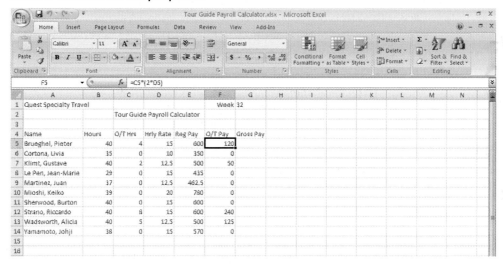

TABLE A-2: Excel arithmetic operators

operator	purpose	example
+	Addition	=A5+A7
-	Subtraction or negation	=A5-10
*	Multiplication	=A5*A7
/	Division	=A5/A7
%	Percent	=35%
^ (caret)	Exponent	=6^2 (same as 6^2)

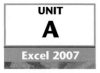

Entering Labels and Values and Using AutoSum

To enter content in a cell, you can type on the formula bar or directly in the cell itself. When entering content in a worksheet, you should start by entering all the labels first. **Labels** are entries that contain text and numerical information not used in calculations, such as "2009 Sales" or "Travel Expenses." Labels help you identify data in worksheet rows and columns, making your worksheet easier to understand. **Values** are numbers, formulas, and functions that can be used in calculations. To enter a calculation, you type an equal sign (=) plus the formula for the calculation; some examples of an Excel calculation are "=2+2" and "=C5+C6." Functions are Excel's built-in formulas; you learn more about them in the next unit. You want to enter some information in the Tour Guide Payroll Calculator workbook, and use a very simple function to total a range of cells.

STEPS

1. **Click cell A15, then click in the formula bar**

   Notice that the **mode indicator** on the status bar now reads "Edit," indicating you are in Edit mode. You are in Edit mode any time you are entering or changing the contents of a cell.

2. **Type Totals, then click the Enter button ✓ on the formula bar**

   Clicking the Enter button accepts the entry. The new text is left-aligned. Labels are left-aligned by default, and values are right-aligned by default. Excel recognizes an entry as a value if it is a number or it begins with one of these symbols: +, -, =, @, #, or $. When a cell contains both text and numbers, Excel recognizes it as a label.

3. **Click cell B15**

   You want this cell to total the hours worked by all the tour guides. You might think you need to create a formula that looks like this: =B5+B6+B7+B8+B9+B10+B11+B12+B13+B14. However, there's an easier way to achieve this result.

4. **Click the AutoSum button Σ in the Editing group on the Home tab of the Ribbon**

   The SUM function is inserted in your formula, and a suggested range appears in parentheses, as shown in Figure A-7. A **function** is a built-in formula; it includes the **arguments** (the information necessary to calculate an answer), as well as cell references and other unique information. Clicking the AutoSum button sums the adjacent range (that is, the cells next to the active cell) above or to the left, though you can adjust the range if necessary. Using the SUM function is quicker than entering a formula, and using the range B5:B14 is more efficient than entering individual cell references.

5. **Click ✓**

   Excel calculates the total contained in cells B5:B14 and displays the result, 378, in cell B15. The cell actually contains the formula =SUM(B5:B14), and the result is displayed.

6. **Click cell C13, type 6, then press [Enter]**

   The number 6 is right-aligned, the cell pointer moves to cell C14 and the value in cell F13 changes.

7. **Click cell C18, type Average Gross Pay, then press [Enter]**

   The new label is entered in cell C18. The contents appear to spill into the empty cells to the right.

8. **Click and hold cell B15, drag the mouse pointer to cell G15, click the Fill button 🔽 in the Editing group, then click Right in the Fill menu**

   Calculated values appear in the selected range, as shown in Figure A-8. Each filled cell contains a formula that sums the range of cells above. The Fill button fills cells based on the first number sequence in the range.

9. **Save your work**

FIGURE A-7: Creating a formula using the AutoSum button

AutoSum button

Formula in selected cell

Outline of cells included in formula

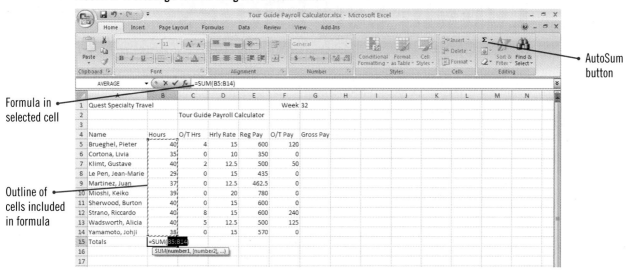

FIGURE A-8: Calculated values

Ribbon

Home tab

In cell C18, contents appear to spill into empty adjacent cells

Fill button

Formula in cell B15 is copied to selected adjacent cells

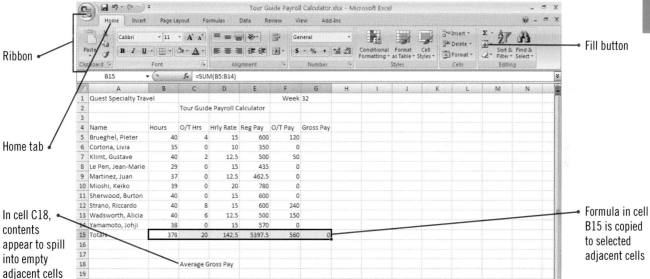

Navigating a worksheet

With over a million cells available in a worksheet, it is important to know how to move around in, or **navigate**, a worksheet. You can use the arrow keys on the keyboard [↑], [↓], [←], or [→] to move a cell at a time, or press [Page Up] or [Page Down] to move a screen at a time. To move a screen to the left press [Alt][Page Up]; to move a screen to the right press [Alt][Page Down]. You can also use the mouse pointer to click the desired cell. If the desired cell is not visible in the worksheet window, use the scroll bars or the Go To command by clicking the Find & Select button in the Editing group on the Home tab of the Ribbon. To quickly jump to the first cell in a worksheet press [Ctrl][Home]; to jump to the last cell, press [Ctrl][End].

Editing Cell Entries

You can change, or **edit**, the contents of an active cell at any time. To do so, double-click the cell, click in the formula bar, or just start typing. Excel switches to Edit mode when you are making cell entries. Different pointers, shown in Table A-3, guide you through the editing process. You noticed some errors in the worksheet and want to make corrections. The first error is in cell A5, which contains a misspelled name.

STEPS

> **QUICK TIP**
> Pressing [Enter] also accepts the cell entry, but moves the cell pointer down one cell.

> **QUICK TIP**
> On some keyboards, you might need to press an "F Lock" key to enable the function keys.

> **QUICK TIP**
> The Undo button allows you to reverse up to 100 previous actions, one at a time.

1. **Click cell A5, then click to the right of P in the formula bar**

   As soon as you click in the formula bar, a blinking vertical line called the **insertion point** appears on the formula bar at the location where new text will be inserted. See Figure A-9. The mouse pointer changes to I when you point anywhere in the formula bar.

2. **Press [Delete], then click the Enter button ☑ on the formula bar**

   Clicking the Enter button accepts the edit, and the spelling of the employee's first name is corrected. You can also press [Enter] or [Tab] to accept an edit.

3. **Click cell B6, then press [F2]**

   Excel switches to Edit mode, and the insertion point blinks in the cell. Pressing [F2] activates the cell for editing directly in the cell instead of the formula bar. Some people prefer editing right in the cell instead of using the formula bar, but it's simply a matter of preference; the results in the worksheet are the same.

4. **Press [Backspace], type 8, then press [Enter]**

   The value in the cell changes from 35 to 38, and cell B7 becomes the active cell. Did you notice that the calculations in cells B15 and E15 also changed? That's because those cells contain formulas that include cell B6 in their calculations. If you make a mistake when editing, you can click the Cancel button ☒ on the formula bar *before* pressing [Enter] to confirm the cell entry. The Enter and Cancel buttons appear only when you're in Edit mode. If you notice the mistake *after* you have confirmed the cell entry, click the Undo button ↶ on the Quick Access toolbar.

5. **Click cell A9, press [F2], press and hold [Shift], press [Home], then release [Shift]**

   Pressing and holding [Shift] lets you select text using the keyboard. Pressing [Home] moves the cursor to the beginning of the cell; pressing [End] would move the cursor to the end or the cell.

6. **Type Maez, Javier, then press [Enter]**

   When text is selected, typing deletes it and replaces it with the new text.

7. **Double-click cell C12, press [Delete], type 4, then click ☑**

   Double-clicking a cell activates it for editing directly in the cell. Compare your screen to Figure A-10.

8. **Save your work**

   Your changes to the workbook are saved.

Recovering a lost workbook file

Sometimes while you are using Excel, you may experience a power failure or your computer may "freeze," making it impossible to continue working. If this type of interruption occurs, Excel has a built-in recovery feature that allows you to open and save files that were open at the time of the interruption. When you restart Excel after an interruption, File Recovery mode automatically starts and tries to make any necessary repairs. If you need to use a corrupted workbook, you can try and repair it manually by clicking the Office button, then clicking Open. Select the workbook file you want to repair, click the Open list arrow, then click Open and Repair.

FIGURE A-9: Worksheet in Edit mode

Enter button
Active cell
Insertion point
Mode indicator

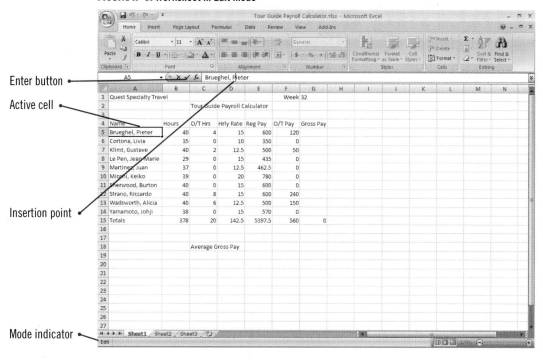

FIGURE A-10: Edited worksheet

Edited label
Edited value

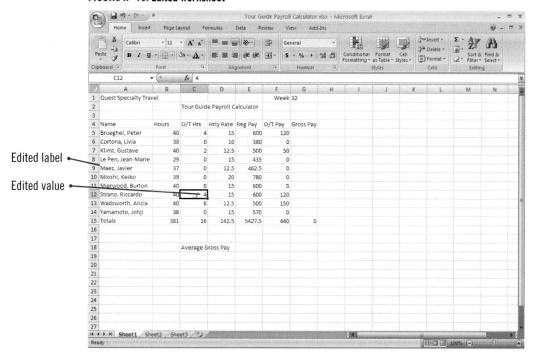

TABLE A-3: Common pointers in Excel

name	pointer	use to
Normal	⊹	Select a cell or range; indicates Ready mode
Copy	⬉⁺	Create a duplicate of the selected cell(s)
Fill handle	➕	Create an alphanumeric series in a range
I-beam	I	Edit contents of formula bar
Move	⬉	Change the location of the selected cell(s)

Entering and Editing a Simple Formula

You use formulas in Excel to perform calculations such as adding, multiplying, and averaging. Formulas in an Excel worksheet start with the equal sign (=), also called the **formula prefix**, followed by cell addresses, range names, and values, along with calculation operators. **Calculation operators** indicate what type of calculation you want to perform on the cells, ranges or values. They can include **arithmetic operators**, which perform mathematical calculations such as adding and subtracting, **comparison operators**, which compare values for the purpose of true/false results, **text concatenation operators**, which join strings of text in different cells, and **reference operators**, which enable you to use ranges in calculations. You want to create a formula in the worksheet that calculates gross pay for each employee.

STEPS

1. **Click cell G5**

   This is the first cell where you want to insert the formula. To calculate gross pay, you need to add regular pay and overtime pay. For employee Peter Brueghel, regular pay appears in cell E5 and overtime pay appears in cell F5.

2. **Type =, click cell E5, type +, then click cell F5**

   Compare your formula bar to Figure A-11. The blue and green cell references in cell G5 correspond to the colored cell outlines. When entering a formula, it's a good idea to use cell references instead of values whenever you can. That way, if you later change a value in a cell (if, for example, Peter's regular pay changes to 615), any formula that includes this information reflects accurate, up-to-date results.

3. **Click the Enter button ☑ on the formula bar**

   The results of the formula =E5+F5, 720, appear in cell G5. This same value appears in cell G15 because cell G15 contains a formula that totals the values in cells G5:G14, and there are no other values now.

4. **Click cell F5**

   The formula in this cell calculates overtime pay by multiplying overtime hours (C5) times twice the regular hourly rate (2*D5). You want to edit this formula to reflect a new overtime pay rate.

5. **Click to the right of 2 in the formula bar, then type .5 as shown in Figure A-12**

   The formula that calculates overtime pay has been edited.

6. **Click ☑ on the formula bar**

   Compare your screen to Figure A-13. Notice that the calculated values in cells G5, F15, and G15 have all changed to reflect your edits to cell F5.

7. **Save your work**

Understanding named ranges

It can be difficult to remember the cell locations of critical information in a worksheet, but using cell names can make this task much easier. You can name a single cell or range of contiguous, or touching, cells. For example, you might name a cell that contains data on average gross pay "AVG_GP" instead of trying to remember the cell address C18. A named range must begin with a letter or an underscore. It cannot contain any spaces or be the same as a built-in name, such as a function or another object (such as a different named range) in the workbook. To name a range, select the cell(s) you want to name, click the name box in the formula bar, type the name you want to use, then press [Enter]. You can also name a range by clicking the Formulas tab, clicking the Define Name list arrow in the Defined Names group, then clicking Define Name. Type the new range name in the Name text box of the New Name dialog box, verify the selected range, then click OK. When you use a named range in a formula, the named range appears, rather than the cell address. You can also create a named range using the contents of a cell already in the range. Select the range containing the text you want to use as a name, then click Create from Selection button in the Defined Names group. The Create Names from Selection dialog box opens. Choose the location of the name you want to use, then click OK.

FIGURE A-11: Simple formula in a worksheet

Cell outline color corresponds to cell reference

Referenced cells are inserted in formula

Mode indicator changes to Point

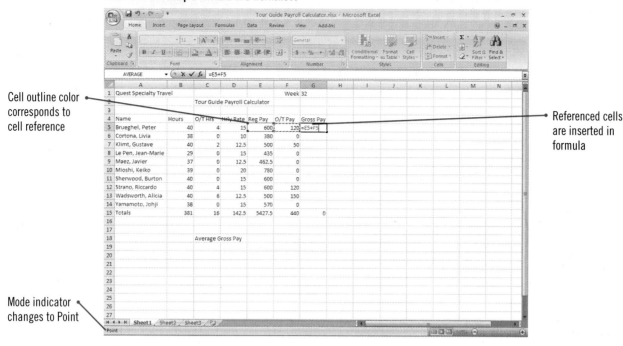

FIGURE A-12: Edited formula in a worksheet

Edited value

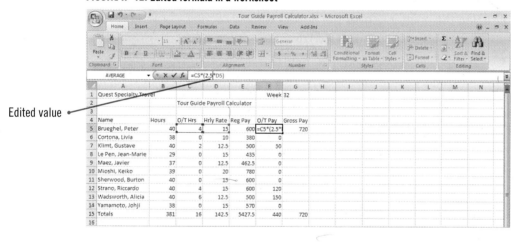

FIGURE A-13: Edited formula with changes

Edited formula results in changes to these other cells

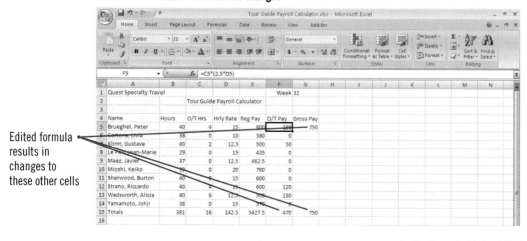

Switching Worksheet Views

You can change your view of the worksheet window at any time, using either the View tab on the Ribbon or the View buttons on the status bar. Changing your view does not affect the contents of a worksheet; it just makes it easier for you to focus on different tasks, such as entering content or preparing a worksheet for printing. The View tab includes a variety of viewing options, such as View buttons, zoom controls, and the ability to show or hide worksheet elements such as gridlines. The status bar offers fewer View options, but can be more convenient to use. ▰▰▰ You want to make some final adjustments to your worksheet, including adding a header so the document looks more polished.

STEPS

QUICK TIP

Although a work-sheet can contain more than a million rows and columns, the current docu-ment contains only as many pages as necessary for the current project.

1. **Click the View tab on the Ribbon, then click the Page Layout View button in the Workbook Views group**

   The view switches from the default view, Normal, to Page Layout view. **Normal view** shows the worksheet without including certain details like headers and footers or tools like rulers and a page number indicator; it's great for creating and editing a worksheet, but may not be detailed enough when you want to put the finishing touches on a document. **Page Layout View** provides a more accurate view of how a worksheet will look when printed, as shown in Figure A-14. The margins of the page are displayed, along with a text box for the header. A footer text box appears at the bottom of the page, but your screen may not be large enough to view it without scrolling. Above and to the left of the page are rulers. Part of an additional page appears to the right of this page, but it is dimmed, indicating that it does not contain any data. A page number indicator on the status bar tells you the current page and the total number of pages in this worksheet.

2. **Drag the pointer 🗘 over the header *without clicking***

   The header is made up of three text boxes: left, center, and right.

QUICK TIP

You can change header and footer information using the Header & Footer Tools Design tab that opens when a header or footer is active. For example, you can insert the date by clicking the Current Date button in the Header & Footer Elements group, or the time by clicking the Current Time button.

3. **Click the left header text box, type Quest Specialty Travel, click the center text box, type Tour Guide Payroll Calculator, click the right header text box, then type Week 32**

   The new text appears in the text boxes, as shown in Figure A-15.

4. **Select the range A1:G2, then press [Delete]**

   The duplicate information you just entered in the header is deleted from cells in the worksheet.

5. **Click the Ruler checkbox in the Show/Hide group on the View tab, then click the Gridlines checkbox**

   The rulers and the gridlines are hidden. By default, gridlines in a worksheet do not print, so hiding them gives you a more accurate image of your final document.

6. **Click the Page Break Preview button 🖳 on the status bar, then click OK in the Welcome to Page Break Preview dialog box, if necessary**

   Your view changes to **Page Break Preview**, which displays a reduced view of each page of your worksheet, along with page break indicators that you can drag to include more or less information on a page.

7. **Drag the bottom page break indicator to the bottom of row 21**

   See Figure A-16. When you're working on a large worksheet with multiple pages, sometimes you need to adjust where pages break; in this worksheet, however, the information all fits comfortably on one page.

QUICK TIP

Once you view a worksheet in Page Break Preview, the page break indica-tors appear as dot-ted lines after you switch back to Normal view.

8. **Click the View tab if necessary, click Page Layout in the Workbook Views group, click the Ruler checkbox in the Show/Hide group in the View tab, then click the Gridlines checkbox**

   The rulers and gridlines are no longer hidden. You can show or hide View tab items in any view.

9. **Save your work**

FIGURE A-14: Page Layout View

Ruler checkbox

Gridlines checkbox

Workbook Views group

Header text box

Vertical ruler

Horizontal ruler

Additional dimmed page

Current page and total number of pages

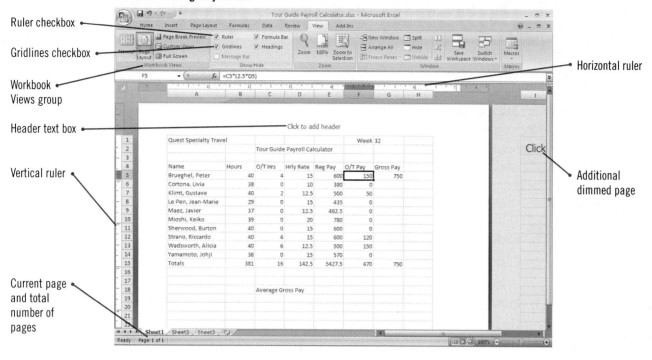

FIGURE A-15: Header boxes

Header areas

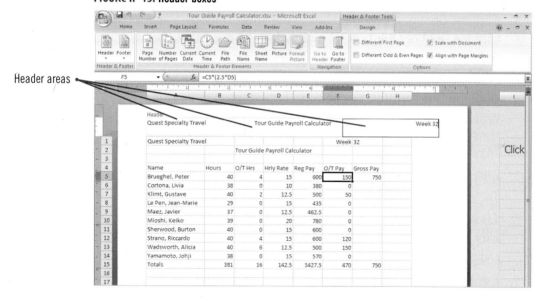

FIGURE A-16: Page Break Preview

Blue outline indicates print area

Bottom page break indicator

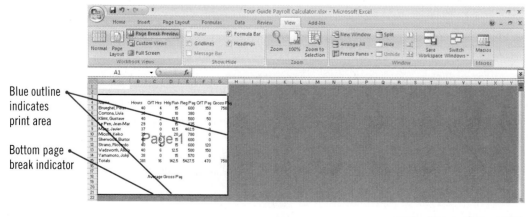

Choosing Print Options

Before printing a document, you may want to review it using the Page Layout tab and Print Preview to fine-tune your printed output. You should also review your settings in the Print dialog box, to make sure you are printing the desired number of copies and using the correct printer. Tools on the Page Layout tab include a Page Setup group, where you can adjust print orientation (the direction in which the content prints across the page), paper size, and page breaks. The Scale to Fit group makes it possible to fit a large amount of data on a single page without making changes to individual margins. In the Sheet Options group, you can turn on and off gridlines and column/row headings. Reviewing your final worksheet in Print Preview shows you exactly how the worksheet will look when printed. You are ready to prepare your worksheet for printing.

STEPS

1. **Click cell A21, type your name, then press [Enter]**

2. **Click the Page Layout tab on the Ribbon**
   Compare your screen to Figure A-17. The dotted line indicates the **print area**, the area to be printed.

> **QUICK TIP**
> You can use the Zoom slider at any time to enlarge your view of specific areas of your worksheet.

3. **Click the Orientation button in the Page Setup group, then click Landscape**
   The paper orientation changes to **landscape**, so the contents will print across the length of the page instead of across the width.

4. **Click the Orientation button in the Page Setup group, then click Portrait**
   The orientation returns to **portrait**, so the contents will print across the width of the page.

5. **Click the Gridlines View checkbox in the Sheet Options group on the Page Layout tab, click the Gridlines Print checkbox to select it if necessary, then save your work**
   Printing gridlines makes the data easier to read, but the gridlines will not print unless the Gridlines Print checkbox is checked.

> **QUICK TIP**
> You can print your worksheet using the default settings by clicking the Office button, pointing to Print, then clicking Quick Print.

6. **Click the Office button, point to Print, then click Print Preview**
   Print Preview shows exactly how your printed copy will look. You can print from this view by clicking the Print button on the Ribbon, or close Print Preview without printing by clicking the Close Print Preview button.

7. **Click the Zoom button in the Zoom group on the Print Preview tab**
   The image of your worksheet is enlarged. Compare your screen to Figure A-18.

> **QUICK TIP**
> To change the active printer, click the Name list arrow, then choose a different printer.

8. **Click the Print button in the Print group, compare your settings to Figure A-19, then click OK**
   One copy of the worksheet prints.

9. **Exit Excel**

Printing worksheet formulas

Sometimes you need to keep a record of all the formulas in a worksheet. You might want to do this to see exactly how you came up with a complex calculation, so you can explain it to others. You can do this by printing out the formulas in a worksheet rather than the results of those calculations. To do so, open the workbook containing the formulas you want to print. Click the Office button, then click Excel Options. Click Advanced in the left pane, scroll to the Display options for this worksheet section, click the list arrow and select the entire workbook or the sheet in which you want the formulas displayed, click the Show formulas in cells instead of their calculated results checkbox, then click OK.

FIGURE A-17: Worksheet with Portrait orientation

Page Layout tab

Scale field

Dotted line
surrounds
print area

Your name
appears here

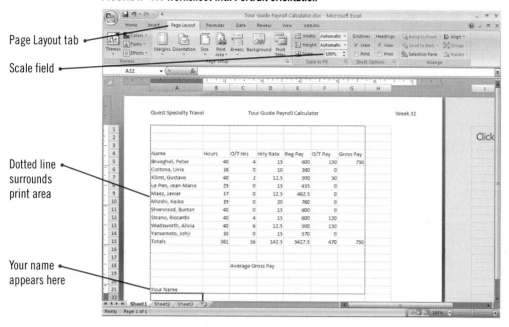

FIGURE A-18: Worksheet in Print Preview

Print button

Zoom button

Close Print
Preview button

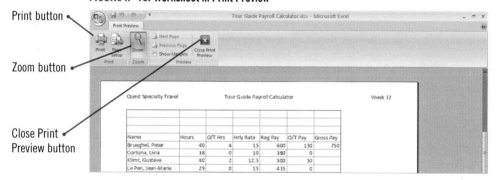

FIGURE A-19: Print dialog box

Active printer: yours
will be different

Choose which
pages to print

Number of
copies field

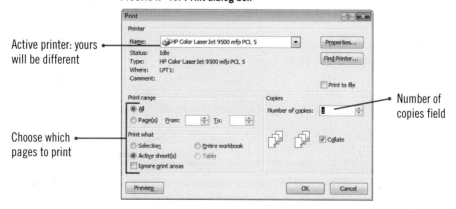

Scaling to fit

If you have a large amount of data that you want to fit to a single sheet of paper, but you don't want to spend a lot of time trying to adjust the margins and other settings, use the Fit to option in the Page Setup dialog box. Open this dialog box by clicking the launcher in the Scale to Fit group in the Page Layout tab. Make sure the Page tab is selected, then click the Fit to option button. Select the number of pages you want the worksheet to fit on, then click OK. If you're ready to print, click Print and the Print dialog box will open. Select the pages you want to print and the number of copies you want, then click OK.

Practice

If you have a SAM user profile, you may have access to hands-on instruction, practice, and assessment of the skills covered in this unit. Log in to your SAM account (http://sam2007.course.com/) to launch any assigned training activities or exams that relate to the skills covered in this unit.

▼ CONCEPTS REVIEW

Label the elements of the Excel worksheet window shown in Figure A-20.

FIGURE A-20

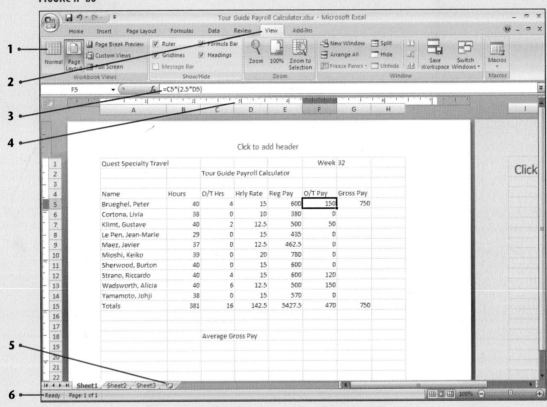

Match each term with the statement that best describes it.

7. Cell

8. Normal View

9. Workbook

10. Name Box

11. Formula prefix

12. Orientation

a. Direction in which contents of page will print

b. Equal sign preceding a formula

c. File consisting of one or more worksheets

d. Default view in Excel

e. Part of the Excel program window that displays the active cell address

f. Intersection of a column and a row

Select the best answer from the list of choices.

13. In Excel, order of precedence determines:

   a. The order in which worksheets are printed.
   b. The colors used to distinguish cell references.
   c. The order in which calculations are performed.
   d. How values are multiplied.

14. The maximum number of worksheets you can include in a workbook is:

   a. 3.
   b. 250.
   c. 255.
   d. Unlimited.

15. A selection of multiple cells is called a:

   a. Group.
   b. Range.
   c. Reference.
   d. Package.

16. Using a cell address in a formula is known as:

   a. Formularizing.
   b. Prefixing.
   c. Cell referencing.
   d. Cell mathematics.

17. Which worksheet view shows how your worksheet will look when printed?

   a. Page Layout
   b. Data
   c. Review
   d. View

18. Which button should you click if you want to print formulas in a worksheet?

   a. Save button
   b. Fill button
   c. Any button on the Quick Access Toolbar
   d. Office button

19. Clicking the launcher in the Scale to Fit group on the Page Layout tab opens which dialog box?

   a. Print
   b. Scale to Fit
   c. Width/Height
   d. Page Setup

20. In which view can you see the header and footer areas of a worksheet?

   a. Normal View
   b. Page Layout View
   c. Page Break Preview
   d. Header/Footer View

21. Which key can you press to switch to Edit mode?

   a. [F1]
   b. [F2]
   c. [F4]
   d. [F6]

▼ SKILLS REVIEW

1. **Understand spreadsheet software.**

   a. What is the difference between a workbook and a worksheet?
   b. Identify five common business uses for electronic spreadsheets.
   c. What is 'what-if' analysis?

2. **Tour the Excel 2007 window.**

   a. Start Excel.
   b. Open the file EX A-2.xlsx from the drive and folder where you store your Data Files, then save it as Weather Statistics.
   c. Locate the formula bar, the Sheet tabs, the mode indicator, and the cell pointer.

3. **Understand formulas.**

   a. What is the average high temperature of the listed cities? (*Hint*: Select the range B5:G5 and use the status bar.)
   b. What formula would you create to calculate the difference in altitude between Chicago and Phoenix?

4. **Enter labels and values and use AutoSum.**

   a. Click cell H7, then use the AutoSum button to calculate the total rainfall.
   b. Click cell H8, then use the AutoSum button to calculate the total snowfall.
   c. Save your changes to the file.

5. **Edit cell entries.**

   a. Use the [F2] key to correct the spelling of Sante Fe in a worksheet cell (the correct spelling is Santa Fe).
   b. Click cell A12, then type your name.
   c. Save your changes.

6. Enter and edit a simple formula.

a. Change the value 41 in cell B8 to 52.

b. Change the value 35 in cell C7 to 35.4.

c. Select the range B10:G10, then use the Fill button in the Editing group on the Home tab to fill the formula to the remaining cells in the selection. (*Hint*: If you see a warning icon, click it, then click Ignore Error.)

d. Save your changes.

7. Switch worksheet views.

a. Click the View tab on the Ribbon, then switch to Page Layout view.

b. Add the header Average Annual Weather Statistics to the center header box.

c. Add your name to the right header box.

d. Delete the contents of cell A1.

e. Delete the contents of cell A12.

f. Save your changes.

8. Choose Print options.

a. Use the Page Layout tab to change the orientation to Portrait.

b. Turn off gridlines by deselecting both the Gridlines View and Gridlines Print checkboxes in the Sheet Options group.

c. View the worksheet in Print Preview, then zoom in to enlarge the preview. Compare your screen to Figure A-21.

d. Open the Print dialog box, then print one copy of the worksheet.

e. Save your changes, then close the workbook.

FIGURE A-21

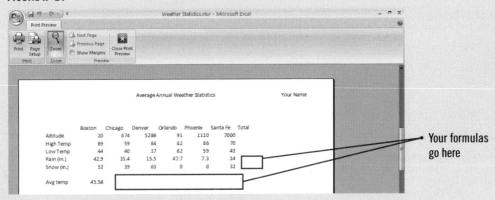

▼ INDEPENDENT CHALLENGE 1

A local real estate office has hired you to help them make the transition to using Excel in their office. They would like to list their properties in a worksheet. You've started a worksheet for this project that contains labels but no data.

a. Open the file EX A-3.xlsx from where you store your Data Files, then save it as Real Estate Listings.

b. Enter the data shown in Table A-4 in columns A, C, D, and E (the property address information should spill into column B).

TABLE A-4

Property Address	Price	Bedrooms	Bathrooms
1507 Cactus Lane	350000	3	2.5
32 California Lane	325000	3	4
60 Pottery Lane	475500	2	2
902 Fortunata Drive	295000	4	3
Total			

▼ INDEPENDENT CHALLENGE 1 (CONTINUED)

c. Use Page Layout View to create a header with the following components: a title in the center and your name on the right.

d. Create formulas for totals in cells C6:E6.

e. Save your changes, then preview your work and compare it to Figure A-22.

f. Print the worksheet.

g. Close the worksheet and exit Excel.

FIGURE A-22

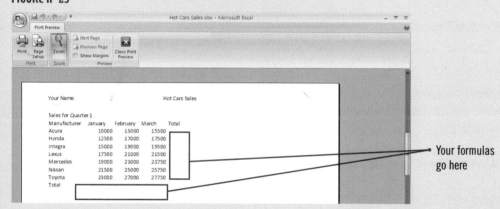

Your formulas go here

▼ INDEPENDENT CHALLENGE 2

FIGURE A-23

Your formulas go here

You are the General Manager for Hot Cars, a small auto parts supplier. Although the company is just three years old, it is expanding rapidly, and you are continually looking for ways to save time. You recently began using Excel to manage and maintain data on inventory and sales, which has greatly helped you to track information accurately and efficiently.

a. Start Excel.

b. Save a new workbook as **Hot Cars Sales** in the drive and folder where you store your Data Files.

c. Switch to an appropriate view, then add a header that contains your name in the left header text box and a title in the center header text box.

d. Using Figure A-23 as a guide, create labels for at least seven car manufacturers and sales for three months. Include other labels as appropriate. The car manufacturers should be in column A, and the months in columns B, C, and D. A Total row should be beneath the data, and a Total column should be in column E.

e. Enter values of your choice for the monthly sales for each manufacturer.

f. Add a formula in the Total column to calculate total monthly sales for each manufacturer. Add formulas at the bottom of each column of values to calculate the total for that column. Remember that you can use the SUM function to save time.

g. Save your changes, preview the worksheet, then print it.

Excel 2007

▼ INDEPENDENT CHALLENGE 2 (CONTINUED)

Advanced Challenge Exercise

- Create a label two rows beneath the data in column A that says 15% increase.
- Create a formula in the row containing the 15% increase label that calculates a 15% increase in total monthly sales.
- Save the workbook.
- Display the formulas in the worksheet, then print a copy of the worksheet with formulas displayed.

h. Close the workbook(s) and exit Excel.

▼ INDEPENDENT CHALLENGE 3

FIGURE A-24

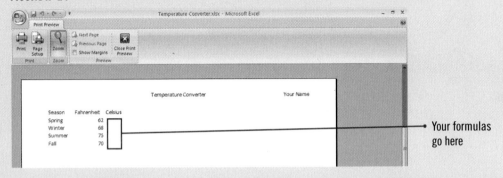

This Independent Challenge requires an Internet connection. Your office is starting a branch in Paris and you think it would be helpful to create a worksheet that can be used to convert Fahrenheit temperatures to Celsius, to help employees who are unfamiliar with this type of temperature measurement.

a. Start Excel, then save a blank workbook as Temperature Converter in the drive and folder where you store your Data Files.

b. Create column and row titles using Figure A-24 as a guide.

c. Create labels for each of the seasons.

d. In the appropriate cells, enter what you determine to be an ideal indoor temperature for each season.

e. Use your Web browser to find out the conversion rate for Fahrenheit to Celsius. (*Hint*: Use your favorite search engine to search on a term such as "temperature conversion.")

f. In the appropriate cells, create an equation that calculates the conversion of the Fahrenheit temperature you entered into a Celsius temperature.

g. Preview the worksheet in Page Layout View, adding your name to the header, as well as a meaningful title.

h. Save your work, then print the worksheet.

i. Close the file, then exit Excel.

▼ REAL LIFE INDEPENDENT CHALLENGE

FIGURE A-25

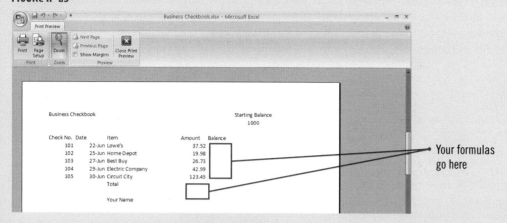

You've decided to quit your day job and turn your favorite hobby into a business. You've set up a small business selling the product or service of your choice. You want to use Excel to keep track of your many start-up costs.

a. Start Excel, open the file EX A-4.xlsx from the drive and folder where you store your Data Files, then save it as **Business Checkbook**.

b. Type check numbers (using your choice of a starting number) in cells A5 through A9.

c. Create sample data for the date, item, and amount in cells B5 through D9.

d. Save your work.

Advanced Challenge Exercise

- ■ Use Help to find out about creating a series of numbers.
- ■ Delete the contents of cells A5:A9.
- ■ Create a series of numbers in cells A5:A9.
- ■ In cell C15, type a brief description of how you created the series.
- ■ Save the workbook.

e. Create formulas in cells E5:E9 that calculate a running balance. (*Hint:* For the first check, the running balance equals the starting balance minus a check; for the following checks, the running balance equals the previous balance value minus each check value.)

f. Create a formula in cell D10 that totals the amount of the checks.

g. Enter your name in cell C12, then compare your screen to Figure A-25.

h. Save your changes to the file, preview and print the worksheet, then exit Excel.

▼ VISUAL WORKSHOP

Open the file EX A-5.xlsx from the drive and folder where you store your Data Files, then save it as **Inventory Items**. Using the skills you learned in this unit, modify your worksheet so it matches Figure A-26. Enter formulas in cells D4 through D13 and in cells B14 and C14. Use the AutoSum button to make entering your formulas easier. Add your name in the left header text box, then print one copy of the worksheet once with the formulas not displayed, and one copy with the formulas displayed.

FIGURE A-26

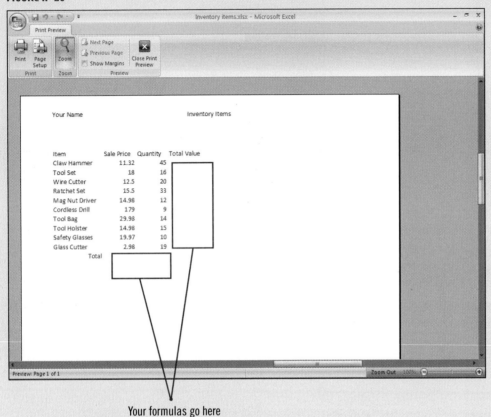

Your formulas go here

Working with Formulas and Functions

Files You Will Need:

EX B-1.xlsx
EX B-2.xlsx
EX B-3.xlsx
EX B-4.xlsx

Using your knowledge of Excel basics, you can expand your worksheets to include more complex formulas and functions. To work more efficiently, you can copy and move existing formulas into other cells instead of manually retyping the same information. When copying or moving, you can also control how cell references are handled, so that your formulas always reference the intended cells. Grace Wong, vice president of finance at Quest Specialty Travel, needs to analyze tour revenue for the current year. She has asked you to prepare a worksheet that summarizes this revenue data and includes some statistical analysis. She would also like you to perform some what-if analysis, to see what quarterly revenues would look like with various projected increases.

OBJECTIVES

Create a complex formula

Insert a function

Type a function

Copy and move cell entries

Understand relative and absolute cell references

Copy formulas with relative cell references

Copy formulas with absolute cell references

Round a value with a function

Creating a Complex Formula

A **complex formula** is one that uses more than one arithmetic operator. You might, for example, need to create a formula that uses addition and multiplication. You can use arithmetic operators to separate tasks within a complex equation. In formulas containing more than one arithmetic operator, Excel uses the standard order of precedence rules to determine which operation to perform first. You can change the order of precedence in a formula by using parentheses around the part you want to calculate first. For example, the formula =4+2*5 equals 14, because the order of precedence dictates that multiplication is performed before addition. However, the formula =(4+2)*5 equals 30, because the parentheses cause 4+2 to be calculated first. You want to create a formula that calculates a 20% increase in tour revenue.

STEPS

1. **Start Excel, open the file EX B-1.xlsx from the drive and folder where you store your Data Files, then save it as** Tour Revenue Analysis

2. **Click cell B14, type =, click cell B12, then type +**
   In this first part of the formula, you are creating references to the total for Quarter 1.

3. **Click cell B12, then type *.2**
   The second part of this formula adds a 20% increase (B12*.2) to the original value of the cell. Compare your worksheet to Figure B-1.

4. **Click the Enter button ✔ on the formula bar**
   The result, 386122.344, appears in cell B14.

5. **Press [Tab], type =, click cell C12, type +, click cell C12, type *.2, then click ✔**
   The result, 410969.712, appears in cell C14.

6. **Drag the ✛ pointer from cell C14 to cell E14, click the Fill button 🔲▾ in the Editing group on the Home tab of the Ribbon, then click Right**
   The calculated values appear in the selected range, as shown in Figure B-2.

7. **Save your work**

Reviewing the order of precedence

When you work with formulas that contain more than one operator, the order of precedence is very important because it affects the final value. For example, you might think the formula 4+2*5 equals 30, but because the order of precedence dictates that multiplication is performed before addition, the actual result is 14. If a formula contains two or more operators, such as 4+.55/4000*25, Excel performs the calculations in a particular sequence based on the following rules: Operations inside parentheses are calculated before any other operations. Reference operators (such as ranges) are calculated first. Exponents are calculated next, then any multiplication and division—progressing from left to right. Finally, addition and subtraction are calculated from left to right. In the example 4+.55/4000*25, Excel performs the arithmetic operations by first dividing 4000 into .55, then multiplying the result by 25, then adding 4. You can change the order of calculations by using parentheses. For example, in the formula (4+.55)/4000*25, Excel would first add 4 and .55, then divide that amount by 4000, then finally multiply by 25.

FIGURE B-1: Formula containing multiple arithmetic operators

Complex formula

Mode indicator

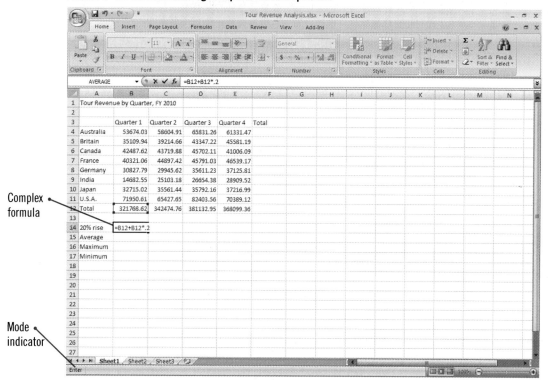

FIGURE B-2: Complex formulas in worksheet

Formula in cell C14 copied to cells D14 and E14

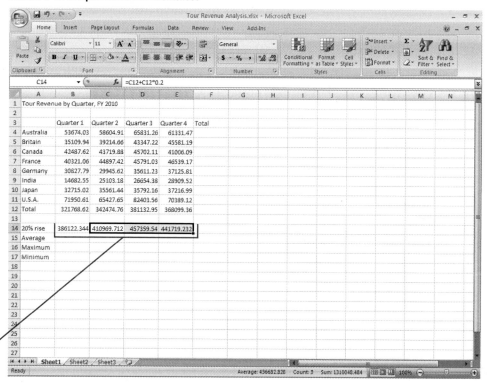

Inserting a Function

Functions are predefined worksheet formulas that enable you to perform complex calculations easily. You can use the Insert Function button on the formula bar to choose a function from a dialog box. In addition to using the AutoSum button on the Ribbon to quickly insert the SUM function, you can click the AutoSum button list arrow to enter other frequently used functions, such as Average. Functions are organized into categories, such as Financial, Date & Time, and Statistical, based on their purpose. You can insert a function on its own, or as part of another formula. For example, you have used the SUM function on its own to add a range of cells. You could also use the SUM function within a formula that adds a range of cells and then multiplies the total by a decimal. If you use a function alone, it always begins with the formula prefix = (the equal sign). ░░░░░ You need to calculate the average sales for the first quarter of the year, and decide to use a function to do so.

STEPS

QUICK TIP

When using the Insert Function button or the AutoSum button list arrow, it is not necessary to type the equal sign (=); Excel adds it as necessary.

1. **Click cell B15**

   This is the cell where you want to enter the calculation that averages revenue for the first quarter. You want to use the Insert Function dialog box to enter this function.

2. **Click the Insert Function button** f_x **on the formula bar**

   An equal sign (=) is inserted in the active cell and in the formula bar, and the Insert Function dialog box opens, as shown in Figure B-3. In this dialog box, you specify the function you want to add by clicking it in the Select a function list. The Select a function list initially displays recently used functions. If you don't see the function you want, you can click the Or select a category list arrow to choose the desired category or, if you're not sure what category to choose, you can type the function name or a description in the Search for a function field. The AVERAGE function is a statistical function, but you don't need to open the Statistical category because this function appears in the Most Recently Used list.

QUICK TIP

To learn about a function, click it in the Select a function list. Read the arguments and format required for the function.

3. **Click AVERAGE, if necessary, read the information that appears under the list, then click OK**

   The Function Arguments dialog box opens, where you define the range of cells you want to average.

QUICK TIP

When selecting a range, remember to select all the cells between and including the two references in the range.

4. **Click the Collapse button** 🔢 **in the Number1 field of the Function Arguments dialog box, drag the ✛ pointer to select the range B4:B11, release the mouse button, then click the Expand button** 🔲

   Clicking the Collapse button minimizes the dialog box so you can select cells in the worksheet. When you click the Expand button, the dialog box is restored, as shown in Figure B-4. You can also begin dragging in the worksheet to automatically minimize the dialog box; after you select the desired range, the dialog box is restored.

5. **Click OK**

   The Function Arguments dialog box closes and the calculated value displays in cell C15. The average revenue per country for Quarter 1 is 40221.0775.

6. **Click cell C15, click the AutoSum button list arrow** Σ ▾ **in the Editing group on the Home tab, then click Average**

   A ScreenTip beneath cell C15 displays the arguments needed to complete the function. The text number1 is shown in boldface type, telling you that the next step is to supply the first cell in the group you want to average. You want to average a range of cells.

7. **Drag ✛ to select the range C4:C11, then click the Enter button** ✔ **on the formula bar**

   The average revenue per country for the second quarter appears in cell C15.

8. **Select the range C15:E15, click the Fill button** 📋▾ **in the Editing group, then click Right**

   The formula in cell C15 is copied to the rest of the selected range, as shown in Figure B-5.

9. **Save your work**

FIGURE B-3: Insert Function dialog box

Search for a function field

Your list of recently used functions may differ

Or select a category list arrow

Description of selected function

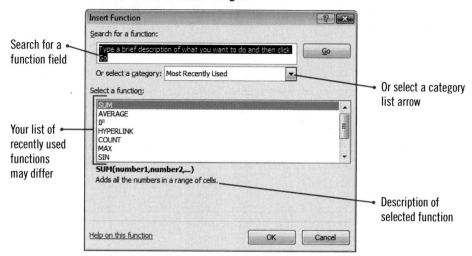

FIGURE B-4: Expanded Function Arguments dialog box

Function in formula bar

Insert Function button

Argument

Drag title bar of dialog box to move it if necessary

Description and argument format of selected function

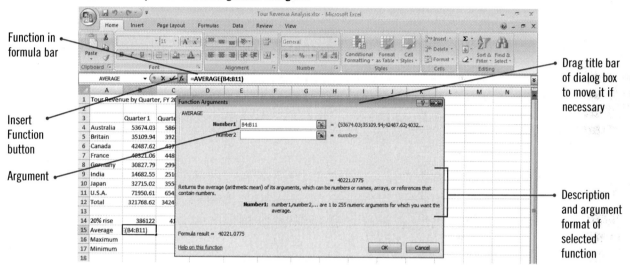

FIGURE B-5: Average function in worksheet

Completed function appears in formula bar

Formula in cell C15 copied to cells D15 and E15

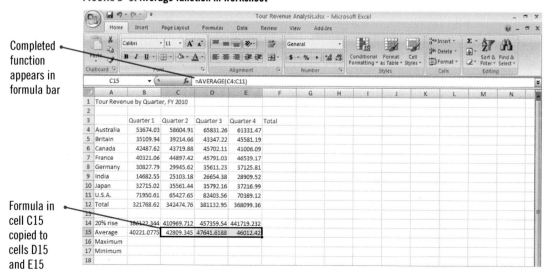

Typing a Function

In addition to entering a function using the Insert Function dialog box or the AutoSum button on the Ribbon, you can manually type the function into a cell and complete the arguments needed. This method requires that you know the name and initial characters of the function, but can be faster than opening several dialog boxes. Experienced Excel users often prefer this method, but it is only an alternative, not better or more correct than any other method. The AutoComplete feature makes it easier to enter function names because it suggests functions depending on the first letters you type. ▓▓▓▓ You want to calculate the maximum and minimum quarterly sales in your worksheet, and decide to manually enter these statistical functions.

1. **Click cell B16, type =, then type m**

   Since you are manually typing this function, it is necessary to begin with the equal sign (=). The AutoComplete feature displays a list of function names beginning with M. Once you type an equal sign in a cell, each letter you type acts as a trigger to activate the AutoComplete feature. This feature minimizes the amount of typing you need to do to enter a function, and reduces typing and syntax errors.

   > **QUICK TIP**
   > You can single-click any function in the AutoComplete list to open a Screentip describing the selected function.

2. **Click MAX in the list**

   A Screentip appears, describing the function.

3. **Double-click MAX**

   The function is added to the cell and a Screentip appears beneath the cell to help you complete the formula. See Figure B-6.

4. **Select the range B4:B11, as shown in Figure B-7, then click the Enter button ☑ on the formula bar**

   The result, 71950.61, appears in cell B16. When you completed the entry, the closing parenthesis was automatically added to the formula.

5. **Click cell B17, type =, type m, then double-click MIN**

   The argument for the MIN function appears in the cell.

6. **Select the range B4:B11, then press [Enter]**

   The result, 14682.55, appears in cell B17.

7. **Select the range B16:E17, click the Fill button list arrow ▣▾ in the Editing group, then click Right**

   The maximum and minimum values for all of the quarters display in the selected range, as shown in Figure B-8.

8. **Save your work**

Using the COUNT and COUNTA functions

When you select a range, a count of cells in the range that are not blank appears in the status bar. For example, if you select the range A1:A5 and only cells A1 and A2 contain data, the status bar displays "Count: 2." To count nonblank cells more precisely, or to incorporate these calculations in a worksheet, you can use the COUNT and COUNTA functions. COUNT returns the number of cells that contain numeric data, including numbers, dates, and formulas. COUNTA returns the number of cells that contain any data at all, even text or a blank space. For example, the formula =COUNT(A1:A5) returns the number of cells in the range that contain numeric data, and the formula =COUNTA(A1:A5) returns the number of cells in the range that are not blank.

FIGURE B-6: MAX function in progress

13					
14	20% rise	386122.344	410969.712	457359.54	441719.232
15	Average	40221.0775	42809.345	47641.6188	46012.42
16	Maximum	=MAX(			
17	Minimum	MAX(number1, [number2], ...)			
18					

FIGURE B-7: Completing the MAX function

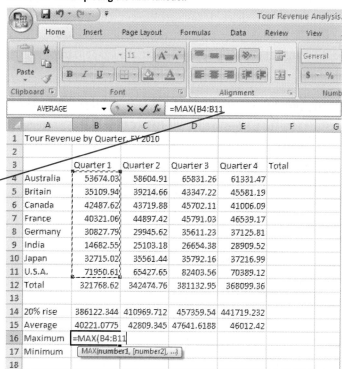

Closing parenthesis will be added automatically when you accept entry

FIGURE B-8: Completed MAX and MIN functions

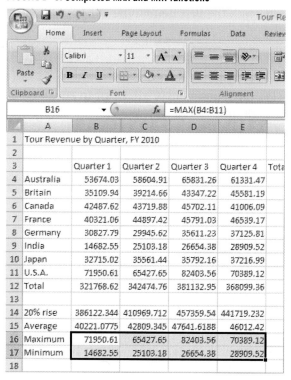

Copying and Moving Cell Entries

You can copy or move cells and ranges (or the contents within them) from one location to another using the Cut, Copy, and Paste buttons; the fill handle in the lower-right corner of the active cell; or the drag-and-drop feature. When you copy cells, the original data remains in the original location; when you cut or move it, the original data is deleted. You can also cut, copy, and paste cells or ranges from one worksheet to another. ━━━ In addition to the 20% rise in tour revenue, you also want to show a 30% rise. Rather than retype this information, you copy and move the labels in these cells.

STEPS

1. **Select the range B3:E3, then click the Copy button 🖺 in the Clipboard group**

   The selected range (B3:E3) is copied to the **Office Clipboard**, a temporary storage area that holds the selections you copy or cut. A moving border surrounds the selected range until you press [Esc] or copy an additional item to the Clipboard. Notice that the information you copied remains in the selected range; if you had cut instead of copied, the information would have been deleted once it was pasted.

2. **Click the launcher 🖾 in the Clipboard group, click cell B19, then click the Paste button in the Clipboard group**

   The Office Clipboard pane opens, as shown in Figure B-9. Your Clipboard may contain additional items. When pasting an item from the Clipboard into the worksheet, you only need to specify the upper-left cell of the range where you want to paste the selection.

3. **Press [Delete]**

   The selected cells are empty. You have decided to paste the cells in a different row. You can repeatedly paste an item from the Office Clipboard as many times as you like, as long as the item remains in the Clipboard.

4. **Click cell B20 , click the first item in the Office Clipboard, then click the Close button on the Clipboard pane**

   Cells B20:E20 contain the copied labels.

5. **Click cell A14 , press and hold [Ctrl], point to any edge of the cell until the pointer changes to ▸, drag ▸ to cell A21, then release [Ctrl]**

   As you drag, the pointer changes to ▸, as shown in Figure B-10.

6. **Click to the right of 2 in the formula bar, press [Backspace] , type 3, then press [Enter]**

7. **Click cell B21, type =, click cell B12 , type *1.3, then click ✔ on the formula bar**

   This new formula calculates a 30% increase of the revenue for Quarter 1, though using a different method from what you used previously. Anything you multiply by 1.3 returns an amount that's 130% of the original amount, or a 30% increase. Compare your screen to Figure B-11.

8. **Save your work**

FIGURE B-9: Copied data in Clipboard

Paste button

Copy button

Clipboard launcher

Item in Clipboard

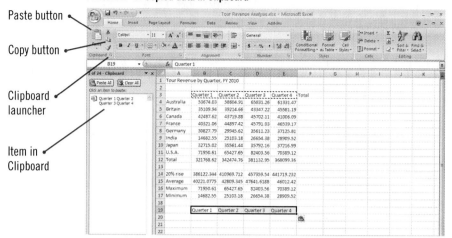

FIGURE B-10: Copying cell contents with drag-and-drop

Cell contents being copied

Plus (+) indicates copying in progress

Indicates new location of copy

FIGURE B-11: Formula to calculate 30% increase

Formula calculates 30% increase

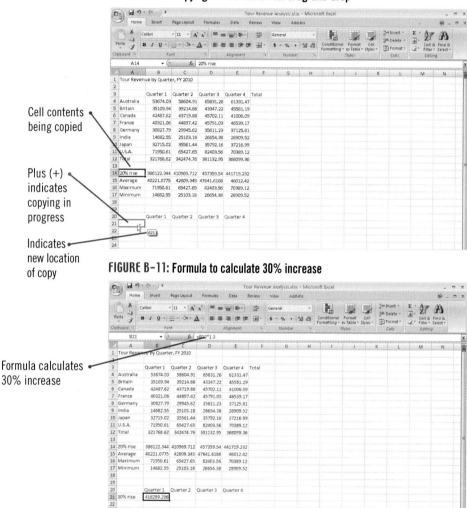

Inserting and deleting selected cells

As you add formulas to your workbook, you may need to insert or delete cells. When you do this, Excel automatically adjusts cell references to reflect their new locations. To insert cells, click the Insert button list arrow in the Cells group on the Home tab, then click Insert Cells. The Insert dialog box opens, asking if you want to insert a cell and move the selected cell down or to the right of the new one. To delete one or more selected cells, click the Delete button list arrow in the Cells group, click Delete Cells, and in the Delete dialog box, indicate which way you want to move the adjacent cells. When using this option, be careful not to disturb row or column alignment that may be necessary to maintain the accuracy of cell references in the worksheet. Click the Insert or Delete button to add/delete a single cell.

Understanding Relative and Absolute Cell References

As you work in Excel, you may want to reuse formulas in different parts of a worksheet to reduce the amount of data you have to retype. For example, you might want to include a what-if analysis in one part of a worksheet showing a set of sales projections if sales increase by 10%, and another analysis in another part of the worksheet showing projections if sales increase by 50%; you can copy the formulas from one section to another and just change the "1" to a "5". But when you copy formulas, it is important to make sure that they refer to the correct cells. To do this, you need to understand the difference between relative and absolute cell references. ████ You plan to reuse formulas in different parts of your worksheets, so you want to understand relative and absolute cell references.

DETAILS

- **Use relative references when you want to preserve the relationship to the formula location**

  When you create a formula that references other cells, Excel normally does not "record" the exact cell address. Instead, it looks at the relationship that cell has to the cell containing the formula. For example, in Figure B-12, cell F5 contains the formula: =SUM(B5:E5). When Excel retrieves values to calculate the formula in cell F5, it actually looks for "the cell four columns to the left of the formula," which in this case is cell B5. This way, if you copy the cell to a new location, such as cell F6, the results will reflect the new formula location, and will automatically retrieve the values in cells B6, C6, D6, and E6. These are **relative cell references**, because Excel is recording the input cells *in relation to* or *relative to* the formula cell.

  In most cases, you want to use relative cell references when copying or moving, so this is the Excel default. In Figure B-12, the formulas in F5:F12 and in B13:F13 contain relative cell references. They total the "four cells to the left of" or the "eight cells above" the formulas.

- **Use absolute cell references when you want to preserve the exact cell address in a formula**

  There are times when you want Excel to retrieve formula information from a specific cell, and you don't want the cell address in the formula to change when you copy it to a new location. For example, you might have a price in a specific cell that you want to use in all formulas, regardless of their location. If you used relative cell referencing, the formula results would be incorrect, because Excel would use a different cell every time you copied the formula. Therefore you need to use an **absolute cell reference** , a reference that does not change when you copy the formula.

  You create an absolute cell reference by placing a $ (dollar sign) in front of both the column letter and the row number of the cell address. You can either type the dollar sign when typing the cell address in a formula (for example, "=C12*B16"), or you can select a cell address on the formula bar and then press [F4] and the dollar signs are added automatically. Figure B-13 show formulas containing both absolute and relative references. The formulas in cells B19 to E26 use absolute cell references to refer to a potential sales increase of 50%, shown in cell B16.

FIGURE B-12: Formulas containing relative references

Formula containing relative references

Copied formulas adjust to preserve relationship of formula to referenced cells

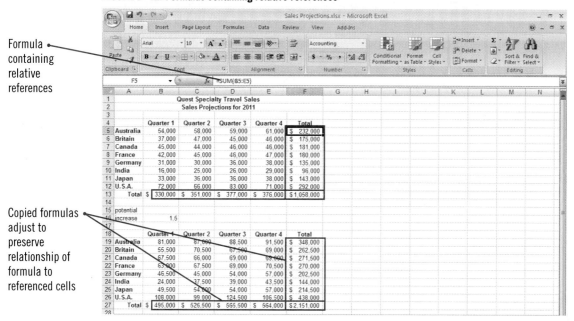

FIGURE B-13: Formulas containing absolute and relative references

Cell referenced in absolute formulas

Relative references in copied formulas adjust

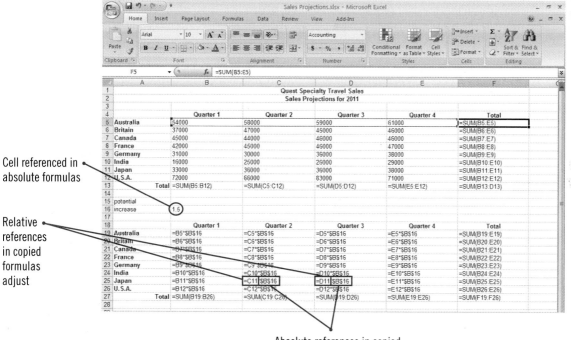

Absolute references in copied formulas do not adjust

Using a mixed reference

Sometimes when you copy a formula, you want to change the row reference, but keep the column reference the same. This type of cell referencing combines elements of both absolute and relative referencing and is called a **mixed reference**. For example, when copied, a formula containing the mixed reference C$14 would change the column letter relative to its new location, but not the row number.

In the mixed reference $C14, the column letter would not change, but the row number would be updated relative to its location. Like the absolute reference, a mixed reference can be created using the [F4] function key. With each press of the [F4] key, you cycle through all the possible combinations of relative, absolute, and mixed references (C14, C$14, $C14, C14).

Copying Formulas with Relative Cell References

Copying and moving a cell allows you to reuse a formula you've already created. Copying cells is usually faster than retyping the formulas in them, and helps to prevent typing errors. You can use the Copy and Paste commands or the fill handle to copy formulas. The Fill button list arrow can also be used to fill cells containing formulas going left, right, up, down, and in series. If the cells you are copying contain relative cell references and you want to maintain the relative referencing, you don't need to make any changes to the cells before copying them. ▰▰▰▰ You want to copy the formula in cell B21, which calculates the 30% increase in quarterly sales for quarter 1, to cells C21 through E21. You also want to create formulas to calculate total sales for each tour country.

1. **Click cell B21, if necessary, then click the Copy button ▤ in the Clipboard group**
   The formula for calculating the 30% sales increase during Quarter 1 is copied to the Clipboard. Notice that the formula =B12*1.3 appears in the formula bar and a moving border surrounds the active cell.

2. **Click cell C21, then click the Paste button in the Clipboard group**
   The formula from cell B21 is copied into cell C21, where the new result of 445217.188 appears. Notice in the formula bar that the cell references have changed, so that cell C12 is referenced in the formula. This formula contains a relative cell reference, which tells Excel to substitute new cell references within the copied formulas as necessary. This maintains the same relationship between the new cells containing the formula and the cells within the formula. In this case, Excel adjusted the formula so that cell C12—the cell reference nine rows above C21—replaced cell B12, the cell reference nine rows above B21. You can drag the fill handle in a cell to copy cells or to continue a series of data (such as Quarter 1, Quarter 2, etc.) based on previous cells. This option is called **Auto Fill**.

3. **Point to the fill handle in cell C21 until the pointer changes to ✚, press and hold the left mouse button, drag ✚ to select the range C21:E21, then release the mouse button**
   See Figure B-14. A formula similar to the one in cell C21 now appears in the range D21:E21. After you release the mouse button, the **Auto Fill Options button** appears, so you can fill the cells with only specific elements of the copied cell if you wish.

4. **Click cell F4, click the AutoSum button Σ in the Editing group, then click the Enter button ✓ on the formula bar**

5. **Click ▤ in the Clipboard group, select the range F5:F6, then click Paste**
   See Figure B-15. After you release the mouse button, the **Paste Options button** appears, so you can paste only specific elements of the copied selection if you wish. The formula for calculating quarterly revenue for tours in Britain appears in the formula bar. You would like totals to appear in cells F7:F11. The Fill command in the Editing group can be used to copy the formula into the remaining cells.

6. **Select the range F6:F11**

7. **Click the Fill button list arrow ▤▾ in the Editing group, then click Down**
   The formulas are copied to each cell. Compare your worksheet to Figure B-16.

8. **Save your work**

QUICK TIP

To specify components of the copied cell or range prior to pasting, click the Paste button list arrow in the Clipboard group, then click Paste Special. You can selectively copy formulas, values, or other choices.

QUICK TIP

You can use the Paste button in the Clipboard group of the Home tab to paste specific elements of a selection; click the Paste button arrow, then click an option in the list, such as Transpose (to paste column data as rows and row data as columns), No Borders (to remove any borders around pasted cells), or Paste Special (to open the Paste Special dialog box, where the complete set of paste options is available).

FIGURE B-14: Copying a formula with the fill handle

Paste button list arrow

Auto Fill Options button

Fill handle

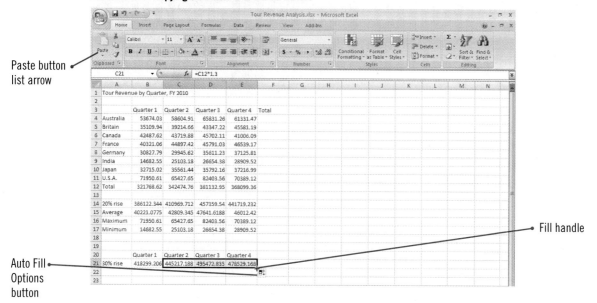

FIGURE B-15: The results of using the Paste button

Paste Options button

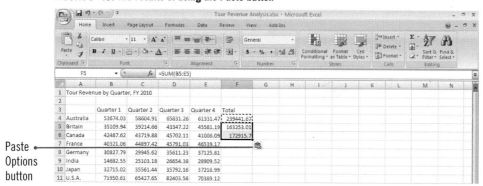

FIGURE B-16: Copying cells using Fill Down

Fill button list arrow

Filled cells

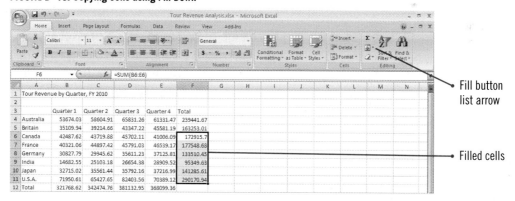

Using Auto Fill options

When you use the fill handle to copy cells, the Auto Fill Options button appears. Auto Fill options differ depending on what you are copying. If you had selected cells containing a series (such as "Monday" and "Tuesday") and then used the fill handle, you would see options for continuing the series (such as "Wednesday" and "Thursday") or for simply pasting the copied cells. Clicking the Auto Fill Options button opens a list that lets you choose from the following options: Copy Cells, Fill Series (if applicable), Fill Formatting Only, or Fill Without Formatting. Choosing Copy Cells means that the cell and its formatting will be copied. The Fill Formatting Only option copies only the formatting attributes, but not the formula and its cell references. The Fill Without Formatting option copies the formula and its cell references, but no formatting attributes. Copy Cells is the default option when using the fill handle to copy a formula, so if you want to copy the cell, its references and formatting, you can ignore this button.

Copying Formulas with Absolute Cell References

When copying formulas, you might want one or more cell references in the formula to remain unchanged in relation to the formula. In such an instance, you need to apply an absolute cell reference before copying the formula, to preserve the specific cell address when the formula is copied. You create an absolute reference by placing a dollar sign ($) before the row letter and column number of the address (for example A1). ▓▓▓▓▓ You need to do some what-if analysis to see how various sales percentage increases might affect total revenues. You decide to add a column that calculates a possible increase in the total tour revenue, and then change the percentage to see various potential results.

1. **Click cell H1, type Change, then press [→]**

2. **Type 1.1, then press [Enter]**
   You store the increase factor that will be used in the what-if analysis in this cell. The value 1.1 can be used to calculate a 10% increase; anything you multiply by 1.1 returns an amount that's 110% of the original amount, or a 10% increase.

3. **Click cell H3, type What if?, then press [Enter]**

4. **In cell H4, type =, click F4, type *, click cell I1, then click the Enter button ☑ on the formula bar**
   The result, 263385.8, appears in cell H4. This value represents the total annual revenue for Australia if there is a 10% increase. You want to perform a what-if analysis for all the tour countries.

5. **Drag the fill handle of cell H4 to extend the selection to cell H11**
   The resulting values in the range H5:H11 are all zeros, which is not the result you wanted. See Figure B-17. Because you used relative cell addressing in cell H4, the copied formula adjusted so that the formula in cell H5 is =F5*I2. Because there is no value in cell I2, the result is 0, an error. You need to use an absolute reference in the formula to keep the formula from adjusting itself. That way, it will always reference cell I1.

6. **Click cell H4, press [F2] to change to Edit mode, then press [F4]**
   When you press [F2], the range finder outlines the arguments of the equation in blue and green. When you press [F4], dollar signs are inserted in the cell address, changing the I1 cell reference to an absolute reference.

7. **Click ☑, then drag ✚ to extend the selection to range H4:H11**
   The formula correctly contains an absolute cell reference, and the value of H4 remains unchanged. The correct values for a 10% increase appear in cells H4:H11. You now want to see a 20% increase in sales.

8. **Click cell I1, type 1.2, then click ☑**
   The values in the range H4:H11 change to reflect the 20% increase. Compare your worksheet to Figure B-18.

9. **Save your work**

FIGURE B-17: Creating an absolute reference in formula

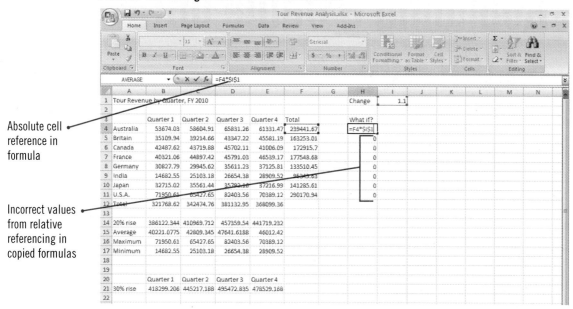

Absolute cell reference in formula

Incorrect values from relative referencing in copied formulas

FIGURE B-18: What-if analysis with modified change factor

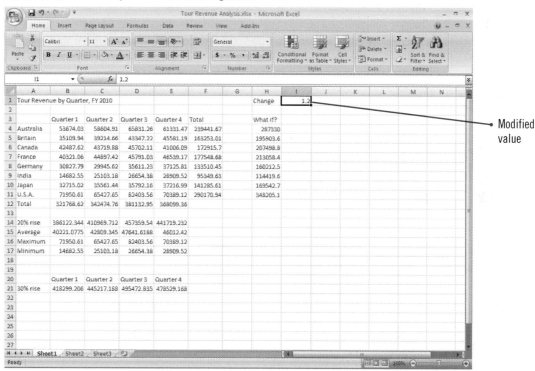

Modified value

Using the fill handle for sequential text or values

Often, you need to fill cells with sequential text: months of the year, days of the week, years, or text plus a number (Quarter 1, Quarter 2,...). For example, you might want to create a worksheet that calculates data for every month of the year. Using the fill handle, you can quickly and easily create labels for the months of the year just by typing January in a cell. Drag the fill handle from the cell containing January until you have all the monthly labels you need. You can easily fill cells using sequences by dragging the fill handle. As you drag the fill handle, Excel automatically extends the existing sequence. (The content of the last filled cell appears in the ScreenTip.) Use the Fill button list arrow in the Editing group, then click Series to examine all the fill series options for the current selection.

Rounding a Value with a Function

The more you explore features and tools in Excel, the more ways you'll find to simplify your work and convey information more efficiently. For example, cells containing financial data are often easier to read if they contain fewer decimals than those that appear by default. You can achieve this result by using the ROUND function, to round down your results. ▓▓▓▓▓ In your worksheet, you'd like to round the cells showing the 20% rise in sales to show fewer digits; after all, it's not important to show cents in the projections, only whole dollars. You want Excel to round the calculated value to the nearest integer. You decide to edit cell B14 so it includes the ROUND function, and then copy the edited formula into the other formulas in this row.

STEPS

1. **Click cell B14, then click to the right of = on the formula bar**

   You want to position the function at the beginning of the formula, before any values or arguments.

2. **Type RO**

   AutoComplete displays a list of functions beginning with RO.

3. **Double-click ROUND in the AutoComplete list**

   The new function and an opening parenthesis are added to the formula, as shown in Figure B-19. A few additional modifications are needed to complete your edit of the formula. You need to indicate the number of digits to which the function should round numbers down, and you also need to add a closing parenthesis around the set of arguments that come after the ROUND function.

4. **Press [END], type ,0), then click the Enter button ☑ on the formula bar**

   The comma separates the arguments within the formula, and 0 indicates that you don't want any decimals to appear in the calculated value. When you complete the edit, the parenthesis at either end of the formula briefly become bold, indicating that the formula has the correct number of open and closed parentheses and is balanced.

5. **Click the fill handle of cell B14, then drag the ✚ pointer to cell E14**

   When you release the mouse button, the formula in cell B14 is copied to the selected range. All the values are rounded to display no decimals. Compare your worksheet to Figure B-20.

6. **Click cell A25, type your name, then click ☑ on the formula bar**

7. **Save your work, preview and print the worksheet, then exit Excel**

FIGURE B-19: Adding a function to an existing formula

ROUND function and opening parenthesis inserted in formula

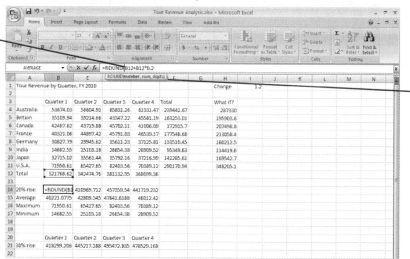

ScreenTip indicates what information is needed

FIGURE B-20: Function added to formula

Function surrounds existing formula

Calculated values with no decimals

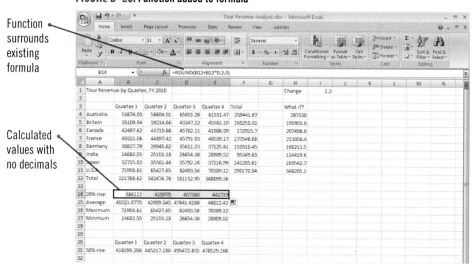

Creating a new workbook using a template

Excel **templates** are predesigned workbook files intended to save time when you create common documents such as balance sheets, expense statements, loan amortizations, sales invoices, or timecards. They contain labels, values, formulas, and formatting, so when you use a template all you have to do is customize it with your own information. Excel comes with many templates, and you can also create your own or find additional templates on the Web. Unlike a typical workbook, which has the file extension .xlsx, a template has the extension .xltx. To create a workbook using a template, click the Office button, then click New. The New Workbook dialog box opens. The Blank Workbook template is selected by default, because this is the template used to create a blank workbook with no content or special formatting. The left pane lists templates installed on your computer as well as many categories of templates available through Microsoft Office Online. Click a category, find the template you want, as shown in Figure B-21, click Download, then click Continue. A new workbook is created based on the template, so when you save the new file in the default format, it will have the

regular .xlsx extension. To save a workbook of your own as a template, open the Save As dialog box, then click the Save as type list arrow and change the file type to Excel Template.

FIGURE B-21: New Workbook dialog box

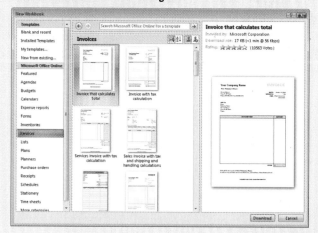

Practice

If you have a SAM user profile, you may have access to hands-on instruction, practice, and assessment of the skills covered in this unit. Log in to your SAM account (http://sam2007.course.com/) to launch any assigned training activities or exams that relate to the skills covered in this unit.

▼ CONCEPTS REVIEW

Label each element of the Excel worksheet window shown in Figure B-22.

FIGURE B-22

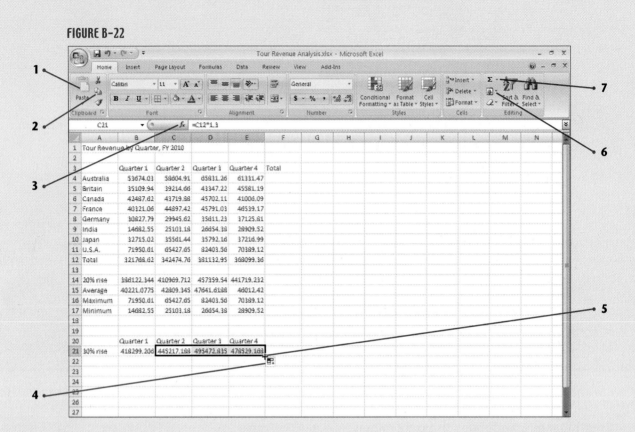

Match each term or button with the statement that best describes it.

8. **Launcher**

9. **Formula AutoComplete**

10. **Drag-and-drop**

11. **Fill handle**

12. **[Delete]**

a. Clears the contents of selected cells

b. Item on the Ribbon that opens a dialog box or task pane

c. Lets you move data from one cell to another without using the Clipboard

d. Displays an alphabetical list of functions from which you can choose

e. Lets you copy cell contents or continue a series of data into a range of selected cells

Select the best answer from the list of choices.

13. **What type of cell reference changes when it is copied?**
    a. Circular
    b. Absolute
    c. Relative
    d. Specified

14. **What type of cell reference is C$19?**
    a. Relative
    b. Absolute
    c. Mixed
    d. Certain

15. **Which key do you press to convert a relative cell reference to an absolute cell reference?**
    a. [F2]
    b. [F4]
    c. [F5]
    d. [F6]

16. **You can use any of the following features to enter a function *except*:**
    a. Insert Function button.
    b. Formula AutoComplete.
    c. AutoSum button list arrow.
    d. Clipboard.

17. **Which key do you press to copy while dragging-and-dropping selected cells?**
    a. [Alt]
    b. [Ctrl]
    c. [F2]
    d. [Tab]

1. Create a complex formula.

  a. Open the file EX B-2.xlsx from the drive and folder where you store your Data Files, then save it as **Candy Supply Company Inventory**.

  b. In cell B11, create a complex formula that calculates a 30% decrease in the total number of cases of Snickers bars.

  c. Use the Fill button to copy this formula into cell C11 through cell E11, as shown in Figure B-23.

  d. Save your work.

FIGURE B-23

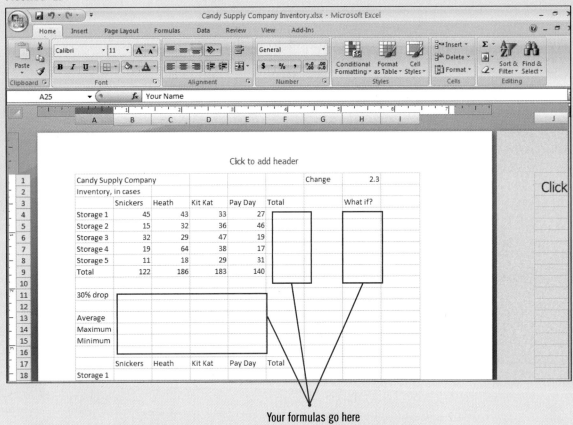

Your formulas go here

2. Insert a function.

  a. Use the AutoSum button to create a formula in cell B13 that averages the number of cases of Snickers bars in each storage area. (*Hint*: Click the AutoSum button list arrow to open a list of available functions.)

  b. Use the Insert Function button to create a formula in cell B14 that calculates the most cases of Snickers bars in a storage area.

  c. Use the AutoSum button to create a formula in cell B15 that calculates the minimum number of cases of Snickers bars in a storage area.

  d. Save your work.

3. Type a function.

  a. In cell C13, type a formula that includes a function to average the number of cases of Heath bars. (*Hint*: Use AutoComplete to enter the function.)

  b. In cell C14, type a formula that includes a function to calculate the maximum number of cases of Heath bars in a storage area.

  c. In cell C15, type a formula that includes a function to calculate the minimum number of cases of Heath bars in a storage area.

  d. Save your work.

4. **Copy and move cell entries.**
   a. Select the range B3:F3.
   b. Copy the selection into the Clipboard.
   c. Open the Clipboard task pane, then paste the selection into cell B17.
   d. Select the range A4:A9.
   e. Use the drag-and-drop method to copy the selection to cell A18. (*Hint*: The results should fill the range A18:A23.)
   f. Select the range H1:I1.
   g. Move the selection using the drag-and-drop method to cell G1.
   h. Save your work.

5. **Understand relative and absolute cell referencess.**
   a. Write a brief description of the difference between relative and absolute references.
   b. List at least three situations in which you think a business might use an absolute reference in its calculations. Examples can include calculations for different types of worksheets, such as timecards, invoices, and budgets.

6. **Copy formulas with relative cell references.**
   a. Select the range C13:C15.
   b. Use the fill handle to copy these cells to the range D13:E15.
   c. Calculate the total in cell F4.
   d. Use the Fill button to copy the formula in cell F4 down to cells F5:F9.
   e. Use the fill handle to copy the formula in cell E11 to cell F11.
   f. Save your work.

7. **Copy formulas with absolute cell references.**
   a. In cell H1, enter the value 1.575.
   b. In cell H4, create a formula that multiplies F4 and an absolute reference to cell H1.
   c. Use the fill handle to copy the formula in cell H4 to cells H5 and H6.
   d. Use the Copy and Paste buttons to copy the formula in cell H4 to cells H7 and H8.
   e. Change the amount in cell H1 to 2.3.
   f. Save your work.

8. **Round a value with a function.**
   a. Click cell H4.
   b. Edit this formula to include the ROUND function showing one digit.
   c. Use the fill handle to copy the formula in cell H4 to the range H5:H8.
   d. Enter your name in cell A25, then compare your work to Figure B-23.
   e. Save, preview, print, and close the workbook, then exit Excel.

▼ INDEPENDENT CHALLENGE 1

You are thinking of starting a small breakfast and lunch diner. Before you begin, you need to evaluate what you think your monthly expenses will be. You've started a workbook, but need to complete the entries and add formulas.

a. Open the file EX B-3.xlsx from the drive and folder where you store your Data Files, then save it as **Estimated Diner Expenses**.

b. Make up your own expense data and enter it in cells B4:B10. (Monthly sales are included in the worksheet.)

c. Create a formula in cell C4 that calculates the annual rent.

d. Copy the formula in cell C4 to the range C5:C10.

e. Move the label in cell A15 to cell A14.

f. Create a formula in cells B11 and C11 that totals the expenses.

g. Create a formula in cell C13 that calculates annual sales.

h. Create a formula in cell B14 that determines whether you will make a profit or loss, then copy the formula into cell C14.

i. Copy the labels in cells B3:C3 to cells E3:F3.

j. Type **Projection increase** in cell G1, then type **.2** in cell I1.

k. Create a formula in cell E4 that calculates an increase in the monthly rent by the amount in cell I1. You will be copying this formula to other cells, so you'll need to use an absolute reference.

l. Create a formula in cell F4 that calculates an annual increase based on the calculation in cell E4.

m. Create formulas in cells E13 and E14 and cells F13 and F14 that calculates monthly and annual sales and profit/loss based on the increase in cell E4.

n. Copy the formulas in cells E4:F4 in the remaining monthly and annual expenses.

o. Change the projection increase to **.15**, then compare your work to the sample in Figure B-24.

p. Enter your name in a cell in the worksheet.

q. Save your work, preview and print the worksheets, then close the workbook and exit Excel.

FIGURE B-24

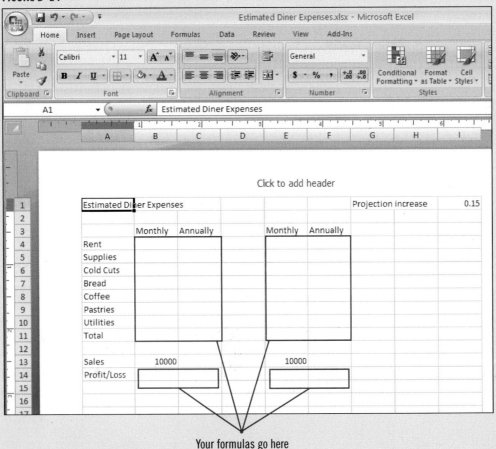

Working with Formulas and Functions

▼ INDEPENDENT CHALLENGE 2

The Pamper Yourself Salon & Day Spa is a small, growing spa that has hired you to organize its accounting records using Excel. The owners want you to track the company's expenses. Before you were hired, one of the bookkeepers began entering last year's expenses in a workbook, but the analysis was never completed.

a. Start Excel, open the file EX B-4.xlsx from the drive and folder where you store your Data Files, then save it as **Pamper Yourself Finances**. The worksheet includes labels for functions such as the Average, Maximum, and Minimum amounts of each of the expenses in the worksheet.

b. Think about what information would be important for the bookkeeping staff to know.

c. Create formulas in the Total column and row using the Sum function.

d. Create formulas in the Average, Maximum, and Minimum columns and rows using the method of your choice.

e. Save your work, then compare your worksheet to the sample shown in Figure B-25.

Advanced Challenge Exercise

■ Create the label **Expense categories** in cell B19.

■ In cell A19, create a formula using the COUNT function that determines the total number of expense categories listed per quarter.

■ Save the workbook.

f. Enter your name in cell A25.

g. Preview the worksheet, then print it.

h. Save your work, then close the workbook and exit Excel.

FIGURE B-25

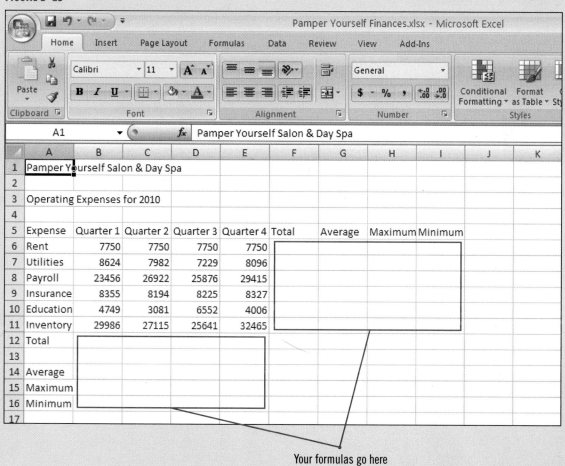

Your formulas go here

▼ INDEPENDENT CHALLENGE 3

As the accounting manager of a locally-owned clothing store, it is your responsibility to calculate and submit accrued sales tax payments on a monthly basis to the state government. You've decided to use an Excel workbook to make these calculations.

a. Start Excel, then save a new, blank workbook to the drive and folder where you store your Data Files as **Sales Tax Calculations**.

b. Decide on the layout for all columns and rows. The worksheet will contain data for four stores, which you can name by store number, neighborhood, or another method of your choice. For each store, you will calculate total sales tax based on the local sales tax rate. You'll also calculate total tax owed for all four stores.

c. Make up sales data for at least four stores.

d. Enter the rate to be used to calculate the sales tax, using your own local rate.

e. Create formulas to calculate the sales tax owed for each store. If you don't know the local tax rate, use **6.5%**.

f. Create a formula to total all the owed sales tax, then compare your work to the sample shown in Figure B-26.

Advanced Challenge Exercise

- Use the ROUND function to eliminate any decimals in the sales tax figures for each store and the total due.
- Save the workbook.

g. Add your name to the header.

h. Save your work, preview and print each worksheet, then close the workbook and exit Excel.

FIGURE B-26

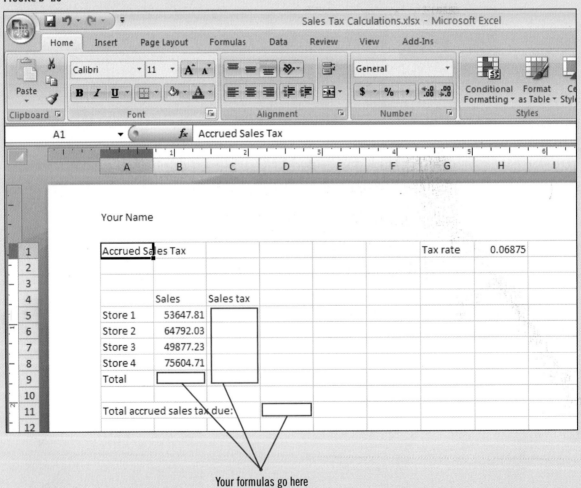

Working with Formulas and Functions

▼ REAL LIFE INDEPENDENT CHALLENGE

Many of your friends are purchasing homes, and you are thinking about taking the plunge yourself. As you begin the round of open houses and realtors' listings, you notice that there are many fees associated with buying a home. Some fees are based on a percentage of the purchase price and others are a flat fee; overall, they seem to represent a substantial amount above the purchase prices you see listed. You've seen three houses so far that interest you; one is moderately priced, one is more expensive, and the third is still more expensive. You decide to create an Excel workbook to figure out the real cost of buying each one.

a. Find out the typical cost or percentage rate of at least three fees that are usually charged when buying a home and taking out a mortgage. (*Hint*: If you have access to the Internet you can research the topic of home-buying on the Web, or you can ask friends about standard rates or percentages for items such as title insurance, credit reports, and inspection fees.)

FIGURE B-27

b. Start Excel, then save a new, blank workbook to the drive and folder where you store your Data Files as **Home Purchase Fees**.

c. Create labels and enter data for three homes. If you enter this information across the columns in your worksheet, you should have one column for each house, with the purchase price in the cell below each label. Be sure to enter a different purchase price for each house.

d. Create labels for the Fees column and for an Amount or Rate column. Enter the information on the three fees you have researched.

e. In each house column, enter formulas that calculate the fee for each item. The formulas (and use of absolute or relative referencing) will vary depending on whether the charges are a flat fee or based on a percentage of the purchase price.

f. Total the fees for each house, create formulas that add the total fees to the purchase price, then compare your work to the sample in Figure B-27.

g. Enter a title for the worksheet in the header.

h. Enter your name in the header, preview the worksheet, then print it.

i. Save your work, then close the file and exit Excel.

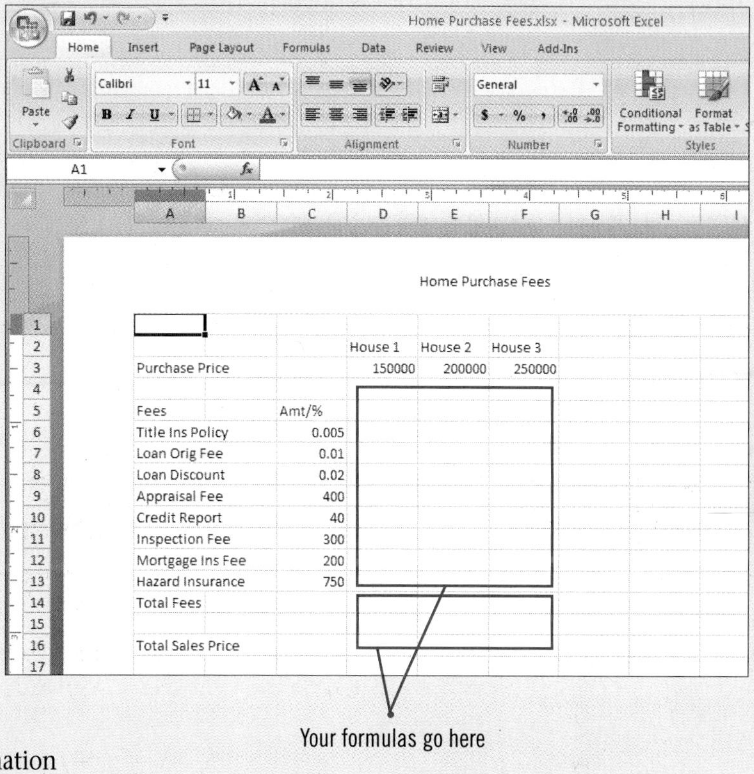

▼ VISUAL WORKSHOP

Create the worksheet shown in Figure B-28 using the skills you learned in this unit. Save the workbook as **Sales Analysis** to the drive and folder where you store your Data Files. Enter your name in the header as shown, then preview and print one copy of the worksheet. Print a second copy of the worksheet with the formulas showing.

FIGURE B-28

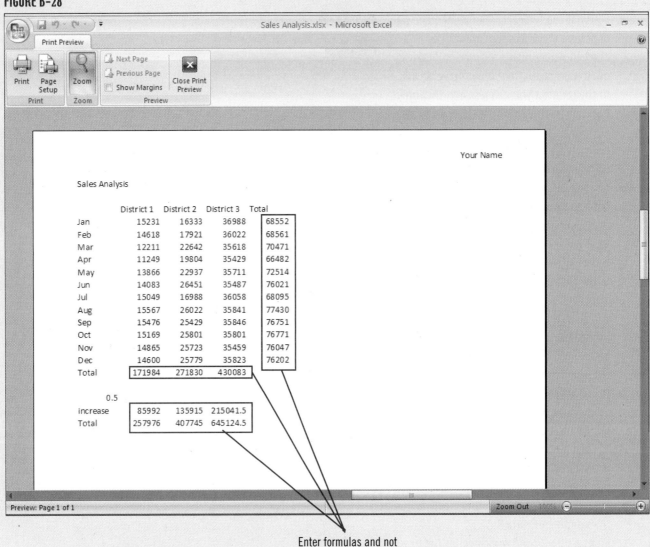

Enter formulas and not values in these cells

Working with Formulas and Functions

Formatting a Worksheet

You can use formatting features to make a worksheet more attractive or easier to read, and to emphasize key data. You can apply different formatting attributes such as colors, font styles, and font sizes to the cell contents, you can adjust column width and row height, and you can insert or delete columns and rows. You can also apply conditional formatting so that cells meeting certain criteria are formatted differently. This makes it easy to emphasize selected information, such as sales that exceed or fall below a certain threshold. The marketing managers at QST have requested information on advertising expenses for all QST locations during the past four quarters. Grace Wong has created a worksheet listing this information. She asks you to format the worksheet to make it easier to read and to call attention to important data.

OBJECTIVES

Format values

Change font and font size

Change attributes and alignment

Adjust column width

Insert and delete rows and columns

Apply colors, patterns, and borders

Apply conditional formatting

Name and move a sheet

Check spelling

Formatting Values

The **format** of a cell determines how the labels and values look—for example, whether the contents appear boldfaced, italicized, or with dollar signs and commas. Formatting changes only the appearance of a value or label; it does not alter the actual data in any way. To format a cell or range, first you select it, then you apply the formatting using the Ribbon or a keyboard shortcut. You can apply formatting before or after you enter data in a cell or range. 🔷🔷🔷🔷 Grace has provided you with a worksheet that lists individual advertising expenses, and you're ready to improve its appearance and readability. You decide to start by formatting some of the values so they display as currency, percentages, and dates.

STEPS

1. **Start Excel, open the file EX C-1.xlsx from the drive and folder where you store your Data Files, save it as** QST Advertising Expenses, **click the** View tab **on the Ribbon, then click the** Page Layout button

    This worksheet is difficult to interpret because all the information looks the same. In some columns, the contents appear cut off because there is too much data to fit given the current column width. You decide not to widen the columns yet, because the other changes you plan to make might affect column width and row height. The first thing you want to do is format the data showing the cost of each ad.

> **QUICK TIP**
>
> You can apply a different currency format, such as Euros or British Pounds, by clicking the Accounting Number Format Button arrow, then clicking a different currency type.

2. **Select the range E4:E32, then click the** Accounting Number Format button **$ in the Number group on the Home tab**

    The default Accounting Number format adds dollar signs and two decimal places to the data, as shown in Figure C-1. Formatting this data in accounting format makes it easier to recognize. Excel automatically resizes the column to display the new formatting. The Accounting and Currency formats are both used for monetary values, but the Accounting format aligns currency symbols and decimal points of numbers in a column.

> **QUICK TIP**
>
> Select any range of contiguous cells by clicking the top-left cell, pressing and holding [Shift], then clicking the bottom-right cell. Add a row to the selected range by continuing to hold down [Shift] and pressing [↓]; add a column by pressing [→].

3. **Select the range G4:I32, then click the** Comma Style button **❜ in the Number group**

    The values in columns G, H, and I display the Comma Style format, which does not include a dollar sign but can be useful for some types of accounting data.

4. **Select the range J4:J32, click the** Number Format list arrow, **click** Percentage, **then click the** Increase Decimal button **🔢 in the Number group**

    The data in the % of Total column is now formatted with a percent sign (%) and three decimal places. The Format list arrow lets you choose from popular number formats and shows an example of what the selected cell or cells would look like in each format (when multiple cells are selected, the example is based on the first cell in the range). Each time you click the Increase Decimal button, you add one decimal place; clicking the button twice would add two decimal places.

5. **Click the** Decrease Decimal button **🔢 in the Number group twice**

    Two decimal places are removed.

6. **Select the range B4:B31, click the** launcher **🔳 in the Number group**

    The Format Cells dialog box opens with the Date category already selected on the Number tab.

7. **Select the first** 14-Mar-01 **format in the Type list box as shown in Figure C-2, then click** OK

    The dates in column B appear in the 14-Mar-01 format. The second 14-Mar-01 format in the list displays all days in two digits (it adds a leading zero if the day is only a single-digit number), while the one you chose displays single-digit days without a leading zero. You can also open the Format Cells dialog box by right-clicking a selected range.

> **QUICK TIP**
>
> Make sure you examine formatted data to confirm that you have applied the appropriate formatting; for example, dates should not have a currency format, and monetary values should not have a date format.

8. **Select the range C4:C31, right-click the range, click** Format Cells **on the shortcut menu, click** 14-Mar **in the Type list box in the Format Cells dialog box, then click** OK

    Compare your worksheet to Figure C-3.

9. **Press [Ctrl][Home], then save your work**

Formatting a Worksheet

FIGURE C-1: Advertising expense worksheet

Number Format list arrow

Accounting Number Format button

Commands in Number group change the appearance of numbers

Format as Table button

Decrease Decimal button

Increase Decimal button

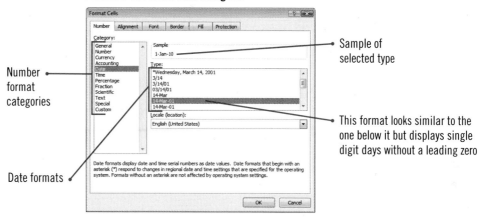

FIGURE C-2: Format Cells dialog box

Number format categories

Date formats

Sample of selected type

This format looks similar to the one below it but displays single digit days without a leading zero

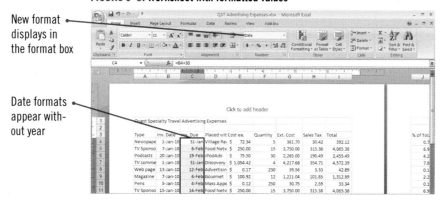

FIGURE C-3: Worksheet with formatted values

New format displays in the format box

Date formats appear without year

Formatting as a table

Excel includes 60 predefined table styles to make it easy to format selected worksheet cells as a table. You can apply table styles to any range of cells that you want to format quickly, or even to an entire worksheet, but they're especially useful for those ranges with labels in the left column and top rows, and totals in the bottom row or right column. To apply a table style, select the data to be formatted or click anywhere within the intended range (Excel can automatically detect a range of cells), click the Format as Table button in the Styles group on the Home tab, then click a style in the gallery, as shown in Figure C-4. Table styles are organized in three categories (Light, Medium, and Dark). Once you click a style, Excel confirms the range selection, then applies the style. Once you have formatted a range as a table, you can use Live Preview to preview with different choices by pointing to any style in the Table Styles gallery.

FIGURE C-4: Table Styles gallery

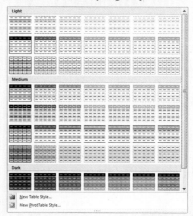

UNIT
C
Excel 2007

Changing Font and Font Size

A **font** is the name for a collection of characters (letters, numerals, symbols, and punctuation marks) with a similar, specific design. The **font size** is the physical size of the text, measured in units called points. A **point** is equal to 1/72 of an inch. The default font in Excel is 11-point Calibri. Table C-1 shows several fonts in different sizes. You can change the font and font size of any cell or range using the Ribbon, the Format Cells dialog box, or the Mini toolbar. You can open the Format Cells dialog box by clicking the launcher in the Font, Alignment, or Number group on the Home tab, or by right-clicking a selection, then clicking Format Cells in the shortcut menu. The Mini toolbar opens when you right-click a cell or range. You want to change the font and size of the labels and the worksheet title so that they stand out more from the data.

STEPS

1. **Right-click cell A1, click Format Cells on the shortcut menu, then click the Font tab in the Format Cells dialog box if necessary**
   See Figure C-5.

QUICK TIP
To preview font and font size changes directly in selected cells, use the Font group on the Home tab; Live Preview shows font, font size, font color, and fill color when you hover the mouse pointer over selections in these lists and palettes.

2. **Scroll down in the Font list to see an alphabetical listing of the fonts available on your computer, click Times New Roman in the Font list box, click 20 in the Size list box, preview the results in the Preview area, then click OK**
   The title appears in 20-point Times New Roman, and the Font group on the Home tab displays the new font and size information.

3. **Click the Increase Font Size button A⁺ in the Font group twice**
   The size of the title increases to 24-point.

QUICK TIP
You can also format an entire row by clicking the row indicator button (or an entire column by clicking the column indicator button).

4. **Select the range A3:J3, right-click, then click the Font list arrow on the Mini toolbar**
   The Mini toolbar includes the most commonly used formatting tools, so it's great for making quick formatting changes. Notice that the font names on this font list are displayed in the font they represent.

QUICK TIP
Once you click the Font list arrow, you can quickly move to a font in the list by typing the first few characters of its name.

5. **Click Times New Roman, click the Font Size list arrow, then click 14**
   The Mini toolbar closes when you move the pointer away from the selection. Compare your worksheet to Figure C-6. Notice that some of the column headings are now too wide to appear fully in the column. Excel does not automatically adjust column widths to accommodate cell formatting; you have to adjust column widths manually. You'll learn to do this in a later lesson.

6. **Save your work**

TABLE C-1: Examples of fonts and font sizes

font	12 point	24 point
Calibri	Excel	Excel
Playbill	Excel	Excel
Comic Sans MS	Excel	Excel
Times New Roman	Excel	Excel

Formatting a Worksheet

FIGURE C-5: Font tab in the Format Cells dialog box

Currently selected font

Available fonts might differ on your computer

Effects options

Type a custom font size or select from the list

Font style options

Preview area shows sample of selected formatting

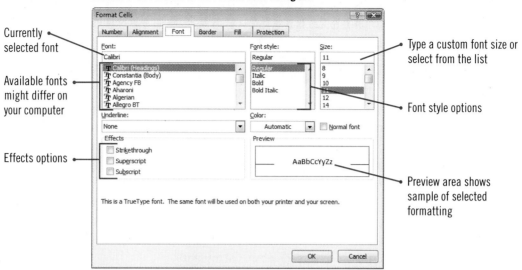

FIGURE C-6: Worksheet with formatted title and labels

Font and size of active cell or range

Title appears in 24-point Times New Roman

Column headings now 14-point Times New Roman

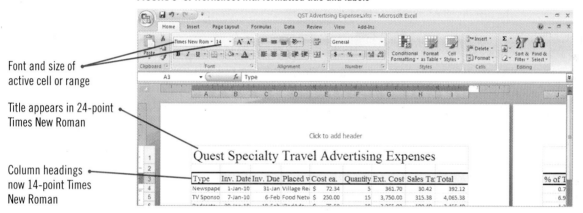

Inserting and adjusting clip art and other images

You can illustrate your worksheets using clip art and other images. A **clip** is an individual media file, such as art, sound, animation, or a movie. **Clip art** refers to images such as a corporate logo, a picture, or a photo. Microsoft Office comes with many clips available for your use. To add a clip to a worksheet, click Clip Art in the Illustrations group on the Insert tab. The Clip Art task pane opens. Here you can search for clips by typing one or more keywords (words related to your subject) in the Search for text box, then click Go. Clips that relate to your keywords appear in the Clip Art task pane, as shown in Figure C-7. (If you have a standard Office installation and an active Internet connection, you will see many clips available through Microsoft Office Online in addition to those on your computer.) Click the image you want, and it is inserted at the location of the active cell. You can also add your own images to a worksheet by clicking the Insert tab on the Ribbon, then clicking the Picture button. Navigate to the file you want, then click Insert Picture from File. To resize an image, drag any corner sizing handle. To move an image, point inside the clip until the pointer changes to ✛, then drag it to a new location.

FIGURE C-7: Results of Clip Art search

Type keyword(s) here

Click to begin search

Changing Attributes and Alignment

Attributes are styling formats such as bold, italic, and underlining that you can apply to affect the way text and numbers look in a worksheet. You can "paint" or copy a cell's format into other cells by using the Format Painter button in the Clipboard group on the Home tab of the Ribbon. This is similar to using copy and paste, but instead of copying cell contents, it copies only the cell's formatting. You can also change the **alignment** of labels and values in cells to be left, right, or center. You can apply attributes and alignment options using the Home tab, the Format Cells dialog box, or the Mini toolbar. See Table C-2 for a description of common attribute and alignment buttons that are available on the Home tab of the Ribbon and the Mini toolbar. You want to further enhance the worksheet's appearance by adding bold and underline formatting and centering some of the labels.

STEPS

1. **Press [Ctrl][Home], then click the Bold button** B **in the Font group**
   The title in cell A1 appears in bold.

2. **Click cell A3, then click the Underline button** U **in the Font group**
   The column heading is now underlined, though this may be difficult to see with the cell selected.

3. **Click the Italic button** I **in the Font group, then click** B
   The heading now appears in boldface, underlined, italic type. Notice that the Bold, Italic, and Underline buttons in the Font group are all selected.

4. **Click** I
   The italic attribute is removed from cell A3, but the bold and underline attributes remain.

5. **Click the Format Painter button** ✔ **in the Clipboard group, then select the range B3:J3**
   The formatting in cell A3 is copied to the rest of the labels in the column headings. You can turn off the Format Painter by pressing [Esc] or by clicking ✔. You decide the title would look better if it were centered over the data columns.

6. **Select the range A1:J1, then click the Merge & Center button** ▦ **in the Alignment group**
   The Merge & Center button creates one cell out of the 10 cells across the row, then centers the text in that newly created large cell. The title "Quest Specialty Travel Advertising Expenses" is centered across the 10 columns you selected. You can change the alignment within individual cells using buttons on the Home tab; you can split merged cells into their original components by selecting the merged cells, then clicking the Merge & Center button.

7. **Select the range A3:J3, right-click, then click the Center button** ≡ **on the Mini toolbar**
   Compare your screen to Figure C-8. Although they may be difficult to read, notice that all the headings are centered within their cells.

8. **Save your work**

FIGURE C-8: Worksheet with formatting attributes applied

Formatting buttons selected

Merge & Center button

Center button

Title centered across columns

Column headings centered, bold and underlined

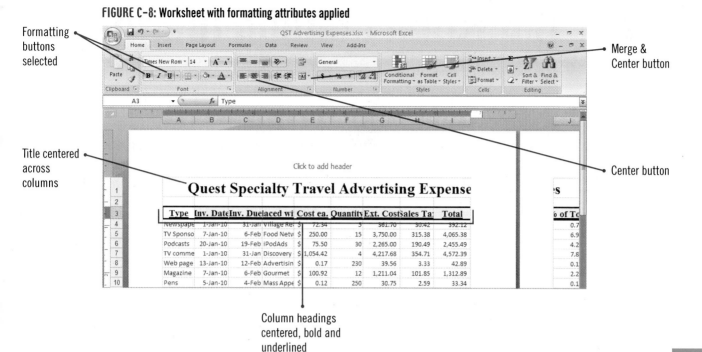

Rotating and indenting cell entries

In addition to applying fonts and formatting attributes, you can rotate or indent data within a cell to further change its appearance. You can rotate text within a cell by altering its alignment. To change alignment, select the cells you want to modify, then click the launcher in the Alignment group to open the Alignment tab of the Format Cells dialog box. Click a position in the Orientation box or type a number in the Degrees text box to change from the default horizontal alignment, then click OK. You can indent cell contents using the Increase Indent button on the Alignment group on the Home tab on the Ribbon, which moves cell contents to the right one space, or the Decrease Indent button, which moves cell contents to the left one space.

TABLE C-2: Common attribute and alignment buttons

button	description	button	description
B	Bolds text		Aligns text at the left edge of the cell
I	Italicizes text		Centers text horizontally within the cell
U	Underlines text		Aligns text at the right edge of the cell
	Adds lines or borders		Centers text across columns, and combines two or more selected, adjacent cells into one cell

Adjusting Column Width

As you format a worksheet, you might need to adjust the width of one or more columns to accommodate text or larger font size or style. The default column width is 8.43 characters wide, a little less than one inch. With Excel, you can adjust the width of one or more columns by using the mouse, the Ribbon, or the shortcut menu. Using the mouse, you can drag or double-click the right edge of a column heading. The Ribbon and shortcut menu include commands for making more detailed width adjustments. Table C-3 describes common column adjustment commands. You notice that some of the labels in column A don't fit in the cells. You want to adjust the widths of the columns so that the labels appear in their entirety.

STEPS

1. **Position the mouse pointer on the line between the column A and column B headings until it changes to ↔**

   See Figure C-9. The **column heading** is the box at the top of each column containing a letter. Before you can adjust column width using the mouse, you need to position the pointer on the right edge of the column you want to adjust. The entries for TV commercials are the widest in the column.

   > **QUICK TIP**
   > To reset columns to the default width, click the column headings to select the columns, click the Format button in the Cells group, click Default Width, then click OK in the Standard Width dialog box.

2. **Click and drag the ↔ to the right until the column displays the TV commercials entries fully**

3. **Position the pointer on the column line between columns B and C until it changes to ↔, then double-click**

   Column B automatically widens to fit the widest entry, in this case, the column label. Double-clicking activates the **AutoFit** feature, which automatically resizes a column so it accommodates the widest entry in a cell.

4. **Use AutoFit to resize columns C, D, and J**

   > **QUICK TIP**
   > If a column heading is selected, you can change the width of the column by right-clicking, then clicking Column Width in the shortcut menu.

5. **Select the range F5:I5**

   You can change the width of multiple columns at once, by first selecting either the column headings or at least one cell in each column.

6. **Click the Format button in the Cells group, then click Column Width**

   The Column Width dialog box opens. Column width measurement is based on the number of characters that will fit in the column when formatted in the Normal font and font size (in this case, 11 pt Calibri).

   > **QUICK TIP**
   > If "#######" appears after you adjust a column of values, the column is too narrow to display the contents; increase the column width until the values appear.

7. **Drag the dialog box by its title bar if its placement obscures your view of the worksheet, type .91" in the Column width text box, then click OK**

   The widths of columns F, G, H, and I change to reflect the new setting. See Figure C-10.

8. **Save your work**

Changing row height

Changing row height is as easy as changing column width. Row height is calculated in points, the same units of measure used for fonts. The row height must exceed the size of the font you are using. Normally, you don't need to adjust row heights manually, because row height adjusts automatically to accommodate other formatting changes. If you format something in a row to be a larger point size, Excel adjusts the row to fit the largest point size in the row. However, you have just as many options for changing row height as you do column width. Using the mouse, you can place the ↕ pointer on the line dividing the row heading from the heading below, and dragging to the desired height; double-clicking the line autofits the row height where necessary. You can also select one or more rows, then use the Row Height command on the shortcut menu, or the Row Height or AutoFit Row Height command on the Format button in the Cells group on the Home tab.

FIGURE C-9: Preparing to change the column width

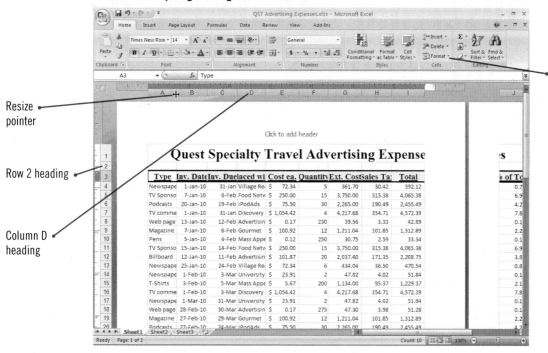

Click to change
column or row
formatting

Resize
pointer

Row 2 heading

Column D
heading

FIGURE C-10: Worksheet with column widths adjusted

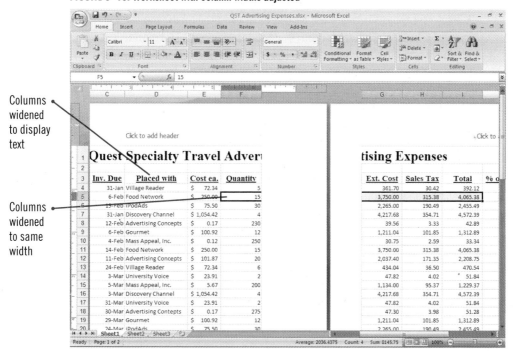

Columns
widened
to display
text

Columns
widened
to same
width

TABLE C-3: Common column formatting commands

command	description	available using
Column Width	Sets the width to a specific number of characters	Format button, shortcut menu
AutoFit Column Width	Fits to the widest entry in a column	Format button, mouse
Hide & Unhide	Hides or displays hidden column(s)	Format button, shortcut menu
Default Width	Changes the default column width for current worksheet	Format button

Inserting and Deleting Rows and Columns

As you modify a worksheet, you might find it necessary to insert or delete rows and columns to keep your worksheet current. For example, you might need to insert rows to accommodate new inventory products or remove a column of yearly totals that are no longer necessary. When you insert a new row, the contents of the worksheet shift down from the newly inserted row. When you insert a new column, the contents of the worksheet shift to the right from the point of the new column. Excel inserts rows above the cell pointer and inserts columns to the left of the cell pointer. To insert multiple rows, drag across row headings to select the same number of rows as you want to insert. ▨▨▨▨ You want to improve the overall appearance of the worksheet by inserting a row between the last row of data and the totals. Also, you have learned that row 27 and column J need to be deleted from the worksheet.

STEPS

1. **Right-click cell A32, then click Insert on the shortcut menu**

   The Insert dialog box opens. See Figure C-11. You can choose to insert a column or a row, or you can shift the data in the cells in the active column right or in the active row down. An additional row between the last row of data and the totals will visually separate the totals.

2. **Click the Entire row option button, then click OK**

   A blank row appears between the Billboard data and the totals, and the formula result in cell E33 has not changed. The Insert Options button 🖋 appears beside cell A33. Pointing to the button displays a list arrow, which you can click and then choose from the following options: Format Same As Above, Format Same As Below, or Clear Formatting. You want the default formatting, Same as Above.

3. **Click the row 27 heading**

   All of row 27 is selected, as shown in Figure C-12.

4. **Click the Delete button in the Cells group; *do not click the button arrow***

   Excel deletes row 27, and all rows below this shift up one row. You must use the Delete button or the Delete command on the shortcut menu to delete a row or column; pressing [Delete] on the keyboard removes only the *contents* of a selected row or column.

5. **Click the column J heading**

   The percentage information is calculated elsewhere and is no longer necessary in this worksheet.

6. **Click the Delete button in the Cells group**

   Excel deletes column J. The remaining columns to the right shift left one column.

7. **Save your work**

Hiding and unhiding columns and rows

When you don't want data in a column or row to be visible, but you don't want to delete it, you can hide the column or row. To hide a selected column, click the Format button in the Cells group, point to Hide & Unhide, then click Hide Columns. A hidden column is indicated by a dark black vertical line in its original position. This black line disappears when you click elsewhere in the worksheet. You can display a hidden column by selecting the columns on either side of the hidden column, clicking the Format button in the Cells group, pointing to Hide & Unhide, and then clicking Unhide Columns. (To hide or unhide one or more rows, substitute Hide Rows and Unhide Rows for the Hide Columns and Unhide Columns commands.)

FIGURE C-11: Insert dialog box

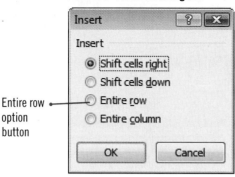

Entire row option button

FIGURE C-12: Worksheet with row 27 selected

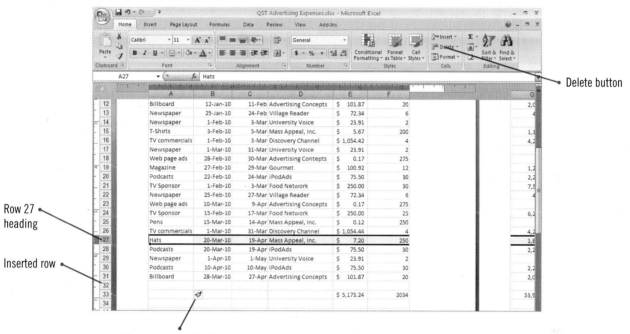

Delete button

Row 27 heading

Inserted row

On your screen, the Insert Options button might appear in a different location

Adding and editing comments

Much of your work in Excel may be in collaboration with teammates with whom you share worksheets. You can share ideas with other worksheet users by adding comments within selected cells. To include a comment in a worksheet, click the cell where you want to place the comment, click the Review tab on the Ribbon, then click the New Comment button in the Comments group. A resizable text box containing the computer user's name opens in which you can type your comments. A small, red triangle appears in the upper-right corner of a cell containing a comment. If comments are not already displayed in a workbook, other users can point to the triangle to display the comment. To see all worksheet comments, as shown in Figure C-13, click the Show All Comments button in the Comments group. To edit a comment, click the cell containing the comment, then click the Edit Comment button in the Comments group. To delete a comment, click the cell containing the comment, then click the Delete button in the Comments group.

FIGURE C-13: Comments in worksheet

Excel 2007

Applying Colors, Patterns, and Borders

You can use colors, patterns, and borders to enhance the overall appearance of a worksheet and to make it easier to read. You can add these enhancements by using the Border and Fill Color buttons in the Font group on the Home tab of the Ribbon and on the Mini toolbar, or by using the Fill tab and the Border tab in the Format Cells dialog box. You can apply a color to the background of a cell or a range, or to cell contents, and you can apply a pattern to a cell or range. You can apply borders to all the cells in a worksheet or only to selected cells to call attention to selected information. To save time, you can also apply **cell styles**, predesigned combinations of formatting attributes. You want to add a pattern, a border, and color to the title of the worksheet to give the worksheet a more professional appearance.

STEPS

1. **Select cell A1, click the Fill Color list arrow button** in the Font group, then hover the pointer over the Turquoise, Accent 2 color (first row, sixth column from the left)

   See Figure C-14. Live Preview shows you how the color will look *before* you apply it.

QUICK TIP

When you change fill or font color, the color on the Fill Color and Font Color buttons changes to the last color you selected.

2. **Click the Turquoise, Accent 2 color (first row, sixth column from the left)**

   The color is applied to the background or fill of this cell. (Remember that cell A1 spans columns A through I because the Merge and Center command was applied.)

3. **Right-click cell A1, then click Format Cells on the shortcut menu**

   The Format Cells dialog box opens. Adding a pattern to cells can add to the visual interest of your worksheet. To format an entire row or column at once, click the row heading or column heading button.

QUICK TIP

Use fill colors and patterns sparingly. Too many colors can be distracting or make it hard to see which information is important.

4. **Click the Fill tab, click the Pattern Style list arrow, click the 6.25% Gray style (first row, sixth column from the left), then click OK**

5. **Click the Borders list arrow** in the Font group, then click Thick Bottom Border

   Unlike underlining, which is a text-formatting tool, borders extend to the width of the cell, and can appear at the bottom of the cell, at the top, or on either side. It can be difficult to see a border when the cell is selected.

QUICK TIP

You can also create custom cell borders. Click the Borders list arrow in the Font group, click More Borders, then click the individual border buttons to create borders or boxes.

6. **Select the range A3:I3, click the Font Color list arrow** in the Font group, then click the Blue, Accent 1 color (first Theme color row, fifth column from the left) on the palette

   The new color is applied to the selected range.

7. **Select the range J1:K1, click the Cell Styles button in the Styles group, then click the Neutral button (first row, fourth column from the left) on the palette**

   The font and color change in the range, as shown in Figure C-15.

8. **Save your work**

FIGURE C-14: Viewing fill color using Live Preview

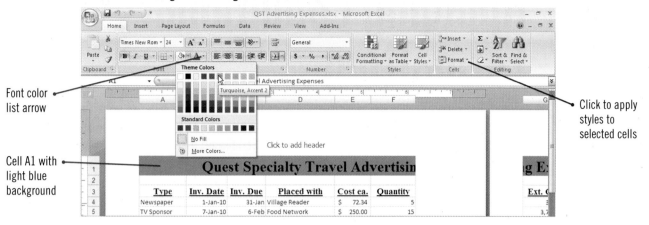

Font color list arrow

Cell A1 with light blue background

Click to apply styles to selected cells

FIGURE C-15: Worksheet with color, patterns, border, and style applied

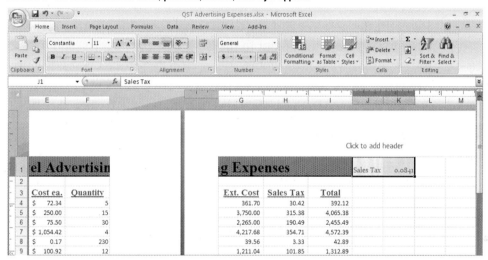

Saving time with themes and cell styles

You can save yourself time by formatting with themes and cell styles. A **theme** is a predefined set of attributes that gives your Excel worksheet a professional look. Formatting choices included in a theme are colors, fonts, and line and fill effects. A theme can be applied using the Themes button in the Themes group on the Page Layout tab on the Ribbon, as shown in Figure C-16. **Cell styles** are sets of attributes based on themes, so they are automatically updated if you change a theme. For example, if you apply the 20% - Accent1 cell style to cell A1 in a worksheet that has no theme applied, the fill color changes to light blue and the font changes to Constantia. If you change the theme of the worksheet to Metro, cell A1's fill color changes to light green and the font changes to Corbel, because these are the attributes that coordinate with the selected theme. Using themes and cell styles makes it easier to ensure that your worksheets are consistent and saves you from a lot of reformatting every time you make a change.

FIGURE C-16: Themes gallery

Applying Conditional Formatting

So far, you've used formatting to change the appearance of different types of data, such as dates, dollar amounts, worksheet titles, and column labels. But you can also use formatting to highlight important aspects of the data itself. For example, you can apply formatting that automatically changes the font color to red for any cells where ad costs exceed $100 and to green where ad costs are below $50. This type of formatting is called **conditional formatting** because Excel automatically applies different formats depending on conditions you specify. If the data meets your conditions, Excel applies the formats you specify. The formatting is updated if you change data in the worksheet. Data bars are a type of conditional formatting that visually illustrate differences among values.  Grace is concerned about advertising costs exceeding yearly budget. You decide to use conditional formatting to highlight certain trends and patterns in the data, so it's easy to spot the most expensive expenditures.

STEPS

1. **Select the range I4:I30, click the Conditional Formatting button in the Styles group, point to Data Bars, then point to the Light Blue Data Bar (second row, second from left)**
   Live Preview shows how this formatting will appear in the worksheet, as shown in Figure C-17. Notice that the length of the bar in each cell reflects its value relative to other cells in the selection.

2. **Preview the Green Data Bar (first row, second from left), then click it**

QUICK TIP
You can apply an Icon Set to a selected range by clicking the Conditional Formatting button in the Styles group, then pointing to Icon Sets; icons appear within the cells to illustrate differences in values.

3. **Select the range G4:G30, click the Conditional Formatting button in the Styles group, then point to Highlight Cells Rules**
   The Conditional Formatting menu displays choices for creating different types of formatting rules. For example, you can create a rule for values that are greater than a certain amount, less than a certain amount, or between two amounts.

4. **Click Between**
   The Between dialog box opens. Depending on the choice you made in the Highlight Cells Rules menu (such as "Greater Than" or "Less Than"), this dialog box displays different input boxes. You can define multiple different conditions and then assign formatting attributes to each one. You define the condition first. The default setting for the first condition is "Cell Value Is" "between." The value can be a constant, formula, cell reference, or date. The formatting default format is exactly what you want: Light Red Fill with Dark Red Text.

QUICK TIP
You can copy conditional formats the same way you copy other formats.

5. **Type 2000 in the first text box, type 4000 in the second text box, compare your settings to Figure C-18, then click OK**
   All cells with values between 2000 and 4000 in column G appear with a light red fill and dark red text.

6. **Click cell G7, type 3975.55, then press [Enter]**
   When the value in cell G7 changes, the formatting also changes, because the new value meets the condition to apply the format. Compare your results to Figure C-19.

7. **Press [Ctrl][Home] to select cell A1, then save your work**

Managing conditional formatting rules

If you create a conditional formatting rule and then want to change the conditions to reflect a different value or format, you don't need to create a new rule; instead, you can modify the rule using the Rule Manager. Select the cell(s) containing conditional formatting, click the Conditional Formatting button in the Styles group, then click Manage Rules. The Conditional Formatting Rules Manager dialog box opens. Select the rules you want to edit or delete, click Edit Rule, modify the settings in the Edit the Rule Description area, click OK, then click OK again to close the dialog box. The rule is modified, and the new conditions are applied to the selected cells.

FIGURE C-17: Previewing a Data Bar

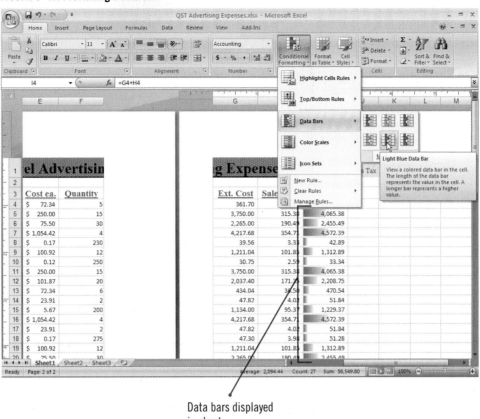

Data bars displayed
in sheet

FIGURE C-18: Setting conditions in Between dialog box

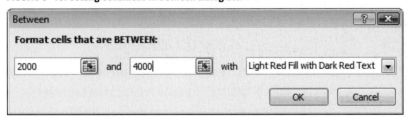

FIGURE C-19: Results of Conditional Formatting

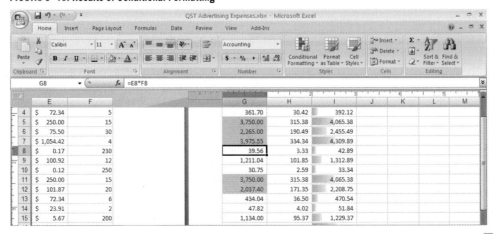

Naming and Moving a Sheet

By default, an Excel workbook initially contains three worksheets, named Sheet1, Sheet2, and Sheet3. The sheet name appears on the sheet tab at the bottom of the worksheet. When you open a workbook, the first worksheet is the active sheet. To move from sheet to sheet, you can click any sheet tab at the bottom of the worksheet window. The sheet tab scrolling buttons, located to the left of the sheet tabs, are useful when a workbook contains too many sheet tabs to display at once. To make it easier to identify the sheets in a workbook, you can rename each sheet and add color to the tabs. You can also organize them in a logical way. For instance, to better track performance goals, you could name each workbook sheet for an individual salesperson, and you could move the sheets so they appeared in alphabetical order. ▓▓▓ In the current worksheet, Sheet1 contains information on advertising expenses. Sheet2 contains an advertising budget, and Sheet3 contains no data. You want to name the two sheets in the workbook to reflect their contents, add color to a sheet tab to easily distinguish one from the other, and change their order.

STEPS

1. **Click the Sheet2 tab**

   Sheet2 becomes active, appearing in front of the Sheet1 tab; this is the worksheet that contains the budgeted expenses. See Figure C-20.

2. **Click the Sheet1 tab**

   Sheet1, which contains the actual expenses, becomes active again.

3. **Double-click the Sheet2 tab, type Budget, then press [Enter]**

   The new name for Sheet2 automatically replaces the default name on the tab. Worksheet names can have up to 31 characters, including spaces and punctuation.

4. **Right-click the Budget tab, point to Tab Color on the shortcut menu, then click the Bright Green, Accent 4, Lighter 80% color (second row, third column from the right) as shown in Figure C-21**

   The tab color changes to a bright green gradient.

5. **Double-click the Sheet1 tab, type Actual, then press [Enter]**

   Notice that the color of the Budget tab changes depending on whether it is the active tab; when the Actual tab is active, the color of the Budget tab changes to solid bright green. You decide to rearrange the order of the sheets, so that the Budget tab is to the left of the Actual tab.

6. **Click the Budget sheet tab, hold down the mouse button, drag it to the left of the Actual sheet tab, as shown in Figure C-22, then release the mouse button**

   As you drag, the pointer changes to ▯, the sheet relocation pointer, and a small, black triangle shows its position. The first sheet in the workbook is now the Budget sheet. See Figure C-23. To see hidden sheets, click the far left tab scrolling button to display the first sheet tab; click the far right navigation button to display the last sheet tab. The left and right buttons move one sheet in their respective directions.

7. **Click the Actual sheet tab, then enter your name in the left-side header box**

8. **Click the Page Layout tab on the Ribbon, click the Orientation button in the Page Setup group, then click Landscape**

9. **Press [Ctrl][Home], then save your work**

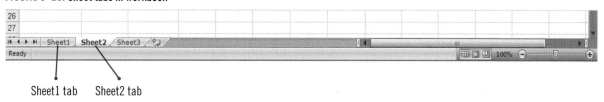
FIGURE C-20: Sheet tabs in workbook

Sheet1 tab   Sheet2 tab

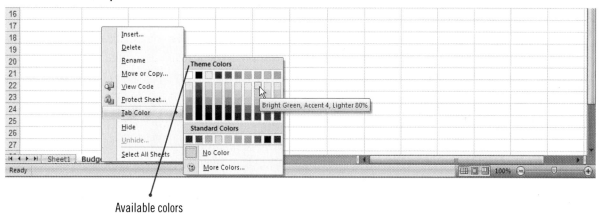
FIGURE C-21: Tab Color palette

Available colors

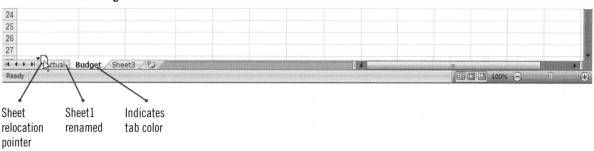
FIGURE C-22: Sheet during move

Sheet
relocation
pointer

Sheet1
renamed

Indicates
tab color

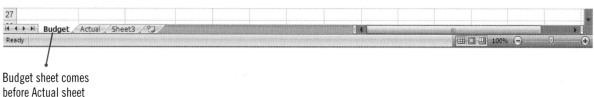
FIGURE C-23: Reordered sheets

Budget sheet comes
before Actual sheet

Copying worksheets

There are times when you may want to copy a worksheet. For example, a workbook might contain a sheet with Quarter 1 expenses, and you want to use that sheet as the basis for a sheet containing Quarter 2 expenses. To copy a sheet within the same workbook, press and hold [Ctrl], drag the sheet tab to the desired tab location, release the mouse button, then release [Ctrl]. A duplicate sheet appears with the same name as the copied sheet followed by "(2)" indicating it is a copy. You can then rename the sheet to a more meaningful name. To copy a sheet to a different workbook, both the source and destination workbooks must be open. Select the sheet to copy or move, right-click the sheet tab, then click Move or Copy in the shortcut menu. Complete the information in the Move or Copy dialog box. Be sure to click the Create a copy check box if you are copying rather than moving the worksheet. Carefully check your calculation results whenever you move or copy a worksheet.

Checking Spelling

Excel includes a spelling checker to help you ensure that the words in your worksheet are spelled correctly. The spelling checker scans your worksheet, displays words it doesn't find in its built-in dictionary, and suggests replacements when they are available. To check other sheets in a multiple-sheet workbook, you need to display each sheet and run the spelling checker again. Because the built-in dictionary cannot possibly include all the words that anyone needs, you can add words to the dictionary, such as your company name, an acronym, or an unusual technical term. Once you add a word or term, the spelling checker will no longer consider that word misspelled. Any words you've added to the dictionary using Word, Access, or PowerPoint are also available in Excel. Another feature, AutoCorrect, automatically corrects some spelling errors as you type. ▓▓▓▓ Before you distribute this workbook to Grace and the marketing managers, you check its spelling.

STEPS

1. **Click the Review tab on the Ribbon, then click the Spelling button in the Proofing group**

   The Spelling: English (U.S.) dialog box opens, as shown in Figure C-24, with "iPodAds" selected as the first misspelled word in the worksheet. For any word, you have the option to Ignore this case of the flagged word, Ignore All cases of the flagged word, or Add the word to the dictionary.

2. **Click Ignore All**

   Next, the spelling checker finds the word "Contepts" and suggests "Concepts" as an alternative.

3. **Verify that the word Concepts is selected in the Suggestions list, then click Change**

   When no more incorrect words are found, Excel displays a message indicating that all the words on the worksheet have been checked.

4. **Click OK**

5. **Click the Home tab, click Find & Select in the Editing group, then click Replace**

   The Find and Replace dialog box opens. You can use this dialog box to replace a word or phrase. It might be a misspelling that the Spelling Checker didn't recognize as wrong, such as a word that wasn't corrected with the spelling checker, or simply something you want to change. Grace has just told you that each instance of 'Billboard' in the worksheet should be changed to 'Sign'.

6. **Type Billboard in the Find what text box, press [Tab], then type Sign in the Replace with text box**

   Compare your dialog box to Figure C-25.

7. **Click Replace All, click OK to close the warning box, then click Close to close the Find and Replace dialog box**

   Excel has made two replacements.

8. **Save your work, view the Actual sheet in Print Preview, click the Page Setup button on the Ribbon, fit the worksheet to one page, then return to Print Preview**

   Compare your worksheet to Figure C-26.

9. **Print one copy of the worksheet, close it, then exit Excel**

E-mailing a workbook

You can send an entire workbook from within Excel using your installed email program, such as Microsoft Office Outlook or Outlook Express. To send a workbook as an e-mail message attachment, open the workbook, click the Office button 🗔, point to Send, then click E-mail. An email message opens with the workbook automatically attached; the filename appears in the Attached field. Complete the To and optional Cc fields, include a message if you wish, then click Send.

FIGURE C-24: Spelling: English dialog box

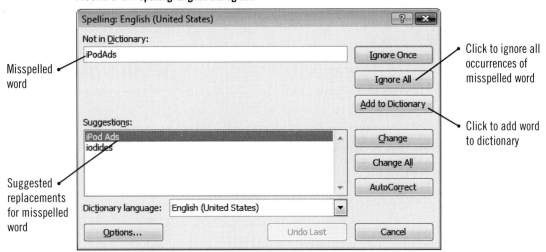

Misspelled word

Suggested replacements for misspelled word

Click to ignore all occurrences of misspelled word

Click to add word to dictionary

FIGURE C-25: Find and Replace dialog box

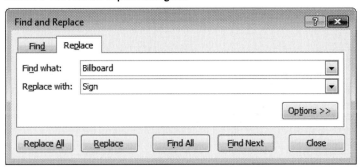

FIGURE C-26: Viewing worksheet in Print Preview

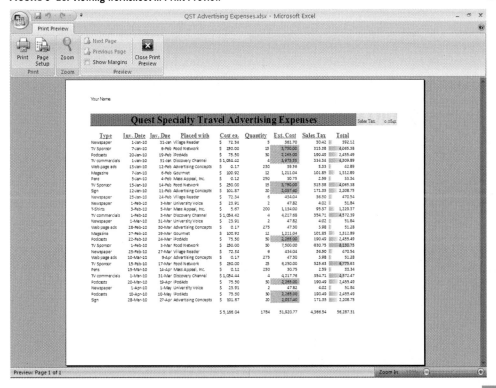

Practice

If you have a SAM user profile, you may have access to hands-on instruction, practice, and assessment of the skills covered in this unit. Log in to your SAM account (http://sam2007.course.com/) to launch any assigned training activities or exams that relate to the skills covered in this unit.

▼ CONCEPTS REVIEW

Label each element of the Excel worksheet window shown in Figure C-27.

FIGURE C-27

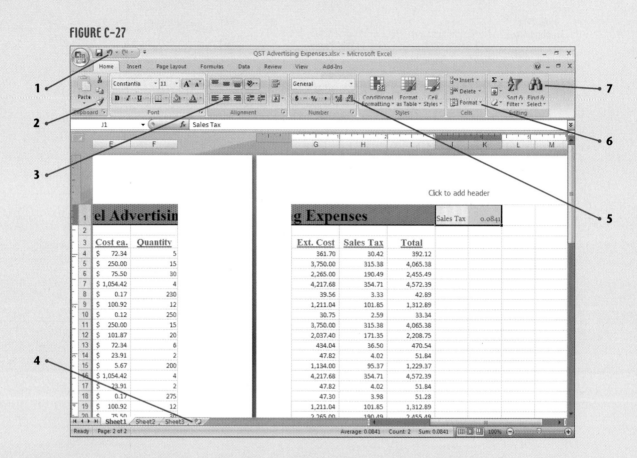

Match each command or button with the statement that best describes it.

8. **Spelling & Grammar button**

9. ☐

10. ☐

11. **[Ctrl][Home]**

12. **Conditional Formatting**

13. **[Delete]**

a. Erases the contents of a cell

b. Changes formatting of a cell based on cell contents

c. Moves cell pointer to cell A1

d. Checks for apparent misspellings in a worksheet

e. Displays options for erasing the contents of a cell

f. Centers cell contents over multiple cells

Select the best answer from the list of choices.

14. **Which of the following is an example of an accounting number format?**
    a. 5555
    c. 55.55%
    b. $5,555.55
    d. 5,555.55

15. **What feature is used to delete a conditional formatting rule?**
    a. Rule Reminder
    c. Rule Manager
    b. Conditional Rule Manager
    d. Format Manager

16. **Which button removes boldface formatting from selected cells?**
    a. *I*
    c. (decimal button)
    b. **B**
    d. **B**

17. **Which button opens the Format Cells dialog box?**
    a. (dialog launcher)
    c. **B**
    b. (format painter)
    d. (undo)

18. **What is the name of the feature used to resize a column to accommodate its widest entry?**
    a. AutoFormat
    c. AutoResize
    b. AutoFit
    d. AutoRefit

19. **Which button increases the number of decimal places in selected cells?**
    a. (indent)
    c. (decrease decimal)
    b. (increase decimal)
    d. (indent)

20. **Which button applies multiple formatting styles to selected cells?**
    a. (undo)
    c. (cell styles)
    b. (format painter)
    d. (copy)

▼ SKILLS REVIEW

1. **Format values.**
   a. Start Excel, open the file EX C-2.xlsx from the drive and folder where you store your Data Files, then save it as Health Insurance Premiums.
   b. Enter a formula in cell B10 that totals the number of employees.
   c. Create a formula in cell C5 that calculates the monthly insurance premium for the accounting department. (*Hint*: Make sure you use the correct type of cell reference in the formula. To calculate the monthly premium, multiply the number of employees by the monthly premium.)
   d. Copy the formula in cell C5 to the range C6:C10.
   e. Format the range C5:C10 using the Accounting Number Format.
   f. Change the format of the range C6:C9 to the Comma Style.
   g. Reduce the number of decimals to 0 in cell B14, using a button in the Number group.
   h. Save your work.

2. **Change fonts and font sizes.**
   a. Select the range of cells containing the column labels (in row 4).
   b. Change the font of the selection to Times New Roman.
   c. Increase the font size of the selection to 12 points.
   d. Increase the font size of the label in cell A1 to 14 points.
   e. Save your changes.

3. **Change attributes and alignment.**
   a. Apply the bold and italic attributes to the worksheet title QST Corporate Office.
   b. Use the Merge & Center button to center the Health Insurance Premiums label over columns A through C.
   c. Apply the italic attribute to the Health Insurance Premiums label.
   d. Add the bold attribute to the labels in row 4.
   e. Use the Format Painter to copy the format in cell A4 to the range A5:A10.
   f. Apply the format in cell C10 to cell B14.

    g. Change the alignment of cell A10 to Align Right.

    h. Select the range of cells containing the column titles, then center them.

    i. Remove the italic attribute from the Health Insurance Premiums label, then increase the font size to 14.

    j. Move the Health Insurance Premiums label to cell A3, then add the bold and underline attributes.

    k. Add a bottom double border to the cell in the last cell in the Total column, above the calculated total value.

    l. Save your changes.

4. Adjust column width.

    a. Resize column C to a width of 10.71.

    b. Use the AutoFit feature to resize columns A and B.

    c. Clear the contents of cell A13 (do not delete the cell).

    d. Change the text in cell A14 to Monthly Insurance Premium, then change the width of the column to 25.

    e. Resize any remaining columns as needed to view all the data.

    f. Save your changes.

5. Insert and delete rows and columns.

    a. Insert a new row between rows 5 and 6.

    b. Add a new department—Humanitarian Aid—in the newly inserted row. Enter 5 for the Employees.

    c. Copy the formula in cell C5 to C6.

    d. Add the following comment to cell A6: New department. Display the comment, then drag to move it out of the way, if necessary.

    e. Add a new column between the Department and Employees columns with the title Family Coverage, then resize the column using AutoFit.

    f. Delete the Legal row.

    g. Move the value in cell C14 to B14.

    h. Save your changes.

6. Apply colors, patterns, and borders.

    a. Add an outside border around the range A4:D10.

    b. Apply the Aqua, Accent 5, Lighter 80% fill color to the labels in the Department column (do not include the Total label).

    c. Apply the Orange, Accent 6, Lighter 60% fill color to the range A4:D4.

    d. Change the color of the font in the range A4:D4 to Red, Accent 2, Darker 25%.

    e. Add a 12.5% Gray pattern style to cell A1.

    f. Format the range A14:B14 with a pattern style of Thin Diagonal Stripes, a fill color of Dark Blue, Text 2, Lighter 40%, then apply the bold attribute.

    g. Save your changes.

7. Apply conditional formatting.

    a. Select the range D5:D9, then create a conditional format that changes cell contents to green fill with dark green text if the value is between 4000 and 7000.

    b. Select the range C5:C9, then create a conditional format that changes cell contents to red text if the number of employees exceeds 10.

    c. Select the range C5:C9, then create a blue data bar.

    d. Use the Rule Manager to modify the conditional format in cell C5 to display the cell contents in bold red text.

    e. Copy the format in cell C5 to the range in C6:C9.

    f. Merge and center the title over columns A-D.

8. Name and move a sheet.

    a. Name the Sheet 1 tab Insurance Data.

    b. Name the Sheet 3 tab Employee Data.

    c. Change the Insurance Data tab color to Red, Accent 2, Lighter 40%.

    d. Change the Employee Data tab color to Aqua, Accent 5, Lighter 40%.

▼ SKILLS REVIEW (CONTINUED)

e. Move the Employee Data sheet so it comes after (to the right of) the Insurance Data sheet.

f. Make the Insurance Data sheet active, enter your name in cell A20, then save your work.

9. Check spelling.

a. Move the cell pointer to cell A1.

b. Use the Find & Select feature to replace the Accounting label in cell A5 with Accounting/Legal.

c. Check the spelling in the worksheet using the spelling checker, and correct any spelling errors.

d. Save your changes.

e. Preview and print the Insurance Data sheet, compare your work to Figure C-28, then close the workbook and exit Excel.

FIGURE C-28

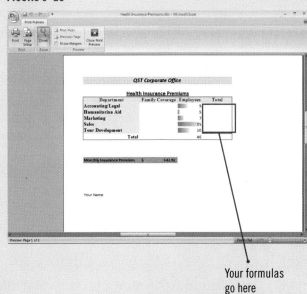

Your formulas go here

▼ INDEPENDENT CHALLENGE 1

You run a freelance accounting business, and one of your newest clients is Lovely Locks, a small beauty salon. Now that you've converted the salon's accounting records to Excel, the manager would like you to work on an analysis of the inventory. Although more items will be added later, the worksheet has enough items for you to begin your modifications.

a. Start Excel, open the file EX C-3.xlsx from the drive and folder where you store your Data Files, then save it as **Lovely Locks Inventory**.

b. Create a formula in cell E4 that calculates the value of the on-hand inventory, based on the price paid for the item, in cell B4. Format the cell in the Comma Style.

c. Use an absolute reference to calculate the sale price of the item in cell F4, using the markup value shown in cell I1.

d. Copy the formulas created above into the range E5:F14; first convert any necessary cell references to absolute so that the formulas work correctly.

e. Add the bold attribute to the column headings, and italicize the items in column A.

f. Make sure all columns are wide enough to display the data and headings.

g. Format the Sale Price column so it displays the Accounting Number Format with two decimal places.

h. Change the Price Paid column so it displays the Comma style with two decimal places.

i. Add a row under #2 Curlers for **Nail files**, price paid **$0.31**, sold individually **(each)**, with **56** on hand.

j. Verify that all the formulas in the worksheet are correct. Adjust any items as needed, and check the spelling.

k. Use conditional formatting to call attention to items with a quantity of less than 20 on hand. Use yellow fill with dark yellow text.

l. Create an icon set for the range D4:D15 using the symbols of your choosing.

m. Add an outside border around the data in the Item column.

n. Delete the row containing the Pins item.

o. Enter your name in an empty cell below the data, then save the file.

p. Preview and print the worksheet, compare your work to the sample of page 1 shown in Figure C-29, close the workbook, then exit Excel.

FIGURE C-29

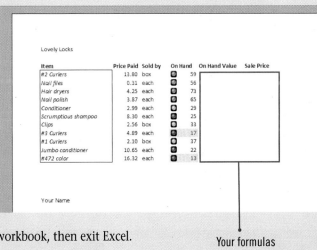

Your formulas go here

▼ INDEPENDENT CHALLENGE 2

You volunteer several hours each week with the Assistance League of South Bend, and are in charge of maintaining the membership list. You're currently planning a mailing campaign to members in certain regions of the city. You also want to create renewal letters for members whose membership expires soon. You decide to format the list to enhance the appearance of the worksheet and make your upcoming tasks easier to plan.

a. Start Excel, open the file EX C-4.xlsx from the drive and folder where you store your Data Files, then save it as South Bend Assistance League.

b. Remove any blank columns.

c. Create a conditional format in the Zip Code column so that entries greater than 46649 appear in light red fill with dark red text.

d. Make all columns wide enough to fit their data and headings.

e. Use formatting enhancements, such as fonts, font sizes, and text attributes, to make the worksheet more attractive.

f. Center-align the column labels.

g. Use conditional formatting so that entries for Year of Membership Expiration that are between 2011 and 2013 appear in a bold, contrasting color.

h. Adjust any items as necessary, then check the spelling.

i. Change the name of the Sheet 1 tab to one that reflects the sheet's contents, then add a tab color of your choice.

j. Enter your name in an empty cell, then save your work.

k. Before printing, preview the worksheet, make any final changes you think necessary, then print a copy. Compare your work to the sample shown in Figure C-30.

l. Close the workbook, then exit Excel.

FIGURE C-30

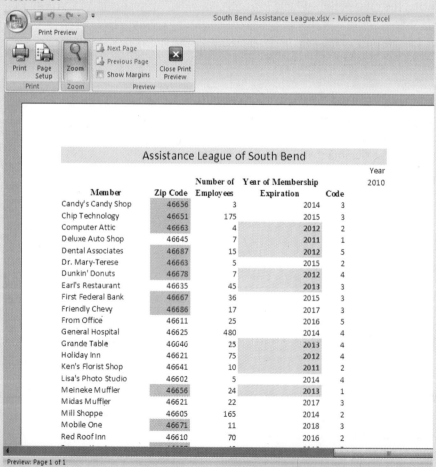

▼ INDEPENDENT CHALLENGE 3

Fine Line Writing Instruments is a Chicago-based company that manufactures high-quality pens and markers. As the finance manager, one of your responsibilities is to analyze the monthly reports from your five district sales offices. Your boss, Joanne Bennington, has just asked you to prepare a quarterly sales report for an upcoming meeting. Because several top executives will be attending this meeting, Joanne reminds you that the report must look professional. In particular, she asks you to emphasize the company's surge in profits during the last month and to highlight the fact that the Northeastern district continues to outpace the other districts.

a. Plan a worksheet that shows the company's sales during the first quarter. Assume that all pens are the same price. Make sure you plan to include:

- The number of pens sold (units sold) and the associated revenues (total sales) for each of the five district sales offices. The five sales districts are: Northeastern, Midwestern, Southeastern, Southern, and Western.
- Calculations that show month-by-month totals for January, February, and March, and a three-month cumulative total.
- Calculations that show each district's share of sales (percent of Total Sales).
- Labels that reflect the month-by-month data as well as the cumulative data.
- Formatting enhancements and data bars that emphasize the recent month's sales surge and the Northeastern district's sales leadership.

b. Ask yourself the following questions about the organization and formatting of the worksheet: What worksheet title and labels do you need, and where should they appear? How can you calculate the totals? What formulas can you copy to save time and keystrokes? Do any of these formulas need to use an absolute reference? How do you show dollar amounts? What information should be shown in bold? Do you need to use more than one font? Should you use more than one point size?

c. Start Excel, then save a new, blank workbook as **Fine Line Writing Instruments** to the drive and folder where you store your Data Files.

d. Build the worksheet with your own price and sales data. Enter the titles and labels first, then enter the numbers and formulas. You can use the information in Table C-4 to get started.

e. Adjust the column widths as necessary.

f. Change the height of row 1 to 33 points.

g. Format labels and values, and change the attributes and alignment if necessary.

h. Resize columns and adjust the formatting as necessary.

i. Add data bars for the monthly Units Sold columns.

j. Add a column that calculates a 25% increase in sales dollars. Use an absolute cell reference in this calculation. (*Hint:* Make sure the current formatting is applied to the new information.)

TABLE C-4

Fine Line Writing Instruments										
1st Quarter Sales Report										
		January		February		March		Total		
Office	Price	Units Sold	Sales	Units Sold	Sales	Units Sold	Sales	Units Sold	Sales	
Northeastern										
Midwestern										
Southeastern										
Southern										
Western										

▼ INDEPENDENT CHALLENGE 3 (CONTINUED)

Advanced Challenge Exercise

- Use the Format as Table feature to add a table style of your choice to the data.
- Insert a clip art image related to pens in an appropriate location, adjusting its size and position as necessary.
- Save your work.

l. Enter your name in an empty cell.

m. Check the spelling in the workbook, then save your work.

n. Preview, compare your work to Figure C-31, then print the worksheet in landscape orientation.

o. Close the workbook file, then exit Excel.

FIGURE C-31

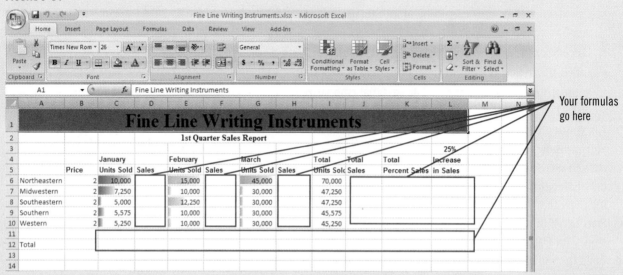

▼ REAL LIFE INDEPENDENT CHALLENGE

***Note*: This project requires an Internet connection.**

You are saving up to take an international trip you have always dreamed about. You plan to visit seven different countries over the course of two months, and budgeting an identical spending allowance in each country. To help work toward your goal, you want to create a worksheet that calculates the amount of native currency you will have in each country. You want the workbook to reflect the currency information for each country.

a. Start Excel, then save a new, blank workbook as World Tour Budget to the drive and folder where you store your Data Files.

b. Think of seven countries you would like to visit, then enter column and row labels for your worksheet. (*Hint*: You may wish to include row labels for each country, plus column labels for the country, the $1 equivalent in native currency, the total amount of native currency you'll have in each country, and the name of each country's monetary unit.)

c. Decide how much money you want to bring to each country (for example, $1000), and enter that in the worksheet.

d. Use your favorite search engine to find your own information sources on currency conversions for the countries you plan to visit.

e. Enter the cash equivalent to $1 in U.S. dollars for each country in your list. Also include the name of the currency used in each country.

f. Create an equation that calculates the amount of native currency you will have in each country, using an absolute cell reference in the formula.

g. Format the entries in column B with three decimal places and in column C with two decimal places, using the correct currency unit for each country. (*Hint*: Use the Number tab in the Format cells dialog box; choose the appropriate currency format from the Symbol list, using two decimal places.)

h. Create a conditional format that changes the font attributes of the calculated amount in the "$1,000 US" column to bold and red if the amount exceeds 500 units of the local currency.

i. Merge and center the title over the column headings.

j. Add any formatting attributes to the column headings, and resize the columns as necessary.

k. Add a background color to the title.

Advanced Challenge Exercise

■ Modify the conditional format in the "$1,000 US" column so that entries between 1500 and 3999 display in red, boldface type, and entries above 4000 appear in blue, boldface type.

■ Delete all the unused sheets in the workbook.

■ Save your work as **World Tour Budget ACE** where you store your Data Files.

■ If you have access to an e-mail account, e-mail this workbook to your instructor as an attachment.

l. Enter your name in the header of the worksheet.

m. Spell check, save, preview and compare your work to Figure C-32, then print the worksheet.

n. Close the workbook and exit Excel.

FIGURE C-32

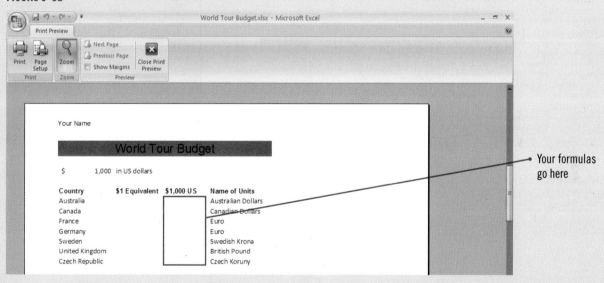

▼ VISUAL WORKSHOP

Open the file EX C-5.xlsx from the drive and folder where you store your Data Files, then save it as **Top Notch Personnel**. Use the skills you learned in this unit to format the worksheet so it looks like the one shown in Figure C-33. Create a conditional format in the Level column so that entries greater than 3 appear in red text. Create an additional conditional format in the Review Cycle column so that any value equal to 4 appears in green bold text. Replace the Accounting department label with Legal. (*Hint*: The only additional font used in this exercise is 16-point Times New Roman in row 1.) Enter your name in cell A25, check the spelling in the worksheet, then save and print your work.

FIGURE C-33

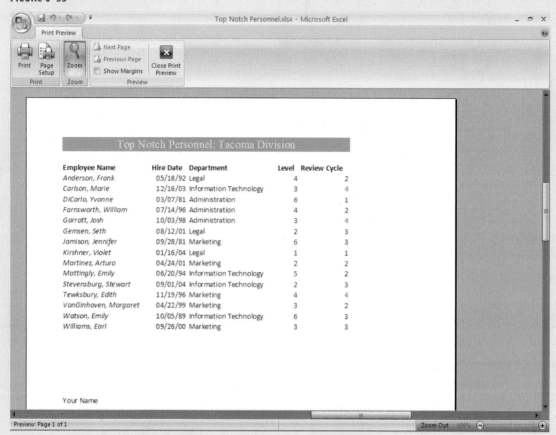

Working with Charts

Files You Will Need:

EX D-1.xlsx
EX D-2.xlsx
EX D-3.xlsx
EX D-4.xlsx
EX D-5.xlsx
EX D-6.xlsx

Worksheets provide an effective layout for calculating and organizing data, but the grid layout is not always the best format for presenting your work to others. To display information so it's easier to interpret, you can create a chart. **Charts**, often called graphs, present information in a pictorial format, making it easier to see patterns, trends, and relationships. In this unit, you learn how to create a chart, how to edit the chart and change the chart type, how to add text annotations and arrows, and how to preview and print the chart. At the upcoming annual meeting, Grace Wong wants to emphasize a growth trend at Quest Specialty Travel. She asks you to create a chart showing the increase in company revenues over the past four quarters.

OBJECTIVES

Plan a chart
Create a chart
Move and resize a chart
Change the chart design
Change the chart layout
Format a chart
Annotate and draw on a chart
Create a pie chart

Planning a Chart

Before creating a chart, you need to plan the information you want your chart to show and how you want it to look. Planning ahead helps you to decide what type of chart to create and how to organize the data. Understanding the parts of a chart makes it easier to format it and change specific elements so that the chart best illustrates your data. In preparation for creating the chart for Grace's presentation, you identify your goals for the chart and plan it.

DETAILS

Use the following guidelines to plan the chart:

- **Determine the purpose of the chart and identify the data relationships you want to communicate graphically**

  You want to create a chart that shows quarterly revenues throughout Quest Specialty Travel. This worksheet data is shown in Figure D-1. In the first quarter, the Marketing department launched an international advertising campaign. The campaign resulted in greatly increased sales starting in the second quarter. You want to create a chart for the annual meeting that illustrates the increase and compares sales across the quarters for each location.

- **Determine the results you want to see, and decide which chart type is most appropriate**

  Different chart types display data in distinctive ways. For example, a pie chart compares parts to the whole, so it's useful for showing what proportion of a budget amount was spent on print ads relative to what was spent on direct mail or radio commercials. A line chart, in contrast, is best for showing trends over time. To choose the best chart type for your data, you should first decide how you want your data displayed and interpreted. Table D-1 describes several different types of charts you can create in Excel and their corresponding buttons on the Insert tab of the Ribbon. Because you want to compare QST revenues in multiple locations over a period of four quarters, you decide to use a column chart.

- **Identify the worksheet data you want the chart to illustrate**

  Sometimes you use all the data in a worksheet to create a chart, while at other times you may need to select a range within the sheet. The worksheet from which you are creating your chart contains revenue data for the past year. You will need to use all the quarterly data contained in the worksheet.

- **Understand the elements of a chart**

  The chart shown in Figure D-2 contains basic elements of a chart. In the figure, QST locations are on the horizontal axis (also called the **x-axis**) and monthly sales are on the vertical axis (also called the **y-axis**). The horizontal axis is also called the **category axis** because it often contains the names of data groups, such as locations, months, or years. The vertical axis is also called the **value axis** because it often contains numerical values that help you interpret the size of chart elements. (3-D charts also contain a **z-axis**, for comparing data across both categories and values.) The area inside the horizontal and vertical axes is the **plot area**. The **tick marks** at the left edge of the vertical axis and **gridlines** (extending across the plot area) create a scale of measure for each value. Each value in a cell you select for your chart is a **data point**. In any chart, a **data marker** visually represents each data point, which in this case is a column. A collection of related data points is a **data series**. In this chart, there are four data series (Quarter 1, Quarter 2, Quarter 3, and Quarter 4), so you include a **legend** to make it easy to identify them.

FIGURE D-1: Worksheet containing revenue data

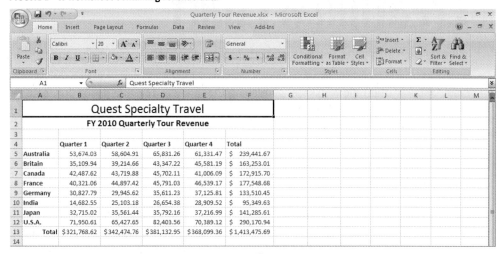

FIGURE D-2: Chart elements

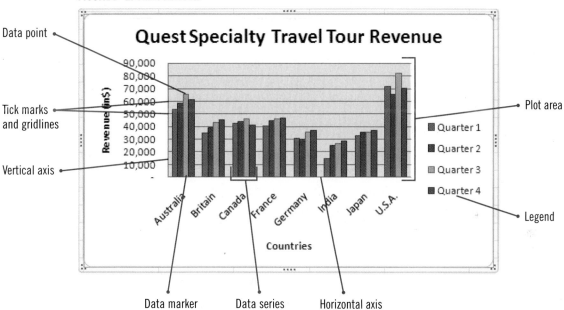

TABLE D-1: Common chart types

type	button	description
Column		Compares distinct object levels using a vertical format; the Excel default; sometimes referred to as a bar chart in other spreadsheet programs
Line		Compares trends over even time intervals; looks similar to an area chart, but does not emphasize total
Pie		Compares sizes of pieces as part of a whole; used for a single series of numbers
Bar		Compares distinct object levels using a horizontal format; sometimes referred to as a horizontal bar chart in other spreadsheet programs
Area		Shows how individual volume changes over time in relation to total volume
Scatter		Compares trends over uneven time or measurement intervals; used in scientific and engineering disciplines for trend spotting and extrapolation

Creating a Chart

To create a chart in Excel, you first select the range in a worksheet containing the data you want to chart. Once you've selected a range, you can use buttons on the Insert tab of the Ribbon to create and modify a chart. ░░░░░░ Using the worksheet containing the quarterly revenue data, you create a chart that shows the growth trend that occurred.

STEPS

1. **Start Excel, open the file EX D-1.xlsx from the drive and folder where you store your Data Files, then save it as** Quarterly Tour Revenue

   You want the chart to include the quarterly tour revenue figures, as well as quarter and country labels. You don't include the Total column and row because the quarterly figures make up the totals, and these figures would skew the chart.

2. **Select the range A4:E12, then click the** Insert tab **on the Ribbon**

   The Insert tab contains groups for inserting various types of objects, including charts. The Charts group includes buttons for each major chart type, plus an Other Charts button for additional chart types, such as stock charts for charting stock market data.

3. **Click the** Column chart button, **then click the** Clustered Column button **on the Column palette, as shown in Figure D-3**

   The chart is inserted in the center of the worksheet, and three contextual Chart Tools tabs open on the Ribbon: Design, Layout, and Format. On the Design tab, which is currently in front, you can quickly change the chart type, chart layout, and chart format and you can swap the data between the columns and rows. Currently, the countries are charted along the horizontal axis, with the quarterly revenues charted along the y-axis. This lets you easily compare quarterly revenues for each country.

4. **Click the** Switch Row/Column button **in the Data group on the Chart Tools Design tab**

   Clicking this button switches the data in the columns and rows, as shown in Figure D-4, so that the quarterly revenues are charted along the horizontal axis and the countries are plotted as the data points.

5. **Click the** Undo button ↶ **on the Quick Access toolbar**

   The chart returns to its original configuration.

6. **Click the** Chart Tools Layout tab, **click the** Chart Title button **in the Labels group, then click** Above Chart **on the palette**

   A title placeholder appears above the chart.

7. **Click anywhere in the** Chart Title text box, **press [Ctrl][A] to select the text, type** Quarterly Tour Revenue, **then click anywhere in the chart to deselect the title**

   Adding a title helps identify the chart. This chart is known as an **embedded** chart because it's inserted directly in the current worksheet. The **sizing handles**, the small series of dots at the corners and sides of the chart's border, indicate that the chart is selected. See Figure D-5. Your chart might be in a different location on the worksheet and may look slightly different; you will move and resize it in the next lesson. Any time a chart is selected, as it is now, a blue border surrounds the worksheet data range, a purple border surrounds the row labels, and a green border surrounds the column labels. Embedding a chart in the current sheet is the default selection when creating a chart, but you can also place a chart on a different sheet in the workbook, or on a newly created chart sheet. A **chart sheet** is a sheet in a workbook that contains only a chart, which is linked to the workbook data.

8. **Save your work**

FIGURE D-3: Column chart palette

Clustered Column chart type

Column chart types

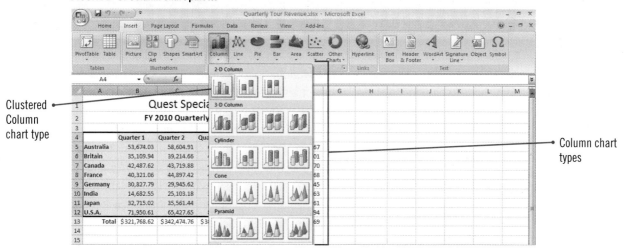

FIGURE D-4: Clustered Column chart with rows and columns switched

Undo button

Switch Row/Column button

Column labels

Row labels

Data range

Selected chart object

Chart Tools tabs

Legend

Quarter labels on horizontal axis

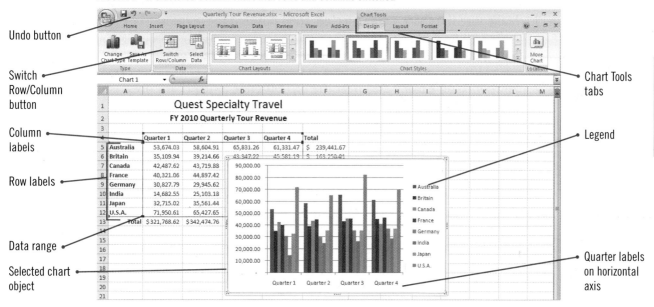

FIGURE D-5: Chart with rows and columns restored and title added

Title

Sizing handles

Country labels on horizontal axis

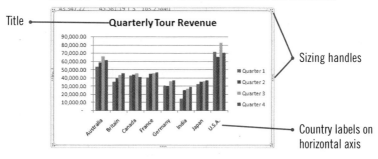

Using the contextual Chart Tools tabs

When a chart is selected, the three contextual Chart Tools tabs (Design, Layout, and Format) appear on the Ribbon. These tabs help guide you through developing and perfecting your chart. Using the Design tab, you can change overall color schemes and positioning of objects within the chart as well as the data range and configuration used for the chart. The Layout tab is used to add and modify chart elements, such as titles and labels, and for adding graphics,

such as pictures, shapes, and text boxes. The Format tab lets you format objects such as shapes and text, arrange multiple objects so they are layered attractively, and resize any object to exact specifications. While these tabs organize chart tools in a logical order, it is not necessary to use them in the order in which they appear. In other words, you can jump from the Design tab to the Format tab, back to Design, then to Layout, if you wish.

Moving and Resizing a Chart

Charts are graphics, or drawn objects, and are not located in a specific cell or at a specific range address. An **object** is an independent element on a worksheet. You can select an object by clicking within its borders; sizing handles around the object indicate it is selected. You can move a selected chart object anywhere on a worksheet without affecting formulas or data in the worksheet. However, any data changed in the worksheet is automatically updated in the chart. You can resize a chart to improve its appearance by dragging its sizing handles. You can even move a chart to a different sheet, and it will still reflect the original data. Chart objects contain other objects, such as a title and legend, which you can move and resize. In addition to repositioning chart elements to set locations using commands on the Layout tab, you can freely move any object using the mouse. Simply select it, then drag it or cut and paste it to a new location. When the mouse pointer hovers over any chart object, the name of the selected object appears on screen as a ScreenTip. You want to resize the chart, position it below the worksheet data, and move the legend.

STEPS

QUICK TIP

If you want to delete a chart, select it, then press [Delete].

1. **Make sure the chart is still selected, then position the pointer over the chart**

   The pointer shape indicates that you can move the chart object or use a sizing handle to resize it. For a table of commonly used graphic object pointers, refer to Table D-2.

TROUBLE

If you do not drag a blank area on the chart, you might inadvertently move a chart element instead of the whole chart; if this happens, undo the action and try again.

2. **Position on a blank area near the top left edge of the chart, press and hold the left mouse button, drag the chart until its upper left corner is at the upper left corner of cell A16, then release the mouse button**

   As you drag the chart, you can see an outline representing the chart's perimeter. The chart appears in the new location.

3. **Position the pointer on the right-middle sizing handle until it changes to ↔, then drag the right edge of the chart to the right edge of column G**

   The chart is widened. See Figure D-6.

QUICK TIP

To resize a chart object to exact specification, select the object, click the Chart Tools Format tab on the Ribbon, then enter the desired height and width in the Size group.

4. **Position the pointer over the upper-middle sizing handle until it changes to ↕, then drag it to the top edge of row 15**

5. **Scroll down if necessary so row 26 is visible, position the pointer over the lower-middle sizing handle until it changes to ↕, then drag the bottom border of the chart to the bottom border of row 26**

   You can move any object on a chart. You want to align the top of the legend with the top of the plot area.

QUICK TIP

Although the sizing handles on objects within a chart look different from the sizing handles that surround a chart, they function the same way.

6. **Click the legend to select it, press and hold [Shift], drag the legend up using so the dotted outline is approximately ¼" above the top of the plot area, then release [Shift]**

   When you click the legend, sizing handles appear around it and "Legend" appears as a ScreenTip when the pointer hovers over the object. As you drag, a dotted outline of the legend border appears. Pressing and holding the [Shift] key holds the horizontal position of the legend as you move it vertically.

7. **Click cell A12, type United States, click the Enter button ✓ on the formula bar, use AutoFit to resize column A, then press [Ctrl][Home]**

   The axis label changes to reflect the updated cell contents, as shown in Figure D-7. Changing any data in the worksheet modifies corresponding text or values in the chart. Because the chart is no longer selected, the Chart Tools tabs no longer appear on the Ribbon.

8. **Save your work**

FIGURE D-6: Moved and resized chart

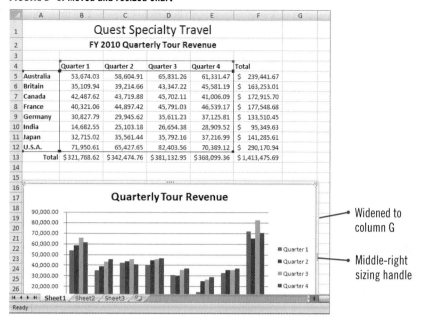

Widened to column G

Middle-right sizing handle

FIGURE D-7: Worksheet with modified legend and label

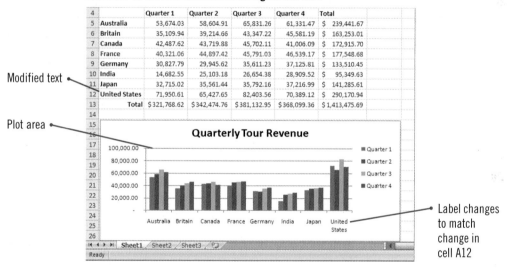

Modified text

Plot area

Label changes to match change in cell A12

TABLE D-2: Common graphic object pointers

name	pointer	use	name	pointer	use
Diagonal resizing	⤢ or ⤡	Change chart shape	I-beam	I	Edit chart text from corners
Draw	+	Create shapes	Move chart	⁺‡	Change chart location
Horizontal resizing	⇔	Change chart shape from left to right	Vertical resizing	↕	Change chart shape from top to bottom

Moving an embedded chart to a sheet

Suppose you have created an embedded chart that you decide would look better on a chart sheet. You can make this change without recreating the entire chart. To do so, first select the chart, click the Chart Tools Design tab, then click the Move Chart button in the Location group. The Move Chart dialog box opens. If the chart is embedded, click the New sheet option button, then click OK. If the chart is on its own sheet, click the Object in option button, then click OK.

Changing the Chart Design

Once you've created a chart, it's easy to modify the design. You can change data values in the worksheet, and the chart is automatically updated to reflect the new data. Each of the Chart Tools tabs can be used to make specific changes in a chart. Using the Chart Tools Design tab, you can change the chart type in the Type group, modify the data range and configuration in the Data group, change the layout of objects in the Chart Layouts group, choose from coordinating color schemes in the Chart Styles group, and move the location of the chart in the Location group. The layouts in the Chart Styles group offer preconfigured arrangements of objects in your chart, such as a legend, title, or gridlines; these layouts offer an alternative to manually making formatting and design changes. ██████ You look over your worksheet and realize the data for the United States in Quarter 2 and Quarter 4 is incorrect. After you correct this data, you want to see how the same data looks using different chart layouts and types.

STEPS

1. **Click cell C12, type 75432.29, press [Tab] twice, type 84295.27, then press [Enter]**

   In the worksheet, the United States entries for Quarter 2 and Quarter 4 reflect the increased sales figures. See Figure D-8. The totals in column F and row 13 are also updated.

> **QUICK TIP**
>
> You can see more layout choices by clicking the More button in the Chart Layouts group.

2. **Select the chart by clicking a blank area within the chart border, click the Chart Tools Design tab on the Ribbon, then click the Layout 3 button in the Chart Layouts group**

   The legend moves to the bottom of the chart. You prefer the original layout.

3. **Click the Undo button 🔄 on the Quick Access toolbar, then click the Change Chart Type button in the Type group**

   The Change Chart Type dialog box opens, as shown in Figure D-9, where you can choose from all available chart type categories and types. The left pane lists the available categories, and the right pane shows the individual chart types. An orange border surrounds the currently selected chart type.

> **QUICK TIP**
>
> If you plan to print a chart on a black-and-white printer, you may wish to change to a black-and-white chart style, so you can see how the output will look as you work.

4. **Click Bar in the left pane of the Change Chart Type dialog box, confirm that the Clustered Bar chart type is selected, then click OK**

   The column chart changes to a clustered bar chart. See Figure D-10. You look at the bar chart, then decide to see if the large increase in sales is more apparent if you use a three-dimensional column chart.

5. **Click the Change Chart Type button in the Type group, click Column in the left pane of the Change Chart Type dialog box, click 3-D Clustered Column (fourth from the left in the first row), then click OK**

   A three-dimensional column chart appears. You notice that the three-dimensional column format is more crowded than the two-dimensional format, but it gives you a sense of volume.

> **QUICK TIP**
>
> You can also use the Undo button on the Quick Access toolbar to return to a previous chart type.

6. **Click the Change Chart Type button in the Type group, click the Clustered Column button (first from the left, first row), then click OK**

7. **Click the Style 3 button in the Chart Styles group**

   The columns change to shades of blue. You prefer the previous color scheme.

8. **Click 🔄 in the Quick Access toolbar, then save your work**

Creating a Combination Chart

You can apply a chart type to an existing data series in a chart, to create a combination chart. In the existing chart, select the data series that you want plotted on a secondary axis, then open the Format dialog box (use the shortcut menu, or click Format Selection in the Current Selection group of the Format tab on the Ribbon). In the Format dialog box, click Series Options, if necessary, click the Secondary Axis option button under Plot Series On, then click Close. Click the Layout tab on the Ribbon, click Axes in the Axes group, then click the type of secondary axis you want and where you want it to appear. To finish, click the Change Chart Type button in the Type group on the Design tab, then select a chart type for the secondary axis.

FIGURE D-8: Worksheet with modified data

Modified data

Adjusted data points

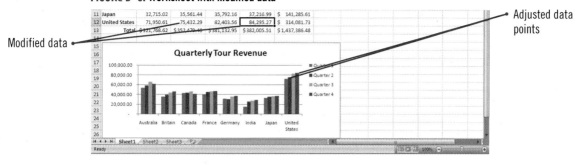

FIGURE D-9: Change Chart Type dialog box

Currently selected chart type

Bar category

Chart type categories

FIGURE D-10: Column chart changed to bar chart

Change Chart Type button

Move Chart button

Click More button to see additional chart layouts

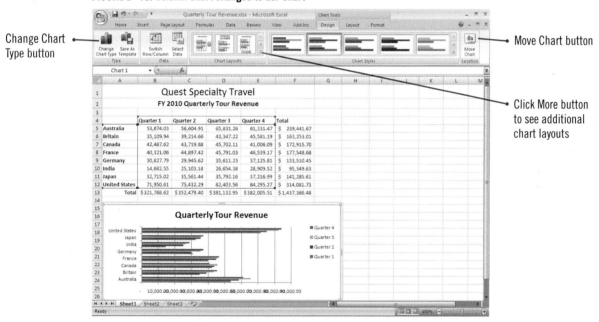

Working with a 3-D chart

Excel includes true 3-D chart types as well as chart types formatted in 3-D. In a true 3-D chart, a third axis, called the **z-axis**, lets you compare data points across both categories and values. The z-axis runs along the depth of the chart, so it appears to advance from the back of the chart. To create a true 3-D chart, look for chart subtypes that begin with "3-D," such as 3-D Column. Charts that are formatted in 3-D contain only two axes but their graphics give the illusion of three-dimensionality. For example, the Clustered Column in 3-D chart displays columns in a 3-D format, but does not include a z-axis that you can modify. To create a chart that is only formatted in 3-D, look for chart subtypes that end with "in 3-D." In a 3-D chart, other data series in the same chart can sometimes obscure columns or bars, but you can rotate the chart to obtain a better view. Right-click the chart, then click 3-D Rotation. The Format Chart Area dialog box opens, with the 3-D Rotation category active. This dialog box can also be used to modify fill, line, line style, shadow, and 3-D format. The 3-D Rotation options let you choose the orientation and perspective of the chart area, plot area, walls, and floor for a 3-D chart. You can use these rotation options to improve the appearance of plotted data within a chart. The 3-D Format options let you choose what three-dimensional effects you would like to apply to select chart elements. (Not all 3-D Format options are available on all charts.)

Changing the Chart Layout

Changing chart layout involves adding, removing, and modifying individual chart elements such as the chart title, plot area, gridlines, and data series. While the Chart Tools Design tab includes preconfigured chart layouts you can apply, the Chart Tools Layout tab makes it easy to create and modify individual chart objects. Using buttons on this tab, you can also add shapes and additional text to a chart, add and modify labels, change the display of axes, and modify the fill behind the plot area. You can also eliminate or change the look of gridlines. **Gridlines** are the horizontal and vertical lines in the chart that enable the eye to follow the value on an axis. You can create titles for the horizontal and vertical axes, add graphics, or add background color. You can even format the text you use in a chart. *⬛⬛⬛⬛⬛* You want to make some layout changes in the chart, to make sure it's easy to interpret and improve its general appearance.

STEPS

QUICK TIP
The Chart Tools tabs appear on the Ribbon only when a chart or one of its objects is selected.

1. **With the chart still selected, click the** Chart Tools Layout tab **on the Ribbon, click the** Gridlines button **in the Axes group, point to** Primary Horizontal Gridlines, **then click** None
The gridlines that extend from the value axis tick marks across the chart's plot area are removed from the chart, as shown in Figure D-11.

2. **Click the** Gridlines button **in the Axes group, point to** Primary Horizontal Gridlines, **then click** Major & Minor Gridlines
Both major and minor gridlines now appear in the chart. **Minor gridlines** show the values between the tick marks. You can change the color of the columns to better distinguish the data series.

3. **Click the** Axis Titles button **in the Labels group, point to** Primary Horizontal Axis Title, **click** Title Below Axis, **triple-click the** axis title, **then type** Tour Countries
Descriptive text on the category axis helps readers understand the chart.

4. **Click the** Axis Titles button **in the Labels group, point to** Primary Vertical Axis Title, **then click** Rotated Title
A placeholder for the vertical axis title is added to the left of the vertical axis.

QUICK TIP
You can also edit text in a chart element by positioning the pointer over the selected text box until it changes to ⬚, click the text box, then edit the text.

5. **Triple-click the** vertical axis title, **then type** Revenue (in $)
The text "Revenue (in $)" appears to the left of the vertical axis, as shown in Figure D-12.

6. **Right-click the** horizontal axis labels ("Australia", "Britain", etc.), **click the** Font list **on the Mini toolbar, click** Times New Roman, **click the** Font Size list **on the Mini toolbar, then click** 8
The font of the horizontal axis text changes to Times New Roman, and the font size decreases, making more of the plot area visible.

QUICK TIP
You can move any title to a new position by clicking an edge of the object then dragging it.

7. **Right-click the** vertical axis labels, **click the** Font list **on the Mini toolbar, click** Times New Roman, **click the** Font Size list **on the Mini toolbar, then click** 8

8. **Right-click the** chart title ("Quarterly Tour Revenue"), **click** Format Chart Title **on the shortcut menu, click** Border Color **in the left pane, then click the** Solid line option button **in the right pane**
Adding a solid border is the first step to creating a shadow box that surrounds the title. You can only add a shadow to a text box that has a border.

9. **Click** Shadow **in the left pane, click the** Presets list arrow, **click the** Offset Diagonal Bottom Right **(first row, first from the left) style in the Outer group, click** Close, **then save your work**
A border with a drop shadow surrounds the title. Compare your work to Figure D-13.

FIGURE D-11: Gridlines removed from chart

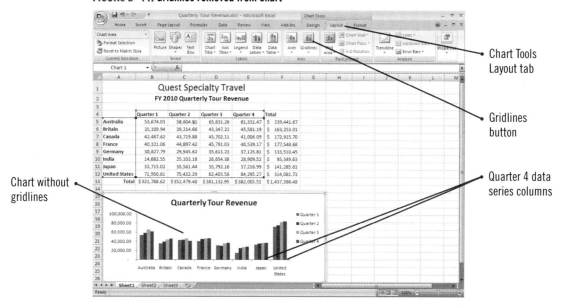

Chart Tools Layout tab

Gridlines button

Quarter 4 data series columns

Chart without gridlines

FIGURE D-12: Axes titles added to chart

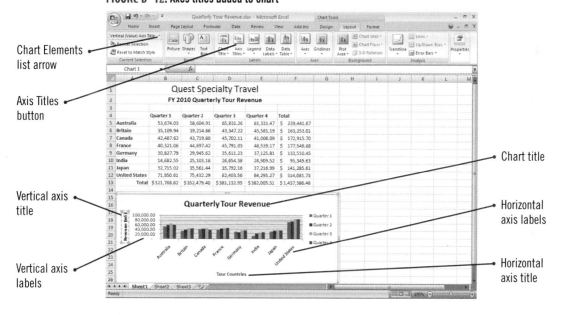

Chart Elements list arrow

Axis Titles button

Vertical axis title

Vertical axis labels

Chart title

Horizontal axis labels

Horizontal axis title

FIGURE D-13: Enhanced chart

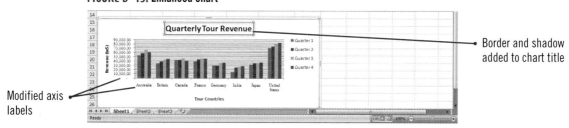

Border and shadow added to chart title

Modified axis labels

Adding data labels to a chart

There are times when your audience might benefit by seeing data labels on a chart. These labels can indicate the series name, category name, and/or the value of one or more data points. Once your chart is selected, you can add this information to your chart by clicking the Data Labels button in the Labels group in the Chart Tools Layout tab on the Ribbon. Once you have added the data labels, you can apply formatting to them or delete individual data labels. Delete individual data labels by clicking them until handles surround the set you want to delete, then press [Delete].

Formatting a Chart

Formatting a chart can make it easier to read and understand. Many formatting enhancements can be made using the Chart Tools Format tab. You can change colors in a specific data series or you can apply a style to a series using the Shape Styles group. Styles make it possible to apply multiple formats, such as an outline, fill color, and text color, all with a single click. You can also make individual selections of fill color, outline, and other effects using the Shape Styles group. WordArt, which lets you create curved or stylized text, can be created using the WordArt Styles group. You want to improve the appearance of the chart by creating titles for the horizontal and vertical axes and adding a drop shadow to the chart title.

STEPS

1. **With the chart selected, click the Chart Tools Format tab on the Ribbon, then click any column in the Quarter 4 data series**

   The Chart Tools Format tab opens, and handles surround each column in the Quarter 4 data series, indicating that the entire series is selected.

2. **Click the Format Selection button in the Current Selection group**

3. **Click Fill in the left pane of the Format Data Series dialog box, then click the Solid fill option button**

4. **Click the Color list arrow [icon], click Orange, Accent 6 (first row, tenth from the left) as shown in Figure D-14, then click Close**

   All the columns for the series become orange, and the legend changes to match the new color. You can also change the color of selected objects by applying a shape style.

5. **Click any column in the Quarter 3 data series**

   Handles surround each column in the Quarter 3 data series.

6. **Click the More button [icon] on the Shape Styles gallery, then hover the pointer over the Moderate Effect – Accent 3 button (fifth row, fourth from the left) as shown in Figure D-15**

7. **Click the Subtle Effect – Accent 3 button (fourth row, fourth from the left) in the palette**

   The color for the data series changes, as shown in Figure D-16.

8. **Save your work**

Changing alignment in axis text and titles

The buttons on the Chart Tools Layout tab provide a few options for aligning axis text and titles, but you can customize the position and rotation to exact specifications using the Format dialog box. You can modify the alignment of axis text to make it fit better within the plot area. With a chart selected, right-click the axis text you want to modify, then click Format Axis on the shortcut menu. The Format Axis dialog box opens for the selected element. Click Alignment, then select the appropriate option. You can create a custom angle by clicking the Text direction list arrow, clicking Horizontal, then selecting the number of degrees from the Custom angle text box. When you have made the desired changes, click Close.

FIGURE D-14: Format Data Series dialog box

Click Border Color to control line display

Click Shadow to control shadow settings

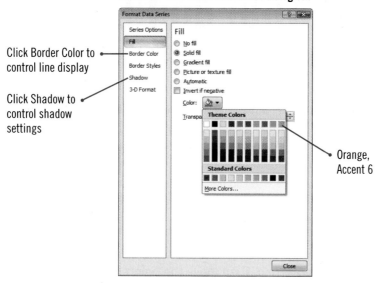

Orange, Accent 6

FIGURE D-15: Chart with formatted data series

Subtle Effect – Accent 3

Moderate Effect – Accent 3

In Step 6, point to this style

Live Preview of current style

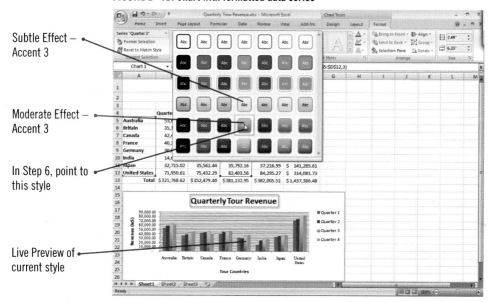

FIGURE D-16: Color of data series changed

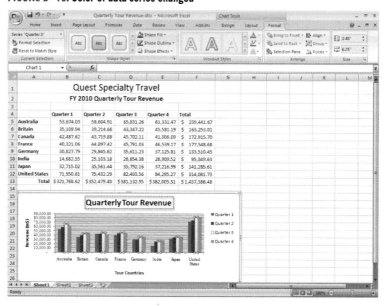

Annotating and Drawing on a Chart

You can add text annotations and graphics to a chart to point out critical information. **Text annotations** are labels that further describe your data. You can also draw lines and arrows that point to the exact locations you want to emphasize. Shapes such as arrows and boxes can be added from the Illustrations group on the Insert tab or from the Insert group on the Chart Tools Layout group on the Ribbon. These groups are also used to Insert pictures and clip art. 📧📧 You want to call attention to the India tour revenue increases, so you decide to add a text annotation and an arrow to this information in the chart.

STEPS

1. **Make sure the chart is selected, click the** Chart Tools Layout tab, **click the** Text Box button **in the Insert group, then move the pointer over the worksheet**
   The pointer changes to ↓, indicating that you can begin typing text by clicking.

QUICK TIP

You can also insert text by clicking the Text Box button in the Text group in the Insert tab.

2. **Click to the right of the chart (anywhere** outside **the chart boundary)**
   A text box is added to the worksheet, and the Drawing Tools Format tab opens, so that you can format the new object. First you need to type the text.

3. **Type** Great improvement
   The text appears in a selected text box on the worksheet and the chart is no longer selected, as shown in Figure D-17. Your text box may be in a different location; this is not important, because you'll move the annotation in the next step.

4. **Point to an edge of the text box so that the pointer changes to** 🕂, **drag the** text box **into the chart to the left of the chart title, as shown in Figure D-18, then release the mouse button**
   You want to add a simple arrow shape in the chart.

QUICK TIP

To annotate a chart, you can also use the Callouts category of the Shapes palette in either the Illustrations group on the Insert tab or the Insert group on the Chart Tools Layout tab.

5. **Click the** chart **to select it, click the** Chart Tools Layout tab, **click the** Shapes button **in the Insert group, click the** Arrow shape **in the Lines category, then move the pointer over the chart**
   The pointer changes to ╋, and the status bar displays "Click and drag to insert an AutoShape." When you draw an arrow, the point farthest from where you start has the arrowhead. When ╋ is near the text box handles, the handles turn red. The red handles act as an anchor for the arrow.

6. **Position** ╋ **at the** red square **to the right of the t in the word "improvement" (in the text box), press and hold the** left mouse button, **drag the line to the** Quarter 2 column **in the India series, then release the mouse button**
   An arrow points to India's second quarter revenue, and the Drawing Tools Format tab displays options for working with this new object. You can resize, format, or delete it just like any other object in a chart.

7. **Click the** Shape Outline list arrow **in the Shape Styles group, point to** Weight, **then click** 1½ pt
   Compare your finished chart to Figure D-19.

8. **Save your work**

FIGURE D-17: Text box added

Drawing Tools
Format tab

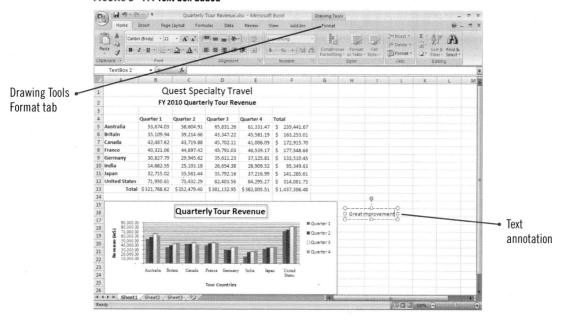

Text
annotation

FIGURE D-18: Text annotation on chart

Text annotation

FIGURE D-19: Drawn object added to chart

Arrow added and
formatted

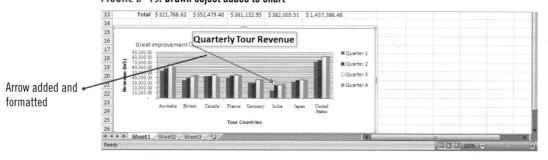

Adding SmartArt graphics

In addition to charts, annotations, and drawn objects, you can create a variety of diagrams using SmartArt. Diagram types include List, Process, Cycle, Hierarchy, Relationship, Matrix, and Pyramid. To insert SmartArt, click the SmartArt button in the Illustrations group on the Insert tab on the Ribbon. Click the category of SmartArt you want to create from the left panel, then click the style from the center panel. The right panel shows a sample of the selection you've chosen, as shown in Figure D-20. The diagram appears on the worksheet as an embedded object with sizing handles. An additional window opens where you can enter the diagram text.

FIGURE D-20: Choose a SmartArt Graphic dialog box

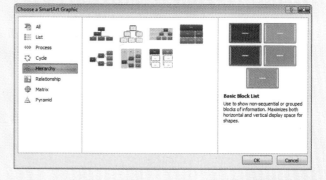

Creating a Pie Chart

You can create multiple charts based on the same worksheet data. While a column chart may illustrate certain important aspects of your worksheet data, you may find you want to create an additional chart to emphasize a different point. Depending on the type of chart you create, you have additional options for calling attention to trends and patterns. For example, if you create a pie chart, you can emphasize one data point by **exploding**, or pulling that slice away from, the pie chart. When you're ready to print a chart, you can preview it just as you do a worksheet, to check the output before committing it to paper. You can print a chart by itself or as part of the worksheet. ▓▓▓ At an upcoming meeting, Grace plans to discuss the total tour revenue and which countries need improvement. You want to create a pie chart she can use to illustrate total revenue. Finally, you want to print the worksheet and the charts.

STEPS

1. **Select the range A5:A12, press and hold [Ctrl], select the range F5:F12, click the Insert tab, click the Pie button in the Charts group, then click the Pie in 3-D button in the gallery**

   The new chart appears in the center of the worksheet. You can move the chart and quickly format it using a Chart Layout.

2. **Drag the chart so its top left corner is at the top left corner of cell G1, then click the Layout 2 button in the Chart Layouts group**

3. **Click the slice for the India data point, click again so it is the only data point selected, right-click, then click Format Data Point**

   The Format Data Point dialog box opens, as shown in Figure D-21. You can use the Point Explosion slider to control the distance a pie slice moves or you can type a value in the Point Explosion text box.

4. **Double-click 0 in the Point Explosion text box, type 40, then click Close**

   Compare your chart to Figure D-22. You decide to preview the chart and data before you print.

5. **Drag the bottom edge of the chart so it is close to the top of row 15, if necessary**

6. **Click cell A1, switch to Page Layout view, type Your Name in the left-hand header box, then click cell A1**

   You decide the chart and data would fit better on the page if they were printed in **landscape** orientation— that is, with the text running the long way on the page.

7. **Click the Page Layout tab, click the Orientation button in the Page Setup group, then click Landscape**

8. **Open the Print Preview window, click the Page Setup button on the Print Preview tab, click the Fit to option button, make sure the contents are set to fit to 1 page wide by 1 page tall, then click OK**

   The data and chart are positioned horizontally on a single page. See Figure D-23. The printer you have selected may affect the appearance of your preview screen, and if you do not have a color printer installed, the image will appear in black & white.

9. **Click the Print button on the Print Preview tab, print one copy of the page, save and close the workbook, then exit Excel**

FIGURE D-21: Format Data Point dialog box

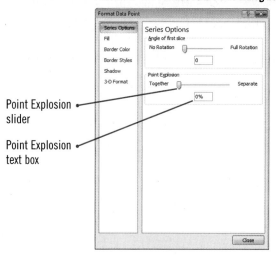

Point Explosion slider

Point Explosion text box

FIGURE D-22: Exploded pie slice

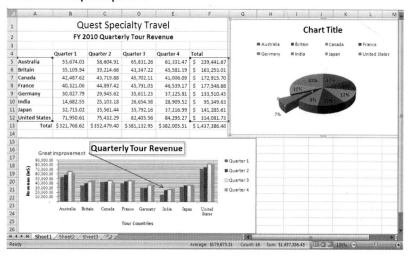

FIGURE D-23: Landscape view of completed charts

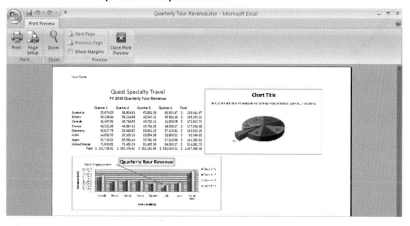

Using the Page Setup dialog box for a chart

When a chart is selected (or a chart sheet is active) and the Print Preview window is open, you can make modifications by clicking Page Setup in the Print group on the Print Preview tab. The Page Setup dialog box does not display all the options normally available. For example, the Center on page options (in the Margins tab) are not always available, and the Scaling options (in the Page tab) are grayed out.

You can also use the Show Margins checkbox in the Preview group of the Print Preview tab to accurately position a chart on the page. Margin lines appear on the screen and show you exactly how the margins appear on the page. The exact placement appears in the status bar when you press and hold the mouse button on the margin line. You can drag the lines to the exact settings you want.

Practice

If you have a SAM user profile, you may have access to hands-on instruction, practice, and assessment of the skills covered in this unit. Log in to your SAM account (http://sam2007.course.com/) to launch any assigned training activities or exams that relate to the skills covered in this unit.

▼ CONCEPTS REVIEW

Label each element of the Excel chart shown in Figure D-24.

FIGURE D-24

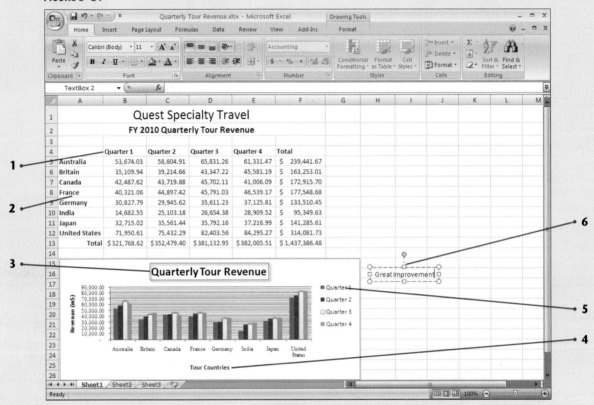

Match each chart type with the statement that best describes it.

7. Line	**a.** Compares trends over even time intervals
8. Pie	**b.** Shows how volume changes over time
9. Area	**c.** Compares data over time the Excel default
10. Column	**d.** Displays a column and line chart using different scales of measurement
11. Combination	**e.** Compares data as parts of a whole

Select the best answer from the list of choices.

12. Which tab on the Ribbon do you use to create a chart?

  a. Design   **c.** Page Layout

  b. Insert   **d.** Format

13. Which tab appears only when a chart is selected?

  a. Insert   **c.** Review

  b. Chart Tools Format   **d.** Page Layout

14. Which pointer do you use to resize a chart object?

  a. $+$ **c.** $\downarrow$

  b. I **d.** $\updownarrow$

15. How do you move an embedded chart to a chart sheet?

  a. Click a button on the Chart Tools Design tab.

  b. Drag the chart to the sheet tab.

  c. Delete the chart, switch to a different sheet, then create a new chart.

  d. Use the Copy and Paste buttons on the Ribbon.

16. The object in a chart that identifies patterns used for each data series is a(n):

  a. Data marker.   **c.** Organizer

  b. Data point.   **d.** Legend.

17. A collection of related data points in a chart is called a:

  a. Data series.   **c.** Cell address.

  b. Data tick.   **d.** Value title.

▼ SKILLS REVIEW

1. Plan a chart.

  a. Start Excel, open the Data File EX D-2.xlsx from the drive and folder where you store your Data Files, then save it as **Departmental Software Usage**.

  b. Describe the type of chart you would use to plot this data.

  c. What chart type would you use to compare total company expenses by department?

  d. What term is used to describe each value in a worksheet range selected for a chart?

2. Create a chart.

  a. In the worksheet, select the range containing all the data and headings.

  b. Click the Insert tab, if necessary.

  c. Create a clustered column chart, then add the chart title **Software Usage, by Department** above the chart.

  d. Save your work.

3. Move and resize a chart.

  a. Make sure the chart is still selected.

  b. Move the chart beneath the data.

  c. Resize the chart so it extends to the left edge of column I.

  d. Use the Chart Tools Layout tab to move the legend below the charted data.

  e. Resize the chart so its bottom edge is at the top of row 25.

  f. Save your work.

4. Change the chart design.

  a. Change the value in cell B3 to 25. Observe the change in the chart.

  b. Select the chart.

  c. Use the Chart Layouts group on the Chart Tools Design tab to change to Layout 7, then undo the change.

  d. Use the Change Chart Type button on the Chart Tools Design tab to change the chart to a clustered bar chart.

  e. Change the chart to a 3-D clustered column chart , then change it back to a clustered column chart.

  f. Save your work.

5. Change the chart layout.

   a. Use the Layout tab to turn off the displayed gridlines in the chart.

   b. Change the font used in the horizontal and vertical axes labels to Times New Roman.

   c. Turn on the major gridlines for both the horizontal and vertical axes.

   d. Change the chart title's font to Times New Roman, with a font size of 20.

   e. Enter Departments as the horizontal axis title.

   f. Enter Number of Users as the vertical axis title. (*Hint*: Use a rotated title)

   g. Change the font size of the horizontal axis to 10, if necessary, and the font to Times New Roman.

   h. Change the font size of the vertical axis labels to 10, if necessary, and the font to Times New Roman.

   i. Change Personnel in the column heading to Human Resources. (*Hint*: Change the label in the worksheet, then resize the column.)

   j. Change the font size of the legend to 14.

   k. Add an offset diagonal bottom-right outer drop shadow to the chart title. (*Hint*: Use a solid line border in the default color.)

   l. Save your work.

6. Format a chart.

   a. Make sure the chart is selected, then select the Format tab, if necessary.

   b. Change the color of the Excel data series to Olive Green, Accent 3 Darker 50%.

   c. Change the shape effect of the Excel data series to Bevel – Circle.

   d. Save your work.

7. Annotate and draw on a chart.

   a. Make sure the chart is selected, then create the text annotation Needs more users.

   b. Position the text annotation so the 'N' in 'Needs' is positioned approximately below the 't' in 'Software'.

   c. Use the Shapes group on the Insert tab to create a 1½ pt weight arrow that points to the Excel users in the Design Department.

   d. Deselect the chart.

   e. Save your work.

8. Create a pie chart.

   a. Select the range A1:F2, then create a 3-D pie chart.

   b. Drag the 3-D pie chart beneath the existing chart.

   c. Change the chart title to Excel Users.

   d. Apply Chart Style 26 to the chart.

   e. Explode the Human Resources slice from the pie chart at 25%.

   f. In the worksheet, enter your name in the left section of the header.

g. View the worksheet and charts in the Print Preview window, make sure all the contents fit on one page, then compare your work to Figure D-25.

h. Save your work.

i. Close the workbook, then exit Excel.

FIGURE D-25

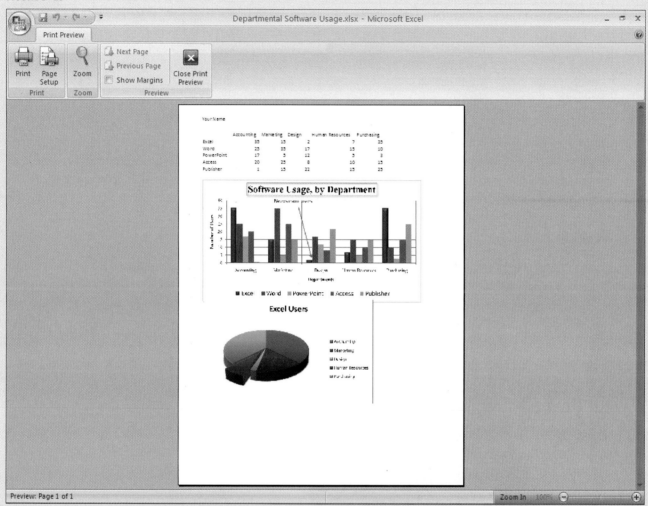

▼ INDEPENDENT CHALLENGE 1

You are the operations manager for the Springfield Theater Group in Massachusetts. Each year the group applies to various state and federal agencies for matching funds. For this year's funding proposal, you need to create charts to document the number of productions in previous years.

a. Start Excel, open the file EX D-3.xlsx from the drive and folder where you store your Data Files, then save it as **Springfield Theater Group**.

b. Take some time to plan your charts. Which type of chart or charts might best illustrate the information you need to display? What kind of chart enhancements do you want to use? Will a 3-D effect make your chart easier to understand?

c. Create a clustered column chart for the data.

d. If you wish, change at least one of the colors used in a data series.

e. Make the appropriate modifications to the chart to make it easy to read and understand, and visually attractive. Include chart titles, legends, and value and category axis titles, using the suggestions in Table D-3.

TABLE D-3

suggested chart enhancements for a column chart	
Title	Types and Number of Plays
Legend	Year 1, Year 2, Year 3, Year 4
Vertical axis title	Number of Plays
Horizontal axis title	Play Types

f. Create at least two additional charts for the same data to show how different chart types display the same data. Place each new chart on its own sheet in the workbook, and name the sheet according to the type of chart you created. One of the additional charts should be a pie chart; the other is up to you. Modify each new chart as necessary to improve its appearance and effectiveness. Compare your chart to the sample in Figure D-26.

FIGURE D-26

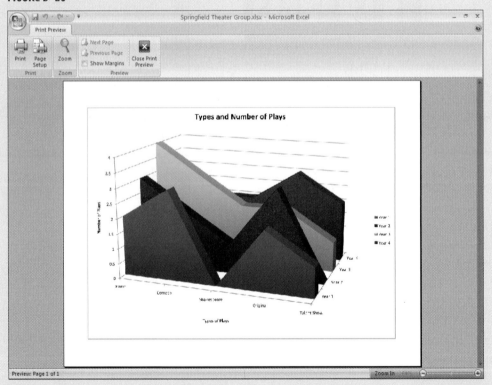

g. Enter your name in the worksheet header.

h. Save your work. Before printing, preview the workbook in Print Preview, then adjust any items as necessary.

i. Print the worksheet (charts and data).

j. Close the workbook, then exit Excel.

▼ INDEPENDENT CHALLENGE 2

FIGURE D-27

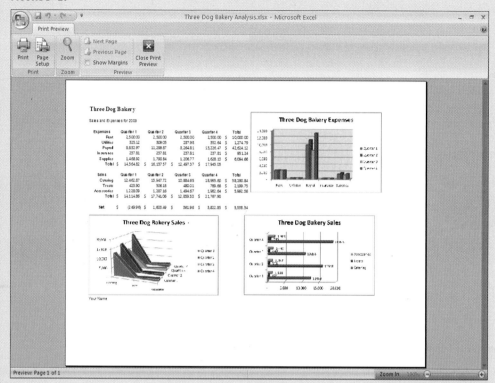

You work at Three Dog Bakery, a locally-owned bakery for dogs. One of your responsibilities at the bakery is to manage the company's sales and expenses using Excel. Another is to convince the current staff that Excel can help them make daily operating decisions more easily and efficiently. To do this, you've decided to create charts using the previous year's operating expenses, including rent, utilities, and payroll. The manager will use these charts at the next monthly meeting.

a. Start Excel, open the Data File EX D-4.xlsx from the drive and folder where you store your Data Files, then save it as **Three Dog Bakery Analysis**.

b. Decide which data in the worksheet should be charted. What type of chart or charts are best suited for the information you need to show? What kinds of chart enhancements are necessary?

c. Create a 3-D column chart (with the data series in rows) on the worksheet, showing the expense data for all four quarters. (*Hint*: Do not include the totals.)

d. Change the scale of the vertical axis (Expense data) so no decimals are displayed. (*Hint*: Right-click the scale you want to modify, click Format Axis, click Number category, change the number of decimal places, then click Close.)

e. Using the sales data, create two charts on this worksheet that illustrate trends in the data. (*Hint*: Move each chart to a new location on the worksheet, then deselect it before creating the next one.)

f. In one chart of the sales data, add data labels, then add chart titles as you see fit.

g. Make any necessary formatting changes to make the charts look more attractive, then enter your name in a worksheet cell.

h. Save your work.

i. Before printing, preview each chart, and adjust any items as needed. Fit the charts to a single page, then print one copy. Compare your work to the sample in Figure D-27.

j. Close the workbook, then exit Excel.

▼ INDEPENDENT CHALLENGE 3

FIGURE D-28

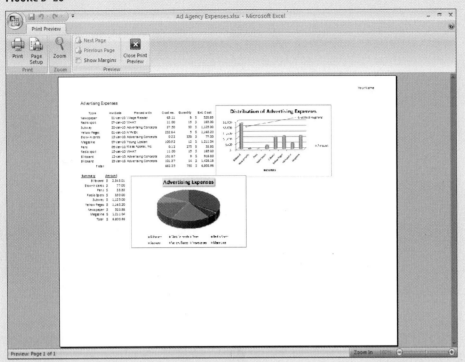

You are working as an account representative at the Inspiration Ad Agency. You have been examining the expenses charged to clients of the firm. The board of directors wants to examine certain advertising expenses and has asked you to prepare charts that can be used in this evaluation. In particular, you want to see how dollar amounts compare among the different expenses, and you also want to see how expenses compare with each other proportional to the total budget.

a. Start Excel, open the Data File EX D-5.xlsx from the drive and folder where you store your Data Files, then save it as **Ad Agency Expenses**.

b. Choose three types of charts that seem best suited to illustrate the data in the range A16:B24. What kinds of chart enhancements are necessary?

c. Create at least two different types of charts that show the distribution of advertising expenses. (*Hint*: Move each chart to a new location on the same worksheet.) One of the charts should be a 3-D pie chart.

d. Add annotated text and arrows highlighting important data, such as the largest expense.

e. Change the color of at least one data series in at least one of the charts.

f. Add chart titles and category and value axis titles where appropriate. Format the titles with a font of your choice. Place a drop shadow around the chart title in at least one chart.

g. Add your name to a section of the header, then save your work.

h. View the file in Print Preview. Adjust any items as needed. Be sure the charts are all visible on the page. Compare your work to the sample in Figure D-28.

Advanced Challenge Exercise

- Explode a slice from the 3-D pie chart.
- Add a data label to the exploded pie slice.
- Change the number format of labels in the non-pie charts so no decimals are displayed.
- Modify the scale of the vertical axis in one of the charts. (*Hint*: Right-click the vertical axis, click Format Axis, then click Axis Options.)
- Save your work, then view it in Print Preview.

i. Print the charts, close the workbook, then exit Excel.

▼ REAL LIFE INDEPENDENT CHALLENGE

FIGURE D-29

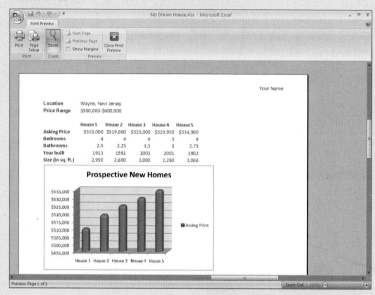

Note: This project requires an Internet connection.

A cash inheritance from a distant relative has finally been deposited in your bank account, and you have decided to quit your job and relocate to the town of your dreams. You have a good idea where you'd like to live and decide to use the Web to see what sort of houses are currently available.

a. Start Excel, then save a new, blank workbook as **My Dream House** to the drive and folder where you save your Data Files.

b. Decide on where you would like to live, and use your favorite search engine to find information sources on homes for sale in that area.

c. Determine a price range and features within the home. Find data for at least five homes that meet your location and price requirements, and enter them in the worksheet. See Table D-4 below for suggested data layout.

d. Format the data so it looks attractive and professional.

e. Create any type of column chart, using only the House and Asking Price data. Place it on the same worksheet as the data. Include a descriptive title.

f. Change the colors in the chart, using the Chart Style of your choice.

g. Enter your name in a section of the header.

TABLE D-4

location					
price range					
	House 1	House 2	House 3	House 4	House 5
Asking price					
Bedrooms					
Bathrooms					
Year built					
Size (in sq. ft.)					

h. Save the workbook. Preview the chart(s) and change margins and/or orientation as necessary. Compare your work to the sample chart shown in Figure D-29.

i. Print your worksheet(s), including the data and chart(s), making setup modifications as necessary.

Advanced Challenge Exercise

- Change the chart type to a Clustered Column chart.
- Create a combination chart that plots the asking price on one axis and the size of the home on the other axis. (*Hint*: Use Help to get tips on how to chart with a secondary axis.)

j. Close the workbook, then exit Excel.

▼ VISUAL WORKSHOP

Open the Data File EX D-6.xlsx from the drive and folder where you store your Data Files, then save it as **Projected Project Revenue**. Modify the worksheet data so it looks like Figure D-30, then create and modify two charts to match the ones shown in the figure. You will need to make formatting, layout, and design changes once you create the charts. Enter your name in the left section of the header, then save, preview, and print your results.

FIGURE D-30

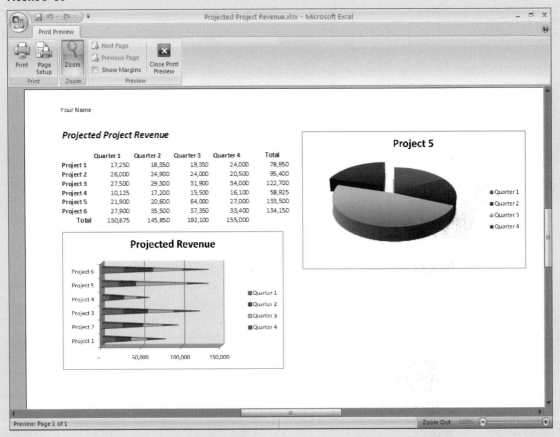

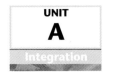

Integrating Word and Excel

Now that you have experienced the power of Word and Excel, you need to learn how to use these two programs together to create sophisticated documents that incorporate data from both programs. For example, you can prepare a report in Word that contains a chart you created in Excel. Any changes you make to the chart in Excel also appear in the chart contained in the Word report. You can also copy words and numbers between Word and Excel, and you can insert a Word file into an Excel workbook. You integrate data between programs to save time and effort so you can work more effectively. Instead of recreating the same information in different programs, you create the information once in one program and then reuse it in other programs. You are working as an assistant to Mary Lou Jacobs, the general manager of QST Vancouver, one of the two Canadian branches of Quest Specialty Travel. Mary Lou has asked you to use Word and Excel to create a report and a price list.

OBJECTIVES

Integrate data between Word and Excel
Copy data from Excel to Word
Copy a chart from Excel to Word
Create linked objects
Embed a Word file in Excel

Integrating Data Between Word and Excel

Microsoft Office programs are designed to work together through a process called **integration**. When you integrate data from multiple Office programs, you work with both a source file and a destination file. The **source file** is the file from which the information is copied or used. The **destination file** is the file that receives the copied information. You can choose from three integration methods: pasting, linking, and embedding. As the operations assistant at QST Vancouver, you often create documents such as reports and price lists that include data from both Word and Excel. You decide to review some of the ways in which you integrate data between the two programs.

DETAILS

You can integrate Word and Excel by:

- **Copying and pasting data from the Clipboard**

  You use the Copy and Paste commands to duplicate **objects** such as text selections, values, and pictures from one program and place them into another program. When you copy and paste an object, changes that you make to the object in the source file do not appear in the destination file. The report shown in Figure A-1 was created in Word and includes two objects that were copied from Excel—the photograph that appears to the right of the document title and the shaded table under the document subtitle.

- **Linking data**

  Sometimes you want to "connect" the data that is included in two or more files. For example, suppose you copy the contents of a cell containing a formula from an Excel spreadsheet and paste it into a Word document. When you change the values referenced in the formula in Excel, you want the corresponding values to change in the Word document. You use the Link command from the Paste Special dialog box to create a **link** between selected data in two files. You use the term **linked object** to refer to the connected data. In the report shown in Figure A-1, the value 75% is a linked object. If this percentage changes in the Excel workbook, the linked percentage in the Word document also changes.

- **Copying charts**

  When you copy a chart from Excel and paste it into Word using the Paste command, Word automatically creates a link to the original chart. In the report shown in Figure A-1, the column chart is copied from Excel. When the chart values are updated in Excel, the same chart values are updated in the chart copied to Word.

- **Embedding objects**

  You can **embed**, or place a copy of, the contents of a Word file into an Excel worksheet. You edit the embedded object by double-clicking it and using Word program tools to change text and formatting. This process changes the embedded copy of the Word object in Excel, but does not affect the original source document that was created in Word. Similarly, any changes to the source Word document are not reflected in the embedded copy in Excel. In the price list shown in Figure A-2, the text that describes the QST tours was inserted in Excel as an embedded Word file.

Understanding Object Linking and Embedding (OLE)

The term **Object Linking and Embedding (OLE)** refers to the technology that Microsoft uses to allow you to integrate data between programs. You create an object in one program and then you can choose to either link the object or embed it in another program. The difference between linking and embedding relates to where the object is stored and how you update the object after you place it in a document. A linked object in a destination file is an image of an object contained in a source file. Both objects share a single source, which means you update the object only in the source file.

When you embed an object that you created in another program, you include a copy of the object in a destination file. To update the object, you double-click it in the destination file and then use the tools of the source program to make changes. You cannot edit the source object using the tools of the destination program.

FIGURE A-1: Word report with objects copied from Excel

Table object
copied from
Excel

Photograph copied
from Excel

Chart linked to
Excel source chart

75% is a linked value

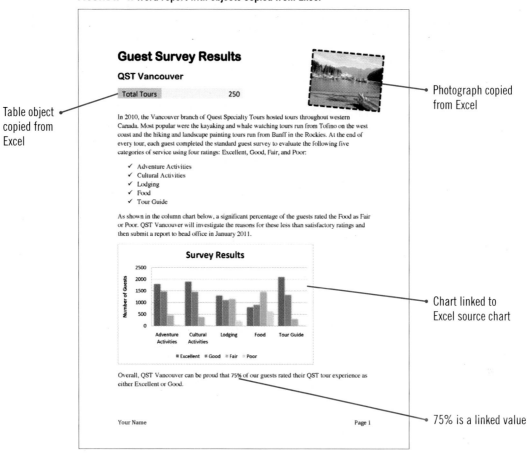

FIGURE A-2: Excel price list with embedded Word file

Text inserted
directly from
a Word file

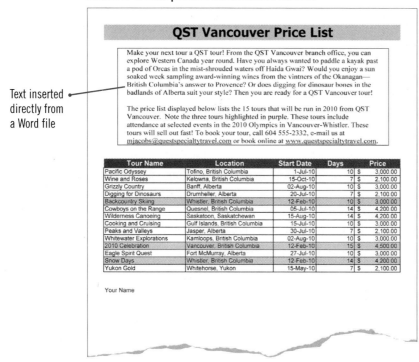

Copying Data from Excel to Word

You use the Copy and Paste commands when you want to copy an item such as a line of text, a value, or an object such as a chart or picture from one program to another program. The procedure is the same as the one you use to copy and paste an object from one location in a document to another location in the same document. When you copy an object from one program to another, the copied object retains the formatting of the original object and usually does not change when the original object is changed. The exception occurs when you copy and paste a chart, which you will learn about in the next lesson. Mary Lou Jacobs, the general manager of QST Vancouver, has summarized survey data in an Excel worksheet and created a report in Word to describe the survey results. She asks you to copy two objects from the Excel spreadsheet and paste them into the Word report.

STEPS

1. **Start Excel, open the file INT A-1.xlsx from the drive and folder where you store your Data Files, then save it as QST Vancouver Survey Data**

    The values in the range B7:F10 represent the total number of responses in each of the four rating categories for the tours that QST operated out of Vancouver in 2010.

2. **Start Word, open the file INT A-2.docx from the drive and folder where you store your Data Files, then save it as QST Vancouver Survey Report**

    The Word report contains text that describes the results of the survey.

3. **Move the mouse pointer over the Excel program button on the taskbar as shown in Figure A-3, then click the Excel program button to switch to Excel**

    When you point to the Excel program button, the program name and filename appear in a ScreenTip.

4. **On the Home tab, click the launcher 🔲 in the Clipboard group**

    > **TROUBLE**
    > If items already appear in the Clipboard task pane, click Clear All.

    The Clipboard task pane opens to the left of the spreadsheet window. You use the Clipboard when you want to copy and paste more than one item from one program to another program. You can "collect" up to 24 items to the Clipboard and then switch to the other program to paste them.

5. **Click the photograph, click the Copy button 🔲 in the Clipboard group, select the range A4:C4, then click 🔲**

    Both items now appear on the Clipboard, as shown in Figure A-4. When you place multiple items on the Clipboard, newer items appear at the top of the list and older items move down.

6. **Click the Word program button on the taskbar, click the launcher 🔲 in the Clipboard group, verify that the insertion point is to the left of the title, then click the photograph on the Clipboard**

    You pasted the photograph to the left of the document title.

7. **Click in the blank space below QST Vancouver, click Total Tours 250 on the Clipboard, then click the Close button on the Clipboard task pane**

    You pasted the object as a table below the document subtitle. When you use the Copy and Paste commands, the program retains the formatting of the copied object by default.

8. **Right-click the photograph in the Word document, point to Text Wrapping, click Square, then drag the photograph to the right of the title, as shown in Figure A-5**

9. **Click anywhere in the document to deselect the photograph, then save the document**

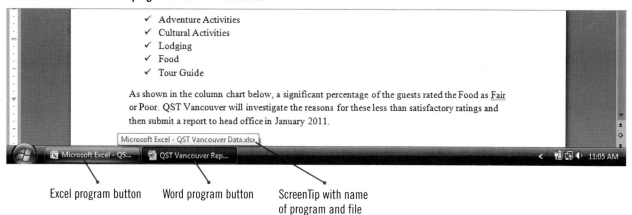

Excel program button   Word program button   ScreenTip with name of program and file

FIGURE A-4: Two items collected on the Clipboard

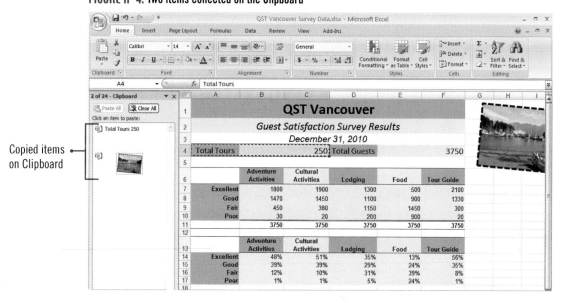

Copied items on Clipboard

FIGURE A-5: Picture positioned in the Word report

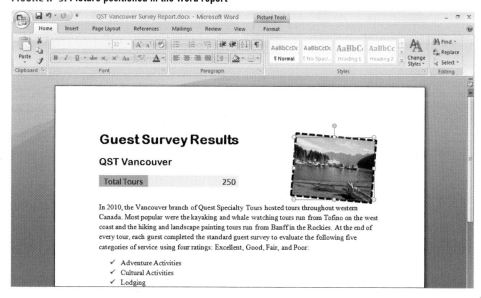

Copying a Chart from Excel to Word

You use the Copy and Paste buttons to create a link between a chart that you copy from Excel and paste into a document in Word. When you change the data in the source file, the linked data also changes in the destination file. You need to copy a column chart representing survey results from Excel and paste it into the Word report. By default, the copied chart will be linked to the chart in the Excel report.

STEPS

1. **Click the Excel program button on the taskbar, then close the Clipboard task pane**

2. **Scroll down to view the column chart, click the chart to select it, then click the Copy button in the Clipboard group**

QUICK TIP
To paste a chart without linking it, choose the Paste as Picture command.

3. **Switch to Word, click below the second paragraph (which ends with January 2011), click the Paste button in the Clipboard group, then click the Paste Options button in the lower right corner of the pasted chart as shown in Figure A-6**

   In the list of Paste options, the option to link to the chart is selected by default.

4. **Switch to Excel, then note the position of the bars for the Food category in the column chart**

   At present, the "Poor" column is quite high compared to the "Poor" columns for the other categories.

5. **Scroll up, click cell E7, type 1200, press [Enter], click cell E10, type 200, then press [Enter]**

   In the chart, the Excellent column in the Food category has grown and the Poor column has shrunk.

6. **Switch to Word**

   As shown in Figure A-7, the bars for the Food category in the column chart have changed in the linked chart to reflect the changes you made to the chart in Excel.

TROUBLE
The Excel window may appear to the left of the Word window on your screen.

7. **Right-click any edge of the column chart in Word, then click Edit Data**

   The Word and Excel windows are resized and repositioned so that they appear side by side. Any changes you make to the chart data in Excel will be immediately visible in the linked chart in the Word document.

8. **Click the chart in Excel, click the Design tab, click Quick Styles, then click Style 12 (the second red style in the fourth column)**

   As shown in Figure A-8, the color of the columns in the Excel chart changes to red and the color of the columns in the chart copied to Word do not change. When you link a chart from Excel to Word, you can update only the chart data, not the chart style.

9. **Maximize the Excel window, save the workbook, switch to Word, maximize the window, then save the document**

FIGURE A-6: Paste options

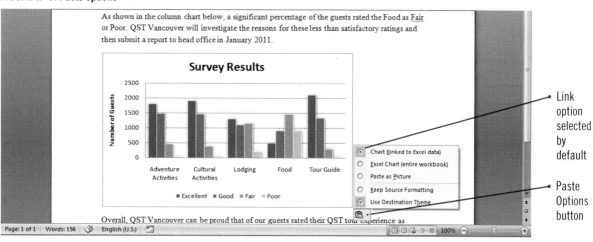

Link option selected by default

Paste Options button

FIGURE A-7: Linked chart updated in Word

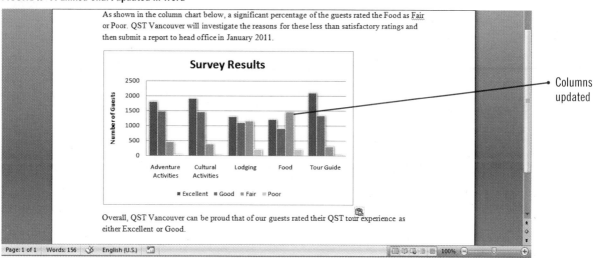

Columns updated

FIGURE A-8: Chart style not applied to linked object

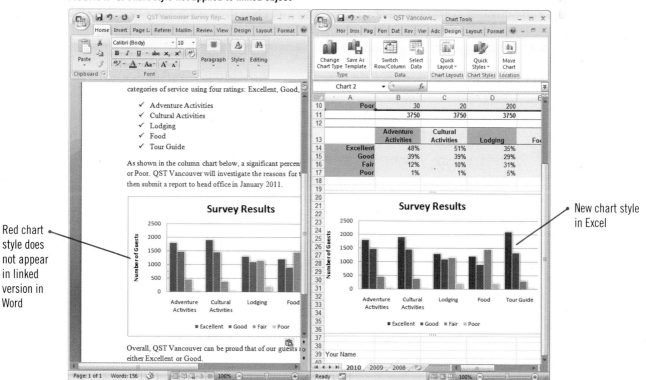

Red chart style does not appear in linked version in Word

New chart style in Excel

Creating Linked Objects

To link data other than a chart, you use the Copy button and the Paste Special command to create a link between the source file and the destination file. The Paste Special command also lets you choose one of several formats for the linked object. ▓▓▓▓ You need your report to include a figure that represents the average tour ratings. You decide to link the report with the source file data so that you can update the data in both files when new information becomes available.

STEPS

1. **Switch to Excel, click cell G14, type the formula** =AVERAGE(B14:F14), **press [Enter], click cell G14, then drag its fill handle to cell G17 to enter the remaining three percentages**

   The value 44% appears in cell G14 to indicate that, on average, 44% of the responses were Excellent. Only 3% of the responses were Poor.

2. **Click cell F19, type Good/Excellent, press [Tab], in cell G19, type the formula** =G14+G15, **then press [Enter]**

   The value 78% appears in cell G19, indicating that 78% of guests rated their tour experience as Good or Excellent.

3. **Click cell G19, click the Copy button** 📋 **in the Clipboard group, switch to Word, scroll to the last paragraph (which starts with Overall, QST Vancouver...), then click just to the left of the word "of" following the phrase "can be proud that"**

   You have positioned the insertion point at the location where you want to paste the contents of cell G19 from Excel.

4. **Click the Paste list arrow in the Clipboard Group, then click Paste Special**

   The Paste Special dialog box opens, as shown in Figure A-9. In this dialog box, you can choose to paste the value as a link and you can choose how you want the pasted value to appear in the destination file.

5. **Click the Paste link option button, click Unformatted Text, click OK, then press [Spacebar] once**

   You decide to test the link.

6. **Switch to Excel, click cell E7, type 800, press [Enter], click cell E10, type 600, then press [Enter]**

   The Good/Excellent rating is now 75%.

7. **Switch to Word, right-click 78% in the last paragraph, then click Update Link**

   Each time you change a linked value in the source file, you need to update the link in the destination file.

8. **Type your name where indicated in the Word footer, view the report in Print Preview, compare it to Figure A-10, print a copy of the report, then save and close the document**

9. **In Excel, type your name where indicated in cell A39, print a copy of the worksheet, then save and close the workbook**

FIGURE A-9: Paste Special dialog box

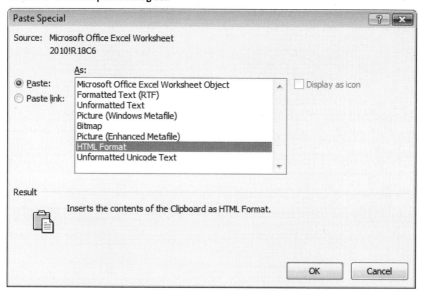

FIGURE A-10: Completed report in Print Preview

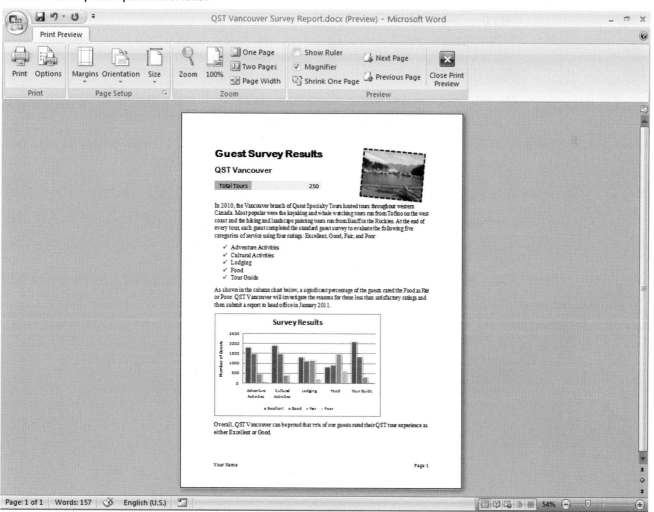

Embedding a Word File in Excel

You can embed an entire file that you create in one Office program into a document created in another Office program. You can then edit the embedded file by double-clicking it in the destination program to open the source program. You use the tools of the source program to make changes. Table A-1 summarizes the four ways in which you integrated data between Word and Excel in this unit. 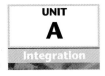 You have created a price list in Excel, but before you print it for distribution at an upcoming meeting at QST Vancouver, you decide to include some explanatory text that you have stored in a Word document.

STEPS

1. **In Excel, open the file INT A-3.xlsx from the drive and folder where you store your Data Files, save it as QST Vancouver Price List; in Word, open the file INT A-4.docx from where you store your Data Files, save it as QST Vancouver 2010 Tours, then close it**

2. **In Excel, click cell G3, click the Insert tab, then click the Object button in the Text group**
    The Object dialog box opens. Here you can choose to create a new object or you can insert an object from a file.

    ### TROUBLE
    If the file extension .docx does not appear after the file-name, you can enable this option in Windows. To do this, click the Start button, click Control Panel, click Appearance and Personalization, click Folder Options, click the View tab, and then remove the check mark next to Hide extensions for known file types.

3. **Click the Create from File tab, click Browse, navigate to where you stored the QST Vancouver 2010 Tours file, double-click QST Vancouver 2010 Tours.docx, then click OK**
    The text from the Word document appears in a box that starts in cell G3. You can choose to insert the Word object anywhere in the spreadsheet and then move it. When you insert an object from another program such as Word, you sometimes need to reposition the current workbook contents to accommodate the inserted object.

4. **Select the range A6:E20, move the mouse pointer over any border of the selection to show the ‡ pointer, then drag the selection down to cell A18**

5. **Move the mouse pointer over the border of the box containing the Word text to show the ‡ pointer, then drag the selection to cell A3 as shown In Figure A-11**

6. **Double-click the box containing the Word text**
    Because the object is embedded, the Word ribbon and tabs appear within the Excel window, which means you can use the tools from the source program (Word) to edit it. The title bar shows the name of the Excel file because you are working within the destination file to edit the embedded object.

7. **Click the Select button in the Editing group, click Select All, click the launcher ▣ in the Paragraph group, click the Left text box in the Indentation section, type .2, press [Tab], type .2 in the Right text box, then click OK**

8. **Select 10 in the first line of paragraph 2, type 15, compare the edited object to Figure A-12, then click outside the object to return to Excel**
    The embedded object is updated in Excel. The text in the source file is not updated because the source file is not linked to the destination file.

9. **Type your name where indicated in cell A35, print the worksheet, then save and close the workbook**

FIGURE A-11: Embedded Word file positioned in Excel

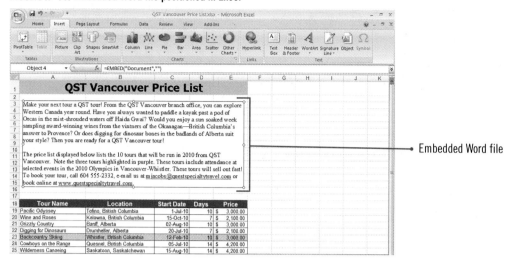

Embedded Word file

FIGURE A-12: Embedded object updated in Excel

Title bar shows that Excel is the destination program

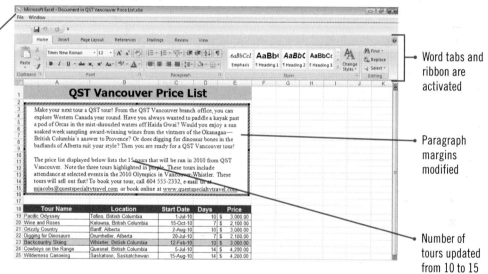

Word tabs and ribbon are activated

Paragraph margins modified

Number of tours updated from 10 to 15

TABLE A-1: Unit A integration tasks

object	command	source program	destination program	result	connection	page no.
Cell	Copy/Paste	Excel	Word	Object with Excel formatting	Pasted: no link	4
Chart	Copy/Paste	Excel	Word	Object with Excel formatting	Linked	6
Cell	Copy/Paste Special/Paste Link	Excel	Word	Text or object: Formatting varies depending on formatting option chosen	Linked	8
File	Insert/Object/ Create from File	Word	Excel	Text box containing the Word file: to update, double-click and update using Word tools within the Excel destination file	Embedded: no link	10

Practice

▼ CONCEPTS REVIEW

Match each term with the statement that best describes it.

1. Integration
2. Destination file
3. Paste Special
4. Source file
5. Linked object

a. The file containing information that is copied and often linked to a different file
b. The ability to use information across multiple programs
c. Within a document, an element that maintains a connection to a different file
d. The file that receives the information copied from a different file
e. Used to create a connection between an object copied from one file to another file

Select the best answer from the list of choices.

6. Which of the following commands do you use when you do not need to maintain a link between an object copied from one file to another file?
   a. Copy and Insert
   b. Copy and Paste Special
   c. Insert File
   d. Copy and Paste

7. Which of the following objects is, by default, pasted as a link in the destination file?
   a. Excel chart pasted into Word
   b. Word text pasted into Excel
   c. Excel values pasted into Word
   d. Picture pasted from Excel to Word

8. In Word, which tab contains the Paste button?
   a. Review
   b. References
   c. Insert
   d. Home

9. Which of the following options do you select when you want to insert the entire contents of a Word file into Excel?
   a. Create File
   b. Copy and Paste
   c. Create from File
   d. Copy and Paste Special

▼ SKILLS REVIEW

1. **Copy data from Excel to Word.**
   a. Start Excel, open the file INT A-5.xlsx from the drive and folder where you store your Data Files, then save it as **Language Arts Data**.
   b. Start Word, open the file INT A-6.docx from the drive and folder where you store your Data Files, then save it as **Language Arts Report**.
   c. Switch to Excel, open the Clipboard, then click Clear All, if necessary.
   d. Select cell A1, then copy the contents to the Clipboard.
   e. Select the range A3:A7, then copy the contents to the Clipboard.
   f. Switch to Word, open the Clipboard, paste the Language Arts object at the top of the document (at the current position of the insertion point), add an additional blank line, then center the inserted text.

g. Paste the Subject Areas object on the line above paragraph 2 (which starts with "Students in the Helena...").

h. Close the Clipboard, then save the document.

2. Copy a Chart from Excel to Word

a. Switch to Excel, close the Clipboard, then copy the bar chart.

b. Switch to Word, then paste the bar chart below the second text paragraph (which ends with "and State scores.").

c. Switch to Excel, then note the position of the bars for the Creative Writing category.

d. Change the value in cell B7 to 65, then switch to Word.

e. Use the Edit Data command to display both the source and destination documents side by side.

f. In Excel, change the value in cell B4 to 30, click the chart to select it, then use the Quick Styles button on the Chart Styles group on the Design tab to apply chart Style 23 (a teal color).

g. Maximize the Excel window, then save the workbook.

h. Switch to Word, maximize the Word window, verify that the chart data has changed and that the chart formatting has not changed, then save the document.

3. Create Linked Objects

a. Switch to Excel, enter Difference in cell D3, then enter the formula =B4-C4 in cell D4.

b. Use the Fill handle to copy the formula to the range D5:D7.

c. Select the range A3:D7, copy it, switch to Word, then use the Paste Special command to paste the cells as a link below paragraph 3 (which ends with "state-wide."), using the Formatted Text (RTF) selection.

d. In Excel, copy cell D7, switch to Word, click to the left of "points" in the last paragraph, then use Paste Special to paste the cell as a link using the Unformatted Text selection.

e. Insert a space following the pasted value.

f. In Excel, change the value in cell B7 to 85.

g. In Word, update the pasted table, then update the pasted value in the last paragraph.

h. Enter your name where indicated in the footer in Word, view the report in Print Preview and compare it to Figure A-13, print a copy of the Word report, then save and close the Word report.

i. In Excel, enter your name in cell A30 where indicated, print a copy of the Excel worksheet, then save and close the workbook.

4. Embed a Word file in Excel

a. In Excel, open the file INT A-7.xlsx from the drive and folder where you store your Data Files, then save it as Montana Art Workshops Revenue.

b. In Word, open the file INT A-8.docx from the drive and folder where you store your Data Files, save it as Montana Art Workshops, then close it.

c. In Excel, in cell H5, insert the Word file Montana Art Workshops as an embedded file.

d. Select the range A8:F15, then move it to cell A20.

e. Position the box containing the Word text so it its upper left corner is in cell A3.

f. Double-click the box containing the Word text, select all the text in the Word document, then change the font color to Orange, Accent 6, Darker 50%, and apply bold formatting.

FIGURE A-13

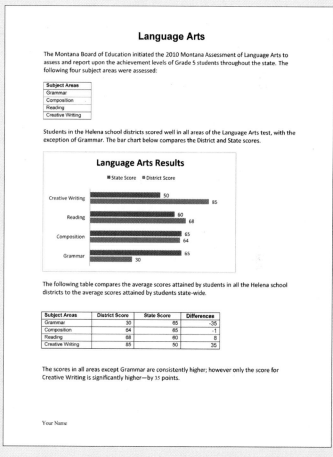

▼ SKILLS REVIEW (CONTINUED)

g. Change $15.00 to $12.00 in paragraph 1, then change "Fun with Acrylics" to **Basic Oil Painting** in paragraph 2.

h. Click outside the embedded object to return to Excel, compare your screen to Figure A-14, enter your name in cell A30, print a copy, then save and close the workbook.

FIGURE A-14

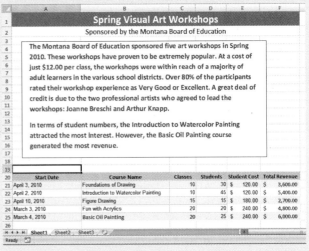

▼ INDEPENDENT CHALLENGE 1

As a member of the Carmel Arts Commission in Carmel, California, you are responsible for compiling the minutes of the commission's quarterly meetings. You have already written most of the text required for the minutes. Now you need to insert data from Excel that shows how much money was raised from various fundraising activities.

a. Start Word, open the file INT A-9.docx from the drive and folder where you store your Data Files, save it as **Carmel Arts Commission Minutes**, start Excel, open the file INT A-10.xlsx from the drive and folder where you store your Data Files, then save it as **Carmel Arts Commission Data**.

b. In Excel, open the Clipboard, clear all items if necessary, then copy the photograph and cell A2.

c. In Word, open the Clipboard and paste the photograph at the top of the Word document, then paste cell A2 below the document title.

d. Change the text wrapping of the picture to Square, position the photograph to the right of the document title, center the pasted text between the left and right margins, if necessary, then add a blank line above it.

e. Copy the Fundraising Revenue chart from Excel, paste it in the appropriate area in the Word report, then add additional blank lines where needed.

f. In Excel, change the number of participants in the perennials sale to **700**.

g. In Excel, copy the contents of cell E7, switch to Word, select XX in the bulleted list below the chart, paste the value as a link using the Unformatted Text selection.

h. In Excel, click cell G7, then calculate the total funds raised by adding the contents of the range B7:F7.

i. In cell B8, enter the formula **=B7/G7**, use [F4] to make cell G7 absolute, then copy the formula to the range C8:F8.

j. Copy cell E8, switch to Word, select ZZ in the bulleted list below the chart, paste the value as a link using the Unformatted Text selection, then if necessary add a space after the pasted object.

k. In Excel, change the number of participants in the perennials sale to **900**, then verify that the links are updated. If the links do not update, click the Office button, point to Prepare, click Edit Links to Files, click Update Now, then click Close.

l. Type your name in the Word footer, save the file, print a copy, exit Word, save and close the Excel workbook, then exit Excel.

▼ INDEPENDENT CHALLENGE 2

You work at a summer camp in Minnesota that provides teens with training in leadership and communication skills. You have collected data about the camp enrollment from 2005 to 2010 in an Excel workbook. Now you need to prepare the workbook for distribution at an upcoming meeting with local businesspeople who are interested in sponsoring the camp. You want to include text in the workbook that you have stored in a Word document.

a. Start Excel, open the file INT A-11.xlsx from the drive and folder where you store your Data Files, then save it as **Lake Country Camp Report**.

b. Start Word, open the file INT A-12.docx from the drive and folder where you store your Data Files, save it as **Lake Country Camp Information**, then close it.

c. In a blank area of the Excel worksheet, insert the Camp Information file as an embedded object.

d. Adjust the positions of the Excel data and the box containing the Word text so that the Word text appears above the Excel data and below the title.

▼ INDEPENDENT CHALLENGE 2 (CONTINUED)

e. In Excel, insert a formula just below the data that calculates the total enrollment for Leadership Training and Communication Skills.

f. To the right of "Communication Skills," enter and format **Total**, then calculate the total enrollment for both camps for each year and the total for all camps from 2005 to 2010.

g. Note the Total enrollment value, edit the embedded Word document so that the text is indented by .3" from the left and right margins, then type the correct total enrollment figure in the embedded paragraph.

h. Enter your name in cell A22 in Excel, save the Excel workbook, print a copy, then close the workbook.

▼ INDEPENDENT CHALLENGE 3

You own Gardens Galore, a landscaping business in Charlotte, North Carolina. You have entered the projected income and expenses in Excel. Now you need to link objects to the company's sales summary in Word.

a. Start Excel, open the file INT A-13.xlsx from the drive and folder where you store your Data Files, then save it as **Gardens Galore Sales Data**.

b. In cell B15, calculate the Cost of Sales by multiplying the Sales Amount by 60%. (*Hint*: In your formula, multiply the value in cell B6 times .6.) Copy the formula to the range C15:E15.

c. In cell B18, calculate the total profit or loss by subtracting the total expenses from the total income for the month, then copy the formula to the range C18:F18. You should see $21,700 in cell F18.

d. Save the workbook, switch to Word, open the file INT A-14.docx from the drive and folder where you store your Data Files, then save it as **Gardens Galore Sales Report**.

e. Select EXPENSES in the paragraph under Projected Expenses, switch to Excel, then copy the value in cell F16 and paste it as a link (as Unformatted Text) in Word.

f. Use the same procedure to copy the INCOME and PROFIT amounts from Excel to the appropriate locations in the Word document. Make sure you paste the copied values as links in Unformatted Text.

g. Copy the pie chart from Excel and paste it into the Word document below the first paragraph after Projected Expenses.

h. Click to the left of the pie chart to select it, click the Center button, then add a blank line above and below the chart.

i. In Excel, note the percentages in the pie chart, then increase the salaries expense for June to 15,000 and for July to 12,000, then change the sales income for both April and May to 25,000. Note how the percentages change in the pie chart.

j. In Excel, open the Clipboard, copy the heading in cell A1 and the picture of the flowers to the Clipboard, then add your name to cell A42.

k. In Word, open the Clipboard, paste the two objects as shown in Figure A-15, center the title, then modify the text wrapping of the photograph and position it as shown.

l. If necessary, update the values in the Projected Expenses and Projected Income paragraphs, add your name to the document footer, print a copy of the sales report, compare it to Figure A-15, then save and close the Word and Excel files.

FIGURE A-15

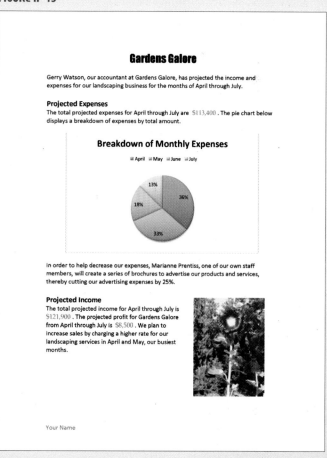

Using the Data Files INT A-15.xlsx and INT A-16.docx, create the price list shown in Figure A-16. Use formulas to calculate the prices and totals for Two-Packs and Four-Packs. Save the workbook as **Essential Epicure Price List** and save the Word document as **Essential Epicure Information**. Embed the Word document into the Excel workbook, position the inserted file and the price list in Excel as shown in Figure A-16, then add any necessary content and format the embedded Word object as shown in Figure A-16. (*Hint*: The indentation on both sides of the text is .3, and the type size is 14 point.) Add your name to the Excel worksheet, print a copy of the price list, then close all files and programs.

FIGURE A-16

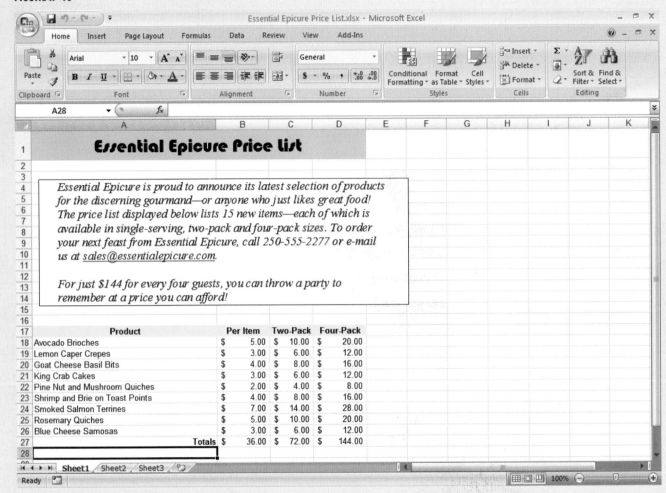

Getting Started with Access 2007

In this unit, you will learn the purpose, advantages, and terminology of Microsoft Office Access 2007, the relational database program in Microsoft Office 2007. You will create and modify tables, the basic building blocks of an Access relational database. You'll also navigate, enter, update, preview, and print data. Mark Rock is the tour developer for United States group travel at Quest Specialty Travel (QST), a tour company that specializes in cultural tourism and adventure travel. Mark uses Access to store, maintain, and analyze customer and tour information.

OBJECTIVES

Understand relational databases

Open a database

Enter data

Edit data

Create a database

Create a table

Create primary keys

Relate two tables

Print a datasheet

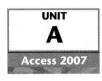

Understanding Relational Databases

Microsoft Office Access 2007 is relational database software that runs on the Windows operating system. You use **relational database software** to manage data that is organized into lists, such as information about customers, products, vendors, employees, projects, or sales. Many small companies track customer, inventory, and sales information in a spreadsheet program such as Microsoft Office Excel. While Excel does offer some list management features, Access provides many more tools and advantages, mainly due to the "relational" nature of the lists that Access manages. Table A-1 compares the two programs. You and Mark Rock review the advantages of database software over spreadsheets for managing lists of information.

DETAILS

The advantages of using Access for database management include:

- **Duplicate data is minimized**

  Figures A-1 and A-2 compare how you might store sales data in a single Excel spreadsheet list versus three related Access tables. Note that with Access, you do not have to reenter information such as a customer's name and address or product description every time a sale is made, because lists can be linked, or "related," in relational database software.

- **Information is more accurate, reliable, and consistent because duplicate data is minimized**

  The relational nature of data stored in an Access database allows you to minimize duplicate data entry, which creates more accurate, reliable, and consistent information.

- **Data entry is faster and easier using Access forms**

  Data entry forms (screen layouts) make data entry faster and easier than entering data in a spreadsheet.

- **Information can be viewed and sorted in many ways using Access queries, forms, and reports**

  In Access, you can save queries (questions about the data), data entry forms, and reports, allowing you to use them over and over without performing extra work to re-create a particular view of the data.

- **Information is more secure using Access passwords and security features**

  Access databases can be password protected, and users can be given different privileges to view or update data.

- **Several users can share and edit information simultaneously**

  Unlike spreadsheets or word processing documents, Access databases are inherently multiuser. More than one person can be entering, updating, and analyzing data at the same time.

FIGURE A-1: Using a spreadsheet to organize sales data

	A	B	C	D	E	F	G	H	I	J	K	L	M	N	O	P
1	Cust No	First	Last	Street	City	State	Zip	Phone	Date	Invoice	Product No	Artist	Name	Format	Tracks	Cost
2	1	Kusong	Tse	222 Elm	Topeka	KS	66111	913-555-0000	8/1/2006	8111	11-222	Michael Smith	Always	CD	14	15
3	2	Paige	Denver	400 Oak	Lenexa	MO	60023	816-555-8877	8/1/2006	8112	11-222	Michael Smith	Always	CD	14	15
4	1	Kusong	Tse	222 Elm	Topeka	KS	66111	913-555-0000	8/2/2006	8113	22-333	Gold Flakes	Avalon	CD	13	14
5	3	Caitlyn	Baily	111 Ash	Ames	IA	50010	515-555-3333	8/3/2006	8114	22-333	Gold Flakes	Avalon	CD	13	14
6	2	Paige	Denver	400 Oak	Lenexa	MO	60023	816-555-8877	8/4/2006	8115	44-1111	Lungwort	Sounds	CD	15	13
7	3	Caitlyn	Baily	111 Ash	Ames	IA	50010	515-555-3333	8/4/2006	8116	44-1111	Lungwort	Sounds	CD	15	13
8	4	Max	Royal	500 Pine	Manilla	NE	55123	827-555-4422	8/5/2006	8117	44-1111	Lungwort	Sounds	CD	15	13
9																

Duplicate customer data is entered each time an existing customer makes an additional purchase

Duplicate product data is entered each time the same product is sold more than once

FIGURE A-2: Using a relational database to organize sales data

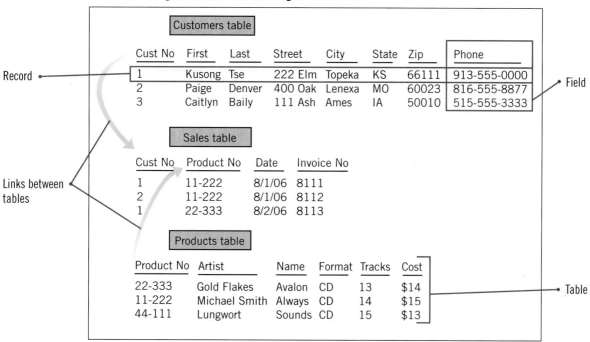

Record · — Field
Links between tables
Table

Customers table

Cust No	First	Last	Street	City	State	Zip	Phone
1	Kusong	Tse	222 Elm	Topeka	KS	66111	913-555-0000
2	Paige	Denver	400 Oak	Lenexa	MO	60023	816-555-8877
3	Caitlyn	Baily	111 Ash	Ames	IA	50010	515-555-3333

Sales table

Cust No	Product No	Date	Invoice No
1	11-222	8/1/06	8111
2	11-222	8/1/06	8112
1	22-333	8/2/06	8113

Products table

Product No	Artist	Name	Format	Tracks	Cost
22-333	Gold Flakes	Avalon	CD	13	$14
11-222	Michael Smith	Always	CD	14	$15
44-111	Lungwort	Sounds	CD	15	$13

TABLE A-1: Comparing Excel to Access

feature	Excel	Access
Layout	Provides a natural tabular layout for easy data entry	Provides a natural tabular layout as well as the ability to create customized data entry screens
Storage	Limited to approximately 65,000 records per sheet	Stores any number of records up to 2 GB
Linked tables	Manages single lists of information	Allows links between lists of information to reduce data redundancy
Reporting	Limited to the current spreadsheet arrangement of data	Creates and saves multiple presentations of data
Security	Limited to file security options such as marking the file "read-only" or protecting a range of cells	Allows users to access only the records and fields they need
Multiuser capabilities	Does not easily allow multiple users to simultaneously enter and update data	Allows multiple users to simultaneously enter and update data
Data entry	Provides limited data entry screens	Provides the ability to create extensive data entry screens called forms

Opening a Database

You can start Access from the Start menu, which opens when you click the Start button on the Windows taskbar, or from an Access shortcut icon on the desktop. Access opens to the Getting Started with Microsoft Office Access page, which shows different ways to work with Access. To open a specific database in Access, you can click a database in the Open Recent Database list or click the More link to navigate to a different database. You can also start Access and open a database at the same time by opening the database directly from a My Computer or Windows Explorer window. ![] Mark Rock has entered some tour information in a database called Quest-A. He asks you to start Access and review this database.

STEPS

1. **Start Access**

   Access starts and opens the Getting Started with Microsoft Office Access page, shown in Figure A-3, which helps you create a new database from a template, create a new blank database, or open an existing database.

2. **Click the More link in the Open Recent Database list, navigate to the drive and folder where you store your Data Files, click the Quest-A.accdb database file, click Open, then click the Maximize button ▣ if the Access window is not already maximized**

   The Quest-A database contains two tables of data named States and Tours.

3. **In the Navigation Pane, double-click the Tours table to open it, then click ▣ on the Tours table**

   The Tours table opens in Datasheet View, as shown in Figure A-4. **Tables** are the fundamental building blocks of a relational database because they store all of the data. **Datasheet View** displays the data in a table in a spreadsheet-like view of fields and records called the **datasheet**. The Tours datasheet contains six fields and 21 records. **Field names** are listed at the top of each column. Important database terminology is summarized in Table A-2.

4. **In the Navigation Pane, double-click the States table to open it**

   The States table contains only two fields, StateAbbreviation and StateName, and four records. By using a separate States table, you only need to enter full state names such as Colorado and Florida once, rather than every time you enter a record for a particular state in the Tours table. The Tours and States tables are linked together via the common StateAbbreviation field. Later in this unit, you learn more about how multiple lists of information, defined as tables in Access, are linked to create relational databases.

FIGURE A-3: Getting Started with Microsoft Office Access page

Additional database template categories from Microsoft Office Online

Featured database templates

Open Recent Database list

More link

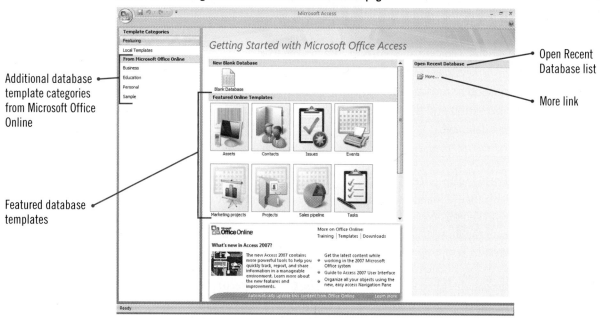

FIGURE A-4: Tours table

Shutter Bar Open/Close button

Navigation Pane showing tables

Each row is a record

Field names

Tours table open in Datasheet View

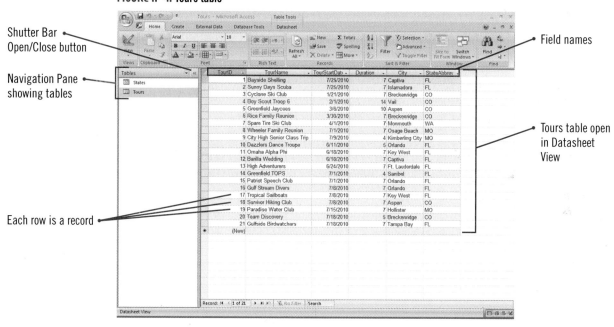

TABLE A-2: Important database terminology

term	description
Field	The smallest unit of data organization; consists of a specific category of data such as a customer's name, city, state, or phone number
Record	A group of related fields that describe a person, place, or thing
Key field	A field that contains unique information for each record, such as a customer number for a customer
Table	A collection of records for a single subject
Database	A collection of tables associated with a general topic
Relational database	An Access database with multiple tables that are linked together by a common field
Objects	The parts of an Access database that help you view, edit, manage, and analyze the data, such as **tables**, **queries**, **forms**, **reports**, **macros**, and **modules**

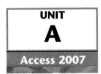

Entering Data

Your skill in navigating and entering data is a key to your success with a relational database. You use either mouse or keystroke techniques to navigate the data in the table's datasheet, which displays fields as columns and records as rows. ▰▰▰▰▰ Mark Rock has developed some new tours for Quest Specialty Travel, and asks you to add this tour information by entering new records in the States and Tours tables of the Quest-A database.

STEPS

1. **Press [Tab] twice, then press [Enter] twice**

    Both the [Tab] and [Enter] keys move the focus to the next field. The **focus** refers to which data you would edit if you started typing. The field name and record selector button for the field and record that have the focus are highlighted with a different color. When you navigate to the last field of the record, pressing [Tab] or [Enter] advances the focus to the first field of the next record. You can also use the Next record ▶ and Previous record ◀ **navigation buttons** on the navigation bar in the lower-left corner of the datasheet to navigate the records. The **Current Record** text box on the navigation bar tells you the number of the current record as well as the total number of records in the datasheet.

2. **Click the StateAbbrev field below WA to position the insertion point to enter a new record**

    You can also use the New (blank) record button ▦ on the navigation bar to move to a new record. You enter new records at the end of the datasheet. You learn how to sort and reorder them later. A complete list of navigation keystrokes is shown in Table A-3.

3. **Type CA, press [Tab], then type California**

    Access saves data automatically as you move among records or within the database. With the California record entered in the States table, you're ready to enter a new tour record in the Tours table.

4. **Double-click the Tours table in the Navigation Pane, click (New) in the last row, press [Enter] to advance to the TourName field, type Perfect Waves, press [Enter], type 7/16/10, press [Enter], type 5, press [Enter], type Hunt Beach, press [Enter], type CA, then press [Enter]**

    The new tour record you entered is shown in Figure A-5. The TourID field is an **AutoNumber** field, which means that Access automatically enters the next consecutive number into the field as it creates the record.

Changing from Navigation mode to Edit mode

If you navigate to another area of the datasheet by clicking with the mouse pointer instead of pressing [Tab] or [Enter], you change from **Navigation mode** to Edit mode. In **Edit mode**, Access assumes that you are trying to make changes to the current field value, so keystrokes such as [Ctrl][End], [Ctrl][Home], [←], and [→] move the insertion point *within* the field. To return to Navigation mode, press [Tab] or [Enter] (thus moving the focus to the next field), or press [↑] or [↓] (thus moving the focus to a different record).

FIGURE A-5: New record in the Tours table

Record selector box for TourID 16

Current focus

Navigation bar

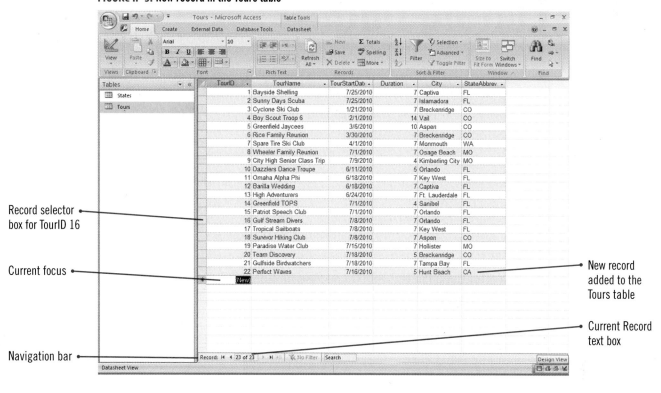

New record added to the Tours table

Current Record text box

TABLE A-3: Navigation mode keyboard shortcuts

shortcut key	moves to the
[Tab], [Enter], or [→]	Next field of the current record
[Shift][Tab] or [←]	Previous field of the current record
[Home]	First field of the current record
[End]	Last field of the current record
[Ctrl][Home] or [F5]	First field of the first record
[Ctrl][End]	Last field of the last record
[↑]	Current field of the previous record
[↓]	Current field of the next record

Editing Data

Updating existing information is another critical data management task. To change the contents of an existing record, click the field you want to change, then type the new information. You can delete unwanted data by clicking the field and using [Backspace] or [Delete] to delete text to the left or right of the insertion point. Other data-entry keystrokes are summarized in Table A-4. Mark Rock asks you to make some corrections to the records in the Tours table.

STEPS

1. **Double-click Dance in the TourName field of the TourID 10 record, and press the [Delete] key twice**

   You deleted both the word "Dance" and the extra space between "Dazzlers" and "Troupe." Access automatically saves new records and changes to existing data as soon as you move to another record or close the datasheet.

2. **Click after Barilla in the TourName field of TourID 12 record, and type -Cavuto**

   When you are editing a record, the **edit record symbol**, which looks like a small pencil, appears in the record selector box to the left of the current record, as shown in Figure A-6, to indicate you are in Edit mode.

3. **Double-click Speech in the TourID 15 record, and type Debate**

   You use the same editing techniques in an Access datasheet that you use in an Excel spreadsheet or Word document.

4. **Click the TourStartDate field in the TourID 22 record, click the Calendar icon, then navigate to and click August 27, 2010**

   The **calendar picker**, a pop-up calendar from which you can choose dates for a date field, is a new feature for Access 2007. You can also type the date directly into the field as 8/27/2010.

5. **Press [Esc]**

   Pressing [Esc] once removes the current field's editing changes, so the TourStartDate changes back to 7/16/2010. Pressing [Esc] twice removes all changes to the current record. Once you move to another record, the edits are saved, you return to Navigation mode, and you can no longer use [Esc] to remove editing changes to the current record. You can, however, click the Undo button on the Quick Access toolbar to undo the last change you made.

   > **QUICK TIP**
   > The ScreenTip for the Undo button displays the action you can undo.

6. **Click the record selector for the TourID 16 record, click the Delete button in the Records group on the Home tab, then click Yes**

   A message warns that you cannot undo a record deletion operation. Notice that the Undo button is dimmed, indicating that it cannot be used now.

7. **Click the Close button on the title bar to close both the Quest-A.accdb database and Access 2007**

   Because Access saves data as you work in a database, you are not prompted to save data when you close the database or the Access itself.

Resizing and moving datasheet columns

You can resize the width of a field in a datasheet by dragging the **column separator**, the thin line that separates the field names to the left or right. The pointer changes to ↔ as you make the field wider or narrower. Release the mouse button when you have resized the field. To adjust the column width to accommodate the widest entry in the field, double-click the column separator. To move a column, click the field name to select the entire column, then drag the field name left or right.

Access 8   Getting Started with Access 2007

FIGURE A-6: Edit mode

Edit record symbol

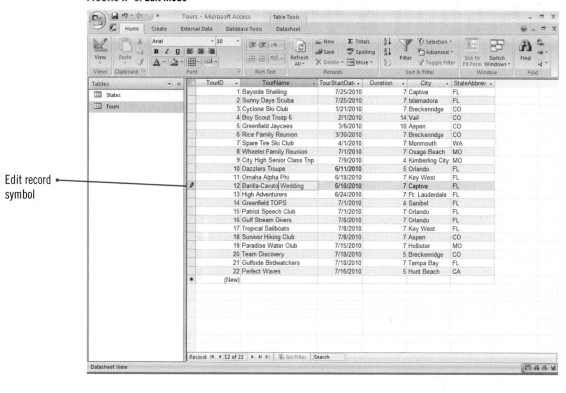

TABLE A-4: Edit mode keyboard shortcuts

editing keystroke	action
[Backspace]	Deletes one character to the left of the insertion point
[Delete]	Deletes one character to the right of the insertion point
[F2]	Switches between Edit and Navigation mode
[Esc]	Undoes the change to the current field
[Esc][Esc]	Undoes all changes to the current record
[F7]	Starts the spell check feature
[Ctrl][']	Inserts the value from the same field in the previous record into the current field
[Ctrl][;]	Inserts the current date in a Date field

Creating a Database

You can create a new database using an Access **template**, a sample database provided within the Microsoft Access program, or you can start with a blank database to create a database from scratch. Your decision depends on whether Access has a template that closely resembles the type of data you plan to manage. If it does, building your own database from a template might be faster than creating the database from scratch. Regardless of which method you use, you can always modify the database later, tailoring it to meet your specific needs. Mark Rock wants to organize Quest's clients, prospects, and vendors, and asks you to create an Access database to track contacts. You'll use the Contacts template to get started.

STEPS

QUICK TIP

To create a new blank database, double-click the Blank Database icon.

TROUBLE

If an Access Help window or Security Warning bar opens, close it. If a Microsoft Office Genuine Advantage dialog box opens, click Continue.

1. **Start Access**

   The "Getting Started with Microsoft Office Access" page opens, which you can use to create a database from a template. Some templates are stored on your computer when you install Access, and others are available from Microsoft Office Online.

2. **In the Navigation Pane, click** Personal, **click** Contacts, **then click** Download

   The Contact List form opens, as shown in Figure A-7.

3. **Enter** your own name **and** e-mail address **for the first record, use** school information **for the Business Phone and Company field, use** Student **for the Job Title field, then press [Enter]**

   Although you are entering this record in an Access **form** (an easy-to-use data entry screen) instead of directly in a table, the data is stored in the underlying table.

4. **Click the** Shutter Bar Open/Close button ≫ **at the top of the Navigation Pane, then click the** Supporting Objects button

   The **Navigation Pane** provides a way to move between objects (tables, queries, forms, and reports) in the database. Tables are the most important objects because they physically store all of the data. Table A-5 defines the four primary Access objects—tables, queries, forms, and reports—and the icon that identifies each in the Navigation Pane. When you created this database, the Contacts template not only created the Contact List form you used to enter your name, but also the Contact Details form and two reports, Contact Phone List and Contact Address Book. The "supporting" objects are the Contacts table and the Contacts Extended query. Tables and queries are considered "supporting" objects because they define the fields that are displayed in forms and reports.

TROUBLE

If the Contact List form still shows your last name, click the Contacts table tab, then click anywhere in the new record below your name to save the changes to your name.

5. **Double-click the** Contacts table **in the Navigation Pane, double-click** your last name **in the Last Name field, type** Johnson, **then press [↓] to move away from that record**

   The Contacts table appears with the record you entered using the Contact List form. All data is physically stored in Access table objects, even if it is entered through a query or form. Any changes made to the data in any object are dynamically tied to every other object. Data is automatically saved as you move from record to record.

6. **Click the** Contact List tab

   The data you edited in the Contacts table is automatically reflected in the Contact List form. The same is true of all other objects, such as reports.

TROUBLE

If the Contact Phone List report still shows your last name instead of "Johnson," close the report by right-clicking its tab and clicking Close, then double-click the report in the Navigation Pane to reopen it.

7. **Double-click the** Contact Phone List report **in the Navigation Pane**

   All reports that depend on this data are automatically updated, as shown in Figure A-8.

8. **Click the** Close button ✕ **on the title bar to close both the Contacts database and Access 2007**

FIGURE A-7: Contact List form provided by the Contacts template

Shutter Bar Open/Close button

Form icon

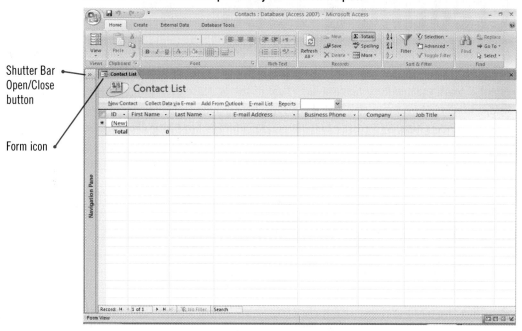

FIGURE A-8: Contact Phone List report provided by the Contacts template

Objects in the Contact database

Data edited in the Contacts table is updated in the Contact Phone List report

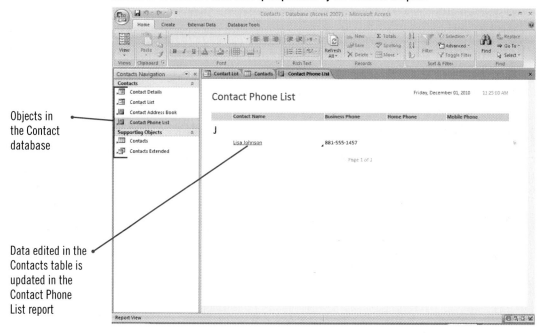

TABLE A-5: Access objects and their purpose

object	Navigation Pane icon	purpose
Table		Contains all of the raw data within the database in a spreadsheet-like view; tables are linked with a common field to create a relational database, which minimizes redundant data
Query		Allows the user to select a subset of fields or records from one or more tables; queries are created when a user has a question about the data
Form		Provides an easy-to-use data entry screen
Report		Provides a professional printout of data that can contain enhancements such as headers, footers, graphics, and calculations on groups of records

Creating a Table

After establishing your database, you often need to create a new table. You can use one of the table templates Access provides or you can create your own table from scratch. Creating a table consists of three essential tasks: meaningfully naming each field in the table, selecting an appropriate data type for each field, and naming the table itself. The **data type** determines what kind of data can be entered into a field, such as numbers, text, or dates. Data types are described in Table A-6. Mark Rock asks you to create a small table that lists the different types of tours Quest offers, such as Educational, Adventure, and Cultural. Because Access does not have a template for such a table, you'll create the table yourself.

STEPS

1. **Reopen the Quest-A.accdb database, enable content if prompted, click the Create tab on the Ribbon, click the Table button, then click the Maximize button** 🔲

   A new, blank table datasheet appears, as shown in Figure A-9, with one sample field named ID that has an AutoNumber data type. You don't need this sample field in the table, so you can rename the first field and use it to identify tour categories.

2. **Click the ID field name, then click the Rename button on the Datasheet tab**

   ID in the column header is highlighted, allowing you to enter a new field name.

3. **Type Category, then press [↓]**

   The new field, renamed Category, is now the first field. With the field named appropriately, the next step is to choose the correct data type for the field. Currently, the field has an AutoNumber data type, but because this field will store the name of each tour category, you need to change its data type to Text.

4. **Click the Data Type list arrow (which currently displays AutoNumber) on the Datasheet tab, then click Text**

   For this table, you want to create one more field called TourDescription that also has a Text data type because it will store text descriptions of each tour.

QUICK TIP

Widen the TourDescription field by dragging the resize pointer ↔ to resize the column.

5. **Double-click Add New Field, type TourDescription, then press [↓]**

   Because Text is the default data type for new fields, the TourDescription field has already been assigned with the correct data type.

6. **Click the blank cell below the Category field, type Adventure, then enter the remaining records as shown in Figure A-10**

   After naming the fields, assigning the data types, and entering the data, you save the table with an appropriate name. Table1 is the default name, but it is not very descriptive. You cannot rename a table that is open, so you'll close it and give it a descriptive name when prompted.

TROUBLE

The Close Window button for the table is on the Ribbon (not on the title bar). You can also click the Office button, then click Close to close the table.

7. **Click the Close Window button** ✕ **for the new table, click Yes, type TourCategories, then click OK**

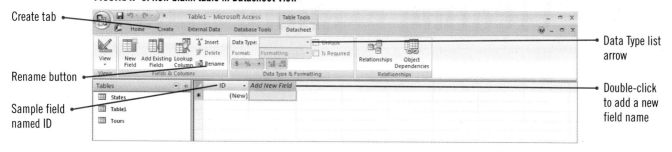

FIGURE A-9: New blank table in Datasheet View

Create tab

Rename button

Sample field named ID

Data Type list arrow

Double-click to add a new field name

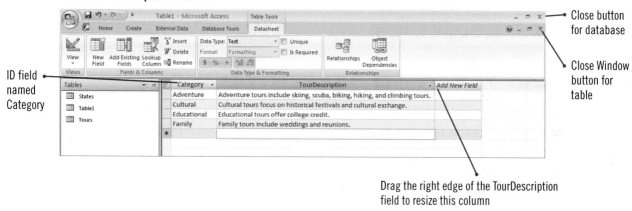

FIGURE A-10: Complete datasheet

ID field named Category

Close button for database

Close Window button for table

Drag the right edge of the TourDescription field to resize this column

TABLE A-6: Data types

data type	description of data	size
Text	Text information or combinations of text and numbers, such as a street address, name, or phone number	Up to 255 characters
Memo	Lengthy text, such as comments or notes	Up to 65,535 characters
Number	Numeric information, such as quantities	Several sizes available to store numbers with varying degrees of precision
Date/Time	Dates and times	Size controlled by Access to accommodate dates and times across thousands of years (for example, 1/1/1850 and 1/1/2150 are valid dates)
Currency	Monetary values	Size controlled by Access; accommodates up to 15 digits to the left of the decimal point and four digits to the right
AutoNumber	Integers assigned by Access to sequentially order each record added to a table	Size controlled by Access
Yes/No	Only one of two values stored (Yes/No, On/Off, True/False)	Size controlled by Access
OLE Object	Office and Windows files that can be linked or embedded (OLE) such as pictures, sound clips, documents, or spreadsheets	Up to 2 GB
Attachment	Any supported file type including .jpg images, spreadsheets, and documents (new for Office 2007)	Up to 1 GB
Hyperlink	Web and e-mail addresses	Size controlled by Access

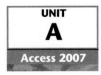

Creating Primary Keys

The **primary key field** of a table serves two important purposes. First, it contains data that uniquely identifies each record. No two records can have the exact same entry in the field designated as the primary key field. Secondly, the primary key field helps relate one table to another in a **one-to-many relationship**, where one record from one table is related to many records in the second table. For example, one state record in the States table might be related to many tours in the Tours table. In the States table, StateAbbreviation is the primary key field. This field is duplicated in the Tours table, providing the link between one state and many tours. The primary key field is always on the "one" side of a one-to-many relationship between two tables. **█████** Mark Rock asks you to check that a primary key field has been appropriately identified for each table.

STEPS

1. **Double-click Tours in the Navigation Pane, maximize the window, then click the Design View button on the Home tab**

   Design View, as shown in Figure A-11, is used to modify and define field properties that are not available in Datasheet View. You see many of a field's **properties** (characteristics that define a field) in the lower half of Design View. Some field properties, such as Field Name and Data Type, can be specified in either Datasheet View or Design View. Specifying the primary key field requires that you work in Design View.

2. **Click the TourID field if it is not already selected, then click the Primary Key button on the Design tab**

   A field designated as the primary key field for a table appears with the key icon, as shown in Figure A-12.

3. **Close and save the Tours table**

   Next, you'll use Design View to set the primary key fields for the other two tables.

4. **Double-click States in the Navigation Pane, click the Design View button, click StateAbbreviation if it is not already selected, click the Primary Key button, then close and save the States table**

   You'll use the Category field as the primary key field in the TourCategories table.

5. **Double-click TourCategories in the Navigation Pane, click the Design View button, make sure the Category field is the primary key, then close the TourCategories table**

   Now that each table has been modified to contain an appropriate primary key field, you no longer have to worry that two tour records in the Tours table could be assigned the same TourID, two states in the States table could be given the same StateAbbreviation, or two tour categories could be assigned to the same Category. In other words, assigning an appropriate primary key field to each table helps prevent you from entering incorrect and duplicate records. The second purpose of the primary key field is to help tie tables together in one-to-many relationships, which you learn about in the next lesson.

FIGURE A-11: Design View of the Tours table

Primary Key button

View button

Field Properties pane

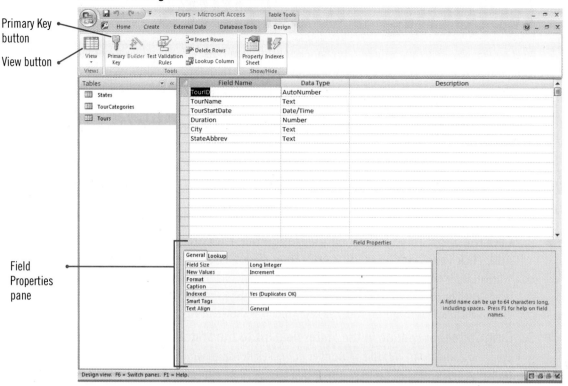

FIGURE A-12: TourID is set as the primary key field

Save button

Primary key field symbol

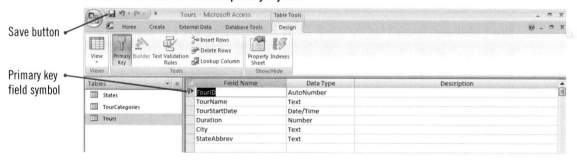

Learning about field properties

Properties are the characteristics that define the field. Two properties are required for every field: Field Name and Data Type. Many other properties, such as Field Size, Format, Caption, and Default Value, are defined in the Field Properties pane in the lower half of a table's Design View. As you add more property entries, you are generally restricting the amount or type of data that can be entered in the field, which increases data entry accuracy. For example, you might change the Field Size property for a State field to 2 in order to eliminate an incorrect entry such as FLL. Field properties change depending on the data type of the selected field. For example, there is no Field Size property for date fields, because Access controls the size of fields with a Date/Time data type.

Access 2007

Relating Two Tables

After you create tables and establish primary key fields, you must link the tables together in one-to-many relationships before you can build queries, forms, or reports that display fields from more than one table. A one-to-many relationship between two tables means that one record from the first table is related to many records in the second table. You use a common linking field, which is always the primary key field in the table on the "one" side of the relationship, to establish this connection. Mark Rock mentions that he plans to create reports that include tour, category, and state information. To help in creating the reports, you define the one-to-many relationships between the tables of the Quest-A database.

STEPS

1. **Click the Database Tools tab on the Ribbon, then click the Relationships button**

> **QUICK TIP**
> Drag the table's title bar to move the field list.

2. **Click the Show Table button on the Design tab, click States, click Add, click Tours, click Add, click TourCategories, click Add, then click Close**

   With all three tables visible in the Relationships window, you're ready to link them together. Each table is represented by a small **field list** window that displays the names of the fields in the table. The primary key field in each table is identified with the key symbol, as shown in Figure A-13.

> **QUICK TIP**
> Drag the bottom border of the field list to display all of the fields.

3. **Drag StateAbbreviation in the States field list to the StateAbbrev field in the Tours field list**

   Dragging a field from one table to another in the Relationships window links the two tables by the selected fields and opens the Edit Relationships dialog box, as shown in Figure A-14. **Referential integrity**, a set of Access rules that govern data entry, helps ensure data accuracy.

> **QUICK TIP**
> Right-click a relationship line, then click Delete if you need to delete a relationship and start over.

4. **Click the Enforce Referential Integrity check box in the Edit Relationships dialog box, then click Create**

   The **one-to-many line** shows the link between the StateAbbreviation field of the States table (the "one" side) and the StateAbbrev field of the Tours table (the "many" side, indicated by the **infinity symbol**). Similarly, you need to create a one-to-many relationship between the TourCategories table and the Tours table, so that one category can be associated with many tours. However, because these tables do not have a common field, you must establish one before you can join the tables.

5. **Right-click the Tours field list, click Table Design, click the cell below StateAbbrev, type Category, then press [Tab] to specify the default Text data type**

   A field added to the "many" table to help establish a one-to-many relationship is called the **foreign key field**. Now that you created the foreign key field for the link between the Tours and TourCategories, you can join the tables in a one-to-many relationship.

6. **Close and save the Tours table, drag the Category field from the TourCategories table to the Category field of the Tours table, then click Create in the Edit Relationships dialog box**

   The final Relationships window should look like Figure A-15. The relationship line between the Tours and TourCategories tables is also a one-to-many relationship, but the "one" and "many" symbols do not appear because you did not establish referential integrity on this relationship. The primary key field for the Tours table is TourID, but because it participates on the "many" side of two different one-to-many relationships, it contains two foreign key fields, StateAbbrev and Category.

7. **Close and save the Relationships window**

FIGURE A-13: Relationships window

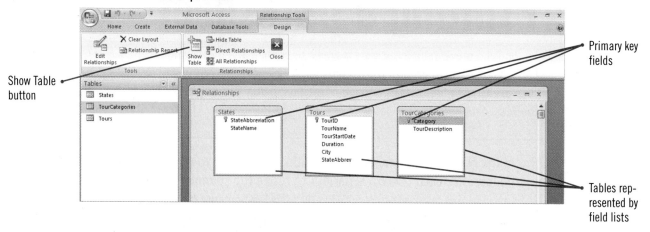

Show Table button

Primary key fields

Tables represented by field lists

FIGURE A-14: Edit Relationships dialog box

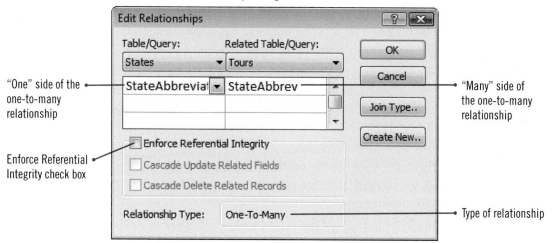

"One" side of the one-to-many relationship

Enforce Referential Integrity check box

"Many" side of the one-to-many relationship

Type of relationship

FIGURE A-15: Final Relationships window

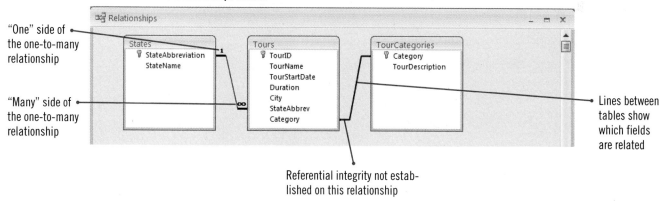

"One" side of the one-to-many relationship

"Many" side of the one-to-many relationship

Lines between tables show which fields are related

Referential integrity not established on this relationship

Enforcing referential integrity

Referential integrity is a set of rules that helps reduce invalid entries and orphan records. An **orphan record** is a record in the "many" table that doesn't have a matching entry in the linking field of the "one" table. With referential integrity enforced on a one-to-many relationship, you cannot enter a value in a foreign key field of the "many" table that does not have a match in the linking field of the "one" table. Referential integrity also prevents you from deleting a record in the "one" table if a matching entry exists in the foreign key field of the "many" table. You should enforce referential integrity on all one-to-many relationships if possible. If you are working with a database that already contains orphan records, you cannot enforce referential integrity on that relationship.

Printing a Datasheet

Printing and previewing Access data is similar to printing and previewing other types of Office documents. Previewing helps you see how the document will look when printed so you can make printing adjustments, such as changing the margins or page orientation, before printing it. ▓▓▓▓ Mark Rock asks you to print the Tours datasheet.

STEPS

1. **In the Navigation Pane, double-click the Tours table to open it in Datasheet View, then double-click each column separator to resize the columns to their best fit**

   One more new tour needs to be added to the list before you print it—a family reunion.

2. **Add a new record with your last name's Reunion in the TourName field, today's date in the TourStartDate field, 4 in the Duration field, your hometown in the City field, FL in the StateAbbrev field, and Family in the Category field**

   You decide to preview the datasheet before printing it to make sure it fits on one sheet of paper.

3. **Click the Office button ⬤, point to Print, then click Print Preview**

   The Tours table appears on a miniature page, as shown in Figure A-16, formatted as it will look when you print it. By previewing the datasheet, you realize that it is too wide to print on one page. (The Category and StateAbbrev fields do not appear on page 1.) You decide to try **landscape orientation** (11 inches wide by 8.5 inches tall) rather than the default **portrait orientation** (8.5 inches wide by 11 inches tall) to see if the printout fits on one page.

4. **Click the Landscape button on the Print Preview tab**

   The navigation buttons on the navigation bar in the lower-left corner in Figure A-17 are dim, indicating that the printout fits on one page.

> **QUICK TIP**
> Click the Close Print Preview button on the Print Preview tab to close the preview window and return to Datasheet View.

5. **Click the Print button on the Print Preview tab, then click OK**

   If you need to change printing options, you can use the Page Setup dialog box.

6. **Click the Close button ⊠ on the title bar to close both the Quest-A.accdb database and Access 2007**

FIGURE A-16: Datasheet in print preview—portrait orientation

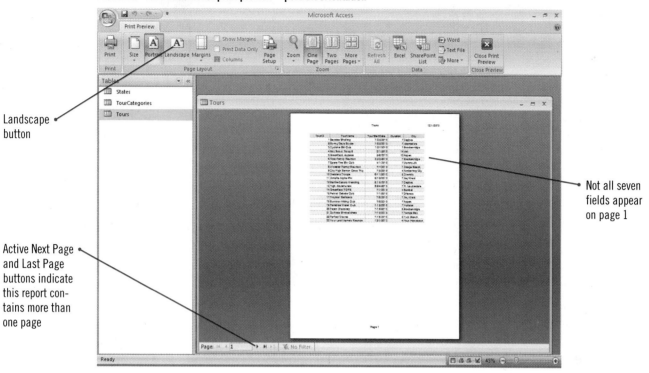

Landscape button

Not all seven fields appear on page 1

Active Next Page and Last Page buttons indicate this report contains more than one page

FIGURE A-17: Datasheet in print preview—landscape orientation

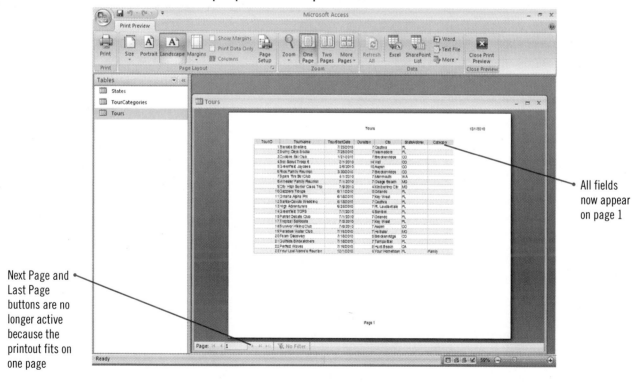

All fields now appear on page 1

Next Page and Last Page buttons are no longer active because the printout fits on one page

Practice

If you have a SAM user profile, you may have access to hands-on instruction, practice, and assessment of the skills covered in this unit. Log in to your SAM account (http://sam2007.course.com/) to launch any assigned training activities or exams that relate to the skills covered in this unit.

▼ CONCEPTS REVIEW

Label each element of the Access window shown in Figure A-18.

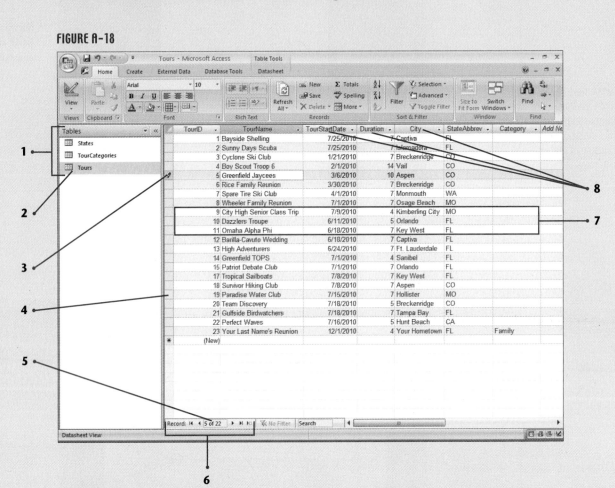

FIGURE A-18

Match each term with the statement that best describes it.

9. **Objects**

10. **Table**

11. **Record**

12. **Field**

13. **Datasheet**

14. **Form**

15. **Edit record symbol**

a. Seven types of these are contained in an Access database and are used to enter, enhance, and use the data within the database

b. A collection of records for a single subject, such as all the customer records

c. A small pencil icon that appears in the record selector box

d. A spreadsheet-like grid that displays fields as columns and records as rows

e. A group of related fields for one item, such as all of the demographic information for one customer

f. A category of information in a table, such as a customer's name, city, or state

g. An Access object that provides an easy-to-use data entry screen

Select the best answer from the list of choices.

16. **Which of the following is *not* a typical benefit of relational databases?**
    a. More accurate data
    b. Automatic correction of data as it is entered
    c. Faster information retrieval
    d. Minimized duplicate data entry

17. **Which of the following is *not* an advantage of managing data with relational database software such as Access versus spreadsheet software such as Excel?**
    a. Uses a single table to store all data
    b. Reduces duplicate data entry
    c. Provides greater security
    d. Allows multiple users to enter data simultaneously

18. **The object that creates a professional printout of data that includes headers, footers, and graphics is the:**
    a. Query.
    b. Table.
    c. Report.
    d. Form.

19. **The object that contains all of the database data is the:**
    a. Report.
    b. Form.
    c. Page.
    d. Table.

20. **What can you use to quickly create a new database?**
    a. Template
    b. Object
    c. Module
    d. Form

▼ SKILLS REVIEW

1. **Understand relational databases.**
   a. Identify five advantages of managing database information in Access versus using a spreadsheet.
   b. Explain how a relational database organizes data to minimize redundant information. Use an example involving a database with two related tables, Customers and States, in your explanation.

2. **Open a database.**
   a. Explain the relationship between a field, a record, a table, and a database.
   b. Start Access.
   c. Open the RealEstate-A.accdb database from the drive and folder where you store your Data Files. Enable content if a Security Warning message appears.
   d. Open each of the three tables. On a sheet of paper, complete the following table:

table name	number of records	number of fields

3. **Enter data.**
   a. Enter the following records into the Agents table, then print it. Tab through the AgentNo field as it is defined with an AutoNumber data type and it automatically increments as you enter the rest of the data in the record.

AgentNo	AgentFirst	AgentLast	AgentPhone	AgencyNo
(10)	(Your first name)	(Your last name)	555-888-9999	1
(11)	(Your instructor's first name)	(Your instructor's last name)	555-888-5555	3

b. Enter the following record into the Agencies table, then print it. Tab through the AgencyNo field because it is an AutoNumber field.

AgencyNo	AgencyName	Street	City	State	Zip	AgencyPhone
(4)	(Your last name) Realty	(Your school's street address)	(Your school's city)	(Your school's state)	(Your school's zip code)	555-888-4444

4. Edit data.

a. Open the Listings table datasheet.

b. Change the Area field for ListingNo 7 from Shell Knob to Ozark Mountain.

c. Change the SqFt field for ListingNo 14 from 3500 to 5500.

d. Delete the record for ListingNo 6. Resize the columns to their best fit. Your Listings table datasheet should look similar to the one in Figure A-19.

FIGURE A-19

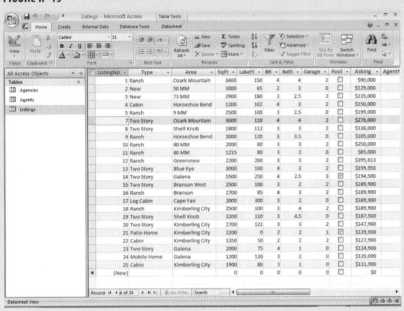

e. Enter one new record, using your own last name in the Area field, then print the first page only of the datasheet in landscape orientation. (*Hint*: Click the Pages option button in the Print dialog box, then enter 1 in both the From and To boxes.)

f. Close the RealEstate-A.accdb database and Access 2007.

5. Create a database.

a. Open Access 2007, then use the Students database template in the Education category to create a new database. This requires you to be connected to the Internet. Close any windows that open before the database does.

b. In the Student List form that opens, enter your first and last names. Use any valid entries for the E-mail Address, Business Phone, Company, and Job Title fields.

c. Print the record.

d. Expand the Navigation Pane, then use it to complete the following table on a sheet of paper to identify the number and names of the objects that were automatically created by the Students database template. The first row is completed for you.

object type	number created	names of the objects
Tables	2	Students, Guardians
Queries		
Forms		
Reports		

6. Create a table.

a. Create a new table called States with the following fields and data types:

StateName   Text

StateAbbreviation   Text

b. Enter your own state in the first record.

c. Close the States table, close the Students.accdb database, then exit Access 2007.

7. Create primary keys.

a. Open the RealEstate-A.accdb database used in earlier steps. Enable content if prompted.

b. Open the Agencies table in Design View, then set AgencyNo as the primary key field.

c. Open the Agents table in Design View, then set AgentNo as the primary key field.

d. Open the Listings table in Design View, then set ListingNo as the primary key field.

e. Save all your changes.

f. On another sheet of paper, answer the following questions:

Why is a field with an AutoNumber data type a good candidate for the primary key field for that table?

Why is a field with an AutoNumber data type *not* a good candidate for the foreign key field for a one-to-many relationship?

8. Relate two tables.

a. In the Relationships window, set a one-to-many relationship between the Agencies and Agents table, using the common AgencyNo field. Apply referential integrity to this relationship.

b. In the Relationships window, set a one-to-many relationship between the Agents and Listings table, using the common AgentNo field. Apply referential integrity to this relationship.

c. Click the Relationship Report button on the Design tab, then print the report that is created.

d. Close the Relationships report without saving changes, then close the Relationships window.

9. Print a datasheet.

a. Preview and print the Agencies table datasheet in landscape orientation.

b. Preview and print the Agents table datasheet in landscape orientation.

c. Close the RealEstate-A.accdb database, and exit Access 2007.

▼ INDEPENDENT CHALLENGE 1

Review the following twelve examples of database tables:

- Telephone directory
- Encyclopedia
- College course offerings
- Shopping catalog
- Restaurant menu
- International product inventory
- Cookbook
- Party guest list
- Movie listing
- Members of the U.S. House of Representatives
- Islands of the Caribbean
- Ancient wonders of the world

For each example, write a brief answer for the following.

a. What field names would you expect to find in each table?

b. Provide an example of two possible records for each table.

▼ INDEPENDENT CHALLENGE 2

You are working with several civic groups to coordinate a community-wide cleanup effort. You have started a database called Recycle-A that tracks the clubs, their trash deposits, and the trash collection centers that are participating.

- **a.** Start Access, then open the **Recycle-A.accdb** database from the drive and folder where you store your Data Files.
- **b.** Open each table's datasheet, and write the number of records and fields in each of the tables.
- **c.** In the Centers table datasheet, modify the ContactFirst and ContactLast names for the Trash Can record to your name.
- **d.** Preview the Centers table datasheet in landscape orientation, print the datasheet if your instructor requests it, then close the table.
- **e.** Open the Relationships window and complete the following table on a sheet of paper:

type of relationship	table on the "one" side of the relationship	table on the "many" side of the relationship	linking field name in the "one" table	linking field name in the "many" table
One-to-many				
One-to-many				

Advanced Challenge Exercise

- ■ Open the datasheet for the Clubs table. Click the expand button to the left of each record (which looks like a small plus sign) to view related records from the Deposits table.
- ■ Close the datasheet for the Clubs table. Open the datasheet for the Centers table. Click the expand button to the left of each record to view related records from the Deposits table.

- **f.** Close the Centers table, close the Recycle-A.accdb database, then exit Access.

▼ INDEPENDENT CHALLENGE 3

You are working for an advertising agency that provides advertising media for small and large businesses in the Midwestern United States. You have started a database called Media-A which tracks your company's customers.

- **a.** Start Access and open the **Media-A.accdb** database from the drive and folder where you store your Data Files. Enable content as needed.
- **b.** Add a new record to the Customers table, using your own first and last names, **$7,788.99** in the YTDSales field, and any reasonable entry for the rest of the fields.
- **c.** Edit the Rocket Laboratory record. The Company name should be **Johnson County Labs**, and the Street value should be **2145 College St**.
- **d.** Preview the Customers datasheet in landscape orientation, print the datasheet if your instructor requests it, then close the table.
- **e.** Create a States table with two fields, **StateName** and **StateAbbreviation**, both with a Text data type.
- **f.** Enter at least three records into the States table, making sure that all of the states used in the Customers datasheet are entered in the States table. This includes Kansas KS, Missouri MO, and any other state you entered in previous steps.
- **g.** In Design View, set the StateAbbreviation field as the primary key field, then save and close the States table.

▼ INDEPENDENT CHALLENGE 3 (CONTINUED)

Advanced Challenge Exercise

- Open the Relationships window, add both table field lists to the window, then expand the size of the Customers field list so that all fields are visible.
- Drag the StateAbbreviation field from the States table to the State field of the Customers table, to create a one-to-many relationship between the two tables. Enforce referential integrity on the relationship. If you are unable to enforce referential integrity, it means that there is a value in the State field of the Customers table that doesn't have a match in the StateAbbreviation field of the States table. Open both datasheets, making sure every state in the Customers table is also represented in the States table, close all datasheets, and reestablish the one-to-many relationship between the two tables with referential integrity.

- Click the Relationship Report button on the Design tab, then print the report that is created.
- Close the Relationships report without saving changes, then close the Relationships window.

h. Close the Media-A.accdb database, then exit Access 2007.

▼ REAL LIFE INDEPENDENT CHALLENGE

This Independent Challenge requires an Internet connection.

Now that you've learned about Microsoft Access and relational databases, brainstorm how you might use an Access database in your daily life or career. Start by visiting the Microsoft Web site, and explore what's new about Access 2007.

a. Connect to the Internet, and use your browser to go to your favorite search engine. Use the keywords "benefits of a relational database" or "benefits of Microsoft Access" to find articles that discuss the benefits of organizing data in a relational database.

b. Read several articles about the benefits of organizing data in a relational database such as Access, identifying three distinct benefits. As you read the articles, list all of the terminology unfamiliar to you as well, identifying at least five items.

c. Using a search engine or a Web site that provides a computer glossary such as *www.whatis.com* or *www.webopedia.com*, look up the definition of the five or more new terms you have identified.

d. Using the research you have conducted on the Web, create a one-page document that lists the three benefits of using a relational database you identified in Step b as well as the five or more technical terms that you researched in Step c. In order to document the original sources of your information, be sure to list the Internet Web page addresses (URLs such as *www.microsoft.com*) for each source you reference for benefits and definitions.

e. Apply this research to a job you have had or would like to secure in the future. In one paragraph, describe the job and give at least one example of how Access might be used to manage data important to that job. In a second paragraph, discuss how the benefits of using a relational database might apply to this example.

▼ VISUAL WORKSHOP

Open the **Basketball-A.accdb** database from the drive and folder where you store your Data Files, then open the Players table datasheet. Modify the first three records in the existing Players table to reflect the changes shown in the First, Last, and Height fields of Figure A-20. Note that your name should be entered in the First and Last fields of the first record. Resize all columns to show all data, print the first page of the datasheet in landscape orientation, close the Players table, close the Basketball-A.accdb database, then exit Access.

FIGURE A-20

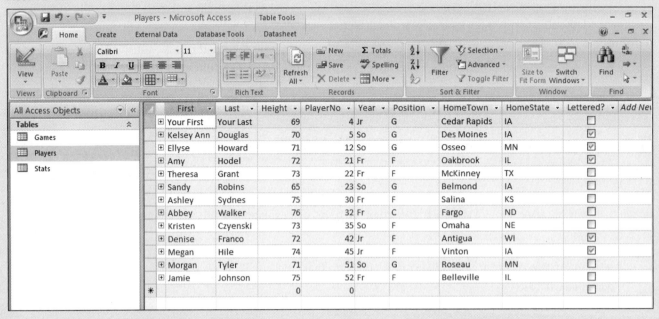

First	Last	Height	PlayerNo	Year	Position	HomeTown	HomeState	Lettered?	Add Nev
Your First	Your Last	69	4	Jr	G	Cedar Rapids	IA	☐	
Kelsey Ann	Douglas	70	5	So	G	Des Moines	IA	☑	
Ellyse	Howard	71	12	So	G	Osseo	MN	☑	
Amy	Hodel	72	21	Fr	F	Oakbrook	IL	☑	
Theresa	Grant	73	22	Fr	F	McKinney	TX	☐	
Sandy	Robins	65	23	So	G	Belmond	IA	☐	
Ashley	Sydnes	75	30	Fr	F	Salina	KS	☐	
Abbey	Walker	76	32	Fr	C	Fargo	ND	☐	
Kristen	Czyenski	73	35	So	F	Omaha	NE	☐	
Denise	Franco	72	42	Jr	F	Antigua	WI	☑	
Megan	Hile	74	45	Jr	F	Vinton	IA	☑	
Morgan	Tyler	71	51	So	G	Roseau	MN	☐	
Jamie	Johnson	75	52	Fr	F	Belleville	IL	☐	
		0	0					☐	

Building and Using Queries

Files You Will Need:

Quest-B.accdb

RealEstate-B.accdb

Vet-B.accdb

Membership-B.accdb

Recycle-B.accdb

Capitals-B.accdb

Basketball-B.accdb

You build queries in an Access database to ask "questions" about data, such as which adventure tours are scheduled for June or what types of tours take place in California. Queries present the answer in a datasheet, which you can sort, filter, and format. Because queries are stored in the database, they can be used multiple times. Each time a query is opened, it presents a current view of the latest updates to the database. Mark Rock, tour developer for U.S. group travel at Quest Travel Services, has several questions about the customer and tour information in the Quest database. You'll develop queries to provide Mark with up-to-date answers.

OBJECTIVES

Create a query

Use Query Design View

Modify queries

Sort and find data

Filter data

Apply AND criteria

Apply OR criteria

Format a datasheet

Creating a Query

A **query** allows you to select a subset of fields and records from one or more tables and then present the selected data as a single datasheet. A major benefit of working with data through a query is that you can focus on the information you need to answer your questions, rather than navigating the fields and records from many large tables. You can enter, edit, and navigate data in a query datasheet just like a table datasheet. However, keep in mind that Access data is physically stored only in tables, even though you can view and edit it through other Access objects such as queries and forms. Because a query doesn't physically store the data, a query datasheet is sometimes called a **logical view** of the data. Technically, a query is a set of **SQL** (Structured Query Language) instructions, but because Access provides several easy-to-use query tools, knowledge of SQL is not required to build or use Access queries. ██████ You use the Simple Query Wizard to build a query to display a few fields from the States and Tours tables in one datasheet.

STEPS

1. **Start Access, open the Quest-B.accdb database, then enable content, if prompted**

   Access provides several tools to create a new query. One way is to use the **Simple Query Wizard**, which prompts you for information needed to create a new query.

2. **Click the Create tab on the Ribbon, click the Query Wizard button, then click OK to start the Simple Query Wizard**

   The first Simple Query Wizard dialog box opens, prompting you to select the fields you want to view in the new query.

3. **Click the Tables/Queries list arrow, click Table: Tours, double-click TourName, double-click City, then double-click Category**

   So far, you've selected three fields from the Tours table for this query. You also want to add the full state name, a field stored only in the States table.

4. **Click the Tables/Queries list arrow, click Table: States, then double-click StateName**

   You've selected three fields from the Tours table and one from the States table for your new query, as shown in Figure B-1. Because the Tours and States tables are linked together in this database by a common field (StateAbbrev), you can create queries by selecting individual fields from each of the linked tables to present a datasheet with a subset of desired fields.

5. **Click Next, select Tours Query, type ToursByState in the text box, click Finish, then maximize the datasheet**

   The ToursByState datasheet opens, displaying three fields from the Tours table and the StateName field from the States table, as shown in Figure B-2.

FIGURE B-1: Selecting fields in the Simple Query Wizard

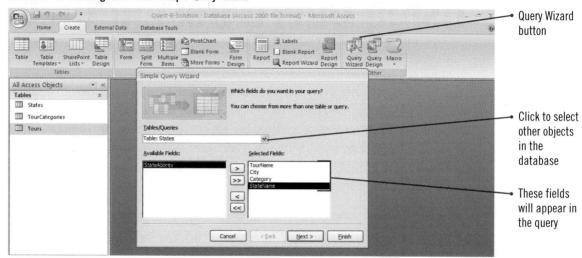

Query Wizard button

Click to select other objects in the database

These fields will appear in the query

FIGURE B-2: ToursByState query datasheet

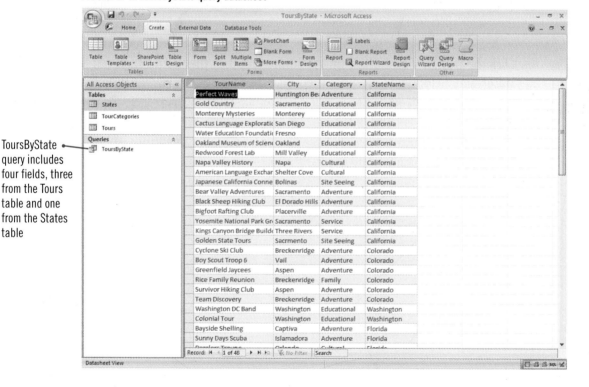

ToursByState query includes four fields, three from the Tours table and one from the States table

Using Query Design View

You use **Query Design View** to add, delete, or move the fields in an existing query, to specify sort orders, or to add **criteria** to limit the number of records shown in the resulting datasheet. (Criteria are limiting conditions you set in Query Design View.) You can also use Query Design View to create a new query from scratch. Query Design View presents the fields you can use for that query in small windows called **field lists**. If the fields of two or more related tables are used in the query, the relationship between two tables is displayed with a **join line** identifying which fields are used to establish the relationship. ██████ Mark Rock asks you to print a list of Adventure tours in Colorado. You use Query Design View to modify the existing ToursByState query to meet his request.

STEPS

1. **Click the Home tab on the Ribbon, then click the Design View button to switch to Query Design View for the ToursByState query**

   The Query Design View opens as shown in Figure B-3, showing the field lists for the States and Tours tables in the upper pane of the window, as well as the one-to-many relationship established between the two tables via the common StateAbbrev field. The four fields you previously requested for this query are displayed in the **query design grid** in the lower pane of the window.

   QUICK TIP

   Query criteria are not case sensitive.

2. **Click the first Criteria cell for the Category field, then type adventure**

   By adding the word "adventure" to the first Criteria cell for the Category field, only those records with this value in the Category field will be displayed in the datasheet.

3. **Click the Datasheet View button on the Design tab to switch to Datasheet View**

   The resulting datasheet lists the Adventure tours. To further narrow this list to tours in Colorado, you return to Query Design View and enter more criteria.

   TROUBLE

   If you see more than five records, return to Query Design View and make sure your criteria are on the same row.

4. **Click the Design View button on the Home tab, click the first Criteria cell for the StateName field, type Colorado, then click the Datasheet View button on the Design tab**

   Now only five records are displayed, as only five of the Adventure tours are in the state of Colorado, as shown in Figure B-4. You want to save this query with a different name.

5. **Click the Office button ⊕, click Save As, type ColoradoAdventures, then click OK**

   Now two queries are included in the Queries list on the Navigation Pane: ToursByState and ColoradoAdventures.

FIGURE B-3: Query Design View of the TourByState query

Datasheet View button

Field list for States table

Query design grid

Field list for Tours table

Criteria cell for Category field

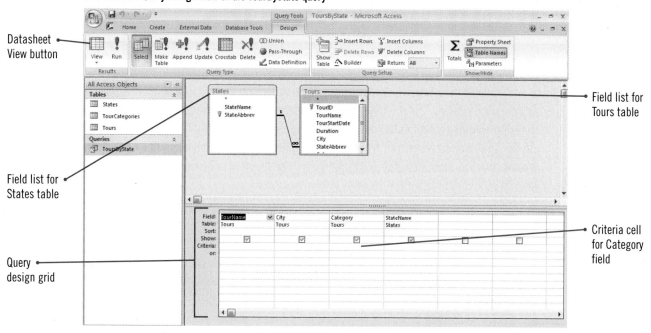

FIGURE B-4: ColoradoAdventures datasheet

Category equals Adventure

StateName equals Colorado

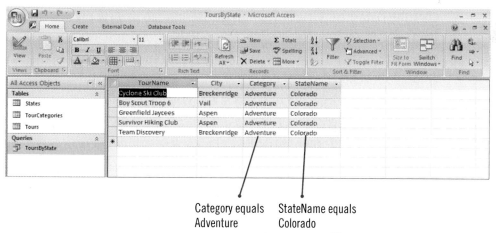

Modifying Queries

To modify an existing query, you work in Query Design View. The upper pane of the Query Design View window shows the field lists for the tables used by the query. You use the lower pane of Query Design View to add, delete, or change the order of the fields shown on the datasheet. You also use the lower pane to add criteria to narrow the number of records selected, to define sort orders, and to build calculated fields. To delete or move a field in the query grid, you select it by clicking its field selector. The **field selector** is the thin gray bar above each field in the query grid. ▰▰▰▰ You want to add more fields and make other modifications to the ColoradoAdventures query. Use Query Design View to make the changes.

STEPS

1. **Click the Design View button on the Home tab**

    You want to move the StateName field to the third field position, immediately after the City field.

2. **Click the field selector for the StateName field to select it, then drag the StateName field selector one column to the left to position StateName between the City and Category fields**

    A black vertical line appears to help you visualize where you are repositioning the field. You also want to sort the records in ascending order based on the TourName field.

3. **Click the Sort cell for the TourName field, click the list arrow, then click Ascending**

    Defining the sort order in Query Design View allows you to permanently save the sort order with the query object so that every time you open the query, the specified sort is applied. Selecting an ascending sort order for the TourName field lists the query results in alphabetic order (A-Z) by TourName. You also want to add the TourStartDate and Duration fields to this query so they appear immediately after the TourName field.

4. **Drag the TourStartDate field from the Tours field list to the second column, then drag the Duration field from the Tours field list to the third column**

    The existing fields in the query grid move to the right to accommodate the addition of new fields to the grid, as shown in Figure B-5.

5. **Click the Datasheet View button on the Design tab to view the selected data**

    The datasheet is shown in Figure B-6. Note the order of the fields and sort order of the records.

6. **Change Discovery in the Team Discovery record to your last name, then save the ColoradoAdventures query**

7. **Click the Office button 🔘, point to Print, click Print Preview, click the Landscape button on the Print Preview tab, click the Print button, then click OK**

8. **Close Print Preview, then close the ColoradoAdventures query**

FIGURE B-5: Modified query in Design View

TourStartDate
inserted as
second field

Ascending
sort order
selected

Duration
inserted as
third field

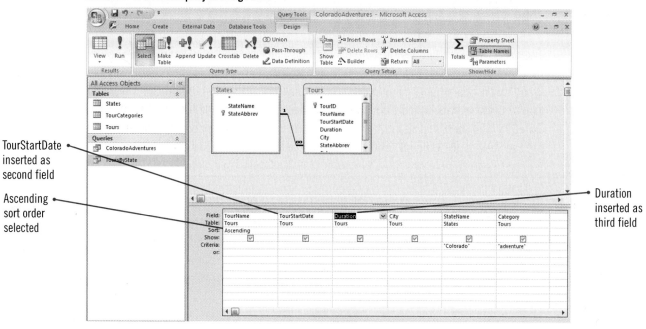

FIGURE B-6: Modified datasheet

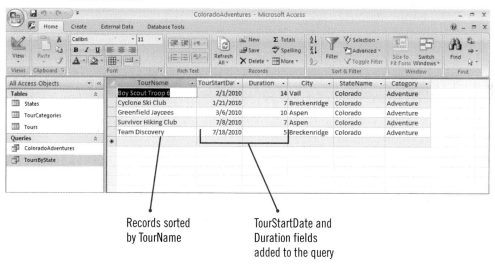

Records sorted
by TourName

TourStartDate and
Duration fields
added to the query

Adding or deleting a table to a query

You might want to add a table's field list to the upper pane of Query Design View in order to select fields from that table for the query. To add a new table to Query Design View, click the Design tab on the Ribbon, click the Show Table button, then add the desired table(s). To delete an unneeded table from Query Design View, click its title bar, then press [Delete].

Sorting and Finding Data

The Access sort and find features are handy tools that help you quickly organize and find data. Table B-1 describes the Sort and Find buttons on the Home tab. Besides using these buttons, you can also click the list arrow on a datasheet's column heading, and then click a sorting option. Sorting and finding data works exactly the same way in table and query datasheets. ▄▄▟▟▓ Mark Rock asks you to provide a list of tours sorted by TourStartDate, and then by Duration. He also asks you to correct two tours by changing the entry of "Site Seeing" to "Cultural" in the Category field.

STEPS

QUICK TIP

Click the Navigation Pane list arrow, then make sure All Access Objects is checked to show all tables, queries, and other objects.

1. **Double-click Tours in the Navigation Pane to open the Tours datasheet, then maximize the window**

   By default, records in a table datasheet are sorted on the primary key field. For the Tours table, the primary key field is the TourID field.

QUICK TIP

A sort arrow appears next to the field name by which the datasheet is sorted.

2. **Click any value in the TourStartDate field, then click the Ascending button ⬇ on the Home tab**

   The records are re-sorted based on the TourStartDate field. Notice that some tours start on the same date. You can specify a second sort order to further sort the records that have the same date in the TourStartDate field.

TROUBLE

To clear the current sort order, click the Clear All Sorts button ⬇.

3. **Drag across the TourStartDate and Duration field selector buttons to select both columns, then click ⬇**

   The records are now listed in ascending order, first by TourStartDate, then by the values in the Duration field, as shown in Figure B-7. Sort orders always work left to right, so you might need to rearrange the fields before applying a sort order that uses more than one field. Your next task is to replace all occurrences of "Site Seeing" with "Cultural" in the Category field.

TROUBLE

If your find and replace did not work correctly, click the Undo button ⬅ and repeat step 4.

4. **Click the Category column heading to select that field, click the Replace button 🔲 on the Home tab, type Site Seeing in the Find What box, press [Tab], type Cultural in the Replace With box, click Find Next to find the first occurrence of Site Seeing, click Replace, click Replace again to replace the next occurrence of "Site Seeing," then click Cancel**

   Access replaced two occurrences of "Site Seeing" with "Cultural" in the Category field, as shown in Figure B-8.

5. **Replace Rice in the TourID 26 record with your last name, then print the first page of the Tours datasheet**

6. **Save the Tours table**

   If you close a datasheet without saving the changes, the records return to the original sort order based on the values in the primary key field. If you close a datasheet and save layout changes, the last sort order is saved.

FIGURE B-7: Tours datasheet sorted by TourStartDate and Duration fields

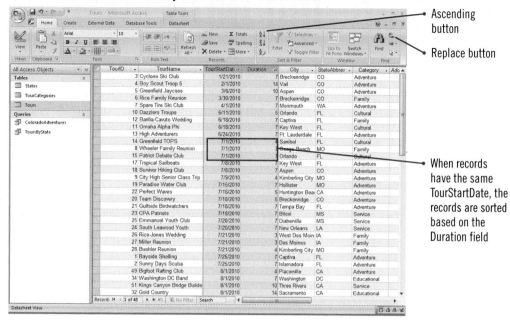

Ascending button

Replace button

When records have the same TourStartDate, the records are sorted based on the Duration field

FIGURE B-8: "Site Seeing" replaced with "Cultural" in the Category field

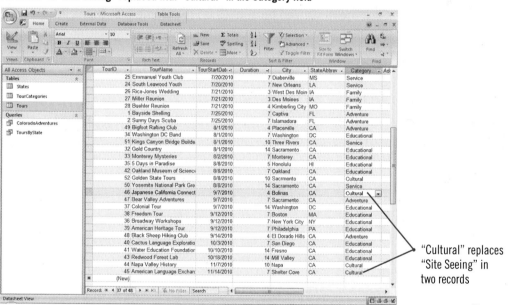

"Cultural" replaces "Site Seeing" in two records

TABLE B-1: Sort and Find buttons

name	button	purpose
Ascending		Sorts records based on the selected field in ascending order (0 to 9, A to Z)
Descending		Sorts records based on the selected field in descending order (Z to A, 9 to 0)
Clear All Sorts		Removes the current sort order
Find		Opens the Find and Replace dialog box, which allows you to find data in a single field or in the entire datasheet
Replace		Opens the Find and Replace dialog box, which allows you to find and replace data
Go To		Helps you navigate to the first, previous, last, or new record
Select		Helps you select a single record or all records in a datasheet

Filtering Data

Filtering a table or query datasheet temporarily displays only those records that match given criteria. Recall that criteria are limiting conditions you set. For example, you might want to show only those tours in the state of Florida, or those tours with a duration of less than seven days. While filters provide a quick and easy way to display a subset of records in the current datasheet, they are not nearly as powerful or flexible as queries. For example, a query is a saved object within the database, whereas filters are temporary. Filters are removed when the datasheet is closed, but if you want to apply a filter over and over again, you can save it as a query. Table B-2 compares filters and queries. ▰▰▰▰▰ Mark Rock asks you to find all Adventure tours offered in the month of July. You can filter the Tours datasheet to provide this information.

STEPS

QUICK TIP

You can also click the list arrow on a column heading, click the Select All check box to clear all the check boxes, then click the value to use as the filter.

1. **Click any occurrence of Adventure in the Category field, click the Selection button ▒ on the Home tab, then click Equals "Adventure"**

Seventeen records are selected, as shown in Figure B-9. Filtering by a given field value, called **Filter By Selection**, is a fast and easy way to filter the records for an exact match. To filter for comparative data (for example, where TourStartDate is *equal to or greater than* 7/1/2010), you must use the **Filter By Form** feature. Filter buttons are summarized in Table B-3.

QUICK TIP

To save a filter permanently as a query object, click the Advanced button, then click Save As Query.

2. **Click the Advanced button ▒ on the Home tab, then click Filter By Form**

The Filter by Form window opens. The previous Filter By Selection criterion, "Adventure" in the Category field, is still in the grid. Access distinguishes between text and numeric entries by placing quotation marks around text criteria.

QUICK TIP

If you need to clear previous criteria, click the Advanced button, then click Clear Grid.

3. **Click the TourStartDate cell, then type 7/*/2010 as shown in Figure B-10**

Filter by Form also allows you to apply two or more criteria at the same time. An asterisk (*) in the day position of the date criterion works as a wildcard, selecting any date in the month of July (the seventh month) in the year 2010.

4. **Click the Toggle Filter button ▒ on the Home tab**

The datasheet redisplays all nine records that match both filter criteria, as shown in Figure B-11. Note that filter icons appear next to the TourStartDate and Category field names as both fields are involved in the filter.

QUICK TIP

Be sure to remove existing filters before applying a completely new filter, or you filter the current subset of records instead of applying the filter to the entire datasheet.

5. **Change Bayside in TourID 1 to your last name, then print the filtered datasheet**

To remove the current filter, you click the Toggle Filter button.

6. **Click ▒ to remove the filter, then save and close the Tours datasheet**

Using wildcard characters

To search for a pattern, you can use a **wildcard** character to represent any character in the criteria entry. Use a ? (question mark) to search for any single character and an * (asterisk) to search for any number of characters. Wildcard characters are often used with the Like operator. For example, the criterion Like "12/*/10" would find all dates in December of 2010, and the criterion Like "F*" would find all entries that start with the letter F.

FIGURE B-9: Filtering for Adventure records

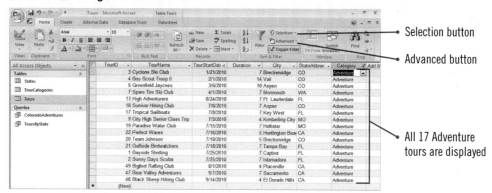

Selection button

Advanced button

All 17 Adventure tours are displayed

FIGURE B-10: Filter by Form window

Adding a criterion to display records with a TourStartDate in July, 2010

Toggle Filter button

"Adventure" criterion still in Category field

FIGURE B-11: Filtering for Adventure records in July, 2010

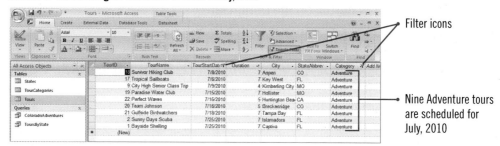

Filter icons

Nine Adventure tours are scheduled for July, 2010

TABLE B-2: Filters versus queries

characteristics	filters	queries
Are saved as an object in the database	No	Yes
Can be used to select a subset of records in a datasheet	Yes	Yes
Can be used to select a subset of fields in a datasheet	No	Yes
Resulting datasheet used to enter and edit data	Yes	Yes
Resulting datasheet used to sort, filter, and find records	Yes	Yes
Commonly used as the source of data for a form or report	No	Yes
Can calculate sums, averages, counts, and other types of summary statistics across records	No	Yes
Can be used to create calculated fields	No	Yes

TABLE B-3: Filter buttons

name	button	purpose
Filter		Provides a list of values in the selected field by which to customize a filter
Selection		Filters records that equal, do not equal, or are otherwise compared to the current value
Advanced		Provides advanced filter features such as Filter By Form, Save As Query, and Clear Grid
Toggle Filter		Applies or removes the current filter

Applying AND Criteria

As you have seen, you can limit the number of records that appear on a query datasheet by entering criteria into Query Design View. Criteria are tests, or limiting conditions, for which the record must be true to be selected for a datasheet. To create **AND criteria**, which means that *all* criteria must be true in order for the record to be selected, enter two or more criteria on the *same* Criteria row of the query design grid. Mark Rock asks you to provide a list of all educational tours in the state of California with a duration of greater than seven days. Use Query Design View to create the query with AND criteria to meet his request.

STEPS

QUICK TIP

Drag the bottom border of the Tours field list down to display all of the fields. The scroll bar disappears when all fields are displayed.

1. **Click the Create tab on the Ribbon, click the Query Design button, double-click Tours, click Close in the Show Table dialog box, then maximize the query window**

   You want to add four fields to this query.

2. **Double-click TourName, double-click Duration, double-click StateAbbrev, and double-click Category to add these fields to the query grid**

   Start by adding criteria to select only those records in California. Because you are using the StateAbbrev field, you need to use the two-letter state abbreviation for California, CA, as the Criteria entry.

3. **Click the first Criteria cell for the StateAbbrev field, type CA, then click the Datasheet View button on the Design tab**

   Querying for only those tours in the state of California selects 16 records. Next, you add criteria to select only those records in the Educational category.

4. **Click the Design View button on the Home tab to switch to Query Design View, click the first Criteria cell for the Category field, type Educational, then click the Datasheet View button on the Design tab**

   Criteria added to the same line of the query design grid are AND criteria. When entered on the same line, each criterion must be true for the record to appear in the resulting datasheet. Querying for both California and Educational tours selects six records. Every time you add AND criteria, you *narrow* the number of records that are selected because the record must be true for *all* criteria.

5. **Click the Design View button on the Home tab, click the first Criteria cell for the Duration field, then type >7, as shown in Figure B-12**

   Access assists you with **criteria syntax**, rules by which criteria need to be entered. Access automatically adds quotation marks around text criteria in Text fields and pound signs (#) around date criteria in Date/Time fields. The criteria in Number, Currency, and Yes/No fields are not surrounded by any characters. See Table B-4 for more information about comparison operators such as > (greater than).

TROUBLE

If your datasheet doesn't match Figure B-13, return to Query Design View and compare your criteria to that of Figure B-12.

6. **Click the Datasheet View button on the Design tab**

   The third AND criterion further narrows the number of records selected to three, as shown in Figure B-13.

7. **Click the Save button 🖫 on the Quick Access toolbar, type CaliforniaEducational as the query name, then click OK**

   The query is saved with the new name, CaliforniaEducational, as a new object in the Quest-B database.

Searching for blank fields

Is Null and **Is Not Null** are two other types of common criteria. The Is Null criterion finds all records where no entry has been made in the field. Is Not Null finds all records where there is any entry in the field, even if the entry is 0. Primary key fields cannot have a null entry.

FIGURE B-12: Query Design View with criteria on one row (AND criteria)

Datasheet View button

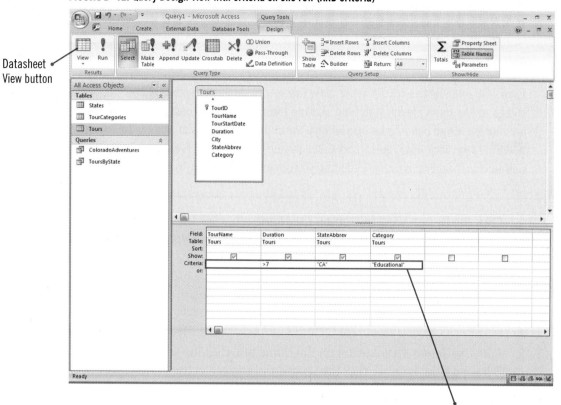

Criteria for displaying Educational tours in California that are longer than one week

FIGURE B-13: Datasheet of CaliforniaEducational query

Design View button

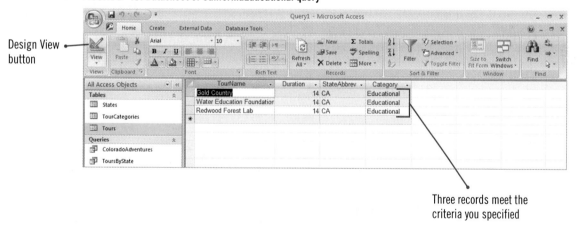

Three records meet the criteria you specified

TABLE B-4: Comparison operators

operator	description	expression	meaning
>	Greater than	>500	Numbers greater than 500
>=	Greater than or equal to	>=500	Numbers greater than or equal to 500
<	Less than	<"Braveheart"	Names from A to Braveheart, but not Braveheart
<=	Less than or equal to	<="Bridgewater"	Names from A through Bridgewater, inclusive
<>	Not equal to	<>"Fontanelle"	Any name except for Fontanelle

Applying OR Criteria

To create **OR criteria**, which means that *any one* criterion must be true in order for the record to be selected, enter two or more criteria on the *different* Criteria rows of the query design grid. To create OR criteria for the *same field*, enter the two criteria in the same Criteria cell separated by the OR operator. As you add rows of OR criteria to the query design grid, you *increase* the number of records selected for the resulting datasheet because the record needs to be true for *only one* of the criteria rows in order to be selected for the datasheet. Mark Rock asks you to add Cultural tours longer than seven days in duration from the state of California to the previous query. To do this, you can modify the query to employ OR criteria to add the records.

STEPS

1. **Click the Design View button on the Home tab, click the second Criteria cell in the Category field, type cultural, then click the Datasheet View button on the Design tab**

   The query added all of the tours with "Cultural" in the Category field to the datasheet, as specified by the second row of the query grid in Query Design View. Because each row of the query grid is evaluated separately, the fact that three criteria were entered in the first row is of no consequence to the second row. In order for the second row to also apply three criteria—Cultural, California, and duration of greater than 7—three criteria must be entered in the second row. In other words, the criteria in one row have no effect on the criteria of other rows.

2. **Click the Design View button on the Home tab, click the second Criteria cell in the Duration field, type >7, click the second Criteria cell in the StateAbbrev field, then type CA**

   Query Design View should look like Figure B-14.

3. **Click the Datasheet View button on the Design tab**

   Five records were selected that meet all three criteria as entered in row one OR row two of the query grid, as shown in Figure B-15.

4. **Edit the Gold Country record to be your last name Country, then save, print, and close the datasheet**

   Because the CaliforniaEducational query now selects both educational and cultural records, you rename it.

5. **Right-click CaliforniaEducational in the Navigation Pane, click Rename on the shortcut menu, type CaliforniaEducationalCultural to rename the query, then press [Enter]**

Building and Using Queries

FIGURE B-14: Query Design View with criteria on two rows (OR criteria)

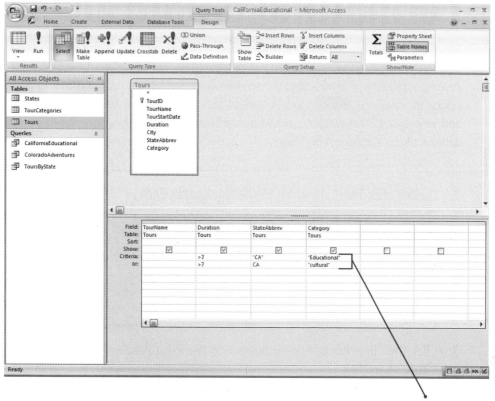

OR criteria on two rows
in the design grid

FIGURE B-15: Datasheet of CaliforniaEducationalCultural query

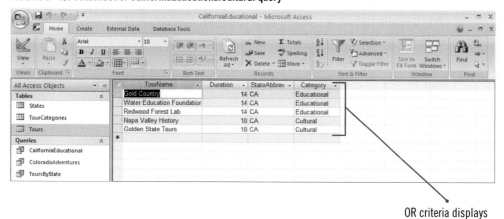

OR criteria displays
five records

Formatting a Datasheet

Although the primary Access tool to create professional printouts is the report object, you can print a datasheet as well. Although a datasheet printout does not allow you to add custom headers, footers, images, or subtotals as reports do, you can apply some formatting, such as changing the font size, font face, colors, and gridlines. ⬛⬛⬛ Mark Rock has asked you to create a printout of the different tour categories and their descriptions, which is stored in the TourCategories table. You can format the TourCategories datasheet before printing it for Mark.

STEPS

1. **Double-click TourCategories in the Navigation Pane**

   The TourCategories datasheet opens. Before applying new formatting enhancements, you preview the default printout.

2. **Click the Office button ⬤, point to Print, click Print Preview, then click the top edge of the paper to zoom in**

   The preview window displays the layout of the printout, as shown in Figure B-16. By default, the printout of a datasheet contains the object name and current date in the header. The page number is in the footer. You decide to increase the size of the font and data before printing.

3. **Click the Close Print Preview button on the Print Preview tab, click the Font Size list arrow, then click 12**

   A larger font size often makes a printout easier to read. You also need to adjust the width of the Description column to its best fit.

4. **Double-click the column separator to the right of the Description field**

   Double-clicking the column (field) separator automatically adjusts the width of the column to the widest entry in the datasheet.

5. **Click the Alternate Fill/Back Color button arrow ⬚ ▾ on the Home tab, then click Yellow**

   For datasheet printouts, alternating the background color of each row makes the printout easier to read, as shown in Figure B-17. You want to add one more new category, Sports, before printing the datasheet.

6. **Type Sports in the Category field for a new record, then type (any valid and unique description) for this category in the Description field**

7. **Preview the datasheet again, click the Print button on the Print Preview tab, then click OK in the Print dialog box**

8. **Save and close the TourCategories datasheet, close the Quest-B.accdb database, then exit Access**

FIGURE B-16: Default printout of a datasheet

Print Preview tab

Close Print Preview button

TourCategories datasheet in Print Preview

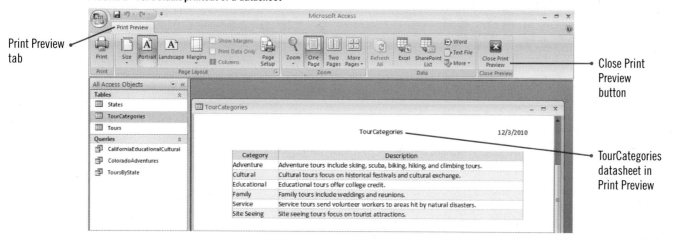

FIGURE B-17: Formatted datasheet

Font Size list arrow

Alternate Fill/Back Color button

Font size increased to 12, Description field resized, and Yellow alternate color applied

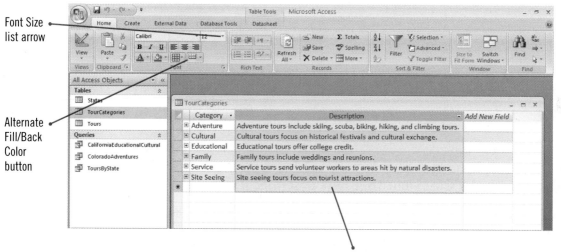

Practice

▼ CONCEPTS REVIEW

Label each element of the Access window shown in Figure B-18.

FIGURE B-18

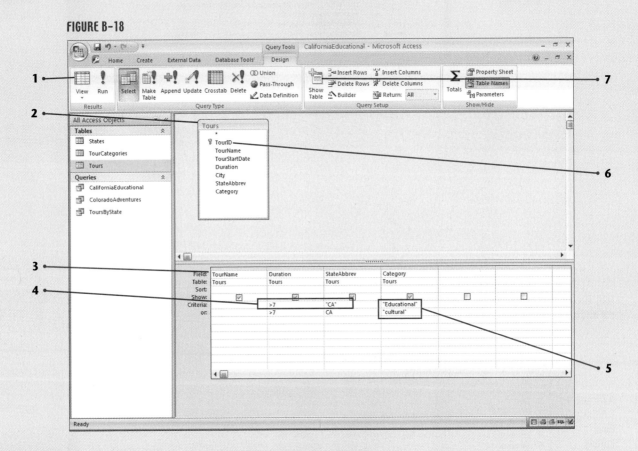

Match each term with the statement that best describes it.

8. Query grid
9. Criteria
10. Filter
11. Syntax
12. Query
13. Sorting
14. Wildcard
15. Is Null

a. Creates a datasheet of selected fields and records from one or more tables
b. Creates a temporary subset of records
c. Limiting conditions used to narrow the number of records that appear on a datasheet
d. Used to search for a pattern
e. Criterion that finds all records where no entry has been made in the field
f. The lower pane in Query Design View
g. Putting records in ascending or descending order based on the values of a field
h. Rules that determine how criteria is entered

Select the best answer from the list of choices.

16. The rules by which criteria need to be entered in the query grid are referred to as:
- **a.** Syntax.
- **b.** Hyperlink.
- **c.** Field lists.
- **d.** Formatting.

17. SQL stands for which of the following?
- **a.** Standard Query Language
- **b.** Structured Query Language
- **c.** Special Query Listing
- **d.** Simple Query Listing

18. A query is sometimes called a "logical view" of data because:
- **a.** You can create queries with the Logical Query Wizard.
- **b.** Queries contain logical criteria.
- **c.** Query naming conventions are logical.
- **d.** Queries do not store data, they only display a view of data.

19. Which of the following describes OR criteria?
- **a.** Using two or more rows of the query grid to select only those records that meet given criteria
- **b.** Selecting a subset of fields and/or records to view as a datasheet from one or more tables
- **c.** Reorganizing the records in either ascending or descending order based on the contents of one or more fields
- **d.** Using multiple fields in the query design grid

20. Which of the following is *not* true about a query?
- **a.** A query is the same thing as a filter.
- **b.** A query can be used to create calculated fields.
- **c.** A query can be used to create summary statistics.
- **d.** A query can be used to enter and edit data.

▼ SKILLS REVIEW

1. Create a query.
- **a.** Open the RealEstate-B.accdb database from the drive and folder where you store your Data Files. Enable content if you are prompted with a Security Alert message.
- **b.** Create a new query using the Simple Query Wizard. Select the AgentFirst and AgentLast names from the Agents table, and select the Type, SqFt, and Asking fields from the Listings table. Select all details, and title the query AgentListings.
- **c.** Choose any record with Michelle Litten's name and change it to your own. As soon as you save the changes by moving to another record, all three of Michelle's records update to your name. Although Michelle Litten was entered only once in the database, her agent number was linked to three different listings in the Listings table, which selects her name three times out of the Agents table for this query.

2. Use Query Design View.
- **a.** Open the AgentListings query in Query Design View.
- **b.** Enter criteria to display only homes with an Asking price of greater than $200,000. (*Hint*: Enter the value in the criterion as 200000 without a comma. Also, don't forget the greater than operator, >.) Display the datasheet.
- **c.** In Query Design View, sort the records in ascending order based on the AgentLast field, then display and print the datasheet.
- **d.** Save and close the AgentListings query.

3. Modify queries.

a. Open the ListingsMasterList query in Datasheet View.

b. Switch to Query Design View, then add the AgencyName field from the Agencies table to the first column in the query grid.

c. Add the AgentFirst field to the third column.

d. Add ascending sort orders to the AgentLast and AgentFirst fields, then display the datasheet.

e. Print, save, and close the ListingsMasterList query.

4. Sort and find data.

a. Open the Listings table datasheet.

b. Select both the SqFt and LakeFt fields, then sort the records in descending order.

c. In the Area field, find all occurrences of Shell Knob, replace them with Shell City, then close the Find and Replace dialog box.

d. Enter your own last name in the Area field of the first record, then print only the first page of the datasheet.

5. Filter data.

a. Filter the Listings datasheet for only those records where the Type field equals Two Story.

b. Apply an advanced filter by form to further narrow the records so that only the Two Story listings with an Asking Price of greater than or equal to $194,500 are selected.

c. Print the datasheet, then close the Listings datasheet without saving changes.

6. Apply AND criteria.

a. Open the ListingsMasterList query in Query Design View.

b. Enter criteria to select all of the listings in the Shell City area with three or more baths. Display the datasheet and save the changes.

c. Print the ListingsMasterList datasheet in landscape orientation.

7. Apply OR criteria.

a. Open the ListingsMasterList query in Query Design View.

b. In addition to the existing criteria, include criteria to select all listings in Kimberling City with three or more baths, so that both Shell City and Kimberling City records with three or more baths are selected. Display the datasheet, compare it to Figure B-19, and save the changes.

FIGURE B-19

AgencyName	AgentLast	AgentFirst	ListingNo	Type	Area	SqFt	BR	Bath	Asking
Camden and Camden Realtors	Fye	Donna	20	Two Story	Kimberling City	2700	3	3	$147,900
Camden and Camden Realtors	Fye	Donna	19	Two Story	Shell City	3200	3	4.5	$187,500
Camden and Camden Realtors	Pledge	Shari	18	Ranch	Kimberling City	2500	3	4	$189,900
Sun and Ski Realtors	StudentLast	StudentFirst	8	Two Story	Shell City	1800	3	3	$138,000
*			(New)						

The order of the records might differ, depending on your name

c. Print the ListingsMasterList datasheet in landscape orientation, then save and close the ListingsMasterList query.

8. Format a datasheet.

a. Open the Agents table datasheet and apply the Arial Narrow font and a 14-point font size.

b. Resize all columns so that all data and field names are visible.

c. Apply a Light Gray 2 alternate fill/back color.

d. Print the datasheet, then save and close the Agents datasheet.

e. Close the RealEstate-B.accdb database, then exit Access.

▼ INDEPENDENT CHALLENGE 1

You have built an Access database to track the veterinarians and clinics where they work in your area.

a. Start Access, open the **Vet-B.accdb** database from the drive and folder where you store your Data Files, enable content if prompted, then open the Vets table datasheet.

b. Open the Clinics datasheet, review the data in both datasheets, then close them.

c. Using the Simple Query Wizard, select the Last and First fields from the Vets table, and select the ClinicName and Phone fields from the Clinics table. Title the query **ClinicListing**, then view and maximize the datasheet.

d. Sort the records in ascending order by Last name, then First name. Review the values in the Last field, and determine if the First sort order was needed.

e. Find Cooper in the Last field, and replace it with **Chen**.

f. Find any occurrence of Leawood Animal Clinic in the ClinicName field, and change Leawood to **Emergency**.

g. In Query Design View, add criteria to select only Emergency Animal Clinic or Animal Haven in the ClinicName field.

h. Display the datasheet, change Vicki Kowalewski's name to your own, then save and print the ClinicListing datasheet.

i. Close the ClinicListing datasheet and the Vet-B.accdb database, and exit Access.

▼ INDEPENDENT CHALLENGE 2

You have built an Access database to track membership in a community service club. The database tracks member names and addresses as well as their status in the club, which moves from rank to rank as the members contribute increased hours of service to the community.

a. Start Access, open the **Membership-B.accdb** database from the drive and folder where you store your Data Files, enable content if prompted, open the Members and Status table datasheets to review the data, then close them.

b. In Query Design View, build a query with the following fields: LName and FName from the Members table, and StatusLevel from the Status table.

c. View the datasheet, then return to Query Design View.

d. In Query Design View, add criteria to select only those members with a silver or gold StatusLevel. Apply an ascending sort order on the LName and FName fields, then view the datasheet.

e. Return to Query Design View, add an ascending sort order to StatusLevel, then rearrange the fields in the query grid so that the StatusLevel field is the first sort order, LName the second, and FName the third. View the datasheet.

f. Save the query with the name **GoldSilver**.

g. Return to Query Design View, then add the Phone field as the fourth field in the query. View the datasheet, shown in Figure B-20.

h. Enter your own name in the first record, widen all columns so that all data is visible, then print the datasheet.

i. Save and close the GoldSilver query, then close the Membership-B.accdb database, and exit Access.

FIGURE B-20

▼ INDEPENDENT CHALLENGE 3

You have built an Access database to organize the deposits at a recycling center. Various clubs regularly deposit recyclable material, which is measured in pounds when the deposits are made.

a. Start Access, open the **Recycle-B.accdb** database from the drive and folder where you store your Data Files, then enable content if prompted.

b. Open the Clubs table datasheet to review this data, then close it. Open the Centers table datasheet to review this data, then close it.

c. Review the Deposits datasheet, then filter the datasheet for records where the Weight value is greater than or equal to 100.

d. Apply an alternate light gray fill/back color of your choice, print the datasheet, then save and close the Deposits datasheet.

e. Using either the Query Wizard or Query Design View, create a query with the following fields: Deposit Number, Deposit Date, and Weight from the Deposits table; Name from the Centers table; and Name from the Clubs table. Note that in the Simple Query Wizard's field list and in the query datasheet, when two fields from different tables have the same name, the fields are distinguished by adding the table name and a period before the field name.

f. Name the query **DepositList**. Sort the records in ascending order by Deposit Number.

g. Change any occurrence of "Adair" in the "Adair County Landfill" entry in the Centers.Name field to your last name, then print the datasheet.

h. Save and close the DepositList query.

Advanced Challenge Exercise

- Compare the printout of the Deposits table datasheet and the DepositList query. In a document, answer the following questions:
  - What common field links the Deposits table to the Centers table? (*Hint*: Use the Relationships window if the answer is not apparent from the printouts.)
  - What common field links the Deposits table to the Clubs table? (*Hint*: Use the Relationships window if needed.)
  - Why do you think that number fields are often used as the common field to link two tables in a one-to-many relationship, as opposed to text fields?
  - How many times is each center name and each club name physically entered in the database?
  - Why do many center names and club names appear many times on the DepositList query?

i. Close the Recycle-B.accdb database, then exit Access.

▼ REAL LIFE INDEPENDENT CHALLENGE

You can use an Access database to record and track your experiences, such as places you've visited. Suppose that your passion for travel includes a plan to visit the capitals of all 50 states. A database is provided with your Data Files that includes one table listing each state and capital, and another table of people from each state that you can contact for more information about state information.

a. Start Access, open the **Capitals-B.accdb** database from the drive and folder where you store your Data Files, then enable content if prompted.

b. Open both the Contacts and States datasheets to review their data, then close them.

c. In the States table, add a new field to track information about each state that you are personally interested in. Options include recording the current state population, state bird, primary tourist attraction, largest city, or any other fact about each state you choose.

d. Research and enter correct data for the new field you created in step c, for both your home state and another state that you are interested in, then print the States datasheet.

e. Using either Query Design View or the Simple Query Wizard, create a query with the following fields: StateName and Capital from the States table, and LName and FName from the Contacts table. Save the query as **StateContacts**, then display the datasheet.

f. Use Query Design View to add three ascending sort orders on these fields—StateName, then LName, then FName— then display the datasheet.

g. Use Query Design View to add a criterion to select only records from the state of New York, then display the datasheet.

h. Edit Ablany to correct the spelling of New York's state capital, Albany. Navigate to a new record so that the edit is saved in the database.

i. Format the datasheet to a 14-point font size, Times New Roman font face, and a Light Blue 1 alternate fill/back color.

j. Save the revised query with the name NewYorkContacts.

k. Change the name of the first record to your name, then print the datasheet.

Advanced Challenge Exercise

This Advanced Challenge Exercise requires an Internet connection.

- Use the Web to research state mottos.
- Create a Text field in the States table called Motto and enter the motto for at least five different states, including New York.
- In Query Design View of the NewYorkContacts query, add the Motto field as the fifth column of the query.
- View the datasheet, widen the motto field as necessary, as shown in Figure B-21, then print the NewYorkContacts query.
- Close the NewYorkContacts query without saving changes.

l. Close the Capitals-B.accdb database, then exit Access.

FIGURE B-21

▼ VISUAL WORKSHOP

Open the Basketball-B.accdb database from the drive and folder where you store your Data Files, and enable content if prompted. Create a query based on the Players, Stats, and Games tables as shown in Figure B-22. Criteria has been added so that only those records where the Reb-O (offensive rebounds) and Reb-D (defensive rebounds) field values are equal to or greater than 1, and the 3P (three pointer) field values are equal to or greater than 2. The records are also sorted. A Light Gray 1 alternate fill/back color has been applied. Change the name of Kelsey Douglas to your own name before printing, save the query with the name HighPerformers, then close the query, the Basketball-B.accdb database, and Access.

FIGURE B-22

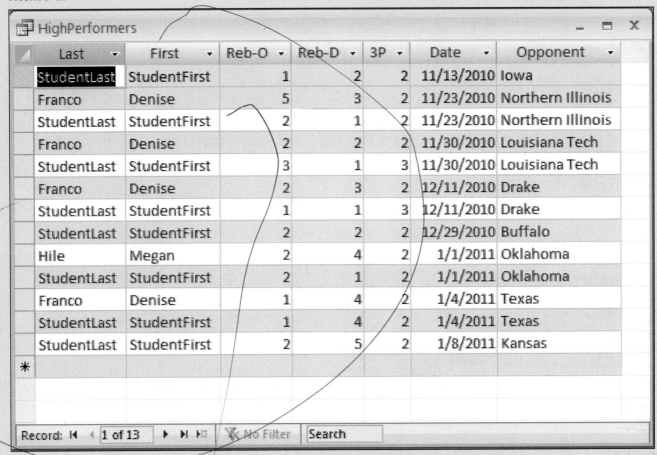

Last	First	Reb-O	Reb-D	3P	Date	Opponent
StudentLast	StudentFirst	1	2	2	11/13/2010	Iowa
Franco	Denise	5	3	2	11/23/2010	Northern Illinois
StudentLast	StudentFirst	2	1	2	11/23/2010	Northern Illinois
Franco	Denise	2	2	2	11/30/2010	Louisiana Tech
StudentLast	StudentFirst	3	1	3	11/30/2010	Louisiana Tech
Franco	Denise	2	3	2	12/11/2010	Drake
StudentLast	StudentFirst	1	1	3	12/11/2010	Drake
StudentLast	StudentFirst	2	2	2	12/29/2010	Buffalo
Hile	Megan	2	4	2	1/1/2011	Oklahoma
StudentLast	StudentFirst	2	1	2	1/1/2011	Oklahoma
Franco	Denise	1	4	2	1/4/2011	Texas
StudentLast	StudentFirst	1	4	2	1/4/2011	Texas
StudentLast	StudentFirst	2	5	2	1/8/2011	Kansas

Record: 1 of 13   No Filter   Search

Using Forms

Files You Will Need:

Quest-C.accdb
RealEstate-C.accdb
Vet-C.accdb
Membership-C.accdb
Recycle-C.accdb
States-C.accdb
Basketball-C.accdb
QSTLogo.jpg
house.jpg
dog.jpg

Although you can enter and edit data on datasheets, most database designers develop and build forms as the primary method for users to interact with a database. In a datasheet, sometimes you have to scroll left or right to see all of the fields, which is inconvenient and time consuming. A form solves these problems by allowing you to organize the fields on the screen in any arrangement. A form also supports graphical elements such as pictures, buttons, and tabs, which make data entry faster and more accurate. Mark Rock, a tour developer at Quest Specialty Travel, asks you to create forms to make tour information easier to access, enter, and update in the Quest Access database.

OBJECTIVES

Create a form

Use Form Layout View

Use Form Design View

Add fields to a form

Modify form controls

Create calculations

Modify tab order

Insert an image

Creating a Form

A **form** is an Access database object that allows you to arrange the fields of a record in any layout so you can enter, edit, and delete records. A form provides an easy-to-use data entry and navigation screen. Forms provide many productivity and security benefits for the **user**, who is primarily interested in entering, editing, and analyzing the data in the database. As the **database designer**, the person responsible for building and maintaining tables, queries, forms, and reports, you also need direct access to all database objects, and use the Navigation Pane for this purpose. Users should not be able to access all the objects in a database—imagine how disastrous it would be if they accidentally deleted an entire table of data. You can prevent these types of problems by providing users with only the functionality they need in easy-to-use, well-designed forms. Mark Rock asks you to build a form to enter and maintain tour information.

STEPS

1. **Start Access, open the Quest-C.accdb database, then enable content if prompted**

   You can use many methods to create a new form, but the Form Wizard is a popular way to get started. The **Form Wizard** is an Access tool that prompts you for information it needs to create a new form, such as the layout, style, title, and record source for the form.

2. **Click the Create tab on the Ribbon, click the Tours table in the Navigation Pane, click the More Forms button, then click the Form Wizard**

   The Form Wizard starts, prompting you to select the fields for this form from the table you selected.

3. **Click the Select All Fields button `>>`**

   You could now select more fields from other tables. In this case, you can base the new form only on the fields of the Tours table.

4. **Click Next, click the Columnar option button, click Next, click the Flow style, click Next, type Tours Entry Form as the title, click Finish, then maximize the form window**

   The Tours Entry Form opens in **Form View**, as shown in Figure C-1. The field names are shown as labels in the first column, and text boxes that display data from the underlying record source appear in the second column. You can enter, edit, find, sort, and filter records using Form View.

5. **Click Cyclone Ski Club in the TourName text box, click the Ascending button `↑` on the Home tab, then click the Next record button `▶` on the navigation bar to move to the second record**

   Numbers sort before letters in a Text field, so the tour named *5 Days in Paradise* appears before *American Heritage Tour*. Information about the current record number and total number of records appears in the navigation bar, just as it does in a datasheet.

6. **Click the New (blank) record button `▶*` on the navigation bar, then enter the record shown in Figure C-2**

   Note that when you click in the TourStartDate text box, a small calendar icon appears to the right of the record. You can type a date directly into a date text box or click the **calendar icon** to select a date from a pop-up calendar. Similarly, when you work in the Category field, you can either type a value directly into the text box or click the list arrow to select an option from the drop-down list. Every item on the form, such as a label or text box, is called a **control**. Table C-1 summarizes the most common form controls as well as whether they are **bound** (display data) or **unbound** (do not display data).

FIGURE C-1: Tours Entry Form in Form View

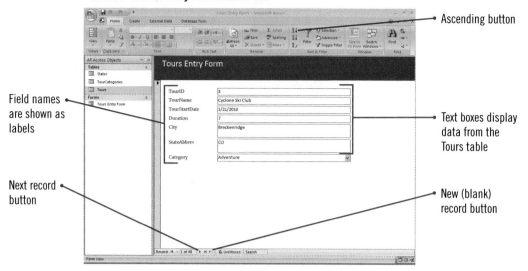

Ascending button

Field names are shown as labels

Text boxes display data from the Tours table

Next record button

New (blank) record button

FIGURE C-2: Adding a new record in the Tours Entry Form

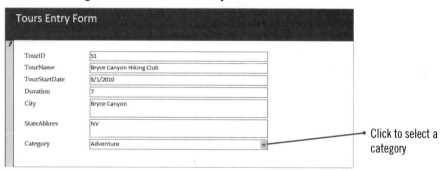

Click to select a category

TABLE C-1: Form controls

name	used to	bound	unbound
Label	Provide consistent descriptive text as you navigate from record to record; the label is the most common type of unbound control and can also be used as a hyperlink to another database object, external file, or Web page		x
Text box	Display, edit, or enter data for each record from an underlying record source; the text box is the most common type of bound control	x	
List box	Display a list of possible data entries	x	
Combo box	Display a list of possible data entries for a field, and provide a text box for an entry from the keyboard; combines the list box and text box controls	x	
Tab control	Create a three-dimensional aspect to a form		x
Check box	Display "yes" or "no" answers for a field; if the box is checked, it means "yes"	x	
Toggle button	Display "yes" or "no" answers for a field; if the button is pressed, it means "yes"	x	
Option button	Display a choice for a field	x	
Option group	Display and organize choices (usually presented as option buttons) for a field	x	
Bound object frame	Display data stored by an OLE (object linking and embedding) field, such as a picture	x	
Unbound object frame	Display a picture or clip art image that doesn't change from record to record		x
Line and Rectangle	Draw lines and rectangles on the form		x
Command button	Provide an easy way to initiate a command or run a macro		x

Using Form Layout View

Layout View, new to Access 2007, lets you make some design changes to the form while you are browsing the data. For example, you can add or delete a field to the form or change formatting characteristics such as fonts and colors. ▓▓▓▓ Mark Rock asks you to make several design changes to the Tours Entry Form. You can make these changes in Layout View.

STEPS

1. **Click the** TourID value, **click the** Ascending button 🔼 **on the Home tab, click the** View button arrow, **then click** Layout View

   In Layout View, you can move through the records, but you cannot enter or edit the data as you can in Form View.

2. **Click the** First record button ◀ **on the navigation bar to move to the first record, click the** Next record button ▶ **to move to the second record, click the** TourID label **to select it, then click** between the words Tour and ID and press [Spacebar]

   You often use Layout View to make minor design changes such as revising labels and changing formatting characteristics.

3. **Continue editing the labels to add spaces, as shown in Figure C-3**

   You also want to bold the first two labels, Tour ID and Tour Name, to make them more visible.

4. **Click the** Tour ID label, **click the** Bold button **B** **on the Format tab, click the** Tour Name label, **then click** **B**

   Often, you want to apply the same formatting enhancement to multiple controls. For example, you decide to narrow all of the text boxes. You select all the text boxes at the same time before applying the change.

5. **Click the** Tour ID text box **(it currently displays 2), then press and hold [Shift] while clicking each of the** other five text boxes and one combo box **in that column**

   With all seven controls selected, any change you make to one control is made to all.

6. **Drag the** right edge of the controls **to the left to make them approximately half as wide**

   Your Layout View for the Tours Entry Form should look like Figure C-4.

FIGURE C-3: Using Layout View to modify form labels

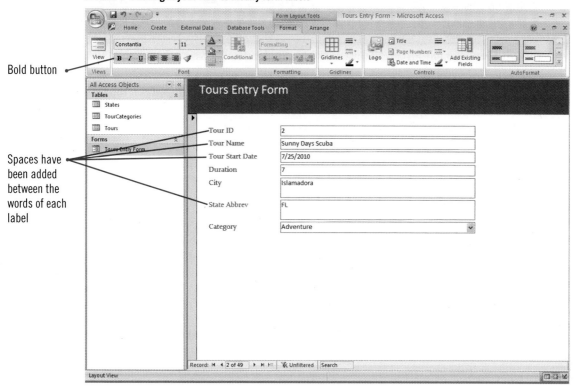

Bold button

Spaces have been added between the words of each label

FIGURE C-4: Final Layout View for the Tours Entry Form

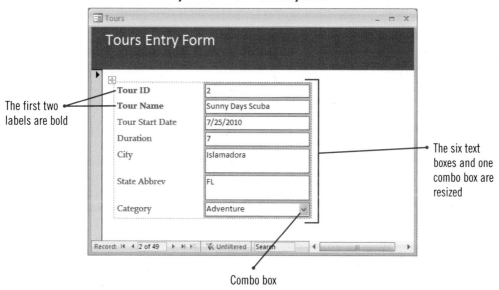

The first two labels are bold

The six text boxes and one combo box are resized

Combo box

Using Form Design View

Design View of a form is devoted to working with the detailed structure of the form. Unlike Form View and Layout View, Design View displays no data, but rather provides full access to all of a form's structural and design modifications. In fact, Design View is the only place where you can modify certain structural elements such as the Form Header and Footer sections. ▂▂▂▂ Mark Rock likes the design changes you've made so far, but asks that you add a title to the form that appears when it is printed. To do so, you add a title as a label in the Form Header section in Design View.

STEPS

QUICK TIP

Another way to open an object in Design View is to right-click it in the Navigation Pane, then click Design View on the shortcut menu.

1. **Click the View button arrow on the Home tab, then click Design View**

   In Design View, you can work with additional form sections such as the Form Header and Form Footer. The vertical and horizontal **rulers** help you position controls on the form. In Design View, you can add new controls to the form such as labels, combo boxes, and check boxes that are found on the Design tab of the Ribbon.

TROUBLE

If you do not see sizing handles on the Tours Entry Form label, click the label to select it.

2. **Click the Label button on the Design tab, click below the Tours Entry Form label in the Form Header, type Quest Specialty Travel, then press [Enter]**

   With the label in position, as shown in Figure C-5, you change the font color and size so it is more visible. **Sizing handles**, small squares that surround the label, identify which control is currently selected.

3. **With the Quest Specialty Travel label still selected, click the Font Color button arrow 🅰 ▾, then click the white box**

   The white font color is more readable, but the label would be easier to read if it were larger, so you decide to increase the font size.

4. **With the Quest Specialty Travel label still selected, click the Font Size list arrow [▾], click 18, then double-click a sizing handle to expand the label to automatically fit the entire entry**

   When you work with controls, the mouse pointer shape is very important. The shapes indicate whether dragging the mouse will select, move, or resize controls. Pointer shapes are summarized in Table C-2. With the Quest Specialty Travel label formatted appropriately, it's time to save your changes and review the form in Form View, where the users will work with it.

5. **Click the Save button 🖫 on the Quick Access toolbar, then click the Form View button ▦ on the Design tab**

   The updated Tours Entry Form is shown in Figure C-6.

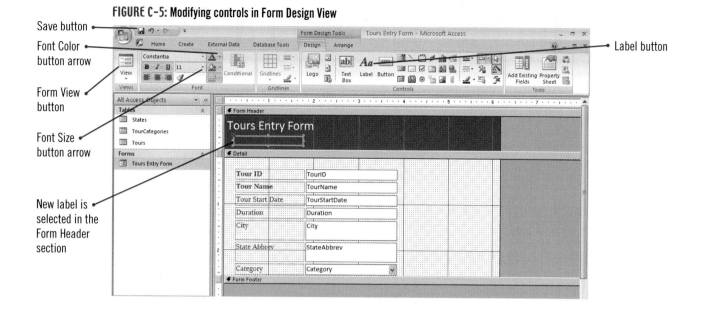

FIGURE C-5: Modifying controls in Form Design View

Save button
Font Color button arrow
Form View button
Font Size button arrow
Label button
New label is selected in the Form Header section

FIGURE C-6: Updated Tours Entry Form in Form View

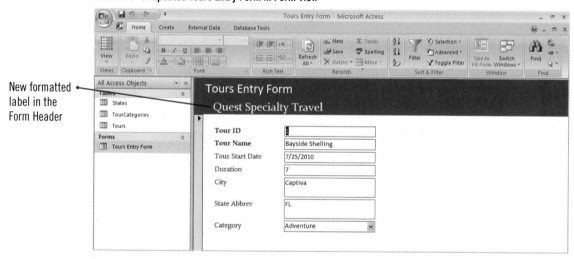

New formatted label in the Form Header

TABLE C-2: Mouse pointer shapes in Form Design View

shape	when does this shape appear?	action
�	When you point to any unselected control on the form (the default mouse pointer)	Single-clicking with this mouse pointer *selects* a control
✛	When you point to the edge of a selected control (but not when you are pointing to a sizing handle)	Dragging one control with this mouse pointer moves all selected controls
✛	When you point to the larger sizing handle in the upper-left corner of a selected control	Dragging the larger sizing handle moves *only the single control* where the pointer is currently positioned, not other controls that may also be selected
↕ ↔ ⤢ ⤡	When you point to any sizing handle (except the larger one in the upper-left corner)	Dragging with one of these mouse pointers *resizes* the control

Adding Fields to a Form

Adding and deleting fields to an existing form is a common activity. You can add or delete fields from a form in either Layout View or Design View using the Field List window. The **Field List** window lists the database tables and the fields they contain. To add a field to the form, drag it from the Field List to the desired location on the form. To delete a field on a form, click the field to select it, then press the [Delete] key. Deleting a field from a form does not delete it from the underlying table or have any effect on the data contained in the field. You can toggle the Field List on and off using the Add Existing Fields button. [icon] Mark Rock asks you to add the state name to the Tours Entry Form, as some of the users might not be familiar with all of the two-letter state abbreviations. You can use Layout View and the Field List window to accomplish this goal.

STEPS

1. **Click the Layout View button ▦ on the Home tab, click the Format tab if it is not already selected, then click the Add Existing Fields button**

   The Field List pane opens in Layout View, as shown in Figure C-7. Notice that the Field List is divided into an upper section, which shows the tables and fields within those tables that are used for the form, and the lower section, which shows related tables. The expand/collapse button to the left of the table names allows you to expand (show) the fields within the table or collapse (hide) them. The StateName field is in the States table in the lower section of the Field List.

2. **Click the expand button ⊞ to the left of the States table, then drag the StateName field to the position between the StateAbbrev and Category fields on the form**

   The form expands to accommodate the addition of the StateName label and text box by moving the Category label and text box down. When you add a new field to a form, two controls are generated: a label to describe the data that shows the field name, and a text box to display the contents of the field. With the field in place, you modify the label to be consistent with the other labels on the form.

3. **Click the StateName label to select it, click between the words and press [Spacebar] to modify the label to read State Name, then click to the right of Name: and press [Backspace] to delete the colon (:)**

   You also decide to delete the TourID field from the form. Because the TourID field has been defined as an AutoNumber field in the Tours table, it automatically increments as new tour records are entered and does not need to be displayed on this form.

4. **Click the text box that contains the TourID value, then press [Delete]**

   Deleting a field's text box automatically deletes its associated label control.

5. **Click the Save button ▦ on the Quick Access toolbar, then click the Form View button ▦ on the Design tab**

6. **Click the New (blank) record button ▸* in the navigation bar, then enter a new record in the updated form, as shown in Figure C-8**

   Note that after you enter MO in the StateAbbrev text box, the value in the StateName text box will automatically populate with the full state name, Missouri. Because the Tours table is related to the States table through the common State Abbrev field, the state name is automatically selected, or "pulled" out of the State table after you enter the state abbreviation into the Tour record.

FIGURE C-7: Adding controls in Form Layout View

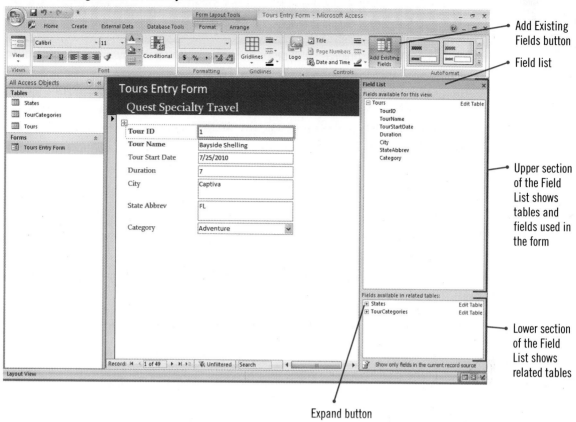

Add Existing Fields button

Field list

Upper section of the Field List shows tables and fields used in the form

Lower section of the Field List shows related tables

Expand button

FIGURE C-8: Updated Tours Entry Form in Form View

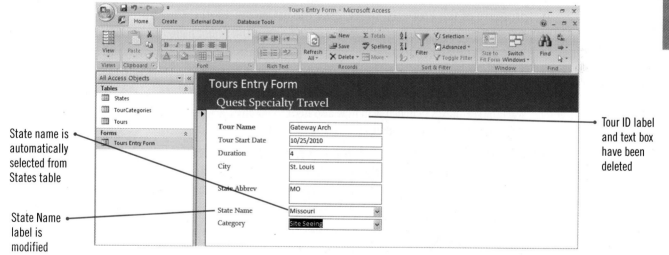

State name is automatically selected from States table

State Name label is modified

Tour ID label and text box have been deleted

Bound versus unbound controls

Controls are said to be either bound or unbound. **Bound controls** are controls that display values from a field such as text boxes and combo boxes. **Unbound controls** do not display data, but rather serve to describe data or enhance the appearance of the form. Labels are the most common type of unbound control, but other types include lines, images, tabs, and command buttons. Another way to distinguish bound from unbound controls is to observe the form as you move from record to record. Because bound controls display data, their contents change as you move through the records, displaying the entry in the field of the current record. Unbound controls such as labels and lines do not change as you move through the records in a form.

Modifying Form Controls

You have already modified one type of form control, the label, by using the formatting buttons on the Ribbon to change font size and color. Some control properties, however, can only be viewed and modified using the control's **Property Sheet**, a comprehensive listing of all **properties** (characteristics) for the selected control. One such property is the **Control Source property**, which determines field **binding** (the field to which a text box is connected). Because Quest offers more adventure tours than any other type of tour, you decide to modify the default value of the Category field to be "Adventure." You work with the control's Property Sheet to modify the default value.

STEPS

1. **Click the** View button arrow **on the Home tab, click** Design View**, click the** Design tab **on the Ribbon if it is not already selected, then click the** Property Sheet button

   The Property Sheet opens, showing you all of the properties for the selected item, which is currently the entire form. The Category field is bound to a **combo box**, which is a combination of a text box and a list of values commonly entered for that field.

2. **Click the** Category combo box**, click the** Data tab **in the Property Sheet, click the** Default Value box**, type** Adventure**, then press** [Enter]

   The Property Sheet should look like Figure C-9. Access often helps you with the rules, or syntax, of entering property values. In this case, it entered quotation marks around "Adventure" to indicate that the default entry is text. You can also use the Property Sheet window to modify the most important property of a text box, its Control Source property, to bind the text box to a field. In the Tours Entry Form, each text box and combo box is already bound to the field name shown in the control. To change this binding, use the Control Source property in the Property Sheet. In this case, you want to switch the order of the Duration and TourStartDate text boxes. You could either move the controls on the form or change their bindings.

QUICK TIP

If you know the field name, you can change a field's Control Source property by directly typing the field name into the text box on the form. You must know the exact field name to use this method.

3. **Click the** TourStartDate text box **to select it, click** TourStartDate **in the Control Source property of the Property Sheet, click the** list arrow**, then click** Duration

   At this point, you have two text boxes bound to the Duration field. Change the second one to bind it to the TourStartDate field.

TROUBLE

Be sure to modify the text boxes on the right, not the labels on the left. If the Expression Builder dialog box opens, click Cancel.

4. **Click the** second Duration text box **to select it, click** Duration **in the Control Source property of the Property Sheet, click the** list arrow**, then click** TourStartDate

   With the text boxes switched, you now also need to modify the descriptive labels on the left. The text displayed in a label is controlled by the Caption property.

5. **Click the** Tour Start Date label **to select it, click the** Format tab **in the Property Sheet, select** Tour Start Date **in the Caption property, type** Duration**, click the** Duration label **to select it, select** Duration **in the Caption property, type** Tour Start Date**, then press** [Enter]

   Don't be overwhelmed by the number of properties available for each control on the form or the number of ways to modify each property. Over time, you will learn about most of these properties, but at first you can make most property changes directly in Form or Layout View, rather than using the Property Sheet itself.

6. **Click the** Save button 🖫 **on the Quick Access toolbar, then click the** Form View button 🖼 **on the Design tab**

   The modified Tours Entry Form is shown in Figure C-10.

FIGURE C-9: Using the Property Sheet

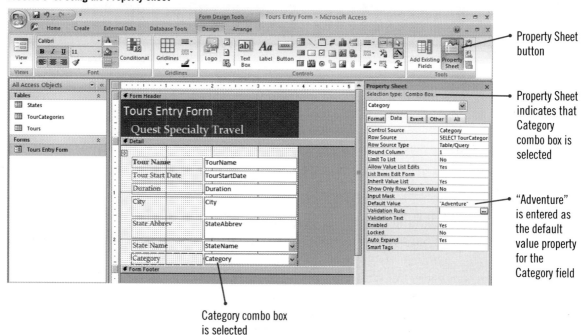

Property Sheet button

Property Sheet indicates that Category combo box is selected

"Adventure" is entered as the default value property for the Category field

Category combo box is selected

FIGURE C-10: Modified Tours Entry Form

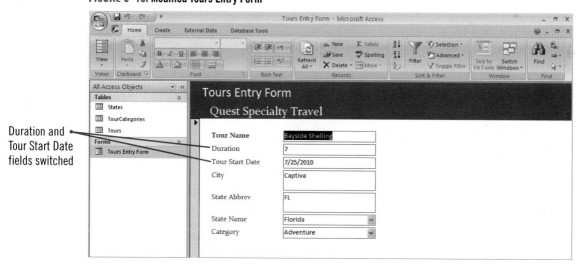

Duration and Tour Start Date fields switched

Creating Calculations

Text boxes are generally used to display data from underlying fields and are therefore *bound* to those fields. A text box control can also display a calculation. To create a calculation in a text box, you enter an **expression**, which consists of an equal sign and a combination of symbols that calculates a result. For example, you could use a text box to calculate sales tax or commission. Or, you could use a text box to combine, or concatenate, the values of two Text fields such as FirstName and LastName. Mark Rock asks you to add a text box to the Tours Entry Form to calculate the tour end date. You can add a text box in Form Design View to accomplish this.

STEPS

1. **Click the View button arrow on the Home tab, click Design View, click the Design tab if it is not already selected, then click the Property Sheet button to close the Property Sheet**
   To add the calculation to determine the tour end date (the tour start date plus the duration), start by adding a text box to the form.

2. **Click the Text Box button on the Design tab, then click to the right of the TourStartDate text box on the form**
   Adding a new text box automatically adds a new label to the left of the new text box. The form also widens to accommodate new controls. The number in the default caption of the label identifies how many controls you have previously added to the form. You don't need this label, so you can delete it.

> **TROUBLE**
> The number in your label might vary, based on previous work done to the form.

3. **Click the Text17 label to the left of the new text box, then press [Delete]**

> **QUICK TIP**
> You can resize controls one **pixel** (picture element) at a time by pressing [Shift] and an arrow key.

4. **Click the new text box to select it, click Unbound, type =[TourStartDate]+[Duration] , press [Enter] , then drag the middle-right sizing handle to the right far enough to view the entire expression, as shown in Figure C-11**
   All expressions entered into a text box start with an equal sign (=). When referencing a field name within an expression, [square brackets]—(not parentheses) and not {curly braces}—surround the field name. In an expression, you must type the field name exactly as it was created in Table Design View, but you do not need to match the capitalization.

> **TROUBLE**
> Move the Start and End Dates label, the TourStartDate text box, and the calculated text box as necessary so that they do not overlap.

5. **Click the Tour Start Date label on the left to select it, click the Tour Start Date text, edit it to read Start and End Dates, then press [Enter]**
   With the new calculation in place and the label modified, a final step before previewing the form is to align the top edges of the two text boxes that display dates.

6. **Click the TourStartDate text box, press [Shift] , click the expression text box to add it to the selection, click the Arrange tab on the Ribbon, then click the Align Top button**
   Now the top edges of the text boxes are perfectly aligned. The Control Alignment buttons on the Layout tab (To Grid, Left, Right, Top, and Bottom) control alignment of two or more controls with respect to one another. Table C-3 shows techniques on how to select more than one control at the same time. The alignment buttons on the Design tab ▤, ▤, and ▤ align text within the edges of the control itself.

7. **Click the Save button ▤ on the Quick Access toolbar, click the Home tab on the Ribbon, click the Form View button ▤, then press [Page Down] to navigate to the Fullington Family Reunion tour, viewing the calculated field as you move through the records**
   The updated Tours Entry Form with the tour date end calculation for the Fullington Family Reunion is shown in Figure C-12.

FIGURE C-11: Adding a text box to calculate a value

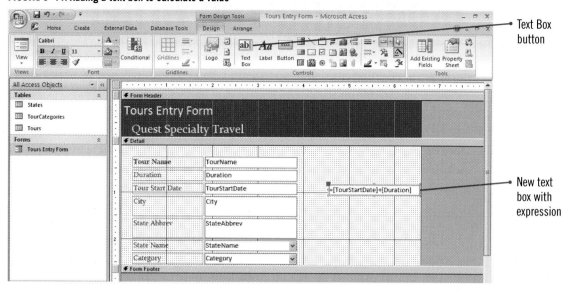

Text Box button

New text box with expression

FIGURE C-12: Displaying the results of a calculation in Form View

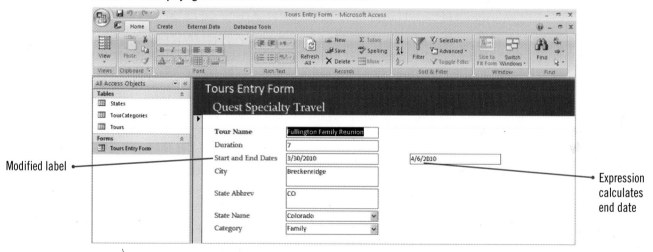

Modified label

Expression calculates end date

TABLE C-3: Selecting more than one control at a time

technique	description
Click, [Shift]+click	Click a control, then press and hold [Shift] while clicking other controls; each one is selected
Drag a selection box	Drag a selection box (an outline box you create by dragging the pointer in Form Design View); every control that is in or is touched by the edges of the box is selected
Click in the ruler	Click in either the horizontal or vertical ruler to select all controls that intersect the selection line
Drag in the ruler	Drag through either the horizontal or vertical ruler to select all controls that intersect the selection line as it is dragged through the ruler

Modifying Tab Order

After positioning all of the controls on the form, you should check the tab order and tab stops. A **tab stop** in Access refers to whether you can tab into a control when entering or editing data, in other words, whether the control can receive the focus. Recall that focus refers to which field would be edited if you started typing. **Tab order** is the order the focus moves as you press [Tab] in Form View. Controls that cannot be bound to fields such as labels and lines cannot have the focus in Form View because they are not used to enter or edit data. By default, all text boxes and combo boxes have a tab stop and are placed in the tab order. You plan to check the tab order of the Tours Entry Form, then change tab stops and tab order as necessary in Design View.

STEPS

1. **Click** Fullington **in the Tour Name text box, then press [Tab] eight times, watching the focus move through the bound controls of the form**

   Currently, focus moves through the first column to the tour end date text box and then to the next record. Because the tour end date text box is a calculated field, you don't want it to receive the focus, as this date is automatically calculated based on the tour start date plus the duration. To remove the tour end date text box from receiving the focus, you remove its tab stop. You also review the tab order before and after this change to observe the difference.

2. **Click the** View button arrow **on the Home tab, click** Design View, **click the** Arrange tab, **click the** Tab Order button, **then click** Detail **in the Section box**

   The Tab Order dialog box allows you to change the tab order of controls by dragging the **row selector**, the box to the left of the field name, up or down. Text17 in Figure C-13 is the name of the text box you added that contains the expression. It can appear anywhere in the list, depending on how you added the field.

3. **Click** Cancel, **click the** new text box with the expression **to select it, click the** Design tab, **then click the** Property Sheet button **to open the Property Sheet**

   The Other tab of the Property Sheet contains the properties you need to change the tab stop and tab order. The **Tab Stop** property determines whether the field accepts focus, and the **Tab Index** property indicates the tab order for the control on the form. Therefore, you can change the tab order property in either the Tab Order dialog box or in the Property Sheet.

4. **Click the** Other tab **in the Property Sheet, then double-click the** Tab Stop property **to change the value from Yes to** No

   While working in this control's Property Sheet, you also decide to rename the text box from Text17 to something more descriptive so that when you reference this control, it also has a meaningful name.

5. **Double-click** Text17 **in the Name property box, then type** TourEndDate

   Your form should look like Figure C-14. With the tab stop modified for the TourEndDate calculation, you're ready to test the new form.

6. **Click the** Form View button **on the Design tab**

7. **Press [Tab] seven times, noticing that you no longer tab into the TourEndDate text box**

8. **Save the Tours Entry Form**

FIGURE C-13: Tab Order dialog box

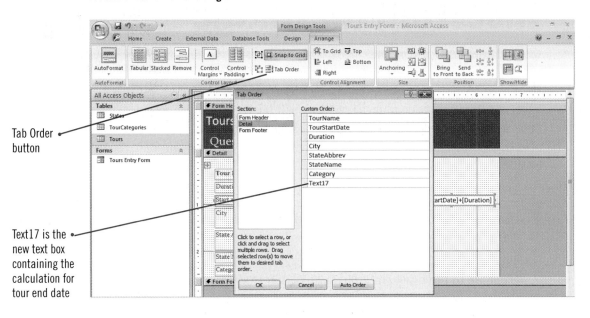

Tab Order button

Text17 is the new text box containing the calculation for tour end date

FIGURE C-14: Modifying tab properties for the selected field

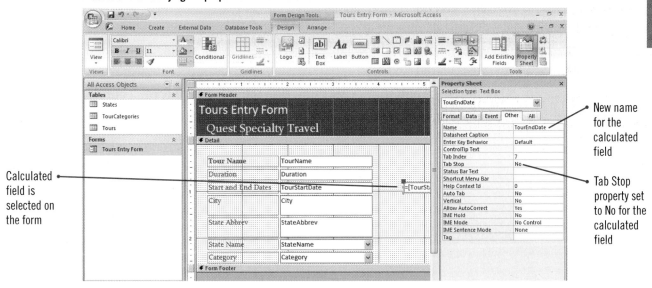

Calculated field is selected on the form

New name for the calculated field

Tab Stop property set to No for the calculated field

Inserting an Image

Graphic images, such as pictures, logos, or clip art, can add style and professionalism to a form. The form section in which you place the images is significant. For example, if you add a company logo to the Form Header section, the image appears at the top of the form in Form View as well as at the top of a printout. If you add the same image to the Detail section, it prints next to each record in a printout because the Detail section is printed for every record. Form sections are described in Table C-4. ▰▰▰▰ Mark Rock suggests that you add the Quest logo and a descriptive title to the top of the form. You plan to add the logo by inserting an unbound image control in the Form Header section.

STEPS

1. **Click the** View button arrow **on the Home tab, click** Design View, **click the** Design tab, **close the Property Sheet, then click the** Logo button

   The Insert Picture dialog box opens, prompting you for the location of the image.

2. **Navigate to the drive and folder where you store your Data Files, then double-click** QSTLogo.jpg

   The Quest logo image is added to the left side of the Form Header. You need to move it to the right so that the two labels are still clearly visible.

3. **With the Quest logo still selected, drag the** logo **to the right, so that the labels and logo in the Form Header section are clearly visible, then drag a** sizing handle **on the logo to display it clearly**

   The Quest logo is inserted into the Form Header in an image control, as shown in Figure C-15. Table C-5 summarizes other types of multimedia controls that you can add to a form. With the form completed, you open it in Form View to observe the changes.

4. **Click the** Save button 🖫 **on the Quick Access toolbar, then click the** Form View **button 🖾 on the Design tab**

   You decide to add one more record.

5. **Enter the new record shown in Figure C-16, using your name in the TourName field**

   Now print only this new record.

6. **Click the** Office button 🔘, **click** Print, **click the** Selected Record(s) option button, **then click** OK

7. **Close the** Tours Entry Form, **close the** Quest-C.accdb **database, then exit Access**

Using Forms

FIGURE C-15: Adding an image to the Form Header section

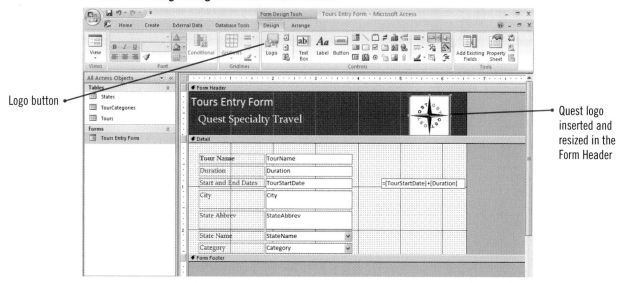

Logo button

Quest logo inserted and resized in the Form Header

FIGURE C-16: Final Tours Entry Form

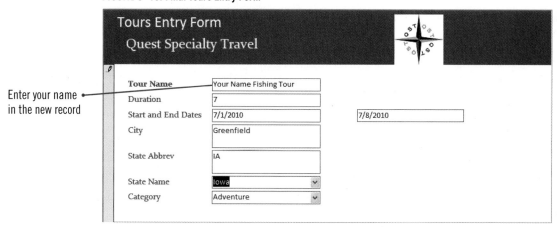

Enter your name in the new record

TABLE C-4: Form sections

section	description
Form Header	Controls placed in the Form Header section print only once at the top of the printout
Detail	Controls placed in the Detail section appear in Form View and print once for every record in the underlying table or query object
Form Footer	Controls placed in the Form Footer section print only once at the end of the printout

TABLE C-5: Multimedia controls

control	button	description
Image		Adds a single piece of clip art, a photo, or a logo to a form
Unbound object frame		Adds a sound clip, movie clip, document, or other type of unbound data (data that isn't stored in a table of the database) to a form
Bound object frame		Displays the contents of a field with an **OLE Object** (object linking and embedding) data type; an OLE Object field might contain pictures, sound clips, documents, or other data created by other software applications

Practice

▼ CONCEPTS REVIEW

Label each element of the Form View shown in Figure C-17.

FIGURE C-17

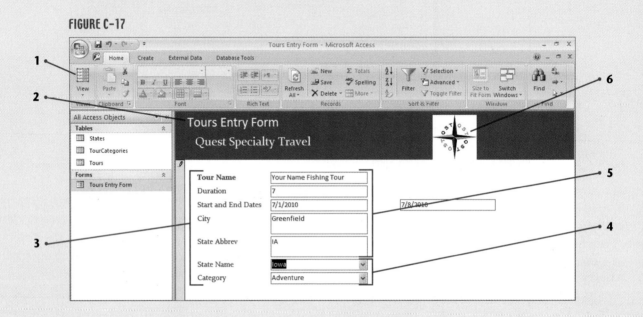

Match each term with the statement that best describes it.

7. **Bound control**

8. **Calculated control**

9. **Detail section**

10. **Form**

11. **Tab order**

12. **Form Footer section**

a. An Access database object that allows you to arrange the fields of a record in any layout and which is used to enter, edit, and delete records

b. The way the focus moves from one bound control to the next in Form View

c. Created by entering an expression in a text box

d. Controls placed here print once for every record in the underlying record source

e. Controls placed here print only once at the end of the printout

f. Used on a form to display data from a field

Select the best answer from the list of choices.

13. Every element on a form is called a(n):
    a. Property.
    b. Tool.
    c. Item.
    d. Control.

14. Which of the following is probably *not* a graphic image?
    a. Logo
    b. Calculation
    c. Clip art
    d. Picture

15. The most common bound control is the:
    a. Text box.
    b. List box.
    c. Combo box.
    d. Label.

16. The most common unbound control is the:
    a. Command button.
    b. Text box.
    c. Label.
    d. Combo box.

17. Which view *cannot* be used to view data?
    a. Layout
    b. Design
    c. Preview
    d. Datasheet

18. Which property helps you bind a text box to a field?
    a. Control Source
    b. Name
    c. Bindings
    d. Bound

19. When you enter a calculation in a text box, the first character is a(n):
    a. Equal sign, =
    b. Left parenthesis, (
    c. Left square bracket, [
    d. Asterisk, *

1. Create a form with the Form Wizard.

 a. Start Access and open the RealEstate-C.accdb database from the drive and folder where you store your Data Files. Enable content if prompted.

 b. Click the Create tab, then use the Form Wizard to create a form based on all of the fields in the Agents table. Use a Columnar layout and an Equity style. Title the form Agent Entry Form.

 c. Add a new record with your name. Note that the AgentNo field is an AutoNumber field and automatically increments as you enter your first and last names. Enter your school's telephone number for the AgentPhone field value, and 4 as the AgencyNo field value.

2. Use Layout View.

 a. Switch to Layout View.

 b. Modify each of the labels in Layout View by adding a space between the words in the labels.

 c. Modify the text color of the labels to be black.

 d. Modify the font size of each label to be 14 points.

 e. Save the form and view it in Form View.

3. Use Form Design View.

 a. Open the Agent Entry Form in Design View.

 b. Add a label with your name to the Form Header section, below the Agent Entry Form label.

 c. Format both labels so that the font size is 22, the font color is white, and they are bold.

 d. Resize the label with your name to display its complete text.

 e. Position the labels so that the left edges are aligned and all text is clearly visible.

 f. Save the form and view it in Form View.

4. Add fields to a form.

 a. Open the form in Layout View.

 b. Open the Field List window if it is not already displayed, then expand the field list for the Agencies table.

 c. Drag the AgencyName field directly under the AgencyNo field on the form.

 d. Delete the AgencyNo label and text box.

 e. Modify the AgencyName: label to add a space between the words and to delete the colon.

 f. Save the form and display it in Form View.

5. Modify form controls.

 a. Open the form in Design View, then open the Property Sheet.

 b. Change the order of the first three controls to AgencyName, AgentLast, and AgentFirst by using their Control Source properties.

 c. Change the text of the first three labels to Agency Name, Agent Last, and Agent First by using their Caption properties.

 d. Save the form, then view it in Form View.

6. Create calculations.

 a. Switch to Design View, then drag the top edge of the Form Footer down about 0.5 inch to make room for a new text box.

 b. Add a text box to the Form Footer section, then delete the accompanying label.

 c. Widen the text box to be almost as wide as the entire form, then enter the following expression into the text box, which will add the words "Agent information for" to the agent's first name, a space, and then the agent's last name.
 ="Agent information for "&[AgentFirst]&" "&[AgentLast]

 d. Save the form, then view it in Form View.

7. Modify tab order.

a. Switch to Form Design View, then open the Property Sheet.

b. Select the new text box with the expression, change the Name property to AgentInfo and change the Tab Stop property to No.

c. Save the form and view it in Form View. Tab through the form to make sure that the tab order is sequential. Use the Tab Order button on the Arrange tab in Form Design View to modify tab order, if necessary.

8. Insert an image.

a. Switch to Form Design or Layout View, then close the Property Sheet.

b. Add the house.jpg image to the right side of the Form Header, then resize the image and labels as necessary.

c. Save, then display the form in Form View. It should look similar to Figure C-18. Display the record with your name in it, then print only that record.

d. Close the Agent Entry Form, close the RealEstate-C.accdb database, then exit Access.

FIGURE C-18

▼ INDEPENDENT CHALLENGE 1

As the office manager of a veterinary association, you need to create a data entry form for new veterinarians.

a. Start Access, then open the Vet-C.accdb database from the drive and folder where you store your Data Files. Enable content if prompted.

b. Using the Form Wizard, create a form that includes all the fields in the Vets table, using the Columnar layout and Solstice style. Title the form Vet Entry Form.

c. Add a record with your own name. Note that the VetNo field is an AutoNumber field and automatically increments. Add yourself to ClinicNo 1.

d. In Form Design View, add a label with your name to the Form Header, below the Vet Entry Form label, in a font color and size that is easily visible.

e. Right-align the text within the four labels in the Detail section so that they are closer to the text boxes they describe. (*Hint:* Use the Align Text Right button on the Design tab.)

f. Add the dog.jpg image to the Form Header section. Move and resize the image so that the entire image as well as both labels are clearly visible.

g. Save the form, then display it in Form View. Print only the record that includes your name, as shown in Figure C-19.

h. Close the Vet Entry Form, close the Vet-C.accdb database, then exit Access.

FIGURE C-19

▼ INDEPENDENT CHALLENGE 2

You have built an Access database to track membership in a community service club. The database tracks member names and addresses as well as their status in the club, which moves from rank to rank as the members contribute increased hours of service to the community.

a. Start Access, then open the Membership-C.accdb database from the drive and folder where you store your Data Files. Enable content if prompted.

b. Using the Form Wizard, create a form based on all of the fields of the Members table and only the DuesOwed field in the Status table.

c. View the data by Members, use a Columnar layout and a Trek style, then title the form Membership Entry Form.

d. Enter a new record with your name and the address of your school. Give yourself a StatusNo entry of 1. In the DuesPaid field, enter 75. DuesOwed automatically displays 100 because that value is pulled from the Status table and is based on the entry in the StatusNo field, which links the Members table to the Status table.

e. In Design View, expand the Detail section down about 0.5 inches, then add a text box below DuesOwed with an expression that calculates the balance between DuesOwed and DuesPaid. Change the label for the calculated field to Balance.

f. Right-align all of the labels.

g. Set the Tab Stop property for the calculated field to No, and enter Balance for the Name property.

Advanced Challenge Exercise

- Drag the top edge of the Form Footer down about 0.5 inch to make more room for the form's Detail section.
- Open the field list, then drag the Status field from the Status table in the field list to below the Balance field in the form. Edit the label to delete the colon (:).
- Check the tab order to make sure that the fields receive focus in a logical order.
- If the calculated field or Status text boxes or labels aren't sized or aligned similarly to the rest of the controls on the form, return to Layout or Design View to resize and align them. (*Hint*: Use the Size to Widest button on the Arrange tab to size several selected controls to the widest selection. Use the Align Left and Align Right buttons on the Arrange tab to align the edges of several selected controls.)
- View the form in Form View. It should look like Figure C-20.

h. Save the form, find the record with your name, then print only that record.

i. Close the Membership Entry Form, then close the Membership-C.accdb database and exit Access.

FIGURE C-20

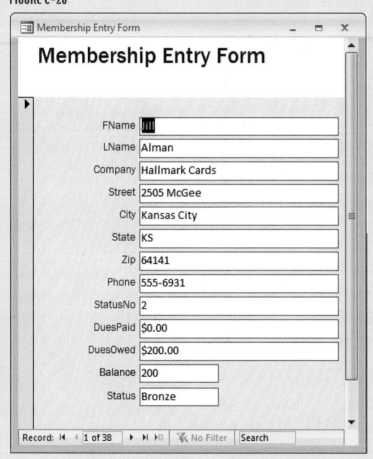

Access 2007

▼ INDEPENDENT CHALLENGE 3

You have built an Access database to organize the deposits at a recycling center. Various clubs regularly deposit recyclable material, which is measured in pounds when the deposits are made.

    a. Open the Recycle-C.accdb database from the drive and folder where you store your Data Files. Enable content if prompted.

    b. Using the Form Wizard, create a form based on all of the fields in the DepositList query. Use the Tabular layout and Urban style, then enter **Deposit List Form** as the title.

    c. Bold each label. Resize the labels and text boxes to be sure they are all wide enough to accommodate all entries in the fields and display the entire label at the top of each column.

    d. Modify the Centers_Name and Clubs_Name labels so they read Center Name and Club Name.

    e. Continue to work in Layout View to drag the bottom edge of the text boxes up, so that they are tall enough to accommodate all of the entries, as shown in Figure C-21, but do not waste any vertical space.

    f. In Form View, change any entry of Jaycees in the Clubs Name to your last name, then print the first page of the form.

Advanced Challenge Exercise

- Using Form View of the Deposit List Form, filter for all records with your name in the Clubs Name field.
- Using Form View of the Deposit List Form, sort the filtered records in ascending order on the Deposit Date field.
- Preview, then print the filtered and sorted records.

    g. Save and close the Deposit List Form, close the Recycle-C.accdb database, then exit Access.

FIGURE C-21

Deposit List Form				
Deposit Number	**Deposit Date**	**Weight**	**Center Name**	**Club Name**
1	1/5/2010	60	Trash Can	Boy Scouts #11
2	1/7/2010	90	Bachman Trash	Oak Hill Patriots
3	2/15/2010	50	Wilson County Landfill	Oak Hill Patriots
4	2/19/2010	30	Bachman Trash	Boy Scouts #11
5	2/22/2010	50	Johnson County Landfill	Girl Scouts #11
6	2/23/2010	100	Wilson County Landfill	Girl Scouts #11
7	3/1/2010	125	Bachman Trash	Lions
8	3/17/2010	60	Trash Can	Boy Scouts #11
9	4/5/2010	115	Trash Can	Lions
10	4/20/2010	105	Trash Can	Boy Scouts #11
11	5/20/2010	90	Bachman Trash	Boy Scouts #11
12	5/21/2010	80	Wilson County Landfill	Jaycees

Record: 1 of 100   No Filter   Search

▼ REAL LIFE INDEPENDENT CHALLENGE

One way you can use an Access database on your own is to record and track your experiences, such as places you've visited. Suppose that your passion for travel includes a dream to visit all 50 states. A database with information about all 50 states is provided with your Data Files, and you can use it to develop a form to help you enter more travel information.

This Independent Challenge requires an Internet connection.

a. Start Access and open the States-C.accdb database from the drive and folder where you store your Data Files. Enable content if prompted.

b. Open the States table datasheet to view the existing information on each state.

c. Add a field to the States table with the name Attractions and a data type of Memo.

d. Create a form based on all of the fields of the States table. Title the form State Entry Form.

e. Using any search engine such as www.google.com or www.yahoo.com, research two states that you'd like to visit.

f. Make entries in the Attractions field of each of your two selected states to store information about the attractions that you'd like to visit in each of those states.

g. Make any other formatting embellishments on the State Entry Form that you desire, then print the record for each of the two states that you updated with information in the Attractions field.

h. Save and close the State Entry Form, close the States-C.accdb database, then exit Access.

Open the **Basketball-C.accdb** database, then use the Form Wizard to create the form as shown in Figure C-22 based on all of the fields in the Games table. Use a Columnar layout and a Foundry style. The label in the Form Header, Basketball Scores, is a font size of 22. The Margin of Victory label and calculation were added in Form Design View. The margin of victory is calculated as the Home Score minus the Opponent Score. Also notice that the labels are right-aligned. Enter the record shown in Figure C-22, using your name as the name of the school. Print only that record.

FIGURE C-22

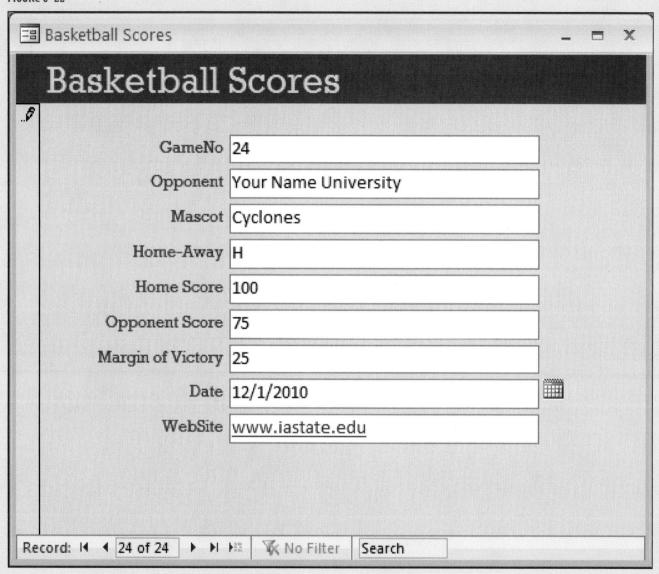

Using Reports

A **report** is an Access object used to create professional-looking printouts. Although you can print a datasheet or form, reports are the primary object you use to print database content because they provide many more data layout options. For example, a report might include formatting embellishments such as multiple fonts and colors, extra graphical elements such as clip art and lines, and multiple headers and footers. Reports are also very powerful data analysis tools. A report can calculate subtotals, averages, counts, or other statistics for groups of records. However, you cannot enter or edit data through a report. Mark Rock, a tour developer at Quest Specialty Travel, asks you to produce some reports to analyze data for Quest meetings.

OBJECTIVES

Preview a report

Use the Report Wizard

Use Report Design View

Use report sections

Add subtotals and counts

Resize and align controls

Format a report

Change page layout

Previewing a Report

When you want to communicate Access information at internal meetings or with customers, the report object helps you professionally format and summarize the data. Creating a report is similar to creating a form—you work with bound, unbound, and calculated controls in Report Design View just as you do in Form Design View. Reports, however, have more sections than forms. A **section** determines where and how often controls in that section print in the final report. Table D-1 shows more information on report sections. ▨▨▨▨▨ You and Mark Rock preview a completed report that illustrates many features of Access reports.

STEPS

1. **Start Access, open the Quest-D.accdb database, then enable content if prompted**

   The Quest-D database already contains two reports named Tour Descriptions and Tours By Category. You'll open the Tours By Category report in **Report View**, a view that maximizes the amount of data you can see on the screen.

TROUBLE
If you do not see any reports in the Navigation Pane, click the Reports button in the Navigation Pane.

2. **Double-click the Tours By Category report in the Navigation Pane, then double-click the title bar of the report to maximize it**

   The Tours By Category report appears in Report View, as shown in Figure D-1. The Tours By Category report shows all of the tours for each state within each category. In the Adventure category, four tours are in California and five tours are in Colorado.

3. **Double-click California in the State column, then attempt to type Oregon**

   Reports are **read-only** objects, meaning that they read and display data, but cannot be used to change (write to) data. Like forms, a report always displays the most up-to-date data that is stored in only one type of Access object, tables. Switching to **Print Preview** shows you how the report prints on a sheet of paper.

4. **Click the View button arrow on the Home tab, then click Print Preview**

   Print Preview shows you the report as it appears on a full sheet of paper, including margins. You can zoom in and out to increase or decrease the magnification of the image by clicking the report.

5. **Click the report once to view an entire sheet of paper, then click the Next Page button ▶ on the navigation bar to advance to the second page of the report**

   The second page of the Tours By Category report appears in Print Preview, as shown in Figure D-2. On the second page, you can clearly see how the records are grouped together by the value in the Category field, then by State, and finally sorted in ascending order on the Start Date field.

6. **Click the Close Print Preview button, then close the Tours By Category report**

Using Reports

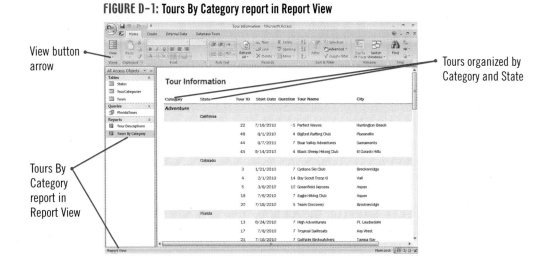

FIGURE D-1: Tours By Category report in Report View

View button arrow

Tours organized by Category and State

Tours By Category report in Report View

FIGURE D-2: Second page of the Tours By Category report in Print Preview

Report is grouped by Category, then State, and then sorted on Start Date

Close Print Preview button

Second page of the report

Next Page button

TABLE D-1: Report sections

section	where does this section print?	which controls are most commonly placed in this section?
Report Header	At the top of the first page of the report	Label controls containing the report title; can also include clip art, a logo image, or a line separating the title from the rest of the report
Page Header	At the top of every page (but below the Report Header on page one)	Text box controls containing a page number or date expression
Group Header	Before every group of records	Text box controls for the field by which the records are grouped
Detail	Once for every record	Text box controls for the rest of the fields in the recordset (the table or query upon which the report is built)
Group Footer	After every group of records	Text box controls containing calculated expressions, such as subtotals or counts, for the records in that group
Page Footer	At the bottom of every page	Text box controls containing a page number or date expression
Report Footer	At the end of the entire report	Text box controls containing expressions such as grand totals or counts that calculate a value for all of the records in the report

Using the Report Wizard

You can create reports in Access by using the **Report Wizard**, a tool that asks questions to guide you through the initial development of the report, similar to the Form Wizard. Your responses to the Report Wizard determine the record source, style, and layout of the report. The **record source** is the table or query that defines the fields and records displayed on the report. The Report Wizard also helps you sort, group, and analyze the records. ░░░░░ You plan to use the Report Wizard to create a report similar to the Tours By Category report. This time, however, you want to group the tours by state.

1. **Click the Create tab on the Ribbon, then click the Report Wizard button**

   The Report Wizard starts, prompting you to select the fields you want on the report. You can select fields from one or more tables or queries.

2. **Click the Tables/Queries list arrow, click Table: States, double-click the StateName field, click the Tables/Queries list arrow, click Table: Tours, click the Select All Fields button ☒, click StateAbbrev in the Selected Fields list, then click the Remove Field button ☒**

   By selecting the StateName field from the States table, and all fields from the Tours table except the StateAbbrev field, you have all of the fields you need for the report—including the full state name stored in the States table, instead of the two-letter state abbreviation used in the Tours table—as shown in Figure D-3.

3. **Click Next, then click by States if it is not already selected**

   Choosing "by States" groups the records together within each state. In addition to record-grouping options, the Report Wizard asks if you want to sort the records within each group. You can use the Report Wizard to specify up to four fields to sort in either ascending or descending order.

4. **Click Next, click Next again to add no grouping levels, click the first sort list arrow, click TourName, then click Next**

   The last questions in the wizard deal with report appearance and creating a report title.

5. **Click the Stepped option button, click the Portrait option button, click Next, click the Apex style, click Next, type Tours By State for the report title, click Finish, then maximize the Print Preview window**

   The Tours By State report opens in Print Preview, as shown in Figure D-4. The records are grouped by state, the first state being California, and then sorted in ascending order by the TourName field within each state.

6. **Scroll down to see the second grouping section on the report for the state of Colorado, click the Close Print Preview button on the Print Preview tab, then save and close the report**

   Closing Print Preview displays the report in either Report View, Layout View, or Design View, depending upon which view you used last.

FIGURE D-3: Selecting fields for a report using the Report Wizard

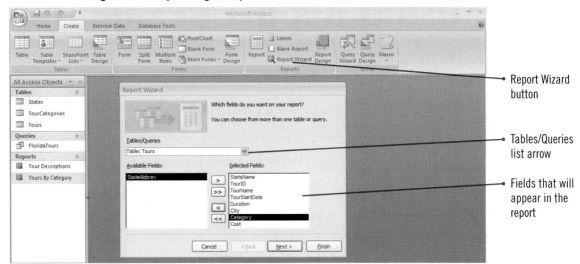

Report Wizard button

Tables/Queries list arrow

Fields that will appear in the report

FIGURE D-4: Tours By State report in Print Preview

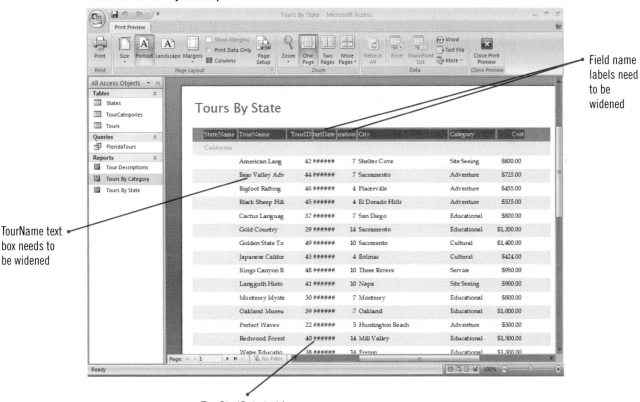

Field name labels need to be widened

TourName text box needs to be widened

TourStartDate text box needs to be widened

Using Report Design View

Like forms, reports have multiple views—including Report View, Layout View, Design View, and Print Preview—that you can use for various activities. Design View is the most complicated view because it allows you to make the most changes to the report. ░░░░░ Mark Rock asks you to create a new report that lists all of the tours from Florida in descending order by cost.

STEPS

1. **Click the** Create tab **on the Ribbon, click the** Report Design button, **then maximize the window**

   Design View opens with a blank report design surface. When building a report from scratch in Report Design View, the first task is to select the object (table or query) on which to base the report. The **Record Source** property of the report determines the object that the report is based on, which provides the fields and records displayed on the report.

2. **Click the** Property Sheet button **on the Design tab, click the** Data tab, **click the** Record Source list arrow, **then click** FloridaTours

   The FloridaTours query contains all of the fields in the Tours table as well as criteria to select only those records from the state of Florida. By choosing this query for the Record Source property, the report will display only Florida tours. Now add the fields from the FloridaTours query to the report.

3. **Click the** Add Existing Fields button **on the Design tab, click the** Show only fields in the current record source link **at the bottom of the Field List window, click** TourName, **press and hold** [Shift], **click the** Cost field, **release** [Shift], **then drag the** fields **to the middle of the Detail section**

   Report Design View should look similar to Figure D-5.

4. **Click the** View button arrow **on the Design tab, click** Print Preview, **then click the** Next Page button ▶ **on the navigation bar several times to page through the report**

   Right now, only one record prints per page, making the report very long. You can return to Design View and modify the report to make it more compact.

5. **Click the** Close Print Preview button **on the Print Preview tab to return to Design View, close the Field List window, then click a blank spot in the report**

   You can save space by arranging the fields across the page in a row (instead of in a vertical column), with the field labels appearing above the text boxes.

6. **Right-click the** TourName label, **click** Cut **on the shortcut menu, right-click the** Page Header section, **then click** Paste **on the shortcut menu**

   Moving the TourName label to the Page Header section means it prints once per page.

7. **Use the** Move pointer ✛ **to drag the** TourName text box **under the TourName label in the Detail section, then cut, paste, and move controls as shown in Figure D-6**

   All of the labels are now positioned in the Page Header section so that they appear only once per page, and all of the text box controls are positioned in the Detail section.

8. **Drag the** top edge of the Page Footer section **up to the bottom edge of the text boxes, click the** Save button 🖫 **on the Quick Access toolbar, type** Tours In Florida, **click OK, click the** View button arrow **on the Design tab, then click** Print Preview

   Because the Detail section prints once per record, eliminating blank space in this section removes extra blank space in the report overall.

9. **Click the** Close Print Preview button **on the Print Preview tab, then close the** Tours In Florida **report**

FIGURE D-5: Adding fields to Report Design View

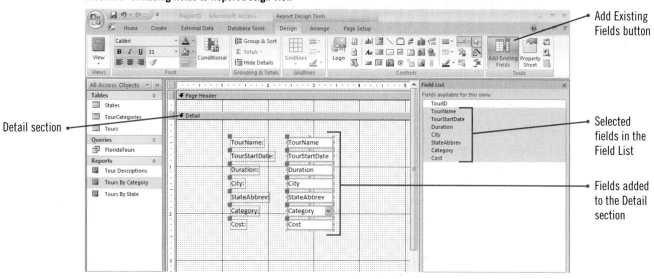

Detail section

Add Existing Fields button

Selected fields in the Field List

Fields added to the Detail section

FIGURE D-6: Redesigning a report in Report Design View

All of the labels are positioned in the Page Header section

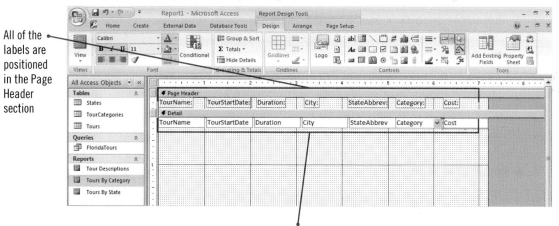

All of the text boxes are positioned in the Detail section

Using Report Sections

Grouping means to sort records in a particular order *plus* provide a header or footer section before or after each group. For example, if you group records by the State field, the grouping sections are called the State Header and State Footer. The State Header section appears once for each state in the report, immediately before the records in that state. The State Footer section also appears once for each state in the report, immediately after the records for that state. ▓▓▓ The records in the Tours By State report are currently grouped by state. Mark Rock asks you to further group the records by category within each state.

STEPS

1. **Right-click the Tours By State report in the Navigation Pane, click Design View, then maximize the report**

   To change sorting or grouping options for a report, you need to work in Report Design View.

2. **Click the Design tab on the Ribbon if it is not already selected, then click the Group & Sort button**

   The Group, Sort, and Total pane opens, as shown in Figure D-7. Currently, the records are grouped by the StateAbbreviation field and further sorted by the TourName field. To add the Category field as a grouping field within each state, you work with the Group, Sort, and Total pane.

3. **Click the Add a group button in the Group, Sort, and Total pane; click the select field list arrow if the field list window doesn't automatically appear; then click Category**

   A Category Header section appears on the report. In addition to grouping the records by both the StateAbbreviation and Category fields, you want to count the number of records in each group later so that, as an example, you can find out how many Adventure tours are in California. You open the Category Footer section and then add an expression to calculate this information to the Category Footer section.

4. **Click the More button on the Group on Category bar, click the without a footer section list arrow, then click with a footer section**

   A Category Footer section is added to the report. You want to group the records by state, then category, and then sort them within each category by TourName. To accomplish this you need to switch the order of the TourName and Category fields in the Group, Sort, and Total pane.

5. **With the Group on Category bar still selected, click the Move up button ⬆**

   With the Category Header and Footer sections open and in correct position, you're ready to add controls to those sections to further enhance the report. First, move the Category text box to the Category Header section so that it displays once per new category, rather than once for every record.

6. **Right-click the Category combo box in the Detail section, click Cut on the shortcut menu, right-click the Category Header section bar, then click Paste**

7. **Save the report, click the View button arrow, then click Print Preview**

   The Tours By State report should look similar to Figure D-8. Notice that the values in the Category field now appear once per category, before the records in each category are listed.

FIGURE D-7: Group, Sort, and Total pane

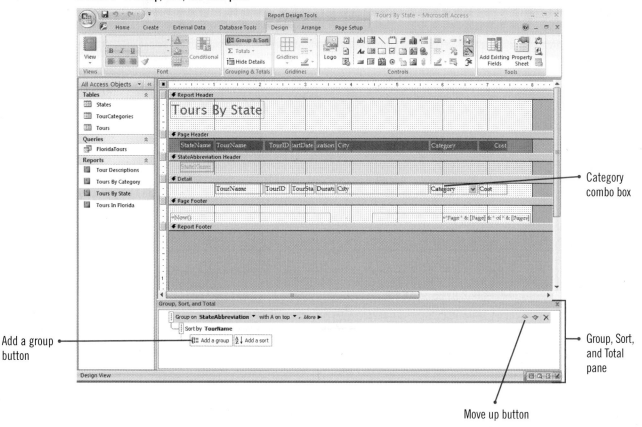

Add a group button

Category combo box

Group, Sort, and Total pane

Move up button

FIGURE D-8: Tours By State report with Category Header and Footer sections

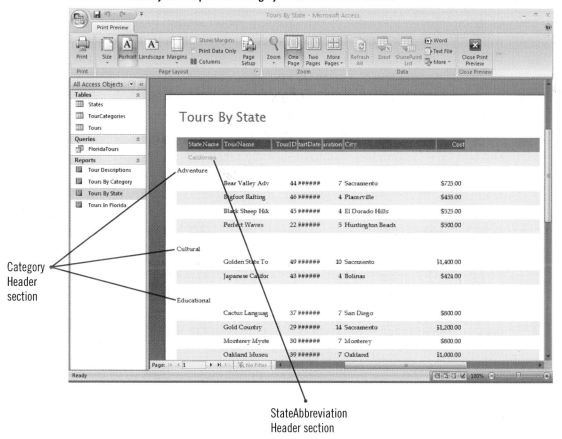

Category Header section

StateAbbreviation Header section

Adding Subtotals and Counts

In a report, you create a **calculation** by entering an expression into a text box. When a report is previewed or printed, the expression is evaluated and the resulting calculation is placed on the report. An **expression** is a combination of field names, operators (such as +, –, /, and *), and functions that result in a single value. A **function** is a built-in formula, such as Sum or Count, that helps you quickly create a calculation. Table D-2 lists examples of common expressions that use Access functions. Notice that every expression starts with an equal sign (=), and when it uses a function, the arguments for the function are placed in (parentheses). **Arguments** are the pieces of information that the function needs to create the final answer. When an argument is a field name, the field name must be surrounded by [square brackets]. 〰〰〰 Mark Rock asks you to add a calculation to the Tours By State report to count the number of records in each category within each state.

1. **Click the** Close Print Preview button **on the Print Preview tab to return to Report Design View**

    Now you can add two controls to the Category Footer section—a label and a text box—to describe and calculate the total count of records within each category within each state.

QUICK TIP

To add only a descriptive label to the report, use the Label button *Aa* on the Design tab.

2. **Click the** Text Box button abl **on the Design tab, then click in the** Category Footer **section below the City text box**

    Adding a new text box automatically adds a new label as well. First, you modify the label to identify the calculation you want to add to the text box, then you enter the appropriate expression to count the records in the text box.

TROUBLE

Depending on your activity in Report Design View, you may get a different number in the Text##: label. The number corresponds to the number of controls that have been added to this report.

3. **Click the new** Text19 label **to select the label, double-click the** Text19 **entry to select the text, type** Count of records, **then press [Enter]**

4. **Click the** Unbound text box **in the Category Footer section to select it, click** Unbound **within the text box, type** =Count([TourName]), **then press [Enter]**

    The Count function counts the values in the TourName field, as shown in Figure D-9. To add numeric values in a Number or Currency field, you use the Sum function, as in =Sum([Price]).

5. **Click the** Save button 💾 **on the Quick Access toolbar, click the** View button arrow, **then click** Print Preview

    The new label and calculation in the Category Footer section correctly identify how many records are in each category within each state. To calculate how many records are in each state, you can copy the controls from the Category Footer section to the StateAbbreviation Footer section. First, you need to open the StateAbbreviation Footer section.

6. **Click the** Close Print Preview button **on the Print Preview tab; click the** More button **for the StateAbbreviation group in the Group, Sort, and Total pane; click the** without a footer section list arrow; **then click** with a footer section

    With the State Footer section open in Report Design View, you can now add controls to this section.

7. **Right-click the** text box with the Count expression **in the Category Footer section, click** Copy **on the shortcut menu, right-click the** StateAbbreviation Footer, **click** Paste, **then press [→] enough times to position the controls in the StateAbbreviation Footer section directly below those in the Category Footer section**

TROUBLE

Click the Next Page button ▶ to view page 2 if the footer for the state of California doesn't appear at the bottom of page 1.

8. **Click** 💾, **click the** View button arrow, **click** Print Preview, **then scroll to the bottom of the first page to see the footer for the state of California**

    As shown in Figure D-10, 16 records were counted for the California group, but some of the data is not displayed correctly. You widen and align controls in the next lesson.

FIGURE D-9: Counting records in the Category Footer

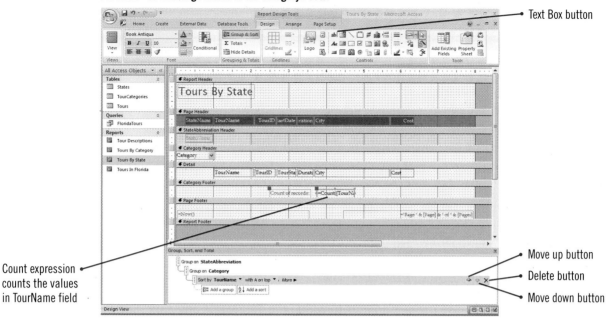

Text Box button

Count expression counts the values in TourName field

Move up button

Delete button

Move down button

FIGURE D-10: Previewing the new group footer calculations

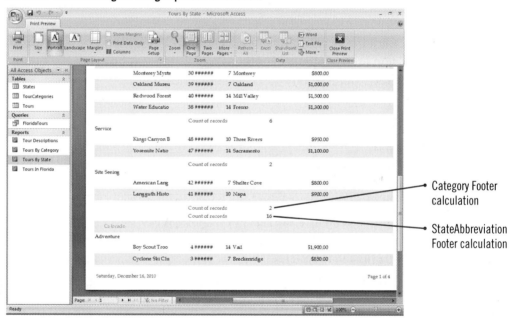

Category Footer calculation

StateAbbreviation Footer calculation

TABLE D-2: Sample Access expressions

sample expression	description
=Sum([Salary])	Uses the **Sum function** to add up the values in the Salary field
=[Price] * 1.05	Multiplies the Price field by 1.05 (adds 5% to the Price field)
=[Subtotal] + [Shipping]	Adds the value of the Subtotal field to the value of the Shipping field
=Avg([Freight])	Uses the **Avg function** to display an average of the values in the Freight field
=Date()	Uses the **Date function** to display the current date in the form of mm-dd-yy
="Page " &[Page]	Displays the word Page, a space, and the result of the [Page] field, an Access field that contains the current page number
=[FirstName]& " " &[LastName]	Displays the value of the FirstName and LastName fields in one control, separated by a space
=Left([ProductNumber],2)	Uses the **Left function** to display the first two characters in the ProductNumber field

Resizing and Aligning Controls

After you add information to the appropriate section of a report, you might also want to align the data on the report. Aligning controls in precise columns and rows makes the information easier to read. There are two different types of **alignment** commands. You can left-, right-, or center-align a control *within its own border* using the Align Text Left, ▤, Center ▤, and Align Text Right ▤ buttons on the Design tab. You can also align the edges of controls *with respect to one another* using the Align Left ▣, Align Right ▤, Align Top ▥, and Align Bottom ▥ buttons on the Arrange tab. ▨▨ You decide to widen and align several controls in the Category and State Footer sections to improve the readability of your report.

If you make a mistake, click the Undo button ↺ on the Quick Access toolbar.

1. **Click the** Close Print Preview button **on the Print Preview tab to return to Design View, then use the** ←→ **pointer to widen the** TourName **and** TourStartDate **fields as shown in Figure D-11**

   When you add, move, or resize controls, they often need to be realigned. You decide to align the expressions that count records directly under the Cost text box.

Be sure to select the text boxes that contain expressions, and not the labels.

2. **Click the** Cost text box, **press and hold [Shift], click the** text box with the Count expression **in the Category Footer as well as the** text box with the Count expression **in the** StateAbbreviation Footer, **then release [Shift]**

   With these three controls selected, you want to align the right edge of the controls *with respect to each other*.

3. **With the three controls still selected, click the** Arrange tab **on the Ribbon, then click the** Align Right button ▤

   With the expressions aligned, you want to move the labels in the footer sections below the City text box in the Detail section.

You can also click or drag through the horizontal or vertical rulers to select all controls that intersect with the selection line.

4. **Point to the upper-left sizing handle of the** Count of records label **in the Category Footer, drag it to the right to position it just to the left of the expression it describes, then repeat this action to move the label in the StateAbbreviation Footer closer to the expression it describes**

If the entire state name is not displayed, return to Report Design View and widen the StateName field in the StateAbbreviation Header section.

5. **Click the** Save button 🖫 **on the Quick Access toolbar, click the** Home tab, **click the** View button arrow, **click** Print Preview, **then scroll to the bottom of the first page to see the footer for the state of California as shown in Figure D-12**

6. **Click the** Close Print Preview button **on the Print Preview toolbar, then close the** Tours By State **report**

FIGURE D-11: Widening controls

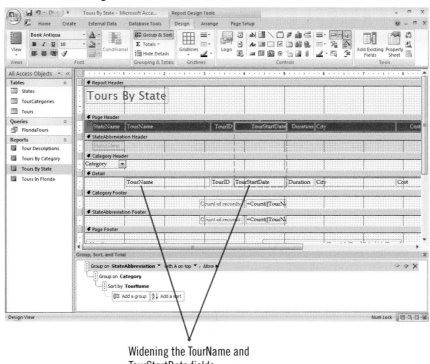

Widening the TourName and
TourStartDate fields

FIGURE D-12: Previewing the widened and aligned controls

TourName and
TourStartDate
fields are wide
enough to show
field values

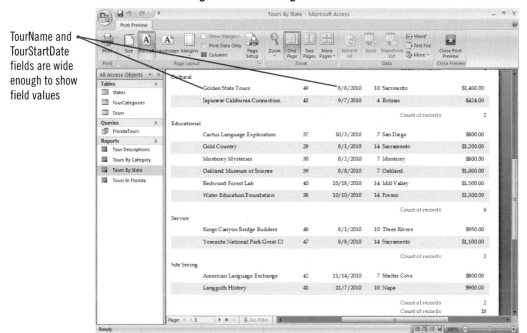

Precisely moving and resizing controls

You can move and resize controls using the mouse, but precise movements are often easier to accomplish using the keyboard. Pressing the arrow keys while holding [Ctrl] moves selected controls one **pixel** (picture element) at a time in the direction of the arrow. Pressing the arrow keys while holding [Shift] resizes selected controls one pixel at a time.

Formatting a Report

Formatting refers to enhancing the appearance of the information. Table D-3 lists several of the most popular formatting commands found on the Design tab. Although the Report Wizard automatically applies many formatting embellishments, you often want to improve the appearance of the report to fit your particular needs. ▓▓▓▓▓ When reviewing the Tour Descriptions report with Mark, you decide to format several sections to improve the appearance of the report.

STEPS

1. **Right-click the** Tour Descriptions report **in the Navigation Pane, click** Print Preview, **maximize the report, then click the** report **to zoom in**

   You decide to lighten the background of the Page Header section to the same shade as the Category Header section. You also want to darken the text color of the Page Header section to black. You can make some formatting changes in Layout View, which shows data, but Report Design View provides the best access to formatting and other design changes.

2. **Click the** Close Print Preview button **on the Print Preview toolbar, right-click the** Tour Descriptions report, **click** Design View, **maximize the report, then click the** Page Header section bar **to select it**

   The **Back Color** property determines the color of the section background. It is represented as a hexadecimal number (which uses both numbers 0–9 and letters A–F) in the Back Color property on the Format tab of the property sheet, or you can modify it using the Fill/Back Color button on the Ribbon. Avoid relying too heavily on color formatting. Background shades often become solid black boxes when printed on a black-and-white printer or fax machine.

QUICK TIP

When the color on the Fill/Back Color 🪣, Font Color 🅰, or Line Color ✎ button displays the color you want, click the button to apply that color.

3. **Click the** Fill/Back Color button arrow 🪣▾ **on the Design tab, then click** Aqua Blue 1 **(the second to last box in the second from the top row) in the Standard Colors list**

   With the background color of the Page Header section lightened, the white labels in the Page Header section are now very difficult to read.

4. **Click the** vertical ruler **to the left of the labels in the Page Header section to select them, click the** Font Color button arrow 🅰▾, **then click** Automatic

   The report in Design View should look like Figure D-13. You also want to add a label to the Report Footer section to identify yourself.

QUICK TIP

The quick keystroke for Undo is [Ctrl][Z]. The quick keystroke for Redo is [Ctrl][Y].

5. **Drag the** bottom edge **of the Report Footer down about 0.5 inches, click the** Label button 🅰🅰 **on the Design tab, click at the** 1-inch mark **in the Report Footer, then type** Created by your name

6. **Save, preview, then print the Tour Descriptions report**

   The final formatted Tour Descriptions report should look like Figure D-14.

7. **Close Print Preview, then close the** Tour Descriptions report

FIGURE D-13: Formatting a report

Font color of labels in Page Header section has been changed to automatic (black)

Label button

Bottom edge of the Report Footer section

Back color of Page Header section has been changed to Aqua Blue 1

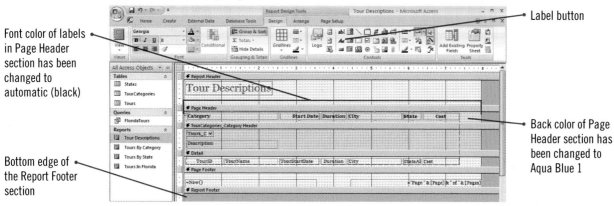

FIGURE D-14: Formatted Tour Descriptions report

Font color is automatic (black)

Back color is Aqua Blue 1

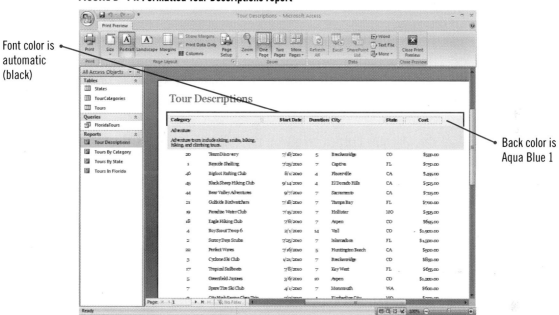

TABLE D-3: Useful formatting commands

button	button name	description
B	Bold	Toggles bold on or off for the selected control(s)
I	Italic	Toggles italics on or off for the selected control(s)
U	Underline	Toggles underline on or off for the selected control(s)
	Align Text Left	Left-aligns the selected control(s) within its own border
	Center	Centers the selected control(s) within its own border
	Align Text Right	Right-aligns the selected control(s) within its own border
	Fill/Back Color	Changes the background color of the selected control(s)
	Alternate Fill/Back Color	Changes the background color of alternate records in the selected section
A	Font Color	Changes the text color of the selected control(s)
	Line Color	Changes the border color of the selected control(s)
	Line Thickness	Changes the border style of the selected control(s)
	Line Type	Changes the special visual effect of the selected control(s)

Changing Page Layout

To fit all of the information on a report on a sheet of paper, you might need to change page layout options such as margins or page orientation. If a report contains many columns, for example, you might want to expand the print area by narrowing the margins. **Page orientation** refers to printing the report in either a **portrait** (8.5 inches wide by 11 inches tall) or **landscape** (11 inches wide by 8.5 inches tall) direction. Most of the page layout options such as paper size, paper orientation, and margins are accessible in Print Preview. ▓▓▓▓▓ Mark Rock asks you to print the Tours By State report. You preview it and make any page layout changes needed before printing it.

STEPS

1. **In the Navigation Pane, double-click the Tours By State report to open it in Report View, then maximize the report**

   In examining the report, you see that you need more horizontal space on the page to display all of the labels and field values properly. One way to provide more horizontal space on the report is to switch from portrait to landscape orientation.

2. **Click the View button arrow, click Print Preview, click the Landscape button on the Print Preview tab, then click the preview to zoom out to see an entire page**

   With the report in landscape orientation, you decide that wider margins would center the data to make it look better.

3. **Click the Margins button arrow on the Print Preview tab, then click Wide**

   Wide margins provide a one-inch top and bottom margin and at least a 0.75-inch left and right margin, as shown in Figure D-15.

4. **Close Print Preview, then switch to Report Design View**

   Carefully view the labels in the Page Header section, noting which ones need to be widened to display the entire entry.

5. **Use your moving, resizing, aligning, and previewing skills to make the report look like Figure D-16 in Print Preview**

   Your report doesn't have to look exactly like Figure D-16, but make sure that all of the labels are wide enough to display the text within them. To increase your productivity, use the [Shift] key to click and select more than one control at a time before you move, resize, or align them. You might need to move between Report Design View and Print Preview, making several adjustments before you are satisfied with your report.

QUICK TIP

If you want your name on the print-out, switch to Report Design View and add your name as a label to the Page Header section.

6. **When finished improving the layout, save it, click the Office button ⊙, click Print, click the From box, type 1, click the To box, type 1, then click OK**

7. **Close the Tours By State report, close the Quest-D.accdb database, then exit Access**

FIGURE D-15: Changing the margins of the Tours By State report

Landscape button

Margins button

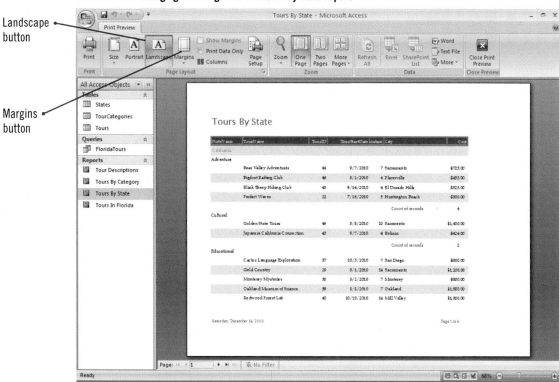

FIGURE D-16: Previewing the final Tours By State report

All labels and text boxes are widened to clearly see all values

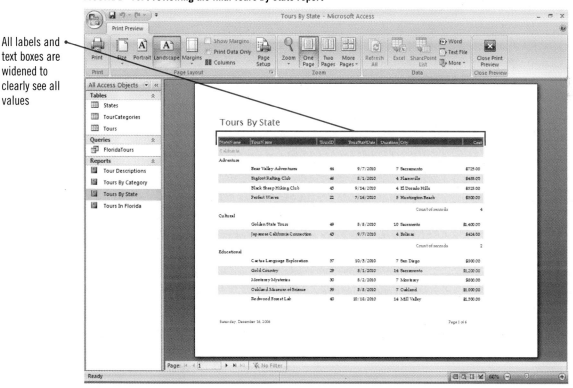

Practice

▼ CONCEPTS REVIEW

Label each element of the Report Design View window shown in Figure D-17.

FIGURE D-17

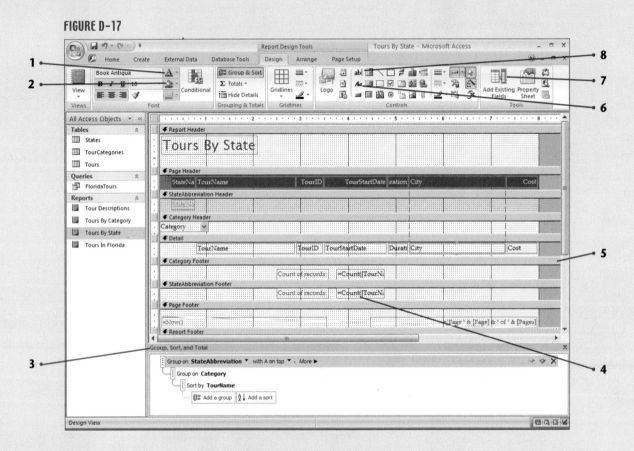

Match each term with the statement that best describes it.

9. **Expression**	a. Prints once for every record
10. **Section**	b. Used to identify which fields and records are passed to the report
11. **Detail section**	c. Enhancing the appearance of information displayed in the report
12. **Record Source property**	d. Sorting records *plus* providing a section
13. **Formatting**	e. Determines where a control appears on the report and how often it prints
14. **Grouping**	f. A combination of field names, operators, and functions that result in a single value before and after the group of records

Select the best answer from the list of choices.

15. You press and hold which key to select more than one control in Report Design View?
    a. [Alt]
    b. [Ctrl]
    c. [Shift]
    d. [Tab]

16. Which type of control is most commonly placed in the Detail section?
    a. Combo box
    b. Label
    c. List box
    d. Text box

17. Which type of control is most commonly placed in the Page Header section?
    a. Bound image
    b. Combo box
    c. Command button
    d. Label

18. A calculated expression is most often placed in which report section?
    a. Layout
    b. Formulas
    c. Group Footer
    d. Report Header

19. Which of the following would be the appropriate expression to count the number of records using the FirstName field?
    a. =Count([FirstName])
    b. =Count[FirstName]
    c. =Count(FirstName)
    d. =Count{FirstName}

20. To align the edges of several controls with respect to one another, you use the alignment commands on the:
    a. Formatting tab.
    b. Design tab.
    c. Print Preview ribbon.
    d. Arrange tab.

21. Which of the following *cannot* be changed in Print Preview?
    a. Font size
    b. Margins
    c. Paper orientation
    d. Paper size

▼ SKILLS REVIEW

1. Preview a report.

a. Start Access and open the RealEstate-D.accdb database from the drive and folder where you store your Data Files. Enable content if prompted.

b. Open the Agencies table and change A1 to your own last name in the A1 Realtors record, then close the Agencies table.

c. Open the Agency Listings report in Print Preview, then print the report.

d. On the printout, identify these sections:
- Report Header
- Page Header, Page Footer
- Detail

e. On the printout, identify the two Group Header sections as well as the field used to group the records. You can use Report Design View to confirm your answers, if needed.

f. Close the Agency Listings report.

2. Use the Report Wizard.

a. Use the Report Wizard to create a report based on the AgentLast and AgentPhone fields from the Agents table, and all the fields except the ListingNo, Pool, and AgentNo field from the Listings table.

b. View the data by Agents, then group it by the Type field. (*Hint:* Click Type, then click the > button.) Sort the records in descending order by the Asking field.

c. Use a Block layout and a Landscape orientation.

d. Use a Solstice style and title the report Agent Listings by Type.

e. Preview the first page of the new report. Notice which fields and field names are displayed completely and which need more space.

3. Use Report Design View.

a. In Report Design View, widen the AgentLast label in the Page Header section to begin at the left edge of the page. This automatically widens the AgentLast text box in the Detail section.

b. Modify the AgentLast label in the Page Header section to read Agent.

c. Narrow the Bath label and corresponding text box to be half as wide as they currently appear.

d. Switch between Print Preview and Report Design View to move and resize other labels in the Page Header section, so that the caption of each label is clearly visible. (*Hint:* If you make a mistake, click the Undo button.)

e. Preview the first page of the new report, switching between Report Design View and Print Preview to size all controls in a way that makes all data visible. Do not design the report to exceed the width of one landscape sheet of paper.

f. Save and close the Agent Listings by Type report, open the Agents table in Datasheet View, then enter your last name in place of Hughes in the Gordon Hughes record. Close the Agents table.

g. Reopen the Agent Listings by Type report, then print the first page.

4. Use report sections.

a. In Report Design View of the Agent Listings by Type report, expand the size of the Type Header section about 0.5 inches.

b. Cut the Type field from the Detail section, then paste it in the Type Header section.

c. Increase the font size of the Type text box to 14, then resize the control so that it is about three inches wide and tall enough for the larger text.

d. Open the Group, Sort, and Total pane by clicking the Group & Sort button, and remove the AgentNo grouping level by clicking the Delete button on the right edge of the Group on AgentNo bar.

e. Open a Group Footer section for the Type field.

f. Close the Group, Sort, and Total pane, then preview the report.

5. Add subtotals and counts.

    a. In Report Design View, add a text box control to the Type Footer section, just below the Asking text box in the Detail section. Change the label to read **Subtotal of Asking Price:** and enter the expression **=Sum([Asking])** in the text box.

    b. Copy and paste the text box that contains the =Sum([Asking]) expression, so that two copies of the text box and accompanying label appear in the Type Footer section.

    c. Modify the second text box to read **=Avg([Asking])**, and the second label to read **Average Asking Price:**.

    d. Open the Property Sheet for the =Avg([Asking]) expression, and on the Format tab, change the Format property to Currency and the Decimal Places property to 0.

    e. Open the Property Sheet for the =Sum([Asking]) expression, and on the Format tab, change the Format property to Currency and the Decimal Places property to 0.

    f. Open the Property Sheet for the Asking text box in the Detail section, and on the Format tab, change the Format property to Currency and the Decimal Places property to 0.

    g. Preview the report to view the new subtotals in the Type Footer section.

6. Resize and align controls.

    a. In Report Design View, right-align the right edges of the Asking, the =Sum([Asking]), and the =Avg([Asking]) text boxes.

    b. Right-align the text within the labels to the left of the expression text boxes in the Type Footer section, and also align the right edges of the labels with respect to one another.

    c. Save and preview the report.

7. Format a report.

    a. Switch to Report Design View and change the font of the label in the Report Header to Freestyle Script, 36 points.

    b. Double-click a sizing handle on the label in the Report Header to expand it to accommodate the entire label. Be sure to double-click a sizing handle of the label, not the label itself, which opens the property sheet.

    c. Change the background color of the Page Header section to Light Gray 1 on the Fill/Back Color palette.

    d. Click the Detail section bar, and apply a Light Gray 1 background color using the Alternate Fill/Back Color palette.

    e. Save and preview the report.

8. **Change page layout.**

    a. Use Report Design View to move the text box in the Page Footer section that calculates the page number to the left, so that no controls on the page extend beyond the 9-inch marker on the horizontal ruler.

    b. Drag the right edge of the report to the left, so that it is no wider than nine inches.

    c. Save the report, then switch to Print Preview. The first page of the report should look like Figure D-18. Your fonts and colors might look different.

    d. Change the margins to Normal (.75-inch top and bottom, .35-inch left and right), then print the first page of the report.

    e. Close and save the Agent Listings by Type report.

    f. Close the RealEstate-D.accdb database, then exit Access.

FIGURE D-18

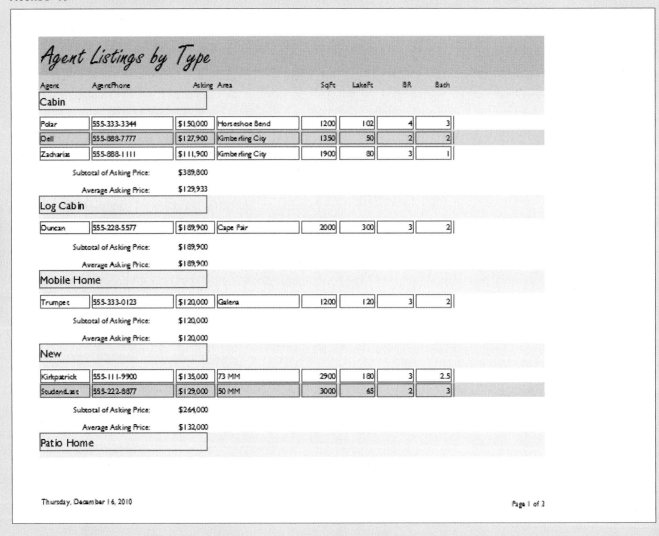

▼ INDEPENDENT CHALLENGE 1

As the office manager of a veterinary association, you need to create a report showing membership in the association.

a. Start Access, then open the **Vet-D.accdb** database from the drive and folder where you store your Data Files. Enable content if prompted.

b. Use the Report Wizard to create a report with the First and Last fields from the Vets table, and all the fields except for ClinicNo from the Clinics table.

c. View your data by Clinics, do not add any more grouping levels, and sort in ascending order by Last.

d. Use the Stepped layout, Portrait orientation, and Flow style.

e. Name the report **Clinic Membership**.

f. In Report Design View, expand the size of the Address1 label and text box to be about two inches wide. Be careful not to expand any controls beyond the 8-inch right edge of the report.

g. Open the Group, Sort, and Total pane, then add a ClinicNo Footer section.

h. Add a text box to the ClinicNo Footer section, just below the Last text box.

i. Modify the caption of the label to the left of the new text box in the ClinicNo Footer section to read **Count:**, move the label close to the text box, and right-align the text within the label.

j. Enter an expression in the new text box in the ClinicNo Footer section to count the values in the Last field, **=Count([Last])**, and left-align the values within the text box.

k. Add a label to the Report Header section to display your name. Format the label to be black text and 12 points, and expand the label to display your entire name as needed.

l. Using Report Design View to make modifications and Print Preview to review them, modify the controls as necessary to display all of the data clearly, then save the report and print the first page. Be careful not to expand beyond the 8-inch mark on the horizontal ruler in Report Design View, or the report will be wider than a sheet of paper in portrait orientation. The report should look similar to Figure D-19. Your fonts and colors might look different.

m. Close the Clinic Membership report, close the Vet-D.accdb database, then exit Access.

FIGURE D-19

ClinicName	Address1	City	State	Zip	Phone	Last	First
Veterinary Specialists	**17053 South 71 Highway**	**Belton**	**MO**	**64012**	**(816) 555-4000**		
						Garver	Mark
						Major	Mark
						Manheim	Thomas
						Stewart	Frank
						Count: 4	
Animal Haven	**204 East North Avenue**	**Belton**	**MO**	**64012**	**(816) 555-7900**		
						Chernoble	Selbert
						Kowalewski	Vicki
						Newhart	Darryl
						Sanderson	Anne
						Sellers	Kenneth
						Count: 5	

Clinic Membership — Student Name

▼ INDEPENDENT CHALLENGE 2

You have built an Access database to track membership in a community service club. The database tracks member names and addresses as well as their status in the club, which moves from rank to rank as the members contribute increased hours of service to the community.

a. Start Access and open the Membership-D.accdb database from the drive and folder where you store your Data Files. Enable content if prompted.

b. Open the Members table and change the name of Traci Kalvert to your name, then close the Members table.

c. Use the Report Wizard to create a report using the Status and DuesOwed fields from the Status table, and the FName, LName, and DuesPaid fields from the Members table.

d. View the data by Status. Do not add any more grouping fields, and sort the records in ascending order by LName.

e. Use an Outline layout, Portrait orientation, and Civic style.

f. Title the report Dues Analysis, then preview the report.

g. In Report Design View, use the Group, Sort, and Total pane to open the StatusNo Footer section.

h. Add a text box to the StatusNo Footer section, just below the DuesPaid text box. Change the label to Count: and the expression in the text box to =Count([DuesPaid]).

i. Expand the StatusNo Footer section as necessary, and add a second text box to the StatusNo Footer section, just below the first. Change the label to Subtotal: and the expression in the text box to =Sum([DuesPaid]).

j. Apply two property changes to the =Sum([DuesPaid]) text box. The Format property should be set to Currency and the Decimal Places property should be set to 2.

Advanced Challenge Exercise

- Expand the StatusNo Footer section as necessary, and add a third text box to the StatusNo Footer section, just below the second. Change the label to Dues Owed Less Dues Paid:.
- Change the text box expression to =Count([DuesPaid])*[DuesOwed]–Sum([DuesPaid]).
- Apply two property changes to the new text box. The Format property should be set to Currency and the Decimal Places property should be set to 2.

k. Align the right edges of the DuesPaid text box in the Detail section and all text boxes in the StatusNo Footer section. Also, right-align all data within these controls.

l. Align the right edges of the labels in the StatusNo Footer section.

m. Apply an Aqua Blue 1 Alternate Fill/Back color to the StatusNo Header, and a Dark Blue font color to the label in the Report Header.

n. Save, then preview the Dues Analysis report. The report should look similar to Figure D-20. Your fonts and colors might look different.

o. Print the first page of the Dues Analysis report, then close it.

p. Close the Membership-D.accdb database, then exit Access.

FIGURE D-20

Dues Analysis

Status	New	
DuesOwed	$100.00	

LName	FName	DuesPaid
Lang	Brad	$50.00
Larson	Kristen	$50.00
Martin	Jerry	$50.00
Parton	Jeanette	$0.00
Student	StudentFirst	$100.00
Yode	Kathy	$100.00

Count		6
Subtotal:		$350.00
Dues Owed Less Dues Paid:		$250.00

▼ INDEPENDENT CHALLENGE 3

You have built an Access database to organize the deposits at a recycling center. Various clubs regularly deposit recyclable material, which is measured in pounds when the deposits are made.

a. Start Access and open the **Recycle-D.accdb** database from the drive and folder where you store your Data Files. Enable content if prompted.

b. Open the Centers table, change Johnson in Johnson County Landfill to your own last name, then close the table.

c. Use the Report Wizard to create a report with the Name field from the Centers table, and the Deposit Date and Weight from the Deposits table.

d. View the data by Centers, do not add any more grouping levels, and sort the records in ascending order by Deposit Date.

e. Click the Summary Options button in the Report Wizard dialog box that also prompts for sort orders, and click the Sum check box for the Weight field.

f. Use a Stepped layout, a Portrait orientation, and a Flow style. Title the report **Deposit Totals**.

g. View the report in Print Preview, then switch to Report Design View and widen the Name text box. Switch between Print Preview and Report Design View to widen and then observe the Name text box. Widen it enough to make all trash center names visible.

h. In Report Design View, delete the long, top text box in the Center Number Footer section that starts with ="Summary.

i. Right-align the right edge of the Sum label in the Center Number Footer section with the Deposit Date text box in the Detail section.

j. Left-align the left edge of the =Sum([Weight]) text box in the Center Number Footer section with the Weight text box in the Detail section.

k. Save, preview, and then print the first page of the report. It should look similar to Figure D-21. Your fonts and colors might look different.

FIGURE D-21

Deposit Totals		
Name	Deposit Date	Weight
Trash Can		
	1/5/2010	60
	2/5/2010	80
	2/17/2010	50
	2/24/2010	80
	3/17/2010	60
	4/5/2010	115
	4/20/2010	105
	7/12/2010	85
	7/13/2010	95

Advanced Challenge Exercise

- In Report Design View, add Deposit Date as a grouping field, and move it above Deposit Date used as a sorting field.
- Open the Deposit Date Footer section, then change the by entire value option to by year.
- Add the Deposit Date field to the Deposit Date Header section, then change the Format property for the Deposit Date text box to **yyyy** (four-digit year format) and the Deposit Date label to **Year:**.
- Copy the controls from the Center Number Footer section, and paste them in the Deposit Date Footer section.
- Change the label in the Deposit Date Footer section from Sum to **Yearly Sum**. Change the label in the Center Number Footer section from Sum to **Center Sum**.
- Align the right edge of the label in the Deposit Date Footer section with the label in the Center Number Footer section, and the right edge of the text box in the Deposit Date Footer section with the right edge of the text box in the Center Number Footer section. Also, right-align the data within each of these four controls.
- Save and preview the report, then print the first page, a portion of which is shown in Figure D-22.

1. Close the Deposit Totals report, close the Recycle-D.accdb database, then exit Access.

FIGURE D-22

Deposit Totals

Name	Deposit Date	Weight
Trash Can		
Year: 2010		
	1/5/2010	60
	2/5/2010	80
	2/17/2010	50
	2/24/2010	80
	3/17/2010	60
	4/5/2010	115
	4/20/2010	105
	7/12/2010	85
	7/13/2010	95
	8/21/2010	205
	11/2/2010	80
	12/8/2010	80
	Yearly Sum	1095

▼ REAL LIFE INDEPENDENT CHALLENGE

One way you can use an Access database on your own is to help you study information. Suppose you have a passion for geography and want to memorize all 50 U.S. state capitals and mottos. A database with information about all 50 states is provided with your Data Files, and you can use it to develop a report to study this information.

a. Start Access and open the **States-D.accdb** database from the drive and folder where you store your Data Files. Enable content if prompted.

b. Use the Report Wizard to create a report that lists all four fields in the States table, sorted by StateName, using a Tabular layout, a Portrait orientation, and a None style. Title the report **State Trivia**.

c. Widen all controls as necessary to display all of the data in each field, but do not extend the report beyond the width of the paper in portrait orientation.

d. Add a line control to the top edge of the Detail section, just above the text boxes in the Detail section, to separate the states with a line, as shown in Figure D-23.

e. Add your name as a label to the Report Header section.

f. Save the report, then preview and print it.

g. Close the State Trivia report, close the States.accdb database, then exit Access.

FIGURE D-23

State Trivia

StateName	StateAbbrev	Capital	Motto
Alabama	AL	Montgomery	We dare to defend our rights
Alaska	AK	Juneau	North to the future
Arizona	AZ	Phoenix	God enriches
Arkansas	AR	Little Rock	The people rule
California	CA	Sacramento	I have found it
Colorado	CO	Denver	Nothing without Providence
Connecticut	CT	Hartford	He who transplanted sustains
Delaware	DE	Dover	Liberty and independence
Florida	FL	Tallahassee	In God we trust
Georgia	GA	Atlanta	Wisdom, justice, and moderation
Hawaii	HI	Honolulu	The life of the land is perpetuated in righteousness
Idaho	ID	Boise	Let it be perpetual
Illinois	IL	Springfield	State sovereignty, national union

Open the **Basketball-D.accdb** database from the drive and folder where you store your Data Files and enable content if prompted. First, enter your own name instead of Heidi Harmon in the Players table. Your goal is to create the report shown in Figure D-24. Choose the First, Last, HomeTown, and HomeState fields from the Players table and the FG, 3P, and FT fields from the Stats table. View the data by Players, do not add any more grouping levels, and do not add any more sorting levels. When the Report Wizard prompts you for sort orders, click the Summary Options button and choose Sum for the FG, 3P, and FT fields. Use a Block layout, a Portrait orientation, a Solstice style, and title the report **Points per Player**. In Report Design View, delete the long text box calculation in the PlayerNo Footer section, and move and align the =Sum([FG]), =Sum([3P]), and =Sum([FT]) calculations in the PlayerNo Footer directly under the text boxes that they sum in the Detail section. Cut the First, Last, HomeTown, and HomeState text boxes from the Detail section, then paste them in the PlayerNoHeader section. Make sure that no Alternate Fill/Back color is applied to the Detail section. (Select the Detail section, then choose No Color for the Alternate Fill/Back color.) Move and resize all controls as needed.

FIGURE D-24

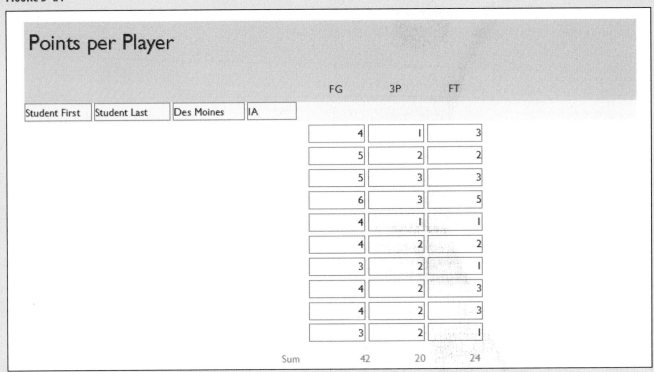

Integrating Word, Excel, and Access

As the administrator of a business, your typical to-do list might include creating sales charts, ordering new products, completing purchase orders, and producing proposals to obtain new contracts. You can use integration techniques in the Office suite to accomplish such diverse tasks quickly and easily. A good strategy is to build an Access database that contains customer and supplier names and addresses, inventory information, and sales records. You can then link data in the Access database to an Excel workbook and to a Word report. When you update information in the Access database, the linked information in the Excel and Word files also changes. Mary Lou Jacobs, general manager of Quest Specialty Travel Vancouver, one of the two Canadian QST branches, often needs to compile reports that include data from files created in Word, Excel, and Access. She asks you to help her integrate the information from these data sources into one document.

OBJECTIVES

Integrate data among Word, Excel, and Access

Import an Excel worksheet into Access

Copy a Word table to Access

Link an Access table to Excel and Word

Link an Access table to Word

Integrating Data Among Word, Excel, and Access

You can increase efficiency by integrating the information you create in Word, Excel, and Access so that it works together. For example, you can enter data into an Access database, make calculations using that data in Excel, and then create a report in Word that incorporates the Excel data and the Access table. You can also import data from an Excel spreadsheet into Access and copy a table created in Word into an Access table. ▰▰▰▰▰ Mary Lou Jacobs needs to create a database containing information about the tours that QST Vancouver runs. She then needs to include some of this information in a report that she creates in Word. Before you create this report, you decide to review some of the ways in which information can be shared among Access, Word, and Excel.

DETAILS

You can integrate Word, Excel, and Access by:

- **Importing an Excel worksheet into Access**

  You can enter data directly into an Access database table or you can import data from other sources such as an Excel workbook, another Access database, or even a text file. You use the Get External Data command in Access to import data from an outside source. Figure B-1 shows how data entered in an Excel file appears when imported into a new table in an Access database. During the import process, you can change the field names and even data types of selected fields.

- **Copying a Word table into Access**

  Sometimes you may create a table in Word that contains data you also wish to include in an Access database. To save time, you can copy the table from Word and paste it into a new Access table or into an existing Access table.

- **Linking an Access table to Excel and Word**

  You link an Access table to Excel and then to Word when you want the data in all three applications to always remain current. First, you use the Copy and Paste Special commands to copy an Access table and paste it into Excel as a link. You can then make calculations using Excel tools that are not available in Access. Any changes you make to the data in Access are also reflected in the linked Excel copy. However, you cannot change the structure of the linked Access table in Excel. For example, you cannot delete any of the columns or rows that contain copied text. The data used in the Excel calculations is linked to the source file in Access. When the data in Access is changed, the results of the formulas in Excel also change.

  Once you have made calculations based on the data in Excel, you can then copy the data from Excel and paste it as a link into Word. When you change the data in Access, the data in both the Excel and the Word files also changes. Figure B-2 shows a Word document that contains two tables. The top table is linked to both Excel and Access. The table was copied from Access and pasted as a link into Excel, additional calculations were made in Excel, and finally the table was copied to the Word report and pasted as a link.

- **Linking an Access table to Word**

  You can use the Copy and Paste Special commands to copy a table from Access and then paste it as a link into a Word document. You can then format the linked table attractively. In Figure B-2 the bottom table was copied from Access, pasted as a link in Word, and then reformatted.

FIGURE B-1: Excel data imported to an Access table

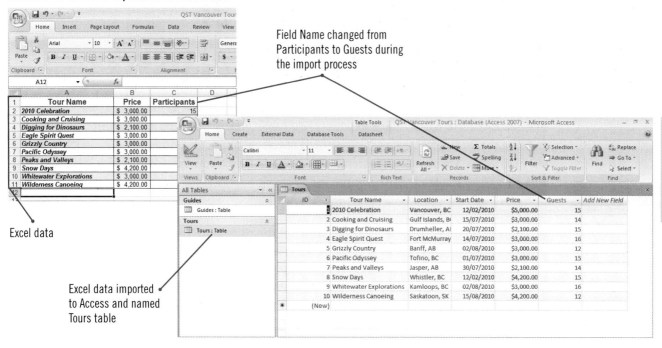

Field Name changed from Participants to Guests during the import process

Excel data

Excel data imported to Access and named Tours table

FIGURE B-2: Word report with links to Excel and Access

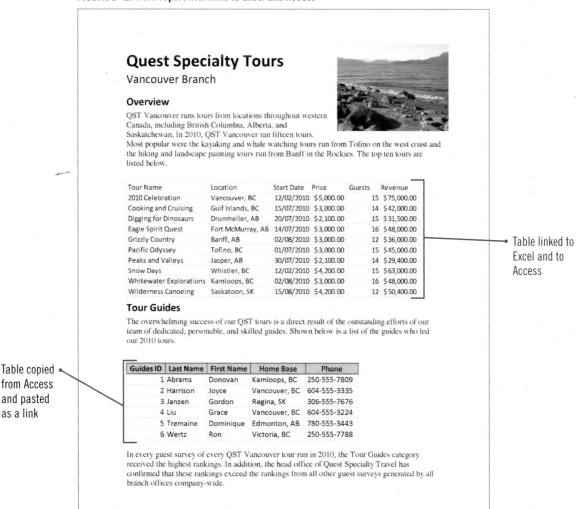

Table linked to Excel and to Access

Table copied from Access and pasted as a link

Importing an Excel Worksheet into Access

You can minimize typing time by importing data directly into a table in an Access database. You can then add additional records to the table and delete field names and data that you do not need. You can choose to import the Excel data directly into a new table or you can append the data to an existing table. Mary Lou Jacobs, the general manager of QST Vancouver, has already entered data about the top ten tours run from QST Vancouver in 2010. She asks you to import this table into a new Access database.

STEPS

1. **Start Excel, open the file** INT B-1.xlsx **from the drive and folder where you store your Data Files, then save it as** QST Vancouver Tour Prices

   The Excel workbook contains a list of the top ten tours offered by QST Vancouver in 2010. A workbook that you plan to export from Excel into Access should contain only the data that you want to appear in the Access table; you need to remove titles, subtitles, charts, and any other extraneous data.

2. **Move the mouse pointer to the left of row 1, click to select row 1, click the** right mouse button, **click** Delete, **then save and close the workbook**

3. **Start Access, click** Blank Database, **select the contents of the File Name text box, type** QST Vancouver Tours, **click the** Browse button ☞, **navigate to the drive and folder where you store your Data Files, click** OK, **then click** Create

   A new database opens in Access.

   > **TROUBLE**
   > Be sure to click the Excel button in the Import group, not the Export group.

4. **Click the** External Data tab, **click the** Excel button **in the Import group, click** Browse, **then navigate to the drive and folder where you stored the QST Vancouver Tour Prices file**

5. **Click** QST Vancouver Tour Prices, **then click** Open

   In the Get External Data – Excel Spreadsheet dialog box shown in Figure B-3, you can choose from among three options. When you select the first or second option, any change you make to the data in the Excel source file will not be made to the data imported to Access. If you choose the third option, the imported Excel source file is linked to the data imported to Access.

6. **Click** OK **to accept the default option and start the Import Spreadsheet Wizard, click** Next **to accept Sheet1 as the location for the imported data, then verify that the** First Row Contains Column Headings check box **is selected**

   The column headings in the Excel spreadsheet become field names in the Access table. A preview of the Access table appears, with the column names shown in gray.

   > **QUICK TIP**
   > In this dialog box, you can also change the data types of imported data.

7. **Click** Next, **click the** Participants column **to select it, then type** Guests **as shown in Figure B-4**

   The field name changes in the Field Name text box and the table preview.

8. **Click** Next, **click** Next **to let Access set the primary key, type** Tours **as the table name, click** Finish, **then click** Close

   Access creates a new table called Tours. You can work with this table in the same way you work with any table you create in Access.

9. **Double-click** Tours : Table **in the list of database objects, widen the Tour Name column, then compare the table to Figure B-5**

   The imported Excel data now appears in a new Access table. You chose to import the data without links, so any changes you make to the Excel source data will not be reflected in the Access table.

FIGURE B-3: Options in the Get External Data dialog box

The file path will be different on your computer

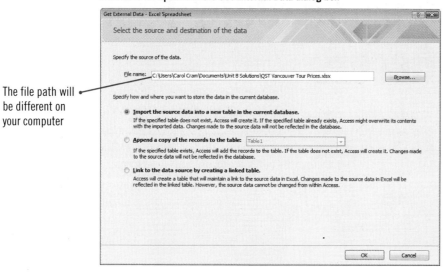

FIGURE B-4: Changing field names in an imported table

Guests entered in the Field Name box

Field name changes in column heading

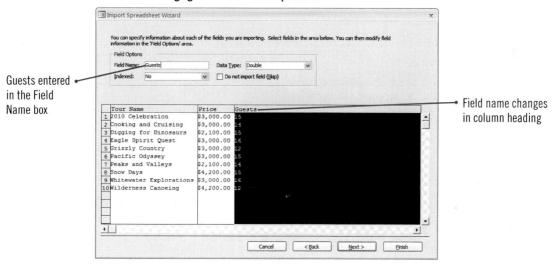

FIGURE B-5: Excel table imported to Access

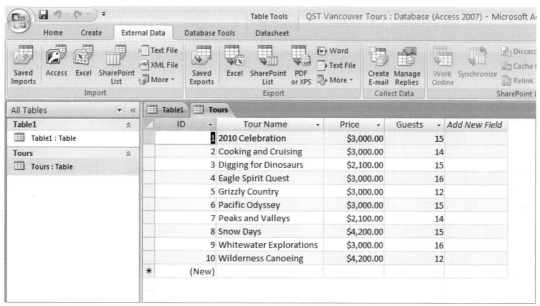

Copying a Word Table to Access

When you have entered data into a Word table and then want to make it part of a database, you can copy the table from Word and paste it into Access. The source Word table and the destination Access table are not linked, so any changes you make to one table do not affect the other table. If you want to paste a Word table into an Access table that already contains records, you need to make sure that the Word table contains the same number of records as the Access table. You can also paste a Word table into a new, blank Access table. ⬛⬛⬛⬛ Mary Lou has given you a Word document containing two tables that she wants you to incorporate into the Word report. One table contains tour information that was not included in the tour list you imported into Access from Excel, and the other table contains tour guide information.

STEPS

1. **Start Word, open the file INT B-2.docx from the drive and folder where you store your Data Files, then save it as QST Vancouver Tour Information**

   The top table contains tour information and the bottom table lists the tour guides who work from the QST Vancouver office.

2. **Move the mouse pointer over the upper-left corner of the top table, click the table select button ⊞, then click the Copy button ⬚ in the Clipboard group**

   You copied the selected table to the Clipboard.

3. **Click the Microsoft Access program button on the taskbar, then click Add New Field in the Tours table as shown in Figure B-6**

   The first blank column is selected. You want to insert the data from the Word table into the Tours database table. When you add data from one table to an existing table, you need to make sure that the number of records is the same in both tables.

4. **Click the Home tab, click the Paste button, then click Yes**

   Ten records are pasted into the Tours table in Access. You do not need the names of the tours to appear twice in the database table. When you copy data from another source and paste it into an Access table, you can delete fields and records in the same way you can in Access.

5. **Click anywhere in the table, right-click Tour Name1, click Delete Column, then click Yes**

   The table would be easier to read if the Location and Start Date fields appeared before the Price field.

6. **Click the View button to switch to Design view, select the last two rows (Location and Start Date), then drag them above the Price row as shown in Figure B-7**

7. **Close the Tours table, then click Yes to save it**

   A blank table called Table1 : Table appears in Datasheet view. You can copy a table directly from Word into a new blank table in Access.

8. **Switch to Word, select the table containing the list of tour guides, click the Copy button ⬚ in the Clipboard group, switch to Access, click the Paste button, then click Yes**

   The six records are pasted into a new Access table.

9. **Double-click ID, type Guides ID as shown in Figure B-8, press [Enter], close the table, click Yes, type Guides, click OK, then switch to Word and close the QST Vancouver Tour Information file**

   You created a new table using data imported from a Word table, and named it Guides.

FIGURE B-6: Selecting the location for copied data

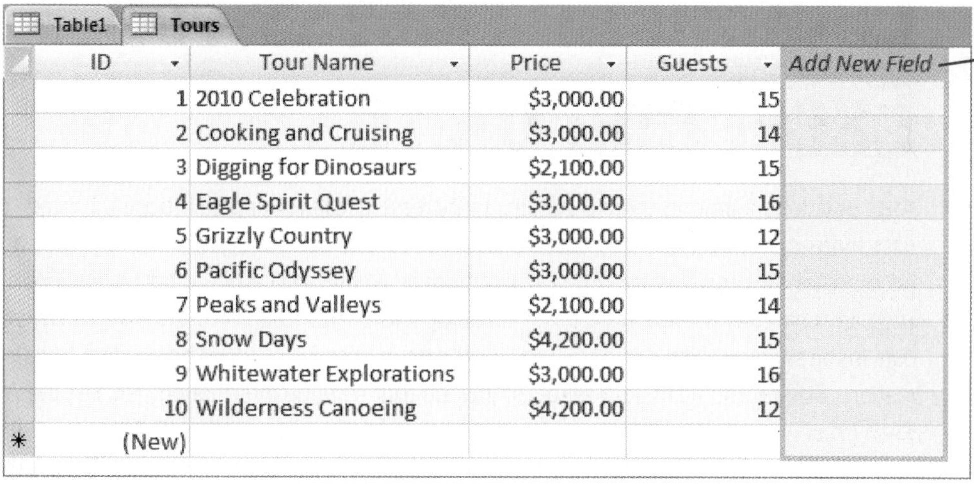

ID	Tour Name	Price	Guests	Add New Field
1	2010 Celebration	$3,000.00	15	
2	Cooking and Cruising	$3,000.00	14	
3	Digging for Dinosaurs	$2,100.00	15	
4	Eagle Spirit Quest	$3,000.00	16	
5	Grizzly Country	$3,000.00	12	
6	Pacific Odyssey	$3,000.00	15	
7	Peaks and Valleys	$2,100.00	14	
8	Snow Days	$4,200.00	15	
9	Whitewater Explorations	$3,000.00	16	
10	Wilderness Canoeing	$4,200.00	12	
*	(New)			

Add New Field selected

FIGURE B-7: Repositioning fields in Design view

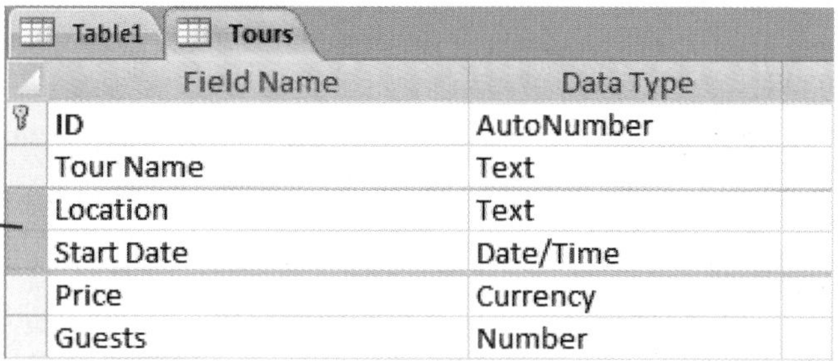

Field Name	Data Type
ID	AutoNumber
Tour Name	Text
Location	Text
Start Date	Date/Time
Price	Currency
Guests	Number

Location and Start Date moved above Price

FIGURE B-8: Renaming the ID field

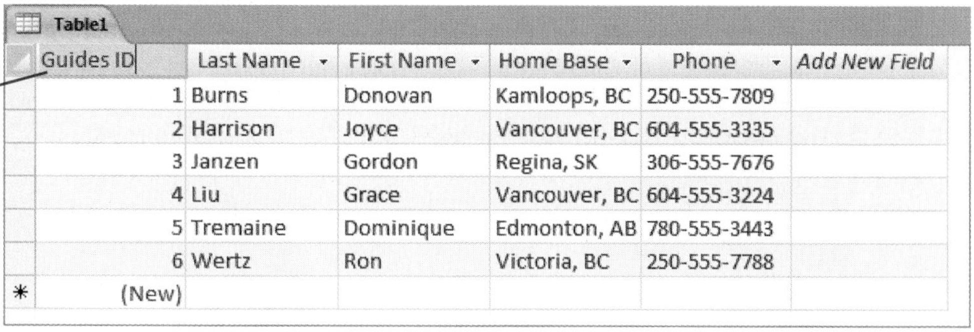

Guides ID	Last Name	First Name	Home Base	Phone	Add New Field
1	Burns	Donovan	Kamloops, BC	250-555-7809	
2	Harrison	Joyce	Vancouver, BC	604-555-3335	
3	Janzen	Gordon	Regina, SK	306-555-7676	
4	Liu	Grace	Vancouver, BC	604-555-3224	
5	Tremaine	Dominique	Edmonton, AB	780-555-3443	
6	Wertz	Ron	Victoria, BC	250-555-7788	
*	(New)				

Guides ID entered

Linking an Access Table to Excel and Word

You can link data among three programs to increase efficiency and to reduce the need to enter the same data more than once. You can use the Copy and Paste Special commands to create a link between an Access database object and an Excel destination file where you can perform calculations and create charts. You can then copy the Excel data, calculations, and charts to a Word document. When you change the data in the source Access database, the linked data in both Excel and Word update to reflect the new information. ▰▰▰▰ You want your report to include tour revenue information. You link the Access Tours table to an Excel worksheet, calculate the tour revenue using Excel tools, then link the calculation results to the tour report in Word. When you change the price of a tour in Access, the price will update in the table you copied to Excel and the table you copied to Word.

STEPS

1. **Switch to Access, click the Tours table in the list of database objects if necessary, then click the Copy button 🖺 in the Clipboard group**

2. **Create a new workbook in Excel, click the Paste button list arrow, then click Paste Link**

   The Tours table appears in Excel. You cannot delete any of the rows or columns in the pasted data in Excel because it is linked to the Access source table. However, you can modify cell formatting and you can perform calculations based on the pasted data.

3. **Adjust the widths of columns B and C so all the data is visible**

   In the copied table, the dates appear in code form and need to be assigned a number format so they are meaningful.

4. **Select the range D2:D11, click the Number Format list arrow, then select Short Date**

5. **Click cell G1, type Revenue, press [Enter], type the formula =E2*F2, press [Enter], then copy the formula to the range G3:G11**

6. **With the range G2:G11 still selected, press and hold [Ctrl], select the range E2:E11, release [Ctrl], click the Accounting Number Format button $, click a blank cell, then save the workbook as QST Vancouver Tour Revenue**

   The values in columns E and G are formatted in the Accounting format as shown in Figure B-9.

7. **Select the range B1:G11, click the Copy button 🖺 in the Clipboard group, switch to Word, open the file INT B-3.docx from the drive and folder where you store your Data Files, then save it as QST Vancouver Tour Report**

   The report contains information about the tours run from QST Vancouver in 2010. Placeholders show where you will paste two tables.

8. **Select the text TOURS TABLE, click the Paste button list arrow, then click Paste Special**

9. **Click the Paste link option button, click Microsoft Office Excel Worksheet Object, click OK, press [Enter] if necessary to add a space under the pasted table, then save the document**

   The table appears as shown in Figure B-10. This table is linked to the table you copied from Excel, which in turn is linked to the table you copied from Access. Table B-1 describes the differences between the three Paste options you have used in these lessons.

FIGURE B-9: Copied data formatted in Excel

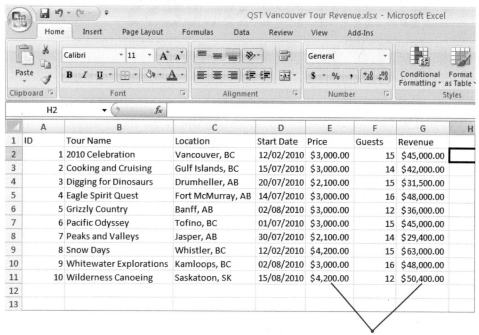

Accounting Number Format

FIGURE B-10: Excel data pasted in Word

Linked table

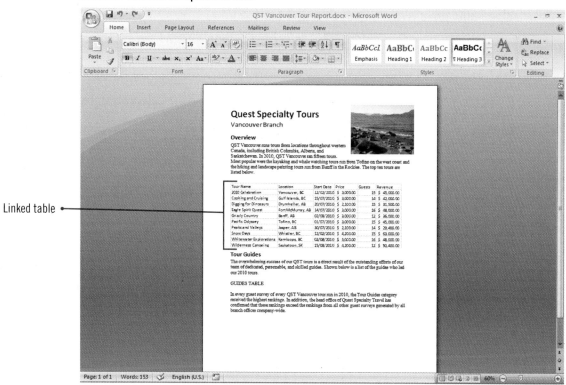

TABLE B-1: Paste Options

command	location	use to
Paste	Paste button in Word and Excel	Paste an object without creating a link. The exception is a chart. When you copy a chart from Excel and paste it into Word, the chart is, by default, linked to the source file in Excel
Paste Special	Paste button list in Word and Excel	Paste an object when you want to create a link or you want to select from a variety of formatting options for the pasted object, whether linked or not
Paste Link	Paste button list in Excel	Paste an object such as a copied table from Access into Excel as a link

Linking an Access Table to Word

If you don't need to use Excel to make calculations based on Access data, you can copy an Access table and paste it directly into Word as a link. When you update the source Access table, the linked data is also updated in Word. You can also use Word tools to modify the formatting of the pasted table so that the table is attractive and communicates the data clearly. Table B-2 summarizes the integration tasks you performed in this unit. ▓▓▓▓▓ The Word report needs to contain a list of the tour guides. You copy the Guides table from Access and then paste it into Word as a link. You then test the links you have created among Access, Word, and Excel by updating data in Access.

STEPS

1. **Switch to Access, click the Guides table in the list of database objects, click the Copy button 📋 in the Clipboard group, then switch to Word**

2. **Select the text GUIDES TABLE below paragraph 2, click the Paste button list arrow, click Paste Special, click the Paste link option button, click Formatted Text (RTF), then click OK**
   The Guides table is pasted as formatted text in Word. You decide to test the links you created.

3. **Switch to Access, open the Tours table, select $3,000.00 in record 1 (2010 Celebration), type 5000, press [Enter], then close the table**

4. **Open the Guides table, select Burns in record 1, type Abrams, press [Enter], then close the table**
   When you modify data in Access, the data in the linked Excel and Word files also changes.

5. **Switch to Excel, verify that the total revenue from the 2010 Celebration tour is now $75,000.00, then save the workbook**

6. **Switch to Word, right-click the Tours table, click Update Link, then verify that the 2010 Celebration tour revenue is now $75,000 as shown in the completed report in Figure B-11**

7. **Double-click any word outside the Tours table to exit the table, right-click the Guides table, then click Update Field**

8. **Select the Guides table, then double-click any column divider**
   The name of the first guide changes from Donovan Burns to Donovan Abrams, as shown in Figure B-11, and the table columns are adjusted so that all the text is visible and easy to read.

9. **Type your name where indicated in the footer, print a copy of the Word report, then save and close the document**

10. **Save and close all open files and programs**

> **TROUBLE**
> If the value did not update, click the Microsoft Office button, point to Prepare, click Edit Links to Files, click Update Values, then click Close.

> **TROUBLE**
> If the value did not update, click the Microsoft Office button, point to Prepare, click Edit Links to Files, click the second link, then click Update Now.

Opening linked files and enabling content

When you open files created in different applications, you need to open them in the order in which they were created. For example, if you wish to change the Word report and need to maintain links, open the Access database first, followed by the Excel workbook. In Excel, click Options to the right of the security warning, then click the Enable this content option button. You can then open the Word report. When you open the Word report, click Yes to update links.

Quest Specialty Tours
Vancouver Branch

Overview

QST Vancouver runs tours from locations throughout western Canada, including British Columbia, Alberta, and Saskatchewan. In 2010, QST Vancouver ran fifteen tours. Most popular were the kayaking and whale watching tours run from Tofino on the west coast and the hiking and landscape painting tours run from Banff in the Rockies. The top ten tours are listed below.

Tour Name	Location	Start Date	Price	Guests	Revenue
2010 Celebration	Vancouver, BC	12/02/2010	$ 5,000.00	15	$ 75,000.00
Cooking and Cruising	Gulf Islands, BC	15/07/2010	$ 3,000.00	14	$ 42,000.00
Digging for Dinosaurs	Drumheller, AB	20/07/2010	$ 2,100.00	15	$ 31,500.00
Eagle Spirit Quest	Fort McMurray, AB	14/07/2010	$ 3,000.00	16	$ 48,000.00
Grizzly Country	Banff, AB	02/08/2010	$ 3,000.00	12	$ 36,000.00
Pacific Odyssey	Tofino, BC	01/07/2010	$ 3,000.00	15	$ 45,000.00
Peaks and Valleys	Jasper, AB	30/07/2010	$ 2,100.00	14	$ 29,400.00
Snow Days	Whistler, BC	12/02/2010	$ 4,200.00	15	$ 63,000.00
Whitewater Explorations	Kamloops, BC	02/08/2010	$ 3,000.00	16	$ 48,000.00
Wilderness Canoeing	Saskatoon, SK	15/08/2010	$ 4,200.00	12	$ 50,400.00

Revenue updated to $75,000

Tour Guides

The overwhelming success of our QST tours is a direct result of the outstanding efforts of our team of dedicated, personable, and skilled guides. Shown below is a list of the guides who led our 2010 tours.

Guides ID	Last Name	First Name	Home Base	Phone
1	Abrams	Donovan	Kamloops, BC	250-555-7809
2	Harrison	Joyce	Vancouver, BC	604-555-3335
3	Janzen	Gordon	Regina, SK	306-555-7676
4	Liu	Grace	Vancouver, BC	604-555-3224
5	Tremaine	Dominique	Edmonton, AB	780-555-3443
6	Wertz	Ron	Victoria, BC	250-555-7788

Burns changed to Abrams

In every guest survey of every QST Vancouver tour run in 2010, the Tour Guides category received the highest rankings. In addition, the head office of Quest Specialty Travel has confirmed that these rankings exceed the rankings from all other guest surveys generated by all branch offices company-wide.

Your Name

TABLE B-2: Unit B integration tasks

object	commands	source program(s)	destination program	result	connection	page no.
Excel file	External Data/Import Excel Spreadsheet	Excel	Access	Excel spreadsheet is imported into a new table in Access; the spreadsheet must contain only the rows and columns required for the Access table	None	20
Word table	Copy/Paste	Word	Access	Word table is pasted in a new or existing table in Access; if an existing table, the Word table should contain the same number of records as the Access table	None	22
Access table	Copy/Paste Link	Access	Excel	Access table is pasted into Excel as a link; the linked data can be formatted in Excel but cannot be modified or deleted	Linked	24
Linked Access table in Excel	Copy/Paste Link	Access and Excel	Word	Access table is linked to Excel and then to Word; changes made in Access appear in Excel and Word	Linked	24
Access table	Copy/Paste Special/Paste Link	Access	Word	Access table is pasted into Word and can be formatted using Word tools	Linked	26

Practice

If you have a SAM user profile, you may have access to hands-on instruction, practice, and assessment of the skills covered in this unit. Log in to your SAM account (http://sam2007.course.com/) to launch any assigned training activities or exams that relate to the skills covered in this unit.

▼ CONCEPTS REVIEW

Match each term with the statement that best describes it.

1. **Paste Link**
2. **Add New Field**
3. **Formatted Text (RTF)**
4. **Update**
5. **Column headings**

a. To change linked data in a destination file to match data in the source file
b. In Access, click to import data into an existing Access table
c. Excel labels that become field names in an Access table
d. Selection used to retain divisions of columns and rows in a pasted table
e. Option to select in Excel to maintain a connection with a pasted Access table

Select the best answer from the list of choices.

6. **In Access, which of the following tabs do you select when you want to import data into an Access table?**
   a. Insert
   b. Insert File
   c. Database Tools
   d. External Data

7. **Which command(s) do you use to copy a table from Access and paste it into Excel as a link?**
   a. Import
   b. Copy/Paste
   c. Copy/Paste Link
   d. Copy/Link

8. **Why would you copy a table from Access and paste it as a link in Excel?**
   a. To remove selected columns
   b. To change selected data
   c. To use selected data in calculations
   d. To modify the number of records

9. **In Word, which option do you select to paste a copied table so that the structure of the table is maintained?**
   a. Unformatted Text
   b. HTML Text
   c. Formatted Text
   d. Formatted Text (RTF)

▼ SKILLS REVIEW

1. **Import an Excel worksheet into Access.**
   a. Start Excel, open the file INT B-4.xlsx from the drive and folder where you store your Data Files, then save it as **Picture Perfect Image List**.
   b. Delete rows 1 and 2, then save and close the workbook.
   c. Start Access, then create a new database called **Picture Perfect Inventory**.
   d. In Access, import the file **Picture Perfect Image List.xlsx** file from Excel as external data.
   e. In the Import Spreadsheet wizard, change the name of the Title field to **Image Title**, then name the new table **Images**.
   f. View the Images table, then widen columns as necessary.

2. Copy a Word table to Access

  a. Start Word, open the file INT B-5.docx from the drive and folder where you store your Data Files, then save it as **Picture Perfect Information**.

  b. Select the top table (which contains the list of images), copy it, then switch to Access.

  c. Paste the table in the Images table, then delete the duplicate column.

  d. In Design view, move the Category and Artist fields above the Price field, then save and close the table.

  e. In Word, select the table containing the top-selling products, copy the table, then paste it as a new table in Access.

  f. Change the ID field to **Product ID**, then close the table and name it **Products**.

  g. In Word, close the Picture Perfect Information file.

3. Link an Access table to Excel

  a. In Access, copy the Images table.

  b. Create a new Excel workbook, paste the Images table as a link, save the workbook as **Picture Perfect Inventory Data**, then adjust column widths where necessary.

  c. Enter **Total Value** in cell G1, adjust the column width, then in cell G2, enter a formula to multiply the Price by the Print Run.

  d. Copy the formula to the range G3:G16, then format the values in columns E and G in the Accounting format.

  e. Copy the range B1:G16, switch to Word, open the file INT B-6.docx from the drive and folder where you store your Data Files, then save it as **Picture Perfect Inventory Report**.

  f. In the Word document select POSTCARD LIST, then paste the copied data as a linked Microsoft Office Excel Worksheet Object, add a blank line above the Price List heading, then save the document.

4. Link an Access table to Word

  a. In Access, copy the Products table, switch to Word, then select the PRICE LIST placeholder.

  b. Paste the copied table as a linked Formatted Text (RTF) object, then save the document.

  c. In Access, open the Images table, change the print run for Western Rain to **100** units, then close the table.

  d. Open the Products table, change the title Green Horizons to **Blue Horizons**, then close the table.

  e. In Excel, verify that the total inventory value for Western Rain has changed from $250 to $500.

  f. In Word, update the link to the table that lists the postcard images (the top table), then click outside the table.

  g. Update the data in the Product table (the lower table), select the table, then double-click a column divider to set the column widths. (*Hint*: If the value does not update, click the Office button, point to Prepare, click Edit Links to Files, click the link, then click Update Now.)

  h. Type your name where indicated in the footer, print a copy of the report, compare it to Figure B-12, then save and close the document.

  i. Save and close all open files and programs.

FIGURE B-12

Picture Perfect Reproductions

Art Postcard Sales

Picture Perfect Reproductions recently began selling postcard reproductions of work by some of its gallery artists. Sales have been brisk, particularly to tourists during the summer months. The table below lists the current stock of postcard images by the top-selling artists in each of five categories. The top-selling category is abstracts.

Image Title	Category	Artist	Price	Print Run	Total Value
Western Rain	Abstract	Merilee Blake	$ 5.00	100	$ 500.00
Tracers	Abstract	Petra Watson	$ 6.00	30	$ 180.00
Figurations	Abstract	Fabrizio Bacci	$ 7.00	32	$ 224.00
Nocturne	Abstract	Ed Sloan	$ 5.00	50	$ 250.00
Forest Currents	Abstract	Donald Watson	$ 5.00	60	$ 300.00
Beach Classic	Abstract	Merilee Blake	$ 7.00	70	$ 490.00
Two Dancers	Figurative	Donald Watson	$ 5.50	48	$ 264.00
Totem	Figurative	Frank Lewis	$ 7.00	30	$ 210.00
Dripping Cedars	Landscape	Merilee Blake	$ 5.75	20	$ 115.00
Gabriola Passage	Landscape	Beth Sawyer	$ 6.00	40	$ 240.00
Forest Markings	Landscape	Hiromi Tanaka	$ 7.00	25	$ 175.00
Forest Path Near Barbizon	Landscape	Henri Ducasse	$ 5.00	50	$ 250.00
Debris of War	Photography	Heinrich Strubel	$ 4.50	40	$ 180.00
Kensington Gardens	Photography	Jenny Smith	$ 7.00	50	$ 350.00
Signs of Struggle	Still Life	Petra Watson	$ 5.00	50	$ 250.00

Price List

The price list shown below lists the top five products sold by *Picture Perfect Reproductions*. Three product categories are represented: Clothing, Posters, and Sundries. The Sundries category includes such items as mouse pads, mugs, tote bags, pens, and jigsaw puzzles.

Product ID	Title	Description	Category	Price
1	Blue Horizons	T-shirt	Clothing	$45.00
2	Far Horizons	Mouse pad	Sundry	$12.00
3	Mountain Wall	Mug	Sundry	$6.00
4	Jagged Cliffs	Sweatshirt	Clothing	$55.00
5	Figurations	Framed Poster	Poster	$60.00

Your Name

▼ INDEPENDENT CHALLENGE 1

Lakeside Computing provides computer consulting and repair services to computer users in Minneapolis. You have just started working for the company and have been asked to build a database that the owner can use to keep track of contracts. The owner would also like you to create a report that analyzes sales trends.

a. Start Excel, open the file INT B-7.xlsx from the drive and folder where you store your Data Files, then save it as **Lakeside Computing Sales Data**.

b. Delete any rows and objects that cannot be imported into Access, then save and close the workbook.

c. Create a database in Access called **Lakeside Computing**.

d. Import the Excel file Lakeside Computing Sales Data into the Access database; change the Type field name to **Category**, and name the new table **Contracts**.

e. Start Word, open the file INT B-8.docx from the drive and folder where you store your Data Files, save it as **Lakeside Computing Technicians**, copy the table, close the document, then paste the table into the Contracts table in Access.

f. Delete the Date1, Client Name1, and Type columns from the pasted information, move Technician field above the Category field, then widen columns if necessary.

g. Copy the Contracts table, paste it as a linked file in a new Excel workbook, then adjust column widths as necessary.

h. Calculate the total revenue from each contract based on an hourly rate of $75. (*Hint*: Add two new columns—one called "Rate" with "75" entered for each record and one called "Total" with the formula entered for each record.)

i. Format the data in column B with the Short Date style, format the values in columns G and H with the Accounting Number format, then save the Excel workbook as **Lakeside Computing Contract Fees**.

j. In Word, set up a new document and enter the text shown in Figure B-13, then save it as **Lakeside Computing Contracts**. Format the title in 22 point and the subtitle in 16 point.

k. Copy cells B1 to H11 from Excel, paste them as a link using the Microsoft Office Excel Worksheet Object option below the text paragraph in the Lakeside Computing Contracts document, then save the document.

l. In the Contracts table in Access, change the number of hours for the March 1 contract to 10, verify that the March 1 revenue has changed from $375 to $750 in the Excel file, then update the worksheet object in the Word file. (*Hint*: You may need to wait a few minutes for the updated values to appear in the Excel and Word files. To speed up the updating in either program, click the Office button, point to Prepare, click Edit Links to Files, then select and update the link.)

m. Select the worksheet object in Word, then apply an outside border. (*Hint*: Click the Borders button list arrow, then select Outside Borders.)

n. Add your name below the worksheet object, print a copy of the Word document, then save all files and close all programs.

FIGURE B-13

> ## Lakeside Computing
> ### Spring 2010 Contracts
>
> *Lakeside Computing* provides computer users with a one-stop shop for computer services for PCs and Macs. The table displayed below lists all of the sales *Lakeside Computing* made in the month of July, 2010.

▼ INDEPENDENT CHALLENGE 2

You work for LifeWorks Software, a new company based in Santa Fe, New Mexico that sells software online to customers around the world. The business is growing rapidly and you need to develop a system for keeping track of inventory. You have a price list saved in a Word document. You need to transfer the Word table data into an Access database, then add some new records. You then need to perform some calculations on the data in Excel. Lastly, you verify that when you update data in the Access database, the data in Excel also changes.

a. Start Word, open the file INT B-9.docx from the drive and folder where you store your Data Files, then save it as **LifeWorks Software Price List**.

b. Copy the table, create a new database in Access called **LifeWorks**, then paste the copied table into a new table named **Products**.

c. Add two new records to the Products table with the information in Table B-3.

TABLE B-3

Product	Category	Price
Travel Tips	Entertainment	$29.95
Financial Freedom	Lifestyle	$34.95

d. Close the table, copy it and link it into a new Excel workbook, then add a new column in Excel called **Sales**.

e. Enter **10** as the number of sales for the first four products and **15** as the number of sales for the last eight products.

f. Add a new column called **Revenue**, calculate the total revenue for each product, then save the workbook as **LifeWorks Software Sales**. Format the Price and Revenue values with the Accounting Number format and adjust column widths as necessary.

g. Note the current revenue amount for the Astrology Kit and the Genealogy Genie.

h. In the Access Products table, change the price of the Genealogy Genie to $40.95 and the price of the Astrology Kit to $35.95.

i. In Excel, verify that the values have updated. (*Hint*: You may need to wait a few minutes for the updated value to appear in the Excel file. To speed up the updating, click the Office button, point to Prepare, click Edit Links to Files, then select and update the link.)

j. Insert a new row 1, enter **LifeWorks Software Sales**, center it across the range A1:F1, increase the font size to 18 points, apply bold formatting, then apply the fill color of your choice.

k. Type your name in cell A16, print the workbook, save and close it, then close all programs and files.

▼ INDEPENDENT CHALLENGE 3

Powder Pack Sports sells skis and snowboards from retail outlets at three resorts in California, Idaho, and Colorado. You need to create a report that analyzes the December sales posted by each of the outlets. First, you create a database for Powder Pack Sports from data you copy from an Excel worksheet and a Word document and then you create a report in Word that contains tables linked to the Access database.

a. Start Access, create a new database called **Powder Pack Sports Inventory**, then import the Excel file INT B-10.xlsx. In the Import Spreadsheet wizard, change the name of the Idaho field to **Sun Valley**, the California field to **Mammoth**, and the Colorado field to **Aspen**.

b. Name the new table **Equipment**, then open the table and widen columns as necessary.

c. Copy the Equipment table, paste it into a new Excel workbook as a link, adjust the widths of columns as necessary, then save the workbook as **Powder Pack Sports Sales**.

d. Enter **Total** in cell G1, then in the appropriate cell enter a formula to add the values for Apex Skis sales for the three locations. Copy and paste the formula to calculate the total sales for the remaining products.

e. Enter **Revenue** in cell H1, enter a formula to calculate total revenue for Apex Skis in the appropriate cell, then copy the formula to the appropriate cells for the rest of the products.

f. In cell H15, calculate the total revenue from all products.

g. Enter **Mogul Sales** in cell B16, then in cell C16 enter the formula to add the total revenue from the three Mogul products.

h. Format all dollar amounts in the Accounting Number format, then save the workbook.

i. Copy the range B1:H14, start Word, open the file INT B-11.docx from the drive and folder where you store your Data Files, then save it as **Powder Pack Sports December Sales**.

j. Replace the word SALES with the copied data as a linked object in the Microsoft Office Excel Worksheet Object format.

k. In Excel, copy the value in cell H15, paste it as a linked object into the appropriate area in Word (*Hint*: See paragraph 1) using the Formatted Text (RTF) format.

l. In Excel, copy the value in cell C16, then paste it as a linked object into the appropriate area in Word (*Hint*: See the last paragraph) in the Formatted Text (RTF) format.

m. Verify that the total revenue is $2,057,170.00 and the total Mogul sales are $1,241,800.00.

n. In Access, change the price of the Mogul Snowboard XX to **$3,000**, then close the table, saving your changes.

o. Update the values in Excel, then update the values in the Word memo report. (*Hint*: You may need to wait a few minutes for the updated values to appear in the Excel and Word files. To speed up the updating in either program, click the Office button, point to Prepare, click Edit Links to Files, then select and update each link.)

p. Type your name where indicated in the report footer, print a copy of the report, save and close the document, then save and close all open files and programs.

▼ VISUAL WORKSHOP

Create a new database called **Symphony Software**, then copy the table from the Word file INT B-12.docx into the database as a new table. Name the table **Staff Travel**. Copy the table, then paste it as linked data in a new Excel workbook. Add a new column called **Per Diem**, enter the per diem rate shown in Figure B-14, then calculate the total expenses for each staff person and the total expenses for the company. In the Access source table, change the number of days that Donald Deville was away to 10 and the number of days that Ivan Smith was away to 8, then close the table. In Excel, verify that the appropriate values are updated, then as shown in Figure B-14, add and format a title and subtitle. (*Hint*: The font size of the title is 20 point and the font size of the subtitle is 16 point.) Format data as shown in the figure. Save the workbook as **Symphony Software Travel Expenses**. Include your name under the table, save and print the Excel worksheet, then exit all files and programs.

FIGURE B-14

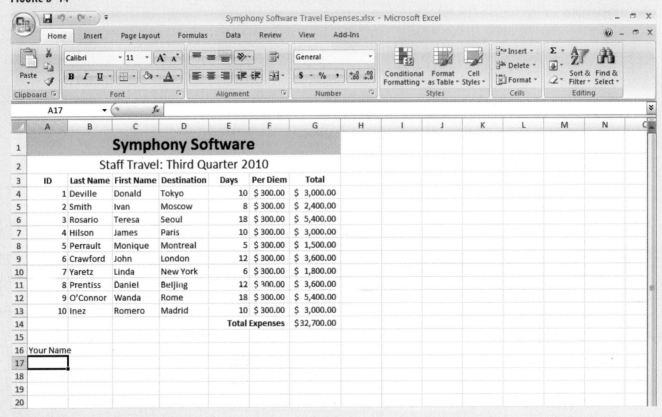

Creating a Presentation in PowerPoint 2007

Microsoft Office PowerPoint 2007 is a powerful computer software program that enables you to create visually dynamic presentations. With PowerPoint, you can create individual slides and display them as a slide show on your computer, a video projector, or over the Internet. Ellen Latsky is the European tour developer for Quest Specialty Travel (QST), an adventure tour company committed to providing travel experiences that immerse travelers into world cultures. One of Ellen's responsibilities is to present new tour ideas for the upcoming travel season at the annual sales meeting held at the company's corporate offices. As a newly hired summer intern, Ellen has asked you to get acquainted with PowerPoint and then start work on the new tour ideas presentation.

OBJECTIVES

Define presentation software

Plan an effective presentation

Examine the PowerPoint window

Enter slide text

Add a new slide

Apply a design theme

Compare presentation views

Print a PowerPoint presentation

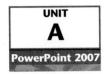
Defining Presentation Software

Presentation software is a computer program you use to organize and present information to others. Whether you are explaining a new product or moderating a meeting, presentation software can help you effectively communicate your ideas. You can use PowerPoint to create presentations, as well as speaker notes for the presenter and handouts for the audience. Table A-1 explains how your information can be presented using PowerPoint. Ellen wants you to start work on the presentation that she will use to present the new European tour series. Because you are only somewhat familiar with PowerPoint, you get to work exploring its capabilities. Figure A-1 shows how a presentation looks printed as handouts. Figure A-2 shows how the same presentation might look printed as notes pages for a speaker.

DETAILS

You can easily complete the following tasks using PowerPoint:

- **Enter and edit text easily**

  Text editing and formatting commands in PowerPoint are organized by the task you are performing at the time, so you can enter, edit, and format text information simply and efficiently to produce the best results in the least amount of time.

- **Change the appearance of information**

  PowerPoint has many effects that can transform the way text, graphics, and slides appear. By exploring some of these capabilities, you discover how easy it is to change the appearance of your presentation.

- **Organize and arrange information**

  Once you start using PowerPoint, you won't have to spend much time making sure your information is correct and in the right order. With PowerPoint, you can quickly and easily rearrange and modify text, graphics, and slides in your presentation.

- **Incorporate information from other sources**

  Often, when you create presentations, you use information from a variety of sources. With PowerPoint, you can import text, photographs, numerical data, and facts from files created in such programs as Microsoft Word, Corel WordPerfect, Adobe Photoshop, Microsoft Excel, and Microsoft Access. You can also import graphic images from a variety of sources such as the Internet, other computers, a digital camera, or other graphics programs.

- **Present information in a variety of ways**

  With PowerPoint, you can present information using a variety of methods. For example, you can print handout pages or an outline of your presentation for audience members. You can display your presentation as an electronic slide show using your computer, or if you are presenting to a large group, you can use a video projector and a large screen. If you want to reach an even wider audience, you can publish the presentation to the Internet so people anywhere in the world can use a browser to view your presentation.

- **Collaborate on a presentation with others**

  PowerPoint makes it easy to collaborate with colleagues and coworkers to create a presentation using the Internet. You can use your e-mail program to send a presentation as an attachment to a colleague for feedback. If you have a large number of people that need to collaborate on a presentation, you can set up a shared workspace on the Internet so everyone in your group has access to the presentation.

FIGURE A-1: PowerPoint Handout

FIGURE A-2: PowerPoint Notes page

+ Pacific means peaceful; named by Magellan in 1520.
+ Largest and deepest of the world's oceans.
+ Covers more than one-third of the earth's surface.
+ Contains more than 30,000 islands.

TABLE A-1: Presenting information using PowerPoint

method	description
On-screen presentations	Run a slide show from your computer or through a video projector to a large screen
Notes	Print a page with the image of a slide and notes about each slide for yourself or your audience
Audience handouts	Print handouts with one, two, three, four, six, or nine slides on a page
Online meetings	View or work on a presentation with your colleagues in real time
Outline pages	Print a text outline of your presentation to highlight the main points
Overheads	Print PowerPoint slides directly to transparencies using a standard printer

Planning an Effective Presentation

Before you create a presentation, you need to have a basic idea of the information you want to communicate. PowerPoint is a powerful and flexible program that gives you the ability to start a presentation simply by entering the text of your message. If you have a design or theme you want to use, you can start the presentation by working on the design. In most cases you'll probably enter the text of your presentation into PowerPoint first and then tailor the design to the message and audience. When preparing your presentation, you need to keep in mind not only to whom you are giving it, but also where you are giving it. It is important to know what equipment you will need, such as a sound system, computer, or projector. 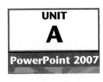 Use the planning guidelines below to help plan an effective presentation. Figure A-3 illustrates a storyboard for a well thought-out presentation.

DETAILS

In planning a presentation, it is important to:

- **Determine and outline the message you want to communicate**

  The more time you take developing the message and outline of your presentation, the better your presentation will be. A presentation with a clear message that reads like a story and is illustrated with visual aids will have the greatest impact on your audience. Start the presentation by describing the tour development goals, defining focus group data, and stating the tour strategy objectives. See Figure A-3.

- **Verify the audience and the delivery location**

  Audience and delivery location should be major factors in the type of presentation you create. For example, a presentation you develop for a staff meeting that is held in a conference room would not necessarily need to be as elaborate or detailed as a presentation that you develop for a large audience held in an auditorium. Room lighting, natural light, screen position, and room layout all affect how the audience responds to your presentation. This presentation will be delivered in a small auditorium to QST's management and sales team.

- **Determine the type of output**

  Output choices for a presentation include black-and-white or color handouts, on-screen slide show, or an online meeting. Consider the time demands and computer equipment availability as you decide which output types to produce. Because you are speaking in a small auditorium to a large group and have access to a computer and projection equipment, you decide that an on-screen slide show is the best output choice for your presentation.

- **Determine the design**

  Visual appeal, graphics, and design work to communicate your message. You can choose one of the professionally designed themes that come with PowerPoint, modify one of these themes, or create one of your own. You decide to choose one of PowerPoint's design themes to convey the new tour information.

- **Decide what additional materials will be useful in the presentation**

  You need to prepare not only the slides themselves but also supplementary materials, including speaker notes and handouts for the audience. You use speaker notes to help remember key details, and you pass out handouts for the audience to use as a reference during the presentation.

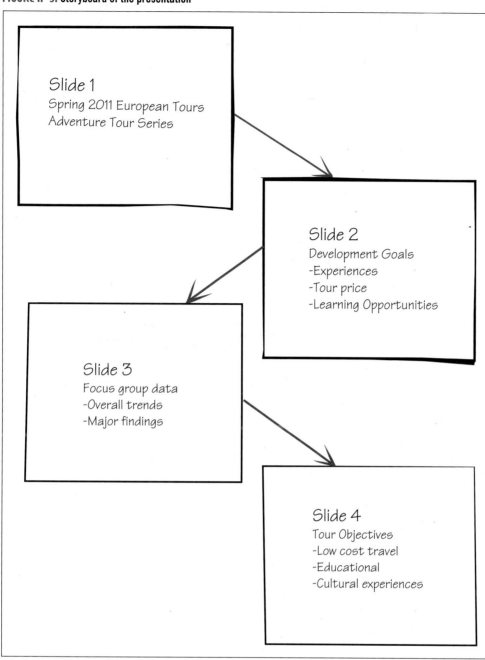

Slide 1
Spring 2011 European Tours
Adventure Tour Series

Slide 2
Development Goals
-Experiences
-Tour price
-Learning Opportunities

Slide 3
Focus group data
-Overall trends
-Major findings

Slide 4
Tour Objectives
-Low cost travel
-Educational
-Cultural experiences

Understanding copyright

Intellectual property is any idea or creation of the human mind. Copyright law is a type of intellectual property law that protects works of authorship, including books, Web pages, computer games, music, artwork, and photographs. Copyright protects the expression of an idea, but not the underlying facts or concepts. In other words, the general subject matter is not protected, but how you express it is, such as when several people photograph the same sunset. Copyright attaches to any original work of authorship *as soon* as it is created, you *do not* have to register it with the Copyright Office or display the copyright symbol, ©.

Fair use is an exception to copyright and permits the public to use copyrighted material for certain purposes without obtaining prior consent from the owner. Determining whether fair use applies to a work depends on its purpose, the nature of the work, how much of the work you want to copy, and the effect on the work's value. Unauthorized use of protected work (such as downloading a photo or a song from the Web) is known as copyright infringement, and can lead to legal action.

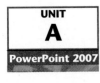

UNIT
A
PowerPoint 2007

Examining the PowerPoint Window

When you first start PowerPoint, a blank slide appears in the PowerPoint window. PowerPoint has different **views** that allow you to see your presentation in different forms. By default, the PowerPoint window opens in **Normal view**, which is the primary view that you use to write, edit, and design your presentation. Normal view is divided into three areas called **panes**: the pane on the left contains the Outline and Slides tabs, the large pane is the Slide pane, and the small pane below the Slide pane is the Notes pane. You move around in each pane using the scroll bars. **▓▓▓▓** The PowerPoint window and the specific parts of Normal view are described below.

TROUBLE
If you have trouble finding Microsoft PowerPoint 2007 on the All Programs menu, check with your instructor or technical support person.

1. **Click the Start button ⊕ on the taskbar, point to All Programs, click Microsoft Office, then click Microsoft Office PowerPoint 2007**
   PowerPoint starts and the PowerPoint window opens, as shown in Figure A-4.

   Using Figure A-4 as a guide, examine the elements of the PowerPoint window, then find and compare the elements described below:

   - The **Ribbon**—a wide (toolbar-like) band that runs across the entire PowerPoint window—is a new feature that organizes all of PowerPoint's primary commands. Each set of primary commands is identified by a **tab**; for example, the Home tab is selected by default as shown in Figure A-4. Commands are further arranged into **groups** on the Ribbon based on their function. So, for example, text formatting commands such as Bold, Underline, and Italic are located on the Home tab, in the Font group.
   - The **Outline tab** displays the text of your presentation in the form of an outline, without showing graphics or other visual objects. Using this tab, it is easy to move text on or among slides by dragging text to reorder the information.
   - The **Slides tab** displays the slides of your presentation as small images, called **thumbnails**. You can quickly navigate through the slides in your presentation by clicking the thumbnails on this tab. You can also add, delete, or rearrange slides using this tab.
   - The **Slide pane** displays the current slide in your presentation.
   - The **Notes pane** is used to type text that references a slide's content. You can print these notes and refer to them when you make a presentation or print them as handouts and give them to your audience. The Notes pane is not visible to the audience when you show a slide presentation in Slide Show view.
   - The **Quick Access toolbar** provides immediate access to common commands that you use all the time, such as Save, Undo, and Redo. The Quick Access toolbar is always visible no matter which Ribbon tab you select. This toolbar is fully customizable. Click the Customize Quick Access Toolbar button to add or remove commands.
   - The **View Shortcuts** on the status bar allow you to switch quickly between PowerPoint views.
   - The **status bar**, located at the bottom of the PowerPoint window, shows messages about what you are doing and seeing in PowerPoint, including which slide you are viewing, and the design theme applied to the presentation. In addition, the status bar displays the Zoom slider controls, the **Fit slide to current window button** 🔲, and information on other functionality such as signatures and permissions.
   - The **Zoom slider**, located in the lower-right corner of the status bar, allows you to zoom the slide in and out quickly.

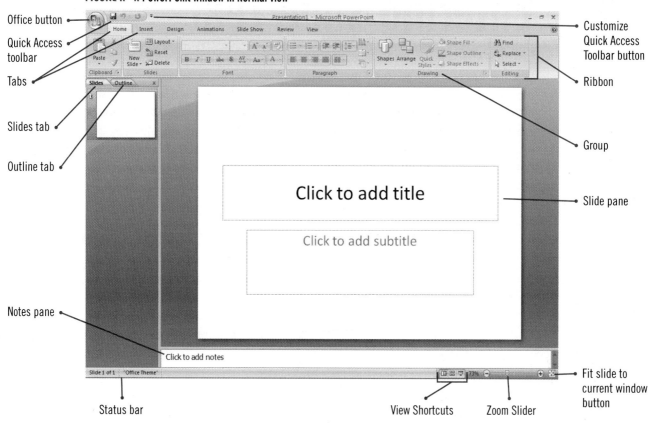

Office button

Quick Access toolbar

Tabs

Slides tab

Outline tab

Notes pane

Status bar

Customize Quick Access Toolbar button

Ribbon

Group

Slide pane

View Shortcuts

Zoom Slider

Fit slide to current window button

Viewing your presentation in grayscale or black and white

Viewing your presentation in grayscale (using shades of gray) or pure black and white is very useful when you are printing a presentation on a black-and-white printer and you want to make sure your presentation prints correctly. To see how your color presentation looks in grayscale or black and white, click the View tab, then click either the Grayscale or Pure Black and White button. Depending on which button you select, the Grayscale or the Black and White tab

appears and the Ribbon displays different settings that you can customize. If you don't like the way an individual object looks in black and white or grayscale, you can change its color. Right-click the object, point to Black and White Setting or Grayscale Setting (depending on which view you are in), and choose from the options on the submenu.

Entering Slide Text

Each time you launch PowerPoint, a new presentation with a blank title slide appears in Normal view. The title slide has two **text placeholders**—boxes with dotted borders—where you enter text. The top text placeholder on the title slide is the **title placeholder**, labeled "Click to add title." The bottom text placeholder on the title slide is the **subtitle text placeholder**, labeled "Click to add subtitle." To enter text in a placeholder, click the placeholder and then type your text. After you enter text in a placeholder, the placeholder becomes a text object. An **object** is any item on a slide that can be modified. Objects are the building blocks that make up a presentation slide. Begin working on your presentation by entering text on the title slide.

STEPS

1. **Move the pointer over the title placeholder labeled** "Click to add title" **in the Slide pane**
   The pointer changes to I when you move the pointer over the placeholder. In PowerPoint, the pointer often changes shape, depending on the task you are trying to accomplish.

2. **Click the** title placeholder **in the Slide pane**
   The **insertion point**, a blinking vertical line, indicates where your text appears when you type in the placeholder. A **selection box** with a dashed line border and sizing handles appears around the placeholder, indicating that it is selected and ready to accept text. See Figure A-5.

   TROUBLE
   If you press a wrong key, press [Backspace] to erase the character.

3. **Type** Spring 2011 European Tour Proposal
   PowerPoint wraps and then center-aligns the title text within the title placeholder, which is now a text object. Notice that the text also appears on the slide thumbnail on the Slides tab.

4. **Click the** subtitle text placeholder **in the Slide pane**
   The subtitle text placeholder is ready to accept text.

5. **Type** Adventure Tour Series, **then press [Enter]**
   The insertion point moves to the next line in the text object.

6. **Type** Your Name, **press [Enter]**, **type** Tour Developer-Europe, **press [Enter] then type** Quest Specialty Travel
   Notice that the AutoFit Options button ⬍ appears near the text object. The AutoFit Options button on your screen indicates that PowerPoint has automatically decreased the size of all the text in the text object so that it fits inside the text object.

7. **Click the** Autofit Options button ⬍, **then click** Stop Fitting Text to This Placeholder **on the shortcut menu**
   The text in the text object changes back to its original size and no longer fits in the text object.

8. **Position** I **to the right of** Series, **drag left to select the entire line of text, press [Backspace], then click outside the text object in a blank area of the slide**
   The Adventure Tour Series line of text is deleted and the Autofit Options button closes, as shown in Figure A-6. Clicking a blank area of the slide deselects all selected objects on the slide.

9. **Click the** Save button 🖫 **on the Quick Access toolbar to open the Save As dialog box, then save the presentation as** QuestA **in the drive and folder where you store your Data Files**

FIGURE A-5: Title text placeholder ready to accept text

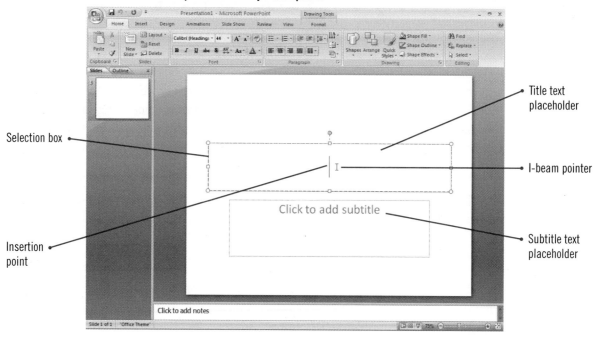

Selection box

Insertion point

Title text placeholder

I-beam pointer

Subtitle text placeholder

FIGURE A-6: Text on title slide

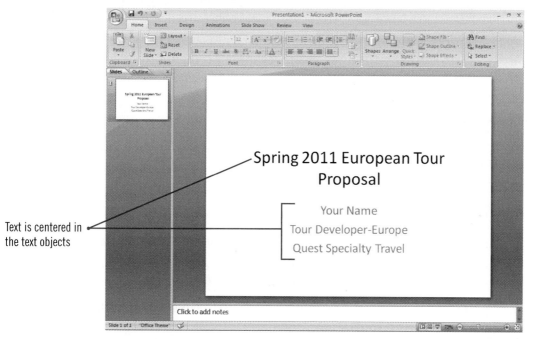

Text is centered in the text objects

Saving fonts with your presentation

When you create a presentation, it uses the fonts that are installed on your computer. If you need to open the presentation on another computer, the fonts might look different if that computer has a different set of fonts. To preserve the look of your presentation on any computer, you can save, or embed, the fonts in your presentation. Click the Office button, then click the PowerPoint Options button. The PowerPoint Options dialog box opens. Click Save in the left pane, then click the Embed fonts in the file check box. Click the Embed all characters option button, then click OK to close the dialog box. Click Save on the Quick Access toolbar. Now the presentation looks the same on any computer that opens it. Using this option, however, significantly increases the size of your presentation, so only use it when necessary. You can freely embed any TrueType font that comes with Windows. You can embed other TrueType fonts only if they have no license restrictions.

Adding a New Slide

Ordinarily when you add a new slide to a presentation, you have a pretty good idea of what you want the slide to look like. For example, you may want to add a slide that has a title over bulleted text and a picture. To help you add a slide like this quickly and easily, PowerPoint provides nine standard slide layouts. A **slide layout** contains text and object placeholders that are arranged in a specific way on the slide. You have already worked with the Title Slide layout in the previous lesson. In the event that a standard slide layout does not meet your needs, you can modify an existing slide layout or create a brand new, custom slide layout. To continue developing the presentation, you create a slide that defines the QST development goals for the new tour series.

STEPS

QUICK TIP

If you know which slide layout you want to use on the new slide, you can click the New Slide list arrow to open the slide layout gallery and then select a specific slide layout.

1. **Click the New Slide button in the Slides group on the Home tab on the Ribbon**

   A new blank slide (now the current slide) appears as the second slide in your presentation as shown in Figure A-7. The new slide in the Slide pane contains a title placeholder and a content placeholder. A **content placeholder** can be used to insert text or objects such as clip art, tables, or charts. Table A-2 describes the content placeholder icons. Notice that the status bar indicates Slide 2 of 2 and that the Slides tab now contains two slide thumbnails. You can easily change the current slide's layout using the Layout button in the Slides group.

2. **Click the Layout button in the Slides group**

   The Layout gallery opens. Each layout is identified by a descriptive name.

3. **Point to the Two Content slide layout, then click the Two Content slide layout**

   A slide layout with a title placeholder and two content placeholders replaces the Title and Content layout for the current slide.

4. **Type Tour Development Goals, then click the left content placeholder**

   The text you type appears in the title placeholder and the insertion point appears at the top of the left content placeholder.

5. **Type Focus on significant experiences, then press [Enter]**

   A new first-level bullet automatically appears when you press [Enter].

6. **Press [Tab]**

   The new first-level bullet indents and becomes a second-level bullet.

QUICK TIP

You can also press [Shift][Tab] to decrease the indent level.

7. **Type Preserve QST values, press [Enter], then click the Decrease List Level button ⊞ in the Paragraph group**

   The Decrease List Level button changes the second-level bullet into a first-level bullet.

8. **Type Price tours reasonably, press [Enter], type Create learning opportunities, press [Enter], then click the Increase List Level button ⊞ in the Paragraph group**

9. **Type Offer local guides, press [Enter], type Provide experts, then click the Save button ⊞ on the Quick Access toolbar**

   The Increase List Level button creates a second-level bullet from a first-level bullet. The Save button saves all of the changes to the file. Compare your screen with Figure A-8.

FIGURE A-7: New blank slide in Normal view

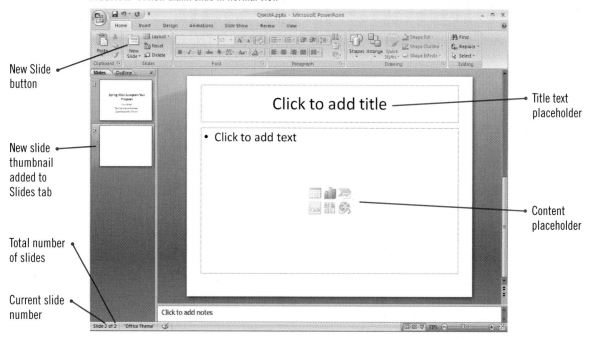

New Slide button

New slide thumbnail added to Slides tab

Total number of slides

Current slide number

Title text placeholder

Content placeholder

FIGURE A-8: New slide with Two Content slide layout

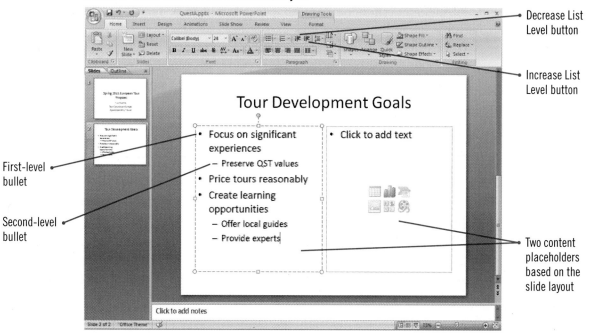

Decrease List Level button

Increase List Level button

First-level bullet

Second-level bullet

Two content placeholders based on the slide layout

TABLE A-2: Content placeholder icons

click this icon	to insert a
	Table
	Graph chart
	Piece of clip art
	Picture from a file
	SmartArt graphic
	Movie or video clip

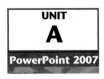
Applying a Design Theme

PowerPoint provides a number of design themes to help you quickly create a professional and contemporary looking presentation. A design **theme** incorporates sets of colors for fill, line, and shadow, called **theme colors**; fonts for titles and other text, called **theme fonts**; and effects for lines and fills, called **theme effects** to create a cohesive look. In most cases, you would apply one theme to an entire presentation; you can, however, apply multiple themes to the same presentation, or even a different theme on each presentation slide. You can use a design theme as is, or you can alter individual elements of the theme as needed. Unless you need to use a specific design theme, such as a company theme or product design theme, it is faster and easier to use one of the themes supplied with PowerPoint. If you design a custom theme, you can save it to use in the future. ▰▰▰ You decide to change the default design theme in the presentation to a new one.

STEPS

1. **Click the** Slide 1 thumbnail **on the Slides tab**

   Slide 1, the title slide, appears in the Slide pane.

2. **Click the** Design tab **on the Ribbon, then point to the** Civic theme **in the Themes group as shown in Figure A-9**

   The Design tab appears and a live preview of the Civic theme is displayed on the slide. A **live preview** allows you to see how your changes affect the slides before actually making the change. The live preview lasts about one minute and then your slide reverts back to its original state. The first (far left) theme thumbnail identifies the current theme applied to the presentation, in this case, the default design theme called the Office Theme. Depending on your monitor resolution and screen size, you can see between five and seven design themes visible in the Themes group. However, there are a total of 20 standard built-in themes available to use.

3. **Slowly move your pointer ▱ over the other design themes, then click the** Themes group down scroll arrow **once**

   A live preview of the theme appears on the slide each time you pass your pointer over the theme thumbnails, and a ScreenTip identifies the theme names.

4. **Move ▱ over the** design themes, **then click the** Metro theme

   The Metro design theme is applied to all the slides in the presentation. Notice the new slide background color, graphic elements, fonts, and text color. You decide that this theme isn't right for this presentation.

5. **Click the** More button ▾ **in the Themes group**

   The Themes gallery window opens. At the top of the gallery window in the This Presentation section are the current theme(s) applied to the presentation. Notice that just the Metro theme is listed here because when you changed the theme in the last step, you replaced the default theme with the Metro theme. The Built-In section identifies all of the standard themes that come with PowerPoint.

6. **Right-click the** Solstice theme **in the Themes group, then click** Apply to Selected Slides

   The Solstice theme is applied only to Slide 1. You like the Solstice theme better and decide to apply it to both slides.

7. **Right-click the** Solstice theme **in the Themes group, then click** Apply to All Slides

   The Solstice theme is applied to both slides. Preview the other slide in the presentation to see how it looks.

8. **Click the** Next Slide button ▾ **at the bottom of the vertical scroll bar**

   Compare your screen to Figure A-10.

9. **Click the** Previous Slide button ▴ **at the bottom of the vertical scroll bar, then save your changes**

> **QUICK TIP**
> One way to apply multiple themes to the same presentation is to click the Slide Sorter button in the status bar, select a slide or a group of slides, then click the theme.

FIGURE A-9: Slide showing a different design theme

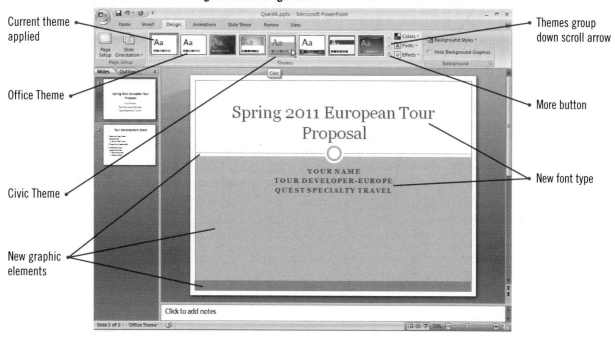

Current theme applied

Office Theme

Civic Theme

New graphic elements

Themes group down scroll arrow

More button

New font type

FIGURE A-10: Presentation with Solstice theme applied

Solstice theme

Solstice theme applied

Previous Slide button

Next Slide button

Customizing themes

You are not limited to using the standard themes PowerPoint provides; you can also modify a theme to create your own custom theme. For example, you might want to incorporate your company's colors on the slide background of the presentation or be able to type using fonts your company uses for brand recognition. To modify an existing theme, you can change the color theme, font theme, or the effects theme and then save it for future use by clicking the Themes group More button, then clicking Save Current Theme. You also have the ability to create a new font theme or a new color theme from scratch by clicking the Theme Fonts button or the Theme Colors button and then clicking Create New Theme Fonts or Create New Theme Colors. You work in the Create New Theme Fonts or Create New Theme Colors dialog box to define the custom theme fonts or colors.

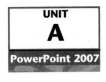
Comparing Presentation Views

PowerPoint has four basic views: Normal view, Slide Sorter view, Notes Page view, and Slide Show view. Each PowerPoint view displays your presentation in a different way and is used for different purposes. Normal view is the primary editing view where you add text, graphics, and other elements to the slides. Slide Sorter view is primarily used to rearrange slides, however, you can also add slide effects and design themes in this view. You use Notes Page view to type notes you want to remember about each slide. Slide Show view displays your presentation filling the computer screen and is the view used to give a presentation. To move easily among three of the PowerPoint views, use the View Shortcuts buttons located in the Status bar next to the Zoom slider. All PowerPoint views can be accessed using the View tab on the Ribbon. Table A-3 provides a brief description of the PowerPoint views. Examine each of the PowerPoint views, starting with Normal view.

STEPS

1. **Click the Outline tab, then click the small slide icon next to Slide 2 in the Outline tab**
   The text for Slide 2 is selected in the Outline tab and Slide 2 appears in the Slide pane as shown in Figure A-11. Notice that the status bar identifies the number of the slide you are viewing, the total number of slides in the presentation, and the name of the applied design theme.

2. **Click the Previous Slide button at the bottom of the vertical scroll bar**
   Slide 1 appears in the Slide pane. The scroll box in the vertical scroll bar moves back up the scroll bar.

3. **Click the Slides tab**
   Thumbnails of the slides in your presentation appear again on the Slides tab. Since the Slides tab is narrower than the Outline tab, the Slide pane enlarges.

   > **QUICK TIP**
   > You can also switch between views using the commands in the Presentation Views group on the View tab.

4. **Click the Slide Sorter button on the status bar**
   A thumbnail of each slide in the presentation appears as shown in Figure A-12. You can examine the flow of your slides and drag any slide or group of slides to rearrange the order of the slides in the presentation.

5. **Double-click Slide 1 in Slide Sorter view**
   Slide 1 appears in Normal view.

6. **Click the Slide Show button on the status bar**
   The first slide fills the entire screen. In this view, you can practice running through your slides as they would appear in the slide show.

   > **QUICK TIP**
   > You can also press [Enter] or [Spacebar] to advance the slide show.

7. **Click the left mouse button to advance through the slides one at a time until you see a black slide, then click once more to return to Normal view**
   The black slide at the end of the slide show indicates that the slide show is finished. At the end of a slide show you automatically return to the slide and PowerPoint view you were in before you ran the slide show, in this case Slide 1 in Normal view.

8. **Click the View tab on the Ribbon, then click the Notes Page button in the Presentation Views group**
   Notes Page view appears, showing a reduced image of the current slide above a large text placeholder. You can enter text in this placeholder and then print the notes page for your own use.

9. **Click the Normal button in the Presentation Views group**

FIGURE A-11: Normal view with the outline tab displayed

Outline tab

Slides tab

Slide icon

Design theme name

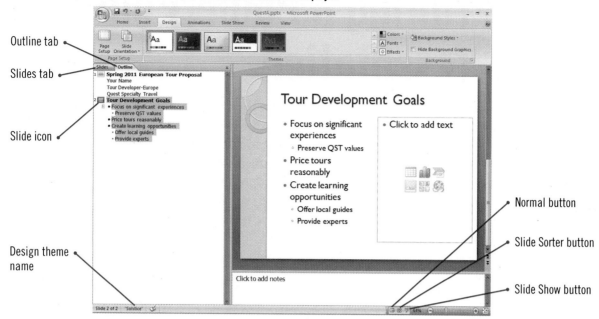

Normal button

Slide Sorter button

Slide Show button

FIGURE A-12: Slide Sorter view

Slide 1

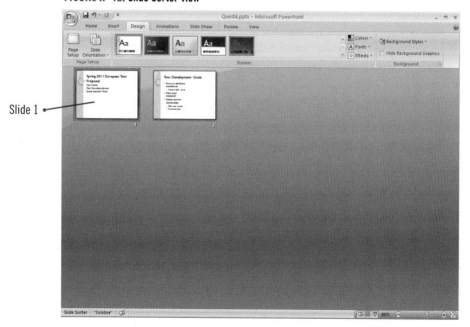

TABLE A-3: PowerPoint views

view name	button	button name	description
Normal	▣	Normal	Displays the Outline and Slides tabs, the Slide pane, and the Notes pane at the same time; use this view to work on your presentation's content, layout, and notes concurrently
Slide Sorter	▦	Slide Sorter	Displays thumbnails of all slides in the order in which they appear in your presentation; use this view to rearrange and add special effects to your slides
Slide Show	▭	Slide Show	Displays your presentation as an electronic slide show
Notes Page	(no View Shortcut button)		Displays a reduced image of the current slide above a large text box where you can enter or view notes

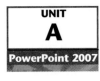

Printing a PowerPoint Presentation

You print your presentation when you want to review your work or when you have completed it and want a hard copy. Reviewing your presentation at different stages of development gives you a better perspective of the overall flow and feel of the presentation. You can also preview your presentation to see exactly how each slide looks before you print the presentation. When you are finished working on your presentation, even if it is not yet complete, you can close the presentation file and exit PowerPoint. ⬛⬛⬛ You are done working on the tour presentation for now. You save and preview the presentation, then you print the slides and notes pages of the presentation so you can review them later. Before leaving for the day, you close the file and exit PowerPoint.

STEPS

1. **Click the Office button 🔘, point to Print, then click Print Preview**

   The Print Preview window opens as shown in Figure A-13. Notice the Print Preview tab appears on the Ribbon, which now displays associated commands for the Print Preview window.

QUICK TIP

To quickly print the presentation with the current Print options, add the Quick Print button to the Quick Access toolbar.

2. **Click the Next Page button in the Preview group, then click the Print button in the Print group**

   You view Slide 2 before opening the Print dialog box. In the Print dialog box, you can specify what you want to print (slides, handouts, notes pages, or outline), the slide range, the number of copies to print, as well as other print options. The default options for the available printer are selected in the dialog box.

3. **Click the Slides option button in the Print range section of the dialog box to select it, type 2 to print only the second slide, then click OK**

   The second slide prints. To save paper when you are reviewing your slides, you can print in handout format, which lets you print up to nine slides per page.

4. **Click the Close Print Preview button in the Preview group, click the Office button 🔘, then click Print**

   The Print dialog box opens again. The options you choose in the Print dialog box remain there until you close the presentation.

QUICK TIP

To print slides appropriate in size for overhead transparencies, click the Design tab, click the Page Setup button in the Page Setup group, click the Slides sized for list arrow, then click Overhead.

5. **Click the All option button in the Print range section, click the Print what list arrow, click Handouts, click the Slides per page list arrow in the Handouts section, then click 3**

6. **Click the Color/grayscale list arrow, click Pure Black and White as shown in Figure A-14, then click OK**

   The presentation prints as handouts showing slide thumbnails next to blank lines. Using the Handouts with three slides per page printing option is a great way to print your presentation when you want to provide a way for audience members to take notes. Printing in pure black and white prints without any gray tones and can save printer toner.

7. **Click the Office button 🔘, then click Close**

   If you have made changes to your presentation, a Microsoft PowerPoint alert box opens asking you if you want to save changes you have made to your presentation file.

8. **Click Yes, if necessary, to close the alert box**

   Your presentation closes.

9. **Click the Office button 🔘, then click the Exit PowerPoint button**

   The PowerPoint program closes, and you return to the Windows desktop.

Creating a Presentation in PowerPoint 2007

Print Preview tab

Print button

The color of the slide changes to reflect the grayscale printer that is attached to the computer

FIGURE A-14: Print dialog box with Handouts selected

Your printer name may be different

Slides option button

Click to select an item to print

Color/grayscale list arrow

Slides per page list arrow

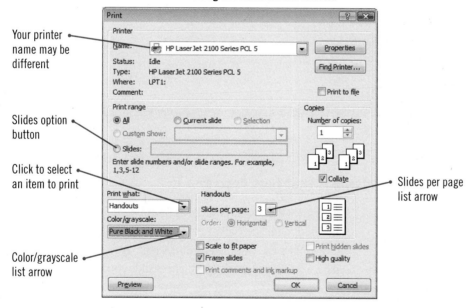

Animating in PowerPoint

Providing emphasis to the information in your presentation can help your audience retain that information. Animating text and other objects is one dramatic way to provide emphasis. Animations make a presentation engaging and enjoyable to watch. You can animate text, shapes, diagrams, charts, and other objects, which provides you a wide variety of options to create a dynamic presentation. You can also add interesting effects to the way slides are presented or transition on the screen. Types of animation effects include flying in or out, fading, and changing color.

Practice

▼ CONCEPTS REVIEW

Label each element of the PowerPoint window shown in Figure A-15.

FIGURE A-15

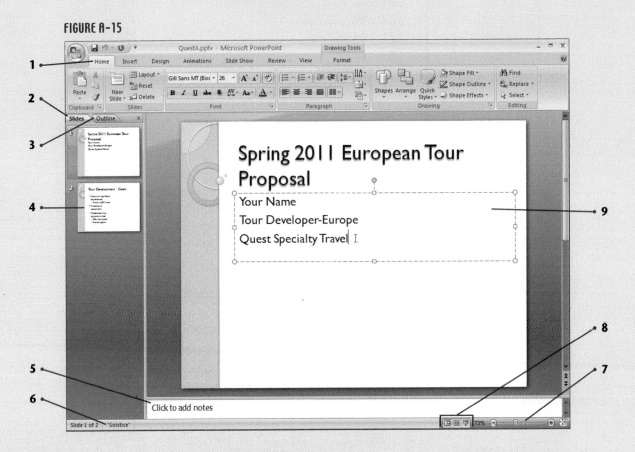

Match each term with the statement that best describes it.

10. **Ribbon**

11. **Normal view**

12. **Slide Sorter view**

13. **Zoom slider**

14. **Notes pane**

a. A view that displays slides as thumbnails

b. Used to organize all of PowerPoint's commands

c. Displays the Outline and Slides tabs, as well as the Slide and Notes panes

d. Used to type text that references slide content

e. Allows you to change the size of the slide in the window

Select the best answer from the list of choices.

15. When you type text in a placeholder, it becomes:
- **a.** A label
- **b.** A text object
- **c.** A text processing object
- **d.** A selection box

16. The buttons you use to switch between the PowerPoint views in the status bar are called:
- **a.** Toolbar buttons
- **b.** View buttons
- **c.** PowerPoint buttons
- **d.** View Shortcuts

17. All of the following are PowerPoint views, except:
- **a.** Notes Page view
- **b.** Outline Page view
- **c.** Normal view
- **d.** Slide Sorter view

18. What does the slide layout do in a presentation?
- **a.** A slide layout defines how all the elements on a slide are arranged.
- **b.** A slide layout automatically applies all the objects you can use on a slide.
- **c.** The slide layout puts all your slides in order.
- **d.** The slide layout enables you to apply a template to the presentation.

19. The view that fills the entire screen with each slide in the presentation is called:
- **a.** Presentation view
- **b.** Slide Sorter view
- **c.** Slide Show view
- **d.** Slide view

20. According to the unit, which of the following is not a guideline for planning a presentation?
- **a.** Determine how much time you need to give the presentation.
- **b.** Determine the purpose of the presentation.
- **c.** Determine what you want to produce when the presentation is finished.
- **d.** Determine which type of output you need to best convey your message.

21. Other than the Slide pane, where else can you enter slide text?
- **a.** Slides tab
- **b.** Outline tab
- **c.** Tab Preview
- **d.** Notes Page view

▼ SKILLS REVIEW

1. Start PowerPoint and examine the PowerPoint window.
- **a.** Start PowerPoint, if necessary.
- **b.** Identify as many elements of the PowerPoint window as you can without referring to the unit material.
- **c.** Be able to describe the purpose or function of each element.
- **d.** For any elements you cannot identify, refer to the unit.

2. Enter slide text.
- **a.** In the Slide pane in Normal view, enter the text **Historic Middle Fork Land & Camps Protection Proposal** in the title placeholder. Refer to Figure A-16 as you complete the slide.
- **b.** In the subtitle text placeholder, enter **Historic Lands Preservation Society**

FIGURE A-16: Slide 1 of the completed presentation

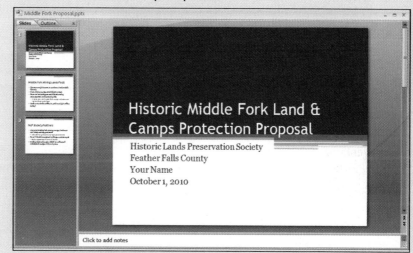

    c. On the next line of the placeholder, enter Feather Falls County.

    d. On the next line of the placeholder, enter Your Name.

    e. On the next line of the placeholder, enter October 1, 2010. Let PowerPoint AutoFit the text in the text object.

    f. Deselect the text object.

    g. Save the presentation using the filename Middle Fork Proposal to the drive and folder where you store your Data Files.

3. Add new slides.

    a. Create a new slide.

    b. Using Figure A-17, enter text on the slide.

    c. Create another new slide.

    d. Using Figure A-18, enter text on the slide.

    e. Save your changes.

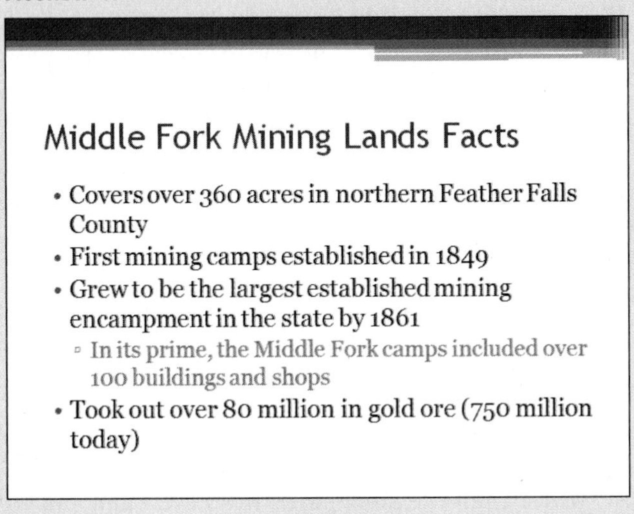

4. Apply a design theme.

    a. Click the Design tab.

    b. Click the Themes group More button, then point to all of the themes.

    c. Locate the Verve theme, then apply it to all the slides.

    d. Move to Slide 1.

    e. Locate the Urban theme, then apply it to Slide 1.

    f. Apply the Urban theme to all of the slides in the presentation.

    g. Use the Next Slide button to move to Slide 3, then save your changes.

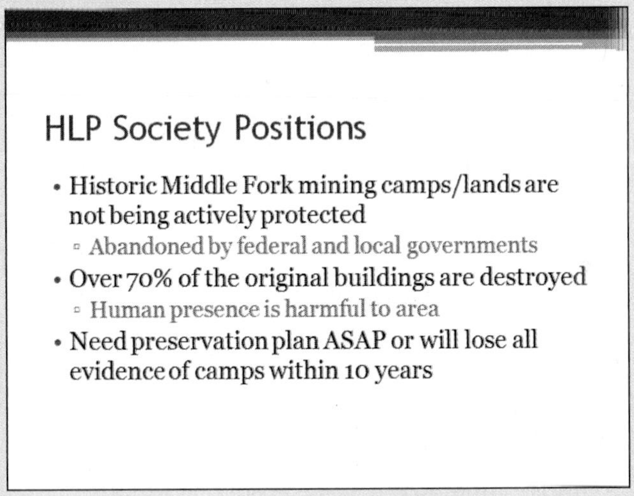

5. Compare presentation views.

    a. Click the View tab.

    b. Click the Slide Sorter button in the Presentation Views group.

    c. Click the Notes Page button in the Presentation Views group, then click the Previous Slide button twice.

    d. Click the Normal button in the Presentation Views group, then click the Slide Show button.

    e. Click until a black screen appears, then click to end the presentation.

    f. Save your changes.

6. Print and close a presentation, and exit PowerPoint.

    a. Print Slide 1 as slides in grayscale. (*Hint*: Click the Current slide option button in the Print dialog box.)

    b. Print all the slides as handouts, 3 slides per page, in pure black and white.

    c. Print the presentation outline.

    d. Close the file, saving your changes.

    e. Exit PowerPoint.

FIGURE A-17

Middle Fork Mining Lands Facts

- Covers over 360 acres in northern Feather Falls County
- First mining camps established in 1849
- Grew to be the largest established mining encampment in the state by 1861
  - In its prime, the Middle Fork camps included over 100 buildings and shops
- Took out over 80 million in gold ore (750 million today)

FIGURE A-18

HLP Society Positions

- Historic Middle Fork mining camps/lands are not being actively protected
  - Abandoned by federal and local governments
- Over 70% of the original buildings are destroyed
  - Human presence is harmful to area
- Need preservation plan ASAP or will lose all evidence of camps within 10 years

▼ INDEPENDENT CHALLENGE 1

You work for Resource Industries, a business that that offers environmental hazard clean up and project management. In an effort to expand the business, your boss has asked you to create a sales presentation that describes the services Resource Industries offers.

a. Start PowerPoint.

b. In the title placeholder on Slide 1, type Resource Industries

c. In the sub-title placeholder, type Professional & Client Services, press [Enter], type Your Name, press [Enter], then type Today's Date

d. Apply the Equity design theme to the slide.

e. Save your presentation with the filename Resource Industries to the drive and folder where you store your Data Files.

f. Use Figures A-19 and A-20 to add two more slides to your presentation. (*Hint*: Slide 2 uses the Comparison layout.)

g. Use the commands on the View tab to switch between all of PowerPoint's views.

h. Preview the presentation using the Print Preview command, print the presentation using the Slides option, save and close the file, then exit PowerPoint.

▼ INDEPENDENT CHALLENGE 2

You have recently been promoted to national sales manager at Windman Power Industries, which manufactures personal watercraft, including items such as paddle boats, canoes, kayaks, sail boats, and rafts. Part of your job is to present company sales figures at a yearly sales meeting. Use the following information as the basis for units sold nationally in your presentation: 797 canoes, 1302 kayaks, 421 paddle boats, 4219 sail boats, 230 rafts. Assume that Windman Power has five sales regions throughout the country: West, East, South, Midwest, and Northeast. Also, assume overall sales rose 22% during the last year and gross sales reached $230 million. The presentation should have at least five slides.

a. Spend some time planning the slides of your presentation. What is the best way to show the information provided? What other information could you add that might be useful for this presentation?

b. Start PowerPoint.

c. Give the presentation an appropriate title on the title slide and enter today's date and your name in the subtitle placeholder.

d. Add slides and enter appropriate slide text.

FIGURE A-19

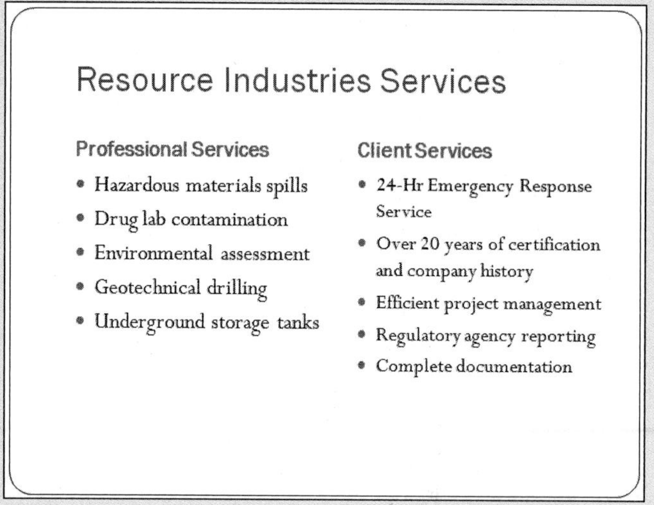

Resource Industries Services

Professional Services
- Hazardous materials spills
- Drug lab contamination
- Environmental assessment
- Geotechnical drilling
- Underground storage tanks

Client Services
- 24-Hr Emergency Response Service
- Over 20 years of certification and company history
- Efficient project management
- Regulatory agency reporting
- Complete documentation

FIGURE A-20

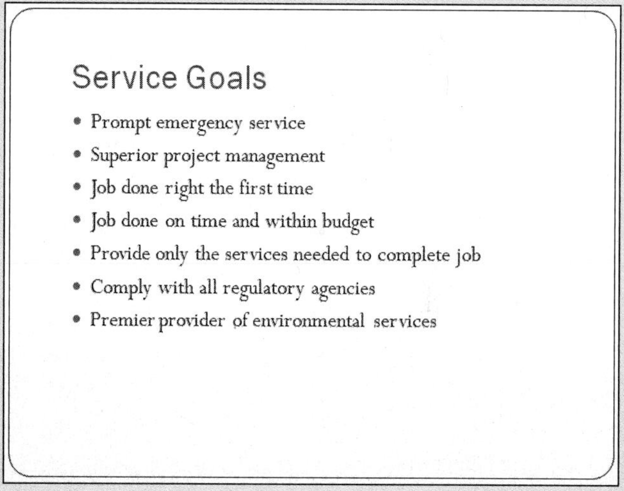

Service Goals
- Prompt emergency service
- Superior project management
- Job done right the first time
- Job done on time and within budget
- Provide only the services needed to complete job
- Comply with all regulatory agencies
- Premier provider of environmental services

e. On the last slide of the presentation, include the following information:

Windman Power Industries

PO Box 777

West Chester, IN 39022

f. Apply a design theme. A typical slide might look like the one shown in Figure A-21.

Advanced Challenge Exercise

- Open the Notes Page view.
- Add notes to three slides.
- Print the Notes Page view for the presentation.

g. Switch views. Run through the slide show at least once.

h. Save your presentation with the filename **Windman** where you store your Data Files.

i. Close the presentation and exit PowerPoint.

FIGURE A-21

An Overall View

Sales Figures
- This year's results!
    - $230 million gross sales
- Comparison to last year
    - $65 million increase in overall sales
- Region by region
    - West-up by 12%
    - East-down by 5%
    - Northeast-up by 6%
    - South-up by 11%
    - Midwest-up by 7%

National Sales
- Product Sales
    - Canoes- 797 units
    - Kayaks- 1302 units
    - Paddle boats- 421 units
    - Sail boats- 4219 units
    - Rafts- 230 units

▼ INDEPENDENT CHALLENGE 3

You work for ThaiMade Trade Co., an emerging company that exports goods from Thailand. The company wants to expand its business globally. The Internet marketing director has asked you to plan and create a PowerPoint presentation that he will use to convey an expanded Internet service that will target Western countries. This new Internet service will allow customers to purchase all kinds of Thai made goods. Sample items for sale include silver and turquoise jewelry, hand crafts, folk art, terra cotta kitchenware, wooden decorative items, and bamboo furniture. Your presentation should contain product information and pricing. Use the Internet, if possible, to research information that will help you formulate your ideas. The presentation should have at least five slides.

a. Spend some time planning the slides of your presentation. What information would a consumer need to have to purchase items on this Web site?

b. Start PowerPoint.

c. Give the presentation an appropriate title on the title slide and enter today's date and your name in the subtitle placeholder.

d. Add slides and enter appropriate slide text.

e. On the last slide of the presentation, type the following information:

ThaiMade Trade Co.

Satrani Condominium Room 214

36/980 Moo 5 Sethup Sub District, Muang district, Chiangmai 50208 Thailand

Tel/Fax: +90-49-39850 Hotline: (03)249347

FIGURE A-22

Fine Jewelry Product List

Silver Jewelry	Turquoise Jewelry
☐ Bracelets	☐ Bracelets
☐ Necklaces	☐ Necklaces
☐ Rings	☐ Rings
☐ Earrings	☐ Earrings
☐ Watches	
☐ Pendants	

f. Apply a design theme. A typical slide might look like the one shown in Figure A-22.

g. Switch views. Run through the slide show at least once.

h. Save your presentation with the filename **ThaiMade** where you store your Data Files.

i. Close the presentation and exit PowerPoint.

▼ REAL LIFE INDEPENDENT CHALLENGE

Every year your college holds a large fund raising event to support a local charity. This year the Student Advisory Committee has chosen to help the East Hills Cerebral Palsy Center. To help them decide what kind of an event to hold this year, the Advisory Committee has appealed to the student body for fund raising ideas. Your idea is to host a regional Bar-B-Q cook off competition that includes local and professional cooking teams. Your idea was chosen as one of the finalist ideas and you need to present your proposal in a meeting of the Advisory Committee.

a. Spend some time planning the slides of your presentation. Assume the following: there are four competition categories (beef brisket, pork shoulder, pork ribs, and chicken); the competition is a two day event; event advertising will be city- and region-wide; local music groups will also be invited; there will be a kids section with games; the event will be held on the college football field. Use the Internet, if possible, to research information that will help you formulate your ideas.

b. Start PowerPoint.

c. Give the presentation an appropriate title on the title slide and enter your name and today's date in the subtitle placeholder.

d. Add slides and enter appropriate slide text. A typical slide might look like the one shown in Figure A-23.

e. View the presentation.

f. Save your presentation with the filename **Bar-B-Q Cookoff** where you store your Data Files.

g. Close the presentation and exit PowerPoint.

FIGURE A-23

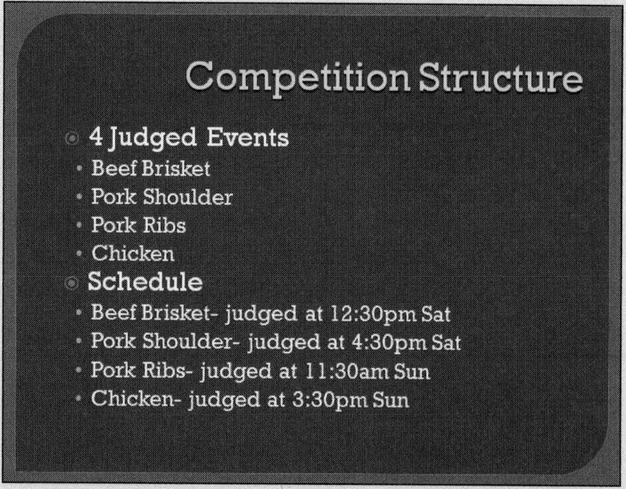

Competition Structure

- 4 Judged Events
  - Beef Brisket
  - Pork Shoulder
  - Pork Ribs
  - Chicken
- Schedule
  - Beef Brisket- judged at 12:30pm Sat
  - Pork Shoulder- judged at 4:30pm Sat
  - Pork Ribs- judged at 11:30am Sun
  - Chicken- judged at 3:30pm Sun

Create the presentation shown in Figures A-24 and A-25. Make sure you include your name on the title slide. Save the presentation as **PackJet Project Tests** where you store your Data Files. Print the slides.

FIGURE A-24

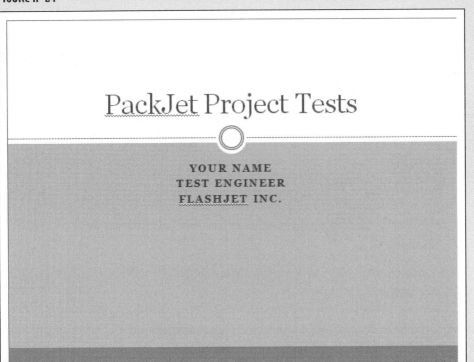

PackJet Project Tests

YOUR NAME
TEST ENGINEER
FLASHJET INC.

FIGURE A-25

Component Tests

- Interface module board
- Security codes
- Flash system codes
  - Temporary access
  - Print reader
- Rocket pack system

Modifying a Presentation

In the previous unit you learned how to enter slide text, add a new slide, and apply a design theme. Now, you are ready to take the next step in creating professional-looking presentations by learning to format text and work with drawn objects. In this unit, you'll enter text in the Outline tab, format text, draw and modify objects, add slide footer information, and check the spelling in the presentation. You continue working on the European tour proposal presentation for Ellen Latsky.

OBJECTIVES

Enter text in the Outline tab

Format text

Convert text to SmartArt

Insert and modify shapes

Edit and duplicate shapes

Align and group objects

Add slide headers and footers

Check spelling in a presentation

Entering Text in the Outline Tab

You can enter presentation text by typing directly on the slide in the Slide pane, or, if you'd rather focus on the presentation text without worrying about the layout, you can enter text in the Outline tab. The outline is organized so that the headings, or slide titles, appear at the top of the outline. Beneath the title, each subpoint, or each line of bulleted text, appears as one or more indented lines under the title. Each indent in the outline creates another level of bulleted text on the slide. ⬛⬛🖰 You switch to the Outline tab to enter text for two more slides in the European tour proposal presentation. Begin by entering more text using the Outline tab.

STEPS

1. **Start PowerPoint, open the presentation** PPT B-1.pptx **from the drive and folder where you store your Data Files, save it as** QuestB, **click the** View tab **on the Ribbon, then click the** Arrange All button **in the Window group**

   The Slide pane, Notes pane, and Slide and Outline tabs are now in their own window with the presentation title at the top.

2. **Click the** Slide 2 thumbnail in the Slides tab, then click the Outline tab

   The Outline tab enlarges to display the text that is on the slides. The slide icon and the text for Slide 2 are highlighted, indicating that it's selected. Notice the number 1 that appears to the left of the first-level bullet for Slide 2, indicating that there are multiple content placeholders on the slide.

3. **Click the** Home tab **on the Ribbon, click the** New Slide button list arrow **in the Slides group, then click** Title and Content

   A new slide, Slide 3, with the Title and Content layout appears as the current slide below Slide 2. A blinking insertion point appears next to the new slide in the Outline tab. See Figure B-1. Text that you enter next to a slide icon becomes the title for that slide.

4. **Type** Focus Group Data Analyzed, **press [Enter], then press [Tab]**

   When you first press [Enter] you create a new slide, but because you want to enter bulleted text on Slide 3 you press [Tab] so that the text you type is entered as bullet text on Slide 3.

5. **Type** Trends, **press [Enter], type** Major Findings, **press [Enter], type** Conclusions, **then press [Enter]**

   The last time you press [Enter], you create a bullet that has no text at the end of this slide.

6. **Press** [Shift][Tab]

   The last bullet that was created on Slide 3 becomes a new slide.

7. **Type** Tour Strategy Objectives, **press** [Ctrl][Enter], **then type the rest of the information on Slide 4 as shown in Figure B-2**

   Pressing [Ctrl][Enter] while the cursor is in the title text object moves the cursor into the content placeholder. Make sure you misspell the word "Utilze" as shown on the slide.

8. **Position the pointer on the** Slide 4 icon in the Outline tab

   The pointer changes to ✥. Slide 4 is out of order.

9. **Drag the** Slide 4 icon up until a horizontal indicator line appears above the Slide 3 icon, **then release the mouse button**

   The fourth slide moves up and switches places with the third slide.

10. **Click the** Slides tab, then save your work

    The Outline tab closes and the Slides tab is now visible in the window.

FIGURE B-1: Outline tab open showing new slide

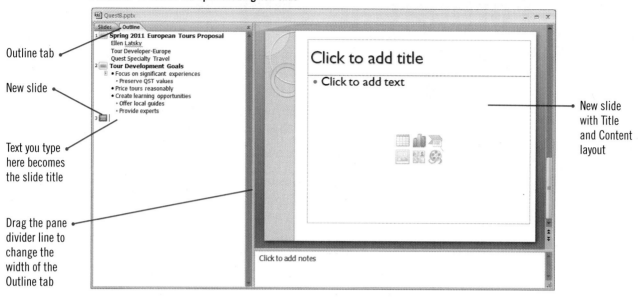

Outline tab

New slide

Text you type here becomes the slide title

Drag the pane divider line to change the width of the Outline tab

New slide with Title and Content layout

FIGURE B-2: Slide 4 with new information

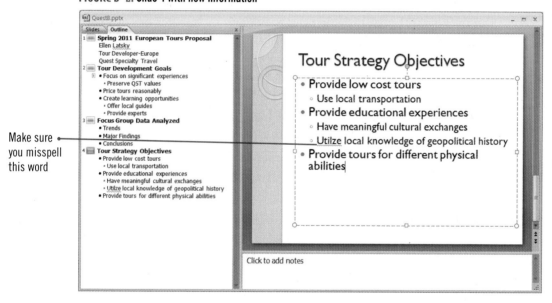

Make sure you misspell this word

Setting permissions

In PowerPoint, you can set specific access permissions for people who review or edit your work, so you have better control over your content. For example, you may want to give a user permission to edit or change your presentation but not allow them to print it. You can also restrict a user by permitting them to view the presentation, without the ability to edit or print the presentation, or you can give the user full access or control of the presentation. To use this feature, you first have to install the Windows Rights Management Services software using the Add or Remove Programs feature in the Control Panel, which installs the Restrict Permissions feature on the Office button. Then, to set user access permissions, click the Office button, point to Prepare, point to Restrict Permission, then click the appropriate option.

Formatting Text

Once you have entered and edited the text in your presentation, you can modify the way the text looks to emphasize your message. Important text should be highlighted in some way to distinguish it from other text or objects on the slide. For example, if you have two text objects on the same slide, you could draw attention to one text object by changing its color, font, or size. ▰▰▰▰ In order to enhance the European tour proposal presentation, you format text on Slide 4.

STEPS

QUICK TIP
Open the PowerPoint Options dialog box to set the option to show or hide the Mini toolbar.

1. **Click the** Slide 4 **thumbnail in the Slides tab, then double-click** Trends **in the text object**

   The word Trends is selected and a small semitransparent Mini toolbar appears above the text. The **Mini toolbar** contains basic text formatting commands, such as bold and italic, and appears when you select text using the mouse. This toolbar makes it quick and easy to format text, especially when the Home tab is not open.

2. **Move the pointer over the** Mini toolbar, **click the** Font Color button list arrow ▣ ▾, **then click the** Dark Red color box **under Standard Colors**

   The text changes color to dark red as shown in Figure B-3. As soon as you move the pointer over the Mini toolbar, the toolbar becomes clearly visible. When you click the Font Color button list arrow, the Font Color gallery appears showing the Theme Colors and Standard Colors. Notice that the Font Color button on the Mini toolbar and the Font Color button on the Home tab change color to reflect the new color choice.

QUICK TIP
You can also select the entire text object by clicking its border when the text object is already selected.

3. **Click outside the text object in a blank area of the slide, press and hold** [Shift], **click the text object, then release** [Shift]

   A selection box with small circles and squares called **sizing handles** appears around the text object. The entire text object is selected, and changes you make now affect all of the text in the text object. If you click a text object without pressing [Shift], a dotted selection box appears, indicating that the object is active and ready to accept text, but the text object itself is not selected. When the whole text object is selected, you can change its size, shape, or other attributes. Changing the color of the text helps emphasize it.

4. **Click the** Font Color button ▣ **in the Font group**

   All of the text in the text object changes to the dark red color.

5. **Click the** Font list arrow **in the Font group**

   A list of available fonts opens with Gill Sans MT, the current font used in the text object, selected at the top of the list with the Theme Fonts.

6. **Click** Arial Narrow

   The Arial Narrow font replaces the original font in the text object. Notice that as you move the pointer over the font names in the font list the text on the slide displays a live preview of the different font choices.

7. **Click the** Text Shadow button ⓢ **in the Font group, click the** Change Case button Aa ▾ **in the Font group, then click** UPPERCASE

   All of the text now displays a gray shadow and is uppercase.

8. **Click the** Bullets button list arrow ☰ ▾ **in the Paragraph group, click** None, **then click the** Center button ☰ **in the Paragraph group**

   The bullets no longer appear next to the text and the text moves to the center of the text box. Compare your screen to Figure B-4.

9. **Click a blank area of the slide outside the text object to deselect it, then save your work**

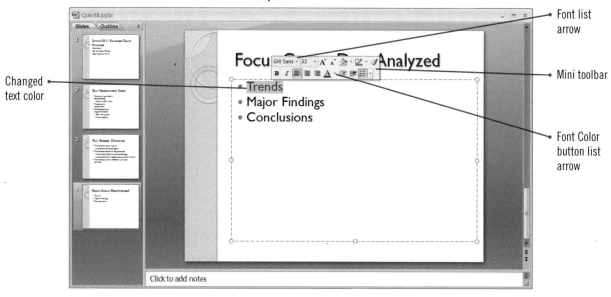

FIGURE B-3: Selected word with Mini toolbar open

Changed text color

Font list arrow

Mini toolbar

Font Color button list arrow

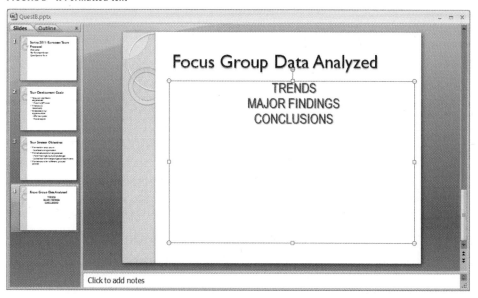

FIGURE B-4: Formatted text

Replacing text and fonts

As you review your presentation, you may decide to replace certain text or fonts throughout the entire presentation using the Replace command. Text can be a word, phrase, or sentence. To replace specific text, click the Home tab on the Ribbon, then click the Replace button in the Editing group. In the Replace dialog box, enter the text you want to replace then enter the text you want to use as its replacement. You can also use the Replace command to replace one font for another. Simply click the Replace button list arrow in the Editing group, then click Replace Fonts to open the Replace Font dialog box.

Converting Text to SmartArt

Sometimes when you are working with text it just doesn't capture your attention, no matter how you dress it up with color or other formatting attributes. The introduction of the SmartArt graphic in PowerPoint 2007 increases your ability to create dynamic-looking text. A **SmartArt** graphic is a professional-quality diagram that visually illustrates text. There are seven basic categories, or types, of SmartArt graphics that illustrate text differently. For example, you can show steps in a process or timeline, show proportional relationships, or show how parts relate to a whole. You can create a SmartArt graphic from scratch or create one by converting existing text you have entered on a slide with a few simple clicks of the mouse. ▄▄▅▅▅ At QST, Ellen wants the text to appear visually dynamic so you convert the text on Slide 4 to a SmartArt graphic.

STEPS

1. **On Slide 4, click anywhere in the text object, then click the Convert to SmartArt Graphic button 📑▾ in the Paragraph group**

   A gallery of SmartArt graphic layouts opens. As with many features in PowerPoint, you can preview how your text will look prior to applying the SmartArt graphic layout by using PowerPoint's Live Preview feature. You can review each SmartArt graphic layout and see how it changes the appearance of text.

2. **Move the pointer over the SmartArt graphic layouts in the gallery**

   Notice how the text becomes part of the graphic and the color and font changes each time you move the pointer over a different graphic layout. SmartArt graphic names appear as ScreenTips.

3. **Click the Basic Timeline layout in the SmartArt graphics gallery**

   A SmartArt graphic appears on the slide in place of the text object and a new SmartArt Tools Design tab opens on the Ribbon as shown in Figure B-5. A SmartArt graphic consists of two parts: the SmartArt graphic itself and a text pane where you type and edit text.

QUICK TIP
The text objects in the SmartArt graphic can be moved and edited like any other text object in PowerPoint.

4. **If necessary, click the Text Pane button in the Create Graphic group to open the text pane, then click each bullet point in the text pane**

   Notice that each time you select a bullet point in the text pane, a selection box appears around the text objects in the SmartArt graphic.

5. **Click the Text Pane button, click the More button ▾ in the Layouts group, then click the Alternating Flow layout**

   The text pane closes and the SmartArt graphic changes to the new graphic layout. You can radically change how the SmartArt graphic looks by applying a SmartArt Style. A **SmartArt Style** is a pre-set combination of simple and 3-D formatting options that follows the presentation theme.

QUICK TIP
Click the Reset Graphic button in the Reset group to revert the SmartArt graphic to its original state.

6. **Move the pointer slowly over the styles in the SmartArt Styles group, then click the More button ▾ in the SmartArt Styles group**

   A live preview of each style is displayed on the SmartArt graphic. The SmartArt styles are organized into sections; the top group offers suggestions for the best match for the document.

7. **Move the pointer over the styles in the 3-D section of the gallery, then click Powder**

   Notice how the new Powder style adds a bevel to the text boxes and makes them semi-transparent. Now move the SmartArt graphic more toward the center of the slide.

8. **Press [left-arrow key] twice, click a blank area of the slide outside the SmartArt graphic object to deselect it, then save your work**

   Compare your screen to Figure B-6.

FIGURE B-5: Text converted to a SmartArt graphic

Text Pane button

More button

Click to open the text pane

Contextual tabs for working with SmartArt graphics

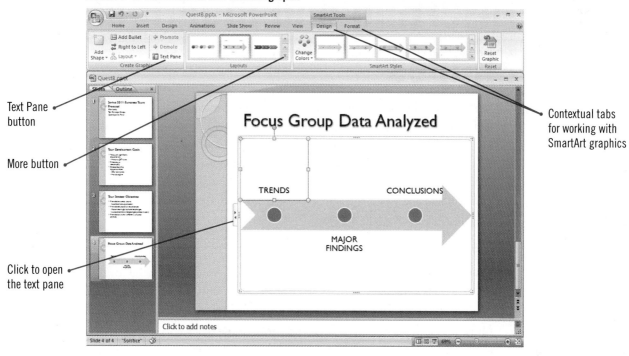

FIGURE B-6: Final SmartArt graphic

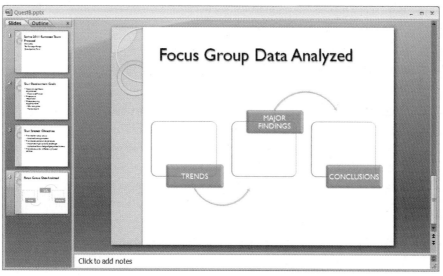

Choosing SmartArt graphics

When choosing a SmartArt graphic to use on your slide, remember that you want the SmartArt graphic to communicate the message of the text effectively; not every SmartArt graphic layout achieves that goal. So, you must consider the type of text you want to illustrate. For example, does the text show steps in a process, does it show a continual process, or does it show non-sequential information? The answer to this question will dictate the type of SmartArt graphic layout you should choose. Also, the amount of text you want to illustrate will have an effect on the SmartArt graphic layout you choose. Most of the time key points will be the text you use in a SmartArt graphic. Finally, some SmartArt graphic layouts are limited by the number of shapes that they can accommodate. So, if you have four points you want to illustrate and you choose a graphic layout with only two shapes, you will not communicate your message correctly. Experiment with the SmartArt graphic layouts until you find the right one, and have fun in the process!

Inserting and Modifying Shapes

In PowerPoint you can insert many different types of shapes including lines, geometric figures, arrows, stars, callouts, and banners to enhance your presentation. You can create single shapes or combine several shapes together to make a more complex figure. You can modify many aspects of a shape including its fill color, line color, and line style, as well as add other effects like shadow, and 3-D effects. Instead of changing individual attributes, you can apply a Quick Style to a shape. A **Quick Style** is a set of formatting options, including line style, fill color, and effects. ⬛⬛⬛⬛ You decide to draw some shapes on Slide 3 of your presentation to complete the slide.

STEPS

1. **Click the Slide 3 thumbnail in the Slides tab**
   Slide 3 appears in the Slide pane.

2. **Press and hold [Shift], click the text object, then release [Shift]**
   The text object is selected.

3. **Position the pointer over the bottom-middle sizing handle, notice the pointer change to ↕, then drag the sizing handle up until the text object looks like Figure B-7**
   The text object decreases in size. When you position the pointer over a sizing handle, it changes to ↕. The pointer points in different directions depending on which sizing handle it is positioned over. When you drag a sizing handle, the pointer changes to ┼, and a faint gray outline appears, representing the size of the text object.

TROUBLE
If you see the Shapes gallery on the Ribbon, you are working at a higher resolution than the figures in this book, skip to step 5.

4. **Click the Shapes button in the Drawing group**
   A gallery of shapes organized by type opens. Notice that there is a section at the top of the gallery where all of the recently used shapes are placed.

5. **Click the Chevron shape ⟫ in the Block Arrows section, position ┼ in the blank area of the slide below the text object, press and hold [Shift], drag down and to the right to create the chevron shape, as shown in Figure B-8, release the mouse button, then release [Shift]**
   A chevron arrow shape appears on the slide, filled with the default color. Pressing [Shift] while you create the object maintains the object's proportions as you change its size. To change the shape style apply a Quick Style from the Shape Styles group.

TROUBLE
If your shape is not approximately the same size as the one shown in Figure B-8, press [Shift] and drag one of the corner sizing handles to resize the object.

6. **Click the Drawing Tools Format tab, click the More button ▾ in the Shape Styles group, move the pointer over the styles in the gallery to review them, then click Moderate Effect — Accent 3**
   A red Quick Style with coordinated gradient fill, line, and shadow color is applied to the shape.

7. **Click the Shape Effects button in the Shape Styles group, then move the pointer over the effects to review them**
   The shape changes every time you move the pointer over a different effect.

8. **Point to Bevel, click Divot, then save your work**

FIGURE B-7: Resized text object

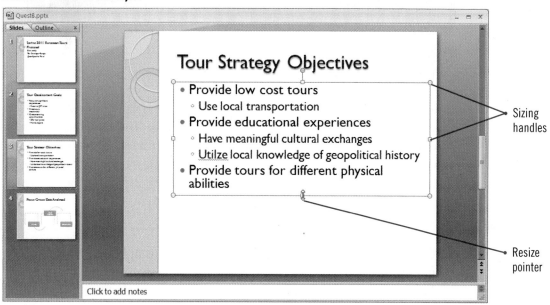

Sizing handles

Resize pointer

FIGURE B-8: Chevron arrow shape

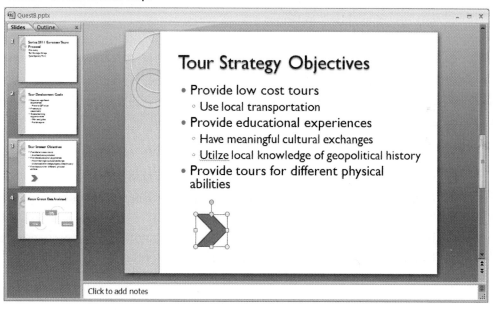

Changing the size and position of shapes

Usually when you resize a shape you can simply drag one of the sizing handles around the outside of the shape, but sometimes you may need to resize a shape more precisely. When you select a shape, the Drawing Tools Format tab appears on the Ribbon, offering you many different formatting options including some sizing commands

located in the Size group. The Width and Height commands in the Size group allow you to change the width and height of a shape. You also have the option to open the Size and Position dialog box, which allows you to change the size of a shape, as well as the rotation, scale, and position of a shape on the slide.

Editing and Duplicating Shapes

Once you have created a shape you still have the ability to refine the aspects of the object. PowerPoint allows you to adjust various aspects of shapes to help change the look of them. For example, if you create a shape with an arrowhead but the head of the arrow does not look quite like you want it to look, you can change it. You can also add text to most PowerPoint shapes, and you can move or copy shapes. You want two identical arrows on Slide 3 to break up the look of the slide. You first change the shape of the arrow you've already created, and then you make a copy of it.

STEPS

1. **Click the arrow shape on Slide 3 to select it, if it is not already selected**

   In addition to sizing handles, two other handles appear on the selected object. You use the **adjustment handle**—a small yellow diamond—to change the appearance of an object. The adjustment handle appears next to the most prominent feature of the object, like the head of an arrow in this case. You use the **rotate handle**—a small green circle—to manually rotate the object.

2. **Press and hold [Shift], drag the right-middle sizing handle on the arrow shape to the right approximately 1/2", release [Shift], then release the mouse button**

3. **Position the pointer over the middle of the selected arrow shape so that it changes to ⁺↖, then drag the arrow shape so that the arrow aligns with the left edge of the text in the text object as shown in Figure B-9**

   A semitransparent copy of the shape appears as you move the arrow shape to help you position it. PowerPoint uses a hidden grid to align objects; it forces objects to "snap" to the grid lines. Make any needed adjustments to the arrow shape position so it looks similar to Figure B-9.

TROUBLE

If you are having trouble making precise adjustments, press and hold [Alt] to turn off the snap to grid feature, then drag the adjustment handle.

4. **Position the pointer over the adjustment handle of the arrow shape so that it changes to ▷, then drag the adjustment handle to the right so it is halfway between the sizing handles**

   The arrow shape appearance changes.

5. **Position ⁺↖ over the arrow shape then press and hold [Ctrl]**

   The pointer changes to ↖, indicating that PowerPoint makes a copy of the arrow shape when you drag the mouse.

6. **Holding [Ctrl], drag the arrow shape to the right until the arrow shape copy is in a blank area of the slide, release the mouse button, then release [Ctrl]**

   An identical copy of the arrow shape appears on the slide.

TROUBLE

If the text does not fit on one line, drag the right-middle sizing handle slightly to the right until the text moves onto one line.

7. **Type Higher**

   The text appears in the selected arrow shape. The text is now part of the shape, so if you move or rotate the object, the text moves with it. Compare your screen with Figure B-10.

8. **Click the other arrow shape, type Aim, then click in a blank area of the slide**

   Clicking a blank area of the slide deselects all objects that are selected.

9. **Save your work**

FIGURE B-9: Slide showing resized shape

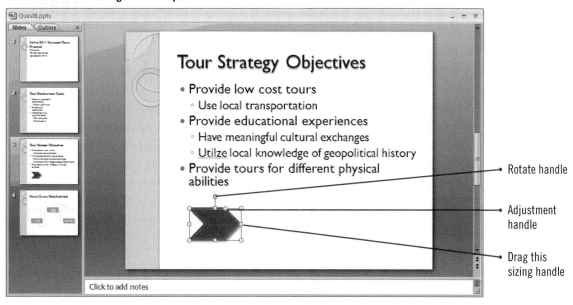

Rotate handle

Adjustment handle

Drag this sizing handle

FIGURE B-10: Slide showing duplicated shape

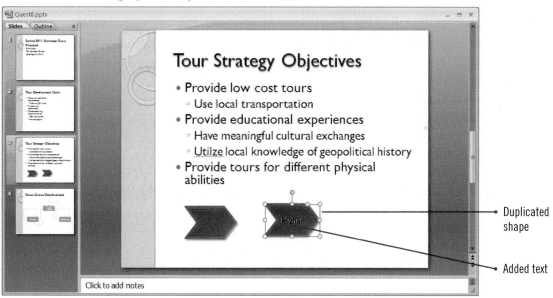

Duplicated shape

Added text

Understanding PowerPoint objects

Every object on a slide, whether it is a text object, a shape, a chart, a picture, or any other object, is stacked on the slide in the order it was created. So, for example, if you add three shapes to a slide, the first shape you create is on the bottom of the stack and the last shape you create is on the top of the stack. Each object, including Title and Content objects, can be moved up or down in the stack depending on how you want the objects to look on the slide. To move an object to the front of the stack, select the object, then click the Bring to Front button in the Arrange group on the Drawing Tools Format tab. To move an object to the back of the stack, click the Send to Back button in the Arrange group on the Drawing Tools Format tab. You can also open the Selection and Visibility pane by clicking the Selection Pane button in the Arrange group to view and rearrange all of the objects on the slide.

Aligning and Grouping Objects

After you are finished creating and modifying your objects, you can position them accurately on the slide to achieve the look you want. Using the Align commands in the Arrange group, you can align objects relative to each other by snapping them to a grid of evenly spaced vertical and horizontal lines. The Group command groups objects into one object, which secures their relative position to each other and makes it easy to edit and move them. The Distribute commands found with the Align commands evenly space objects horizontally or vertically relative to each other or the slide. ▰▰▰▰▰ You are ready to position and group the arrow shapes on Slide 3 to make the slide look consistent and planned.

STEPS

1. **Right-click a blank area of the slide, then click** Grid and Guides **on the shortcut menu**
   The Grid and Guides dialog box opens.

2. **Click the** Display drawing guides on screen check box, **then click** OK
   The PowerPoint guides appear as dotted lines on the slide and intersect at the center of the slide. They help you position the arrow shape.

3. **Position** ⬉ **over the** vertical guide **in a blank area of the slide, press and hold the mouse button until the pointer changes to a measurement guide, then drag the guide to the right until the guide position box reads** 1.00

4. **Position** ✛ **over the** Higher arrow shape **(not over the text in the shape), then drag the** arrow shape **so that the left edge of the selection box touches the vertical guide as shown in Figure B-11**
   The arrow shape attaches or "snaps" to the vertical guide.

5. **With the Higher arrow shape selected, press and hold [Shift], click the** Aim arrow shape, **then release [Shift]**
   The two objects are now selected.

6. **Click the** Drawing Tools Format tab **on the Ribbon, click the** Align button **in the Arrange group, then click** Align Bottom
   The objects are now aligned horizontally along their bottom edges. Notice that the Higher arrow shape moves to align with the Aim arrow shape.

7. **Click the** Group button **in the Arrange group, then click** Group
   The objects group to form one object without losing their individual attributes. Notice that the sizing handles and rotate handle now appear on the outer edge of the grouped object, not around each individual object.

8. **Click the** Align button, **click** Distribute Horizontally, **then click a blank area of the slide**
   The objects are now distributed equally between the edges of the slide. Compare your screen with Figure B-12.

9. **Right-click a blank area of the slide, click** Grid and Guides **on the shortcut menu, click the** Display drawing guides on screen check box, **click** OK, **then save your work**
   The guides are no longer displayed on the slide.

FIGURE B-11: Repositioned shape

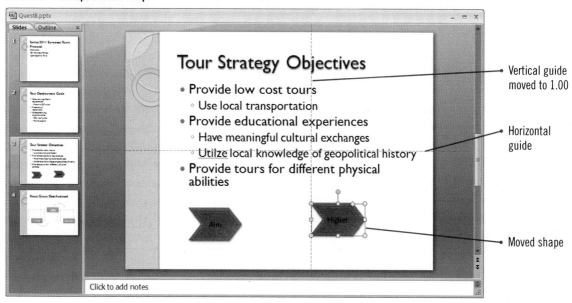

Vertical guide moved to 1.00

Horizontal guide

Moved shape

FIGURE B-12: Aligned and grouped shapes

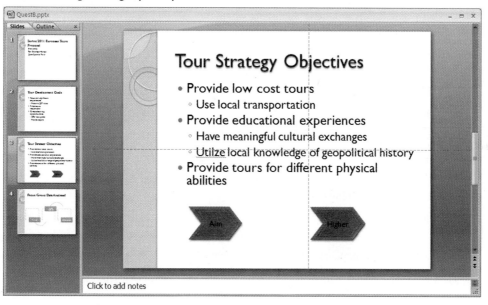

Distributing objects

There are two ways to distribute objects in PowerPoint: relative to each other and relative to the slide edge. If you choose to distribute objects relative to each other, PowerPoint evenly divides the empty space between all of the selected objects. When distributing objects in relation to the slide, PowerPoint evenly splits the empty space from slide edge to slide edge between the selected objects. To distribute objects relative to each other, click the Align button in the Arrange group on the Format tab, then click Align Selected Objects. To distribute objects relative to the slide, click the Align button in the Arrange group on the Format tab, then click Align to Slide.

Adding Slide Headers and Footers

Header and footer text, such as your company or product name, the slide number, and the date, can give your slides a polished look and make it easier for your audience to follow your presentation. On slides, you can add text to the footer; however, notes or handouts can include both header and footer text. Footer information that you apply to the slides of your presentation is visible in the PowerPoint views and when you print the slides. Notes and handouts header and footer text is visible when you print notes pages, handouts, and the outline. ▰▰▰▰▰▰ You add footer text to the slides of the European tour proposal presentation to make it easier for the audience to follow.

STEPS

QUICK TIP

The placement of the footer text objects on the slide is dependent upon the presentation theme.

1. **Click the Insert tab on the Ribbon, then click the Header & Footer button in the Text group**

   The Header and Footer dialog box opens, as shown in Figure B-13. The Header and Footer dialog box has two tabs: a Slide tab and a Notes and Handouts tab. The Slide tab is selected. There are three types of footer text, Date and time, Slide number, and Footer. The rectangles at the bottom of the Preview box identify the default position and status of the three types of footer text placeholders on the slides.

2. **Click the Date and time check box to select it**

   The date and time sub-options are now available and the far-left rectangle at the bottom of the Preview box has a dark border around it, signifying where the date and time information will appear on the slide. The Update automatically date and time option button is selected by default. This option updates the date and time every time you open or print the file.

QUICK TIP

If you want a specific date—such as the original date that the presentation was created—to appear every time you view or print the presen-tation, click the Fixed date option button, then type the date in the Fixed text box.

3. **Click the Update automatically list arrow, then click the fourth option in the list**

   The date format changes to display the month spelled out, the date number, and the four-digit year.

4. **Click the Slide number check box, click the Footer check box, then type Your Name**

   The Preview box now shows that all three footer placeholders are selected.

5. **Click the Don't show on title slide check box**

   Selecting this check box prevents the footer information you entered in the Header and Footer dialog box from appearing on the title slide.

6. **Click Apply to All**

   The dialog box closes and the footer information is applied to all of the slides in your presentation except the title slide. Compare your screen to Figure B-14.

7. **Click the Slide 1 thumbnail in the Slides tab, then click the Header & Footer button in the Text group**

   The Header and Footer dialog box opens again. You want to show your company tag line in the footer on the title slide.

8. **Click the Don't show on title slide check box to deselect it, click the Footer check box, then select the text in the Footer text box**

TROUBLE

If you click Apply to All in Step 9, click the Undo button on the Quick Access toolbar and repeat Steps 7, 8, and 9.

9. **Type "Explore with us...learn from the world", click Apply, then save your work**

   Only the text in the Footer text box appears on the title slide. Clicking Apply applies the footer information to just the current slide.

FIGURE B-13: Header and Footer dialog box

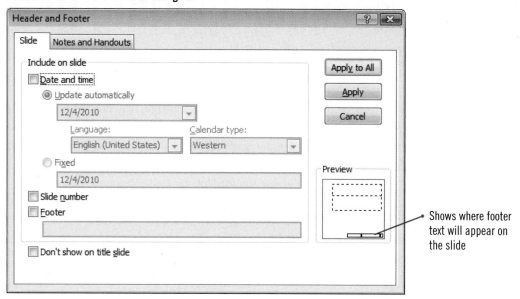

Shows where footer text will appear on the slide

FIGURE B-14: Slide showing footer information

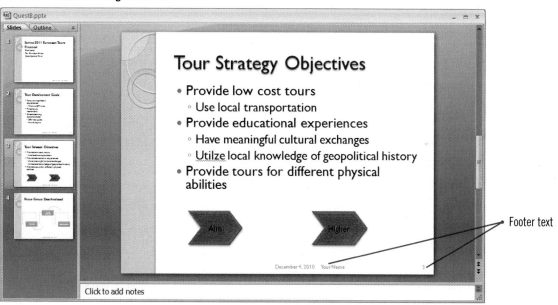

Footer text

Entering and printing notes

You can add notes to your slides when there are certain facts you want to remember during a presentation or when there is information you want to hand out to your audience. Notes do not appear on the slides when you run a slide show. Use the Notes pane in Normal view or Notes Page view to enter notes for your slides. To enter text notes on a slide, click in the Notes pane, then type. If you want to insert graphics as notes, you must use Notes Page view. To open Notes Page view, click the View tab on the Ribbon, then click the Notes Page button in the Presentation Views group. You can print your notes by clicking the Print what list arrow and then clicking Notes Pages in the Print dialog box. The notes page can be a good handout to give your audience to use during the presentation and then after as a reminder. If you don't enter any notes in the Notes pane, and print the notes pages, the slides print as thumbnails with blank lines to the right of the thumbnails to handwrite notes.

Checking Spelling in a Presentation

As your work on the presentation file nears completion, you need to review and proofread your slides thoroughly for errors. You can use the spellchecking feature in PowerPoint to check for and correct spelling errors. This feature compares the spelling of all the words in your presentation against the words contained in PowerPoint's electronic dictionary. You still must proofread your presentation for punctuation, grammar, and word-usage errors because the spellchecker recognizes only misspelled and unknown words, not misused words. For example, the spellchecker would not identify the word "lost" as an error, even if you had intended to type the word "cost." ▓▓▓ Ellen wants to present a professional presentation, one without spelling errors. You're finished working with the European tour proposal presentation for now; this is a good time to check the spelling.

STEPS

TROUBLE
If your spellchecker doesn't find the word "Latsky," then a previous user may have accidentally added it to the custom dictionary. Skip Step 2 and continue with the lesson.

1. **Click the Review tab on the Ribbon, then click the Spelling button in the Proofing group**

   PowerPoint begins to check the spelling in your presentation. When PowerPoint finds a misspelled word or a word it doesn't recognize, the Spelling dialog box opens, as shown in Figure B-15. In this case, PowerPoint does not recognize the name "Latsky" on Slide 1. It suggests that you replace it with the word "Lastly." You want the word to remain as you typed it.

2. **Click Ignore All**

   Clicking Ignore All tells the spellchecker not to stop at and question any more occurrences of this word in this presentation. The next word the spellchecker identifies as an error is the word "Utilze" in the text object on Slide 3. In the Suggestions list box, the spellchecker suggests "Utilize."

QUICK TIP
The spellchecker does not check the text in inserted pictures or objects.

3. **Verify that Utilize Is selected in the Suggestions list box, then click Change**

   If PowerPoint finds any other words it does not recognize, either change or ignore them. When the spellchecker finishes checking your presentation, the Spelling dialog box closes, and an alert box opens with a message that the spelling check is complete.

4. **Click OK**

   The alert box closes. You are satisfied with the presentation so far and you decide to print it. Compare your screen to Figure B-16.

5. **Click the Office button, then click the Print button**

   The Print dialog box opens.

6. **Make sure Slides is selected in the Print what list box, then click the Frame slides check box**

   The slides of your presentation print with a frame around each page.

7. **Click OK in the Print dialog box, then save your presentation**

8. **Click the Office button, then click Exit PowerPoint**

FIGURE B-15: Spelling dialog box

Selected word from Suggestions list

Suggestions list

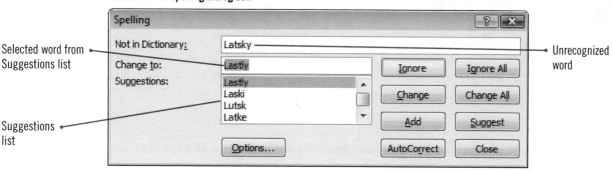

Unrecognized word

FIGURE B-16: Slide showing fixed spelling error

Fixed spelling error

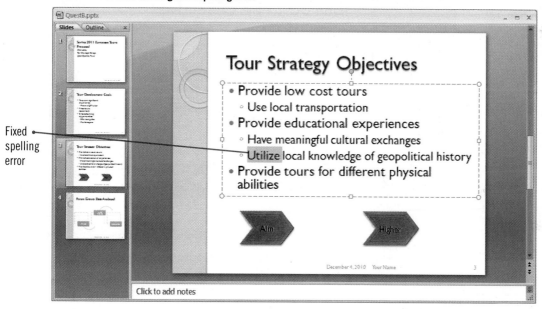

Checking spelling as you type

PowerPoint checks your spelling as you type. If you type a word that is not in the electronic dictionary, a wavy red line appears under it. To correct an error, right-click the misspelled word, then review the suggestions, which appear in the shortcut menu. You can select a suggestion, add the word you typed to your custom dictionary, or ignore it. To turn off automatic spellchecking, click the Office button, then click the PowerPoint Options button to open the PowerPoint Options dialog box. Click the Proofing button, then click the Check spelling as you type check box to deselect it. To temporarily hide the wavy red lines, click the Hide spelling errors check box to select it.

Practice

▼ CONCEPTS REVIEW

Label each element of the PowerPoint window shown in Figure B-17.

FIGURE B-17

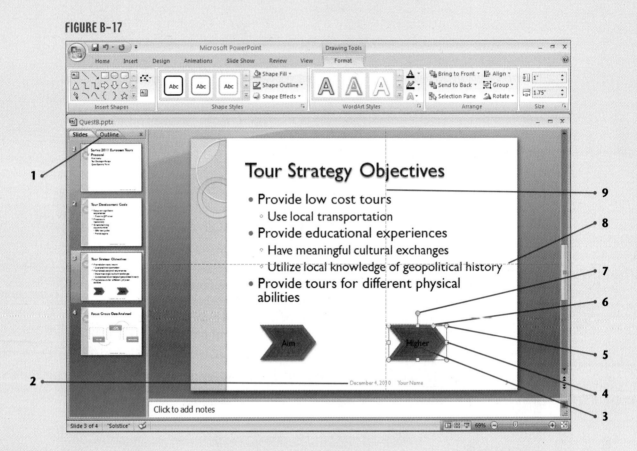

Match each term with the statement that best describes It.

10. **Mini toolbar**
11. **SmartArt graphic**
12. **Adjustment handle**
13. **Quick Style**
14. **Rotate handle**
15. **Sizing handle**

a. A circle or square that appears around a selected object
b. A pre-set combination of formatting options that you apply to an object
c. A formatting toolbar
d. Changes the appearance of an object
e. Allows you to manually rotate an object
f. A diagram that visually illustrates text

Select the best answer from the list of choices.

16. Which of the following statements about the Mini toolbar is incorrect?

   a. It is semitransparent until you move the pointer over it.

   b. It is used to change the layout of a slide.

   c. It is used to format text.

   d. It appears when you select text.

17. Which statement about the PowerPoint spellchecker is true?

   a. PowerPoint only identifies spelling errors when you run the spellchecker.

   b. The spellchecker catches grammar problems.

   c. The spellchecker identifies misspelled and unknown words.

   d. Most misused words are caught by the spellchecker.

18. A professional-quality diagram that visually illustrates text best describes which of the following?

   a. A SmartArt graphic   **c.** A slide layout

   b. A shape   **d.** A content object

19. What does the adjustment handle do to a shape?

   a. Changes the shape to another   **c.** Changes the size of a shape

   b. Changes the rotation of a shape   **d.** Changes the appearance of a shape

20. How do you make a shape smaller?

   a. Drag the adjustment handle.   **c.** Drag the rotate handle.

   b. Drag the sizing handle.   **d.** Drag the shape edge.

21. What would you use to place a shape in a specific position on a slide?

   a. PowerPoint guides   **c.** PowerPoint distribution angles

   b. PowerPoint placeholders   **d.** PowerPoint anchor points

22. What is *not* true about grouped objects?

   a. Grouped objects have one rotate handle.

   b. Sizing handles appear around the grouped object.

   c. Grouped objects lose some of their individual characteristics.

   d. Grouped objects act as one object.

▼ SKILLS REVIEW

1. Enter text in the Outline tab.

   a. Open the presentation PPT B-2.pptx from the drive and folder where you store your Data Files, then save it as TechJet. The completed presentation is shown in Figure B-18.

   b. Create a new slide after Slide 3 with the Title and Content layout.

   c. Open the Outline tab, then type Network Integration.

   d. Press [Enter], press [Tab], type Protocols and Conversions, press [Enter], press [Tab], then type Server codes and routing protocols.

   e. Press [Enter], type File transfer, press [Enter], type Data conversion, press [Enter], then type Platform functionality ratings.

   f. Move Slide 4 to the Slide 3 position.

FIGURE B-18

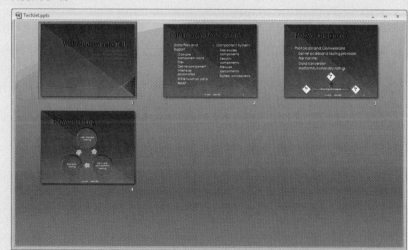

   g. Switch back to the Slides tab.

   h. Save your changes.

2. Format text.

   a. Go to Slide 1.

   b. Select the name Joseph M. Sera, then move the pointer over the Mini toolbar.

   c. Click the Font Color list arrow, then click Orange under Standard Colors.

   d. Using [Shift] select the text object, then change all of the text to the color Orange.

   e. Click the Font Size list arrow, then click 24.

   f. Click the Bold button.

   g. Save your changes.

3. Convert text to SmartArt.

   a. Click the text object on Slide 4.

   b. Apply the Basic Cycle SmartArt graphic layout to the text object.

   c. Click the More button in the SmartArt Styles group, then apply the Inset style to the graphic.

   d. Reposition the diagram to the center of the slide, if necessary.

   e. Click outside the SmartArt graphic in an empty part of the slide.

   f. Save your changes.

4. Insert and modify shapes.

   a. Go to Slide 3.

   b. Using [Shift] select the text object, then drag the bottom-middle sizing handle up to decrease the size of the text object.

   c. Click the Insert tab on the Ribbon, then insert the Left-Right-Up Arrow shape from the Shapes gallery similar to the one in Figure B-19.

   d. Type **Routing protocols**, then click Moderate Effect – Accent 3 in the Shape Styles group.

   e. Click the Shape Effects button in the Shape Styles group, point to Shadow, then click Offset Bottom.

   f. Click the Shape Fill button in the Shape Styles group, point to Gradient, then click Linear Up.

   g. Click a blank area of the slide, then save your changes.

FIGURE B-19

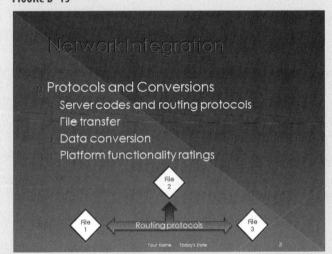

5. Edit and duplicate shapes.

   a. Insert a Diamond shape from the Shapes gallery to the left of the arrow shape.

   b. Click the More button in the Shape Styles group, click Colored Outline – Accent 4, then type **File 1**.

   c. Drag to select the text File 1, click the Home tab, click the Font Size button in the Font group, then click 14.

   d. Using [Ctrl] make two copies of the diamond shape, then change the text in one shape to **File 2** and the text in the other shape to **File 3**.

   e. Move the File 2 diamond shape to the top of the arrow shape and the File 3 diamond shape to the right of the arrow shape, as shown in Figure B-19.

   f. Click a blank area of the slide, then save your changes.

6. Align and group objects.

   a. Hold down [Shift], click the File 1 diamond shape, click the File 3 diamond shape, then release [Shift].

   b. Click the Drawing Tools Format tab if necessary, click Align, click Align Middle.

   c. Hold down [Shift], click the arrow shape, click the File 2 diamond shape, click the Group button in the Arrange group, then click Group.

   d. Click the Align button in the Arrange group, then click Distribute Horizontally.

   e. Save your work.

7. Add slide headers and footers.

   a. Open the Header and Footer dialog box.

   b. In the Slide tab, type today's date into the Fixed text box.

   c. Add the slide number to the footer.

   d. Type your name in the Footer text box.

   e. Apply the footer to all of the slides except the title slide.

   f. Open the Header and Footer dialog box again, then click the Notes and Handouts tab.

   g. Enter today's date in the Fixed text box.

   h. Type the name of your class in the Header text box, then click the Page number check box.

   i. Type your name in the Footer text box.

   j. Apply the header and footer information to all the notes and handouts.

   k. Save your changes.

8. Check spelling in a presentation.

   a. Perform a spelling check on the document and change any misspelled words. Ignore any words that are correctly spelled but that the spellchecker doesn't recognize. There is at least one misspelled word in the presentation.

   b. Save your changes, then close the file and exit PowerPoint.

▼ INDEPENDENT CHALLENGE 1

You are the Director of the Westminster Theater Arts Center in Kansas City, Missouri, and one of your many duties is to raise funds to cover operation costs. One of the primary ways you do this is by speaking to businesses, community clubs, and other organizations throughout the Kansas City region. Every year you speak to many organizations, where you give a short presentation detailing what the theater center plans to do for the coming season. You need to continue working on the presentation you started already.

   a. Start PowerPoint, open the presentation PPT B-3.pptx from the drive and folder where you store your Data Files, and save it as **WTAC 2011**.

   b. Use the Outline tab to enter the following as bulleted text on the Commitment to Excellence slide:

     Study

     Diligence

     Testing

     Excellence

   c. Apply the Verve design theme to the presentation.

   d. Change the font color of each play name on Slide 3 to Yellow.

   e. Change the bulleted text on Slide 5 to the Basic Cycle SmartArt graphic layout, then apply the Polished SmartArt Style.

Advanced Challenge Exercise

   ■ Open the Notes Page view.

   ■ To at least two slides, add notes that relate to the slide content that you think would be important when giving this presentation.

   ■ Save the presentation as **WTAC 2011 ACE** to the drive and folder where you store your Data Files, then print the Notes Page view for the presentation.

   f. Check the spelling in the presentation then view the presentation in Slide Show view.

   g. Add your name as a footer on the notes and handouts, print handouts (three slides per page), and then print the presentation outline.

   h. Save your changes, close your presentation, then exit PowerPoint.

PowerPoint 2007

▼ INDEPENDENT CHALLENGE 2

You are a manager for Schweizerhaus, Ltd., a Swiss mortgage loan company headquartered in Bern, Switzerland. You have been asked by your boss to develop a presentation outlining important details and aspects of the mortgage process for clients and investors. The focus of the presentation is the use of mortgage brokers to secure loans for clients.

a. Start PowerPoint, open the presentation PPT B-4.pptx from the drive and folder where you store your Data Files, and save it as **Loan Broker**.

b. Apply the Technic design theme to the presentation.

c. On Slide 4 select the three shapes, Banks, Mortgage Bankers, and Private Investors, then using the Align command distribute them vertically and align them to their left edges.

d. On Slide 4 select the three shapes, Borrower, Mortgage Broker, and Mortgage Bankers, then using the Align command distribute them horizontally and align them to their bottom edges.

e. Select all of the shapes, then apply Moderate Effect – Accent 2 from the Shape Styles group.

f. Using the Arrow shape from the Shapes gallery, draw a 3pt arrow between all of the shapes as shown in Figure B-20. (*Hint*: Draw one arrow shape, change the line weight to 3 pt using the Shape Outline button, then duplicate the shape.)

g. Create a sixth slide to end the presentation with the following information:
Schweizerhaus, Ltd.
Zieglerstrasse 765, Bern
TEL: 3937095, FAX: 9375719

h. Check the spelling in the presentation, view the presentation in Slide Show view, then view the slides in Slide Sorter view.

i. Add your name as a footer on the notes and hand-outs, print the presentation as handouts (two slides per page), then print the presentation outline.

j. Save your changes, close your presentation, then exit PowerPoint.

FIGURE B-20

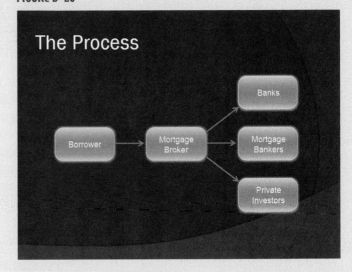

▼ INDEPENDENT CHALLENGE 3

You are an independent distributor of natural foods in Bellingham, Washington. Your business, NorthWest Natural Foods, has grown progressively since its inception five years ago, but sales and profits have leveled off over the last nine months. In an effort to stimulate growth, you decide to acquire All Natural Inc., a major natural food dealer in California, which would allow your company to begin expanding into surrounding states. Use PowerPoint to develop a presentation that you can use to gain a financial backer for the acquisition. Create your own information for the presentation.

a. Start PowerPoint, create a new presentation, then apply the Concourse design theme to the presentation.

b. Enter **A Plan for Growth** as the main title on the title slide, and **NorthWest Natural Foods** as the subtitle.

c. Save the presentation as **NW Natural** to the drive and folder where you store your Data Files.

d. Add five more slides with the following titles: Slide 2-Background; Slide 3-Current Situation; Slide 4-Acquisition Goals; Slide 5-Our Management Team; Slide 6-Funding Required.

e. Enter text into the text placeholders of the slides. Use both the Slide pane and the Outline tab to enter text.

f. Convert text on one slide to a SmartArt graphic, then apply the SmartArt graphic style Subtle Effect.

▼ INDEPENDENT CHALLENGE 3 (CONTINUED)

Advanced Challenge Exercise

- Click the Replace button arrow in the Editing group on the Home tab, then click Replace Fonts.
- Replace the Eras Medium ITC font with the Arial font.
- Save the presentation as **NW Natural ACE** to the drive and folder where you store your Data Files.

g. Check the spelling in the presentation, view the presentation as a slide show, then view the slides in Slide Sorter view.

h. Add your name as a footer on the slides, save your changes, then print the slides.

i. Close your presentation, then exit PowerPoint.

▼ REAL LIFE INDEPENDENT CHALLENGE

Your computer professor at Central State University has been asked by the department head to convert his Applied Technology course into an accelerated course that both students and professional working people can take. Your professor has asked you to help him create a presentation for the class that he can post on the Internet and use as a promotional tool at local businesses. Most of the raw information is already on the slides, you primarily need to jazz it up by adding a theme, and some text formatting.

a. Start PowerPoint, open the presentation PPT B-5.pptx from drive and folder where you store your data files, and save it as **Applied Tech**.

b. Add a new slide after the Course Facts slide with the same layout, type **Course Details** in the title text placeholder, then enter the following as bulleted text in the Outline tab:
Unix/Information Systems
Networking
Applied Methods
Technology Solutions
Software Design
Applications

c. Apply the Origin theme to the presentation.

d. Select the title text object on Slide 1 (*Hint*: Press [Shift] to select the whole object), then change the text color to Dark Red.

e. Change the font of the title text object to Bernard MT Condensed.

f. Change the text on Slide 4 to a SmartArt graphic. The text on this slide is a list so make sure the diagram type you choose is appropriate for the text.

g. Change the style of the SmartArt diagram using one of the SmartArt Styles, then view the presentation in Slide Show view.

h. Add the slide number and your name as a footer on the notes and handouts, print handouts (four slides per page), and then print the presentation outline.

i. Save your changes, close your presentation, then exit PowerPoint.

▼ VISUAL WORKSHOP

Create the presentation shown in Figures B-21 and B-22. Add today's date as the date on the title slide. Save the presentation as Trade Analysis to the drive and folder where you store your Data Files. Review your slides in Slide Show view, then add your name as a footer to the notes and handouts. Print the slides of your presentation, then print the outline. Save your changes, close the presentation, then exit PowerPoint.

FIGURE B-21

FIGURE B-22

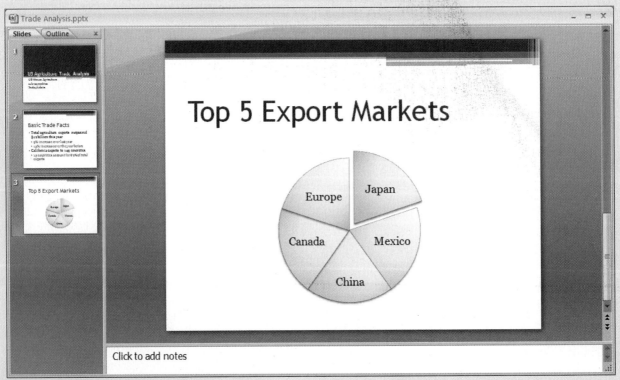

Inserting Objects into a Presentation

A good presenter will make use of visual elements, such as charts, graphics, and photographs, in conjunction with text to help communicate the presentation message. Visual elements keep the presentation interesting and help the audience focus on what the presenter is saying. In this unit, you continue working on the presentation for your boss Ellen Latsky by inserting visual elements, including clip art, a picture, and a chart, into the presentation. You format these objects using PowerPoint's powerful object editing features.

OBJECTIVES

Insert text from Microsoft Word

Insert clip art

Insert and style a picture

Insert a text box

Insert a chart

Enter and edit chart data

Insert a table

Insert and format WordArt

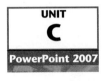

Inserting Text from Microsoft Word

PowerPoint makes it easy to insert text from other sources into a presentation. Documents saved in Microsoft Word format (.docx), Rich Text Format (.rtf), plain text format (.txt), and HTML format (.htm) can be inserted into a presentation. If you have an existing Word document or outline, you can import it into PowerPoint to create a new presentation or use it to insert additional slides in an existing presentation. When you import a Microsoft Word or a Rich Text Format document into a presentation, PowerPoint creates an outline structure based on the styles in the document. For example, a Heading 1 style in the Word document becomes a slide title in PowerPoint and a Heading 2 style becomes the first level of text in a bulleted list. If you insert a plain text format document into a presentation, PowerPoint creates an outline based on the tabs at the beginning of the document's paragraphs. Paragraphs without tabs become slide titles; paragraphs with one tab indent become first-level text in bulleted lists; paragraphs with two tabs become second-level text in bulleted lists; and so on. Ron Dawson, QST's Vice President of Marketing, sent you a Microsoft Word document with data from a focus group study QST held last spring. You use this information in the presentation.

STEPS

1. **Start PowerPoint, open the presentation PPT C-1.pptx from the drive and folder where you store your Data Files, save it as QuestC, click the View tab on the Ribbon, then click the Arrange All button in the Window group**

2. **Click the Outline tab, then click the Slide 4 icon in the Outline tab**
   Slide 4 appears in the Slide pane. Each time you click a slide icon in the Outline tab, the slide title and text are highlighted indicating the slide is selected. Before you insert information into a presentation, you must first designate where you want the information to be placed. In this case, the Word document will be inserted after Slide 4, the selected slide.

3. **Click the Home tab on the Ribbon, click the New Slide button list arrow in the Slides group, then click Slides from Outline**
   The Insert Outline dialog box opens.

4. **Select the Word document file PPT C-2.docx from the drive and folder where you store your Data Files, then click Insert**
   Four new slides (5, 6, 7, and 8) are added to the presentation. See Figure C-1.

5. **Read the text for the new Slide 5 in the Slide pane, then review the text on slides 6, 7, and 8 in the Outline tab**
   After reviewing the text on the new slides, you realize that the information on Slide 8 is not necessary for the presentation.

6. **Click the Slides tab, then right-click the Slide 8 thumbnail**
   A shortcut menu opens displaying a number of common commands. Right-clicking most objects in PowerPoint opens a shortcut menu.

7. **Click Delete Slide on the shortcut menu**
   Slide 8 is deleted from the presentation. The last slide in the presentation displaying a picture placeholder now appears in the Slide pane. You also notice that Slide 6 should come before Slide 5.

8. **Click Slide 6 in the Slides tab, then drag it above Slide 5**
   Slide 6 and Slide 5 change places. Compare your screen to Figure C-2.

9. **Click the Save button ■ on the Quick Access Toolbar**

FIGURE C-1: Outline tab showing imported text

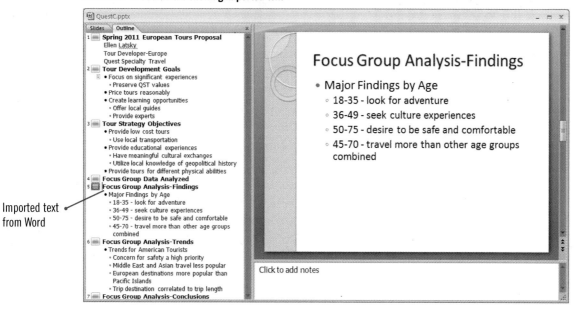

Imported text from Word

FIGURE C-2: Presentation after moving a slide

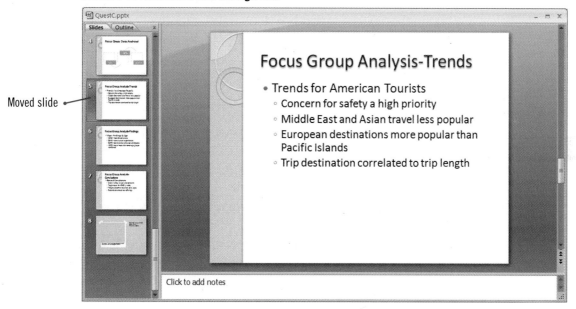

Moved slide

Inserting slides from other presentations

To insert slides from another presentation into the current presentation, click the New Slide button list arrow in the Slides group, then click Reuse Slides. The Reuse Slides task pane opens on the right side of the window. Click the Open a PowerPoint File link, locate the presentation you want to use, then click Open. Click the slide(s) to place them in the presentation. The new slides automatically take on the theme of the current presentation. You can also copy slides from one presentation to another. Open both presentations, change the view of each presentation to Slide Sorter view or use the Arrange All command to see both presentations, select the desired slides, then copy and paste them (or use drag and drop) into the desired presentation.

Inserting Clip Art

PowerPoint has access to many professionally designed graphics, called **clip art**, which you can place in your presentation. In Microsoft Office, clip art and other media files, including photographs, movies, and sounds, are stored in a file index system called the Microsoft Clip Organizer and are identified by descriptive keywords. The Clip Organizer sorts the clip art into groups, including My Collections, Office Collections, and Web Collections. The Office Collections group holds all the media files that come with Microsoft Office. You can customize the Clip Organizer by adding clips to a collection, moving clips from one collection to another, or creating a new collection. As with drawn objects, you can modify clip art images by changing their shape, size, fill, or shading. Clip art is available from many sources outside the Clip Organizer, including the Microsoft Office Online Web site and commercially available collections that you can purchase. ▰▰▰▰ To enhance the QST presentation, you add a clip from the Clip Organizer to one of the slides and then adjust its size and placement.

1. **Click the up scroll arrow in the Slides tab until Slide 2 appears, click the Slide 2 thumbnail, then click the Clip Art icon ▦ in the Content placeholder**

   The Clip Art task pane opens. At the top of the task pane in the Search for text box, you enter a keyword to search for clips that meet that description. You can search for a clip in a specific collection or in all collections. You can also search for a clip that is a specific media type, such as clip art, photographs, movies, or sounds. At the bottom of the task pane, you can click a hyperlink to organize clips, locate other pieces of clip art at the Office Online Web site, or read tips on how to find clip art.

2. **Select any text in the Search for text box, type travel, click the Results should be list arrow, then click the Photographs check box, the Movies check box, and the Sounds check box to remove the check marks**

   Since you are only interested in finding clip art, deselecting the Photographs, Movies, and Sounds check boxes significantly reduces the amount of media PowerPoint needs to search through to produce your results. PowerPoint searches for clips identified by the keyword "travel."

3. **Click the Go button, then click the clip art thumbnail shown in Figure C-3**

   The clip art object appears in the content placeholder and the Picture Tools Format tab appears on the Ribbon. If you don't see the clip shown in Figure C-3, select another one. Although you can change a clip's size by dragging a corner sizing handle, you can also **scale** it to change its size by a specific percentage.

4. **Click the Size and Position dialog box launcher in the Size group, in the Scale section make sure the Lock aspect ratio check box has a check mark, in the Scale section click the Height up arrow until the Height and Width percentages display 110%, then click Close**

   The clip proportionally increases in size.

5. **Click the Picture Border button in the Picture Styles group, then click the Aqua, Accent 1 color box in the top row**

   A light blue border appears around the object.

6. **Click the Picture Border button, point to Weight, then click the 3 pt solid line style**

   The clip now has a 3-point solid border. It appears to be framed.

7. **Drag the clip art object straight down even with the bottom line of text**

   You don't like the new placement of the clip.

8. **Click the Undo button ↺ on the Quick Access toolbar, click a blank area of the slide, then save your changes**

9. **Click the Results should be list arrow in the Clip Art task pane, click the All media types check box, click Go, then click the task pane Close button**

   Now the next time you search for a clip, PowerPoint will search through all media types. Compare the slide on your screen to the slide shown in Figure C-4.

FIGURE C-3: Screen showing Clip Art task pane

Select this clip

Clip Art icon

Click to locate clips on the Office Online Web site

FIGURE C-4: Slide with formatted clip art object

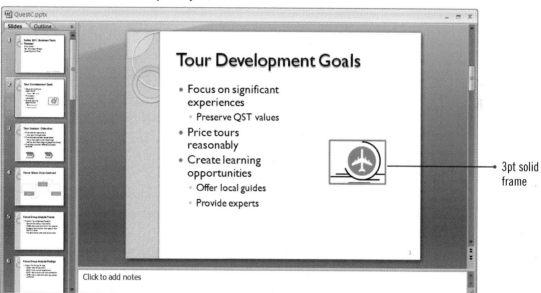

3pt solid frame

Finding more clips online

If you can't find exactly what you want in the Clip Organizer, you can easily download and use clips from the Clip Art and Media Web page in the Microsoft Office Online Web site. To get clips from the Clip Art Web page, click the Clip art on Office Online hyperlink at the bottom of the Clip Art task pane. If your computer is connected to the Internet, this will launch your Web browser and automatically connect you to the Microsoft Office Online Web site. You can search the site by keyword or browse by media type category. Each clip you download is automatically inserted into the Clip Organizer Web Collections folder and appears in the Clip Art task pane.

Inserting and Styling a Picture

In PowerPoint, a **picture** is defined as a digital photograph, a piece of line art or clip art, or other artwork that is created in another program and inserted into a PowerPoint presentation. PowerPoint gives you the ability to insert 17 different types of pictures including JPEG File Interchange Format and BMP Windows Bitmap. As with all objects in PowerPoint, you can format and style inserted pictures to help them fit the theme of your presentation. You can also hide a portion of the picture you don't want visible by **cropping** it. The cropped portion of a picture, unlike other objects such as clip art, is automatically deleted when the presentation is saved unless you change the setting in the Compression Settings dialog box. ▒▒▒▒ QST has a library of pictures from tours available to use in presentations. In this lesson, you insert a picture that has previously been saved to a file, and then you crop it and style it.

STEPS

QUICK TIP

You can also insert a picture by clicking the Picture button in the Illustrations group on the Insert tab.

1. **Click the down scroll arrow in the Slides tab until Slide 8 appears, click the Slide 8 thumbnail, then click the Insert Picture from File icon 🖼 in the content placeholder on the slide**

   The Insert Picture dialog box opens displaying the pictures available in the Pictures folder. The Pictures folder is the default folder.

2. **Select the picture file PPT C-3.jpg from the drive and folder where you store your Data Files, then click Insert**

   The picture appears in the Picture placeholder on the slide and the Picture Tools Format tab opens on the Ribbon. The picture would look better if you cropped some of the beach off the bottom.

3. **Click the Crop button in the Size group, then place the pointer over the bottom-middle sizing handle of the picture**

   The pointer changes to **T**. When the Crop button is active, the sizing handles appear as straight black lines.

4. **Press and hold [Alt], drag the bottom edge of the picture up until the lower-left corner of the picture is at the water line as shown in Figure C-5, then click the Crop button**

   Pressing [Alt] while dragging or drawing an object in PowerPoint overrides the automatic snap-to-grid setting. PowerPoint has a number of picture formatting options, and you decide to experiment with some of them.

5. **Click the Picture Styles More button ⊽, then click Bevel Rectangle (3rd row)**

   The picture changes shape. Notice that this particular style includes an adjustment handle so that you can adjust the shape of the picture.

6. **Click the Recolor button in the Adjust group, click Sepia in the Color Modes section, then click the Slide Show button ⊡ in the status bar**

   The slide fills your screen. After evaluating the slide you conclude that the shape and color changes you've made to the picture don't improve the look of the slide.

7. **Press [Esc], click the Undo button list arrow on the Quick Access toolbar, then click Format Picture**

   All of the formatting changes you made to the picture are removed. The cropped portion of the picture does not change and remains hidden.

8. **Click the Picture Styles More button, click Drop Shadow Rectangle (1st row), click a blank area on the slide, then save your changes**

   Compare your screen to Figure C-6.

FIGURE C-5: Using the cropping pointer to crop a picture

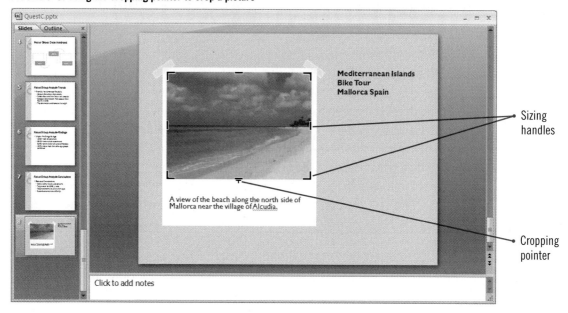

Sizing handles

Cropping pointer

FIGURE C-6: Cropped and styled picture

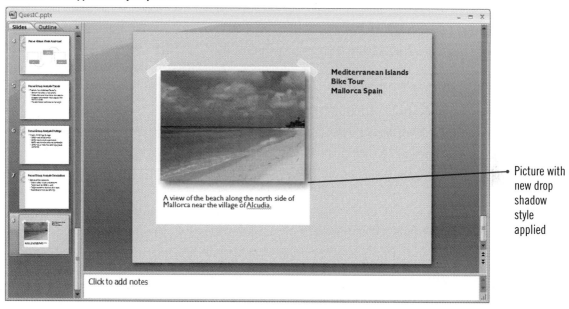

Picture with new drop shadow style applied

Picture compression

By default, all inserted pictures in PowerPoint 2007 are automatically compressed every time you save your presentation. If you want to prohibit the automatic compression of pictures or be able to choose individual pictures to compress, select a picture, then click the Picture Tools Format tab. Click the Compress Pictures button in the Adjust group, then click Options in the Compress Pictures dialog box. The Compression Settings dialog box opens. Notice that PowerPoint compresses pictures every time the presentation is saved and deletes cropped portions of pictures to save space. To compress individual pictures, make sure the top option in the Compression Settings dialog box is deselected, select a picture, click the Compress Pictures button, then click OK. To stop PowerPoint from automatically deleting cropped portions of pictures, deselect the check box next to the Delete cropped areas of pictures option in the Compression Settings dialog box.

PowerPoint 2007

Inserting a Text Box

As you've already learned, you enter text on a slide using a title or content placeholder that is arranged on the slide based on a particular slide layout. Every so often you need additional text on a slide where the traditional placeholder does not place text effectively for your message. You can create an individual text object by clicking the Text Box button in the Text group on the Insert tab on the Ribbon. There are two types of text objects that you can create: a text label, used for a small phrase where text doesn't automatically wrap to the next line inside the box; and a word processing box, used for a sentence or paragraph where the text wraps inside the boundaries of the box. Either type of text box can be formatted and edited just like any other text object. You decide to add a text object to Slide 8 to finish the information about the bike tour. You create a word processing box on the slide, enter text, edit text, and then format the text.

STEPS

1. **Click the Insert tab on the Ribbon, click the Text Box button in the Text group, then move the pointer to the blank area of the slide to the right of the picture**

    The pointer changes to ↓.

QUICK TIP

To create a text label in which text doesn't wrap, click the Text Box button, position ↓ where you want to place the text, click once, then enter your text.

2. **Drag down and toward the right side of the slide about an inch and a half to create a word processing box**

    When you begin dragging, an outline of the text object appears, indicating how large a text object you are drawing. After you release the mouse button, an insertion point appears inside the text object, in this case a word processing box, which indicates that you can enter text. The font and font style appear in the Font group on the Ribbon.

3. **Type Travel from Palma to La Puebla for 135 miles over 6 days**

    Notice that the text object increases in size as your text wraps inside the text object. Your screen should look similar to Figure C-7. After entering the text you realize there is a mistake.

4. **Drag ↓ over the phrase for 135 miles to select it**

5. **Position ⇱ on top of the selected phrase and press and hold the mouse button**

    The pointer changes to ⇱.

QUICK TIP

You can also move text between text objects on a slide and in the Outline tab using this drag-and-drop method.

6. **Drag the selected words to the right of the word Travel in the text object, then release the mouse button**

    A light blue insertion line appears as you drag, indicating where PowerPoint places the text when you release the mouse button. The phrase "for 135 miles" moves after the word "Travel".

7. **Move ⇱ to the edge of the text object, which changes to ⊹, click the text object border, then click the Italic button *I* in the Font group**

    All of the text in the text object is italicized.

8. **Drag the right-middle sizing handle of the text object to the right until the text is on two lines, position ⊹ over the text object edge, then drag it next to the picture caption**

    Your screen should look similar to Figure C-8.

9. **Click a blank area of the slide outside the text object, then save your changes**

FIGURE C-7: New text object

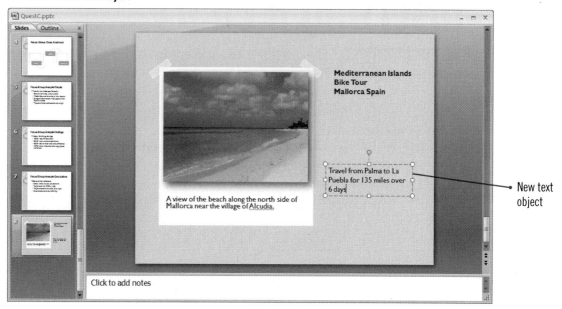

New text object

FIGURE C-8: Formatted text object

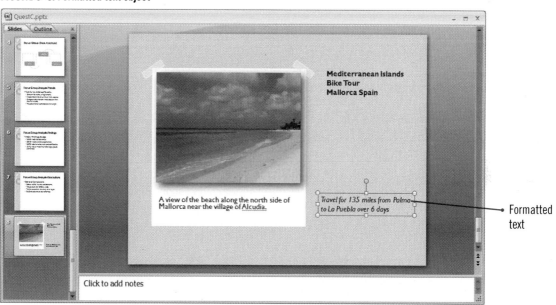

Formatted text

Sending a presentation using e-mail

You can send a copy of a presentation over the Internet to a reviewer for them to edit and add comments. You can use Microsoft Outlook, or any other compatible e-mail program, to send your presentation. Although your e-mail program allows you to attach files, you can send a presentation using Outlook from within PowerPoint. Click the Office button, point to Send, then click Email. Outlook opens and automatically creates an e-mail with the presentation attached to it. The recipient of the presentation can use PowerPoint 2007 or an earlier version of PowerPoint to edit the presentation or add comments. To open a PowerPoint 2007 file in an earlier version of PowerPoint, you must save the presentation as a PowerPoint 97-2003 presentation or install the Compatibility Pack for the Office 2007 Office system files from Microsoft's Web site. Once the presentation is back in your hands, you can view, edit, or delete the reviewer's comments.

Inserting a Chart

Often, the best way to communicate numerical information is with a visual aid such as a chart. If you have Microsoft Excel installed on your computer, PowerPoint uses Excel to create charts. If you don't have Excel installed, a charting program called **Microsoft Graph** opens that you can use to create charts for your slides. A **chart** is the graphical representation of numerical data. Every chart has a corresponding **worksheet** that contains the numerical data displayed by the chart. When you insert a chart object into PowerPoint, you are actually embedding it. An **embedded** object is one that is a part of your presentation (just like any other object you insert into PowerPoint) except that an embedded object's data source can be opened, in this case Excel, for editing purposes. Changes you make to an embedded object in PowerPoint using PowerPoint's features do not affect the data source for the data. ▰▰▰ You insert a chart on a new slide that graphically shows results from an online survey Ellen Latsky conducted.

STEPS

1. **Verify that Slide 8 is selected, click the New Slide button list arrow in the Slides group, then click Title and Content**

   A new slide is added to your presentation with the Title and Content slide layout.

2. **Click the Insert Chart icon 📊 in the Content placeholder**

   The Insert Chart dialog box opens as shown in Figure C-9. Each chart type includes a number of 2-D and 3-D styles. The Column chart type, for example, includes 19 different styles and the Line chart type includes 7 different styles. The Clustered Column chart is the default chart style. For a brief explanation of how each of these chart types graphs data, refer to Table C-1.

3. **Click OK**

   Excel opens in a split window sharing the computer screen with the PowerPoint window as shown in Figure C-10. The PowerPoint window displays the clustered column chart and the Excel window displays sample data in a worksheet. The Chart Tools Design tab on the Ribbon contains commands you use in PowerPoint to work with the chart. The worksheet consists of rows and columns. The intersection of a row and a column is called a **cell**. Cells are referred to by their row and column location; for example, the cell at the intersection of column A and row 1 is called cell A1. Cells in the first or left column contain **axis labels** that identify the data in a row for example, "Category 1" is an axis label. Cells in the first or top row are **legend** names and provide further information about the data. Cells below and to the right of the axis labels and legend names contain the data values that are represented in the chart. Each column and row of data in the worksheet is called a **data series**. Each data series has corresponding **data series markers** in the chart, which are graphical representations such as bars, columns, or pie wedges. The gray boxes with the numbers along the left side of the worksheet are called **row headings**, and the gray boxes with the letters along the top of the worksheet are called **column headings**.

4. **Move the pointer over the worksheet in the Excel window**

   The pointer changes to ⊹. Cell A6 is the **active cell**, which means that it is selected. The active cell has a thick black border around it.

5. **Click cell C4**

   Cell C4 is now the active cell.

6. **Click the Excel Window Close button ⊠ on the title bar**

   The Excel window closes and the PowerPoint window fills the screen. A new chart object appears on the slide displaying the data from the Excel worksheet.

7. **Click in a blank area of the slide to deselect the chart object**

   The Chart Tools Design Ribbon is no longer active.

8. **Click the slide Title placeholder, type On-line Survey Results, then save your changes**

FIGURE C-9: Insert Chart dialog box

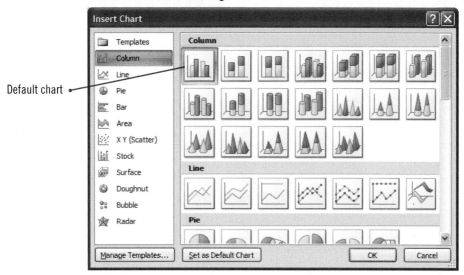

Default chart

FIGURE C-10: The PowerPoint and Excel split windows

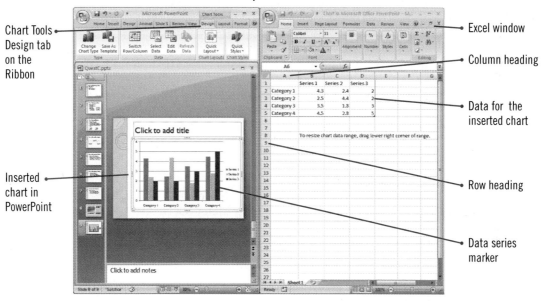

Chart Tools
Design tab
on the
Ribbon

Inserted
chart in
PowerPoint

Excel window

Column heading

Data for the
inserted chart

Row heading

Data series
marker

TABLE C-1: Chart types

chart type	icon looks like	use to
Column		Track values over time or across categories
Line		Track values over time
Pie		Compare individual values to the whole
Bar		Compare values in categories or over time
Area		Show contribution of each data series to the total over time
XY (Scatter)		Compare pairs of values
Stock		Show stock market information or scientific data
Surface		Show value trends across two dimensions
Doughnut		Compare individual values to the whole with multiple series
Bubble		Indicate relative size of data points
Radar		Show changes in values in relation to a center point

Entering and Editing Chart Data

After you insert a chart into your presentation, you need to replace the sample data with the correct information. If you have data in an Excel worksheet or another source, you can import it into Excel; otherwise you can type your own information into the worksheet. As you enter data and make other changes in the Excel worksheet, the chart in PowerPoint automatically reflects the new changes. ▰▰▰ You enter and format the survey data collected by Ellen.

STEPS

1. **Click the chart on Slide 9, click the Chart Tools Design tab on the Ribbon, then click the Edit Data button in the Data group**

   The chart is selected in PowerPoint and the worksheet opens in a separate Excel window. The data in the worksheet needs to be replaced with the correct information.

2. **Click the Series 1 cell, type Safety, press [Tab], type Price, press [Tab], then type Experience**

   The Legend labels are entered. Pressing [Tab] in Excel moves the active cell from left to right one cell at a time in a row. Pressing [Enter] in the worksheet moves the active cell down one cell at a time in a column.

3. **Click the Category 1 cell, type 2 Years Past, press [Enter], type Last Year, press [Enter], then type This Year**

   The axis labels are entered and the chart in the PowerPoint window reflects all the changes.

4. **Enter the remainder of the data shown in Figure C-11 to complete the worksheet, then press [Enter]**

   The sample information in Row 5 of the worksheet is not needed.

5. **Right-click the Row 5 row heading, then click Delete**

   Clicking a row heading selects the entire row. The chart currently shows the rows grouped by year, and the legend represents the columns in the datasheet. It would be more effective if the row data appeared in the legend so you could compare yearly results.

6. **Click the Switch Row/Column button in the Data group in the PowerPoint window**

   You have finished entering data in the Excel worksheet.

7. **Click the Excel window Close button ☒**

   Notice that the height of each column in the chart, as well as the values along the vertical axis, adjust to reflect the numbers you typed. The vertical axis is also called the **Value axis**. The horizontal axis is called the **Category axis**. The column labels are now on the Category axis of the chart, and the row labels are listed in the legend.

8. **Click a blank area on the slide, then save the presentation**

   Compare your chart to Figure C-12.

FIGURE C-11: Worksheet showing chart data

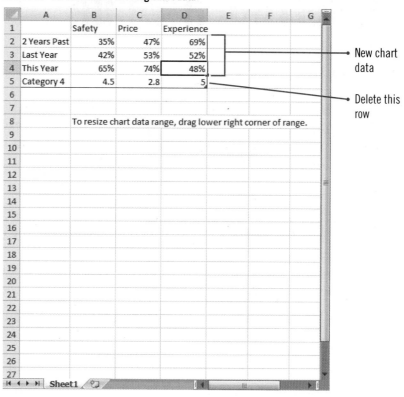

New chart data

Delete this row

To resize chart data range, drag lower right corner of range.

	A	B	C	D
1		Safety	Price	Experience
2	2 Years Past	35%	47%	69%
3	Last Year	42%	53%	52%
4	This Year	65%	74%	48%
5	Category 4	4.5	2.8	5

FIGURE C-12: Formatted chart

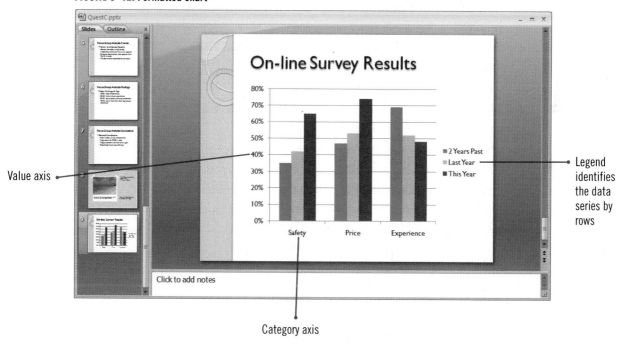

Value axis

Legend identifies the data series by rows

Category axis

Series in rows vs. series in columns

If you have difficulty visualizing what the Switch Row/Column command does, think about what is represented in the legend. **Series in Rows** means that the information in the datasheet rows will be on the Value or vertical axis and is the information shown in the legend.

The column labels will be on the Category or horizontal axis. **Series in Columns** means that the information in the columns becomes the information shown on the Value axis and in the legend; the row labels will be on the horizontal or Category axis.

Inserting a Table

As you create your presentation, you may have some information that would look best organized in rows and columns. For example, if you wanted to compare the basic details of three different cruise tours side by side, a table is ideal for this type of information. Once you have created a table, two new tabs, the Table Tools Design tab and the Table Tools Layout tab, appear on the Ribbon. You can use the Design tab to apply color styles, change cell borders and add cell effects. Using the Layout tab, you can add rows and columns to your table, adjust the size of cells, and align text in the cells. ▓▓▓▓▓ You decide that a table best illustrates the new adventure tour series being proposed by Ellen.

STEPS

1. **Verify that Slide 9 is selected, click the New Slide button list arrow in the Slides group, click Title Only, click the Insert tab on the Ribbon, then click the Table button in the Tables group**

   The Insert Table gallery opens where you can drag the mouse to specify the number of columns and rows you need in the table.

2. **Move the pointer over the grid to select a 4x3 cell area so that 4x3 Table appears in the gallery title bar, then click the lower right corner of the 4x3 grid**

   A table with four columns and three rows appears on the slide, and the Table Tools Design tab opens on the Ribbon. The table has 12 cells. The insertion point is in the first cell of the table and is ready to accept text.

3. **Type Self Guided, press [Tab], type Family, press [Tab], type Cruise, press [Tab], type Extreme, then press [Tab]**

   The text you typed appears in the top four cells of the table. Pressing [Tab] moves the insertion point to the next cell. Pressing [Enter] moves the insertion point to the next line in the cell. Pressing [Tab] in the last row, last column inserts a new row.

4. **Enter the rest of the table information shown in Figure C-13, then drag the right-middle sizing handle slightly to the right**

   The word Mediterranean now fits on one line. The table would look better if it were formatted differently.

5. **Click the Table Styles More button ▼ in the Table Styles group, scroll to the bottom of the gallery, then click Dark Style 1 – Accent 6**

   The background and text color change to reflect the table style you applied.

6. **Click the upper-left cell, click the Table Tools Layout tab, click the Select button in the Table group, click Select Row, then click the Center button ▤ in the Alignment group**

   The text in the top row is centered horizontally in each cell.

7. **Click the Select button in the Table group, click Select Table, then click the Center Vertically button ▤ in the Alignment group**

   The text in the whole table is centered vertically within each cell. The table would look better if all the rows were the same height.

8. **Click the Distribute Rows button ▤ in the Cell Size group, click the Table Tools Design tab, then click the Effects button ▤▾ in the Table Styles group**

   The Table Effects gallery opens. Apply a 3-D effect to the cells so that they stand out.

9. **Point to Cell Bevel, click Cool Slant, drag the table to the center of the blank area of the slide, click the slide title placeholder, type Adventure Series, click a blank area of the slide, then save the presentation**

   The effect makes the cells of the table stand out. Compare your screen with Figure C-14.

FIGURE C-13: The inserted table with data

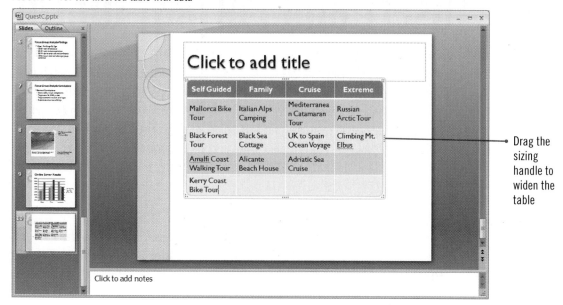

Drag the sizing handle to widen the table

FIGURE C-14: Formatted table

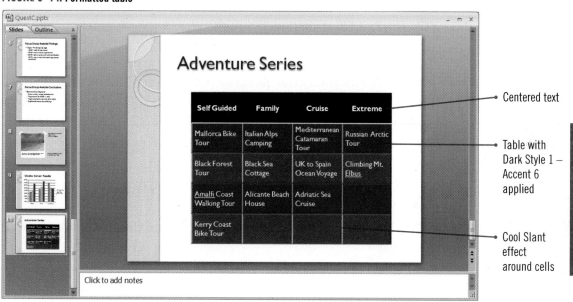

Centered text

Table with Dark Style 1 – Accent 6 applied

Cool Slant effect around cells

Saving slides as graphics

You can save PowerPoint slides as graphics and later use them in other presentations, in graphics programs, and on Web pages. Display the slide you want to save, click the Office button, then click Save As. In the Save As dialog box, click the Save as type list arrow, select the desired graphics format (for example, Web Page (*.htm;*.html), JPEG File Interchange Format (*.jpg), TIFF Tag Image Format (*.tif), or Device Independent Bitmap (*.bmp)), then name the file. Click Save, then click the desired option when the alert box appears asking if you want to save all the slides or only the current slide.

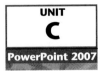
Insert and Format WordArt

As you work to create an interesting presentation, your goal should include making your slides visually appealing. Sometimes plain text can come across as dull and unexciting in a presentation. **WordArt** is a set of decorative text styles, or text effects, that you can apply to any text object to help direct the attention of your audience to a certain piece of information. You can use WordArt in two different ways: you can apply a WordArt text style to an existing text object that converts the text into WordArt, or you can create a new WordArt object. The WordArt text styles and effects include text shadows, reflections, glows, bevels, 3-D rotations, and transformations. ██████ Use WordArt to convert the QST tours tag line on Slide 1 so it is easier to see.

STEPS

1. **Click the Slide 1 thumbnail in the Slides tab, press [Shift], click the footer text object at the bottom of the slide, then drag the Zoom slider to the right until the Zoom percentage reaches 100%**

   Notice how the selected footer text object becomes the focal point as you zoom in. The footer text is hard to see and would look better with a WordArt style applied to it.

QUICK TIP

You can add a new WordArt object to a slide by clicking the Insert tab, then the WordArt button in the Text group.

2. **Click the Drawing Tools Format tab, click the WordArt Styles More button ▼, move your mouse over the WordArt styles in the gallery, then click Gradient Fill – Accent 6, Inner Shadow**

   The WordArt gallery displays all of the WordArt styles, and the Live Preview lets you see how each style would look if applied to the text.

3. **Click the Text Effects button Ⓐ in the WordArt Styles group, point to Reflection, then click Tight Reflection, touching**

   The footer text object is now styled with a WordArt style and a reflection effect. You decide to increase the footer text font and give it a more prominent position on the slide.

4. **Click the Home tab on the Ribbon, click the Increase Font Size button Aˆ in the Font group twice, then drag the left-middle sizing handle to the left until the text is on one line**

   Now the footer text object is easier to read.

5. **Position ╬ over the edge of the text object, drag to position the text object to match Figure C-15**

TROUBLE

Your zoom percentage may be different depending on your screen size and resolution.

6. **Click a blank area of the slide, click the Fit slide to current window button ▣ in the status bar**

   The slide returns to its original zoom percentage of 66%.

7. **Click the Slide Show button � on the status bar, view the presentation, press [Esc] at the end of the slide show, then click the Slide Sorter button ▦ on the status bar**

   Figure C-16 shows the final presentation.

8. **Add your name as a footer to the notes and handouts, save your changes, print the presentation as handouts (four per page), then exit PowerPoint**

FIGURE C-15: Footer text converted to WordArt

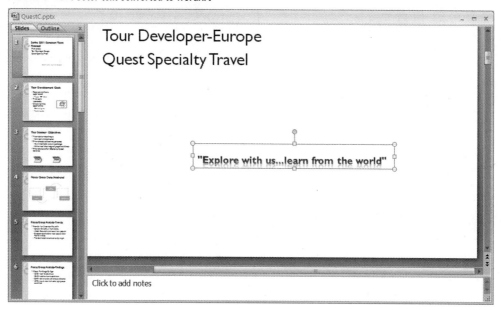

FIGURE C-16: Completed presentation in Slide Sorter view

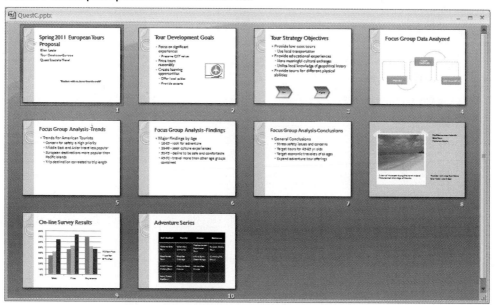

Using content templates from the Web

When you create a presentation, you have the option of using one of the many design themes supplied with PowerPoint, or you can use a template from the Microsoft Office Online Web site. These templates are designed and formatted with sample text, background and text colors, pictures, charts, and other graphic elements. To access a template from the Microsoft Office Online Web site, you need to be connected to the Internet, then click the Microsoft Office button. Click New to open the New Presentation dialog box. Click one of the template categories in the Microsoft

Office Online template list in the left pane, then download and save the template in PowerPoint. Some of the template categories have subcategories that you need to select to display the individual templates. If you don't have access to the Internet or if you want to view more template choices, you can select one of the installed PowerPoint templates. In the New Presentation dialog box, click Installed Templates in the Template Categories list to select one of the installed templates.

Practice

▼ CONCEPTS REVIEW

Label each element of the PowerPoint window shown in Figure C-17.

FIGURE C-17

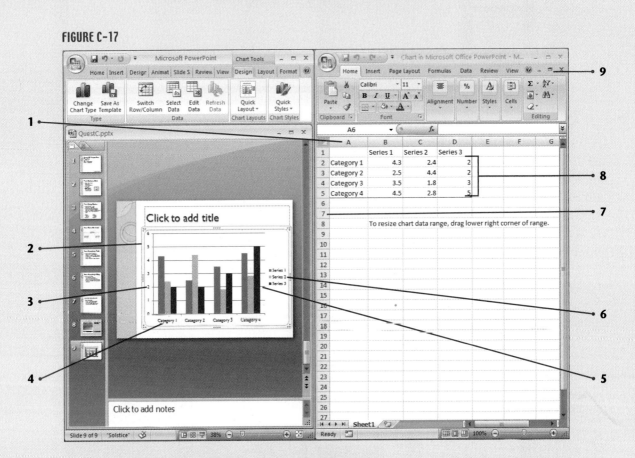

Match each term with the statement that best describes it.

10. **Text label**
11. **Category axis**
12. **Value axis**
13. **Chart**
14. **WordArt**

a. The graphical representation of numerical data
b. A set of decorative styles you can add to text
c. Another name for the vertical axis in a chart
d. A specific type of text object used to enter a small phrase
e. Another name for the horizontal axis in the chart

Select the best answer from the list of choices.

15. Which of the following statements about inserting text from Microsoft Word is *not* true?

   a. Each line of inserted text is placed onto separate slides.

   b. An outline structure is created in PowerPoint based on the Word styles used in the text.

   c. PowerPoint can insert text that has tabs at the end of paragraphs.

   d. You can create a new presentation based on inserted Word text.

16. What is the file index system that stores clip art, photographs, and movies called?

   a. Microsoft Clip Organizer

   b. Office Media Collections

   c. Clip Art Index

   d. WordArt Gallery

17. Hiding a portion of a picture or piece of clip art best describes which of the following actions?

   a. Adjusting

   b. Hiding

   c. Styling

   d. Cropping

18. Where is the numerical data located for a chart?

   a. Table

   b. Legend

   c. Worksheet

   d. Chart

19. An object that has its own data source and becomes a part of your presentation after you insert it best describes which of the following?

   a. A Word outline

   b. An embedded object

   c. A WordArt object

   d. A table

20. According to the book, which of the following objects is ideal to compare data side by side?

   a. Table

   b. Chart

   c. Outline

   d. Grid

21. A set of decorative text styles you apply to text describes which of the following items?

   a. Text labels

   b. Illustrations

   c. WordArt

   d. Gallery

22. What is a column of data in a worksheet called?

   a. Column headings

   b. Data series

   c. Data series markers

   d. Axis labels

▼ SKILLS REVIEW

1. Insert text from Microsoft Word.

   a. Open the file PPT C-4.pptx from the drive and folder where you store your Data Files, then save it as Blue Moon. You will work to create the completed presentation as shown in Figure C-18.

   b. Click Slide 3 in the Slides tab, then use the Slides from Outline command to insert the file PPT C-5.docx from the drive and folder where you store your Data Files.

   c. In the Slides tab, drag Slide 5 above Slide 4.

   d. In the Slides tab, delete Slide 7, Expansion Potential.

2. Insert clip art.

   a. Select Slide 4, then change the slide layout to the Two Content slide layout.

FIGURE C–18

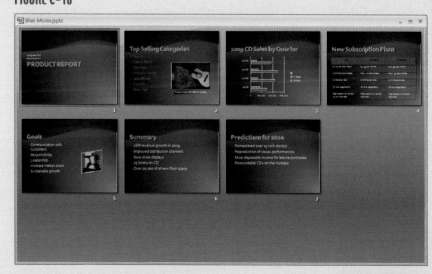

b. Click the clip art icon in the right content placeholder, search for clip art using the keyword **leadership**, then insert the first clip in the Clip Art task pane.

c. In the Size group on the Picture Tools Format Ribbon, use the Shape Width up arrow to change the width to 2.4".

d. Click the Picture Border button, change the color of the clip art border to Gold, Accent 4.

e. Click the Picture Border button, change the weight of the clip art border to 4½ pt.

f. Click the Picture Effects button, point to 3-D Rotation, then click Off Axis 1 Right.

g. Drag the clip art so the bottom lines up with the bottom of the text object, then save your changes.

3. Insert and style a picture.

a. Select Slide 2, then insert the picture **PPT C-6.jpg**.

b. Completely crop the light blue section off the top of the picture, then crop the right side of the picture about ¼".

c. Drag the picture up so it is in the center of the blank area of the slide.

d. Click the Recolor button, then change the picture color to Grayscale.

e. Save your changes.

4. Insert a text box.

a. On Slide 2, insert a text box below the picture.

b. Type **Private submissions for music up 19%**.

c. Delete the word for, then drag the word music after the word Private.

d. Select the text object, then click the Shape Styles More button in the Shape Styles group on the Drawing Tools Format tab.

e. Point to Other Theme Fills, then click Style 11.

f. Center the text object under the picture.

5. Insert a chart.

a. Go to Slide 3, 2009 CD Sales by Quarter, apply the Title and Content slide layout, then insert a Clustered Bar chart.

b. Close Excel.

6. Enter and edit chart data.

a. Show the chart data.

b. Enter the data shown in Table C-2 into the worksheet.

c. Delete the data in Column D, then close Excel.

d. Change the chart style to Style 16 in the Chart Styles group.

e. Save your changes.

TABLE C-2

	U.S. Sales	Int. Sales
1st Qtr	290,957	163,902
2nd Qtr	429,840	125,854
3rd Qtr	485,063	135,927
4th Qtr	365,113	103,750

7. Insert a table.

a. Add a new slide after Slide 3 with the Title and Content layout.

b. Add the slide title **New Subscription Plans**.

c. Insert a table with 3 columns and 6 rows.

d. Enter the information shown in Table C-3, then change the table style to Light Style 2 – Accent 1. (*Hint*: Use the Copy and Paste commands to enter duplicate information in the table.)

e. Center the text in the top row.

TABLE C-3

Basic	Standard	Premium
$1.25 per download	$4.99 per month	$12.95 per month
Unlimited downloads	Max. 12 downloads	Max. 35 downloads
Limited access	Unlimited access	Unlimited access
Online registration	Online registration	Online registration
High-speed connection recommended	High-speed connection required	High-speed connection required

f. In the Table Tools Layout tab, distribute the table rows.

g. Save your changes.

8. Insert and format WordArt.

a. Go to Slide 2, then select the bulleted list text object.

b. Apply the WordArt style Fill – Accent 2, Warm Matte Bevel.

c. View the presentation in Slide Show view, then save your changes.

d. Add your name as a footer to the notes and handouts, print the slides as handouts (3 slides per page).

e. Save your work, close the file, and exit PowerPoint.

▼ INDEPENDENT CHALLENGE 1

You are a financial management consultant for Casey Investments, located in St. Louis, Missouri. One of your responsibilities is to create standardized presentations on different financial investments for use on the company Web site. As part of the presentation for this meeting, you insert some clip art, add a text box, and insert a chart.

a. Open the file PPT C-7.pptx from the drive and folder where you store your Data Files, then save it as Casey.

b. Add your name as the footer on all notes and handouts, then apply the Oriel Design Theme.

c. Insert a clustered column chart on Slide 6, then enter the data in Table C-4 into the worksheet.

d. Format the chart using Style 27.

Advanced Challenge Exercise

■ Click the Chart Tools Layout tab, click the Legend button, then click Show Legend at Top.

■ Click the Chart Tools Format tab, then click the Current Selection list arrow in the Current Selection group, then click Series "3 Year."

■ Click the Shape Fill button list arrow, then click the Orange color under Standard Colors.

TABLE C-4

	1 year	3 year	5 year	7 year
Bonds	4.2%	5.2%	7.9%	6.5%
Stocks	6.9%	8.2%	7.2%	9.6%
Mutual Funds	4.6%	6.0%	7.4%	11.4%

e. Insert clip art of a set of scales on Slide 2, then format as necessary. (*Hint*: Use the keyword scales to search for clips.)

f. On Slide 3, use the Align, and Distribute commands on the Drawing Tools Format tab in the Arrange group to align and distribute the objects so that the shapes are aligned on top and distributed horizontally.

g. Spell check the presentation, then save it.

h. View the slide show. Make changes if necessary.

i. The final presentation should look like Figure C-19.

j. Print the slides as handouts (6 slides per page), then close the presentation, and exit PowerPoint.

FIGURE C-19

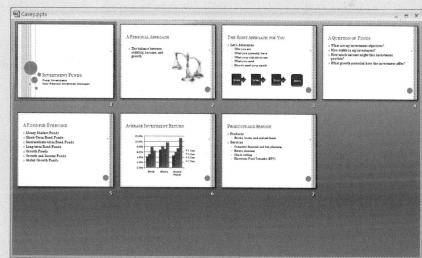

▼ INDEPENDENT CHALLENGE 2

You work for Alcom Home Systems, a company based out of Colorado Springs, Colorado that provides integrated data, security, and voice command systems for homes. You have been asked to enhance a marketing presentation on a new product that the company is going to promote at a large trade fair in Las Vegas. You work on completing a presentation for the show. You insert some clip art, add a text box, and insert a chart.

a. Start PowerPoint, open the file PPT C-8.pptx from the drive and folder where you store your Data Files, and save it as **Alcom**.

b. Add your name and today's date to Slide 1 in the Subtitle text box.

c. Organize the objects on Slide 2 using the Align, Distribute, and Group commands. Add and format additional shapes to enhance the presentation.

d. On Slide 3, style the picture, recolor the picture, and use a picture effect.

e. Apply the Median theme to the presentation.

f. Insert the Word document file **PPT C-9.docx** to create additional slides from an outline after Slide 2.

g. Create a new slide after Slide 4, title the slide **Growth of Integrated Systems**, then insert a chart.

TABLE C-5

	Last Yr.	Current Yr.	Next Yr.
Traditional	91	85	74
Integrated	9	15	26

FIGURE C-20

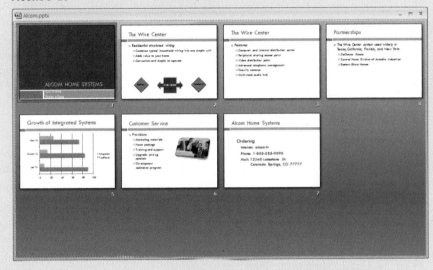

h. Enter the data in Table C-5, then format the chart using at least two formatting commands. Be able to name which formatting commands you applied to the chart.

i. Insert a text box on the Alcom Home Systems slide (Slide 7). Create your own company contact and address information. Format the text box.

j. Spell check, then view the final slide show (refer to Figure C-20). Make any necessary changes.

k. Save the presentation, print the slides as handouts, close the file, and exit PowerPoint.

▼ INDEPENDENT CHALLENGE 3

You work for LearnSource Ltd., a company that produces instructional software to help people learn foreign languages. Once a year, LearnSource holds a meeting with their biggest client, the Department of State, to brief the government on new products and to receive feedback on existing products. Your boss has started a presentation and has asked you to look it over and add other elements to make it look better.

a. Start PowerPoint, open the file PPT C-10.pptx from the drive and folder where you store your Data Files, and save it as **LearnSource**.

b. Add an appropriate design theme to the presentation.

c. Insert the Word outline PPT C-11.docx after the Product Revisions slide.

d. Format the text so that the most important information is the most prominent.

e. Insert an appropriate table on a slide of your choice. Use your own information. (*Hint:* You can convert a bulleted list to a table.)

f. Add at least two appropriate shapes that emphasize slide content. Format the objects using shape styles. If appropriate, use the Align, Distribute, and Group commands to organize your shapes.

▼ INDEPENDENT CHALLENGE 3 (CONTINUED)

Advanced Challenge Exercise (*Internet connection required*)

- Open the Clip Art task pane, then click the Clip art on Office Online link to go to the Microsoft Office Online Web site.
- Insert an appropriate graphic.
- Format the graphic using Picture Tools Format tab.
- Be able to explain how you formatted the graphic object.

FIGURE C-21

g. Spell check and view the final slide show (refer to Figure C-21). Make any necessary changes.

h. Add your name as footer text on the notes and handouts, save the presentation, then print the slides as handouts.

i. Save and close the file, and exit PowerPoint.

▼ REAL LIFE INDEPENDENT CHALLENGE

You are on the Foreign Exchange Commission at your college and one of your responsibilities is to present information on past foreign student exchanges to different organizations on and off campus. You need to create a pictorial presentation that highlights a trip to a different country. Create a presentation using your own pictures or photographs given to you with permission by a friend.

Note: Three photographs (PPT C-12.jpg, PPT C-13.jpg, and PPT C-14.jpg,) from Dijon, France are provided, if necessary to help you complete this Independent Challenge.

a. Start PowerPoint, create a new blank presentation, and save it as Exchange to the drive and folder where you store your Data Files.

FIGURE C-22

b. Locate and insert the pictures you want to use. Place one picture on each slide using the Content with Caption slide layout.

c. Add information about each picture in the text placeholder and enter a slide title. If you use the pictures provided, research Dijon, France using the Internet for relevant information to place on the slides. (*Internet connection required*)

d. Apply an appropriate design theme.

e. Apply an appropriate title and your name to the title slide. Spell check, then view the final slide show (refer to Figure C-22).

f. Add a slide number to the slides and your name as footer text to the notes and handouts, save the presentation, then print the slides and notes pages (if any).

g. Save your work, close the file, and exit PowerPoint.

PowerPoint 2007

Create a one-slide presentation that looks like Figure C-23. The slide layout shown in Figure C-23 is a specific layout designed for pictures. Insert the picture file PPT C-6.jpg to complete this presentation. Add your name as footer to the slide, save the presentation as **Guitar Lessons** to the drive and folder where you store your Data Files, then print the slide.

FIGURE C-23

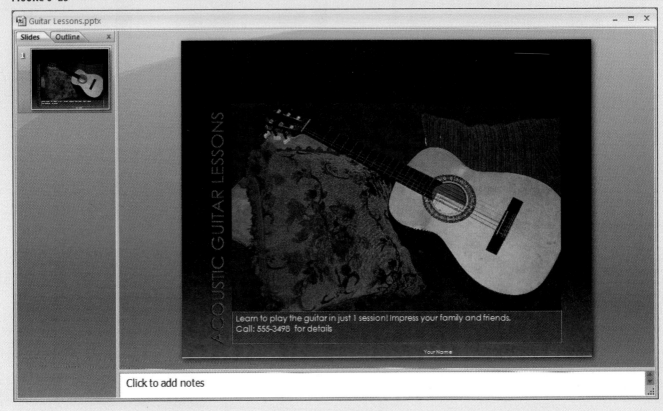

Finishing a Presentation

Though not required, having a consistent professional-looking theme throughout your presentation is optimal if you want to peak and retain your audience's interest in the subject matter you are presenting. PowerPoint helps you achieve a consistent look by providing ways to customize your slides' layout and background. Once you are finished working with the text and other objects of your presentation, you are ready to apply slide show effects, which determine the way the slides and objects on the slides appear in Slide Show view. Ellen has reviewed the presentation and is pleased with the slides you created for the Quest Specialty Travel presentation. You are ready to finalize the layouts and add effects to make the presentation interesting to watch.

OBJECTIVES

Understand masters

Customize background style

Use slide show commands

Set slide show transitions and timings

Set slide animation effects

Inspect a presentation

Evaluate a presentation

Create a design template

Understanding Masters

Each presentation in PowerPoint has a set of **masters**, which store information, including the position and size of text and content placeholders, text styles, background colors, effects, animations, and theme colors. There are three Master views: Slide Master view, Handout Master view, and Notes Master view. Changes made to the Slide Master are reflected on all the slides, changes made to the Notes Master are reflected in the Notes Page view, and changes made to the Handout Master are reflected when you print your presentation using one of the Handout print options. Design elements that you place on the Slide Master appear on every slide in the presentation. For example, you could insert a company logo in the upper-right corner of the slide master and that logo would then appear on every slide in your presentation. Each Slide Master has associated layouts. Changes made to a layout affect all slides that have that layout. ▰▰▰▰ You want to add the company logo to the presentation, so you open your presentation and examine the slide master.

1. **Start PowerPoint, open the presentation** PPT D-1.pptx **from the drive and folder where you store your Data Files, save the presentation as** QuestD, **click the** View tab **on the Ribbon, then click the** Arrange All button **in the Window group**

   The title slide of the presentation appears.

QUICK TIP

You can press and hold [Shift] and click the Normal button on the status bar to display the slide master.

2. **Click the** Slide Master button **in the Presentation Views group, then click the** Solstice Slide Master thumbnail **(first thumbnail) in the left pane**

   The Slide Master view appears with the slide master displayed in the Slide pane as shown in Figure D-1. This master slide is the theme master slide (the Solstice theme in this case). Each master text placeholder identifies the font size, style, color, and position of text placeholders on the slide in Normal view. For example, the Master title placeholder, labeled "Click to edit Master title style," is positioned at the top of the slide and uses a brown, shadowed, 44 pt, Gill Sans MT font. Any objects you place on the slide master will appear on all slides in the presentation. The slide layouts located below the master slide thumbnail in the left pane follow the information in the master slide and changes you make to this master slide, including font changes, are reflected in all of the slide layouts. Each slide layout in the presentation can be modified independently. Each theme comes with its own associated slide masters.

QUICK TIP

When working with slide layouts, you can right-click the thumbnail to open a shortcut list of commands.

3. **Point to each** slide layout **in the left pane, then click the** Title Only Layout thumbnail

   As you point to each slide layout, a ScreenTip appears which identifies each slide layout by name and lists if any of the slides in the presentation are currently using the layout. Three slides are using the Title Only Layout, Slide 4, Slide 9, and Slide 10.

4. **Click the** Solstice Slide Master thumbnail, **click the** Insert tab **on the Ribbon, then click the** Picture button **in the Illustrations group**

   The Insert Picture dialog box opens.

5. **Select the picture file** PPT D-2.jpg **from the drive and folder where you store your Data Files, then click** Insert

   The QST graphic logo appears on the slide master and will appear on all slides in the presentation. The graphic is too large and needs to be repositioned on the slide so you reduce its size and move it to a better location on the slide.

6. **Click the** Shape Width down arrow **in the Size group until** 1.1" **appears, then drag the** graphic **to the upper left corner of the slide**

   Compare your screen to Figure D-2.

7. **Click the** Normal button ▣ **on the status bar, then save your changes**

FIGURE D-1: Slide Master view

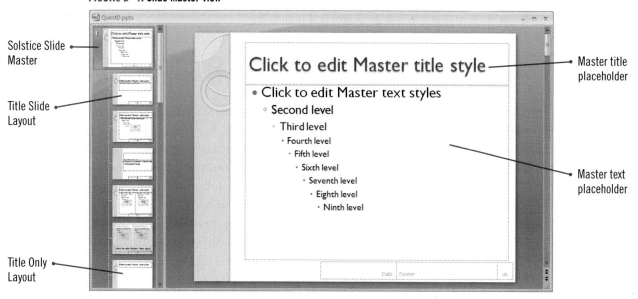

Solstice Slide Master

Title Slide Layout

Title Only Layout

Master title placeholder

Master text placeholder

FIGURE D-2: Graphic added to the slide master

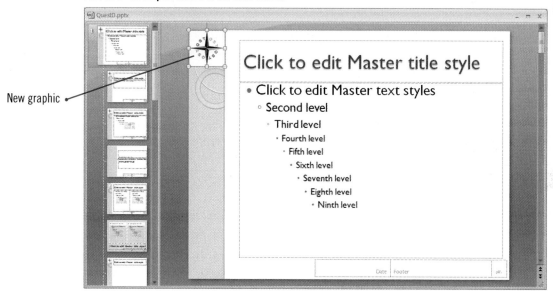

New graphic

Create custom slide layouts

As you work with PowerPoint, you may find that you need to develop a customized slide layout. For example, you may need to create presentations for a client that has slides that display four pictures with a caption underneath each picture. To make everyone's job easier, you create a custom slide layout that includes only the placeholders needed for that particular slide layout. To create a custom slide layout, open Slide Master view, click the Insert Layout button in the Edit Master group. A new slide layout appears in the Slide pane. You can choose to add several different placeholders including

Content, Text, Picture, Chart, Table, SmartArt, Media, and Clip Art. Click the Insert Placeholder button arrow in the Master Layout group, click the placeholder you want to add, drag $+$ to create the placeholder, then position the placeholder on the slide. In Slide Master view, you can add or delete placeholders in any of the slide layouts. You can rename a custom slide layout by clicking the Rename button in the Edit Master group and entering a descriptive name to better identify the layout.

Customizing the Background Style

Every slide in a PowerPoint presentation has a **background**, the area behind the text and graphics. You modify the background to enhance the slides using images and color. A **background graphic** is an object placed on the slide master. You can quickly change the background appearance by applying a background style, which is a set of color variations derived from the theme colors. **Theme colors** are a set of twelve coordinated colors that determine the colors for all slide elements in your presentation including: slide background, text and lines, shadows, title text, fills, accents, and hyperlinks. Every theme, such as Civic and Solstice, has its own set of theme colors. See Table D-1 for a description of the theme colors. ▄▄▟▟ The QST presentation needs some design enhancements. You decide to modify the background of the slides in the presentation by applying a background style.

STEPS

1. **Click the** Design tab **on the Ribbon, then click the** Background Styles button **in the Background group**

   A gallery of background styles opens. Review the different backgrounds using Live Preview.

QUICK TIP

To apply a new background style to only selected slides, select the slides on the Slides tab or in Slide Sorter view, right-click the background style in the Background Styles gallery, then click Apply to Selected Slides.

2. **Move the pointer over each style in the gallery, then click** Style 6

   Figure D-3 shows the new background on Slide 1 of the presentation. Even though you are working in Normal view, the new background style is applied to every slide in the presentation and to the master slide and master slide layouts. The new background style did not appear over the whole slide, which indicates there is a background graphic on the slide master that is preventing you from seeing the entire slide background.

3. **Click the** Hide Background Graphics check box **in the Background group**

   For the selected slide, all the background graphics are hidden from view and only the text objects on the slide remain visible.

4. **Click the** Hide Background Graphics check box **to display the background graphics, click the** Background Styles button, **then click** Format Background

   The Format Background dialog box opens.

QUICK TIP

You can also apply a gradient background style to a shape by right-clicking the shape, then clicking Format Shape in the shortcut menu.

5. **Click the** Type list arrow, **click** Linear, **click the** Direction button, **click** Linear Down, **click** Apply to All, **then click** Close

   The gradient fill of the background style now progresses from dark to light starting at the bottom of the slide and moving to the top. You need to fix the background color of the QST logo graphic so it does not obstruct the slide background graphics.

6. **Press** [Shift], **click the** Normal button ▣ **on the status bar, click the** Solstice Slide Master **thumbnail in the left pane, then click the** QST graphic

   The graphic is selected in the Slide Master view.

7. **Click the** Picture Tools Format tab **on the Ribbon, click the** Recolor button **in the Adjust group, click** Set Transparent Color, **then move the pointer over the slide**

   The pointer changes to the transparent pointer ⃗⃰.

TROUBLE

If the white background does not become transparent, click the Undo button, then repeat the step.

8. **Position** ⃗⃰ **over the** white background **of the QST logo graphic, then click**

   The white background of the QST graphic becomes transparent and the slide background appears behind the graphic.

9. **Click the** Normal button ▣ **on the status bar, then save your work**

   Compare your screen to Figure D-4.

FIGURE D-3: Slide with new background style applied

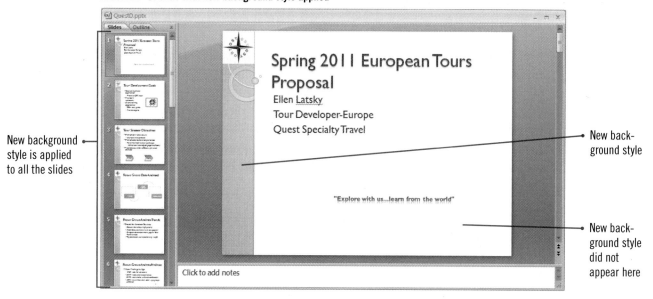

New background style is applied to all the slides

New background style

New background style did not appear here

FIGURE D-4: Finished slide

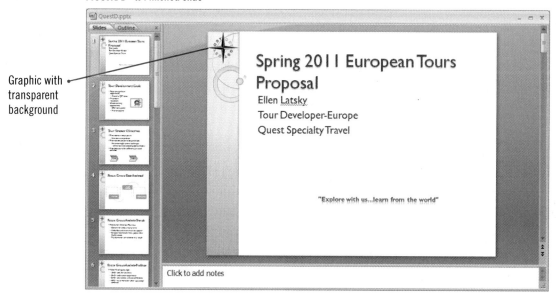

Graphic with transparent background

TABLE D-1: Theme colors

scheme element	description
Background color	Color of the slide's background; fills the slide
Text and lines color	Used for any typed characters and drawn lines; contrasts with the background color
Shadows color	The shadow color for text and other objects; generally a darker shade of the background color
Title text color	Used for slide title; like the text and line colors and contrasts with the background color
Fills color	Used to fill shapes and other objects with color. Contrasts with both the background and the text and line colors
Accent colors	Colors used for other objects on slides, such as bullets
Accent and hyperlink colors	Colors used for accent objects and for hyperlinks you insert
Accent and followed hyperlink color	Color used for accent objects and for hyperlinks after they have been clicked

Using Slide Show Commands

With PowerPoint, you can show a presentation on any compatible computer using Slide Show view. As you've seen, Slide Show view fills your computer screen with the slides of the presentation, showing them one at a time. Once the presentation is in Slide Show view, you can use a number of slide show options to tailor the show to meet your needs. For example, you can draw, or **annotate**, on slides or jump to different slides in other parts of the presentation. ▰▰▰▰ Ellen wants you to learn how to run a slide show and use the slide show options so you can help her when she gives the presentation. You run the slide show of the presentation and practice using some of the custom slide show options.

STEPS

1. **Click the View tab on the Ribbon, then click the Slide Show button in the Presentation Views group**

   The first slide of the presentation fills the screen.

2. **Press [Spacebar]**

   Slide 2 appears on the screen. Pressing [Spacebar] or clicking the left mouse button is the easiest way to move through a slide show. See Table D-2 for other Slide Show view key commands. You can also use the Slide Show shortcut menu for on-screen navigation during a slide show.

3. **Right-click anywhere on the screen, point to Go to Slide on the shortcut menu, then click 8 Mediterranean Islands Bike Tour**

   The slide show jumps to Slide 8. You can highlight or emphasize major points in your presentation by annotating the slide during a slide show using one of PowerPoint's annotation tools.

TROUBLE
The Slide Show toolbar buttons are semitransparent and will blend in with the background color on the slide.

4. **Move the pointer to the bottom left corner of the screen to display the Slide Show toolbar, click the Pen Options menu button 🖊, then click Highlighter**

   The pointer changes to the highlighter pointer ▮.

5. **Drag ▮ to highlight the text below the picture**

   Compare your screen to Figure D-5. While the annotation tool is visible, mouse clicks do not advance the slide show; however, you can still move to the next slide by pressing [Spacebar] or [Enter].

QUICK TIP
You have the option of saving undeleted annotations you create while in Slide Show view when you end or quit the slide show.

6. **Click the Pen Options menu button 🖊 on the Slide Show toolbar, click Erase All Ink on Slide, then press [Ctrl][A]**

   The annotations on Slide 8 are erased and the pointer returns to ⌖ when you press [Ctrl][A].

7. **Click the Slide Show menu button 🖵 on the Slide Show toolbar, point to Go to Slide, then click 10 Adventure Series on the menu**

   Slide 10 appears.

QUICK TIP
If you know the slide number of a slide you want to jump to during a slide show, type the number, then press [Enter].

8. **Press [Home], then press [Enter] to advance through the slide show, then when you see the black slide at the end of the slide show, press [Spacebar]**

   You are returned to Normal view. The black slide indicates the end of the slide show.

FIGURE D-5: Slide 8 in Slide Show view with highlight annotations

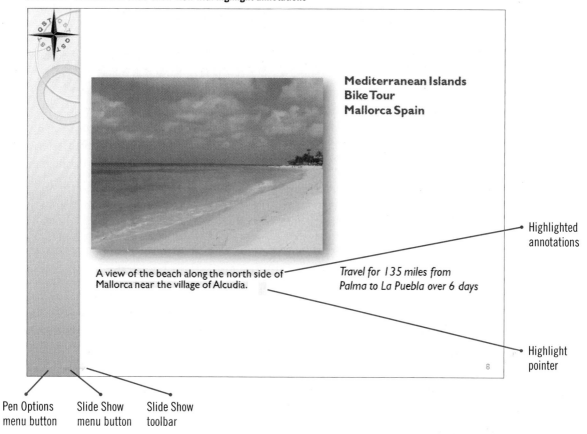

Mediterranean Islands
Bike Tour
Mallorca Spain

A view of the beach along the north side of
Mallorca near the village of Alcudia.

Travel for 135 miles from
Palma to La Puebla over 6 days

Highlighted
annotations

Highlight
pointer

8

Pen Options
menu button

Slide Show
menu button

Slide Show
toolbar

TABLE D-2: Basic Slide Show keyboard controls

control	description
[Enter], [Spacebar], [PgDn], [N], [down arrow key], or [right arrow key]	Advances to the next slide
[E]	Erases the annotation drawing
[Home], [End]	Moves to the first or last slide in the slide show
[H]	Displays a hidden slide
[up arrow key] or [PgUp]	Returns to the previous slide
[W]	Changes the screen to white; press again to return
[S]	Pauses the slide show; press again to continue
[B]	Changes the screen to black; press again to return
[Ctrl][M]	Shows or hides annotations on the slide
[Ctrl][A]	Changes pointer to ⃞
[Esc]	Stops the slide show

Setting Slide Show Transitions and Timings

In a slide show, you can specify how each slide advances in and out of view, and for how long each slide appears on the screen. **Slide transitions** are the special visual and audio effects you apply to a slide that determine how it moves in and out of view during the slide show. **Slide timing**, refers to the amount of time a slide is visible on the screen. Typically, you would set slide timings if you wanted the presentation to automatically progress through the slides during a slide show. Setting the correct slide timing, in this case, is important because it determines how long each slide is visible. Each slide can have a different slide timing. You decide to set slide transitions and 8 second slide timings for all the slides.

STEPS

1. **Make sure Slide 1 is selected, click the Animations tab on the Ribbon, then point to each of the transition options in the Transition to This Slide group**

   A Live Preview of each transition is displayed on the slide. Transitions are organized by type into five groups.

2. **Click the More button in the Transition to This Slide group, then click Box In in the Wipes section (3rd row)**

   The new slide transition plays on the slide and a transition icon appears next to the slide thumbnail in the Slides tab as shown in Figure D-6. The slide transition would have more impact if it were slowed down.

3. **Click the Transition Speed list arrow in the Transition to This Slide group, then click Medium**

   The Box In slide transition plays again at the slower speed. You can apply this transition to all of the slides in the presentation.

4. **Click the Apply To All button in the Transition to This Slide group, then click the Slide Sorter button 🔠 on the status bar**

   All of the slides now have the Box In transition at the medium speed applied to them as identified by the transition icons located below each slide. The options under Advance Slide in the Transition to This Slide group determine how slides progress during a slide show—either by mouse click or automatically by slide timing.

5. **Click the Automatically After up arrow until 00.08 appears in the text box, then click the Apply To All button in the Transition to This Slide group**

   The timing between slides is 8 seconds as indicated by the time under each slide in Slide Sorter view. See Figure D-7. When you run the slide show, each slide will remain on the screen for 8 seconds. You can override a slide's timing and speed up the slide show by pressing [Spacebar], [Enter], or clicking the left mouse button during a slide show.

6. **Click Slide 8, click the Transition Sound list arrow in the Transition to This Slide group, then click Breeze**

   The Breeze sound will now play when Slide 8 appears during the slide show.

7. **Press [Home], click the Slide Show button 🖵 on the status bar, then watch the slide show advance automatically**

8. **When you see the black slide at the end of the slide show, press [Spacebar], then save your changes**

   The slide show ends and returns to Slide Sorter view with Slide 1 selected.

FIGURE D-6: Applied slide transition

Box In slide transition •

More button •

Transition icon •

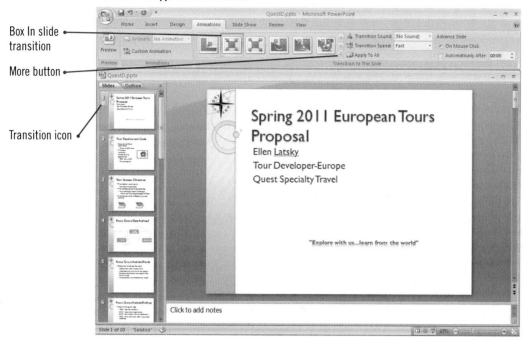

FIGURE D-7: Slide Sorter view showing applied transition and timing

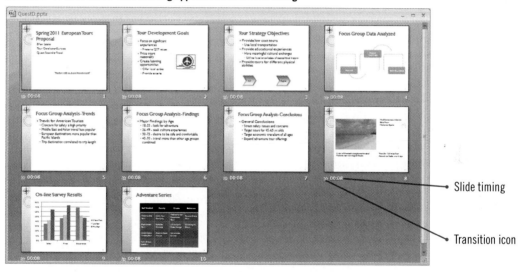

Slide timing •

Transition icon •

Rehearsing slide show timings

You can set different slide timings for each slide. For example, you can have the title slide appear for 20 seconds, the second slide for 1 minute, and so on. You can set timings by clicking the Rehearse Timings button in the Set Up group on the Slide Show tab. Slide Show view opens and the Rehearsal toolbar shown in Figure D-8 opens. It contains buttons to pause between slides and to advance to the next slide. After opening the Rehearsal toolbar, practice giving your presentation. PowerPoint keeps track of how long each slide appears and sets the timing accordingly. You can view your rehearsed timings in Slide Sorter view. The next time you run the slide show, you can use the timings you rehearsed.

FIGURE D-8: Rehearsal toolbar

| Rehearsal ▼ × |
| 0:00:03 0:00:03 |

Total elapsed time for all slides

Move to the next slide

Click to pause

Time elapsed while viewing current slide

Click to reset the clock to zero for the current slide

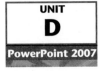
Setting Slide Animation Effects

Animation effects let you control how the objects and main points in your presentation appear on the screen during a slide show. You can set custom animation effects or use one of several standard animation effects. For example, you can apply a Fade by 1st Level Paragraphs animation effect to bulleted text so that each first level bullet appears separately from the others. Using animation effects allows you to control how information flows and what information is emphasized. You can animate text, graphics, sounds, hyperlinks, SmartArt diagrams, charts and individual chart elements. The standard animation effects include Fade, Wipe, and Fly In and can be applied to any selected object. Custom animation effects are organized into four categories, which provide you a wide range of animation choices, such as Ease In and Flicker. Ellen wants you to animate the text and graphics of several slides in the presentation using animation effects.

STEPS

1. **Verify that the** Animations tab **is selected on the Ribbon, double-click** Slide 2 **to view it in Normal view, then click the** body text **object**

   The bullets in the text object can be animated to appear one at a time during a slide show.

2. **Click the** Animate list arrow **in the Animations group, then click** By 1st Level Paragraphs **in the Fade section**

   As you click the animation option a Live Preview of the Box In transition and the Fade animation effect plays.

3. **Click the** Slide Show button **on the status bar, then press [Esc] when you see Slide 3**

   The Fade animation effect, which begins after the slide transition effect, is active on Slide 2. You can also animate other objects on a slide by setting custom animations.

4. **Make sure** Slide 3 **is selected, click the grouped** arrow object **on the slide, then click the** Custom Animation button **in the Animations group**

   The Custom Animation task pane opens.

5. **Click the** Add Effect button **in the Custom Animation task pane, then point to** Entrance

   A submenu of Entrance animation effects appears next to a menu of four animation categories, Entrance, Emphasis, Exit, and Motion Paths as shown in Figure D-9. An Entrance animation effect causes an object to enter the slide with an effect; an Emphasis animation effect causes an object already visible on the slide to have an effect; an Exit animation effect causes an object to leave the slide with an effect; and a Motion Paths animation effect causes an object to move on a specified path on the slide.

6. **Click** More Effects

   The Add Entrance Effect dialog box opens. All of the effects in this dialog box allow an object to enter the slide using a special effect.

7. **Scroll down to the** Exciting section, **click** Glide, **then click** OK

   The arrow object now has the glide effect applied to it as shown in Figure D-10. Notice that the arrow object now has an animation tag and is listed in the Custom Animation task pane as the first object to be animated on the slide. **Animation tags** identify the order in which objects are animated during slide show.

8. **Click the Custom Animation task pane** Close button , **click the** Slide Show tab **on the Ribbon, then click the** From Beginning button **in the Start Slide Show group to run the Slide Show from Slide 1**

   The special effects make the presentation more interesting to view.

9. **When you see the black slide, press [Spacebar], then save your changes**

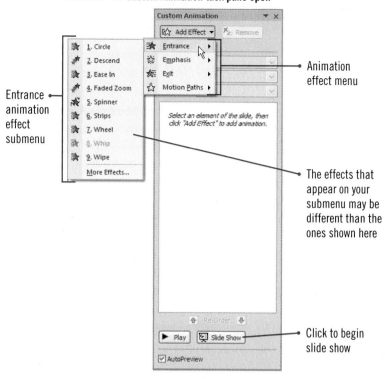

FIGURE D-9: Custom Animation task pane open

Entrance animation effect submenu

Animation effect menu

The effects that appear on your submenu may be different than the ones shown here

Click to begin slide show

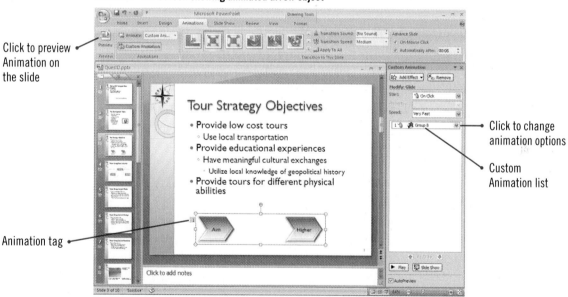

FIGURE D-10: Screen showing animated arrow object

Click to preview Animation on the slide

Click to change animation options

Custom Animation list

Animation tag

Presentation checklist

You should always rehearse your slide show. If possible, rehearse your presentation in the room and with the computer that you will use. Use the following checklist to prepare for the slide show:

- Is **PowerPoint** or **PowerPoint Viewer** installed on the computer?
- Is your **presentation file** on the hard drive of the computer you will be using? Try putting a shortcut for the file on the desktop. Do you have a backup copy of your presentation file on a removable storage device?
- Is the **projection device** working correctly? Can the slides be seen from the back of the room?

- Do you know how to control **room lighting** so that the audience can see both your slides and their handouts and notes? You may want to designate someone to control the lights if the controls are not close to you.
- Will the **computer** be situated so you can advance and annotate the slides yourself? If not, designate someone to advance them for you.
- Do you have enough copies of your **handouts**? Bring extras. Decide when to hand them out, or whether you prefer to have them waiting at the audience members' seats when they enter.

Inspecting a Presentation

Reviewing your presentation can be an important step, not only to find and fix errors, but also to locate and delete private company or personal information and document properties you do not want to share with others. If you share presentations with others, especially over the Internet, it is a good idea to inspect the presentation file using the Document Inspector. The **Document Inspector** looks for hidden data and personal information that is stored in the file itself or in the document properties. Document properties, also known as **metadata**, includes specific data about the presentation, such as the author's name, subject matter, title, who saved the file last, and when the file was created. Other types of information the Document Inspector can locate and remove include: presentation notes, comments, ink annotations, invisible on-slide content, off-slide content, and custom XML data. ▓▓▓▓▓ QST has strict rules about revealing personal and company information in documents. You decide to view and add some document properties, inspect your presentation file, and learn about the Mark as Final command.

STEPS

1. **Click the Office button 🔘, point to Prepare, then click Properties**

   The Document Properties pane opens showing the file location and the title of the presentation. Now enter some descriptive data for this presentation file.

2. **Enter the data shown in Figure D-11, then click the Properties pane Close button**

   This data provides detailed information about the presentation file that you can use to identify and organize your file. You can also use this information as search criteria to locate the file at a later time. You now use the Document Inspector to search for information you might want to delete in the presentation.

3. **Click 🔘, point to Prepare, click Inspect Document, click Yes to save the changes to the document, then read the dialog box**

   The Document Inspector dialog box opens. The Document Inspector searches the presentation file for six different types of information that you might want removed from the presentation before sending it.

4. **Make sure all of the check boxes are selected, then click Inspect**

   The presentation file is reviewed and the Document Inspector dialog box displays the results shown in Figure D-12. Notice that there are three items found: document properties in the Document Properties pane, an off slide object that you created and didn't use, and some reminder notes you wrote yourself in the Notes pane on Slides 8, 9, and 10. You decide to leave the document properties alone but delete the off-slide object, and the notes in the Notes pane for all of the slides.

5. **Click the Off-Slide Content Remove All button, click the Presentation Notes Remove All button, then click Close**

   All of those items are removed from the presentation.

6. **Click 🔘, point to Prepare, click Mark as Final, then click OK in the alert dialog box**

   A dialog box opens. Be sure to read the dialog box to understand what happens to the file and how to recognize a marked-as-final presentation. You decide to proceed with this operation.

7. **Click OK, click the Home tab on the Ribbon, click the Slide 1 thumbnail in the Slides pane, then click anywhere in the title text object**

   Notice that the commands on the Ribbon are dimmed as shown in Figure D-13. Because you marked the file as final, the file is read-only. A **read-only** file is one that can't be edited or modified in any way. Anyone who has received a read-only presentation can edit the presentation by removing the mark as final status. You still want to work on the presentation, so you remove the mark as final status.

8. **Click 🔘, point to Prepare, click Mark as Final, then save your changes**

   The commands on the Ribbon are active again, and the file can now be modified.

FIGURE D-11: Document Properties pane

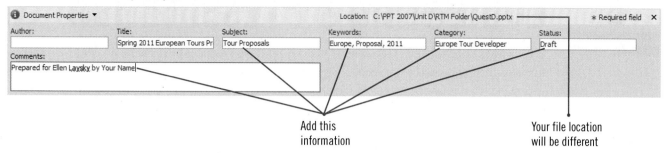

Add this information

Your file location will be different

FIGURE D-12: Document Inspector dialog box

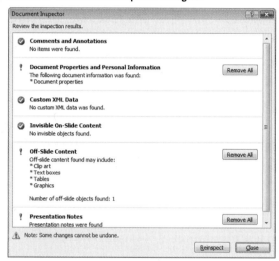

FIGURE D-13: Marked-as-final presentation

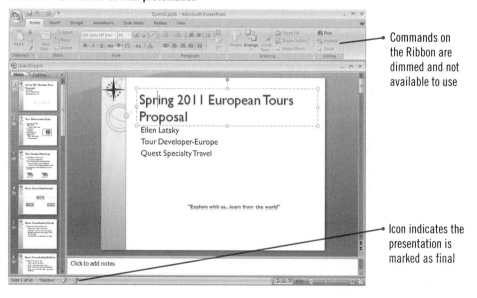

Commands on the Ribbon are dimmed and not available to use

Icon indicates the presentation is marked as final

Digitally sign a presentation

So what is a digital signature and why would you want to use one in PowerPoint? A digital signature is similar to a hand-written signature in that it authenticates your document; however, a digital signature, unlike a hand-written signature, is created using computer cryptography and is not visible within the presentation itself. There are three primary reasons you would add a digital signature to a presentation: one, to authenticate the signer of the document; two, to assure that the content of the presentation has not been changed since it was signed; and three, to assure the origin of the signed document. To add a digital signature, click the Office button, point to Prepare, click Add a Digital Signature, then follow the dialog boxes.

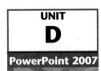

Evaluating a Presentation

As you create a presentation, keep in mind that a good design requires preparation. An effective presentation is focused and visually appealing—easy for the speaker to present and simple for the audience to understand. The visual elements (colors, graphics, and text) can strongly influence the audience's attention and interest and can determine the success of your presentation. See Table D-3 for general information on the impact a visual presentation has on an audience. ▰▰▰ You know Ellen will critique your presentation, so you take the time to evaluate your presentation's effectiveness.

STEPS

1. **Click the Slide Show button ⬚ on the status bar, then press [Spacebar] when the slide show finishes**

2. **Click the Slide Sorter button ⊞ on the status bar**
   You decide that Slide 8 should come after Slide 10.

3. **Drag Slide 8 to the right side of Slide 10, then save your changes**
   Slide 8 is moved to the end of the presentation. The final presentation is shown in Slide Sorter view. Compare your screen to Figure D-14.

4. **Double-click Slide 1, then evaluate your presentation according to the guidelines below**
   Figure D-15 shows a poorly designed slide. Contrast this slide with your presentation as you review the following guidelines.

When evaluating a presentation, it is important to:

- **Keep your message focused**
  Don't put every point you plan to say on your presentation slides. Keep the audience anticipating further explanations to the key points shown in the presentation.

- **Keep your text concise**
  Limit each slide to six words per line and six lines per slide. Use lists and symbols to help prioritize your points visually. Your presentation text provides only the highlights; use notes to give more detailed information. Your presentation focuses attention on the key issues and you supplement the information with further explanation and details during your presentation.

- **Keep the design simple, easy to read, and appropriate for the content**
  A design theme makes the presentation consistent. If you design your own layout, keep it simple and use design elements sparingly. Use similar design elements consistently throughout the presentation; otherwise, your audience may get confused.

- **Choose attractive colors that make the slide easy to read**
  Use contrasting colors for slide background and text to make the text readable. If you are giving an on-screen presentation, you can use almost any combination of colors that look good together.

- **Choose fonts and styles that are easy to read and emphasize important text**
  As a general rule, use no more than two fonts in a presentation and vary the font size, using nothing smaller than 24 points. Use bold and italic attributes selectively.

- **Use visuals to help communicate the message of your presentation**
  Commonly used visuals include clip art, photographs, charts, worksheets, tables, and movies. Whenever possible, replace text with a visual, but be careful not to overcrowd your slides. White space on your slides is OK!

FIGURE D-14: The final presentation in Slide Sorter view

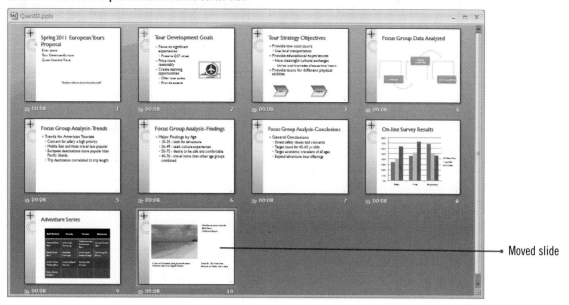

Moved slide

FIGURE D-15: A poorly designed slide

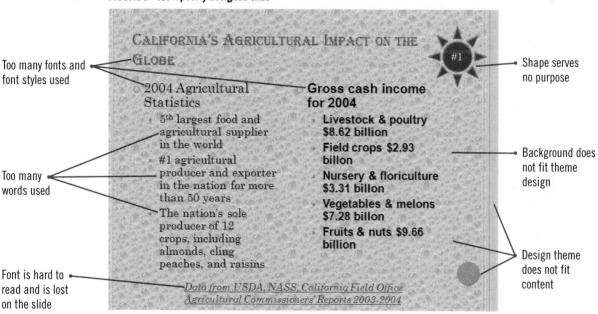

Too many fonts and font styles used

Shape serves no purpose

Too many words used

Background does not fit theme design

Font is hard to read and is lost on the slide

Design theme does not fit content

TABLE D-3: Audience impact from a visual presentation

impact	description
Visual reception	75% of all environmental stimuli is received through visual reception
Learning	55% of what an audience learns comes directly from visual messages
Retention	Combining visual messages with verbal messages can increase memory retention by as much as 30%
Presentation goals	You are twice as likely to achieve your communication objectives using a visual presentation
Meeting length	You are likely to decrease the average meeting length by 26% when you use a visual presentation

Source: Presenters Online, www.presentersonline.com

PowerPoint 2007

Creating a Design Template

When planning the design of your presentation, keep in mind that you are not limited to using just the standard themes PowerPoint provides or the ones you find on the Web. You can customize your presentation using a template. A **template** is a type of presentation file that contains custom design information made to the slide master, slide layouts, and theme. You can create a new template from a blank presentation, or you can modify an existing PowerPoint presentation that you have access to and save it as a template. If you modify an existing presentation, you can keep, change, or delete any color, graphic, or font as necessary. When you are finished creating a new presentation or modifying an existing presentation, you can save it as a template file, which adds the .potx extension to the filename. You can then use your template presentation as the basis for new presentations. ▀▀▀▀ You are finished working on your presentation for now. You want to save the presentation as a template so you and others can use it.

STEPS

QUICK TIP

Presentations saved to the Templates folder appear in the New Presentation dialog box under My Templates.

1. **Click the** Office button 🔘, **point to** Save As, **click** Other Formats, **click the** Save as type **list arrow,** then click PowerPoint Template (*.potx)

   Because this is a template, PowerPoint automatically opens the Templates folder on your hard drive as shown in Figure D-16.

2. **Use the Favorite Link or Folders pane to locate the drive and folder where you store your Data Files, click to select the filename (currently QuestD.potx) in the File name list box, type** QuestD Template, **then click** Save

   The presentation is saved as a PowerPoint template to the drive and folder where you store your Data Files, and the new template presentation appears in the PowerPoint window. The filename in the title bar has a .potx extension which identifies this presentation as a template.

3. **Click the** Slide Sorter button 🔳 **on the status bar, click** Slide 3, **press and hold** [Shift], **click** Slide 10, **release** [Shift], **then click the** Cut button ✂ **in the Clipboard group**

   Slides 3 through 10 are deleted.

4. **Double-click** Slide 2, **press and hold** [Shift], **click the** body text object, **click the** title text object, **right-click the** clip art object, **release** [Shift], **then click** Cut

   The clip art object and the text in the text objects are deleted. Sometimes templates have sample text.

5. **Type** Slide Title Here, **click the content placeholder, type** Bulleted list, **press** [Enter], **press** [Tab], **type** Bulleted list, **click the** Layout button **in the Slides group, then click** Title and Content

   Sample text replaces the text, and the slide layout changes to the Title and Content slide layout.

6. **Click the** Slide 1 thumbnail **in the Slides tab, press** [Shift], **select the three text objects on the slide, then press** [Delete]

   The WordArt object and the text in the text objects are deleted.

7. **Click the** title text placeholder, **type** QST Template, **click the** subtitle placeholder, **type** Subtitle text here, **then save your changes**

8. **Click the** View tab, **then click the** Slide Sorter button **in the Presentation Views group**

   Figure D-17 shows the final template presentation in Slide Sorter view.

9. **Save your work, print the template presentation as** handouts (2 per page), **close the presentation, then exit PowerPoint**

FIGURE D-16: Save As dialog box showing Templates folder

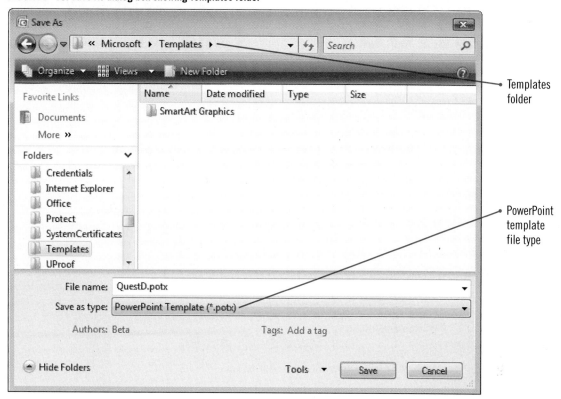

Templates folder

PowerPoint template file type

FIGURE D-17: Completed template presentation in Slide Sorter view

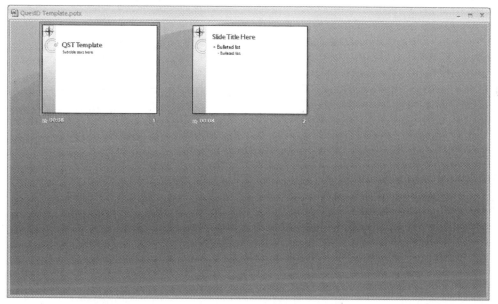

Applying a theme from another presentation

When you apply a theme from one presentation to another, you automatically apply the master layouts, colors and fonts over the existing presentation's theme. To apply a theme from another presentation, open the presentation you want to apply the theme to, click the Design tab, then click the Themes group More button.

Click Browse for Themes, use the Favorite Links or Folders pane to navigate to the presentation whose theme you want to apply. The presentation you select can be a regular presentation or a template with the .potx extension. Click the presentation name, then click Apply.

Practice

SAM If you have a SAM user profile, you may have access to hands-on instruction, practice, and assessment of the skills covered in this unit. Log in to your SAM account (http://sam2007.course.com/) to launch any assigned training activities or exams that relate to the skills covered in this unit.

▼ CONCEPTS REVIEW

Label each element of the PowerPoint window shown in Figure D-18.

FIGURE D-18

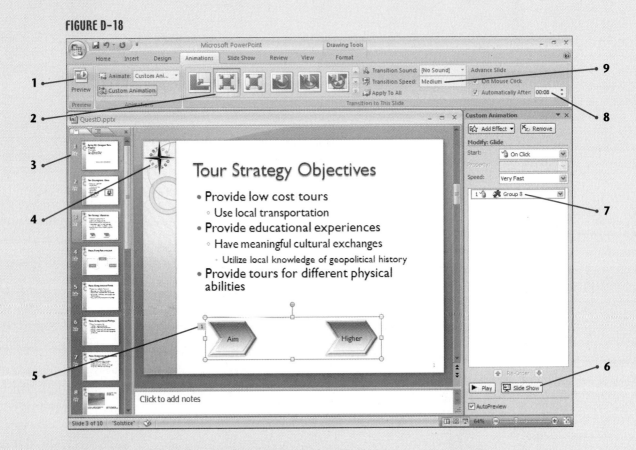

Match each term with the statement that best describes It.

10. **Animation tag**

11. **Background**

12. **Transitions**

13. **Masters**

14. **Metadata**

15. **Annotate**

a. Visual effects that determine how a slide moves in and out of view during a slide show

b. Slides that store theme and placeholder information

c. To draw on a slide during a slide show

d. Includes document properties such as the author's name

e. Identifies the order in which objects are animated

f. The area behind text and graphics

Select the best answer from the list of choices.

16. **Which of the following statements about masters is *not* true?**
    a. Masters store information
    b. Changes made to the slide master are reflected in the handout and notes masters as well
    c. Each slide layout in the presentation has a corresponding slide layout in the Slide Master view
    d. The design theme is placed on the master slide

17. **According to the book, an object placed on the slide master defines which item?**
    a. A background graphic
    b. A logo
    c. A shape
    d. A master placeholder

18. **What is the effect called that determines how a slide moves in and out of view during a slide show?**
    a. Theme
    b. Animation
    c. Timing
    d. Transition

19. **What is the effect called that controls how an object appears on the screen during a slide show?**
    a. Transition
    b. Animation
    c. Path
    d. Template

20. **The Document Inspector can do all of the following *except*,**
    a. look for hidden data
    b. delete metadata
    c. remove on-slide content
    d. locate presentation notes

21. **A PowerPoint file that *can't* be edited or modified defines what type of file?**
    a. A marked as final file
    b. A template file
    c. An inspected file
    d. A file saved in another file format

22. **According to the book, which standard should you follow to evaluate a presentation?**
    a. Slides should include most of the information you wish to present
    b. The message should be outlined in a concise way.
    c. Use many different design elements to keep your audience from getting bored.
    d. Replace visuals with text as often as possible.

23. **Which of the following statements about templates is *not* true?**
    a. The file extension .potx is applied to the PowerPoint file when you save it as a template.
    b. You can create a template from a new presentation.
    c. A template is a type of presentation that contains custom design information.
    d. A template is designed to create custom slide layouts.

▼ SKILLS REVIEW

1. **Understand masters.**
   a. Open the presentation PPT D-3.pptx from the drive and folder where you store your Data Files, then save the presentation as MediaCom.
   b. Open the Slide Master view using the View tab, then click the Civic Slide Master thumbnail.
   c. Insert the picture PPT D-4.jpg, then resize the picture so it is 0.8" wide.

    d. Drag the picture to the upper right corner of the slide within the design frame of the slide, then deselect the picture.

    e. Switch to Normal view, then save your changes.

2. Customize the background style.

    a. Switch to Slide 2, click the Design tab, then open the background styles gallery.

    b. Change the background style to Style 3.

    c. Open the Format Background dialog box.

    d. Set the Transparency to 25%, then apply the background to all of the slides.

    e. Close the dialog box, switch to Slide Master view, then open the Civic Slide Master slide.

    f. Select the inserted picture, then use the Picture Tools Format tab to make its background transparent.

    g. Switch to Normal view, then save your changes.

3. Use slide show commands.

    a. Begin the slide show on Slide 1, then proceed to Slide 4.

    b. Use the Felt Tip Pen to circle the words Early Adopters, Mass Adopters, and Late Adopters.

    c. Use the Pen Options menu button to erase all ink on the slide, then change the pointer back to the Arrow.

    d. Right-click the slide and go to Slide 8, use the Highlighter pointer to highlight each bullet on the slide.

    e. Press [Home], then advance through the slide show, don't save any ink annotations, then save your work.

4. Set slide show transitions and timings.

    a. Go to Slide 1, then apply the Wheel Clockwise, 8 Spokes transition in the Wipes group to all of the slides.

    b. Change the transition speed to slow, then switch to Slide Sorter view.

    c. Change the slide timing to 5 seconds, then apply to all of the slides.

    d. Click Slide 10, then apply the Applause sound.

    e. Click Slide 1, then switch to Normal view.

    f. View the slide show, then save your work.

FIGURE D-19: Completed presentation

5. Set slide show animation effects.

    a. Go to Slide 2, then open the Custom Animation task pane.

    b. Apply the Emphasis Flash Bulb effect to the title text object, then apply the Entrance Unfold effect to both bulleted text objects.

    c. On Slide 3 apply the Emphasis Shimmer effect to the title text object, then apply the Entrance Rise Up effect to the bulleted text object.

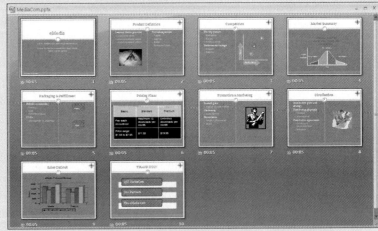

    d. On Slide 4 apply the Entrance Flip effect to the title text object, then apply an Entrance animation effect of your choice from the Exciting group to the six individual objects in the graphic.

    e. Apply animation effects to the rest of the slides in the presentation. Animate all of the text objects and the other objects.

    f. Edit the animations effects as needed, then save your changes.

    g. Compare your presentation to Figure D-19.

6. Inspect a presentation.

a. Open the Document Properties pane, type Internet Product in the Subject text box, then type Review in the Status text box

b. Close the Document Properties pane, then open the Document Inspector dialog box.

c. Make sure the Off-Slide Content check box is selected, then inspect the presentation.

d. Delete the off-slide content, and the presentation notes, then close the dialog box.

e. Save your changes.

7. Evaluate a presentation.

a. Go to Slide 1, then run a slide show.

b. Evaluate the presentation using the points described in the lesson as criteria.

c. Move Slide 6 below Slide 8.

d. Save your work, then print the slides of your presentation.

8. Create a template.

a. Save the presentation as a template (.potx) with the name MediaCom Template to the drive and folder where your Data Files are stored.

b. Delete all slides except Slide 1 and Slide 2.

c. Delete the picture and text on Slide 2, type Slide Title Here in the title text placeholder, type Bulleted List 1 in the left content placeholder, then type Bulleted List 2 in the right content placeholder.

d. Delete the subtitle text object on Slide 1, then type QST MediaCom Template in the title text object in place of the current text.

e. Delete the slide transitions and animations on both slides.

f. Save your work, then print the presentation as handouts, two slides per page.

g. Close the presentation, then exit PowerPoint.

▼ INDEPENDENT CHALLENGE 1

You are a travel consultant for Turner Travel, located in Portland, Oregon. You have been working on a sales presentation that is going to be accessed by customers on the company Web site. You need to finish up what you have been working on by adding transitions, timings, and animation effects to the sales presentation.

a. Open the file PPT D-5.pptx from the drive and folder where you store your Data Files, and save the presentation as TurnerTravel.

b. Add your name as the footer on all slides and handouts.

c. Apply the Fade Through Black slide transitions to all of the slides.

d. Apply the Entrance Glide animation to the title text on each slide.

e. Apply the Emphasis Flicker animation to the bulleted text objects on each slide.

f. Apply the Entrance Thread animation to the table on Slide 8.

g. Apply a 10 second slide timing to each slide, then change the transition speed to Medium.

h. Spell check the presentation, then save it.

i. View the slide show, and evaluate your presentation. Make changes if necessary.

j. Print the slides as handouts (six slides per page), then close the presentation, and exit PowerPoint.

▼ INDEPENDENT CHALLENGE 2

You are a development engineer at FarNorth Sports, Inc., an international sports product design company located in Winnipeg, Manitoba, Canada. FarNorth Sports designs and manufactures items such as bike helmets, bike racks, and kayak paddles, and markets these items primarily to countries in North America and Western Europe. You need to finish the work on a quarterly presentation that outlines the progress of the company's newest technologies by adding animations, customizing the background, and using the Document Inspector.

a. Open the file PPT D-6.pptx from the drive and folder where you store your Data Files, and save the presentation as **FarNorth**.

b. Apply an appropriate design theme, then apply a new slide background style. Make sure the new background style is appropriate for the design theme you have chosen.

c. Apply the Box Out slide transition to all slides, then animate the following objects: the text on Slide 2, the clip art object on Slide 3, the table on Slide 4, and the chart on Slide 6. View the slide show to evaluate the effects you added and make adjustments as necessary.

d. Run the Document Inspector with all options selected, identify what items the Document Inspector finds, close the Document Inspector dialog box, then review the slides to find the items.

e. Add a slide at the end of the presentation that identifies the items the Document Inspector found.

f. Run the Document Inspector again and remove all items except the document properties.

Advanced Challenge Exercise

■ Click the Rehearse Timings button on the Slide Sorter toolbar.
■ Set slide timings for each slide in the presentation.
■ Save new slide timings.

g. Add your name as a footer to the handouts, save your work, then run a slide show to evaluate your presentation.

h. Print the presentation as handouts (four slides per page), then close the presentation and exit PowerPoint.

▼ INDEPENDENT CHALLENGE 3

You work for JB & Associates Financial, a full service investment and pension firm. Your boss wants you to create a presentation on small business pension plan options to be published on the company Web site. You have completed adding the information to the presentation, now you need to add a design theme, format some information, add some animation effects, and add slide timings.

a. Open the file PPT D-7.pptx from the drive and folder where you store your Data Files, and save the presentation as **SBPlans**.

b. Apply an appropriate design theme.

c. Apply animation effects to the following objects: the shapes on Slide 3 and the text and clip art on Slide 5. View the slide show to evaluate the effects you added and make adjustments as necessary.

d. Convert the text on Slide 4 to a Basic Radial SmartArt graphic (Found in the Cycle category).

e. Apply the Polished style to the SmartArt graphic, then change the colors of the graphic to Colorful Range – Accent Colors 2 to 3

f. Switch to Slide 3, align the Sector and Quality arrow shapes to one another, then align the Allocation and Maturity arrow shapes to one another.

g. Adjust the aligned arrow shapes so they are centered on the Buy/Sell oval shape, then apply a 15 second timing to Slides 3–7 and a 5 second timing to Slides 1 and 2.

- Open the Slide Master view, select the last slide layout, then click the Insert Layout button.
- Click the Insert Placeholder button arrow, click Table, then drag a placeholder in the blank area of the master slide layout. (*Hint*: Draw the table placeholder so it takes up most of the blank space in the layout.)
- Return to Normal view, apply the new Custom Layout to Slides 6 and 7. Adjust the placeholder in Slide Master view if necessary.

h. Add your name as a footer to the handouts, save your work, then run a slide show to evaluate your presentation.

i. Print the presentation as handouts (four slides per page), then close the presentation and exit PowerPoint.

▼ REAL LIFE INDEPENDENT CHALLENGE

You work for the operations supervisor at the Southern State University student union. Create a presentation that you can eventually publish to the college Web site that describes all of the services offered at the student union.

a. Plan and create the slide presentation that describes the services and events offered at the student union. To help create content, use the student union at your school or use the Internet to locate information on college student unions. The presentation should contain at least six slides.

b. Use an appropriate design theme.

c. Add clip art and photographs available in the Clip Organizer to help create visual interest.

d. Save the presentation as **SSU Services** to the drive and folder where you store your Data Files. View the slide show and evaluate the contents of your presentation. Make any necessary adjustments.

e. Add transitions, animation effects, and timings to the presentation. View the slide show again to evaluate the effects you added.

f. Add your name as a footer to the handouts. Spell check, save, inspect, and print the presentation as handouts (four slides per page). Compare your finished presentation to Figure D-20.

g. Create a template from this presentation. Delete unnecessary slides and objects, type appropriate sample text if necessary, then save the presentation as **SSU Services Template** to the drive and folder where you store your Data Files.

h. Close the presentation and exit PowerPoint.

FIGURE D-20

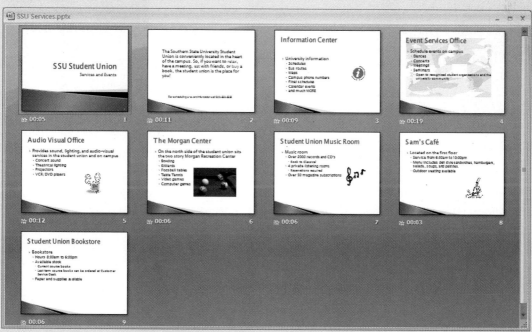

▼ VISUAL WORKSHOP

Open the file PPT D-8.pptx, then save the presentation as a template (.potx) with the filename **Island Travel Template** to the drive and folder where you store your Data Files. Change the presentation to look like Figures D-21 and D-22. Be sure to remove all unnecessary information, objects, and slides from the template presentation. Add your name as a footer to the slides.

FIGURE D-21

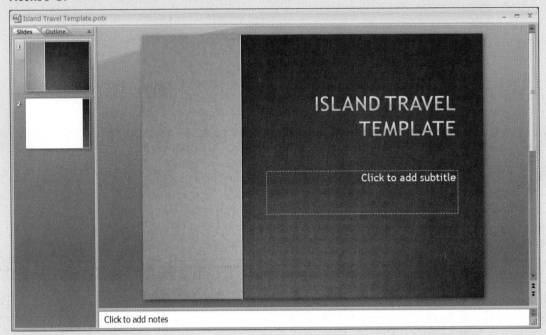

FIGURE D-22

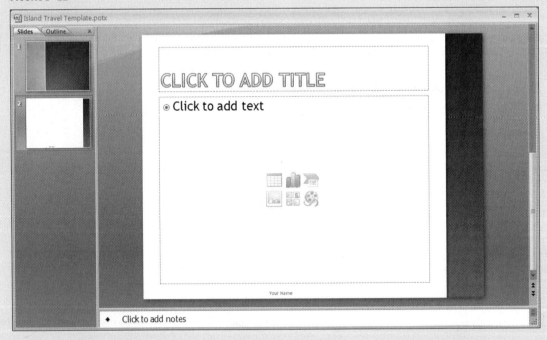

Integrating Word, Excel, Access, and PowerPoint

You can integrate objects that you create in Word, Excel, and Access into PowerPoint presentations that cover a broad spectrum of company activities. For example, you might store information about your customers and products in an Access database, analyze financial information in an Excel workbook, and create sales literature in a Word document. You can combine and then communicate this information to others in the form of a PowerPoint presentation. By creating links between the PowerPoint presentation and the files in the source programs, you can also keep the presentation up to date and ready to go at a moment's notice. █████ You are working as an assistant to Mary Lou Jacobs, the general manager of QST Vancouver, one of the two Canadian branches of Quest Specialty Travel. Mary Lou has asked you to explore how you can use linking and embedding in PowerPoint, and then how to include objects from Word, Excel, and Access in a PowerPoint presentation.

OBJECTIVES

Integrate data among Word, Excel, Access, and PowerPoint

Import a Word outline into PowerPoint

Embed an Excel worksheet in PowerPoint

Link Access and Excel objects to PowerPoint

Manage links

Integrating Data Among Word, Excel, Access, and PowerPoint

You can integrate information into a PowerPoint presentation using the linking and embedding techniques you learned with Word, Excel, and Access. As with those programs, you embed data created in other programs in PowerPoint when you want to be able to edit it from within the destination file. You use linking when you want the linked information in the destination file to update when you change the source file. In addition, you can import a Word outline into PowerPoint to automatically create slides without having to reenter information. █████ The presentation in Figure C-1 includes information originally created in Word, Excel, and Access. Before you create the presentation, you review some of the ways you can integrate information among Word, Excel, Access, and PowerPoint.

You can integrate Word, Excel, Access, and PowerPoint by:

• **Importing a Word outline into PowerPoint**

In the course of your work, you may often create Word documents containing information that you then want to use in a PowerPoint presentation. Instead of retyping the information in PowerPoint, you can save time by importing the information directly from Word into PowerPoint. Figure C-1 shows how a Word outline appears when imported into a PowerPoint presentation. When you import an outline from Word to PowerPoint, you cannot create a link between the two files.

• **Embedding objects**

Recall that when you embed an object, you do not create a link to the source file. However, you can use the source program tools to edit the embedded object within the destination file. An embedded object becomes a part of the PowerPoint file, which means that the file size of the PowerPoint presentation increases relative to the file size of the embedded object. For example, a large embedded object, such as a graphic, will increase the size of the PowerPoint presentation considerably. To embed an object in a PowerPoint presentation, you use the Object command in the Text group on the Insert tab, or you use the Copy command in the source program and the Paste or Paste Special command in PowerPoint. In Figure C-1, the table on Slide 3 is an embedded Excel worksheet object.

To edit an embedded object, you double-click it. The source program starts, and the ribbon and tabs of the source program appear inside the PowerPoint window.

• **Linking objects**

When you link an object to a PowerPoint slide, a representation or picture of the object is placed on the slide instead of the actual object. This representation of the object is connected, or linked, to the original file. The object is still stored in the source file in the source program, unlike an embedded object, which is stored directly on the PowerPoint slide. Any changes you make to a linked object's source file are reflected in the linked object. The pie chart shown on Slide 4 of the presentation in Figure C-1 is linked to values entered in an Excel worksheet, which is in turn linked to data entered in an Access database. The differences between embedding and linking are summarized in Table C-1.

You can open the source file and make changes to the linked object as long as you have access to the source program and to the source file. When you move files among machines or transmit files to other people, make sure they can access both the source programs and the linked files.

FIGURE C-1: PowerPoint presentation with integrated objects

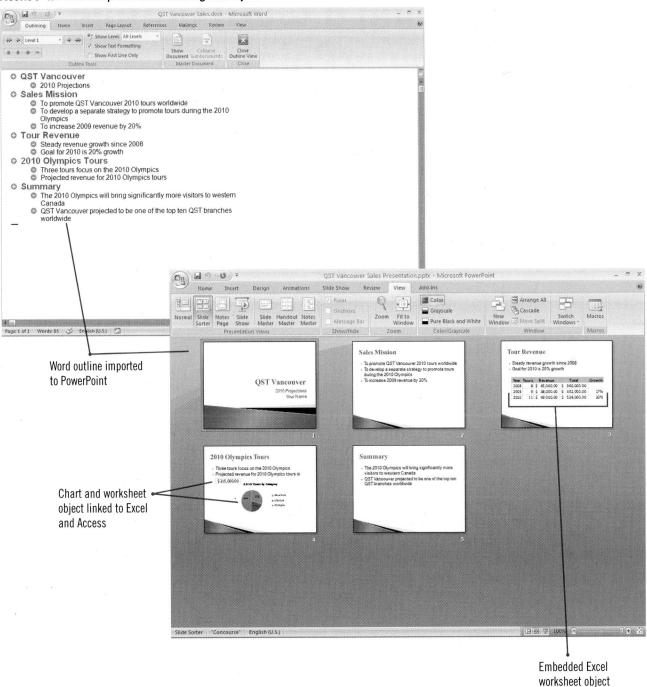

Word outline imported
to PowerPoint

Chart and worksheet
object linked to Excel
and Access

Embedded Excel
worksheet object
is not linked

TABLE C-1: Embedding vs. linking

action	situation
Embed	You are the only user of an object, and you want the object to be a part of your presentation.
Embed	You want to access the object in its source program, even if the source file is not available.
Embed	You want to update the object manually while working in PowerPoint.
Link	You always want your object to include the latest information.
Link	The object's source file is shared on a network or where other users have access to the file and can change it.
Link	You want to keep your presentation file size small.

Importing a Word Outline into PowerPoint

The Word outline you import into PowerPoint must be formatted with heading Quick Styles. PowerPoint imports all text formatted with the Heading 1 Quick Style as a slide title and all text formatted with the Heading 2 Quick Style as a level 1 item in a bulleted list. Any block of text that is not formatted with a heading style is not included in the PowerPoint presentation. If you want to use Word text in a PowerPoint presentation, you can copy a block of text from Word and paste it into PowerPoint, where it will appear in a text box. Mary Lou Jacobs, the general manager of QST Vancouver, has summarized information about the 2010 tours in a Word document. She asks you to use the information in this document as the basis of a PowerPoint presentation.

1. **Start Word, open the file** INT C-1.docx **from the drive and folder where you store your Data Files, then save it as** QST Vancouver Sales

    The Word document contains text that projects tour sales for 2010.

2. **Click the** View tab, **then click the** Outline button

    The document appears in Outline view. All the text in the document, except the text "2010 Projections" following the title, is formatted as a Level 1 or Level 2 heading. Before you import a Word outline into a PowerPoint presentation, you should check to ensure that all the headings and sub-headings are positioned at the correct levels. When you import the outline to PowerPoint, each of the five Level 1 headings becomes a slide title.

3. **Click** 2010 Projections, **then click the** Demote button ⏩ **once**

    The text moves to the right one tab stop and changes from Body text to a Level 2 heading.

4. **Click** Tour Revenue (the fourth bullet below the Sales Mission heading), **click the** Promote button ⏪, **click** Three tours focus on the 2010 Olympics, **then press [Tab]**

5. **Compare your Word outline to Figure C-2, then save and close the document**

6. **Start PowerPoint, then save the blank presentation as** QST Vancouver Sales Presentation **in the drive and folder where you store your Data Files**

7. **Click the** New Slide list arrow, **click** Slides from Outline, **navigate to the location where you stored** QST Vancouver Sales, **then double-click** QST Vancouver Sales.docx

    The Slides tab and the status bar indicate that the presentation now contains six slides. Slides 2 through 6 represent the Level 1 headings in the Word outline that are now slides in the PowerPoint presentation.

8. **Click Slide 1 on the Slides tab, press [Delete], click the** Layout button **in the Slides group, click** Title Slide, **click the** Outline tab **in the left pane, click after** 2010 Projections **on Slide 1, press [Enter], then type your name**

    You change the slide layout for the first slide so that the title of the presentation and your name appear in the middle of the slide.

9. **Click the** Design tab, **select the** Concourse **slide design in the Themes group, then save the presentation**

    The formatted presentation appears as shown in Figure C-3.

FIGURE C-2: Edited outline in Word Outline view

Promote button

Level of currently
selected text

Level 1 headings
start at the left
margin

Demote button

Level 2 headings
appear indented
one tab stop

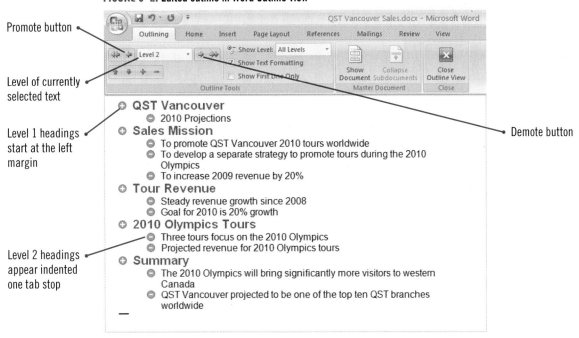

FIGURE C-3: Formatted presentation and Outline tab

Slides tab

Outline tab

Concourse
design

Title slide
layout

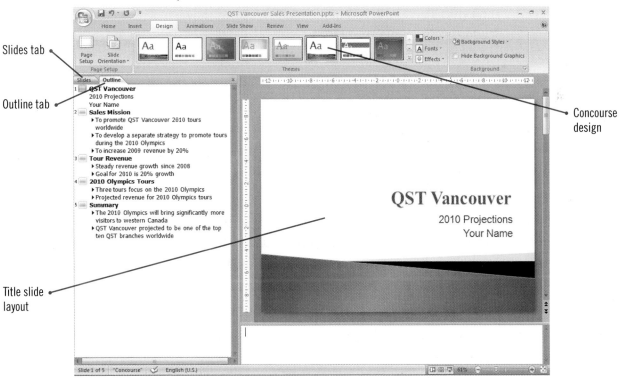

Embedding an Excel Worksheet in PowerPoint

You can use the Object command to embed Excel objects such as worksheets and charts into both Word and PowerPoint documents. When you double-click the embedded object, you can then use the tools of the source program to edit the object. ▰▰▰▰ You want Slide 3 to include a worksheet with calculations that you can update when you obtain new data. You create an Excel worksheet on the slide and then edit it using Excel tools.

1. **Click Tour Revenue in the Outline pane to move to Slide 3, click the Insert tab, click the Object button in the Text group, verify that the Create new option button is selected, scroll to and click Microsoft Office Excel Worksheet, then click OK**

   An Excel worksheet appears on the PowerPoint slide, and the Excel ribbon and tabs appear. The PowerPoint title bar and menu bar appear above the Excel tools, indicating that Excel is operating within PowerPoint. When you embed a worksheet object in a PowerPoint slide, you generally want to show only the cells that contain data.

2. **Drag the lower-right corner handle of the worksheet object up so that only columns A to F and rows 1 to 6 are visible, as shown in Figure C-4**

   You want to clearly see the data you need to enter into the worksheet object.

3. **Click the Select All button in the upper-left corner of the embedded worksheet to select all the worksheet cells, then change the font size to 28 point**

4. **Enter the labels and values in the range A1:D4 as shown in Figure C-5, then adjust the column widths as necessary to show all the data**

5. **Click cell D2, enter the formula =B2*C2, press [Enter], click cell D2, then drag its fill handle to cell D4 to enter the remaining two formulas**

   You need to calculate the percentage change in revenue from 2008 to 2009.

6. **Click cell E3, enter the formula =(D3-D2)/D3, press [Enter], click cell E3, click the Percent Style button ▨, copy the formula to cell E4, then widen the column**

7. **As shown in Figure C-6, bold and horizontally center the labels in row 1, fill the range A1:E1 with Aqua, Accent 5, Lighter 40%, then format the values in columns C and D with the Accounting Number format**

8. **Drag the middle-right sizing handle to column E and the bottom-middle sizing handle up to row 4, if necessary, click outside the worksheet object, then drag the object below the bulleted text and resize it as shown in Figure C-6**

9. **Double-click the worksheet object to show the Excel ribbon and tabs again, change 10 in cell B4 to 11, press [Tab], adjust column widths as necessary, click outside the worksheet object, then save the presentation**

   The percentage growth for 2010 is now 20%.

FIGURE C-4: Resizing the worksheet object

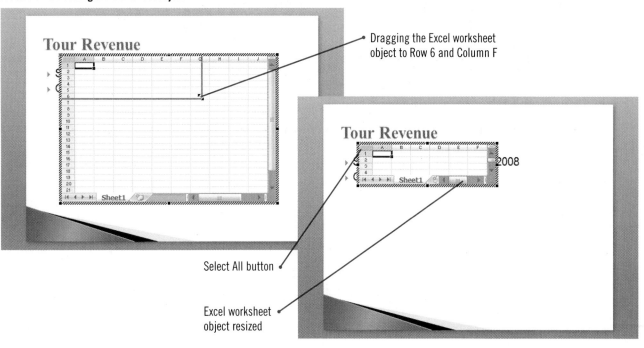

Dragging the Excel worksheet object to Row 6 and Column F

Select All button

Excel worksheet object resized

FIGURE C-5: Labels and values entered in the Excel worksheet object

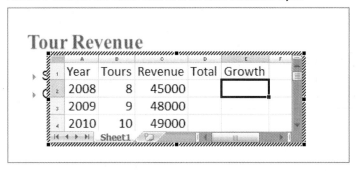

FIGURE C-6: Completed Excel worksheet object

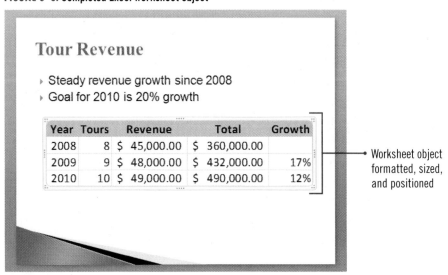

Worksheet object formatted, sized, and positioned

Linking Access and Excel Objects to PowerPoint

In the Unit B integration unit, you learned how to copy a table from Access and then paste it as a link into Excel. When you update the data in the Access table, the linked data in the Excel workbook also updates. You can copy an Access table from Access to PowerPoint; however, you cannot paste the table as a link. To link data from an Access database to a PowerPoint presentation, you first need to copy the data to Excel as a link, and then copy the data from Excel and paste it as a link into PowerPoint. ████ You already have tour data stored in an Access database that you want to include in Mary Lou's PowerPoint presentation for her staff. You want any changes you make to the table in Access also to appear in the PowerPoint presentation.

STEPS

QUICK TIP
To save the database with a new name, click the Office button, point to Save As, click Access 2007 Database, navigate to the drive and folder where you store your Data Files, type the new filename, then click Save.

1. **Start Access, open the file** INT C-2.accdb **from the drive and folder where you store your Data Files, save it as** QST Vancouver 2010 Tours, **double-click the** Tours table, **then examine the column called Category**

   You want the Tours table to be sorted in alphabetical order by Category before you copy it to Excel. You need to create a Query containing the sorted data and then copy the Query datasheet.

2. **Close the Tours table, click the** Create tab, **click the** Query Wizard button, **click OK, click the** Select All button `>>` **to add all the fields in the Tours table to the query, click** Next, **click** Next, **then click** Finish

3. **Click the** Home tab, **click the** View button **in the Views group, click the** Category Sort list arrow, **then select** Ascending **as shown in Figure C-7**

4. **Close and save the Tours query, click** Tours Query **in the list of database objects, then click the** Copy button **in the Clipboard group**

5. **Start Excel, click the** Paste list arrow **in the Clipboard group, click** Paste Link, **widen columns as necessary, click cell** G2, **enter the formula** =E2*F2, **copy the formula to the range** G3:G12, **then format the values in columns E and G with the Accounting format**

6. **Enter the labels and formulas starting in cell** C14 **as shown in Figure C-8, then save the workbook as** QST Vancouver Tour Categories **in the drive and folder where you store your Data Files**

   You calculated the total projected revenue from tours in each of the three tour categories.

7. **Select the range** C14:E15, **click the** Insert tab, **click the** Pie button **in the Charts group, click the** top left pie style, **select** Layout 6 **in the Chart Layouts group, change the chart title to** 2010 Tours by Category, **then move the chart so that it doesn't cover cells containing values**

   You can see that 37% of projected revenue from the tours offered in 2010 will be generated from tours that involve the 2010 Olympics, 37% from Adventure tours, and 26% from Lifestyle tours.

8. **Click the border of the pie chart, click the** Home tab, **click the** Copy button, **switch to the PowerPoint presentation, show Slide 4, click the** Home tab, **click the** Paste button, **then click the** Paste Options button **as shown in Figure C-9**

   The Paste Options list shows that charts copied from Excel are linked by default to the source file.

9. **Click outside of the chart, click a blank area of the chart and drag it below the text, then save the presentation**

   The pie chart is pasted into the PowerPoint slide as a link. The chart you copied to the PowerPoint slide is also linked to the Tours Query datasheet in Access.

FIGURE C-7: Sorting the Category field in Query Design view

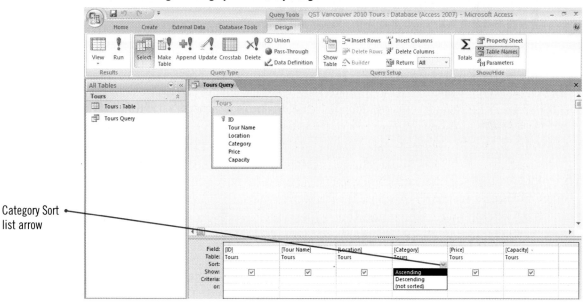

Category Sort list arrow

FIGURE C-8: Formulas to calculate total tours by category

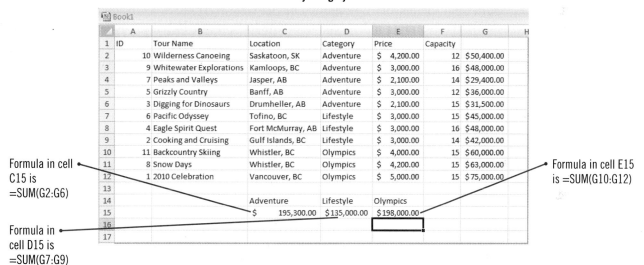

Formula in cell C15 is =SUM(G2:G6)

Formula in cell D15 is =SUM(G7:G9)

Formula in cell E15 is =SUM(G10:G12)

FIGURE C-9: Copying a chart to PowerPoint

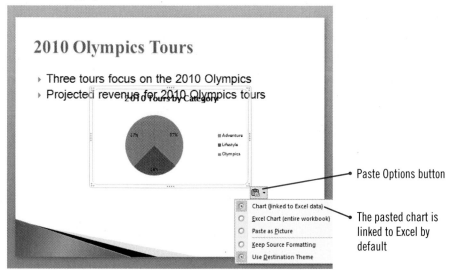

Paste Options button

The pasted chart is linked to Excel by default

Managing Links

You frequently need to manage the links you create between files and programs. You may need to update links manually, find the source of a link, or even break a link. You normally break a link when you need to send a file to another user. In PowerPoint, Word, and Excel, you manage links between files in the Edit Links dialog box, which you access from the Office button. Table C-2 summarizes all the integration tasks you performed in this unit. ▰▰▰▰ You want to modify the chart on Slide 4 of the presentation to reflect changing tour prices, then update the links you've created in the database, the spreadsheet, and the presentation. Finally, you decide to break the links so that you can send the presentation to the Marketing department.

STEPS

1. **Switch to Access, open the Tours Query datasheet, change the price of all three Olympics tours (the last three records) to $6,000, then close the Tours Query datasheet**
   When you change data in the Tours Query datasheet, the corresponding data in the Tours table also changes.

QUICK TIP

The linked values will update in Excel automatically if you wait a few minutes, but you speed up the updating process by updating the values manually in the Edit Links dialog box.

2. **Switch to Excel, click the Office button ⊕, point to Prepare, then click Edit Links to Files**
   The Edit Links dialog box opens as shown in Figure C-10.

3. **Click Update Values, click Close, verify that the Olympics tours now account for 45% of projected tour revenue, save the workbook, then switch to PowerPoint**

4. **Verify that the pie chart is updated in PowerPoint, right-click any label (for example, 45%), use the Mini toolbar to change the font size to 16 point, then change the font size of the legend text to 16 point**
   See Figure C-11. When you insert an Excel chart into a PowerPoint presentation, you usually need to increase the font size of chart objects to make them easy to read.

QUICK TIP

A value that you copy from Excel and paste into PowerPoint as a link is formatted as an object that you can move and resize the same as you would any object.

5. **Switch to Excel, copy cell E15, switch back to PowerPoint, click after tours in the second bulleted item, press [Spacebar], then type is**

6. **Click the Paste button list arrow, click Paste Special, click the Paste link option button, click OK to paste the link as a Microsoft Office Excel Worksheet Object, then move and resize the worksheet object so that it appears as shown in Figure C-12**

TROUBLE

If the value did not update, click the Microsoft Office button, point to Prepare, click Edit Links to Files, click the second link, then click Update Now.

7. **In Access, change the cost of each Olympics tour to $7000, close the table, update the link in Excel, if necessary and widen column G, then verify that the worksheet object in PowerPoint is now $315,000, and the Olympic pie slice is 49%**

8. **In PowerPoint, click the Office button ⊕, point to Prepare, click Edit Links to Files, click the chart link, click Break Link, click the worksheet link, click Break Link, then click Close**
   Now when you change data in the Access file, the linked Excel chart in PowerPoint will not update.

9. **Click the View tab, click the Slide Sorter button, click the Fit to Window button in the Zoom group, compare the completed presentation to Figure C-13, print the presentation as handouts with 6 slides per page, then save and close all open files and programs**

FIGURE C-10: Edit Links dialog box

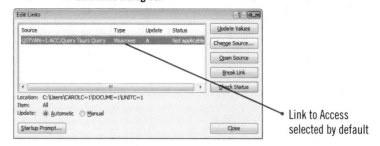

Link to Access selected by default

FIGURE C-11: Data labels resized

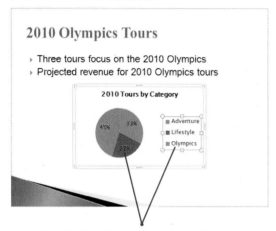

Data labels and legend formatted in 16 point

FIGURE C-12: Sizing and positioning the pasted worksheet object

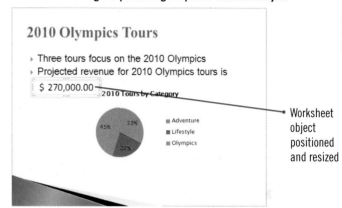

Worksheet object positioned and resized

FIGURE C-13: Completed presentation in Slide Sorter view

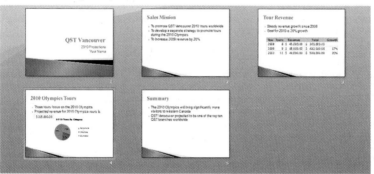

TABLE C-2: Unit C integration tasks

object	commands	source program(s)	destination program	result	connection	page no.
Word outline	In PowerPoint: New Slide/Slides from Outline	Word	PowerPoint	Word outline inserted into PowerPoint; level 1 headings are slide titles and level 2 headings are bulleted items	None	36
Excel worksheet	In PowerPoint: Insert/Object/ Create new	Excel	PowerPoint	Excel worksheet created in PowerPoint, then updated by double-clicking and using Excel tools	Embedded	38
Access query	Copy/Paste Link	Access	Excel	Access query is pasted into Excel as a link; linked data can be formatted in Excel but cannot be modified or deleted	Linked	40
Excel chart	Copy/Paste Link	Access/Excel	PowerPoint	Chart created from linked Access query is pasted into PowerPoint as a link; when the data is updated in Access, data is updated in Excel and PowerPoint	Linked	40

Practice

▼ CONCEPTS REVIEW

Match each term with the statement that best describes it.

1. **Edit links**
2. **Embedded object**
3. **Linked object**
4. **Destination program**
5. **Link**

a. Edit by making changes in the source file
b. The dialog box containing commands to manage connections between files
c. Contains embedded objects that can be edited using the tools of source programs
d. Increases the size of the destination file
e. The best way to share information between programs when the file size of the destination program should remain small

Select the best answer from the list of choices.

6. **Which of the following integration methods do you choose when you want the user to access the object in a source program, even if the source file is not available?**
   a. Link
   b. Paste Special
   c. Embed
   d. Connect

7. **Which button's list arrow do you click to import a Word outline into PowerPoint?**
   a. Import
   b. New Slide
   c. Object
   d. Office

8. **In Word, which view do you work in to prepare text to import into a PowerPoint presentation?**
   a. Draft
   b. Print
   c. Full Screen Reading
   d. Outline

▼ SKILLS REVIEW

1. **Import a Word outline into PowerPoint.**
   a. Start Word, open the file INT C-3.docx from the drive and folder where you store your Data Files, then save it as **Paradise Realty Outline**.
   b. Switch to Outline view, then demote the subheading Bowen Island, British Columbia to Level 2.
   c. Demote the three subheadings: Townhouses, Houses, and Estates to Level 3.
   d. Promote the subheading Property Values to Level 1, then save and close the document.
   e. Start a new presentation in PowerPoint, then save it as **Paradise Realty Presentation** in the drive and folder where you store your Data Files.
   f. Import the Paradise Realty Outline document into PowerPoint.
   g. Delete the blank slide 1, apply the Title Slide layout to the new slide 1, then add your name after the subtitle on Slide 1.
   h. Apply the Oriel slide design, then save the presentation.

2. **Embed an Excel worksheet in PowerPoint.**
   a. Move to Slide 4, delete the placeholder box, then insert a Microsoft Office Excel Worksheet object.
   b. Resize the object so that only columns A to E and rows 1 to 6 are visible.
   c. Change the font size of all the cells to 28 point, enter labels and values as shown in Table C-3, then adjust column widths.
   d. Enter a formula in cell D2 to multiply the number of houses by the average price for the first quarter, copy the formula to the range D3:D5.

e. Bold and center the labels horizontally in row 1, fill the range A1:D1 with Orange, Accent 6, Lighter 40%, format the dollar values in columns C and D with the Accounting format, then widen columns if necessary.

f. Resize the worksheet object so only the cells containing data are visible, then position it below the slide title.

g. Edit the worksheet object by changing the number of houses sold in the third quarter to 5, adjust column widths if necessary, return to PowerPoint, then save the presentation.

TABLE C-3

Quarter	Houses	Average Price	Total
Q1	3	650000	
Q2	1	625000	
Q3	2	550000	
Q4	4	700000	

3. Link Access and Excel objects to PowerPoint.

a. Start Access, open the file INT C-4.accdb from the drive and folder where you store your Data Files, then save it as **Paradise Realty Properties**. (*Hint*: Remember to click Access 2007 Database on the Save As menu.)

b. Create a query called **Properties Query** from the Properties table, containing all fields, that sorts the contents of the Category field in ascending order. (*Hint*: Remember to sort the Category field in Design view.)

c. Close and save the query, copy it, start a new workbook in Excel, then paste the query datasheet as a link.

d. Format the values in column E using the Accounting format, then widen columns as necessary.

e. In the range B16:D17, enter labels and formulas to calculate the total value of all the houses in each of the three categories: Estate, House, and Townhouse, then save the workbook as **Paradise Realty Property Values**.

f. Create a pie chart in the default 2-D style from the range B16:D17; then apply Layout 1.

g. Change the chart title to **Breakdown of Property Values**, copy the chart, then paste it on Slide 5 of the presentation.

4. Manage links.

a. In the Properties Query datasheet in Access, change the price of the two Cowan Point estates (the second and third records in the datasheet) to $2,000,000, then close the query.

b. Switch to Excel, then update the link in the Edit Links dialog box.

c. Switch to PowerPoint, then verify that the link is updated. (*Hint*: The Estates wedge should show 54%.)

d. Change the font size of the labels in the pie chart to 14 pt, then size and position the pie chart so it fills the blank area on the slide attractively. (*Hint*: The label for Townhouse may appear outside the pie wedge, which is acceptable.)

e. In Excel, copy cell B17, then paste it as a linked worksheet object on Slide 5 in PowerPoint.

f. Position the Excel object after "is" and resize it so its font size is comparable to the bullet text.

g. In the Properties Query datasheet in Access, change the price of the Eaglecliff Estate (the first record) to **$2,200,000**.

h. Update the link in Excel, switch to PowerPoint, then verify that the linked worksheet object is updated.

i. Break the links to the Excel chart and worksheet, view the presentation in Slide Sorter view, fit all the slides to the window, compare the presentation to Figure C-14, print it as a handout (six slides to the page), then save and close all open files and programs.

FIGURE C-14

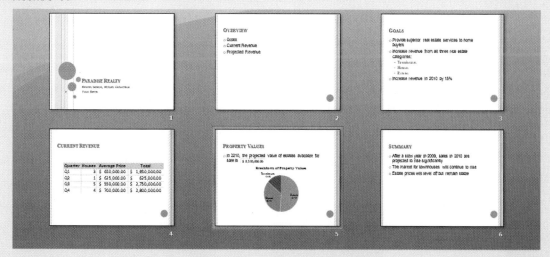

▼ INDEPENDENT CHALLENGE 1

You work at Dog Days, a boutique pet store that sells purebred puppies and dog accessories. You have collected data about recent sales in an Access database and now you need to create a presentation in PowerPoint that contains links to the sales figures. You want to be able to update the links in PowerPoint and so you copy relevant data to an Excel worksheet. You also need to import some of the slides needed for the presentation from a Word outline.

a. In Word, open the file INT C-5.docx from the drive and folder where you store your Data Files, then save it as **Dog Days Outline**.

b. In Outline view, demote the list of the four breeds under the Promotions Level 1 heading to Level 3, then save and close the document.

c. In PowerPoint, open the file INT C-6.pptx, then save it as **Dog Days Presentation**.

d. Insert the Dog Days Outline document into PowerPoint, add your name after the subtitle on Slide 1, delete Slide 2, then apply the Median slide design.

e. On the new Slide 2 (Top Sellers), embed an Excel Worksheet object resized to column C and row 6 with the 22 pt font size and containing the information in Table C-4.

f. Resize columns as necessary, calculate the total revenue in cell B5, format the values with the Accounting format, bold and horizontally center the column labels, add a shaded fill to row 1 using the color of your choice, bold and horizontally right-align Total, resize the worksheet object so only the cells containing labels or values are visible, then position the worksheet object attractively on the slide.

TABLE C-4

Breed	Total Revenue
Wheaten Terrier	24650
Basset Hound	18000
Cavalier King Charles Spaniel	22400
Total	

g. Start Access, open the file INT C-7.accdb from the drive and folder where you store your Data Files, then save it as **Dog Days Database**.

h. Add two new records to the Breeds table as follows: a German Shepherd and a Great Dane. Describe each breed as Large, with sales of 5 dogs and a cost of $500.

i. Create a query called Breeds Query from the Breeds table, using all fields, that sorts the contents of the Size field in ascending order. Save and close the query, copy the query, paste it as a link into a new Excel workbook, then save the workbook as **Dog Days Breed Information** in the drive and folder where you save your Data Files.

j. Calculate the total revenue for each breed in column F, then starting in cell D20, enter labels and formulas to calculate the total revenue from each of the three sizes of dogs.

k. Format all dollar amounts with the Accounting format then use the data in the range D20:F21 to create a pie chart entitled Sales by Dog Size using Layout 6.

l. Move the chart below the data, copy the pie chart, then paste it on the appropriate slide in the presentation. By default the pasted chart is linked to Excel.

m. In Excel copy the total revenue from Medium dogs, then paste it as a linked worksheet object in the appropriate location on Slide 3.

n. Size and position the worksheet object attractively, then increase the font size of the chart labels and the legend labels so that they are easy to read.

o. In Access, change the sale price for the Golden Retriever to $750, then update the links in Excel and PowerPoint.

p. Break the links in PowerPoint, view the presentation in Slide Sorter view, fit it to the window, print a copy of the presentation as a handout (six slides to the page), then save and close all open files and programs.

▼ INDEPENDENT CHALLENGE 2

You are the Assistant Manager at an outdoor equipment store in Boulder, Colorado that specializes in camping, hiking, and mountaineering. The store also maintains an active Web site that sells products internationally. The store's online customers frequently request information about hiking trails in Colorado. To assist these customers, you have created a database of trail information. You have also decided to create a short PowerPoint presentation from information you have stored in Word to inform store employees about the new database. The presentation will include data from the Trails database along with an embedded Excel worksheet and a linked Excel chart.

a. Start Word, open the file INT C-8.docx from the drive and folder where you store your Data Files, save it as **Boulder Outdoor Shop Outline**, then in Outline view demote the subheading "Popular Colorado Trails" to Level 2 and promote the Distances subheading to Level 1.

b. Save and close the document, start a new PowerPoint presentation, save it as **Boulder Outdoor Shop Presentation**, then import the Boulder Outdoor Shop Outline document into the presentation.

c. Delete the blank slide 1, apply the Title Slide layout to the new slide 1, add your name after the subtitle on Slide 1, then apply the slide design of your choice.

d. On Slide 2, embed an Excel Worksheet object displaying 4 columns and 6 rows, with the 24 pt font size and containing the information in Table C-5.

e. Calculate the total sales in cell B5, then in cell C2, enter the formula =B2/B5 to calculate the average percentage of sales attributable to Backpacking/Hiking products. Widen columns as needed to view all the data.

f. Copy the formula to the other two product categories, format values with the Accounting and Percent formats as necessary, then delete XX in the bulleted item and replace it by pasting the appropriate value.

TABLE C-5

Category	Sales	Average
Backpacking/Hiking	340000	
Mountain Biking	560000	
Winter Sports	730000	
Total Sales		

g. Horizontally center and bold the labels in row 1, fill row 1 with the fill color of your choice, right-align and bold Total Sales, position the worksheet object attractively on the slide, then save the presentation.

h. Start Access, open the file INT C-9.accdb from the drive and folder where you store your Data Files, then save it as **Boulder Outdoor Shop Trails Database**.

i. Create a query called **Colorado Trails Query** from all the fields in the Colorado Trails table that sorts the contents of the Type field in ascending order.

j. Close and save the query, copy the query, then paste it as a link into a new Excel workbook that you save as **Boulder Outdoor Shop Trails Information** in the drive and folder where you store your Data Files.

k. Starting in cell D15 of the worksheet, enter labels and formulas to calculate the total miles covered in each of the three trip types: Backpacking, Climb, and Day Hike. (*Hint*: The formula for Backpacking is =SUM(D2:D7).)

l. Create a pie chart, using a layout that shows the total distances covered by each of the three trip types and includes data labels that show both the trip type and the value (for example, Backpacking, 106).

m. Copy the pie chart, then paste it on the appropriate slide in the presentation.

n. Copy cell D16, then paste it as a linked worksheet object so it replaces the YY placeholder. (*Hint*: Move "miles" to the right (use the spacebar) and then size and position the worksheet object so that it fits the space attractively.)

o. In Access, change the distance of the Glacier Gorge hike to 12 miles and the Baker Pass hike to 22 miles.

p. Update links in Excel and PowerPoint, then close the Access database and save and close the Excel workbook.

q. In PowerPoint, break the links, then increase the chart size and the label sizes in the chart as necessary.

r. View the presentation in Slide Sorter view, print a copy of the presentation as a handout (six slides to the page), then save and close all open files and programs.

For a course on tourism in France, you have decided to create a presentation that focuses on popular hotels in various locations. The presentation will contain one slide displaying a pie chart showing the breakdown of hotel guests by location. In Access, open the file INT C-10.accdb from the drive and folder where you store your Data Files, then save it as **France Hotels**. Create a query including all fields that sorts the Hotels table in ascending order by Location. Copy the query and paste it as a link into Excel, then create the 3-D pie chart shown in Figure C-15. Save the Excel workbook as **France Hotels Data**. As shown in the figure, create a one-slide PowerPoint presentation called **France Hotels Presentation**, apply the Title Only slide layout, then paste the pie chart onto the slide. Format the slide as shown and insert clip art. (*Hint*: Use 18 point text for the data labels, add the slide title, use the Verve design, and search clip art for Eiffel Tower.) Switch to Access, change the number of guests who stayed at the Hotel Champs de Mars in Paris to 150, update the links in Excel and PowerPoint, then enter your name in the slide footer. Print the slide, break the link to the PowerPoint presentation, then close all files and exit all programs.

FIGURE C-15

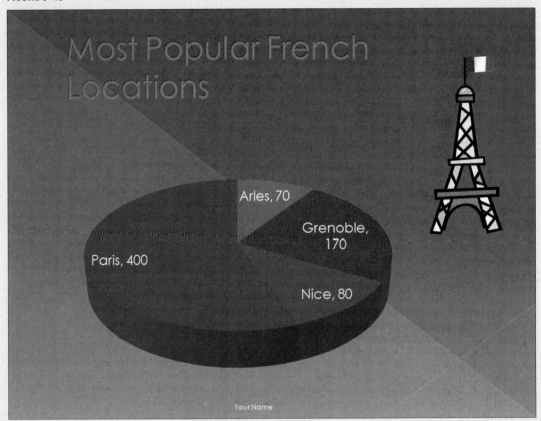

Getting Started with E-Mail

E-mail is an essential communication tool for business and personal correspondence. You can use a desktop information management program like Microsoft Office Outlook 2007, or any of several Web-based e-mail programs, to send and receive e-mail. Once you learn the basic features of e-mail, you will be able to use Outlook or any other e-mail program to manage your e-mail. You are an assistant to Juan Ramirez, the personnel director at Quest Specialty Travel (QST). Much of the correspondence in the company is through e-mail. Juan wants you to learn the basics of e-mail for your job.

OBJECTIVES

Communicate with e-mail

Compile an e-mail address book

Create and send a message

Manage e-mail folders

Receive and reply to a message

Forward a message

Send a message with an attachment

Employ good e-mail practices

Communicating with E-Mail

Electronic mail (e-mail) is the technology that makes it possible for you to send and receive messages through the Internet. The messages sent using e-mail technology are known as **e-mail messages**, or **e-mail** for short. **E-mail software** enables you to send and receive e-mail messages over a network, over an intranet, and over the Internet. A **computer network** is the hardware and software that makes it possible for two or more computers to share information and resources. An **intranet** is a computer network that connects computers in a local area only, such as computers in a company's office. The **Internet** is a network of connected computers and computer networks located around the world. Figure A-1 illustrates how e-mail messages can travel over a network. ▄▄▅▅▅ Quest Specialty Travel employees use e-mail to communicate with each other and with clients because it is fast, reliable, and easy.

DETAILS

E-mail enables you to:

- **Communicate conveniently and efficiently**

  E-mail is an effective way to correspond with coworkers or colleagues. E-mail can be sent from one person to another person or a group of people anywhere in the world. You can send and receive messages directly from any computer with an Internet or network connection. E-mail can also be sent and received from wireless devices such as cell phones and PDAs with e-mail capability. Unlike the postal service, e-mail is delivered almost instantaneously. Recipients do not have to be at their computers at the same time that a message is sent in order to receive the message.

- **Send images and sound as well as text information**

  Messages can be formatted so that they are easy to read and appear professional and attractive. Messages can include graphics in the body of the message to convey visual information. In addition, you can attach files, such as a sound or video, photographs, graphics, spreadsheets, or word-processing documents, to a message.

- **Communicate with several people at once**

  You can create your own electronic address book that stores the names and e-mail addresses of people with whom you frequently communicate. You can then send the same message to more than one person at one time.

- **Ensure the delivery of information**

  With e-mail software such as Outlook, you have the option of receiving a delivery confirmation message when a recipient receives your e-mail. In addition, if you are away and unable to access e-mail because of a vacation or other plans, you can set up an automatic message that is delivered to senders so they are alerted to the fact that you might not receive your e-mail for a specified time period.

- **Correspond from a remote place**

  If you have an Internet connection and communications software, you can connect to your computer from a remote location, and you can send and receive messages from any location. You can sign up with an ISP (Internet service provider) to send and receive e-mail. If you are using Web-based e-mail, you can access your e-mail from any computer that is connected to the Internet from anywhere in the world. You can connect to the Internet using a telephone line or use other, faster technologies including satellite, DSL (Digital Subscriber Line), cable, fiber optic, ISDN (Integrated Services Digital Network), T1, or T3.

- **Organize a record of your communications**

  You can organize the messages you send and receive in a way that best suits your working style. You can store e-mail messages in folders and refer to them again in the future. Organizing your saved messages lets you keep a record of communications, which can be very valuable in managing a project or business. You can also flag messages to give an instant visual cue that distinguishes those messages that require immediate attention from those that can wait. Depending on the service provider, you can download e-mail to your computer or keep it on the provider's Web server. If e-mail is stored on the Web, you can access it from any computer anywhere in the world that has Internet access.

FIGURE A-1: Sending messages with e-mail

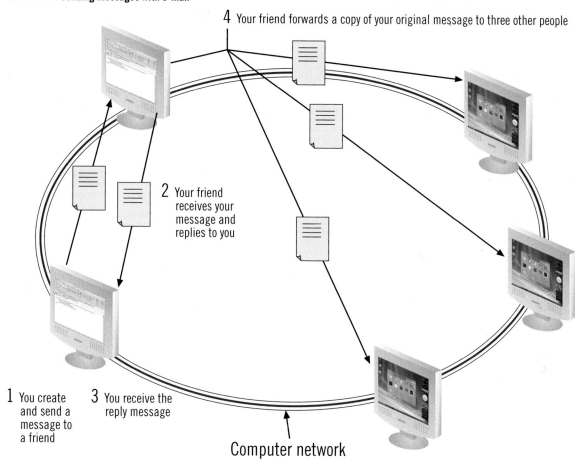

4 Your friend forwards a copy of your original message to three other people

2 Your friend receives your message and replies to you

1 You create and send a message to a friend

3 You receive the reply message

Computer network

The medium is the message

When you communicate with e-mail, take extra care in what you say and how you say it. The recipient of an e-mail message doesn't have the benefit of seeing body language or hearing the tone of voice to interpret the meaning of the message. For example, using all capital letters in the text of a message is the e-mail equivalent of shouting and is not appropriate. Carefully consider the content of a message before you send it, and don't send confidential or sensitive material. Remember, once you send a message, you might not be able to prevent it from being delivered. E-mail is not private; you cannot control who might read the message once it has been sent. Do not write anything in an e-mail that you would not write on a postcard that you send through the postal service. If your e-mail account is a company account, be sure you know the policy on whether or not your company permits the sending of personal messages. All messages you send through an employer's e-mail system have been legally interpreted as property of the company for which you work, so don't assume that your messages are private.

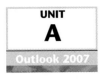
Compiling an E-Mail Address Book

E-mail can be sent from one person to another person or a group of people anywhere in the world. To send and receive e-mail over the Internet using an e-mail program, you must have an e-mail address. Each person has his or her own e-mail address and a password that lets him or her log in to an e-mail program and receive e-mail. To send an e-mail message, you need to know the e-mail address of the person to whom you are sending the message. A person can have more than one e-mail address. ▆▆▆▆ At Quest Specialty Travel, each employee is assigned an e-mail address. As the assistant to the personnel director in the Human Resources department, you maintain a list of all employee e-mail addresses in an electronic address book that you use to distribute information about company policies and events through e-mail. You review the parts of an e-mail address and the benefits of maintaining an e-mail address book.

DETAILS

An e-mail address has three parts:

- **Username**

  The first part of an e-mail address is the username. The username identifies the person who receives the e-mail sent to the e-mail address. At Quest Specialty Travel, as in many companies, universities, or organizations, usernames are assigned and are based on a specified format. At QST, a username is the first initial of the person's first name and the last name. In many e-mail systems, such as those used primarily for personal e-mail, you get to create your username, combining letters and numbers to create a unique username for your e-mail address.

- **@ sign**

  The middle part of an e-mail address is the @ sign, called an "at sign." It separates the username from the service provider or e-mail provider name. Every e-mail address includes an @ sign.

- **Service provider or e-mail provider**

  The last part of the e-mail address is the service provider or e-mail provider. There are many different service providers. For example, the service provider might be the name of the company a person works for or the name of the school where the person goes to school. The service provider generally is a company or organization that provides the connection to the Internet and provides e-mail. The service provider can also be the Web site name for Web-based e-mail. Table A-1 provides some examples of e-mail address formats that are used with different service providers.

The benefits of an e-mail address book include the following:

- **Stores the names and e-mail addresses of people to whom you frequently send e-mail messages**

  Instead of having to remember the address of someone to whom you are sending an e-mail, you can select the name you want from a stored list of names and e-mail addresses. Outlook 2007 and several other e-mail programs refer to the address book entries as "contacts" and place them in a folder called Contacts. When you create a new contact, you enter the person's full name and e-mail address. You may also have the option to enter additional information about that person, including his or her personal and business mailing address, telephone number, cell phone number, Web page, Instant Message address, and even a picture.

- **Reduces errors and makes using e-mail quicker and more convenient**

  Being able to select a contact from your address book saves you from having to type someone's e-mail address each time you want to send a message. It also reduces the chance that your message will not be delivered because you typed the e-mail address incorrectly. In most e-mail programs, if someone sends you a message, you can click the address in the message header to add it directly to your address book without any errors. Figure A-2 shows a sample address book from Outlook 2007.

FIGURE A-2: Address Book

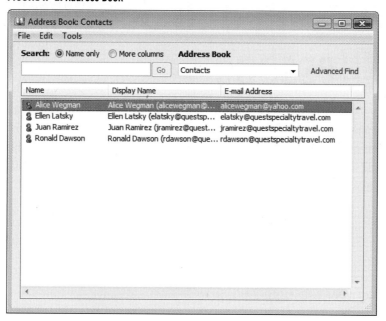

TABLE A-1: E-mail providers and formats for e-mail addresses

e-mail sponsor	example service provider	description of e-mail services	where e-mail is stored	sample e-mail addresses
Corporate or company e-mail	Quest Specialty Travel	A travel company that provides e-mail for employees	Company server, but also can be downloaded to user's computer	username@questspecialtytravel.com
Internet Service Provider: Cable television, voice and data communications company	America Online Comcast Cablevision Earthlink Verizon	Commercial Internet service providers provide Internet access as well as other Internet services, including Web space and several e-mail addresses for subscribers for a monthly fee	ISP server, until user accesses e-mail; then it is downloaded to user's computer	username@aol.com username@comcast.net username@optonline.net username@earthlink.net username@verizon.net
Web based e-mail	Hotmail—Microsoft's Web-based e-mail service Gmail—Google's Web-based e-mail service Yahoo! Mail—Yahoo!'s Web-based e-mail service	Web site that provides free e-mail addresses and service for individuals who sign up	On the Web site e-mail server	username@hotmail.com username@gmail.com username@yahoo.com
Educational institution	Harvard University	Colleges and universities provide e-mail for faculty, staff, and students	On the university e-mail server	username@harvard.edu

Creating and Sending a Message

When you create an e-mail message, you must indicate to whom you are sending the message and specify any people who should receive a copy. You also need to enter a meaningful subject for the message to give its recipients an idea of its content. You write the text of your message in the **message body**. After you create the message, you send it. Outlook 2007 uses Microsoft Word as the default text editor in e-mail messages, which means that you have access to the same text-formatting features in Outlook that you use when you create Word documents. Most e-mail programs use a basic text editor that enables you to do such things as change the color of text, use different fonts, create a bulleted list, and check the spelling of your message. You write and send a message to several employees about an upcoming meeting.

STEPS

QUICK TIP

Make sure you know your username and password so that you can log in to your e-mail program.

1. **Start your e-mail program**

   If you are using Outlook 2007 or another e-mail program, you start the application and then create a message without connecting to the Internet. If your e-mail program is Web-based, such as Hotmail or Gmail, you have to be connected to the Internet to create an e-mail message. You go to the Web site that sponsors your e-mail, and log in to your account.

2. **Click the button or link that allows you to create new mail, such as the** New Mail Message button **or the** Compose Mail button

   All e-mail programs provide a button or link to use to begin writing a new message. There are basic similarities in all programs, in that each new message window or page provides boxes or spaces to enter address information and message content, as shown in Figure A-3.

QUICK TIP

Use the e-mail address of a friend or associate to complete this lesson, or use your own e-mail address.

3. **Enter a** valid e-mail address **in the To text box as the address of the person to whom you are sending the message**

   You can send e-mail to more than one person at one time; just type each e-mail address in the To text box, and separate the addresses with a semi-colon or comma (depending on what your e-mail program requires). Click the To button or the Address Book button to open the address book and select each e-mail address from the address book. If you click names or e-mail addresses in an address book, you are less likely to make an error as you enter addresses. You can send e-mail to recipients even if they are not already in your address book by typing each e-mail address directly in the To text box.

QUICK TIP

Message headers include the names and e-mail addresses of recipients and CC recipients, but not of BCC recipients.

4. **Click the** Cc text box, **then type** a friend's e-mail address **as the e-mail address for a recipient who is to receive a courtesy copy**

   CC stands for courtesy copy. **Courtesy copies** are typically sent to message recipients who need to be aware of the correspondence between the sender and the recipients. BCC, or **blind courtesy copy**, is used when the sender does not want to reveal who he or she has sent courtesy copies to. You can use the address book to enter addresses into the Cc and Bcc text boxes.

5. **Type** Meeting July 10 **in the Subject box as the subject for your message**

   The Subject text box should be a brief statement that indicates the purpose of your message. The subject becomes the title of the message.

QUICK TIP

Although you can write and read messages in Outlook and other programs when you are not online, you must be connected to the Internet to send or receive messages.

6. **Type your** message **in the message window**

   Figure A-4 shows a sample completed message. Many e-mail programs provide a spell-checking program that enables you to make sure that you do not have spelling errors in your message. Messages should be concise and polite. If you want to send a lengthy message, you can consider attaching a file to the message. (You will learn about attaching files later in this unit.)

7. **Click the** Send button **to send your e-mail message**

   Once the message is sent, the message window or Web page closes. Most e-mail programs store a copy of the message in your Sent or Sent Items folder, or give you the option to do so.

FIGURE A-3: New message window

Ribbon (yours might differ)

To text box

Cc text box

Subject text box

Type body of message here

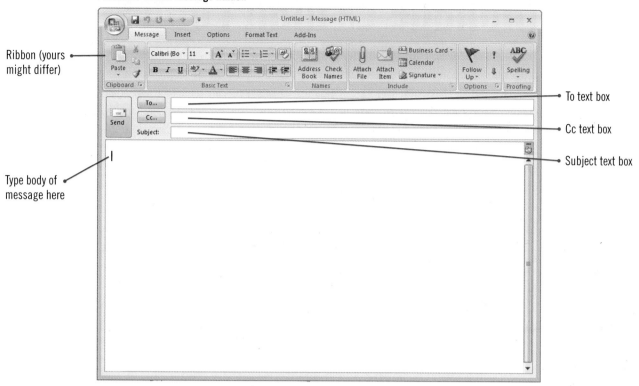

FIGURE A-4: A sample message

Bullets button

Send button

Bulleted list

Subject of message

Body text

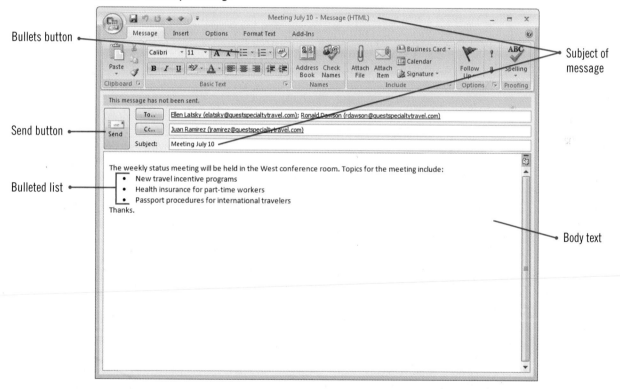

Message headers

A message header contains the basic information about a message. When e-mail travels through the e-mail system, the message header is the first information that you see when you retrieve your e-mail. Message headers include the sender's name and e-mail address, the names and e-mail addresses of recipients and CC recipients, a date and time stamp, and the subject of the message. E-mail programs date-stamp e-mail messages when they are received at the recipient's computer.

Manage E-Mail Folders

Just as files are saved in folders on your computer, e-mail messages can be saved in folders within an e-mail program. Although there are many different e-mail programs, they all provide a way for you to organize and save e-mail messages. You save messages so that you can refer to them again in the future when needed. Most e-mail programs come with several default folders. These include Inbox, Sent Items, Outbox, Deleted Items, and Junk E-mail folders (or folders with similar names). See Figure A-5. In addition, most allow you to create additional personalized folders with meaningful names. Once you save messages, you can sort the messages within the folders to help you find the message you want. ▟▛▙▟ As an employee of the Human Resources department, you send and receive messages on several topics. You organize the e-mail so you can better track the messages you send and receive.

E-mail programs come with the following default folders:

- **Inbox**

    An Inbox is a mail folder that stores all incoming e-mail. All e-mail arrives in the Inbox as it is received. You know who sent the e-mail message because the username or e-mail address and subject line appear in the list of e-mail in your Inbox, as shown in Figure A-6. You will also know when the message came in because your computer puts a date on it, which you can see along with the username and subject line. A closed envelope icon means the message has not been read yet. Many e-mail systems allow you to preview the message header before opening a message. You can organize e-mail by date, sender, subject, and other header data.

- **Sent Items**

    When you send a message, a copy of the message is stored in the Sent Items folder. The Sent Items folder helps you track the messages that you send out. You can change the settings on most e-mail programs so that you do not have to save messages to the Sent Items folder. You may not want to save all sent messages because they take up storage space on your computer.

- **Outbox**

    The Outbox is a temporary storage folder for messages that have not yet been sent. If you are working offline or if you set your e-mail program so that messages do not get sent immediately after you click the Send button, the messages are placed in the Outbox. When you connect to the Internet or click the Send/Receive button, the messages in the Outbox are sent.

- **Deleted Items or Trash**

    When you delete or erase a message from any folder, it is placed in the Deleted Items or Trash folder rather than being immediately and permanently deleted. This means that if you delete a message accidentally, you can find it again. To empty the Deleted Items folder, you have to right-click the folder or click a menu or toolbar button, and then click Empty Deleted Items Folder. Some programs have a special link to click in order to empty the folder. Some Web-based e-mail programs clear out the Trash folder if it gets too full or after messages have been in the folder for a specified period of time.

- **Junk E-mail or Spam**

    Junk e-mail, or spam, is unwanted e-mail that arrives from unsolicited sources. Most junk e-mail is advertising or offensive messages. **Spamming** is the sending of identical or near-identical unsolicited messages to a large number of recipients. Many e-mail programs have filters that identify this type of e-mail and place it in a special folder. This gives you the option of easily deleting the e-mail you don't want. It is possible that a message that you do want may get caught by the spam filter. It is good practice to look at the headers in the Junk E-mail folder before deleting the messages stored there.

FIGURE A-5: Mail Folders

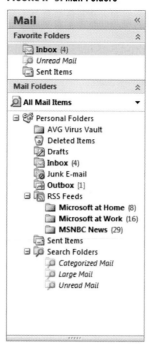

FIGURE A-6: Message headers in Inbox

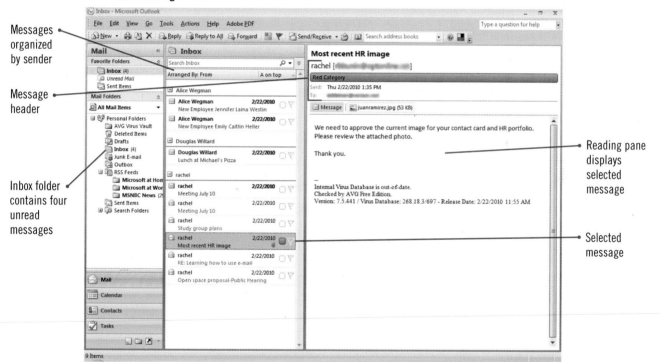

Messages organized by sender

Message header

Inbox folder contains four unread messages

Reading pane displays selected message

Selected message

Sorting the mail

You would be surprised at how quickly your Inbox, Sent Items, and Deleted Items or Trash folders can fill up. How can you manage these? The best way is to create folders for specific projects or people that you know will be "high-volume" for e-mail. For example, if you are working on a special project, create a folder for that project. Any e-mail that you receive or send about the project can be moved into that folder. You can sort e-mail by any message header, such as date, subject, or sender, to find an important message quickly. Once the project is completed, you can archive or delete that folder's e-mail. You should also be mindful as to how much e-mail is accumulating in the Deleted Items or Trash folder. E-mail takes up storage space and if you are running out of storage on your computer, your e-mail is a good place to start cleaning up the hard drive.

Receiving and Replying to a Message

To read a message that arrives in your Inbox, you first select it. Outlook and some other e-mail software programs let you preview each message when it is selected in the Reading or Preview Pane. To open the message in its own window, you can double-click the message header, or right-click the message header, then click Open from the shortcut menu. After reading a message, you can delete it, move it to another folder, flag it for follow-up, or keep it in your Inbox. You can also send a response back to the sender of the message by clicking the Reply button. Or, you can reply simultaneously to the sender of an e-mail message and everyone to whom the original message was sent by clicking the Reply to All button. A reply is a common e-mail activity. ████ You often reply to messages sent to you as you correspond with the staff at QST.

1. **Open a new message window, enter** your e-mail address **in the To text box, type** Learning how to use e-mail **as the subject, then for the body of the message, type** I am sending this message to myself to learn how to send and reply to messages.

You may have to check for mail several times before the e-mail message comes in.

2. **Click the** Send button **in the message window, click the** Send/Receive button **or click the** Get Mail **or** Check Mail **button or link, then open the** Inbox **in the e-mail program**
   When you click the Send/Receive or Get Mail button, your e-mail program checks for any messages in the Outbox that need to be sent and delivers incoming messages to your Inbox. Many e-mail programs deliver e-mail to the Inbox at the time you sign in or log in with your username and password.

3. **Click the** Learning how to use e-mail message **in the Inbox to select it, if necessary**
   You can read the message header to identify the message by subject, date, and sender. If your e-mail has a preview feature, you can preview the message before you open it. In Outlook, the message is shown in the Reading Pane. A preview generally permits you to view the first few lines of a message; you might have to click a link or button to display images. Many programs hide images to protect your privacy, unless you configure the program's settings to accept images for each message in the Inbox.

In Web-based e-mail programs, clicking an e-mail message opens the message. Skip Step 4 if this is the case.

4. **Double-click the** message, **click the** message once, **or click** Open
   You can view the entire message in a new window or Web page, as shown in Figure A-7. When you view a message, you will see buttons for several options available to you after you read the message. One of the options is a Reply button or link. You generally have two options for replying. One is to reply to the original sender. The other is a Reply to All option. When you click Reply to All, you reply to the original sender and all the CC recipients of the original message. BCC recipients are not included in Reply or Reply to All messages.

5. **Click the** Reply button
   A new message window for replying opens. Clicking the Reply button automatically addresses the e-mail to the original sender. The subject line is preceded by "RE:", indicating that the message is a reply. The message header from the original message appears in the message window above the original message. The insertion point is at the top of the message body. See Figure A-8.

Depending on your program preferences, your reply font color might be a color other than black.

6. **Type** I am learning how to use many e-mail features. **in the message body as the reply**
   It is helpful to include the original message in a reply so that the recipient of the message can be reminded of the topic. Depending on how you set up your e-mail program, you can automatically include or exclude the text of the original sender's message in the message body along with the message header.

7. **Click the** Send button **in the message window**
   The message is sent and a copy of it is stored in your Sent Items folder. Most e-mail programs will add a Replied to Message icon next to the original message in the Inbox indicating that you have replied to the message.

8. **Close the original message if necessary to return to the Inbox**

FIGURE A-7: Message opened

Click to reply to original sender only

Click to reply to original sender and all Cc recipients

The addresses on your screen will be different

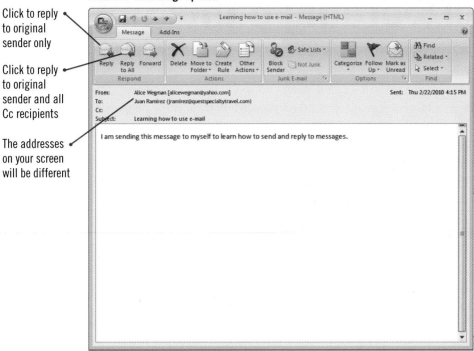

FIGURE A-8: Replying to a message

Address of original sender automatically entered in To box for reply

Indicates a reply e-mail

Insertion point is here for reply text in message

Original message

The addresses on your screen will be different

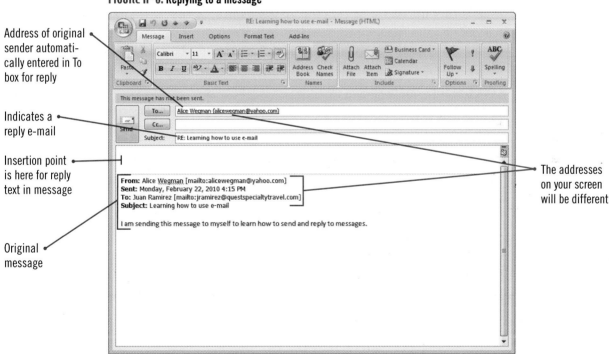

Vacation responses

Most e-mail programs allow you to set up an automatic response or vacation message if you are not going to be able to get your e-mail for a specified period of time. This is a helpful way to let people know that you are not ignoring any e-mail they send, but rather that you are not reading your e-mail. When vacation mode is active, your e-mail program automatically sends out a reply when a message comes in. You determine the parameters and content of the reply message. A typical message might be "Thank you for your message. I am on vacation from July 1–July 10th and will respond to your message when I return." Most e-mail programs only send one Auto Response to each sender each day or within a specified period of time.

Forwarding a Message

You may receive e-mail that you need to send to someone else. Sending a message you have received from one person to someone else is called **forwarding**. When you forward a message, you send it to people who have not already received it – that is, people not in the To or Cc text boxes of the original message. You can include an additional message about the forwarded message in the message body. The subject of the forwarded message stays the same, so it can be organized by subject with any other messages in a string of messages on the same topic and with the same subject heading. In most e-mail programs, you forward a message that you have received to another person by clicking the Forward button. ▰▰▱▱ At QST, you sometimes get e-mail from clients that you forward to the travel agents at their branch offices for their information.

STEPS

1. **Click the Send/Receive button or click the Get Mail or Check Mail button or link in the e-mail program**

   Your e-mail program checks for any messages in the Outbox that need to be sent and delivers messages to your Inbox.

QUICK TIP

Skip Step 3 if clicking the message opens the message rather than selects it.

2. **Click any message in the Inbox that you want to forward to select it, if necessary**

   You read the message header to identify the message. You can see the original recipients of the message by reviewing the header. You can see who, if anyone, got the message by reviewing the e-mail addresses in the To and Cc areas of the header. You will not know who might have received a BCC on the message. You determine if this message needs to be forwarded to anyone.

3. **Double-click the message, click the message once, or click Open to open the message**

   You view the entire message in a new window or Web page. When you view a message, you see buttons for several options available to you after you read the message. One of the options is to use the Forward button to forward the message.

4. **Click the Forward button**

   A new Message window opens containing the original message. Clicking the Forward button does not automatically address the e-mail to anyone; all address fields are blank. The original message is included in the body of the message. The subject line is preceded by "FW:", indicating that the message is a forwarded one. Most e-mail software includes the message header from the original message in the Message window above the original message. The insertion point is at the top of the message window in the To field. You can address this message as you would any new e-mail. You can include multiple recipients, including CC and BCC recipients. If you want to provide a courtesy note explaining the forward, you can click in the message body above the original message header and type a brief note.

5. **Type a friend's e-mail address in the To text box, then type I thought you might like to read this message. in the message body above the forwarded message, as shown in Figure A-9**

6. **Click the Send button in the message window**

   The message is sent, and a copy of it is stored in your Sent Items folder. Most e-mail programs add a Forwarded Message icon next to the original message indicating that you have forwarded the message. Often this is a small arrow pointing to the right.

7. **Close the original message if necessary to return to the Inbox**

New address for forwarded message

Indicates this is a forwarded message

New text for message

Forwarded message

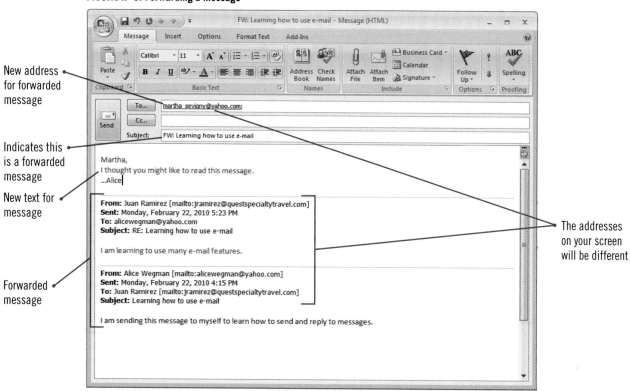

The addresses on your screen will be different

Outlook 2007

Flagging or labeling messages

Most e-mail programs provide a way to identify or categorize e-mail. If you use e-mail for business, school, or personal communication, you will find that you receive many e-mail messages. Some can be read and discarded. Others require additional attention or follow-up. Organizing your e-mail can help you keep up with the many messages you are likely to receive. If you are using Outlook, flags can assist you in your effort to manage your e-mail. If you click the flag icon next to the message, it is marked by default with a red Quick Flag. However, you can use flags of different shades of red to mark messages for different categories of follow-up. In Outlook, flags are available for Today, Tomorrow, This Week, Next Week, No Date and Custom; the Today flag is the darkest shade of red, and the This Week and Next Week flags are the lightest. To apply a flag, select the message you want to flag, click Actions on the menu bar, point to Follow Up, then click the flag you want to use to categorize the message. You can also right-click the message, then point to Follow Up to apply a flag. To select from a list of flag actions and specify a due date in the Custom dialog box, right-click a message, point to Follow Up, then click Add Reminder. If you are using Web-based e-mail, you may have other options for labeling or flagging e-mail.

For example, Gmail provides a way to assign a label to e-mail or to star e-mail for easy sorting or organizing. See Figure A-10.

FIGURE A-10: Flagging messages

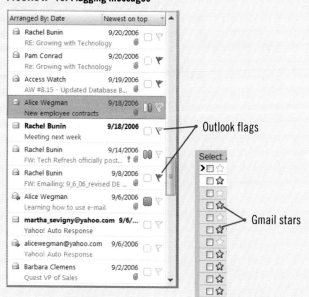

Outlook flags

Gmail stars

Sending a Message with an Attachment

In addition to composing a message by typing in the Message window to send an e-mail message to some-one, you can **attach** a file to an e-mail message. For example, in an office environment, employees can attach Word or Excel documents to e-mail messages so that other employees can open them, make changes to them, and then return them to the original sender or forward them to others for review. You can attach any type of computer file to an e-mail message, including pictures, video clips, and audio clips. Keep in mind that to open an attachment created using a particular software program, the recipient of the attachment must have the appropriate software. 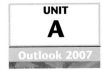 You often send clients' trip photos to people in the office. You also have to send personnel documents to employees throughout the year. Attaching files is a common task in your job in the Human Resources department.

STEPS

1. **In your e-mail program, click the button or link to open a new mail message window, then type your e-mail address in the To text box**

   You can send a message with an attachment to more than one person at one time; just enter each e-mail address in the To text box, separated by a semi-colon or comma, just as you would an e-mail without an attachment. You can also click the Cc text box or Bcc text box, and then enter e-mail addresses for recipients who are to receive a CC or BCC.

2. **Type New Logo in the Subject box as the subject for the message, then type Here is the new logo for you to review. as the message in the message window**

3. **Click the Insert File, Attach File, or Attach button**

   Most e-mail programs provide a way to attach files, but the name of the command or way to access the dia-log box may differ slightly. Once the Attach File or Insert File dialog box opens, files appear in a dialog box as shown in Figure A-11. You may have to click a Browse button to navigate to the file or files you want to attach. Often you can use Thumbnails view in the dialog box to see what the files look like before you attach them to a message.

   TROUBLE

   Attachments such as movies may be too large for some e-mail systems to handle.

4. **Navigate to the drive and folder where you store your Data Files, click QST Logo.jpg, then click Insert, Open, or Attach**

   Most programs will allow you to attach more than one file to a message. Some Internet service providers will limit message size or the number of attachments for one e-mail. Once attached, files appear in the Attach text box or other area of the message window. Often, an icon next to each filename indicates the type of file it is. The numbers in parentheses next to the filenames specify the size of each file. As a rule of thumb, try to keep the total size of attachments below 1 MB. Also, consider the Internet connection speed of the recip-ient's computer. If a recipient does not have a fast Internet connection, a large file could take a long time to download.

5. **Send the message**

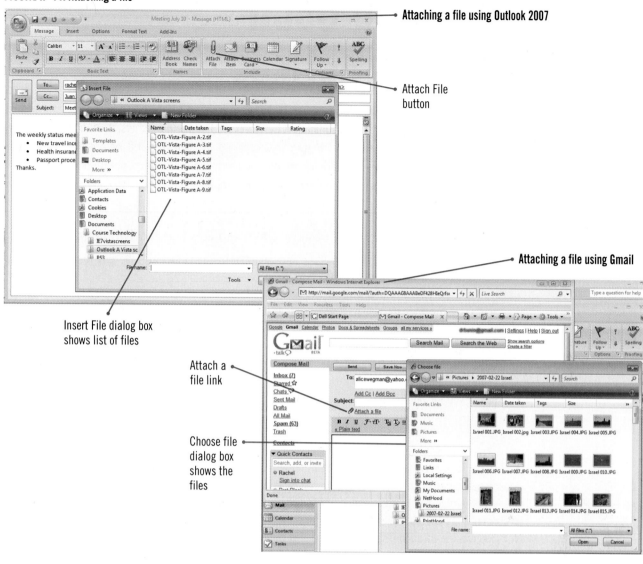

Attaching a file using Outlook 2007

Attach File button

Insert File dialog box shows list of files

Attaching a file using Gmail

Attach a file link

Choose file dialog box shows the files

Options when sending messages

E-mail programs can have several options that affect how messages are delivered. To change these options in Outlook, click the launcher [image] in the Options group on the Message tab in the Message window to open the Message Options dialog box shown in Figure A-12. You can, for example, assign a level of importance and a level of sensitivity so that the reader can prioritize messages. You can also encrypt the message for privacy. If both the sender and recipient are using Outlook, you can add Voting buttons to your message for recipients to use in responding. In addition, when you want to know when a message has been received or read, you can select the Request a delivery receipt for this message check box or the Request a read receipt for this message check box. You can also specify a future date for delivering a message, if the timing of the message is important. Lastly, if you want replies to your message to be sent to a different e-mail address than your own, you can click the Have replies sent to check box and then specify a new destination address for replies.

FIGURE A-12: Outlook 2007 Message Options dialog box

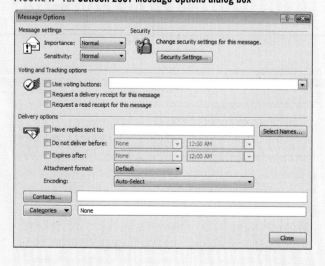

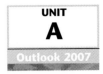
Employing Good E-Mail Practices

E-mail has become the standard for business correspondence. It has also become an accepted standard for personal communication as well as communication between students and teachers. Although it is an easy and fast way to communicate, there are many considerations to keep in mind before sending e-mail. Working in the Human Resources department, you are responsible for corporate policy relating to e-mail. You send out a note that outlines the company policy for e-mail.

DETAILS

The following are good practices to follow when sending and receiving e-mail:

- Always be polite and use proper spelling and grammar in e-mail messages. Be sure to use the spelling checker as a last step before sending messages.
- Unless you have consulted with the recipient and know that they can receive large file attachments, avoid sending any attachment that exceeds 1MB. Consider using compression software to reduce the size of any attachment that exceeds the limit but must be sent.
- Never open an e-mail message unless you know who sent it to you. Keep your spam filter, spyware software, and virus software up-to-date. Be sure to run the virus checker through all received e-mail. Keeping computers safe from viruses and spyware is very important.
- Before you forward a message, consider the contents of the message and the privacy of the person who sent the message. A joke, a story, or anything that is not personal usually can be forwarded without invading the sender's privacy. When you are certain the sender would not mind having his or her message forwarded, you can forward the message to others.
- In very casual correspondence, you can present an informal message by using shortcuts like "LOL" for "laughing out loud" and "BRB!" for "be right back!" However, limit this technique to personal messages. Any e-mail that is intended for professional use or is a reflection on a professional organization should not use shortcuts. See Figure A-13.
- You can use emoticons in your text to show how you are feeling. You create an emoticon by combining more than one keyboard character to make a graphic. The use of emoticons should also be limited to informal e-mail among close colleagues or friends, not professional correspondence. Examples of some popular emoticons are shown in Table A-2.
- When you are finished using an e-mail program, it is good practice to delete e-mail messages that you no longer need. You should delete files periodically from the Sent folder to help manage storage on your computer. It is also good practice to empty the Trash folder. To delete a file, you select a file, then click the Delete button or press the Delete key. To empty the Trash or Deleted Items folder, you right-click the folder, then click Empty Trash or Empty Deleted Items folder. See Figure A-14.

Distribution lists

When using an e-mail program to communicate with friends or coworkers, you may find that you need to send messages to the same group of people on a regular basis. If your address book contains many contacts, it can take time to scroll through all the names to select the ones you want, and you might forget to include someone in an important message. Fortunately, e-mail programs provide an easy way to group your contacts. You can create a **distribution list**, or a **group**, which is a collection of contacts to whom you want to send the same messages. Distribution lists make it possible for you to send a message to the same group without having to select each contact in the group. For example, if you send messages reminding your Human Resources staff of a weekly meeting, you can create a distribution list called "HR-STAFF" that contains the names and e-mail addresses of your staff who must attend the meeting. When you want to send a message to everyone on the team, you simply select HR-STAFF from the address book, instead of selecting each person's name individually. Once a distribution list is created, you can add new members to it, or delete members from it, as necessary. If you change information about a contact that is part of a distribution list, the distribution list is automatically updated.

FIGURE A-13: E-mail shortcuts

BRB – Be right back
LOL – Laughing out loud
IMHO – In my humble opinion
ROFL – Rolling on the floor laughing
Pls – Please
TTYL – Talk to you later
B4 – Before

FIGURE A-14: Confirm before permanently deleting all the items

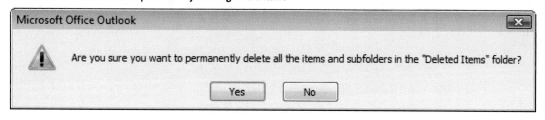

TABLE A-2: Popular emoticons

keys	result	emoticon name
colon and closed parenthesis	:)	smiley
semicolon and closed parenthesis	;)	wink
colon and open parenthesis	:(	sad
colon, dash, capital D	:-D	person laughing
equal sign, dash, o	=-o	surprised
colon, dash, slash	:-\	undecided
8, dash, closed parenthesis	8-)	cool

Practice

If you have a SAM user profile, you may have access to hands-on instruction, practice, and assessment of the skills covered in this unit. Log in to your SAM account (http://sam2007.course.com/) to launch any assigned training activities or exams that relate to the skills covered in this unit.

▼ CONCEPTS REVIEW

Label the elements of the new message window shown in Figure A-15.

FIGURE A-15: New message window

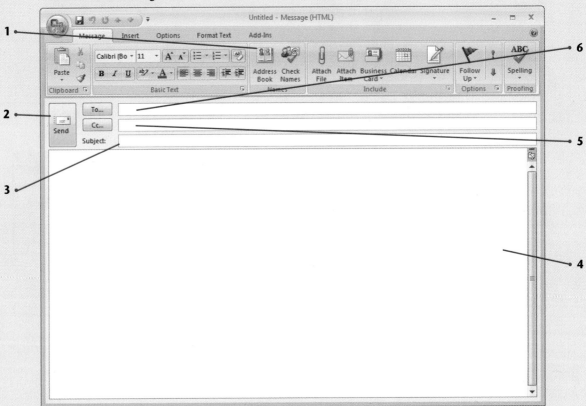

Match each term with the statement that best describes it.

7. **E-mail**

8. **Attachment**

9. **Bcc**

10. **Sent Items folder**

11. **Inbox**

12. **Address book**

a. Stores names and e-mail addresses

b. Stores all e-mail that you send out

c. A computer file that is sent along with an e-mail message

d. Message that is sent and received over a computer network

e. Contains messages you have received

f. Hides e-mail address of recipient to all others

Select the best answer from the list of choices.

13. Any e-mail received as part of large unsolicited mailing is best placed in the _____.

  a. Junk E-Mail or Spam folder
  b. Deleted Items folder
  c. Sent Items folder
  d. Inbox

14. Which of the following statements is true about sending file attachments?

  a. You can only send one attachment with each e-mail message.
  b. Only recipients listed in the To text box will get the attachment.
  c. There is no limit on the size or number of attachments you can send with a message.
  d. Attachments can be files of any type, such as documents, spreadsheets, video, images, and sound files.

15. Which of the following is *not* in the message header?

  a. Mail subject
  b. All To recipients and Cc recipients
  c. Date and time the message was sent
  d. First three lines of the message body

16. To read a message that arrives in your Inbox, you _____.

  a. Click the Inbox header
  b. Double-click or click the message
  c. Click the Read button
  d. Flag the message to read

17. To send an attachment with your e-mail message, you _____.

  a. Click the Attach File or Attach button
  b. Drag the file into the message body
  c. Click Files, then click Insert
  d. You can't attach files to messages

18. When you forward a selected message to another person, the e-mail addresses for the original recipients of the message _____.

  a. Appear in the To text box
  b. Do not appear in any text box
  c. Appear in the Cc text box
  d. Appear in the To text box and the Cc text box

19. To create a new message, you _____.

  a. Click the Inbox button
  b. Click the Create button
  c. Click the New Mail Message button
  d. Click the Send button

20. To send the same message to multiple recipients, which of the following is *not* an option?

  a. Selecting multiple names from the address book
  b. Dragging the message to each of the recipient names in the address book
  c. Creating a distribution list containing the names of the recipients
  d. Entering multiple names in the To text box

▼ SKILLS REVIEW

1. Start Outlook or your e-mail program and view the Inbox.

   a. Start Outlook or your e-mail program.

   b. If necessary, select the mail client part of the program.

   c. Click the Send/Receive button or link to get new e-mail delivered to the Inbox, if necessary.

   d. Open the Inbox to view any new messages.

2. Create and send a message.

   a. Open a new message window.

   b. Click the To text box, then type a friend's e-mail address.

   c. Type your e-mail address in the Cc text box.

   d. Type Travel Incentive Program (TIP) as the Subject of the message.

   e. In the message body, type: The Human Resources Department has approved the annual trip to Belgium as part of the Travel Incentive Program for sales. Congratulations.

   f. Send the message.

3. Manage e-mail folders.

   a. Review the mail folders in your e-mail program.

   b. Look for a Sent Items or Sent folder and see if the Travel Incentive Program message is in that folder.

   c. Open the Deleted Items or Trash folder. See if any e-mail is in that folder.

   d. Review the Spam or Junk E-Mail folder.

4. Receive and reply to a message.

   a. If necessary, click the Send/Receive button to deliver messages to your Inbox.

   b. Display the contents of the Inbox folder.

   c. Open and read the message from yourself.

   d. Click the Reply button.

   e. In the message body, type How exciting. What a great TIP! Belgium is a great place to send the employee with the most sales., then send the message.

5. Forward a message.

   a. Forward the message you received to another friend.

   b. In the top of the forwarded message body, type I just wanted to close the loop on the travel incentive program. Belgium will be the destination this year. (Refer to Figure A-16.)

   c. Send the message.

   d. Close the original message.

FIGURE A-16

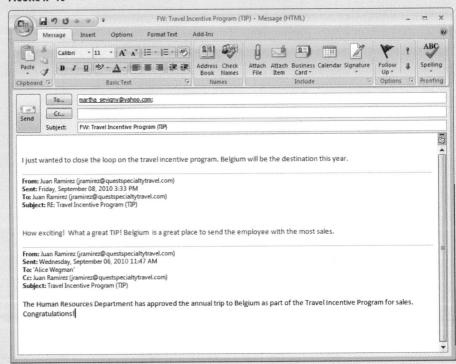

6. Send a message with an attachment.

   a. Create a new e-mail message.

   b. Enter your e-mail address as the message recipient.

   c. Enter your e-mail address in the Cc text box.

   d. Enter Quest Logo as the Subject of the message.

   e. In the message body, type: Here is the logo you requested. Let me know if you need anything else.

   f. Click the Insert File, Attach File, or Attach button or link.

   g. Navigate to the drive and folder where you store your Data Files.

   h. Select the file QST Logo.jpg (see Figure A-17), then click Insert, Open, or Attach (depending on your program).

FIGURE A-17

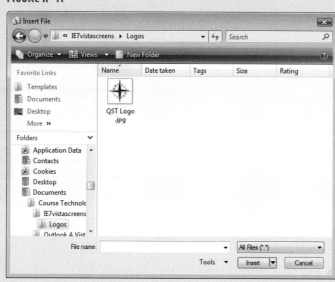

   i. Send the message.

7. Delete items.

   a. Delete all of the messages received in this exercise from the Inbox folder.

   b. Delete all of the messages sent in this exercise from the Sent Items folder.

   c. Empty the Deleted Items folder.

   d. Exit the e-mail program.

▼ INDEPENDENT CHALLENGE 1

You are a member of a planning board in your town. You have been appointed as the chairperson of the committee to investigate a proposal for rezoning a four-block area of downtown as open space. You decide to use e-mail to communicate with the other members of the committee as well as with the local newspaper, the town council, and the mayor.

   a. Start Outlook or your e-mail program.

   b. Open the address book and add yourself as well as three other new contacts to the address book. Use the names and e-mail addresses of classmates, teachers, or friends.

   c. Create a new message and address it to yourself, then use the Cc field to send this message to two of the new contacts.

   d. Type **Open space proposal — Public Hearing** as the Subject of the message.

   e. In the message body, type **There will be a public hearing on Monday at 7:00 p.m. We should prepare our presentation and contact the local newspaper to be sure they carry the story.**

   f. Press [Enter], then type your name. See Figure A-18.

FIGURE A-18

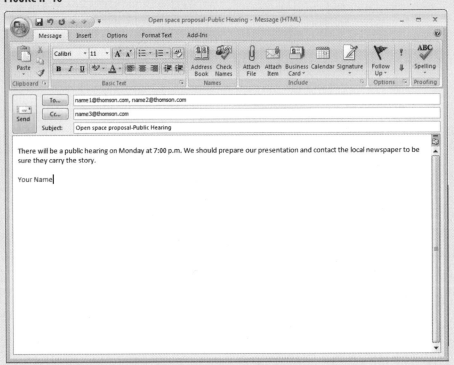

   g. Send the message, then click the Send/Receive button if necessary. Depending on the speed and type of Internet connection you are using, you may need to click the Send/Receive button again, after waiting a few moments, if you do not receive the e-mail in your Inbox the first time you click the Send/Receive button.

   h. Open the message in the Inbox, flag it with a follow-up flag or other symbol, then print it.

Advanced Challenge Exercise

- Forward the message to the person you did not include in the distribution list.
- In the message body, type: **Forgot to include you in this mailing! Please read the message; hope you can be there.**
- Send the message.

   i. Delete all of the messages related to this Independent Challenge from the Inbox folder.

   j. Delete all of the messages related to this Independent Challenge from the Sent Items folder.

   k. Delete the contacts that you added in this Independent Challenge from the Address Book.

   l. Empty the Deleted Items folder.

  m. Exit the e-mail program.

▼ INDEPENDENT CHALLENGE 2

You are planning a study trip to Africa with a group from the university. You have to send e-mail messages with an attachment as you organize this trip.

a. Start Outlook or your e-mail program, then create a new message and address it to two contacts, such as friends, family members, or classmates.

b. Enter your **e-mail address** in the Cc text box.

c. Type **Trip to Namibia** in the Subject text box.

d. Start your word processor and write a brief letter to your friends to encourage them to join you on the adventure. Conclude the document with a personal note about why you want to participate in a study program. Save the document file in the drive and folder where you store your Data Files, using a filename you will remember.

e. Type a short note in the message body of the e-mail to the recipients of the message, telling them that you thought they would like to join you on this trip, and that you are looking forward to them joining you.

f. Attach the word processing document to the message.

g. Send the message, then click the Send/Receive button. Depending on the speed and type of Internet connection you are using, you may need to click the Send/Receive button again, after waiting a few moments, if you do not receive a response e-mail the first time you click the Send/Receive button.

h. Print a copy of the message you receive in response.

Advanced Challenge Exercise

- Locate a picture or graphic image file on your computer that you want to send through e-mail.
- Right-click the picture, point to Send To, then click Mail Recipient on the shortcut menu. (Alternatively, after right-clicking a picture you may see these options: E-mail Picture or E-mail with [e-mail program]. These options will be different depending on your software and system.) Click OK if a dialog box opens asking if you want to make the picture smaller. Click Attach to attach the image to a new message window.
- When a new message window opens, enter your e-mail address in the To text box, then write a brief message in the body of the message.
- Send the message, then read the message and view the picture when it arrives in your Inbox.

i. Delete all of the messages received for this Independent Challenge from your Inbox.

j. Delete all of the messages sent for this Independent Challenge from the Sent Items folder.

k. Empty the Deleted Items folder.

l. Exit Outlook.

▼ VISUAL WORKSHOP

Refer to the e-mail message in Figure A-19 to complete this Visual Workshop. Use your e-mail program to create and then send this message. Be sure to send the message to at least one recipient. Attach a file that you created on your computer. It can be a document, worksheet, image, or database file.

FIGURE A-19

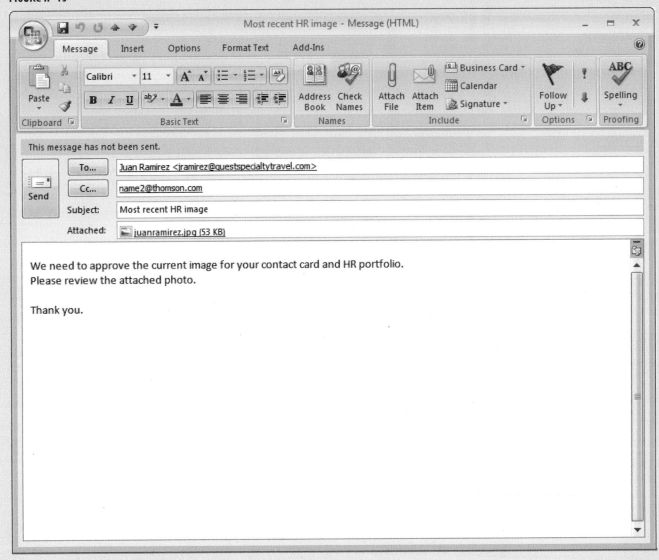

Managing Information Using Outlook

**Files You
Will Need:**

No files needed.

To effectively use Microsoft Office Outlook 2007 in managing your business and personal information, it is important to know not only how to send and receive e-mail, but also how to use the additional modules in Outlook. Outlook integrates several tools, including Mail, Calendar, Contacts, Tasks, Notes, and Journal, to provide you with a uniquely comprehensive information manager. Now that you know how to manage your e-mail, you will learn how Outlook acts as a desktop information manager to help you organize all aspects of your business and personal information.

OBJECTIVES

Start Outlook

Organize e-mail

Organize contacts

Manage appointments

Manage tasks

Create notes

Use the Journal

Apply categories

Starting Outlook

Outlook is a personal information and time management program that is part of the Microsoft Office 2007 suite. Outlook includes several components that work together: Mail, Contacts, Calendar, Tasks, Notes, and Journal. Outlook integrates these components so you can easily manage your schedule and information. The Outlook screen is fully customizable to let you view your contacts, schedule, or mail. The first time you start Outlook you will be prompted to set up a personal **account** that identifies you as a user. If you will be using Outlook for e-mail, you must enter information such as your e-mail address and password, the type of Internet service provider (ISP) you are using, and the incoming and outgoing mail server address for your ISP. More than one account can be set up in a single installation of Outlook. Each user has a username and password to gain access to his or her account. Accounts can be viewed by clicking Tools on the menu bar, then clicking Account Settings. To set up an account in Outlook for the first time, contact your technical resource person for the information you need. ▗▖▗▖ As the assistant to Juan Ramirez in the Human Resources department, you learn Outlook so you can use it for communication and scheduling. Refer to Figure B-1, which shows the Outlook Today window, as you read about how to customize the window.

STEPS

TROUBLE

If Outlook Today is not your default opening screen, click the Shortcuts short-cut in the Navigation Pane, then click Outlook Today on the Shortcuts list to view it.

1. **Click the Start button on the task bar, point to All Programs, click Microsoft Office, then click Microsoft Office Outlook 2007 to start Outlook**

   Outlook Today opens and shows your day at a glance, like an electronic version of a daily planner.

2. **Click View on the menu bar, point to Navigation Pane, then click Normal**

   The options on the View menu enable you to determine how the Navigation Pane, To-Do Bar, Reading Pane and toolbars appear in each of the Outlook modules. In Normal view, the **Navigation Pane** is open on the left side of the screen. In Mail view, it shows the Folder List. It has links and options for other views depending upon the module you are viewing, in addition to the navigation shortcuts. When minimized, the Navigation Pane is reduced to a vertical bar along the side of the Outlook window showing only the module navigation shortcuts.

QUICK TIP

Drag the border between the Folder List and shortcuts in the Navigation Pane to expand or shrink the list and minimize or maximize the shortcuts.

3. **Click View on the menu bar, point to To-Do Bar, then verify that there are checkmarks next to Normal, Date Navigator, Appointments, and Task List**

   The To-Do Bar, see Figure B-1, shows you what you need to do for the day. A calendar called the **Date Navigator** in the To-Do Bar gives you an overview of the month. You can mimimize the To-Do Bar so that it is reduced to a vertical bar on the right side of the window using the View menu, or by clicking the Minimize the To-Do Bar button next to the To-Do Bar Close button. You can also open the To-Do Bar Options dialog box, shown in Figure B-2, and adjust To-Do Bar display options. To open the To-Do Bar Options dialog box, click View on the menu bar, point to To-Do Bar, then click Options.

4. **Click View on the menu bar, point to Toolbars, then verify the checkmarks next to Standard and Web**

5. **Click View on the menu bar, then verify that there is a check mark next to Status Bar**

6. **Click Go on the menu bar, then review the options**

   Mail, Calendar, Contacts, Tasks, Notes, and Journal are the modules in Outlook. You can open any of these modules either by clicking the option on the Go menu or by clicking the shortcut in the Navigation Pane.

7. **Click Go on the menu bar, then click Shortcuts**

   The Navigation Pane now contains a list of shortcuts. You can customize the list to create a shortcut to any folder or group. Outlook Today is a default shortcut.

8. **Click Go on the menu bar, then click Folder List**

   The Folder List in the Navigation Pane displays each folder under Personal Folders with Outlook items specific to your account. See the example Folder List in Figure B-3.

FIGURE B-1: Outlook Today

Click to add new shortcuts to other folders

To-Do Bar

Date Navigator

Navigation Pane

Upcoming appointments

Shortcuts to other views

Upcoming tasks

Shortcuts button   Drag to expand folder list

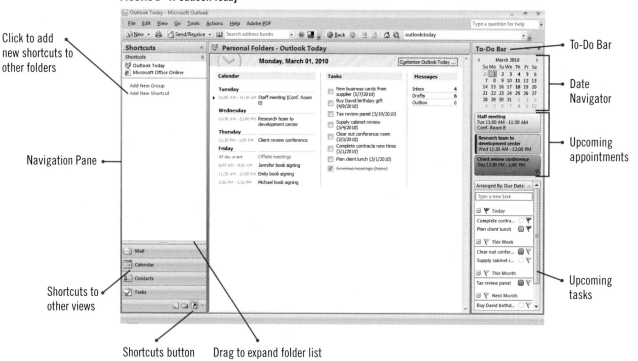

FIGURE B-2: To-Do Bar Options dialog box

FIGURE B-3: Folder List

Calendar folder

Inbox folder

Notes folder

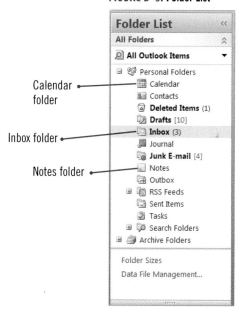

What is RSS?

The Internet has many Web sites that provide an overwhelming amount and variety of information. News sites are updated hourly; some corporations deliver news about products daily; there are entertainment Web sites that provide information about films and shows weekly; and many organizations keep their sites current. To stay on top of all this changing information, you would have to visit each site each day — a seemingly impossible task. Fortunately, there are technologies on the Internet that can help you stay current in topics that interest you. **Really Simple Syndication (RSS)** is a format for "feeding" or "syndicating" news or any content from Web sites to your computer. Outlook provides a way to have this information come directly into an RSS Feeds folder on your desktop. Access to RSS content is free, but you have to subscribe to a Web site that offers RSS feeds. RSS feeds provide subscribers with summaries that link to the full versions of the content. Once you see that you want to read more about the topic, you can click the link to view the article in the Reading Pane. You can organize the RSS feeds by creating folders for each topic or Web site that you subscribe to. The advantage to using RSS is that you may select different types of information from a variety of Web sites and view them all at the same time.

Organizing E-Mail

You have learned many basic features of creating and sending e-mail in any e-mail program, but using Outlook as your e-mail program enables you to take advantage of its features for organizing your e-mail, such as by color, view, or folder. The Inbox folder is where all new e-mail comes in unless you set up rules to deliver e-mail in other folders. A **rule** might specify that all e-mail from a certain person goes into the folder for a specific project. Outlook also has an active Junk E-mail filter that filters out messages that contain certain words. You can add keywords to the Junk E-mail filter to better manage the e-mail that comes into the Inbox. ▓▓▓▓ You will receive e-mail from clients as well as QST employees as you work with Juan Ramirez in the Human Resources department. You set up Outlook to manage the e-mail and learn the many organizational features that make Outlook an excellent personal information manager for your e-mail.

STEPS

1. **Drag the bar above the Mail shortcut in the Navigation Pane down to expand the Folder List, then click the Mail shortcut in the Navigation Pane**

   Outlook Mail is now the active module. You see a list of all Mail folders in the Navigation Pane, divided into sections. The Favorite Folders section contains shortcuts to folders that you use most often. The Mail Folders section shows all available folders, including the Inbox, Deleted Items, Drafts, Junk E-mail, Outbox, RSS Feeds, Sent Items, Search Folders, and Archive Folders. See Figure B-4.

   QUICK TIP

   The Inbox folder appears in both the Favorite Folders list and the Mail Folders list. You can select the folder from either list.

2. **Click the Inbox in the Mail Folders list in the Navigation Pane, click View on the menu bar, point to Reading Pane, then click Right, if necessary**

   The option chosen on the Reading Pane submenu determines where the Reading Pane appears in the window – in this case, on the right. If you have messages in your Inbox, you can use the Reading Pane to view a message without completely opening the message.

3. **Click Actions on the menu bar, point to Junk E-mail, then click Junk E-mail Options**

   The Junk E-mail Options dialog box opens, as shown in Figure B-5. You can specify different levels of junk e-mail protection in this dialog box to keep your Inbox free from spam.

4. **Click the Safe Senders tab, click the Safe Recipients tab, click the Blocked Senders tab, click the International tab, then click Cancel**

   There are many ways you can control the e-mail that you receive. By specifying safe senders and blocked senders, you can be sure that the e-mail you get is the e-mail you want to receive. For example, if you know someone is going to send you e-mail and you don't want the messages to be classified as junk e-mail, you can add that person's e-mail address to your Safe Senders list. If e-mail comes in that you know is offensive or junk, you can add the source address to the Blocked Senders list.

   QUICK TIP

   You can also click Arrange By in the Inbox column header, then, on the list that is displayed, click an option (such as Date) to sort the e-mail by that option.

5. **Click View on the menu bar, then point to Arrange By**

   You can determine how you view the e-mail in any folder. Options include by Date, Conversation, From, To, Categories, Flag, Size, Subject, Type, Attachments, E-mail Account, and Importance.

6. **Click View on the menu bar, point to Current View, then click Messages**

   You can use Outlook to quickly filter your e-mail based on specific criteria, such as who sent you a message or when you received a message.

7. **Click the New button on the Standard toolbar to open the new untitled Message window, as shown in Figure B-6**

8. **If you have set up an e-mail account, enter information into the To text box, the Subject text box, and body of the message, then click the Send button**

   Depending on how your e-mail is setup, a copy might be placed in the Outbox for later mailing. Once the message is sent, a copy of the message is placed in the Sent Items folder.

FIGURE B-4: Outlook Mail

Mail folders

Inbox sorted
by date

Expanded
folder list

Shortcuts
collapsed

Reading Pane
on right

Depending on your
configuration, the
To-Do Bar may be
open to the right of
the Reading Pane

FIGURE B-5: Junk E-mail Options dialog box

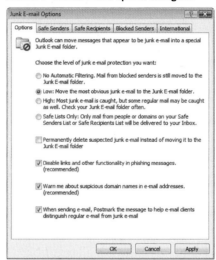

FIGURE B-6: New Message window

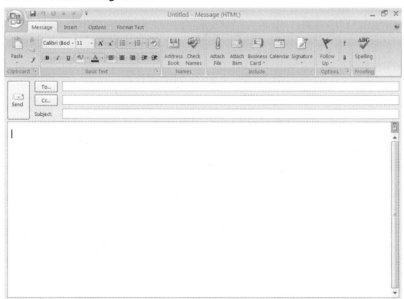

Organizing Contacts

Contacts in Microsoft Outlook enables you to manage all your business and personal contact information. When you create a contact for a person with whom you want to communicate, you store general and detailed information in fields for all Contacts in the Contacts folder. Each field, such as first name, stores specific information. Once you create a contact, you can use the Contacts features to do tasks such as the following: quickly address and send a letter, locate a phone number, make a call, send a meeting request, or e-mail a message. You can sort, group, and filter contacts by any field. You can also easily share contacts within your business or personal community. ▰▰▱▱ You learn about Contacts so you can store all the contact information for employees in Outlook.

STEPS

1. **Click the Contacts shortcut in the Navigation Pane**

   The Navigation Pane changes to Contacts view. You can click an option button in the Current view section to change how you view contacts.

2. **Click the New Contact button on the Standard toolbar**

   See Figure B-7. You enter information for a new contact in each field in the Contact window.

3. **Type your name as the contact's name in the Full Name text box, type Quest Specialty Travel (QST) in the Company text box, type Human Resources Assistant in the Job title text box, then type your Business, Home, and Mobile telephone numbers in the appropriate text boxes**

   If you do not enter a first and last name in the Full Name text box, the Check Full Name dialog box opens so you can enter the full name for the contact, including title, first name, middle name, last name, and suffix. You can click the File as list arrow in the Contact window to choose from several File as options. Outlook allows you to file each contact under different formats, including by first name, last name, company, or job title.

4. **Click the Addresses list arrow, click Business if necessary, click the This is the mailing address check box, then type your address in the Address text box**

   You can store up to three addresses in the Address text box. Choose Business, Home, or Other from the Addresses list, then type the address in the Address text box. If Outlook can't identify an address component that you type in the Address text box, the Check Address dialog box opens for you to verify it.

5. **Type your e-mail address in the E-mail text box**

   You can store up to three e-mail addresses for each contact.

6. **Click the Business Card button in the Options group on the Ribbon to open the Edit Business Card dialog box, click Full Name, Company, Job Title, Business Phone, and Business Address in the Fields list to view the information for each field in the Edit window on the right, then click OK**

   You use the Edit Business Card dialog box to view and edit, when necessary, contact information.

7. **Click the Picture button in the Options group, then click Add Picture to open the Add Contact Picture dialog box**

   You use the Add Contact Picture dialog box to navigate to the drive and folder where the photo is stored, select the photo, and then click Open.

8. **Click Cancel, then click the Details button in the Show group on the Ribbon**

   You can enter a contact's detailed information, including the contact's department, profession, assistant's name, the contact's birthday, anniversary, spouse or partner's name, or even the contact's nickname.

9. **Click the General button in the Show group on the Ribbon, then click the Save & Close button in the Actions group to save and close the contact**

   Figure B-8 shows a completed contact with a business card.

FIGURE B-7: New Contact window

Opens Check Full
Name dialog box

Click to enter up
to three e-mail
addresses

Addresses
list arrow

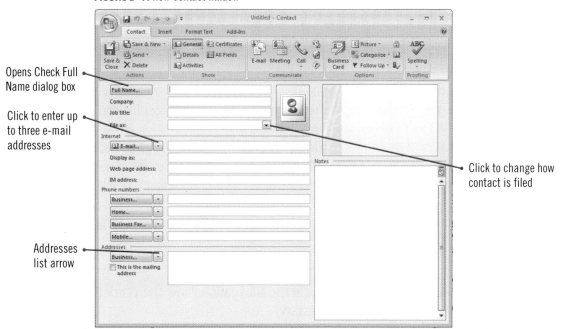

Click to change how
contact is filed

FIGURE B-8: Completed Contact

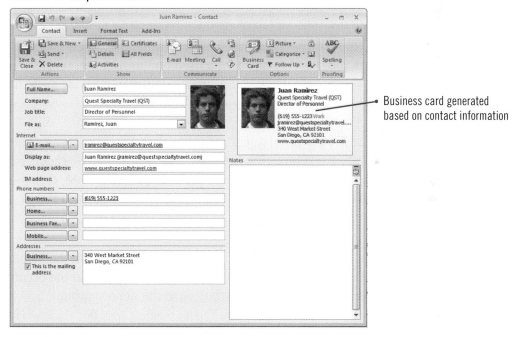

Business card generated
based on contact information

Create a mailing list

You can create a subset of your Contacts folder by filtering the Contacts list. When you **filter** a list, you search for only specific information—for example, only those contacts that live in New Jersey. Using this filtered list and mail merge, you can use Outlook to create a variety of merged documents in Word, such as form letters or mailing labels. You can also use a filtered list and mail merge to send bulk e-mail messages or faxes to your contacts. To filter contacts, click Contacts in the Navigation Pane, click the Customize Current View link in the Navigation Pane to open the Customize View dialog box. Click Filter to open the Filter dialog box, specify the filter criteria, then click OK. Once you have filtered the contacts you want for the merge, click Tools on the menu bar, then click Mail Merge to start the merge. Complete the Mail Merge Contacts dialog box to specify the contacts, fields, and document file to use, and to designate merge options such as document type and whether you want to merge to a new document, a printer, or e-mail.

Managing Appointments

The **Calendar** in Microsoft Outlook provides a convenient, effective way to manage your appointments. Calendar is the electronic equivalent of your desk calendar or pocket calendar. Calendar defines an **appointment** as an activity that does not involve inviting other people or scheduling resources, a **meeting** as an activity you invite people to or reserve resources for, and an **event** as an activity that lasts 24 hours or longer. You can specify the subject and location of the activity and its start and end times. You can also ensure that you do not forget the activity by having Outlook sound a reminder for you prior to the start of the activity. When you create an activity, Outlook notifies you if the new activity conflicts with, or is adjacent to, another scheduled activity. Recurring appointments or events can be set by specifying the recurrence, such as every week, month, or any period of time, and when the recurrence ends. You can view any period of time in Calendar. ▀▀▀▀▀ You will use Outlook to manage the schedule of appointments for Juan Ramirez and the Human Resources department.

STEPS

1. **Click the Calendar shortcut in the Navigation Pane, then click the Week button at the top of the Calendar if necessary**

   The Calendar, as shown in Figure B-9, can be viewed either by day, week, or month. The To-Do Bar, if open, shows the current month in the Date Navigator; if the To-Do Bar is closed, the Date Navigator appears in the Navigation Pane. You can use the Date Navigator in the To-Do Bar or Navigation Pane to quickly view specific dates. Dates with appointments or events appear in bold in the Date Navigator. Tasks for each day appear below the Calendar so you can see what tasks are due on each day.

   QUICK TIP

   To quickly enter an appointment, click the time slot in the Calendar, then type the information directly into it.

2. **Click the New Appointment button on the Standard toolbar**

   An untitled Appointment window opens. See Figure B-10. You can specify the subject and location, and categorize the appointment with a specific color to highlight the appointment type. Recurring appointments are entered once, then you set a recurrence pattern. These appointments are marked by a special indicator.

   QUICK TIP

   When viewing the Calendar, if you click a meeting or appointment, the details appear in the Reading Pane.

3. **Type Review Travel Agendas in the Subject text box, type Conference Room A in the Location text box, click the Start time date list arrow, click the date that is one week from now, click the Start time list arrow, click 9:00 AM, click the Reminder list arrow in the Options group on the Ribbon, then click 1 day**

   If this were a one-time meeting, you could click the Save & Close button in the Actions group and the appointment would be set.

4. **Click the Recurrence button in the Options group on the Ribbon, review the default options, click the End after option button, type 52 in the occurrences text box, click OK, then click the Save & Close button in the Actions group**

   The appointment window closes. This is a recurring event that you attend for at least one year.

5. **Click the Day button at the top of the Calendar, click the Week button, then click the Forward button ⊙ next to the date three times**

   You can view the Calendar by day, week, or month. When you view the calendar by week, you click the Show work week option button at the top of the Calendar to show Monday through Friday only, or you click the Show full week option button to show Sunday through Saturday. In all Calendar views, click the Show As list arrow to set a color bar to the left of the entry to identify the calendar time of the meeting or appointment as Free, Tentative, Busy, or Out of the Office.

6. **Click the Go to Today button on the Standard toolbar to return to today in the Calendar**

7. **Click the New list arrow on the Standard toolbar, then click Meeting Request**

   The Calendar can check the availability of all the invitees and resources for the meetings you want to set up.

8. **Click the Cancel Invitation button in the Actions group on the Meeting tab, close the untitled Appointment window, then click No to saving changes, if necessary**

FIGURE B-9: Calendar for a week

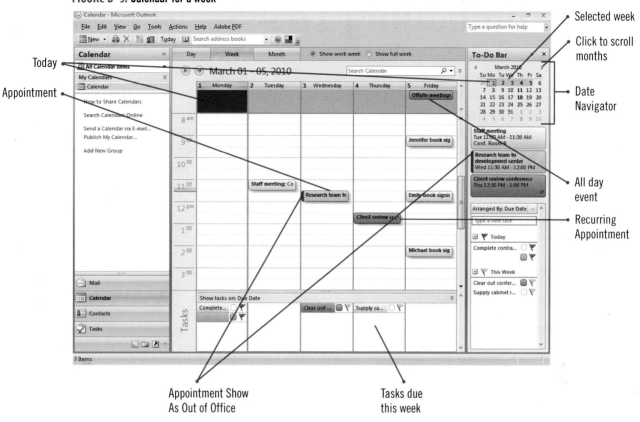

Today

Appointment

Selected week

Click to scroll months

Date Navigator

All day event

Recurring Appointment

Appointment Show As Out of Office

Tasks due this week

FIGURE B-10: New Appointment window

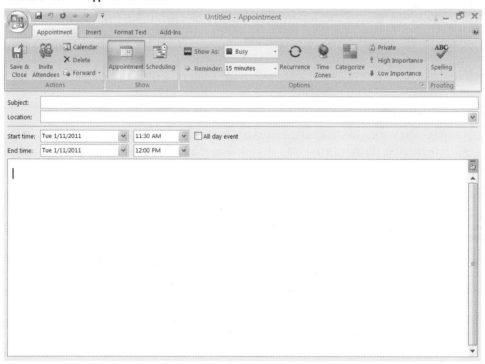

Managing Tasks

Tasks is an Outlook module that is an electronic to-do list. When you have something that has to be done, you can enter it in Tasks. Each task has a subject, a start and due date, and a description. You can also assign a priority to a task. You can mark your progress on tasks by percentage complete, and you can have Outlook create status summary reports in e-mail messages, and then send the summary to anyone on an update list for the task. Tasks can also have reminders. When you are in an Outlook module other than Tasks, your tasks appear at the bottom of the To-Do Bar, if it is open. You can also view the tasks that are due on each date in the Calendar. Similar to meetings and events, tasks can recur. You can also assign a flag and category to each task to help you organize your tasks. ▓▓▓ You always have many tasks that are due as part of your job. A week from tomorrow, the main conference room at the office is being painted, and you have to prepare the room. You enter the task in Outlook to keep track of it.

STEPS

1. **Click the** Tasks shortcut **in the Navigation Pane**

2. **Click the** New Task button **on the Standard toolbar**
   The new untitled Task window opens.

3. **Type** Clear out conference room **in the Subject text box, click the** Start date list arrow, **click the** date **that is one week from today, click the** Priority list arrow, **click** High, **click the** Reminder check box, **click the** Reminder date list arrow, **then click the** date **that is one week from yesterday**

4. **Click the** Categorize button **in the Options group on the Task tab, click** Purple Category **(or the category that is purple, if it has a different name), click** No **in the Rename Category text box if necessary, click the** Follow Up button **in the Options group, then click** Next Week
   The completed task looks like Figure B-11.

QUICK TIP
You can also quickly enter a task by typing in the fields at the top of the To-Do List.

5. **Click the** Save & Close button **in the Actions group on the Task tab**
   You can sort your tasks in several different ways, such as by To-Do Title, Due Date, or Flag Status, by clicking a column header in the task list. Tasks can also be viewed in many ways by clicking the option buttons in the Navigation Pane. Figure B-12 shows Tasks in Simple List view. A few existing tasks appear in the window (your screen may be different).

6. **Click** Actions **on the menu bar, then click** New Task Request
   You can assign tasks to another person and have Outlook automatically update you on the status of the task completion. To assign a task, you fill in the e-mail address of the person to whom you are assigning the task, complete the task details, and then click Send.

7. **Click the** Cancel Assignment button **in the Manage Task group on the Task tab, close the untitled Task window, then click** No **to saving changes, if necessary**

TROUBLE
If the To-Do Bar is not open, click View on the menu bar, click To-Do Bar, then click Normal.

8. **Click the** Calendar shortcut **in the Navigation Pane, click the** Go to Today button **if the calendar does not open to today, then scroll to next week in the Calendar or Date Navigator or until you see the new task you just entered**
   To coordinate your tasks and your appointments, the task list from Tasks is displayed in the Tasks section below the Calendar. The task you just created should appear under the Calendar for next week. You can specify how tasks are organized in the To-Do Bar.

9. **Click the** Arranged By button **above the tasks in the To-Do Bar, then click** Start Date, **if necessary**
   To schedule time to complete a task, simply drag a task from the To-Do Bar to a time block in the Calendar. Any changes you make to a task are reflected in both the To-Do Bar in Calendar and the task list in Tasks.

FIGURE B-11: Task information entered

Purple category

Start and due dates

Reminder is set

Notes about this task

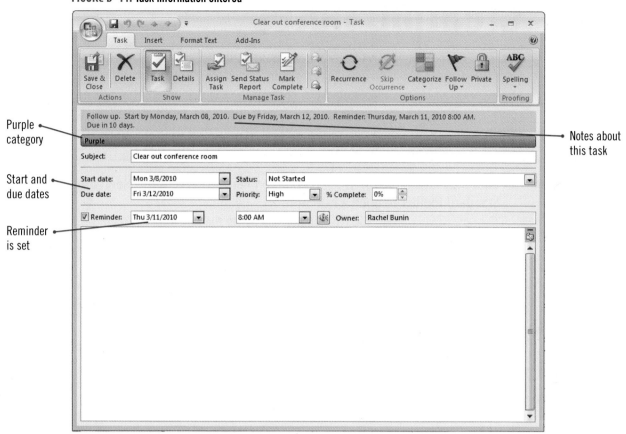

FIGURE B-12: Tasks in Simple List view

Click to enter a new task

Tasks grouped by date due

Due date for task

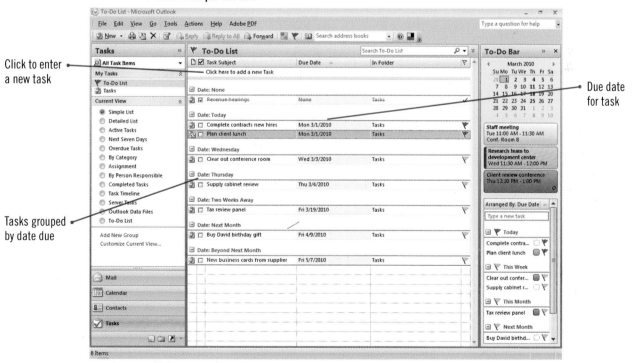

Creating Notes

Notes in Microsoft Outlook is the electronic version of the sticky notes or Post-It™ notes you buy at your local stationery store. Notes created in Outlook are a convenient way to quickly jot down a reminder or an idea. Notes, like tasks and appointments, can be organized and grouped by having categories, contacts, or colors assigned to them. You can also forward a note to share an idea with a colleague. 🔳🔲🔲 You use Notes module in Outlook to quickly write down an idea concerning a new employee at Quest Specialty Travel.

STEPS

QUICK TIP

If a note is covering an area of the window you want to view, click the title bar of the note and drag it to a new location.

1. **Click the Notes shortcut in the Navigation Pane, then click the New Note button on the Standard toolbar to open a new note**

   The Note window opens. You type the note directly in the Note window. The note should begin with a meaningful phrase so that the Notes list displays a clear descriptive title for it.

2. **Type Jennifer Michaels-File new health benefit forms with insurance company**

3. **Click the Note icon in the upper-left corner of the Note window to open a menu**

   You can color-code each note, assign a contact to the note, and forward or print the note. Notes are date and time stamped at the time they are created.

4. **Point to Categorize, then click Purple Category (or the name of the purple category, if necessary)**

   Figure B-13 shows the new note. The Navigation Pane provides many options for viewing the Notes in order to organize them the way you want. If you want to turn a note into an appointment or meeting, you drag the note from the Notes window to the Calendar button in the Navigation Pane. A new appointment window opens with the details from the note filled in the appropriate fields. If you drag the note to the Tasks button in the Navigation Pane, a new task window opens and you can specify a due date and other details.

5. **Close the note**

Sending Business Cards or VCards

You can send contact information over the Internet easily with Outlook. If you know someone has Outlook 2007, you can send a contact business card. In Contacts view, click the contact you want to send, click Actions on the menu bar, then click Send as Business Card. **VCards** are the Internet standard for creating and sharing

virtual business cards. To send a vCard to someone via e-mail, click the contact you want to send as a vCard, click Actions on the menu bar, point to Send Full Contact, then click In Internet Format (vCard). You can also include your vCard with your e-mail signature.

FIGURE B-13: New note

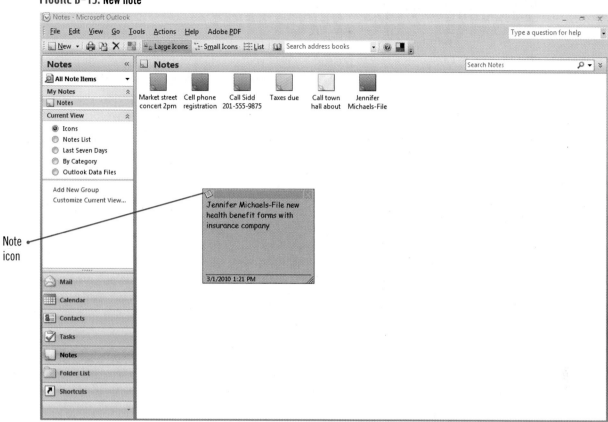

Note icon

Outlook 2007

Customizing Outlook Today

When Outlook Today is open, you can see what is happening in the Calendar, Tasks, and Messages for the day. Outlook Today shows your appointments over a range of time in the Calendar section. It also displays your tasks in one convenient place. In the Customize Outlook Today pane, you can decide to go directly to Outlook Today when Outlook opens, if it does not open automatically. You can also choose to show from one to seven days of appointments in the Calendar section, and you can sort your tasks in Outlook Today by Importance, Due Date, Creation Time, or Start Date, and in ascending or descending order. If you use Outlook for e-mail, Outlook Today displays how many messages are in your Inbox, Outbox, and Drafts folders. You can also add or delete folders from the Messages folder list. To customize Outlook Today, view the Outlook Today page, click the Customize Outlook Today link to the right of the date in Outlook Today and customize the information that appears to fit your personal style and work habits. Pick a different visual appearance for Outlook Today from an available list. Click the Save Changes button in the Customize Outlook Today pane to save any changes you make

Using the Journal

The **Journal** in Outlook is a way to provide a trail of your activities within Microsoft Office. If you turn the Journal on, you can see a timeline of any calls, messages, appointments, or tasks. The Journal also tracks all documents, spreadsheets, databases, presentations, or any Office file that you specify. The Journal may not have been on when you created a spreadsheet or document that you want to be recorded in the Journal. Use Windows Explorer or the desktop to locate the file or item you want to record, then drag the item to the Journal and select the options you want for the entry. ▰▰▰ You use the Journal to help assign documents to contacts.

STEPS

TROUBLE

If the Journal is already on, click Tools on the menu bar, click Options, then click Journal Options to open the Journal Options dialog box.

1. **Click Go on the menu bar, click Journal, then click Yes**

   To turn on the Journal, you specify the Journal options, such as which items to track, in the Journal Options dialog box, shown in Figure B-14. The Journal is displayed as a timeline on your screen. Any activities that have been specified to be tracked appear for each day as icons. You can scroll through the Journal to get an overview of your activities. You can sort or group the activities in the Journal. If you want to recall an event, the Journal is a great tool; you can see any documents that may have been created on a specific day. The Journal folder contains shortcuts to the activities that have been recorded.

TROUBLE

Make sure your e-mail address is listed in your contact information in Contacts so that it will be tracked in the Journal.

2. **Click the E-mail message check box in the Automatically record these items box, click the check box next to your name in the For these contacts list, then click OK**

3. **Click the Mail shortcut in the Navigator Pane, click the New Mail Message button on the Standard toolbar, then send yourself a test message**

QUICK TIP

E-mail is also tracked within Outlook contacts when the Journal is on. Open a contact, then click the Activities button in the Show group on the Contact tab to view any e-mail received from or sent to a contact.

4. **Click Go on the menu bar, click Journal, then review the Journal entry, as shown in Figure B-15**

5. **Click Tools on the menu bar, click Options to open the Options dialog box, then click Journal Options in the Contacts and Notes section of the dialog box**

   You can remove, add, or change Journal options at any time by working in the Journal Options dialog box.

6. **Click to remove the check marks from the E-mail Message check box and from your contact name**

7. **Click OK to close the Journal Options dialog box, then click OK to close the Options dialog box**

FIGURE B-14: Journal Options dialog box

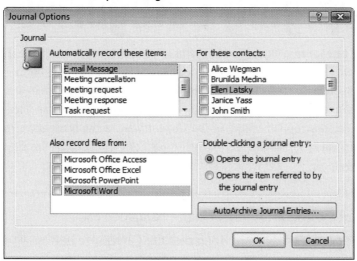

FIGURE B-15: Recorded Journal entry

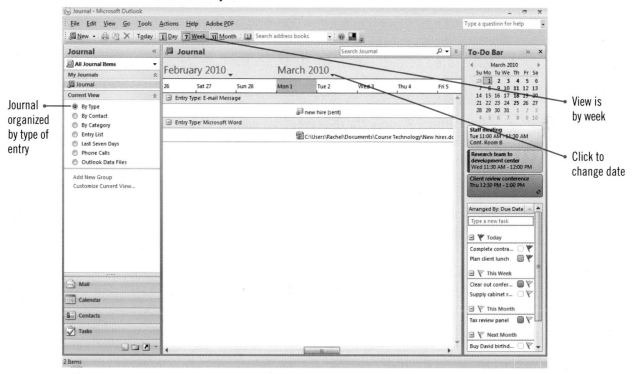

Journal organized by type of entry

View is by week

Click to change date

Applying Categories

You use categories in Outlook to tag items so you can track and organize them by specific criteria. Outlook comes with color categories that are set by default. You can rename the colors as needed. By assigning color categories to contacts, tasks, appointments, notes, or any item in Outlook, you can quickly review all items assigned to a specific category by reviewing the color. You can filter or sort by category. If you click the By Category option button in the Current View of the Navigation Pane, you can see your contacts clearly by category. ⬛⬛⬛⬛ QST wants to use color to help organize information about its contacts and staff. Eventually, you will set up a system to assign colors to contacts and staff based on region.

STEPS

1. **Click the** Contacts shortcut **in the Navigation Pane**

2. **Click your** Contact card, **then click the** Categorize button ⬛ **on the Standard toolbar**
   Outlook comes with six predefined color categories: Purple, Blue, Green, Orange, Red, and Yellow.

3. **Click** Purple Category **(or the name of the purple category, if necessary)**
   Your contact card is now assigned the color purple.

4. **Click the** Calendar shortcut **in the Navigation Pane, scroll to next week, click the** Review Travel Agendas appointment, **click the** Categorize button ⬛ **on the Standard toolbar, then click** Purple Category **(or the category's name)**
   The appointment is also assigned the color purple.

5. **Click the** Contacts shortcut **in the Navigation Pane, then click the** By Category option button **in the Current View section of the Navigation Pane**
   The contacts are grouped by category, as shown in Figure B-16. You can rename categories to be meaningful while retaining the color coding.

6. **Make sure a contact card is selected, click the** Categorize button ⬛ **on the Standard toolbar, then click** All Categories **to open the Color Categories dialog box, as shown in Figure B-17**

QUICK TIP
If you are working on a shared computer, such as in a lab setting, repeat steps 6 and 7 to change the category name back to Purple Category.

7. **Click** Purple Category **(or the category's name), click** Rename, **type** HR Assistant **as the new name, then click** OK
   The name of the purple category changes to "HR Assistant" in the list of contacts by category. As you work on other applications at your computer, you can leave Outlook open so you can refer to your contacts, be reminded of appointments, and track entries in the Journal. However, at the end of the day, it is good practice to close all applications and shut down the computer.

8. **Click** File **on the menu bar, then click** Exit **to exit Outlook**

Coordinating calendars

The Calendar can check the availability of all the people and resources for the meetings you want to set up.

Once you select a meeting time and location, you can send invitations in meeting requests by entering contact names in the To text box, then clicking the Send button. The meeting request arrives in the invitee's Inbox with buttons to Accept, Reject, or Request a change directly in the e-mail message. If an invitee accepts the invitation, a positive e-mail reply is sent back to you, and Outlook posts

the meeting automatically to the invitee's calendar. If you share calendars through a network, you can click the Open a Shared Calendar link in the Navigation Pane to view the calendars of your colleagues. To send a copy of a time period in your calendar to someone through e-mail, click the Send a Calendar via E-mail link in the Navigation Pane, adjust the options in the Send a Calendar via E-mail dialog box, click OK, then address and send the e-mail.

FIGURE B-16: Contacts grouped by category

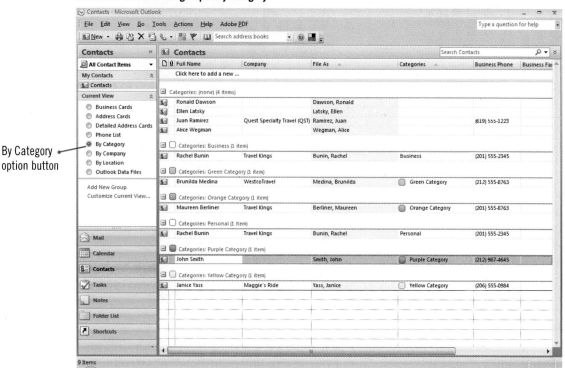

By Category
option button

FIGURE B-17: Color Categories dialog box

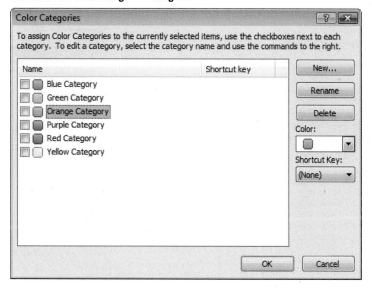

Practice

If you have a SAM user profile, you may have access to hands-on instruction, practice, and assessment of the skills covered in this unit. Log in to your SAM account (http://sam2007.course.com/) to launch any assigned training activities or exams that relate to the skills covered in this unit.

▼ CONCEPTS REVIEW

Label the elements of the Calendar window shown in Figure B-18.

FIGURE B-18

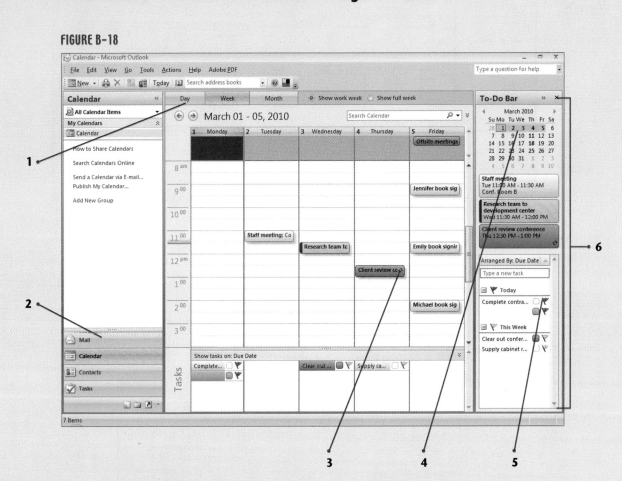

Match each term with the statement that best describes it.

7. Notes   **a.** Track e-mail, documents, activities

8. Tasks   **b.** Keep and track appointments

9. E-mail   **c.** Jot down ideas or reminders

10. Calendar   **d.** Manage a to-do list

11. Journal   **e.** Send and receive messages

Select the best answer from the list of choices.

12. Which of the following is *not* available in Outlook?

a. Mail

b. Notes

c. Calendar

d. Planner

13. To schedule your appointments, meetings, and events, you use _____ .

a. Tasks

b. Notes

c. Contacts

d. Calendar

14. To manage your business and personal to-do list, you use _____ .

a. Tasks

b. Journal

c. Contacts

d. Calendar

15. To track appointments, documents, and activities, you use _____ .

a. Tasks

b. Journal

c. Contacts

d. Calendar

16. The difference between an appointment and an event is that _____ .

a. An event cannot recur

b. An appointment lasts less than 12 hours

c. An event lasts 24 hours or more

d. You cannot categorize an event

17. Which of the following is *not* visible on the To-Do Bar?

a. E-mail in the Inbox

b. An appointment for today

c. Tasks due today

d. Date Navigator

▼ SKILLS REVIEW

1. Start Outlook.
a. Click the Start Button on the taskbar, then start Outlook.

b. Arrange the Outlook window so that the Navigation Pane is in Normal view and contains the folder list, and the To-Do Bar appears on the right side of the screen.

c. Open Mail, then expand the folder list so the Navigation Pane buttons are minimized at the bottom. See Figure B-19.

2. Organize E-mail.
a. View the Inbox.

b. Sort the e-mail in the Inbox by sender, then sort the e-mail in the Inbox by date, most recent on top.

c. Open the Junk E-mail Options dialog box, review the junk e-mail options on the system, then close the dialog box.

d. Open a new message window and write an e-mail message to your instructor or a friend. Include an address in the Cc box, then type **Study group plans** as the subject of the message. As the body of the message, enter a brief message. See Figure B-20.

e. Send the message.

3. Organize contacts.
a. Open Contacts.

b. Open a new untitled Contact window.

c. Create a new contact for a family member.

d. Save and close the contact.

FIGURE B-19

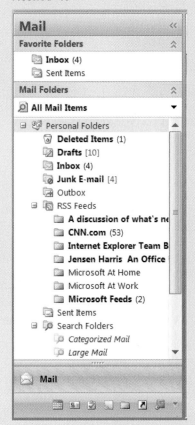

FIGURE B-20

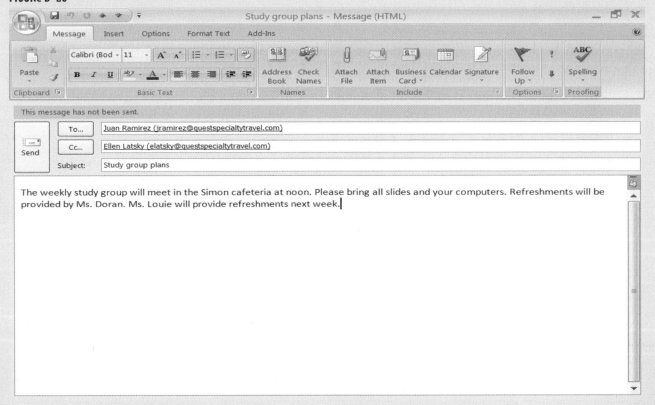

4. Manage appointments.

  a. Open the Calendar.

  b. View the calendar by full week.

  c. View the calendar for today.

  d. Create a new appointment for next week for a two-and-a-half hour lunch meeting with Ruth, Maureen, and Janice at noon in the Stardust Diner.

  e. Set a reminder for two days ahead of the appointment. See Figure B-21.

  f. Save and close the appointment.

FIGURE B-21

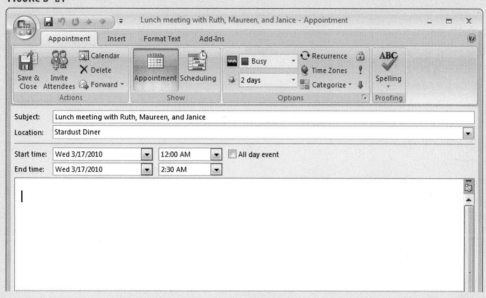

5. Manage tasks.

  a. Open Tasks.

  b. View the task list in Simple List and Detailed List views.

  c. Create a new task, due tomorrow, to buy your friend a birthday gift.

  d. Set a reminder for early morning. See Figure B-22.

  e. Save and close the task.

FIGURE B-22

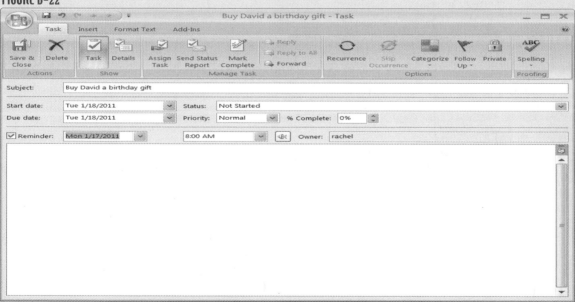

6. Create notes.

   a. Open Notes.

   b. Create a new note reminding you to call town hall about a new town ordinance.

   c. Categorize the note in the Red Category. See Figure B-23.

   d. Close the note.

7. Use the Journal.

   a. Turn on the Journal.

   b. In the Journal Options dialog box, click the E-mail Message check box in the Automatically record these items box and the check box next to your own name in the For these contacts list to have the Journal track your e-mail messages.

   c. Send yourself an e-mail message.

   d. Click Go on the menu bar, then click Journal to view the Journal entry.

   e. Open the Journal Options dialog box, deselect the E-mail Message check box in the Automatically record these items box, then deselect the check box next to your name to turn tracking off.

   f. Close the Journal Options dialog box.

8. Apply categories.

   a. Open Contacts, then assign the Green Category to your Contact card.

   b. Assign a category to the lunch appointment that you created in Step 4.

   c. View Contacts by category. See Figure B-24.

   d. Exit Outlook.

FIGURE B-23

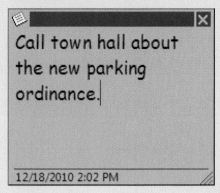

Call town hall about the new parking ordinance.

12/18/2010 2:02 PM

FIGURE B-24

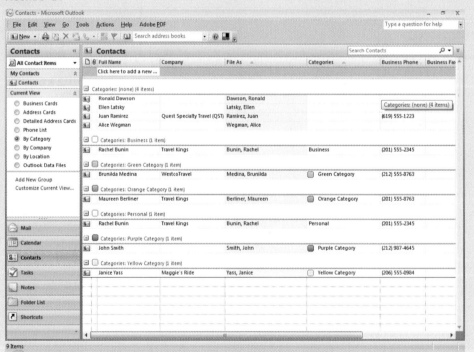

▼ INDEPENDENT CHALLENGE 1

As manager of a sporting goods store, your job is to develop a contact list of all customers that come in the store. The list will be used to send direct mail for future promotions. You created a form for each customer to complete so that you can gather their contact information. The contact information includes first and last name, mailing address, e-mail address, and at least one phone number. Each week you select one customer from the list of new names to receive a small prize package. You need to create the contact list in Outlook and use Outlook to schedule the weekly prize giveaway.

a. Open Contacts in Outlook, and then create five new contact cards. Use your friends' information or make up fictitious names and contact information.

b. Create two notes, each in the Purple category, that remind you of an event in the store.

c. Create a recurring appointment on each Thursday for the next two months to select a winner from the list of new names.

d. Enter two new tasks in the task list. One task is for you to review the employee compensation package, and the other task is for you to review the utility bills. Each task should have a start date of next week, a high priority, and be in the Yellow category.

e. View the Calendar with the To-Do Bar open.

f. Exit Outlook.

▼ INDEPENDENT CHALLENGE 2

Outlook is an integrated information management system that stores information in folders specific to the type of information stored. Outlook stores e-mail in Mail folders, Contacts in Contact folders, and so on. You can create new folders for specific types of information and view them in the folders list. You can also transfer one type of item to another, for example, you can drag a task to the Calendar to create an appointment. The integration of the different types of information is what makes Outlook so powerful. You are going to move items from one Outlook module to another to see how easily you can integrate information.

a. Open Mail in Outlook, drag an e-mail message from the Inbox to the Tasks shortcut on the Navigation Pane, then, in a word processing document or on a piece of paper, explain what happens.

b. Drag an e-mail message from the Inbox to the Notes shortcut in the Navigation Pane, then explain what happens.

c. Open the Calendar, drag an existing appointment from the Calendar to the Tasks shortcut in the Navigation Pane, then explain what happens.

d. Drag the same appointment to the Mail shortcut.

e. View the Contacts list in Address Cards view. Drag a contact card from the Contacts list to the Calendar shortcut in the Navigation Pane, then explain what happens.

Advanced Challenge Exercise

■ Open a new appointment in Calendar, click the Categorize button in the Options group on the Ribbon, then click All Categories.

■ Rename the Purple category to a name of your choice.

■ Rename the Red category to a name of your choice. See Figure B-25.

■ Close the Color Categories dialog box, then close the appointment window.

FIGURE B-25

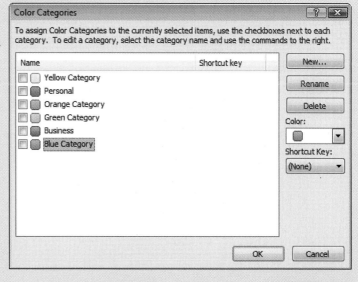

f. View the Contacts list in Business Cards view. Drag a contact card from the Contacts list to the Mail shortcut in the Navigation Pane, then explain what happens.

g. Exit Outlook.

▼ VISUAL WORKSHOP

Start Outlook. First, create a note as shown in Figure B-26, then create an appointment as shown in Figure B-27, using a weekday in the next two weeks as the date for the appointment. Finally, using the same date as for the appointment, create a task as shown in Figure B-28. Note that the dates in the figures will differ from those on your screen.

FIGURE B-26

FIGURE B-27

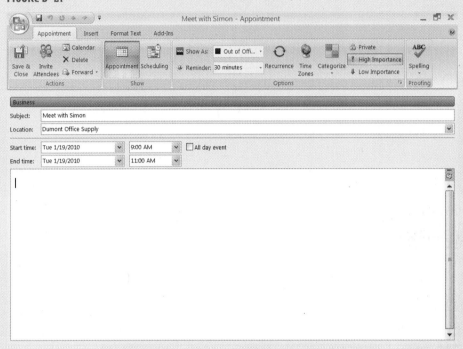

FIGURE B-28

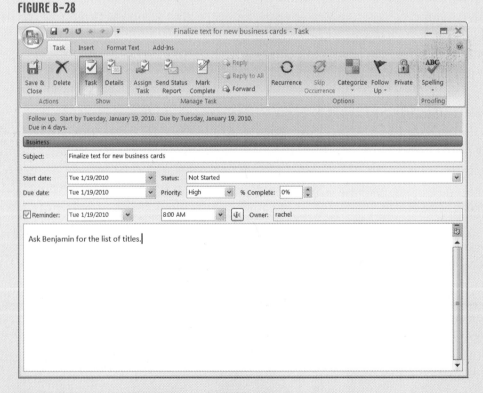

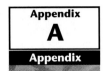

Restoring Defaults in Windows Vista and Disabling and Enabling Windows Aero

Files You Will Need:

No files needed.

Windows Vista is the most recent version of the Windows operating system. An operating system controls the way you work with your computer, supervises running programs, and provides tools for completing your computing tasks. After surveying millions of computer users, Microsoft incorporated their suggestions to make Windows Vista secure, reliable, and easy to use. In fact, Windows Vista is considered the most secure version of Windows yet. Other improvements include a powerful new search feature that lets you quickly search for files and programs from the Start menu and most windows, tools that simplify accessing the Internet, especially with a wireless connection, and multimedia programs that let you enjoy, share, and organize music, photos, and recorded TV. Finally, Windows Vista offers lots of visual appeal with its transparent, three-dimensional design in the Aero experience. This appendix explains how to make sure you are using the Windows Vista default settings for appearance, personalization, security, hardware, and sound and to enable and disable Windows Aero. For more information on Windows Aero, go to *www.microsoft.com/windowsvista/experiences/aero.mspx*.

OBJECTIVES

Restore the defaults in the Appearance and Personalization section

Restore the defaults in the Security section

Restore the defaults in the Hardware and Sound section

Disable Windows Aero

Enable Windows Aero

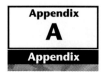

Restoring the Defaults in the Appearance and Personalization Section

The following instructions require a default Windows Vista Ultimate installation and the student logged in with an Administrator account. All of the following settings can be changed by accessing the Control Panel.

STEPS

- To restore the defaults in the Personalization section
    1. Click Start, and then click Control Panel. Click Appearance and Personalization, click Personalization, and then compare your screen to Figure A-1
    2. In the Personalization window, click Windows Color and Appearance, select the Default color, and then click OK
    3. In the Personalization window, click Mouse Pointers. In the Mouse Properties dialog box, on the Pointers tab, select Windows Aero (system scheme) in the Scheme drop-down list, and then click OK
    4. In the Personalization window, click Theme. Select Windows Vista from the Theme drop-down list, and then click OK
    5. In the Personalization window, click Display Settings. In the Display Settings dialog box, drag the Resolution bar to 1024 by 768 pixels, and then click OK

FIGURE A-1

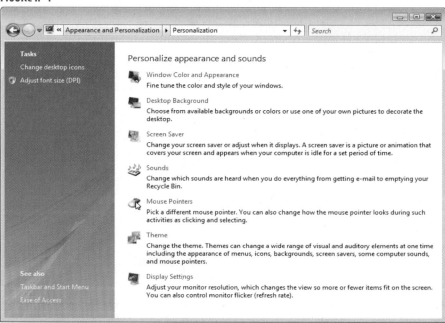

- To restore the defaults in the Taskbar and Start Menu section

    1. Click Start, and then click Control Panel. Click Appearance and Personalization, click Taskbar and Start Menu, and then compare your screen to Figure A-2

    2. In the Taskbar and Start Menu Properties dialog box, on the Taskbar tab, click to select all checkboxes except for "Auto-hide the taskbar"

    3. On the Start Menu tab, click to select the Start menu radio button and check all items in the Privacy section

    4. In the System icons section on the Notification Area tab, click to select all of the checkboxes except for "Power"

    5. On the Toolbars tab, click to select Quick Launch, none of the other items should be checked

    6. Click OK to close the Taskbar and Start Menu Properties dialog box

- To restore the defaults in the Folder Options section

    1. Click Start, and then click Control Panel. Click Appearance and Personalization, click Folder Options, and then compare your screen to Figure A-3

    2. In the Folder Options dialog box, on the General tab, click to select Show preview and filters in the Tasks section, click to select Open each folder in the same window in the Browse folders section, and click to select Double-click to open an item (single-click to select) in the Click items as follows section

    3. On the View tab, click the Reset Folders button, and then click Yes in the Folder views dialog box. Then click the Restore Defaults button

    4. On the Search tab, click the Restore Defaults button

    5. Click OK to close the Folder Options dialog box

- To restore the defaults in the Windows Sidebar Properties section

    1. Click Start, and then click Control Panel. Click Appearance and Personalization, click Windows Sidebar Properties, and then compare your screen to Figure A-4

    2. In the Windows Sidebar Properties dialog box, on the Sidebar tab, click to select Start Sidebar when Windows starts. In the Arrangement section, click to select Right, and then click to select 1 in the Display Sidebar on monitor drop-down list

    3. Click OK to close the Windows Sidebar Properties dialog box

FIGURE A-3

FIGURE A-4

FIGURE A-2

Restoring the Defaults in the Security Section

The following instructions require a default Windows Vista Ultimate installation and the student logged in with an Administrator account. All of the following settings can be changed by accessing the Control Panel.

- To restore the defaults in the Windows Firewall section

  1. Click Start, and then click Control Panel. Click Security, click Windows Firewall, and then compare your screen to Figure A-5

  2. In the Windows Firewall dialog box, click Change settings. If the User Account Control dialog box appears, click Continue

  3. In the Windows Firewall Settings dialog box, click the Advanced tab. Click Restore Defaults, then click Yes in the Restore Defaults Confirmation dialog box

  4. Click OK to close the Windows Firewall Settings dialog box, and then close the Windows Firewall window

- To restore the defaults in the Internet Options section

  1. Click Start, and then click Control Panel. Click Security, click Internet Options, and then compare your screen to Figure A-6

  2. In the Internet Properties dialog box, on the General tab, click the Use default button. Click the Settings button in the Tabs section, and then click the Restore defaults button in the Tabbed Browsing Settings dialog box. Click OK to close the Tabbed Browsing Settings dialog box

  3. On the Security tab of the Internet Properties dialog box, click to uncheck the Enable Protected Mode checkbox, if necessary. Click the Default level button in the Security level for this zone section. If possible, click the Reset all zones to default level button

  4. On the Programs tab, click the Make default button in the Default web browser button for Internet Explorer, if possible. If Office is installed, Microsoft Office Word should be selected in the HTML editor drop-down list

  5. On the Advanced tab, click the Restore advanced settings button in the Settings section. Click the Reset button in the Reset Internet Explorer settings section, and then click Reset in the Reset Internet Explorer Settings dialog box

  6. Click Close to close the Reset Internet Explorer Settings dialog box, and then click OK to close the Internet Properties dialog box

FIGURE A-5

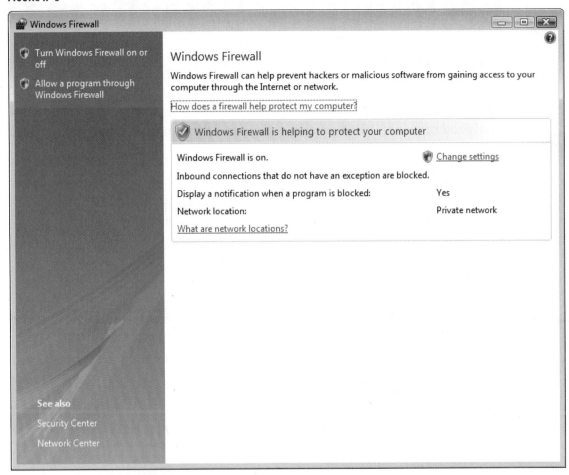

FIGURE A-6

Restoring the Defaults in the Hardware and Sound Section

The following instructions require a default Windows Vista Ultimate installation and the student logged in with an Administrator account. All of the following settings can be changed by accessing the Control Panel.

STEPS

- To restore the defaults in the Autoplay section
  1. Click Start, and then click Control Panel. Click Hardware and Sound, click Autoplay, and then compare your screen to Figure A-7. Scroll down and click the Reset all defaults button in the Devices section at the bottom of the window, and then click Save

- To restore the defaults in the Sound section
  1. Click Start, and then click Control Panel. Click Hardware and Sound, click Sound, and then compare your screen to Figure A-8
  2. In the Sound dialog box, on the Sounds tab, select Windows Default from the Sound Scheme drop-down list, and then click OK

- To restore the defaults in the Mouse section
  1. Click Start, and then click Control Panel. Click Hardware and Sound, click Mouse, and then compare your screen to Figure A-9
  2. In the Mouse Properties dialog box, on the Pointers tab, select Windows Aero (system scheme) from the Scheme drop-down list
  3. Click OK to close the Mouse Properties dialog box

FIGURE A-7

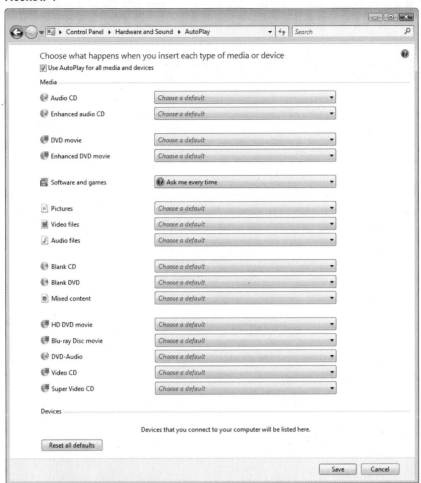

FIGURE A-8

FIGURE A-9

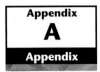

Disabling and Enabling Windows Aero

Unlike prior versions of Windows, Windows Vista provides two distinct user interface experiences: a "basic" experience for entry-level systems and more visually dynamic experience called Windows Aero. Both offer a new and intuitive navigation experience that helps you more easily find and organize your applications and files, but Aero goes further by delivering a truly next-generation desktop experience.

Windows Aero builds on the basic Windows Vista user experience and offers Microsoft's best-designed, highest-performing desktop experience. Using Aero requires a PC with compatible graphics adapter and running a Premium or Business edition of Windows Vista.

The following instructions require a computer capable of running Windows Aero, with a default Windows Vista Ultimate installation and student logged in with an Administrator account.

STEPS

- **To Disable Windows Aero**

We recommend that students using this book disable Windows Aero and restore their operating systems default settings (instructions to follow).

1. **Right-click the desktop, select** Personalize, **and then compare your screen in Figure A-10. Select** Window Color and Appearance, **and then select** Open classic appeareance properties for more color options. **In Appearance Settings dialog box, on the Appearance tab, select any non-Aero scheme (such as** Windows Vista Basic **or** Windows Vista Standard) **in the Color Scheme list, and then click OK. Figure A-11 compares Windows Aero to other color schemes. Note that this book uses Windows Vista Basic as the color scheme**

- **To Enable Windows Aero**

1. **Right-click the desktop, and then select** Personalize. **Select** Window Color and Appearance, **then select** Windows Aero **in the Color scheme list, and then click OK in the Appearance Settings dialog box**

FIGURE A-10

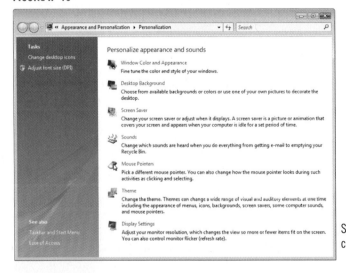

FIGURE A-11

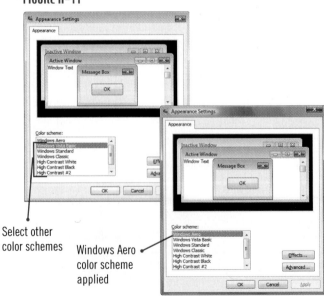

Select other color schemes

Windows Aero color scheme applied

Glossary

3½" disk *See* Floppy disk.

Absolute cell reference In a formula, type of cell address that does not change when you copy the formula; indicated by a dollar sign before the column letter and/or row number. *See also* Relative cell reference.

Accessories Built-in programs that come with Windows Vista and XP, such as the Calculator for performing calculations.

Active The currently available document, program, or object; on the taskbar, the button of the active document appears in a darker shade while the buttons of other open documents are dimmed.

Active cell The cell in which you are currently working.

Active program The program that you are using, differentiated from other open programs by a highlighted program button on the taskbar and a differently colored title bar.

Active window The window that you are currently using, differentiated from other open windows by a differently colored title bar.

Address bar (Windows) A horizontal box near the top of a window that shows your current location in the computer's file hierarchy as a series of links separated by arrows, and that allows you to navigate to other locations on your computer. (Internet Explorer) The area below the toolbar that displays the address of the Web page currently opened.

Adjustment handle A small yellow diamond that changes the appearance of an object's most prominent feature.

Adware Software installed with another program that generates advertising revenue for the program's creator by displaying targeted ads to the program's user.

Align To place an objects' edges or centers on the same plane.

Alignment In Word, the position of text in a document relative to the margins; in Excel, the position of text in a cell relative to the cell edges, such as left, center, or right.

Alignment command In Access, a command used in Layout or Design View for a form or report to either left-, center-, or right-align a value within its control, or to align the top, bottom, right, or left edge of the control with respect to other controls.

American Standard Code for Information Interchange *See* ASCII.

Analog signal A continuous wave signal (sound wave) that can traverse ordinary phone lines.

AND criteria Criteria placed in the same row of the query design grid. All criteria on the same row must be true for a record to appear on the resulting datasheet.

Animation tag Identifies the order an object is animated on a slide during a slide show.

Annotate A freehand drawing on the PowerPoint screen made by using the Annotation tool. You can annotate only in Slide Show view.

Anti-spyware software Software that detects and removes spyware.

Antivirus software Software that searches executable files for the sequences of characters that may cause harm and disinfects the files by erasing or disabling those commands; *also called* virus protection software.

Application software Software that enables you to perform specific computer tasks, such as document production, spreadsheet calculations, database management, and presentation preparation.

Appointment In the Calendar in Outlook, an activity that does not involve inviting other people or scheduling resources.

Architecture The design and construction of a computer; *also called* configuration.

Argument Information that a function uses to create the final answer. Multiple arguments are separated by commas. All of the arguments for a function are surrounded by a single set of parentheses.

Arithmetic operators In a formula, symbols that perform mathematical calculations, such as plus (+), minus (–), multiply (*), divide (/), or exponentiation (^).

ASCII (American Standard Code for Information Interchange) The number system that personal computers use to represent character data.

Attachment A file, such as a picture, audio clip, video clip, document, worksheet, or presentation, that is sent in addition to an e-mail message composed by typing in the Message window.

Attributes Styling characteristics such as bold, italics, and underlining that you can apply to change the way text and numbers look in a worksheet or chart.

AutoComplete A feature that automatically suggests text to insert.

AutoCorrect A feature that automatically detects and corrects typing errors, minor spelling errors, and capitalization, and inserts certain typographical symbols as you type.

AutoFill Options button A feature that lets you fill cells with specific elements of the copied cell (such as formatting).

AutoFit A feature that automatically adjusts the width of a column or the height of a row to accommodate its widest or tallest entry.

Automatic page break A page break that is inserted automatically at the bottom of a page.

Autonumber A field data type in which Access enters a sequential integer for each record added into the datasheet. Numbers cannot be reused even if the record is deleted.

AutoText A feature that stores frequently used text and graphics so they can be easily inserted into a document.

Avg function Built-in Access function used to calculate the average of the values in a given field.

Axis label Text in a chart that identifies data.

.bmp The abbreviation for the bitmap graphics file format.

Back Color property A property that determines the background color of the selected control or section in a form or report.

Back up To save files to another location in case you have computer trouble and lose files.

Background The area behind the text and graphics on a slide.

Background graphic An object placed on the slide master.

Backward-compatible Software feature that enables documents saved in an older version of a program to be opened in a newer version of the program.

Bibliography A list of sources that you consulted or cited while creating a document.

Binary digit (bit) The representation of data as a 1 or 0.

Binding The field binding determines the field to which a bound control in a form or report is connected.

Bit *See* Binary digit.

Bits per second (bps) The unit of measurement for the speed of data transmission.

Blind courtesy copy (BCC) In e-mail, a way to send a message to a recipient who needs to be aware of the correspondence between the sender and the recipients, but is not the primary recipient of the message; used when the sender does not want to reveal who he or she has sent courtesy copies to.

Blog An informal journal that is created by an individual or a group and available to the public on the Internet; short for weblog.

Blogger The person who creates and maintains a blog.

Bluetooth A wireless technology standard that allows electronic devices to use short range radio waves to communicate with one another or connect to the Internet; the radio waves can be transmitted around corners and through walls.

Bold Formatting applied to text to make it thicker and darker.

Boolean filter A word or symbol for locating programs, folders, and files by specifying or more criteria so that you have a greater chance of finding what you need.

Boot process The set of events that occurs between the moment you turn on the computer and the moment you can begin to use the computer.

Booting A process that Windows steps through to get the computer up and running.

Border A line that can be added above, below, or to the sides of a paragraph, text, or table cell; a line that divides the columns and rows of a table.

Bound control A control used in either a form or report to display data from the underlying field; used to edit and enter new data in a form.

bps *See* Bits per second.

Browser A program, such as Microsoft Internet Explorer, designed to access the Internet.

Browser window The specific area on the screen where the current Web page appears.

Building block Reusable piece of formatted content or document part that is stored in a gallery.

Bullet A small graphic symbol used to identify items in a list.

Byte One character of storage space on disk or in RAM.

Cable Plastic-enclosed wires that attach a peripheral device to a computer port.

Cache memory Special high-speed memory chips on the motherboard or CPU that store frequently-accessed and recently-accessed data and commands; *also called* RAM cache *or* CPU cache.

Calculation A new value that is created by entering an expression in a text box on a form or report.

Calculation operators Symbols that indicate what type of calculation to perform on the cells, ranges, or values.

Calendar In Microsoft Outlook, provides a convenient way to manage your appointments and events.

Calendar icon An icon you can click to select a date from a pop-up calendar.

Calendar picker A pop-up calendar from which you can choose dates for a date field.

Card A removable circuit board that is inserted into a slot in the motherboard to expand the capabilities of the motherboard.

Categories In Outlook, a feature used to tag items so you can track and organize them by specific criteria.

Category axis Horizontal axis of a chart, usually containing the names of data groups; in a 2-dimensional chart, also known as the x-axis.

Cathode ray tube monitor *See* CRT monitor.

CD (compact disc) An optical storage device that can contain programs, music, movies, or your own personal files. A CD can store approximately 700 MB of data.

CD-R (compact disc recordable) A CD that on which you can record data with a laser that changes the reflectivity of a dye layer on the blank disk, creating dark spots on the disk's surface that represent the data; once the data is recorded, you cannot erase or modify it.

CD-ROM (compact disc read-only memory) A CD that contains software or music when you purchase it, but you cannot record additional data on it.

CD-RW (compact disc rewritable) A CD on which you can record data as on a CD-R, and then delete or re-record data on it as needed.

Cell The intersection of a column and a row in a worksheet, datasheet, or table.

Cell address The location of a cell, expressed by cell coordinates; for example, the cell address of the cell in column A, row 1 is A1.

Cell pointer A dark rectangle that outlines the active cell.

Cell styles Predesigned combinations of formatting attributes that can be applied to selected cells, to enhance the look of a worksheet.

Center Alignment in which an item is centered between the margins.

Central processing unit (CPU) *See* Microprocessor.

Channel The medium, such as telephone or coaxial cable, over which a message is sent in data communications.

Character spacing Formatting that changes the width or scale of characters, expands or condenses the amount of space between characters, raises or lowers characters relative to the line of text, and adjusts kerning (the space between standard combinations of letters).

Characters per second (cps) The unit of measurement for the speed of dot matrix printers.

Chart A graphical representation of numerical data from a worksheet that make it easier to see patterns, trends, and relationships. Types include 2-D and 3-D column, bar, pie, area, and line charts; *also called* graph.

Chart sheet A separate sheet in a workbook that contains only a chart, which is linked to the workbook data.

Check box A box that turns an option on when checked or off when unchecked.

Chip An integrated circuit embedded in semiconductor material.

Circuit A path along which an electric current travels.

Circuit board A rigid piece of insulating material with circuits on it that control specific functions.

Client A computer networked to and dependent on a server.

Client/server network A network with a server and computers dependent on the server.

Click To quickly press and release the left button on the pointing device; *also called* single-click.

Click and Type A feature that allows you to automatically apply the necessary paragraph formatting to a table, graphic, or text when you insert the item in a blank area of a document in Print Layout or Web Layout view.

Click and type pointer A pointer used to move the insertion point and automatically apply the paragraph formatting necessary to insert text at that location in the document.

Clip A media file, such as a graphic, photograph, sound, movie, or animation, that can be inserted into an Office document.

Clip art A collection of predesigned graphic images that can be inserted into documents, presentations, Web pages, spreadsheets, and other Office files to enhance their appearance.

Clip Organizer A library of art, pictures, sounds, video clips, and animations that all Office applications share.

Clipboard A temporary storage area on your computer's hard disk containing items that are cut or copied from any Office file and are available for pasting. *See also* Office Clipboard and System Clipboard.

Clock speed The pulse of the processor measured in megahertz or gigahertz.

CMOS *See* Complementary metal oxide semiconductor memory.

Collapse button A button that shrinks a portion of a dialog box to hide some settings.

Column break A break that forces text following the break to begin at the top of the next column.

Column heading Shaded boxes located at the top of each column in a worksheet that contain letters identifying each column, such as A, B, etc.

Column separator The thin line that separates the Access field names to the left or right.

Combo box A bound control used to display a list of possible entries for a field in which you can also type an entry from the keyboard. It is a "combination" of the list box and text box controls.

Command An instruction to perform a task.

Command bar Provides buttons for many options, such as printing Web pages, adding Favorites, and searching for information on the Internet.

Command button In a dialog box, a button that carries out or cancels an action. A command button usually has a label that describes its action, such as Cancel or Help. If the label is followed by an ellipsis (...), clicking the button displays another dialog box.

Compact disk *See* CD.

Compact disc read-only memory *See* CD-ROM.

Compact disc recordable *See* CD-R.

Compact disk rewritable *See* CD-RW.

Comparison operators In a calculation, symbols that compare values for the purpose of true/false results.

Compatible The capability of different programs to work together and exchange data.

Complementary metal oxide semiconductor (CMOS) memory A chip installed on the motherboard powered by a battery whose content changes every time you add or remove hardware on your computer system and that is activated during the boot process so it can identify where essential software is stored; *also called* semipermanent memory.

Compress To reduce the size of a file so that it takes up less storage space on a disk.

Computer An electronic device that accepts input, processes data, displays output, and stores data for retrieval later.

Computer network The hardware and software that makes it possible for two or more computers to share information and resources.

Computer system A computer, its peripheral devices, and software.

Computer window The window that shows the drives on your computer and as well as other installed hardware components.

Conditional format A type of cell formatting that changes based on the cell's value or the outcome of a formula.

Configuration *See* Architecture.

Contacts In Microsoft Outlook, enables you to manage all your business and personal contact information.

Content control An interactive object that is embedded in a document you create from a template and which expedites your ability to customize the document with your own information.

Content placeholder In PowerPoint, a slide area that is used to enter text or objects such as clip art, charts, or pictures.

Contextual tab A tab on the Ribbon that appears when needed to complete a specific task; for example, if you select a chart in an Excel workbook or a PowerPoint slide, three contextual Chart Tool tabs (Design, Layout, and Format) appear.

Control Any element on a form or report such as a label, text box, line, or combo box. Controls can be bound, unbound, or calculated.

Control Source property A property of a bound control in a form or report that determines the field to which the control is connected.

Control Panel A set of Windows XP tools used to change computer settings such as desktop colors or mouse settings.

Controller card A card that plugs into a slot on the motherboard and connects to a port to provide an electrical connection to a peripheral device; *also called* expansion card *or* interface card.

Copy To place information onto the Clipboard in order to paste it in another location but also leave it in the original location.

Copy-and-paste operation The feature in document production software that allows you to duplicate selected words and objects somewhere else in the document.

Courtesy copy (CC) In e-mail, a way to send a message to a recipient who needs to be aware of the correspondence between the sender and the recipients, but is not the primary recipient of the message.

cps *See* Characters per second.

CPU *See* Microprocessor.

CPU cache *See* Cache memory.

Criteria Entries (rules and limiting conditions) that determine which records are displayed when finding or filtering records in a datasheet or form, or when building a query.

Criteria syntax Rules by which criteria need to be entered. For example, text criteria syntax requires that the criteria are surrounded by quotation marks (" "). Date criteria are surrounded by pound signs (#).

Crop To hide part of an object, such as clip art, using the Cropping tool or to delete a part of a picture.

CRT (cathode ray tube) monitor A monitor that uses gun-like devices to direct beams of electrons toward the screen to activate dots of color to form an image.

Current record The record that has the focus or is being edited.

Cut To remove information from a file and place it on the Clipboard, usually to be pasted into another location.

Cut and paste To move text or graphics using the Cut and Paste commands.

Cut-and-paste operation The feature in document production software that allow you to delete words and objects from one place in a document and place them somewhere else.

Data The words, numbers, figures, sounds, and graphics that describe people, events, things, and ideas.

Data bus The path between the microprocessor, RAM, and the peripherals along which communication travels.

Data communications The transmission of data from one computer to another or to a peripheral device via a channel using a protocol.

Data file A file created by a user, usually with software, such as a report that you write with a word processing program.

Data marker A graphical representation of a data point, such as a bar or column.

Data point An individual piece of data plotted in a chart.

Data series A column or row in a datasheet. Also, the selected range in a worksheet that Excel converts into a chart.

Data series marker A graphical representation of a data series, such as a bar or column.

Data type A required property for each field that defines the type of data that can be entered in each field. Valid data types include AutoNumber, Text, Number, Currency, Date/Time, OLE Object, and Memo.

Database A collection of information stored on one or more computers organized in a uniform format of records and fields.

Database designer The person responsible for building and maintaining tables, queries, forms, and reports.

Database management software Software you use to collect and manage data.

Datasheet A spreadsheet-like grid that displays fields as columns and records as rows.

Datasheet View A view that lists the records of the object in a datasheet. Tables, queries, and most form objects have a Datasheet View.

Date function A built-in Access function used to display the current date on a form or report; enter the Date function as Date().

Date Navigator A monthly calendar in the To-Do Bar that gives you an overview of the month and enables selection of a specific date to display.

Default Settings preset by the operating system or program.

Delete (Office) To permanently remove an item from a document. (Windows) To place a file or folder in the Recycle Bin, where you can either remove it from the disk permanently or restore it to its original location.

Deleted Items folder The folder that stores items when you delete or erase a message from any mail folder, rather than being immediately, permanently deleted; *also called* trash folder.

Design View A view in which the structure of the object can be manipulated. Every Access object has a Design View.

Desktop The graphical user interface (GUI) displayed on your screen after you start Windows that you use to interact with Windows and other software on your computer.

Desktop computer A personal computer designed to sit compactly on a desk.

Destination file In integration, the file that receives copied information. A Word file that contains an Excel spreadsheet or chart is a destination file.

Details Pane A pane located at the bottom of a window that displays information about the selected disk, drive, folder, or file.

Device A hardware component in your computer system.

Device driver System software that handles the transmission protocol between a computer and its peripheral devices; *also called* driver.

Dialog box A window that opens when a program needs more information to carry out a command.

Dialog box launcher An icon available in many groups on the Ribbon that you can click to open a dialog box or task pane, offering an alternative way to choose commands. *Also called* Launcher.

Digital signal A stop-start signal that your computer outputs.

Digital signature A way to authenticate a computer user's files using computer cryptography. A digital signature is not visible in a file.

Digital subscriber line *See* DSL.

Diskette *See* Floppy disk.

Distribute To evenly divide the space horizontally or vertically between objects relative to each other or the slide edges.

Distribution list A collection of contacts to whom you want to send the same messages; makes it possible for you to send a message to the same group without having to select each contact in the group.

DNS server A computer responsible for directing Internet traffic.

Document An electronic file that you create using a program such as Word or WordPad.

Document Inspector An Office feature that examines a document for hidden data or personal information.

Document production software Software, such as word processing software, desktop publishing software, e-mail editors, and Web authoring software, that assists you in writing and formatting documents, including changing the font and checking the spelling.

Document properties Details about a file, such as author name or the date the file was created, that are used to describe, organize, and search for files.

Document window The portion of a program window that displays all or part of an open document.

Documents folder The folder on your hard drive used to store most of the files you create or receive from others.

Dot matrix printer A printer that transfers ink to paper by striking a ribbon with pins.

Dot pitch (dp) The distance between pixels on a monitor.

Double-click To press and release the left mouse button twice quickly.

dp *See* Dot pitch.

Draft view A view that shows a document without margins, headers and footers, or graphics.

Drag To point to an object, press and hold the left button on the pointing device, move the object to a new location, and then release the left button.

Drag and drop *See* Drag.

Drive A physical location on your computer where you can store files.

Drive name A name for a drive that consists of a letter followed by a colon, such as C: for the hard disk drive.

Driver *See* Device driver.

Drop cap A large dropped initial capital letter that is often used to set off the first paragraph of an article.

Drop-down list button A button that opens a list with one or more options from which you can choose.

DSL (digital subscriber line) A high-speed connection over phone lines.

Dual-core processor A CPU that has two processors on the chip.

DVD An optical storage device that can store up to 15.9 GB of data; was originally an acronym for *digital video disc* and later *digital versatile disc*.

Edit To change the content or format of an existing file.

Edit mode The mode in which Access assumes you are trying to edit a particular field, so keystrokes such as [Ctrl][End], [Ctrl][Home], [↑], and [↓] move the insertion point within the field.

Edit record symbol A pencil-like symbol that appears in the record selector box to the left of the record that is currently being edited in either a datasheet or a form.

Electronic mail (e-mail) The technology that makes it possible for you to send and receive messages through the Internet.

Electronic spreadsheet A computer program that performs calculations and presents numeric data.

E-mail *See* Electronic mail.

E-mail message The message sent using e-mail technology.

E-mail software Enables you to send and receive e-mail messages over a network, within an intranet, and through the Internet.

Embed To place an object such as a text selection, value, or picture created in a source file into a destination file. An embedded object is edited by double-clicking it in the destination file and then using the tools of the source file to make changes. These changes appear only in the embedded object in the destination file, not in the source file.

Embedded chart A chart displayed as an object in a worksheet.

Embedded object An object that is created in one application and inserted to another. Embedded objects remain connected to the original program file in which they were created for easy editing.

Endnote Text that provides additional information or acknowledges sources for text in a document and that appears at the end of a document.

Ergonomic Designed to fit the natural placement of the body to reduce the risk of repetitive-motion injuries.

Ethernet port A port used to connect computers in a LAN or sometimes directly to the Internet; it allows for high-speed data transmission.

Event In the Calendar in Outlook, an activity that lasts 24 hours or longer.

Executable file A file that contains the instructions that tell a computer how to perform a specific task, such as the files that are used during the boot process.

Expand button A button that extends a dialog box to display additional settings.

Expansion card *See* Controller card.

Expansion slot An electrical connector on the motherboard into which a card is plugged; *also called* slot.

Exploding pie slice A slice of a pie chart that has been pulled away from the whole pie, in order to add emphasis.

Expression A combination of values, functions, and operators that calculates to a single value. Access expressions start with an equal sign and are placed in a text box in either Form Design View or Report Design View.

Favorites Center Stores and organizes the links to the Web pages that you want to revisit often. To open the Favorites Center, you click the Favorites Center button on the Command bar.

Field (Word) A code that serves as a placeholder for data that changes in a document, such as a page number. (Access) A piece of information in a record.

Field list A list of the available fields in the table or query that the field list represents.

Field name The name given to each field in a table.

Field selector The button to the left of a field in Table Design View that indicates which field is currently selected. Also the thin gray bar above each field in the query grid.

File An electronic collection of stored data, such as text, a picture, video, or music, that has a unique name, distinguishing it from other files. Word creates word processing files; Excel creates spreadsheet files; Access creates database files; and PowerPoint creates presentation files.

File extension Additional characters assigned by a program added to the end of a filename to identify the type of file.

File hierarchy A logical structure for folders and files that mimics how you would organize files and folders in a filing cabinet.

File management The process of organizing and keeping track of files and folders.

Filename A unique, descriptive name for a file that identifies the file's content. A filename can be no more than 255 characters, including spaces, and can include letters, numbers, and certain symbols.

Filter Used to create a subset of a list, a filter lets you search for only specific information—for example, in Outlook Contacts, filter only for those contacts that live in New Jersey, or in an Access database or an Excel table, filter only for customers whose sales total over a certain amount.

Filter By Form A way to filter data that allows two or more criteria to be specified at the same time.

Filter By Selection A way to filter records for an exact match.

Firewall Hardware or software that prevents other computers on the Internet from accessing a computer or prevents a program on a computer from accessing the Internet.

First line indent A type of indent in which the first line of a paragraph is indented more than the subsequent lines.

Flash drive *See* USB flash storage device.

Flash memory Memory that is similar to ROM except that it can be written to more than once.

Flash memory card A small, portable card encased in hard plastic to which data can be written and rewritten.

Flash storage device A removable storage device that is plugged into a USB port to which data can be written and rewritten; know by other names, including USB drive, jump drive, thumb drive, and flash drive.

Flat panel monitor A lightweight monitor that takes up very little room on the desktop and uses LCD technology to create the image on the screen.

Floating graphic A graphic to which text wrapping has been applied, making the graphic independent of text and able to be moved anywhere on a page.

Floppy disk A flat circle of magnetic oxide-coated plastic enclosed in a hard plastic case that can store 1.44 MB of data; *also called* diskette *or* 3½" disk.

Focus The property that indicates which field would be edited if you were to start typing.

Folder A container for a group of related files. A folder may contain subfolders for organizing files into smaller groups.

Folder name A unique, descriptive name for a folder that identifies what you store in that folder.

Font The typeface or design of a set of characters (letters, numerals, symbols, and punctuation marks), such as Times New Roman.

Font effect Font formatting that applies a special effect to text, such as a shadow, an outline, small caps, or superscript.

Font size The size of text characters, measured in units called points (pts); a point is equal to 1/72 inch.

Footer Information, such as text, a page number, or a graphic, that appears at the bottom of every page in a document or a section.

Footnote Text that provides additional information or acknowledges sources for text in a document and that appears at the bottom of the page on which the note reference mark appears.

Foreign key field In a one-to-many relationship between two tables, the foreign key field is the field in the "many" table that links the table to the primary key field in the "one" table.

Form An Access object that provides an easy-to-use data entry screen that generally shows only one record at a time.

Form View The view of a form object that displays data from the underlying recordset and allows you to enter and update data.

Form Wizard An Access wizard that helps you create a form.

Format (n.) 1) The appearance of text and numbers, including color, font, attributes, borders, and shading. *See also* Number format. 2) The process of preparing a disk so it can store information. (v.) To enhance the appearance of a document by, for example, changing the font or font size or adding borders and shading to a document. Also refers to the process of preparing a disk so it can store information.

Format bar A toolbar in the WordPad window that displays buttons for formatting, or enhancing, the appearance of a document.

Format Painter A feature used to copy the format settings applied to the selected text to other text you want to format the same way.

Formatting marks Nonprinting characters that appear on screen to indicate the ends of paragraphs, tabs, and other formatting elements.

Formula A set of instructions used to perform one or more numeric calculations, such as adding, multiplying, or averaging, on values or cells.

Formula bar The area above the worksheet grid where you enter or edit data in the active cell.

Formula prefix An arithmetic symbol, such as the equal sign (=), used to start a formula.

Forwarding Sending an e-mail message you have received to someone else.

Full Screen Reading view A view that shows only the document text on screen, making it easier to read and annotate.

Function A built-in formula that provides a shortcut for a commonly used calculation, for example, SUM (for calculating a total) or COUNT (for counting items in a list).

Gadget A mini-program on the Windows Sidebar for performing an every day task, such as the Clock gadget for viewing the current time.

Gallery A collection of choices you can browse through to make a selection. Often available with Live Preview.

GB *See* Gigabyte.

GHz *See* Gigahertz.

Gigabyte (G or GB) 1,073,741,824 bytes, or about one billion bytes.

Gigahertz (GHz) One billion cycles per second.

Graph *See* Chart.

Graphic image *See* Image.

Graphical user interface (GUI) A computer environment in which the user manipulates graphics, icons, and dialog boxes to execute commands.

Graphics card The card installed on the motherboard that controls the signals the computer sends to the monitor; *also called* video display adapter *or* video card.

Graphics display A monitor that is capable of displaying graphics by dividing the screen into a matrix of pixels.

Graphics software Software that allows you to create illustrations, diagrams, graphs, and charts.

Gridlines Evenly spaced horizontal and/or vertical lines used in a worksheet or chart to make it easier to read.

Group 1) A collection of related commands on a tab on the Ribbon. 2) A combination of objects that has been changed into a single object so that when you move one of the objects, the others move with it.

Grouping To sort records in a particular order, plus provide a section before and after each group of records.

GUI *See* Graphical user interface.

Gutter Extra space left for a binding at the top, left, or inside margin of a document.

Hand-held computer A small computer designed to fit in the palm of your hand and that generally has fewer capabilities than personal computers.

Hanging indent A type of indent in which the second and subsequent lines of a paragraph are indented more than the first.

Hard copy A printed copy of computer output.

Hard disk A magnetic storage device that contains several magnetic oxide-covered metal platters that are usually sealed in a case inside the computer.

Hard page break *See* Manual page break.

Hardware The physical components of a computer.

Header Information, such as text, a page number, or a graphic, that appears at the top of every page in a document or a section.

Highlighting 1) Transparent color that can be applied to text to call attention to it. 2) When an icon is shaded differently, indicating it is selected. *See also* Select.

Home page The first Web page that opens every time you start Internet Explorer. Also applies to the main page that opens when you first go to a Web site.

Horizontal ruler A ruler that appears at the top of the document window in Print Layout, Draft, and Web Layout view.

Horizontal scroll bar *See* Scroll bar.

Hyperlink Text or a graphic that opens a file, Web page, or other item when clicked. Also known as a link.

I-beam pointer The pointer used to move the insertion point and select text.

Icon A small image on the desktop or in a window that represents a tool, resource, folder, or file you can open and use.

Image A nontextual piece of information such as a picture, piece of clip art, drawn object, or graph. Because images are graphical (and not numbers or letters), they are sometimes referred to as graphical images.

Inactive window An open window you are not currently using.

Inbox A mail folder that stores all incoming mail.

Indent The space between the edge of a line of text or a paragraph and the margin.

Indent marker A marker on the horizontal ruler that shows the indent settings for the active paragraph.

Infinity symbol The symbol that indicates the "many" side of a one-to-many relationship.

Information management software Software that keeps track of schedules, appointments, contacts, and "to-do" lists.

Infrared technology A wireless technology in which devices communicate with one another using infrared light waves; the devices must be positioned so that the infrared ports are pointed directly at one another.

Inkjet printer A printer that sprays ink onto paper and produces output whose quality is comparable to that of a laser printer.

Inline graphic A graphic that is part of a line of text.

Input The data or instructions you type into the computer.

Input and output (I/O) The flow of data from the microprocessor to memory to peripherals and back again.

Input device An instrument, such as a keyboard or a mouse, that you use to enter data and issue commands to the computer.

Insertion point A blinking vertical line that indicates where the next character will appear when text is entered in a Word document, an Excel cell or the formula bar, an Access record, or a text placeholder in PowerPoint.

Instant Search A Windows tool you use to quickly find a folder or file on your computer.

Integrate To incorporate a document and parts of a document created in one program into another program; for example, to incorporate an Excel chart into a PowerPoint slide, or an Access table into a Word document.

Integration The act of inserting and linking information among applications. *See also* Object Linking and Embedding.

Interface The look and feel of a program; for example, the appearance of commands and the way they are organized in the program window.

Interface card *See* Controller card.

Internet A network of connected computers and computer networks located around the world.

Intranet A computer network that connects computers in a local area only, such as computers in a company's office.

I/O *See* Input and output.

Is Not Null A criterion that finds all records in which any entry has been made in the field.

Is Null A criterion that finds all records in which no entry has been made in the field.

Italic Formatting applied to text to make the characters slant to the right.

Join line The line identifying which fields establish the relationship between two related tables.

Journal In Outlook, provides a trail of your activities within Microsoft Office by tracking all documents, spreadsheets, databases, presentations, or any Office file that you specify. When turned on, you can see a timeline of any calls, messages, appointments, or tasks.

Junk e-mail Unwanted mail that arrives from unsolicited sources. *Also called* spam.

Justify Alignment in which an item is flush with both the left and right margins.

K *See* Kilobyte.

KB *See* Kilobyte.

Keyboard The most frequently used input device; consists of three major parts: the main keyboard, the keypads, and the function keys.

Keyboard shortcut A combination of keys or a function key that can be pressed to perform a command (for example, [Ctrl][X] for Cut).

Keyword A descriptive word or phrase you enter to obtain a list of results that includes that word or phrase.

Kilobyte (KB or K) 1,024 bytes, or approximately one thousand bytes.

Labels Descriptive text or other information that identifies spreadsheet rows, columns, or chart data, but are not included in calculations.

LAN *See* Local area network.

Landscape orientation A print setting that positions a document so it spans the widest margins of the page, making the page wider than it is tall.

Laptop computer *See* Notebook computer.

Laser printer A printer that produces high-quality output quickly and efficiently by transferring a temporary laser image onto paper with toner.

Launch To open or start a program on your computer.

Launcher An icon available in many groups on the Ribbon that you can click to open a dialog box or task pane, offering an alternative way to choose commands. *Also called* dialog box launcher.

Layout view An Access view that lets you make some design changes to a form or report while you are browsing the data.

LCD (liquid crystal display) A display technology that creates images by manipulating light within a layer of liquid crystal.

Left-align Alignment in which the item is flush with the left margin.

Left function An Access function that returns a specified number of characters, starting with the left side of a value in a Text field.

Left indent A type of indent in which the left edge of a paragraph is moved in from the left margin.

Legend In a chart, an informative key that explains how information is represented by colors or patterns.

Line spacing The amount of space between lines of text.

Link (Office) A connection created between a source file and a destination file. When an object created in a source file is linked to a destination file, any changes made to the object in the source file also appear in the object contained in the destination file. (Windows) A shortcut for opening a Help topic or a Web site.

Linked object An object such as a text selection, value, or picture that is contained in a destination file and linked to a source file. When a change is made to the linked object in the source file, the change also occurs in the linked object in the destination file. *See also* Link.

Links bar A convenient place to store links to Web pages that you use often. Add a link to the Links bar by dragging the Internet Explorer icon that precedes the URL in the Address bar to the Links bar.

Liquid crystal display *See* LCD.

List box A box in a dialog box containing a list of items; to choose an item, click the list arrow, then click the desired item.

Live Preview A feature that lets you point to a choice in a gallery or palette and see the results in the document without actually clicking the choice.

Live view In Windows Vista, a file icon that displays the actual content in a file on the icon.

Live taskbar thumbnails A Windows Aero feature that displays a small image of the content within open, but not visible windows, including live content such as video.

Local area network (LAN) A network in which the computers and peripheral devices are located relatively close to each other, generally in the same building, and are usually connected with cables.

Lock To lock your user account, then display the Welcome screen.

Lock button A Start menu option that locks your computer.

Lock menu button A Start menu options that displays a list of shut-down options.

Log in To sign in with a user name and password before being able to use a computer.

Log Off To close all windows, programs, and documents, then display the Welcome screen.

Logical view The datasheet of a query is sometimes called a logical view of the data because it is not a copy of the data, but rather, a selected view of data from the underlying tables.

Macro An Access object that stores a collection of keystrokes or commands such as those for printing several reports in a row or providing a toolbar when a form opens.

Magnetic storage device A storage device that stores data as magnetized particles on mylar, a plastic, which is then coated on both sides with magnetic oxide.

Mainframe computer A computer used by larger business and government agencies that provides centralized storage, processing, and management for large amounts of data.

Malware A broad term that describes any program that is intended to cause harm or convey information to others without the owner's permission.

Manual page break A page break inserted to force the text following the break to begin at the top of the next page; *also called* hard page break.

Margin The blank area between the edge of the text and the edge of a page.

Masters In Powerpoint, one of three views that stores information about the presentation theme, fonts, placeholders, and other background objects. The three views are Slide Master view, Handout Master view, and Notes Master view.

Maximize To enlarge a window so it fills the entire screen. The Maximize button is usually located in the upper-right corner of a window.

MB *See* Megabyte.

Meeting In the Calendar in Outlook, an activity you invite people to or reserve resources for.

Megabyte (MB) 1,048,576 bytes, or about one million bytes.

Megahertz (MHz) One million cycles per second.

Memory A set of storage locations on the main circuit board that store instructions and data.

Memory capacity The amount of data that the device can handle at any given time; *also called* storage capacity.

Menu A list of related commands in a program (for example, the File menu).

Menu bar A bar near the top of a program window that provides access to most of a program's features through categories of related commands.

Message body In an e-mail message, where you write the text of your message.

Message header The area that contains the basic information about an e-mail message, including the sender's name and e-mail address, the names and e-mail addresses of recipients and CC recipients, a date and time stamp, and the subject of the message.

Metadata Another name for document properties that includes the author name, the document subject, the document title, and other personal information.

MHz *See* Megahertz.

Microprocessor A silicon chip, located on the motherboard, that is responsible for executing instructions to process data; *also called* processor *or* central processing unit (CPU).

Microsoft Graph A program that creates a chart to graphically depict numerical information when you don't have access to Microsoft Excel.

Microsoft Office Word Help button A button used to access the Word Help system.

Microsoft Windows Vista An operating system.

MIDI (musical instrument digital interface) card A sound card used to record and play back musical data.

Mini toolbar A toolbar that appears faintly above text when you first select it and includes the most commonly used text and paragraph formatting commands.

Minimized window A window that shrinks to a button on the taskbar.

Mirror margins Margins used in documents with facing pages, where the inside and outside margins are mirror images of each other.

Mixed reference Cell reference that combines elements of both absolute and relative referencing.

Mode indicator An area in the lower-left corner of the status bar that informs you of a program's status. For example, when you are entering or changing the contents of a cell, the word 'Edit' appears.

Modem Stands for *mo*dulator-*dem*odulator; a device that converts the digital signals from your computer into analog signals that can traverse ordinary phone lines, and then converts analog signals back into digital signals at the receiving computer.

Module An Access object that stores Visual Basic programming code that extends the functions of automated Access processes.

Monitor The TV-like peripheral device that displays the output from the computer.

Motherboard The main circuit board of the computer on which processing tasks occur.

Mouse A pointing device that has a rolling ball on its underside and two or more buttons for clicking commands; you control the movement of the pointer by moving the entire mouse around on your desk.

Mouse pointer The typically arrow-shaped object on the screen that follows the movement of the mouse. The shape of the mouse pointer changes depending on the program and the task being executed. *See also* Mouse.

Move To change the location of a file by physically placing it in another location.

MP3 player A hand-held computer that is used primarily to play and store music, but that can also be used to watch digital movies and television shows.

Multi-tasking Working with more than one window or program at a time.

Multilevel list A list with an hierarchical structure; an outline.

Multimedia authoring software Software that allows you to record digital sound files, video files, and animations that can be included in presentations and other documents.

Musical instrument digital interface card *See* MIDI card.

Name box Leftmost area of the formula bar that shows the cell reference or name of the active cell.

Named range A range of cells with a meaningful name such as "July Sales" instead of simply the range coordinates such as "C7:G7"; used to make it easier to reference data in a worksheet.

Navigate To move around in a worksheet; for example, you can use the arrow keys on the keyboard to navigate from cell to cell, or press [Page Up] or [Page Down] to move a screen at a time.

Navigation buttons Buttons in the lower-left corner of a datasheet or form that allow you to quickly navigate between the records in the underlying object as well as add a new record.

Navigation mode A mode in which Access assumes that you are trying to move between the fields and records of the datasheet (rather than edit a specific field's contents), so keystrokes such as [Ctrl][Home] and [Ctrl][End] move you to the first and last field of the datasheet.

Navigation Pane (Access) A pane in the Access program window that provides a way to move between objects (tables, queries, forms, reports, macros, and modules) in the database. (Outlook) In Normal view, it is typically on the left side of the screen, showing you the folder list in addition to the navigation shortcuts. (Windows) A pane on the left side of a window that contains links to your personal folders, including the Documents, Pictures, and Music folders.

Negative indent A type of indent in which the left edge of a paragraph is moved to the left of the left margin; *also called* outdent.

Network Two or more computers that share data and resources and which are connected to each other and to peripheral devices.

Network interface card (NIC) The card in a computer on a network that creates a communications channel between the computer and the network.

Network software Software that establishes the communications protocols that will be observed on the network and controls the "traffic flow" as data travels throughout the network.

NIC *See* Network interface card.

Node Any device connected to a network.

Nonvolatile memory *See* Read-only memory.

Normal view (PowerPoint) A presentation view that divides the presentation window into three sections: Slides or Outline tab, Slide pane, and Notes pane. (Excel) Default worksheet view that shows the worksheet without features such as headers and footers; ideal for creating and editing a worksheet, but may not be detailed enough when formatting a document.

Notebook computer A small, lightweight computer designed for portability; *also called* laptop computer.

Notes In Outlook, the electronic version of the sticky notes or Post-It™ notes you buy at your local stationery store; a convenient way to quickly jot down a reminder or an idea.

Notes Page view In PowerPoint, a presentation view that displays a reduced image of the current slide above a large text box where you can type notes.

Notes pane In PowerPoint, the area in Normal view that shows speaker notes for the current slide; also in Notes Page view, the area below the slide image that contains speaker notes.

Notification area An area on the right side of the taskbar that displays the current time as well as icons for open programs, connecting to the Internet, and checking problems identified by Windows Vista.

Number format A format applied to values to express numeric concepts, such as currency, date, and percentage.

Object An item you place or draw in an Office document that can be modified. Objects include drawn lines and shapes, text, clip art, imported pictures, and charts.

Object Linking and Embedding (OLE) The term used to refer to the technology Microsoft uses to allow the integration of data between programs. Linking creates "live" connection between an object in a source file and a linked version in a destination file; embedding places an unconnected copy in the destination file.

Office button An element of Office program windows that provides access to commands for creating, opening, saving, printing, and sharing documents, and to options for personalizing the programs.

Office Clipboard A temporary storage area shared by all Office programs that can be used to cut, copy and paste multiple items within and between programs. The Office Clipboard can hold up to 24 items collected from any Office program. *See also* System Clipboard.

OLE *See* Object linking and embedding.

OLE object In Access, a field data type that stores pointers that tie files, such as pictures, sound clips, or spreadsheets, created in other programs to a record.

One-to-many line The line that appears in the Relationships window and shows which field is duplicated between two tables to serve as the linking field. The one-to-many line displays a "1" next to the field that serves as the "one" side of the relationship and displays an infinity symbol next to the field that serves as the "many" side of the relationship when referential integrity is specified for the relationship. Also called the one-to-many join line.

One-to-many relationship The relationship between two tables in an Access database in which a common field links the tables together. The linking field is called the primary key field in the "one" table of the relationship and the foreign key field in the "many" table of the relationship.

Online collaboration The ability to incorporate feedback or share information across the Internet or a company network or intranet.

Operating environment An operating system that provides a graphical user interface, such as Microsoft Windows and the MAC OS.

Operating system A computer program that controls the basic operation of your computer and the programs you run on it. Windows Vista and Windows XP are examples of operating systems. The operating system allocates system resources, manages storage space, maintains security, detects equipment failure, and controls basic input and output.

Optical storage device A polycarbonate disk coated with a reflective metal on which data is recorded using laser technology as a trail of tiny pits or dark spots in the surface of the disk; the data that these pits or spots represent can then be "read" with a beam of laser light.

Option button A small circle in a dialog box that you click to select an option.

OR criteria In Access, criteria placed on different rows of the query design grid. A record will appear in the resulting datasheet if it is true for any single row.

Orphan The first line of a paragraph when it appears alone at the bottom of a page.

Orphan record A record in the "many" table of a one-to-many relationship that doesn't have a matching entry in the linking field of the "one" table.

Outbox A temporary storage folder for e-mail messages that have not yet been sent.

Outdent *See* Negative indent.

Outline tab In Powerpoint, the section in Normal view that displays your presentation text in the form of an outline, without graphics.

Outline view In Word, view that shows the headings of a document organized as an outline.

Outlook Today Shows your day at a glance, like an electronic version of a daily planner book. When it is open, you can see what is happening in the Calendar, Tasks, and Messages for the day.

Output The result of the computer processing input.

Output device A device, such as a monitor or printer, that displays output.

Page Break Preview A worksheet view that shows page break indicators that you can drag to include more or less information on each page in a worksheet.

Page Layout View Provides an accurate view of how a worksheet will look when printed, including headers and footers.

Page orientation Printing or viewing a page of data in either a portrait (8.5 inches wide by 11 inches tall) or landscape (11 inches wide by 8.5 inches tall) direction.

Pages per minute (ppm) The unit of measurement for the speed of laser and inkjet printers.

PAN *See* Personal area network.

Paragraph spacing The amount of space between paragraphs.

Parallel port A port that transmits data eight bits at a time.

Paste To insert items stored on the Clipboard into a document.

Paste Options button A button that appears next to a pasted object; it allows you to paste only specific elements of the copied selection, such as the formatting or values.

PDA (personal digital assistant) A hand-held computer that is generally used to maintain an electronic appointment book, address book, calculator, and notepad.

Peer-to-peer network A network in which all the computers essentially are equal, and programs and data are distributed among them.

Peripheral device The components of a computer that accomplish its input, output, and storage functions.

Permanent memory *See* Read-only memory.

Personal account In Outlook, identifies you as a user with information such as your e-mail address and password, the type of Internet service provider (ISP) you are using, and the incoming and outgoing mail server address for your ISP.

Personal area network (PAN) A network in which two or more devices communicate directly with each other.

Personal computer A computer typically used by a single user in the home or office for general computing tasks such as word processing, working with photographs or graphics, e-mail, and Internet access.

Personal digital assistant *See* PDA.

Pharm To break into a DNS server and redirect any attempts to access a particular Web site to a spoofed site.

Phish To send e-mails to customers or potential customers of a legitimate Web site asking them to click a link in the e-mail and then verify their personal information, which may then be used for illegal purposes; the link leads to a spoofed site.

Photo editing software Software that allows you to manipulate digital photos.

Picture A digital photograph, or a piece of line art or clip art that is created in another program and is inserted into an Office program.

Pixel (picture element) One of the small dots in a matrix into which a graphics display is divided.

Placeholder In PowerPoint, a dashed line box where you place text or objects.

Plot area In a chart, the area inside the horizontal and vertical axes.

Point 1) A unit of measure used for fonts and row height. One inch equals 72 points, or a point is equal to 1/72nd of an inch. 2) To position the mouse pointer in a particular location on your screen.

Pointer A small arrow or other symbol on the screen controlled by a pointing device.

Pointing device A device, such as a mouse or trackball, that controls the pointer.

Pointing stick A small, eraser-like device embedded among the typing keys on a notebook computer that you push up, left, right, or down to move the pointer; buttons for clicking commands are located in front of the spacebar.

Pop-up A window that opens on your screen as you visit Web sites, generally to advertise products you may or may not want.

Port The interface between a cable and a controller card.

Portable computer card (PC card) A credit card–sized card that plugs directly into a slot in a notebook computer and that can contain additional RAM, a fax modem, or a hard disk drive (similar to a flash storage device).

Portrait orientation A print setting that positions the document on the page so the page is taller than it is wide.

Power button A Start menu option that puts your computer to sleep (your computer appears off and uses very little power).

PowerPoint Viewer A special application designed to run a PowerPoint slide show on any compatible computer that does not have PowerPoint installed.

Ppm *See* Pages per minute.

Presentation software A software program used to organize and present information.

Preview Pane A pane on the right side of a window that shows the actual contents of a selected file without opening a program. Preview may not work for some types of files.

Preview Prior to printing, to see onscreen exactly how the printed document will look.

Primary key field A field that contains unique information for each record. A primary key field cannot contain a null entry.

Print area The dotted line indicating the area to be printed.

Print Layout view A view that shows a document as it will look on a printed page.

Print Preview A view that displays how a document, spreadsheet, database object, or presentation will appear when printed.

Printer The peripheral computer component that produces a hard copy of the text or graphics processed by the computer.

Process To modify data in a computer.

Processor *See* Microprocessor.

Program Task-oriented software that you use for a particular kind of work, such as word processing or database management. Microsoft Access, Microsoft Excel, and Microsoft Word are all programs.

Program button A button on the taskbar that represents an open program or window.

Program tab A single tab on the Ribbon specific to a particular view, such as Print Preview.

Programming language Software used to write computer instructions.

Property (Windows) A characteristic of a specific computer element (such as the mouse, keyboard, or desktop display) that you can customize. (Access) A characteristic that further defines a field (if field properties), control (if control properties), section (if section properties), or object (if object properties).

Property sheet A window that displays an exhaustive list of properties for the chosen control, section, or object within the Form Design View or Report Design View.

Protocol The set of rules that establishes the orderly transfer of data between the sender and the receiver in data communications.

Query An Access object that provides a spreadsheet-like view of the data, similar to that in tables. It may provide the user with a subset of fields and/or records from one or more tables. Queries are created when the user has a "question" about the data in the database.

Query Design grid The bottom pane of the Query Design View window in which you specify the fields, sort order, and limiting criteria for the query.

Query Design View The window in which you develop queries by specifying the fields, sort order, and limiting criteria that determine which fields and records are displayed in the resulting datasheet.

Quick Access toolbar A small, customizable toolbar at the top of an Office program window that contains buttons for commonly used commands such as Save and Undo.

Quick Launch toolbar A toolbar located next to the Start button on the taskbar that contains buttons to start programs and to show the desktop.

Quick Part A reusable piece of content that can be inserted into a document, including a field, document property, preformatted building block.

Quick Style Determines how fonts, colors, and effects of the theme are combined and which color, font, and effect is dominant. A Quick Style can be applied to Smart Art, shapes, or text.

RAM *See* Random access memory.

RAM cache *See* Cache memory.

Random access memory (RAM) Chips on cards plugged into the motherboard that temporarily hold programs and data while the computer is turned on; *also called* volatile memory *or* temporary memory.

Range A selection of two or more cells, such as B5:B14.

Read-only An object property that indicates whether the object can read and display data, but cannot be used to change (write to) data.

Read-only memory (ROM) A chip on the motherboard that is prerecorded with and permanently stores the set of instructions that the computer uses when you turn it on; *also called* nonvolatile memory or permanent memory.

Really Simple Syndication (RSS) A format for feeding or syndicating news or any content from Web sites to your computer.

Receiver The computer or peripheral at the message's destination in data communications.

Record A collection of data items in a database.

Record Source property In a form or report, the property that determines which table or query object contains the fields and records that the form or report will display. It is the most important property of the form or report object. A bound control on a form or report has Control Source property. In this case, the Control Source property identifies the field to which the control is bound.

Recycle Bin A storage area on your computer's hard disk for deleted files, which remain in the Recycle Bin until you empty it. An icon on the desktop provides quick access to the Recycle Bin.

Reference operators Mathematical calculations which enable you to use ranges in calculations.

Referential integrity A set of Access rules that govern data entry and help ensure data accuracy.

Relational database software Software such as Access that is used to manage data organized in a relational database.

Relative cell references In a formula, a type of cell addressing that automatically changes column or row references when cells are copied or moved, to reflect the new location; default type of referencing used in Excel worksheets.

Removable storage Storage media that you can easily transfer from one computer to another, such as DVDs, CDs, or flash drives.

Report An Access object that creates a professional printout of data that may contain such enhancements as headers, footers, and calculations on groups of records.

Report View An Access view that maximizes the amount of data you can see on the screen.

Report Wizard An Access wizard that helps you create a report.

Resizing button A button that you use to adjust the size of a window, such as Maximize, Restore Down, and Minimize.

Resolution The number of pixels that a monitor displays.

Restart To shut down your computer, then start it again.

Ribbon A bar near the top of an Office program window that contains the names of tabs, which contain the most frequently-used Office program commands.

Right-alignment Alignment in which an item is flush with the right margin.

Right-click To press and release the right mouse button once.

Right indent A type of indent in which the right edge of a paragraph is moved in from the right margin.

ROM *See* Read-only memory.

Rotate handle A green circular handle at the top of a selected object that you can drag to rotate the object.

Router A device that controls traffic between network components and usually has a built-in firewall.

Row heading The gray box containing the row number to the left of the row in a worksheet.

Row selector The small square to the left of a field in Table Design View or the Tab Order dialog box. Called the record selector in Datasheet View and Form View.

Rule In Outlook, enables you to organize your mail by setting parameters for incoming mail. For example, you can specify that all mail from a certain person goes into the folder for a specific project.

Ruler (Access) A vertical or horizontal guide that both appear in Form and Report Design View to help you position controls. (Word, WordPad) A horizontal guide at the top of a document window that marks a document's width in 1/8ths of an inch.

Sans serif font A font (such as Calibri) whose characters do not include serifs, which are small strokes at the ends of letters.

Save To store a file permanently on a disk or to overwrite the copy of a file that is stored on a disk with the changes made to the file.

Save As A command used to save a file for the first time or to create a new file with a different filename, leaving the original file intact.

Scale To change the size of a graphic to a specific percentage of its original size.

Scanner A device that transfers the content on a piece of paper into memory; you place a piece of paper on the glass, a beam of light moves across the glass, similar to a photocopier, and stores the image or words on the piece of paper as digital information.

Screen capture A virtual snapshot of your screen, as if you took a picture of it with a camera, which you can paste into a document.

Screen size The diagonal measurement from one corner of the screen to the other.

ScreenTip A label that appears on the screen when you position the mouse pointer over a button, to identify and provide information about a button or a feature.

Scroll To use the scroll bars or the arrow keys to display different parts of a document in the document window.

Scroll arrow The arrow at the end of a scroll bar that is clicked to scroll a document one line at a time, or to scroll a document left and right in the document window.

Scroll bar A bar on the right edge (vertical scroll bar) and bottom edge (horizontal scroll bar) of a document window that allow you to move around in a document that is too large to fit on the screen at once.

Scroll arrow button A button at each end of a scroll bar for adjusting your view in small increments in that direction.

Scroll box A rectangle located in the vertical and horizontal scroll bars that indicates your relative position in a file and that you can drag to view other parts of the file or window. *See also* Scroll bar.

Scroll wheel A wheel on a mouse that you roll to scroll the page on the screen.

SCSI (small computer system interface) port A port that provides an interface for one or more peripheral devices at the same port.

SDRAM *See* Synchronous dynamic RAM.

Search box A screen area used along with the Address bar to help you search for Web sites about a particular topic. Enter a keyword or words in the Search box, then click the Search button to activate the search.

Search criteria One or more pieces of information that helps Windows identify the program, folder, or file you want to locate.

Search engine A special Web site that searches the Internet for Web sites based on words or phrases that you enter.

Section (Access) A location of a form or report that contains controls. The section in which a control is placed determines where and how often the control prints. (Word) A portion of a document that is separated from the rest of the document by section breaks.

Section break A formatting mark inserted to divide a document into sections.

Security The steps a computer owner takes to prevent unauthorized use of or damage to the computer.

Select To highlight an item in order to perform some action on it. *See also* Highlighting.

Selection box A dashed border that appears around a text object or placeholder, indicating that it is ready to accept text.

Semipermanent memory *See* Complementary metal oxide semiconductor memory.

Sender The computer that originates the message in data communications.

Sent Items folder When you send an e-mail message, a copy of the message is stored in this folder to help you track the messages that you send out.

Serial port A port that transmits data one bit at a time.

Series in Columns The information in the columns of a worksheet that are on the Value axis; the row labels are on the Category axis.

Series in Rows The information in the rows of a worksheet that are on the Value axis; the column labels are on the Category axis.

Serif font A font (such as Times New Roman) whose characters include serifs, which are small strokes at the ends of letters.

Server A computer on a network that acts as the central storage location for programs and provides mass storage for most of the data used on the network.

Service provider The organization or company that provides e-mail or Internet access.

Shading A background color or pattern that can be applied to text, tables, or graphics.

Sheet tab Identifies sheets in a workbook and lets you switch between sheets; located below the worksheet grid.

Shortcut A link that you can place in any location that gives you quick access to a file, folder, or program located on your hard disk or network.

Shortcut key *See* Keyboard shortcut.

Shortcut menu A menu that appears when you right-click an item.

Shut down The action you perform when you have finished working with your computer; after you shut down it is safe to turn off your computer.

Sidebar A Windows Vista desktop component that displays gadgets. *See also* Gadget.

Single-click *See* Click.

Single-core processor A CPU with one processor on the chip.

Sizing handles Small squares or dots at each corner of a selected Access control, Excel chart, a graphic, or other object in an Office program. Dragging a sizing handle resizes the object. *Also called* handles.

Sleep To save your work, turn off the monitor, then reduce power consumption to all the hardware components in your computer so it appears off; press any key to use your computer again.

Slide layout This determines how all of the elements on a slide are arranged, including text and content placeholders.

Slide pane The section of Normal view that contains the current slide.

Slide Show view A view that shows a presentation as an electronic slide show; each slide fills the screen.

Slide Sorter view A view that displays a thumbnail of all slides in the order in which they appear in your presentation; used to rearrange slides and slide transitions.

Slides tab The section in Normal View that displays the slides of your presentation as small thumbnails.

Slide timing The amount of time a slide is visible on the screen during a slide show.

Slide transition The special effect that moves one slide off the screen and the next slide on the screen during a slide show. Each slide can have its own transition effect.

Slider An item in a dialog box that you drag to set the degree to which an option is in effect.

Slot *See* Expansion slot.

Small computer system interface port *See* SCSI port.

SmartArt A professional quality graphic diagram supplied with Office 2007 programs that illustrates text using the following structures: List Process, Cycle, Hierarchy, Relationship, Matrix, and Pyramid.

SmartArt Style A pre-set combination of formatting options that follows the design theme that you can apply to a SmartArt graphic.

Soft page break *See* Automatic page break.

Software The intangible components of a computer system, particularly the programs that the computer needs to perform a specific task.

Source file In integration, the file from which information is copied or used. An Excel file inserted into a Word report is a source file. *See also* Destination file.

Spam Unwanted mail that arrives from unsolicited sources. Also called junk e-mail.

Spamming The sending of identical or near-identical unsolicited messages to a large number of recipients. Many e-mail programs have filters that identify this mail and place it in a special folder.

Specifications The technical details about a hardware component.

Spell check The feature in document production software that helps you avoid typographical and grammatical errors.

Spin box A box with two arrows and a text box; allows you to scroll in numerical increments or type a number.

Spoof To create a Web site that looks exactly like another legitimate site on the Web but steals the information people enter.

Spreadsheet software Software that helps you analyze numerical data.

Spyware Software that track a computer user's Internet usage and sends this data back to the company or person that created it, usually without the computer user's permission or knowledge.

SQL (Structured Query Language) A language that provides a standardized way to request information from a relational database system.

Standalone computer A personal computer that is not connected to a network.

Start button A button on the taskbar that you use to start programs, find and open files, access Windows Help and Support Center, and more.

Status bar (Excel) The bar at the bottom of the Excel window that provides information about various keys, commands, and processes.

Status bar (IE7) Located at the bottom of the IE7 window, it displays information about your connection progress whenever you open a new Web page or connect to another Web site, and displays the Web addresses of any links on the Web page when you move your mouse pointer over them.

Status bar (PowerPoint) The bar at the bottom of the PowerPoint window that contains messages about what you are doing and seeing in PowerPoint, such as the current slide number or the current theme.

Status bar (Windows) A horizontal bar at the bottom of a window that displays simple Help information and tips.

Status bar (Word) The bar at the bottom of the Word program window that shows information about the document, including the current page number, the total number of pages in a document, the document word count, and the on/off status of spelling and grammar checking, and contains the view buttons, the Zoom level button and the Zoom slider.

Status indicator Located towards the right side of the status bar, it is animated while a new Web page loads.

Storage capacity *See* Memory capacity.

Store-and-forward technology Technology used in electronic mail wherein messages are stored on a service provider's computer until a recipient logs on to a computer and requests his or her messages. At that time, the messages are forwarded to the recipient's computer.

Strong password A string of at least eight characters of upper and lowercase letters and numbers.

Style A named collection of character and paragraph formats that are stored together and can be applied to text to format it quickly.

Subfolder A folder within another folder for organizing sets of related files into smaller groups.

Subscript A font effect in which text is formatted in a smaller font size and placed below the line of text.

Subtitle text placeholder A box on a PowerPoint title slide reserved for subpoint text.

Suite A group of programs that are bundled together and share a similar interface, making it easy to transfer skills and program content among them.

Sum function A mathematical function that totals values in a field.

Supercomputer The largest and fastest type of computer used by large corporations and government agencies for processing a tremendous volume of data.

Superscript A font effect in which text is formatted in a smaller font size and placed above the line of text.

Switch User To lock your user account and display the Welcome screen so another user can log on.

Symbols Special characters that can be inserted into a document using the Symbol command.

Synchronous dynamic RAM (SDRAM) RAM that is synchronized with the CPU to allow faster access to its contents.

System Clipboard A clipboard that stores only the last item cut or copied from a document. *See also* Clipboard and Office Clipboard.

System resource Any part of the computer system, including memory, storage devices, and the microprocessor, that can be used by a computer program.

System software A collection of programs and data that helps the computer carry out its basic operating tasks.

Tab 1) In Office 2007 programs, a part of the Ribbon that includes groups of buttons for related commands. 2) A place in a dialog box where related commands and options are organized.

Tab leader A line that appears in front of tabbed text.

Tab order The sequence in which the controls on an Access form receive the focus when the user presses [Tab] or [Enter] in Form view.

Tab stop (Word) A location on the horizontal ruler that indicates where to align text. (Access) This refers to whether you can tab into a control when entering or editing data; in other words, whether the control can receive the focus.

Tabbed browsing Allows you to open more than one Web page at a time in a browser window. Click the tab for a Web page to display that Web page in front.

Table (Access) A collection of records for a single subject, such as all of the customer records. (Word, Excel, and PowerPoint) A grid made up of rows and columns of cells that you can fill with text and graphics.

Table style A named set of table format settings that can be applied to a table to format it all at once.

Tablet PC A computer designed for portability that includes the capability of recognizing ordinary handwriting on the screen.

Tabs Identify the current Web page or pages open in the browser; click a tab to view the Web page.

Tag A word or phrase assigned to a file that reminds you of a file's content

Tape A magnetic storage media that provides inexpensive archival storage for large quantities of data.

Task pane A separate section of a window that contains sets of menus, lists, options, and hyperlinks that are used to customize objects.

Taskbar A strip at the bottom of the screen that contains the Start button, Quick Launch toolbar, and clock that shows buttons for the programs that are running.

Tasks In Outlook, the electronic to-do list, whereby each task has a subject, a start and end date, priority, and a description.

TB *See* Terabyte.

Telecommunications The transmission of data over a comparatively long distance using a phone line.

Template An Office file whose content and/or formatting serves as the basis for new files. Each Office application has a special template file extension: .xltx (Excel), .dotx (Word), or .potx (PowerPoint). An Access template must be named Blank.accdb.

Temporary memory *See* Random access memory.

Terabyte (TB) 1,024 GB, or approximately one trillion bytes.

Terminal A computer connected to a network that uses mainframes as a server; it has a keyboard for input and a monitor for output, but processes little or no data on its own.

Terminal emulator A personal computer, workstation, or server that uses special software to imitate a terminal so that it can communicate with a mainframe or supercomputer for complex data processing.

Text annotations Labels added to a chart to draw attention to a particular area.

Text box A rectangular area in a dialog box in which you type text.

Text concatenation operators Mathematical calculations that join strings of text in different cells.

Text label A text box you create using the Text Box button, where the text does not automatically wrap inside the box. Text box text does not appear in the Outline tab.

Text placeholder A box with a dotted border and text that you replace with your own text.

Theme A predefined set of colors, fonts, and line and fill effects that can easily be applied to an Office document a give it a consistent, professional look.

Theme colors The set of 12 coordinated colors in an Office document a color scheme assigns colors for text, lines, fills, accents, hyperlinks, and background.

Thumbnail (PowerPoint) A small image of a slide. Thumbnails are visible on the Slides tab and in Slide Sorter view. (Windows) A smaller image of the actual contents of a file.

Tick marks Notations of a scale of measure on a chart axis.

Title The first line or heading on a slide.

Title bar The bar at the top of the program window that indicates the program name and the name of the current file.

Title placeholder A box on a slide reserved for the title of a presentation or slide.

Title slide The first slide in a presentation.

Toggle button A button that turns a feature on and off.

Toner A powdery substance used by laser printers to transfer a laser image onto paper.

Toolbar A strip with buttons that allow you to activate a command quickly.

Touch pad A touch-sensitive device on a laptop computer that you drag your finger over to control the pointer; buttons for clicking commands are located in front of the touch pad.

Touch pointer A pointer on the screen for performing pointing operations with a finger if touch input is available on your computer.

Trackball A pointing device with a rolling ball on the top side and buttons for clicking commands; you control the movement of the pointer by moving the ball.

Translucency The transparency feature of Windows Aero that enables you to locate content by seeing through one window to the next window.

Trash folder *See* Deleted Items folder.

Unbound Describes a group of controls that do not display data.

Unbound control A control that does not change from record to record and exists only to clarify or enhance the appearance of the form, using elements such as labels, lines, and clip art.

Uniform Resource Locator (URL) The Web page's address; appears in the Address box on the Address bar after you open (or load) the page.

Universal Serial Bus port *See* USB port.

URL (Uniform Resource Locator) A Web address.

USB connector A small, rectangular plug attached to a peripheral device and that you connect to a USB port.

USB drive *See* USB flash storage device.

USB flash drive (also called a pen drive, jump drive, keychain drive, and thumb drive) A popular, removable storage device for folders and files that provides ease of use and portability.

USB flash storage device A popular type of flash memory; *also called* USB drive *or* flash drive *or* flash storage device.

USB (Universal Serial Bus) port A high-speed port to which you can connect a device with a USB connector to have the computer recognize the device and allow you to use it immediately.

User The person primarily interested in entering, editing, and analyzing the data in the database.

User interface A collective term for all the ways you interact with a software program.

Username The first part of an e-mail address that identifies the person who receives the mail that is sent to this e-mail address.

Utility A type of system software that augments the operating system by taking over some of its responsibility for allocating hardware resources.

Value axis In a chart, vertical axis that contains numerical values; in a 2-dimensional chart, also known as the y-axis.

Values Numbers, formulas, and functions used in calculations.

VCards The Internet standard for creating and sharing virtual business cards.

Vertical alignment The position of text in a document relative to the top and bottom margins.

Vertical ruler A ruler that appears on the left side of the document window in Print Layout view.

Vertical scroll bar Appears along the right side of a page window if the page is longer than the window's viewable area; allows you to move the current Web page up or down in the browser window. *See also* Scroll bar.

Video card *See* Graphics card.

Video display adapter *See* Graphics card.

View A way of displaying a document in the document window; each view provides features useful for editing and formatting different types of documents.

View buttons Buttons on the status bar that are used to change document views.

View Shortcuts The buttons at the bottom of the PowerPoint window that you click to switch among views.

Virtual memory Space on the computer's storage devices that simulates additional RAM.

Virus A harmful program that instructs a computer to perform destructive activities, such as erasing a disk drive; variants are called worms and Trojan horses.

Virus protection software *See* Antivirus software.

Volatile memory *See* Random access memory.

Wallpaper The image that fills the desktop background.

WAN *See* Wide area network.

Web Layout view A view that shows a document as it will look when viewed with a Web browser.

Web page A document located on another computer that you can view over the Internet and that often contains words, phrases, and graphics that link to other documents.

Web site A group of Web pages focused on a particular subject.

Web site creation and management software Software that allows you to create and manage Web sites and to see what the Web pages will look like as you create them.

Welcome screen An initial startup screen that displays icons for each user account on the computer.

What-if analysis A decision-making tool in which data is changed and formulas are recalculated, in order to predict various possible outcomes.

Wi-Fi *See* Wireless fidelity.

Wide area network (WAN) A network that connects one or more LAN.

Widow The last line of a paragraph when it is carried over to the top of the following page, separate from the rest of the paragraph.

Wildcard A special character used in criteria to find, filter, and query data. The asterisk (*) stands for any group of characters. For example, the criteria I* in a State field criterion cell would find all records where the state entry was IA, ID, IL, IN, or Iowa. The question mark (?) wildcard stands for only one character.

WiMAX (Worldwide Interoperability for Microwave Access) A standard of wireless communication defined by the IEEE that allows computers to communicate wirelessly over many miles; signals are transmitted from WiMAX towers to a WiMAX receiver in a device.

Window A rectangular frame on a screen that can contain icons, the contents of a file, and/or other usable data.

Windows *See* Microsoft Windows Vista.

Windows 3-D Flip A Windows Aero feature that allows you to display stacked windows at a three-dimensional angle to see even more of the content of all open windows and select the window you want to use.

Windows Aero A Windows Vista feature supported in some editions (or versions) of Windows Vista that enhances the transparency (or translucency) of the Start menu, taskbar, windows, and dialog boxes; enables live taskbar thumbnails, Windows Flip, and Windows 3-D Flip.

Windows Flip A Windows Aero feature that allows you to display a set of thumbnails, or miniature images, of all open windows so that you can select and switch to another window.

Windows Explorer A program that you use to manage files, folders, and shortcuts.

Wireless fidelity The term created by the nonprofit Wi-Fi Alliance to describe networks connected using a standard radio frequency established by the Institute of Electrical and Electronics Engineers (IEEE); frequently referred to as *Wi-Fi*.

Wireless local area network (WLAN) A LAN connected using high frequency radio waves rather than cables.

WLAN *See* Wireless local area network.

Word size The amount of data that is processed by a microprocessor at one time.

Word processing box A text box you create using the Text Box button, where the text automatically wraps inside the box.

Word processing program A software program that includes tools for entering, editing, and formatting text and graphics.

WordArt A set of decorative styles or text effects that is applied to text.

Workbook A collection of related worksheets contained within a single Excel file.

Word-wrap A feature that automatically moves the insertion point to the next line as you type.

Worksheet In spreadsheet software, a page composed of columns and rows that create cells at their intersection; you type data and formulas into cells.

Worksheet window An area of the Excel program window that displays part of the current worksheet; the worksheet window displays only a small fraction of the worksheet, which can contain a total of 1,048,576 rows and 16,384 columns.

Workstation A computer that is connected to the network.

World Wide Web Part of the Internet that consists of Web pages located on different computers around the world.

Worldwide Interoperability for Microwave Access *See* WiMAX.

X-axis The horizontal axis in a chart; because it often shows data categories, such as months, *also called* the category axis.

XML format An acronym that stands for eXtensible Markup Language, which is a language used to structure, store, and send information. Also, the new Word 2007 file format.

Y-axis The vertical axis in a chart; because it often shows numerical values in a 2-dimensional chart, *also called* the value axis.

Z-axis The third axis in a true 3-D chart, lets you compare data points across both categories and values.

Zoom level button A button on the status bar that is used to change the zoom level of the document in the document window.

Zoom slider An adjustment on the status bar that is used to enlarge or decrease the display size of the document in the document window.

Zooming in A feature that makes a document appear bigger, but shows less of it on screen at once; does not affect actual document size.

Zooming out A feature that lets you see more of a document on screen at once, but at a reduced size; does not affect actual document size.

Index